# ROUTLEDGE LIBRARY EDITIONS: JEWISH HISTORY AND IDENTITY

Volume 7

# ORGANIZING RESCUE

# ORGANIZING RESCUE
Jewish National Solidarity in the Modern Period

Edited by
S. ILAN TROEN AND BENJAMIN PINKUS

Taylor & Francis Group

LONDON AND NEW YORK

First published in 1992 by Frank Cass & Co. Ltd

This edition first published in 2020
by Routledge
2 Park Square, Milton Park, Abingdon, Oxon OX14 4RN

and by Routledge
52 Vanderbilt Avenue, New York, NY 10017

*Routledge is an imprint of the Taylor & Francis Group, an informa business*

© 1992 Frank Cass & Co. Ltd

All rights reserved. No part of this book may be reprinted or reproduced or utilised in any form or by any electronic, mechanical, or other means, now known or hereafter invented, including photocopying and recording, or in any information storage or retrieval system, without permission in writing from the publishers.

*Trademark notice*: Product or corporate names may be trademarks or registered trademarks, and are used only for identification and explanation without intent to infringe.

*British Library Cataloguing in Publication Data*
A catalogue record for this book is available from the British Library

ISBN: 978-0-367-44247-7 (Set)
ISBN: 978-1-00-300850-7 (Set) (ebk)
ISBN: 978-0-367-46118-8 (Volume 7) (hbk)
ISBN: 978-0-367-46143-0 (Volume 7) (pbk)
ISBN: 978-1-00-302718-8 (Volume 7) (ebk)

**Publisher's Note**
The publisher has gone to great lengths to ensure the quality of this reprint but points out that some imperfections in the original copies may be apparent.

**Disclaimer**
The publisher has made every effort to trace copyright holders and would welcome correspondence from those they have been unable to trace.

# ORGANIZING RESCUE
# National Jewish Solidarity in the Modern Period

EDITED BY
Selwyn Ilan Troen
and
Benjamin Pinkus

FRANK CASS

*First published in 1992 in Great Britain by*
FRANK CASS & CO. LTD.
Gainsborough House, Gainsborough Road,
London E11 1RS, England

*and in the United States of America by*
FRANK CASS
c/o International Specialized Book Services, Inc.
5602 N.E. Hassalo Street, Portland, Oregon 97213

Copyright © 1992 Frank Cass & Co. Ltd.

British Library Cataloguing in Publication Data

Organizing rescue : national Jewish solidarity in the modern period.
1. Jews, history
I. Troen, Selwyn Ilan   II. Pinkus, Benjamin *1933–*
909.0492408

ISBN 0-7146-3413-1

Library of Congress Cataloging-in-Publication Data

Organizing rescue : national Jewish solidarity in the modern period / edited by Selwyn Ilan Troen and Benjamin Pinkus.
  p.   cm.
  ISBN 0-7146-3413-1
  1. Jews—History—1789–1945.  2. Jews—History—1945–  3. Jews–
–Persecutions—History.  4. Holocaust, Jewish (1939–1945)–
–Influence.  5. Jews—Migrations—History.  6. Refugees, Jewish.
7. Solidarity—Religious aspects—Judaism.  I. Troen, Selwyn Ilan.
II. Pinkus, Benjamin, 1933–
DS125.074    1991
909'.04924—dc20                                  91–9244
                                                  CIP

*All rights reserved. No part of this publication may be reproduced in any form or by any means, electronic, mechanical, photocopying, recording or otherwise, without the prior permission of Frank Cass and Company Limited.*

Typeset by Regent Typesetting, London
Printed by BPCC Wheatons Ltd, Exeter

For Mickey Katzman (of blessed memory) and his brother, Jacob,
in recognition of their commitment to Jewish Solidarity

*Published in cooperation with*
Ben-Gurion Research Centre
Sede Boqer
Ben-Gurion University of the Negev

# CONTENTS

Preface ix

Introductions

1. Organizing the Rescue of Jews in
   the Modern Period     Selwyn Ilan Troen    3

2. The Redemption of Captives in Halakhic
   Tradition: Problems and Policy     Ya'akov Blidstein    20

## PART ONE
## FROM THE DAMASCUS AFFAIR TO THE FIRST WORLD WAR

3. The Crisis as a Factor in Modern Jewish
   Politics, 1840 and 1881–1882     Jonathan Frankel    33

4. Ethnicity and Jewish Solidarity in
   Nineteenth-Century France     Phyllis Cohen Albert    50

5. The *Alliance Israélite Universelle*
   and French Jewish Leadership
   vis-à-vis North African
   Jewry, 1860–1914     Simon Schwarzfuchs    73

6. The Kovno Circle of Rabbi Yitzhak Elhanan
   Spektor: Organizing Western Public
   Opinion over Pogroms in the 1880s     Israel Oppenheim    91

7. German Jews and the Jewish
   Emigration from Russia     Moshe Zimmermann    127

## PART TWO
## WORLD WARS AND THE SHADOW OF THE HOLOCAUST

8. Dr. Nahum Goldmann and
   the Policy of International
   Jewish Organizations     Monty N. Penkower    141

9. Rescue and the Secular Perception:
   American Jewry and the Holocaust     Henry L. Feingold   154

10. German Jewish Refugees in Palestine:
    The Early Years, 1932–1939     Jehuda Reinharz   167

11. The Emotional Elements in Ben-Gurion's
    Relation to the Diaspora during
    the Holocaust     Tuvia Friling   191

12. Activity of the Yishuv on Behalf of
    Iraqi Jewry, 1914–1948     Daphne Tsimhoni   222

13. The American Joint Distribution
    Committee and Polish Jewry 1944–1949     Yosef Litvak   269

## PART THREE
## THE CONTEMPORARY PERIOD

14. Jewish Solidarity and 'Refuge Zionism':
    The Case of B'nai B'rith     Allon Gal   315

15. Diplomacy without Sovereignty:
    The World Jewish Congress Rescue
    Activities     Avi Beker   343

16. Jewish Solidarity in the Integration of
    North African Jews in France     Doris Bensimon   361

17. Israeli Activity on Behalf of Soviet
    Jewry     Benjamin Pinkus   373

18. Jewish Solidarity and the Jews
    of Ethiopia     Ephraim Isaac   403

Notes on Contributors     421

# PREFACE

National solidarity, as manifest in the rescue of Jews by Jews, is a central theme in contemporary Jewish history. The recent immigration of Ethiopian Jewry through Operation Moses and the current renewal of the exodus from the Soviet Union are but the latest chapters in the ongoing saga of the rescue of threatened Jewish communities and their reconstitution elsewhere. In meeting these challenges the State of Israel, in response to the need to save Jews, has joined forces with the multitude of Jewish organizations whose rescue activities long preceded its founding. Scholars and popular writers have described, analysed and evaluated the response of Jews to the persecution of their brethren. Many question why Jews did not organize more effectively to defend communities and assist their survivors. Others focus on the success of attempts at assistance and reconstruction. This volume provides a context for assessing these activities by examining the diversity and change in the patterns of rescue from the mid-nineteenth century to the present.

*Organizing Rescue* brings together interpretive essays and case studies to provide an integrated, historical and comparative framework for asking the following questions: How did the ancient, religiously-anchored injunction of mutual responsibility among Jews evolve into the contemporary commitment to national solidarity? What organizational structures developed to accomplish these ends? How is one to understand and evaluate the efforts made by Jews to defend and preserve communities of their brethren across vast distances and diverse cultural and political systems?

The concept for the book originated in a series of seminars conducted at the Ben-Gurion Research Centre in Sede Boqer which brought together scholarship on the Jewish communities in the Middle East, Europe and the United States in the period between the Holocaust and the establishment of the State of Israel. To expand the focus chronologically and sharpen it thematically, an international seminar was held at Sede Boqer in April 1986 on 'National Jewish Solidarity and the Rescue of Persecuted Jews in Modern Jewish History.'

ORGANIZING RESCUE

Drawing on the contributions of participants together with additional invited papers the following volume was published in somewhat modified form in Hebrew. It is hoped that the present version will bring this timely research to a much wider readership. The conferences took place within the context of the ongoing struggle for Soviet Jewry as well as the excitement of the sudden aliyah of Jews from Ethiopia. At present, there is the prospect of fulfilling the dream of a mass exodus from the Soviet Union.

*Organizing Rescue* is divided into four sections. The Introduction is composed of interpretive essays by Ya'acov Blidstein and Selwyn Troen. Blidstein analyses the origins of Jewish solidarity in Jewish law through the injunction to 'redeem the captives' (*pidyon sh'vuyim*) and its interpretation in rabbinic writings. Troen provides an overview describing the shift from the traditional pattern, in which a local Jewish leader or 'Court Jew' interceded with local authorities on behalf of the community, to rescue activity organized at the national and even international level. This transformation was accompanied by a change from a religious to a secular orientation and a geographical shift in the location of the rescued and the rescuers.

The essays that follow are grouped chronologically into three sections. Part I, From the Damascus Affair to the First World War (1840–1914), deals with the emergence of new patterns of response to the persecution of Jews in Europe, Asia and Africa under the impact of emancipation, nationalism, and anti-semitism. The case studies of Jonathan Frankel, Phyllis Cohen Albert, Simon Schwarzfuchs, Israel Oppenheim and Moshe Zimmermann provide a detailed and multi-faceted analysis of this formative period.

In Part II, World Wars and the Shadow of the Holocaust (1914–1948), Monty N. Penkower, Henry L. Feingold, Jehuda Reinharz, Tuvia Friling, Daphne Tsimhoni and Yosef Litvak deal with the transitional period which brought hope and bitter disillusionment to Jews in Europe and the Middle East. They analyse the crises and dilemmas that faced Jewish communities in old and well-established Jewish centres as well as the response particularly by the new communities in the United States and Palestine.

Part III, The Contemporary Period, illuminates the different manifestations of Jewish national solidarity which developed in response to the Holocaust and the creation of the State of Israel. The essays of Allon Gal, Avi Beker, Doris Bensimon, Benjamin Pinkus, and Ephraim Isaac shed new light on the activities of Jewish

## PREFACE

organizations and of the State of Israel on behalf of threatened Jews. They demonstrate the vitality of the contemporary commitment to Jewish solidarity as expressed in support for a Zionist state fulfilling the promise of the Ingathering of the Exiles together with the cooperation between Israel and the Diaspora on behalf of their persecuted brethren throughout the world.

We are pleased to acknowledge our debt to those who contributed to producing this volume. We are grateful to our colleagues at the Ben-Gurion Research Centre who assisted in organizing the conferences and in producing the Hebrew edition. We would like to express particular thanks to Shaul Shragai, Director of the Centre's Publications Division, for preparing the Hebrew and French articles for English translation and to Dr. Carol Troen for valuable editorial assistance. We also appreciate the cooperation of the University Press of New England for permitting us to include Jonathan Frankel's essay, which was first published in English in *Living with Anti-Semitism; Modern Jewish Responses*, edited by Jehuda Reinharz, and to Duke University Press for allowing us to include Phyllis Cohen Albert's essay, which first appeared in *Mystics, Philosophers, and Politicians: Essays in Jewish Intellectual History in Honor of Alexander Altman*, edited by Jehuda Reinharz and Daniel Swetschinski. The Oxford Centre for Postgraduate Hebrew Studies provided a hospitable venue for completing the text.

Finally, we are grateful for the generous assistance of Mr. Albert Bildner of New York and Mr. George Shrut of Boston, and of Mr. and Mrs. Sidney Corob and Mr. and Mrs. Hyman Kreitman of London who have repeatedly demonstrated a commitment to both Jewish scholarship and to Jewish solidarity.

*Selwyn Ilan Troen and Benjamin Pinkus*

# INTRODUCTIONS

# 1

# Organizing the Rescue of Jews in the Modern Period

## Selwyn Ilan Troen

Jews have maintained their solidarity as a nation despite nearly two millennia of dispersion. Although the modern nation-state has demanded new loyalties which could have replaced traditional ones, ancient ties persist. The bonds that hold modern Jewry together have been severely tested and have proved vital in the commitment of a dispersed people to reach out over vast geographical distances and across diverse political systems. Even though Jews may speak a different language and participate in a different culture, they have continued to understand themselves as brethren and, as such, accept responsibility for one another. The commitment to act on behalf of fellow-Jews has its roots in the centuries-old traditions that have always been part of the Diaspora experience. Nevertheless, the forms of national solidarity have necessarily changed in response to the circumstances in which Jewish communities have found themselves. This volume attempts to examine the ways in which Jewish solidarity has evolved and been expressed in the modern period. In this context, the definition of modernity derives from the patterns of organized communal response that have evolved from the mid-nineteenth century until the present.

Neither the extent of persecutions in the modern period nor the enormous international effort required to deal with them could have been anticipated. The emergence of the modern nation-state and the spread of enlightenment ideas over the past two centuries had suggested different scenarios: Jews would assimilate into the culture of the host nation or, if they chose to maintain their separate identity, would find protection as citizens of the modern, democratic state.[1] These alternatives partly materialized but so did a widespread and unprecedented outbreak of anti-Semitism.

Whereas in the past, local religious and civil authorities or individuals had been responsible for persecution, in the modern period anti-Semitism was transformed and expanded through the agency of the newly-organized nation-states. This occurred in the Russia of the Czars and of the Bolsheviks, in Hitler's Germany, and in many countries of the Middle East. Paradoxically, as the activities of individual Jews and local communities were superseded by newly-organized Jewish national and international organizations, collective pressure on governments – particularly in the enlightened countries of Western Europe and across the Atlantic – combined to make the modern state into a major instrument for rescue. Eventually, through the Zionist movement, the greater part of international Jewry supported the creation of a state of their own to serve both as a guaranteed place of refuge and as a force working on behalf of imperilled communities.

The tradition of solidarity has been part of Jewish history since the injunction to 'redeem the captives' which became incumbent upon Diaspora communities after the destruction of the Second Temple by the Romans in 70 C.E. The identity of the oppressors and the means of rescue have changed through the centuries. Moreover, redemption has come to entail far more than physical rescue. It has come to include extending support for educational, cultural and spiritual activities necessary to ensure the continuity of Jewish life wherever it is threatened. The principle of redemption of the captives, or *pidyon shevuyim* in the Hebrew, expresses the mutual responsibility, solidarity and assistance that have characterized Jewish life through the centuries.[2]

This concept of redemption of the captives has its origins in religious law. While the Bible employs the concept of 'captives' to refer to soldiers who were seized in war, the rabbinic usage embraces innocent civilians taken prisoner under any circumstances. So distinctive have been the circumstances of 'redemption of the captives' for Diaspora Jewry that although it is not included as one of the 613 commandments based on the Bible, rabbinic tradition added this new commandment and endowed it with a special standing in Jewish law. Maimonides, for example, wrote that '*pidyon shevuyim* takes precedence over giving charity to the poor, and there is no greater commandment than charity for the poor, for the captive is among the hungry, the thirsty and the naked, and he stands in danger for his life ... and you have no greater commandment than the redemption of captives.'[3] This statement was built upon a long experience that included the rescue of Jewish

## INTRODUCTION 1: THE RESCUE OF THE JEWS

captives from the hands of brigands and pirates on land and sea or Jews who were unjustly incarcerated in prison. Perhaps the earliest beneficiaries of such assistance were those taken captive by the Romans at the time of the destruction of the Second Temple and during the period of the Bar Kochba revolt. The continued dispersal of Jews throughout the world, and the absence of a central authority that could effectively intercede on their behalf, made individual Jews and whole Jewish communities vulnerable to threats and hostile designs by host societies. *Pidyon shevuyim* necessarily became part of the moral inheritance of Jews for nearly two millenia.

A very limited list of instances when *pidyon shevuyim* was carried out includes: the establishment of a special fund by the community of Alexandria in the ninth to twelfth centuries for the rescue of Jews in Muslim countries who were subject to the threat of seizure while travelling; the attempts to rescue Jews of medieval Christian Europe who were imprisoned as a consequence of the blood libel or simply as a means of extorting money from them or from the larger Jewish community; the organization of rescue funds by the Council of Lithuania during the sixteenth and seventeenth centuries to aid Jewish communities primarily as a consequence of the disorders caused by repeated incursions by the Cossacks and the Tatars from the Crimea and Ukraine; and efforts expended by other European communities on behalf of Venetian Jewry in the seventeenth and the eighteenth centuries whose members had been taken captive by Muslim pirates operating primarily out of North Africa.[4]

The international scope of these activities reveals a well-developed sense of Jewish solidarity that extended beyond the political boundaries in which a particular community was located. For example, Jewish communities in Ottoman countries, particularly Constantinople, organized a substantial international effort on behalf of their brethren in Eastern Europe during the time of the Chmielnicki massacres of 1648–49 and the many troubles that followed in succeeding decades; the Jews from Amsterdam, Austria, Germany, Italy and Lithuania aided captives from the Russo-Polish war of 1654–67 who were dispersed in Ottoman lands; and there were widespread contributions by foreign communities on behalf of Jews who were falsely imprisoned in Poland during the eighteenth century by unscrupulous and ransom-seeking Polish nobles. It is important to note that in all these cases, while funds came from community resources, particularly from the wealthy, the actual negotiations and intercessions were carried on by designated community representatives or by an individual of special prominence or power, such as a leading rabbi or a powerful figure at court – the 'Court Jew.'[5]

The tradition of national solidarity, then, was well-established as Jews confronted the new dangers and opportunities presented in the modern period. In the past, reflecting patterns of demographic dispersal, the great communities around the Mediterranean and Europe, particularly Eastern Europe, were the centres for organized rescue efforts. From the mid-nineteenth century, the growing communities of Western Europe, the United States and, most recently, the State of Israel have undertaken responsibility for mounting such efforts. If, previously, pirates, marauding bands or local nobles had been the source of the greatest danger, in the modern period the new states, as carriers of their own nationalisms or other ideologies, increasingly became the agents of new persecutions and their targets were less individuals than entire sections of the Jewish people. Jews responded to these new conditions even as they remained committed to the two-thousand-year-old imperative to 'redeem the captives.'

This process of adaptation is the topic of this collection of essays. The method for understanding this phenomenon is through a selection of 'case studies' that reflect the range of problems in time and place. The essays that follow describe and analyse the experience of the Jewish people, as victims and as redeemers in Syria, North Africa, Iraq, Ethiopia, Eastern Europe, France, Germany, England, the United States and Israel. It is a large stage with a large cast playing in an apparently unfinished drama. This history may be presented in three acts: from mid-nineteenth century until the First World War; from the First World War to the Second World War and the Holocaust; and from the establishment of the State of Israel to the present.

## FROM THE MID-NINETEENTH CENTURY TO THE FIRST WORLD WAR

The appropriate place for beginning this historical survey is with the response of Western Jewryy to the crises of the mid-nineteenth century. They included the Damascus Affair (1840) when Jews were accused of abducting and murdering for ritual purposes a Capuchin monk serving in Syria; the Mortara Case (1858) when an Italian Jewish child was abducted by the Catholic Church and not returned to his family despite widespread international protest; and the increasing incidents of anti-Semitism in Eastern Europe that

INTRODUCTION 1: THE RESCUE OF THE JEWS

reached critical proportions in the Russian pogroms of 1881–82. Largely in response to these events, modern patterns of solidarity began to take shape, including the establishment of the forerunners of modern international organizations and the development of strategies for action.[6]

During this mid-century period, the rescuers were largely from Western Europe and later from the United States and it was they who created the Alliance Israélite Universelle (Paris, 1860); the Anglo-Jewish Association (1870) and the Joint Foreign Committee of the Board of Deputies (London, 1878); the Hebrew Immigration Aid Society or HIAS (New York, 1884); and the Hilfsverein der deutschen Juden (1901). The location of these organizations and the communities which they sought to rescue reflect the geography and demography of *pidyon shevuyim* in the contemporary period. The 'redeemers' now came from the advanced and powerful states in Western Europe and North America. The 'captives' were increasingly in the Middle East and Eastern Europe.

The Alliance Israélite established the principles by which succeeding organizations have operated. Among its aims were (a) 'to work everywhere for the emancipation and progress of Jews' and (b) to offer effective assistance to Jews suffering from anti-Semitism. These aims were expressed in intensive diplomatic activity on behalf of persecuted communities throughout the world. In the second half of the nineteenth century, the Alliance agenda included agitation on behalf of the Jews of Rumania, Serbia, Russia and even on behalf of the civil rights of Swiss Jews. It invested great energy to aid the Jews of the Ottoman Empire, throughout the Middle East and North Africa. Moreover, in a period of massive Jewish migration, the Alliance actively sought to assist immigrants from Eastern Europe. For the majority who stayed at home, it built an impressive network of schools, particularly throughout North Africa and the Middle East, in Morocco, Tunisia, Algeria, Turkey, Greece, Iraq, Iran, Ethiopia, Egypt, Syria, Lebanon and Palestine. Physical as well as spiritual rescue was its agenda. The Alliance played a major role in the discovery of neglected Jewish communities. For example, it was the Alliance that first established sustained contact with and provided assistance to the Jewish community of Ethiopia.[7]

Since no nationally-based organization was capable of meeting the increasingly urgent needs of Jewish communities in the modern world, Jews of different countries were obliged to coordinate their efforts. Beginning in 1878, the Alliance began to work with the Conjoint Foreign Committee of the Anglo-Jewish Association and the Board of Deputies. Although never as complete as circumstances required, international cooperation could be very effective in times of crisis.

The geographical aspects of crisis and response also reflect political and sociological developments. An important characteristic of these national Jewish relief organizations is that they endeavoured to employ the international power of the countries in which Jews had but recently acquired citizenship on behalf of brethren in distant parts of the world. Active concern for fellow-Jews persisted even though the leadership of these organizations was often avowedly assimilationist and eager to replace certain traditional loyalties to the Jewish community with full participation in the public life of a new community to which they had transferred allegiance. The Alliance Israélite reflected this devotion to ancient loyalties that transcended the boundaries of the modern state in its motto, the ancient Hebrew saying: 'All Israel are comrades.'

The organization of international networks for expressing Jewish solidarity was a phenomenon that is best understood within the context of developments in nineteenth century Western societies. Whereas organizations with an international reach had previously been characteristic only of states, churches and large-scale commercial or business enterprises, during the second part of the nineteenth century a wide variety of political, social, and even scientific and professional organizations developed international frameworks. During the 1850s there were only about three international congresses per year in Western Europe or the United States. By the last decade of the century, more than 100 international meetings were held each year, largely in the new centres of major world powers – Paris, London, Berlin and New York. Herzl's call for a congress of world Jewry to launch the international Zionist movement in 1897 must be seen in this context.[8]

This same period also witnessed the branching out of such initially national movements as the French-based Alliance and the American-sponsored HIAS or, at a later period, the Joint Distribution Committee (1914). In 1936, after a year-long effort, Nahum Goldmann and Stephen Wise were able to convene the World Jewish Congress, a new international organization composed of 37 affiliated groups from 27 countries on five continents, to counter the dangers of Nazism. In 1938, at the ill-fated Évian Conference, where the possibility of finding a refuge for European Jewry was discussed, there were 20 other organizations claiming to represent Jewish rights who came to testify before a council of nations. Nevertheless, while this remarkable effort did not achieve unity, it did signify a widespread and shared commitment to Jewish solidarity.[9]

These new patterns of international organization were also accompanied by changes in leadership. In the past the 'shtadlan,' the 'Court Jew' or outstanding individual had represented his community by interceding with local authorities. In the modern period these individuals have been joined by a far larger base and range of leadership. Modern Jewish leaders include, in addition to those with great wealth or learning, journalists, lawyers, intellectuals, scientists, professionals and businessmen with national and international connections. Indeed, permanent international organizations spawn permanent secretariats and professional workers to manage them. The outstanding contributions and personal interventions of such nineteenth century 'Court Jews' as Moses Montefiore and Adolphe Crémieux in the *cause célèbre* of the Damascus Affair were the last examples of what had for so long been the traditional pattern of community leadership. In the modern period, outstanding individuals generally operate within organizations or at least share responsibility with them.

Nevertheless, Montefiore's and Crémieux's handling of the Damascus Affair presaged the kind of intervention modern Jewish leadership in the Diaspora would seek to achieve. Their strategy was to employ Jewish influence to persuade major Western powers to pressure despotic regimes to change their policies. As Jewish organizations developed and multiplied in the coming generations, they devised ever more effective ways of exerting influence on Western governments on behalf of Jews in other parts of the world. By the end of the century, such pressure was primarily brought to bear on Great Britain, France, Germany and, after the turn of the century, increasingly on the United States.[10]

While assimilated modern Jews took the lead in developing the modern strategies and instruments of rescue, they had no monopoly on them. As early as the 1880s there existed an international network for smuggling information from Eastern Europe for the purpose of influencing Western governments. The earliest recorded effort of this kind was conceived, initiated and carried out in the 1880s by a small group of very traditional, orthodox religious Jews from Kovno. The network they created operated from Eastern Europe to Germany, France and Great Britain. In the course of its activities, it so widened as to incorporate, in addition to leading orthodox rabbis, wealthy and assimilated Jewish leaders as well as journalists and a host of other individuals. The requirements of international organization and activity encouraged cooperation across the internal divides of Jewish society. For over a century one can document such continuity in the patterns of information-gathering and dissemination with the common objective of mobilizing Western public opinion. Indeed, throughout the modern period, the need to educate not only fellow-Jews but righteous gentiles, particularly those who hold the levers of power, has been widely understood throughout the Jewish community.[11]

Solidarity did not mean the willingness to bridge all cultural and social differences within the Jewish world. German Jewry, for example, was all too willing to assist Eastern Jews by protesting against Russian anti-Semitism and by helping emigrating Jews reach safe havens in the West – so long as they were not intending to find refuge in Germany itself. This was in part because they feared that excessive concentrations of Eastern Jews in Germany would compromise their own position. Hence, they were anxious to assist their brethren in going through Germany to find new homes in the United States, the southern hemisphere and even Palestine. Thus assistance was actuated by self-interest as well as by noble philanthropy and feelings of solidarity. These same ambiguities towards Eastern European Jews were exported to the United States and characterized relations within that Jewish community. Nevertheless, the impulse to help, even in this manner, overcame the tendency to divisiveness due to deeply-held beliefs and cultural values. A sense of common destiny and mutual responsibility remained as the dominant, motivating value that engendered national solidarity among a dispersed and increasingly uprooted people.[12]

By the outbreak of the First World War, a remarkably effective international network of organizations had been established. Whole new community networks were established that included schools and hospitals, vocational training agencies, religious institutions and organizations to protect the civil rights of fellow-Jews. Some organizations were created to assist Jews to emigrate to safer lands. Other societies were organized to protect Jews wherever they lived. The agenda facing the Jewish people was extraordinarily large in a world that was undergoing rapid and often violent change. It is altogether remarkable to note the energy and imagination with which Jews met the challenge.

INTRODUCTION 1: THE RESCUE OF THE JEWS

## WORLD WARS AND THE SHADOW OF THE HOLOCAUST

Two far-reaching developments transformed international Jewish life during the interwar period. One was the shift in focus to the Jewish community of the United States as the major source of potential assistance. The other was the emergence of the Jewish community of Palestine as an important factor in international Jewish affairs. The former was a reflection of the growing numbers, wealth and influence of American Jewry in a nation that was becoming the primary world power. The latter was due to the threats to Jewish communities in Central and Eastern Europe under totalitarian regimes and the closing of the gates to America after the 1924 immigration law. As a consequence, Zionism was increasingly perceived as the only practical answer for European Jewry. Moreover, the Yishuv, or the Jewish settlement in Palestine, underwent remarkable development that would transform it from a recipient of aid from abroad to a society capable of acting on behalf of Jewish interests in Palestine and abroad if only in a still limited manner.

The growth of the Jewish community in the United States began in the mid-nineteenth century when, like so many millions of other immigrants, Jews emigrated to the country which they saw as the best hope for physical, economic and political security. Numbering about 20,000 in 1848, the Jewish population grew to about 600,000 in 1870 and added more than another 2,000,000 by the outbreak of the First World War in 1914. By the end of the Second World War, with more than 5,000,000 or about 40 per cent of the world's entire Jewish population, it had become the largest Jewish community in the world.[13]

This numerical growth both necessitated and facilitated the development of communal organizations devoted to providing assistance for Jews at both the local and international level. Particularly after the pogroms in Russia in 1881–82, American Jews modelled their activities on those of the Jewish communities in Britain, France and Germany. Thus, for example, branches of the Russian Refugee Aid Committee were established in New York, Chicago and Philadelphia and other large cities shortly after the arrival of the first refugees. The work of absorption was carried on by the HIAS and scores of local agencies such as orphanages, hospitals, old-age homes, schools, family-aid societies and the like. Many of these local services were supported by federations of local Jewish charities and philanthropies.[14] By 1899, these local federations organized nationally into the National Conference of Jewish Charities. At the same time, international efforts became the province of special associations that were specifically established for such purposes. Their number has so grown that at present there are approximately 400 organizations describing themselves as Zionist and pro-Israel, and about the same number that engage in various other forms of 'overseas aid.' Indeed, such activities have become the dominant feature characterizing the structure of organized Jewish life in America.[15]

Although they are rooted in the American Jewish community, the declarations of purpose of the following major organizations suggest the importance of international solidarity:[16] [Emphasis added in italics]

- American Jewish Congress (1918): 'Works to foster the creative *religious and cultural survival of the Jewish people; to help Israel develop* in peace, freedom, and security; to eliminate all forms of racial and religious bigotry.'
- American Jewish Committee (1906): 'Seeks to prevent infraction of civil and religious rights of Jews *in any part of the world.*'
- World Jewish Congress (1936): 'Seeks to intensify *bonds of world Jewry with Israel as central force in Jewish life, to strengthen solidarity among Jews everywhere and secure their rights, status, and interests as individuals and communities; to encourage development of Jewish social, religious, and cultural life throughout the world and coordinate efforts by Jewish communities and organizations to cope with any Jewish problem* ...'

Furthermore, the names of other organizations convey their fundamental commitment to the rescue of Jewish communities abroad: National Conference on Soviet Jewry (1964); Student Struggle for Soviet Jewry (1964); American Friends of the Alliance Israélite Universelle (1946); American Jewish Joint Distribution Committee (1914); ORT – Organization for Rehabilitation through Training (1924); HIAS – Hebrew Immigrant Aid Society (1884); United Jewish Appeal (1939). It must be added that while the centre for international Jewish activity has passed to the United States, other communities in the world continue to be very active. Noteworthy, by the number of organizations involved, are: Great Britain, France, Brazil, Argentina, and Canada.

The efflorescence of organized activity notwithstanding, effectiveness depended both on its ability to influence the U.S. Government and on the scope of American power. In practice this has

## INTRODUCTION 1: THE RESCUE OF THE JEWS

meant that antagonism between the United States and the Soviet Union has often limited what American Jewry had hoped to accomplish. Moreover, the Jewish agenda suffered in the interwar years when Western society was engulfed by economic problems and the competing aspirations and interests of communist, capitalist and fascist societies. The ability of Jews to influence American policy or that of other Western governments greatly diminished as the narrow exclusive pursuit of national interest took precedence over humanitarian concerns.

In such a context, in which states were the major actors – for good and for evil – it became increasingly apparent that Jews had to have a state of their own. Jews had learned that they could not afford to depend for their survival on their ability to influence even the most enlightened and powerful government. When America and other countries closed their gates in the 1920s, Palestine became the only venue for Jews who were able to escape Europe. As a consequence, the potential significance of the Zionist settlement in Palestine gained widespread recognition and support.[17]

By the outbreak of the Second World War, the Yishuv (the Jewish settlement in Palestine) was fighting for the right of European Jewry to immigrate. It also offered refuge to Jewish communities in the Middle East – among the most settled and ancient Jewish communities in the world – which were being uprooted by a regional revolution. However, the resources of the Yishuv were so limited during the 1930s that painful choices had to be made as priorities were established. For example, it was necessary to negotiate between the competing needs to organize the aliyah of the Iraqi community which had suffered a traumatic pogrom in 1940, to rescue the victims of Nazi-controlled Europe, and to prepare the Yishuv for the expected struggle for independence.[18]

The debate about what should have been done remains very much part of contemporary Jewish history and has raised serious questions about the means and the limits of 'solidarity.' The behaviour of American Jews in the face of the Nazi threat and the Holocaust has been subject to special criticism since it appears to many that they should have been in a position to accomplish far more. Were American Jews unnecessarily inhibited in organizing themselves, in speaking out and in attempting to put pressure on their country's leaders? Or were there real limits on their power to affect the course of history through their host country? These difficult issues continue to require serious examination.[19] However, it is clear that the anxiety over the potential costs of failing to meet national obligations has become a prime force in energizing Jewish solidarity in the post-Holocaust era.

## THE CONTEMPORARY PERIOD

It is likely that most Jews in the years immediately after the creation of the State of Israel believed that the answer to Jewish persecutions had finally been found. Indeed, the State of Israel formalized its purpose as haven and as rescuer in its Declaration of Independence of May, 1948:

> In the year 1897 the First Zionist Congress, inspired by Theodor Herzl's vision of the Jewish State, proclaimed the right of the Jewish people to national revival in their own country ... The Nazi Holocaust, which engulfed millions of Jews in Europe, proved anew the urgency of the reestablishment of the Jewish State, which would solve the problem of Jewish homelessness by opening the gates to all Jews and lifting the Jewish people to equality in the family of nations ... The State of Israel will be open to the immigration of Jews from all countries of their dispersion ...

Finally, there is an appeal for an international effort to ensure that Israel can fulfil its intended role: 'Our call goes out to the Jewish people all over the world to rally to our side in the task of immigration and development and to stand by us in the great struggle for the fulfilment of the dream of generations – the redemption of Israel.'

In fact, Israel did become the major refuge of the modern period. In the three and a half years after declaring Independence in May, 1948, a population of 650,000 absorbed an equal number of immigrants from a war-ravaged Europe and from the volatile and hostile Middle East.[20] Moreover, this host population was itself created by the influx of more than 400,000 who fled Europe after Hitler's rise to power in 1933.[21] The 'Ingathering of the Exiles' is so much part of fundamental state policy that the Cabinet has a Minister assigned to encourage and superintend the realization of this ancient promise.

The aspiration for a Jewish homeland in Israel came to be shared even by groups that had previously been anti-Zionist or non-committal. Established non-Zionist organizations like the B'nai Brith and the American Jewish Committee now expended many of their political and financial resources on behalf of Israel as the best haven. Nevertheless, at present, Israel represents but 27 per cent of world Jewry. The largest community is still in the United States with about 44 per cent.[22] Significant numbers of European refugees chose to remain in Europe, some decided to try to enter the United States and Canada, and still others preferred South America, South Africa and Australia. Similarly, in the 1950s and into the 1960s, large numbers of émigrés from the North African communities of Morocco, Tunisia, Algeria, Libya, Egypt and elsewhere in the Middle East chose to settle in the West rather than in a small, independent, Middle Eastern Jewish State. However disappointing this may be for Zionists, such a pattern of migration has had the positive consequence of contributing to the rebuilding and restructuring of older Jewish communities in the Diaspora. This is eminently true of France which has recently become home to the largest Western European community through the absorption of Jews from former French colonies.[23]

Since the establishment of the State, there have been numerous cases of cooperation between an American-led Diaspora and Israel on behalf of threatened communities. Indeed, the contemporary period is characterized by the dominance of a kind of bipolar system of Jewish solidarity and rescue. This cooperation has become necessary since neither Diaspora Jewry nor Israel has sufficient resources on its own to meet the challenges facing the Jewish people. Israel alone, for example, could not have organized the rescue of Ethiopian Jewry. Hostile relations with Syria and Iran foreclose effective interventions in these countries. Nor is Israel capable of confronting Soviet power. International Jewry, on the other hand, lacks the apparatus provided by sovereignty, especially the advantages of a recognized foreign office or an army, which may be crucial in such cases as the rescue of the hostages at Entebbe. Nevertheless, American-based aid has been extended most generously to settling Jews in Israel even as it has been active in supporting communities from Iran to Northern Africa, Ethiopia and Eastern Europe. Similarly, the State of Israel and the Zionist movement have not only encouraged aliyah but have been engaged in strengthening, both culturally and educationally, Jewish communities throughout the Diaspora – including even that of the United States. In sum, it has now become apparent that it is through the solidarity of Western Jewry with the State of Israel that the injunction to provide for the security and redemption of persecuted Jews throughout the world is being fulfilled.[24]

These realities are causing a transformation in current ideologies. Support for the Jewish state was nearly universal among those committed to the continuing validity of Jewish life in the Diaspora, even among many who had been previously opposed to Zionism. In the West, most Jews now willingly and openly claim that loyalty to their own country is compatible with devotion to Israel. At the same time, the Zionist conception of 'the rejection of the exile' is increasingly difficult to maintain in the face of the vitality of Diaspora life and its contribution to Israel's security and well-being. Thus, Jews throughout the world are trying to accommodate the reality of an ongoing mutual interdependence by going beyond received ideologies.

The ways in which contemporary solidarity operates can be illustrated best by the various strategies implemented on behalf of Soviet Jewry. This community, which is the third largest in the world and the largest in which Jews suffer from persecutions, remains at the centre of international Jewry's concerns. Considerations of *Realpolitik* required Israeli leaders to avoid offending the Soviet Union particularly in the decade after independence. This may have been one of the factors behind the relative silence of Israel during that period. Indeed, until the Six Day War of 1967 behind-the-scenes negotiations and activities superseded public diplomacy or protest. Western Jewry could afford to be less inhibited and took the initiative in organizing international public opinion. In addition, the clamour raised by Soviet Jews themselves after the 1967 war played a most important role in opening the gates of the Soviet Union.[25] Yet, more was necessary. Pressured by the lobbying of numerous Jewish organizations, a sympathetic American Congress enacted laws that encouraged the Soviet Union, as well as other Eastern European countries, to liberalize emigration policies and restrain anti-Semitism. In all of this, the role of an enlightened and aroused gentile public opinion has been crucial.

The dynamics of the rescue of Jewish captives in the contemporary period is well illustrated by the manner in which leading 'refuseniks' have left the Soviet Union. The arrival of Ida Nudel in Israel, on 15 October 1987, dramatically symbolized the current pattern of rescue. This long-suffering and tenacious 'Prisoner of Zion' was brought to Israel on the private plane of a wealthy and assimilated American Jew, Armand Hammer. Waiting to receive her, in addition to thousands of well-wishers and the world press, were the leaders of the Israeli Government, representatives of major international Jewish organizations, and non-Jewish personalities who had become involved with the plight of Soviet Jewry. Awaiting her, too, were the personal congratulations of the leaders of important

INTRODUCTION 1: THE RESCUE OF THE JEWS

Western countries including the United States, Great Britain and France. The rescue of this one individual from the grasp of the Soviet Union was made possible by the resources and the sustained effort of the State of Israel, Western and particularly American Jewry, enlightened non-Jewish public opinion, and the intervention of Western democratic states. When successfully combined, these elements constitute a powerful force for the redemption of modern captives.

In the century and a half since the Damascus Affair, communal responses to the problem of rescue have been revolutionized. The activities of a multitude of associations and the interventions of the State of Israel have replaced the largely personal diplomacy of the leaders of English and French Jewry. Strategies for rescue have evolved together with the development of this organizational structure. The purpose of this book is to trace and examine these transformations.

In the first part of this volume, there are case studies that illustrate and analyse the emergence of international rescue organizations from the middle of the nineteenth century until the First World War. The second part presents essays that deal with how Jews attempted rescue in Europe and the Middle East during massive upheavals in the period of the two World Wars. The studies in the third and final part deal with the Jews of Ethiopia, the Soviet Union, North Africa and France, and illustrate the contemporary context in which the role of Israel and American Jewry has become paramount.

The case studies brought forward here indicate the richness of the topic although they clearly do not exhaust it. By placing these essays in the framework suggested above we have tried to illuminate the modern patterns of Jewish communal response to persecution and the impact of Jewish national solidarity.

NOTES

1. Katz, Jacob, *Out of the Ghetto; the Social Background of Jewish Emancipation 1770–1870* (Cambridge, 1973); Ettinger, Shmuel, 'The Modern Period,' in *A History of the Jewish People* (Cambridge, 1976), ed. H. H. Ben-Sasson, pp.800–33, 847–58; Hertzberg, Arthur, *The French Enlightenment and the Jews* (New York, 1968); Albert, Phyllis Cohen, *The Modernization of French Jewry; Consistory and Community in the Nineteenth Century* (Hanover, N. H., 1977).
2. Bashan, Eliezer, *Captivity and Ransom in Mediterranean Jewish Society, 1391–1830* [Hebrew] (Ramat Gan, 1980), pp.19–28. Bashan's study concludes approximately where this volume begins.
3. Maimonides, *Hilchot Matanot Ani'im*, 8, 10. See Bashan, p.23.

4. Goitein, S. D., *A Mediterranean Society* (Berkeley, 1976), Vols. I–II; Bashan, pp.29 ff.
5. Stern, Selma, *The Court Jew; A Contribution to the History of the Period of Absolutism in Central Europe* (Philadelphia, 1950).
6. Mevorah, Baruch, 'The Consequences of the Damascus Affair on the Development of the Jewish Press, 1840–46' [Hebrew], *Zion*, XXIII–XXIV (1958–59), 46–65; Lipman, Sonia and V.D., *The Century of Moses Montefiore* (Oxford, 1985), Parts II and IV.
7. Chouraqui, André, *L'alliance israélite universelle et la renaissance juive contemporaire, 1860–1960* (Paris, 1965).
8. Luard, Evan, *International Agencies; The Emerging Framework of Interdependence* (London, 1977).
9. Wyman, David, *Paper Walls; America and the Refugee Crisis 1938–1941* (Amherst, 1968), Chapters 1–3; Henry L. Feingold, *The Politics of Rescue; The Roosevelt Administration and the Holocaust, 1938–1945* (New Brunswick, 1970), Chapter 2.
10. The history of the interplay between a major Jewish organization and the American government is captured in Cohen, Naomi, *Not Free to Desist; A History of the American Jewish Committee, 1906–1966* (Philadelphia, 1972).
11. See the following article by Oppenheim, Israel, 'The Kovno Circle of Rabbi Yitzhak Elhanan Spektor; Organizing Public Opinion over Pogroms in the 1880s.'
12. The attitudes of German Jews towards Eastern Jews are complex and under active debate. See Volkov, Shulamit, 'The Dynamics of Dissimilation; Ostjuden and German Jews,' in Reinharz, Jehuda and Walter Schatzberg, *The Jewish Response to German Culture; From the Enlightenment to the Second World War* (Hanover, N.H., 1985), 195–211; Reinharz, Jehuda, *Fatherland or Promised Land; The Dilemma of the German Jew, 1893–1914* (Ann Arbor, 1975), esp. Ch.3; and Aschheim, Steven E., *Brothers and Strangers; The East European Jew in German and German Jewish Consciousness, 1800–1923* (Madison, 1982). Similar problems are to be found in the United States at this time as these attitudes characterized the communal relations between Jews of German origin and immigrants from Eastern Europe. It is well illustrated by the support given by Jacob Schiff to the Galveston Plan and the tensions in creating the New York Kehillah. See, for example, Karp, Abraham, *Haven and Home; A History of the Jews in America* (New York, 1985), chapters 6–9; Goren, Arthur, *New York Jews and the Quest for Community; The Kehillah Experiment, 1908–1912* (New York, 1970), pp.12 ff.
13. Handlin, Oscar and Handlin, Mary, 'A Century of Jewish Immigration to the United States,' *American Jewish Year Book 1948–1949*, Vol.50, pp.1–84.
14. Rischin, Moses, *The Promised City; New York's Jews, 1870–1914* (Cambridge, Mass., 1962); Goren, Arthur, *New York Jews and the Quest for Community*; Lurie, Harry L., *The Jewish Federation Movement in America; A Heritage Affirmed* (Philadelphia, 1961), pp.1–58.
15. *American Jewish Year Book for 1987* (New York, 1987), Vol. 87, pp.367 and ff.
16. The statements of purpose are conveniently collected in the appendix on organizations to be found at the end of recent editions of the *American Jewish Year Book*.
17. Gal, Allon, *David Ben-Gurion – Preparing for a Jewish State; Political Alignment in Response to the White Paper and the Outbreak of World War II, 1938–1941* (Sede Boqer, 1987)[Hebrew].
18. Bauer, Yehuda, *From Diplomacy to Resistance; a History of Jewish Palestine 1939–1945* (Philadelphia, 1970); Porath, Dina, *An Entangled Leadership; the Yishuv and the Holocaust 1942–1945* [Hebrew] (Tel-Aviv, 1987); and Friling, Tuvia, 'Ben-Gurion and the Holocaust of European Jewry 1939–1945; A Stereotype Reexamined,' *Yad Vashem Studies*, Vol. 18, 1987, pp.199–232.
19. Wyman, David, *The Abandonment of the Jews* (New York, 1984); Feingold, Henry L., *The Politics of Rescue*; Penkower, Monty, *The Jews Were Expendable; Free World Diplomacy and the Holocaust* (Chicago, 1983); Morse, Arthur, *While Six*

## INTRODUCTION 1: THE RESCUE OF THE JEWS

*Million Died; A Chronicle of American Apathy* (New York, 1968).
20. 'State of Israel: Aliyah and Absorption,' *Encyclopedia Judaica*, v. 9, p.535.
21. 'Immigration to Palestine and Israel,' *Encyclopedia of Zionism and Israel*, Vol.1, pp.534–8.
22. Schmelz, U. O. and Della Pergola, Sergio, 'World Jewish Population, 1984,' *American Jewish Year Book, 1986* (New York, 1986), pp.350–64.
23. Bensimon, Doris and Della Pergola, Sergio, *La Population juive de France; sociodémographie et identité* (Jerusalem, 1984); Michael M. Laskier, *The Alliance Israélite Universelle and the Jewish Communities of Morocco, 1862–1962* (Albany, 1963).
24. Davis, Moshe, ed., *World Jewry and the State of Israel* (New York, 1977), Part III and Davis, Moshe, ed., *Zionism in Transition* (New York, 1980).
25. Pinkus, Benjamin, *Russian and Soviet Jews; Annals of a National Minority* (Sede Boqer, 1986)[Hebrew], Chapter 6; Orbach, William, *The American Movement to Aid Soviet Jews* (Amherst, 1979).

# 2

# The Redemption of Captives in Halakhic Tradition: Problems and Policy

## Ya'akov Blidstein

Although my topic is the 'redemption of captives' in the Halakha over the generations, I should like at first to widen the scope of the subject somewhat and deal not only with Halakha but also with tradition as a whole. In other words, I shall include not only norms of conduct but also the larger framework into which this activity fits. An attempt to consider the redemption of captives in this broader perspective means that we have to begin with the basic formative experience of the Jewish people, the memory of slavery in the dawn of the nation's history and the redemption from that slavery. The Hebrew term for that redemption, *Geulah*, is derived, it is well known, from the legal sphere and its original meaning was restoration to the bosom of the family ('one of his brothers may redeem him,' Leviticus, xxv, 48) or to the setting in which the person naturally belonged and from which he had been torn. This term was later taken over to the historical and meta-historical plane, and there too *Geulah* signified the return of the whole group to its original bounds, the abolition of the condition of being foreigners and in danger.[1] Even the root of the Hebrew verb, 'to redeem' (p-d-h), has a specially profound semantic significance and deep axiological echoes. Originating in the human-legal sphere, it too expanded perhaps to mean the individual's being rescued by his God from physical danger and also the soul's redemption from the dominion of sin and transgression, and over and over again the verb refers to the entire people's being led out of bondage – 'I [brought thee up out of the land of Egypt and] redeemed thee out of the house of servants' (Micah, vi, 4), says the Lord to his people.

The act of redemption and release from physical confinement is

## INTRODUCTION 2: THE REDEMPTION OF CAPTIVES

thus engraved deep in the national consciousness, and we should not be surprised when a fourteenth-century commentator explained God's identifying himself as the God who led his people out of Egypt (and not as the creator of the world), by referring to the supreme worth of the redemption of captives. Thus the circle is in fact closed: collective *Geulah* is applied in miniature to the rescue of the individual or small group.[2]

It is not my intention to take 'redemption of captives' out of its material and practical context. It is clear that the duty to have the captive freed was a response to simple physical and social needs and it was therefore imposed as a contractual responsibility of a husband towards his wife (the duty of redemption is one of the conditions of the marriage contract) – something that testifies incidentally to the fact that captivity was a fact of life. Redemption was a responsibility of a Jew towards his neighbour, of the community towards its own members and of the Jewish people as a whole towards other parts of the Jewish nation. That a similar responsibility is indeed felt by every human collectivity is well known. The Jewish people, however, whether because of its special socio-historical condition or because of the system of norms it had internalized, does seem to have viewed the redemption of captives as a particularly heavy responsibility and a virtuous and necessary deed.[3] This was of course due to the physical danger involved in captivity, but the classical and halakhic 'captivity' was not always bound up with a threat to life. A Jew confined in a foreign prison for non-payment of a debt is considered to be a 'captive'[4] and it follows, then, that the notion of redemption of captives has a very wide connotation. Restoring someone to his home is no less important and central than his rescue from physical harm, and preservation of identity becomes the equivalent of preservation of life. We should not be surprised to find, therefore, that the medieval sages mandate redemption of captives because the captive is thereby redeemed from sin and enabled to live a free, Jewish, life. This is a consideration in halakhic debates, but it is apparent that it also reflects a significant value stratum.[5]

I

As previously indicated, we had better not stray too far from the concrete and practical connotation of redemption of captives. It would be possible to tell the historical story and point to periods when the Jews carried out this responsibility in a broad and aggressive way and places where the net of Jewish solidarity was spread out to cover wide areas. On the other hand it is possible to point to periods and places when the Jews drew themselves in and reduced their activity. Most important, one can try to clarify and explain the causes of these phenomena. However, I want to emphasize the theoretical side, that is to say the norm itself, its interpretation, the problems of principle it raised and the moral and social decisions it called for.[6]

Here we are face to face with the basic but characteristic paradox. On the one hand, the tradition stresses the duty to get the prisoner out of his prison and demands intensive, uncompromising public exertions to this end. The words of Maimonides guided individuals and communities: 'There is no greater precept laid upon you than the redemption of captives'[7] (and incidentally the Rambam in person carried out what he demanded of others) 'for the captive is a part of the generality of the hungry, the thirsty and the naked and faces a threat to his life. To turn a blind eye to his redemption is to transgress [the precepts] "Thou shalt not harden thy heart" and "Thou shalt not close thy fist" and "Thou shalt not stand idly by the blood of thy neighbour" and "Thou shalt not rule over him with rigour", and to violate the precept "Open thy hand wide to him" and the precepts, "That thy brother live with you", and "Love thy neighbour as thyself" and "Rescue those taken to die" and many other similar things. And there is no greater precept than redemption of captives.' As against this unequivocal stand, however, halakhic literature itself bears witness to the ancient conflict over the nature of the practical implementation of the redemption of captives, and over the relative status of this duty compared with other norms, other values, and competing needs. There is in fact nothing surprising about this, since indeed the halakhic story is always that of confrontation between competing norms and values and of deciding their order of precedence. So on this matter of ours, too, the sages did not rest until they had clarified the question: redemption of prisoners – always? – in all circumstances? At all costs? In sum, it is possible to point to a trend that restricted the possibility of redemption of the captive under pressure from other needs and values and also to a different trend firmly maintaining the primacy of the redemption of the captive. The classic formulation of the restrictive trend is the enactment 'Captives should not be ransomed for more than their value, as a precaution for the good of society.'[8]

The Halakha did try its hand, then, at limiting and restricting, but the attempt was doomed to fail. The trend in favour of rescuing prisoners at all costs won the day in the end, and the halakhic authorities in the main defended this latter principle. There were two reasons for their acting in this way: (a) the attempt to restrict the individual and the community in rescuing prisoners was in the class of edicts that the public cannot accept (the reference is to the public in the more ideal sense, for there is no lack of examples of communities that refused to hold out a helping hand or at least acted in close-fisted fashion); (b) such limitation and restriction was an extreme position which did not treat other values, most honoured in the Halakha, with sufficient seriousness.

That is the tale I wish to tell.

## II

The Mishnah places two basic restrictions on actions for rescuing prisoners: they are not to be ransomed at an exorbitant price, and they are not to be helped to escape, that is to say they are not to be freed by force, but this second restriction already met with resistance in the Mishnaic period itself. The Talmudic interpretation is of the opinion that Rabbi Shimon Ben Gamliel, in the generation after the Bar Kochba revolt, contended that those helping prisoners to escape are restricted only in that they have to free *all of them* and not leave a single captive behind to suffer from the wrath of the captors and the hard conditions that will follow from the freeing of their fellows.[9] At all events, even Rabbi Shimon Ben Gamliel concedes that a captive does not always have to be freed even if it is physically possible, nor does he differ from the Mishnah on the first restriction: captives do not have to be (or ought not to be) redeemed at an exorbitant price. It emerges furthermore that this enactment is binding not only on the public but also on individuals, including members of the captive's family – they too are barred from redeeming him at an exaggerated price.[10]

The reasoning behind all this is clear. The restrictive policy crystallized here derives from concern over the grave long-term consequences of the readiness to pay an exorbitant price, not only as regards raising the price that will be demanded in the future for redeeming prisoners but also the actual encouragement offered to capture members of the community (i.e. Jews) prepared to pay an exorbitant price for them (as indeed testified to in the history of Israel). We have here, therefore, the classic characteristics of a typical piece of halakhic-ethical legislation: (a) the denial of the right of the individual to utilize his power and his private resources as he wishes, so as to prevent broader public harm, and (b) a rejection of a positive act that bears within itself the prospect of future dangers graver than the positive value of the good deed at the present time.

This position, however, comes up against opposition and is narrowed almost to the point of being annulled in spite of its elevated and binding origins. More accurately, it is preserved practically entire in the preeminent codices of Maimonides and the Shulhan Arukh, as if nothing had changed; however, the writers of the *Responsa*, Talmudic interpreters, and many decisors in fact questioned its soundness. The first signs of these doubts over the enactment are already to be seen in the Talmud, which not only gives an account of a man who redeems his daughter at an exaggerated price but even relates how the Tanna, Rabbi Yehoshua, was prepared to redeem a boy from Roman captivity 'for any sum of money demanded' and it is hard not to see here that even if this does not criticize the enactment it in fact ignores it.[11] Furthermore, the Talmud deliberates on the rationale at the base of the enactment: does it stem from the grave long-term consequences of the present exaggerated payment, or is it the damage done to the public purse now which is feared? The focus of this question is whether the enactment restricts both the public and *the private individual*, since it creates a *policy* that does not permit of transgression, or whether the enactment lays down a public standard only, while the private individual remains free to act as he sees fit.[12] The question itself almost invites a much wider breach of the enactment – and in the late Middle Ages the breach was indeed opened in practice:[13] if our enactment is intended to conserve the public purse (and not to influence moves concerning captivity in the future), then *each and every community* is authorized to decide the issue according to its own situation. Therewith the enactment becomes relatively flexible. One way or another, the Mishnah was watered down over the generations. The enactment was not challenged head on, but it 'died the death of a thousand qualifications' (to use the expression of the American philosopher, William James). It would appear that these qualifications do indeed indicate the problematic nature of legislation which demands the certain and immediate sacrifice of the victim (leaving the captive in his prison) for fear of a distant and doubtful danger. The outcome was that observance of the enactment declined.

The Tosafists, for instance[14] (in the twelfth and thirteenth

## INTRODUCTION 2: THE REDEMPTION OF CAPTIVES

centuries), argued that the Mishnaic enactment does imply that the captive was endangered[15] (but that plain 'captivity' in the Mishnah is not a place where the captive's life is really in immediate danger)[16] or if he was a sage (historically, by the way, Jews were more concerned over women and children than over sages, and this despite the trend in halakhic literature in favour of giving precedence to sages)[17] or in time of war, when captivity is not the result of a deliberate choice but results from conditions on the spot where over-payment will not influence the course of events. It is a fair conclusion that this list of qualifications was not produced so as theoretically to reconcile contradictory texts, as it were; it appears rather to reflect the real state of affairs, in which the Mishnaic enactment was not observed to the letter and captives were redeemed at all costs.[18] (It is worth adding, parenthetically, that captors generally demanded – and got – 'exorbitant' prices from people of various nationalities. So a Jew who paid a price of this kind, far more than what the man was worth on the slave market, paid no more than his non-Jewish neighbour did for *his* captive, and from this point of view did not 'over'-pay. The halakhic authorities, however, took the line that the price must be paid in order to free the captive, even if the sum was not only higher than the price of a slave in the market but also higher than the price of a captive who was not a Jew.)[19]

In the centuries that followed new qualifications were added to those I have noted. I have already mentioned the contention of Rabbi Shlomo Luria that it was especially necessary to take into consideration the fact that captivity would prevent a Jew from obeying the religious precepts – a danger that certainly did exist in most cases. The Tosafists' contention that in wartime prisoners are not consciously selected and accordingly Jewish readiness to overpay will not have any influence, was broadened even further; it was now argued that the level of prices had no marked influence at all on the habits of captors. There were even those who (as if in all innocence and ignoring the Halakha ruling) reverted to the idea that the Mishnaic enactment was merely intended to protect the public purse and left the final decision to each community. There were of course halakhic theorists who supported the norm as it stood, but they were a minority. The majority shelved the enactment in practice if not in law.[20]

How are we to interpret this trend? Have we here merely another example of a law's retreat in the face of a social reality too strong to be resisted? True, the classic halakhic codes, Maimonides and the Shulhan Arukh, show hardly any compromise on the strict enactment, and there is, moreover, no doubt that part of the argumentation for shelving the enactment is very weak in the light of the Talmudic and post-Talmudic sources. The sages who presented this argumentation were certainly aware of its weaknesses. Do we not have a drama whose lines are dictated by social conditions, while in their hearts the halakhic jurists themselves are not reconciled to what they are doing?

The truth would seem to be rather different. When we observe that it was precisely the halakhic jurists who initiated and led the effort to redeem captives – and here too the Rambam is a striking example of this in his exertions on behalf of the captives taken after the massacre by Amalric, King of the Crusader Kingdom of Jerusalem, in the city of Bilbeis in 1168 – we become aware that the Mishnaic enactment did not sufficiently oblige these Rabbis to make them say and get them to make the Halakha say what they did not, in fact, want to say. It looks, rather, as if these sages saw themselves bound to uphold the enactment formally, but did not consider it legally just and vital. They no longer agreed that the basic assumption held good and they neither believed that refusal to pay an exorbitant price would produce any long-term benefit, nor saw justification for abandoning a Jew and leaving him physically and spiritually defenceless. This is exactly what the sages are saying when they cast doubt on the possibility of influencing patterns of captivity by refusal to pay exorbitant prices, or when they indicate that these patterns are not influenced at all by the line of conduct adopted by one or another community.

It is, of course, possible to interpret the erosion of the Mishnaic enactment as reflecting the loss of ability to endure suffering, a loss of willingness to sacrifice on behalf of the whole community, a sort of rejection of halakhic responsibility characteristic of life in the Exile with its lack of binding communal and national feeling. So Rabbi Shlomo Luria argued in favour of redeeming the Jew at all costs, adducing the fact that 'Israel in Exile is smaller now and one must hasten to the aid of the remaining remnant lest it burn out in the embers of Israel' (meaning, 'lest the embers of Israel burn out'). But it seems that it is precisely the stand taken by the sages of the early and late Middle Ages which best combines normative values with social ones, while it is precisely the Mishnaic enactment that calls for explanation and justification, and it is a pity that we do not know more about the social conditions which those who laid down the ruling wanted to influence in their day.[21] At all events, the later sages appear to have acted in a balanced and reasonable manner.

INTRODUCTION 2: THE REDEMPTION OF CAPTIVES

## III

I have confined myself to a very particular aspect of the subject of solidarity in tradition and Halakha, and there are certainly other aspects that could and should be expatiated on. I have even restricted myself to the issue centring on the individual and not on the link between any given community and its fellow. I did so because, *inter alia*, the redemption of prisoners is frequently the subject of contemporary discussion. In the light of the survey that I have presented, I wish to close with a brief comment.

Not seldom do we hear that readiness to pay an exaggerated 'price' for prisoners is against Jewish tradition, since 'Captives are not redeemed at more than their price.' We have to remember, however, that the enactment which is the core of this contention was repudiated time and again as inconsistent with the halakhic norms supposed to be the rule governing the real state of affairs. And even in our day, incidentally, there are halakhic authorities who deny that the Mishnah in question has relevance for the reality of the State of Israel and its army. Anyone who wishes to argue that this Mishnah is indeed relevant must of course draw distinctions between different kinds of 'captives' and different kinds of 'prices,' and that is not always a simple matter. For example, is there a difference between civilian hostages and soldiers who have been taken prisoner?

In the end, some will assert that the moral decision laid down in the Mishnah does in fact fit present-day conditions of communications and politics, an epoch that has already long been termed the 'global village,' where everything done (or not done) in one corner of the world is echoed and its lesson learnt in every other corner. Anyone arguing in favour of the validity of the old enactment maintains the assumption of the Mishnah that it is possible to foresee what will happen in this realm and to influence it – and this also means deciding that the long-term prospect justifies short-term suffering, danger, and even loss of life for the individual. This calls for a serious degree of self-scrutiny to ensure that one is acting from a genuine desire to prevent future disaster and not because life is cheap in the present. Clearly, someone who affirms that one must see the analogy between our Mishnah and prisoners-of-war or terror in our day is not just applying the Mishnaic enactment mechanically and simplistically, but is adding a bold new link to the interpretation and implementation of this ancient enactment.

It is not a matter, then, of continuing to apply a Mishnaic enactment endowed with historical continuity. Instead, it is a matter of renewing the enactment under new conditions. In the light of the history of the enactment and its metamorphoses, we realize that this is not something that can be seen as a matter of course, but must be viewed as a decision that still imposes a painful responsibility.

NOTES

1. See I.E. Zeligman, 'Geulah,' *Entsyklopediah Mikra'it*, 2, columns 389–91; D. Daube, *Studies in Biblical Law*, Cambridge, 1941, pp.39–62.
2. See B'hai b-Asher, *Kad ha-Kemah, Tsadaka* (end). See too Midrash T'hilim, 4.
3. A great deal of material on our subject is to be found in E. Bashan's book, *Shviyah v-Padut*, Ramat-Gan, 1980, and also in (Bashan) Sternberg's article in the *Bar-Ilan Annual*, 1968, Vol.5, pp.238–62; see also note 18 below. For antiquity, see S. Baron, *SRHI*, 1, pp.259, 281.
4. Rambam, *Milveh ve-Loveh*, I, 5; and see Bashan, *op.cit.*, p.19, n.1.
5. Yam Shel Shlomo, Gittin, Ch.4, Section 65; Radbaz, Responsa, Part 5, Section 2, 2064. Radbaz suggests the possibility of forced conversion.
6. There is a good summation of the halakhic problem in Shaviv, 'Birurim Behilkhot Pidayon Shvui'im,' *Noam*, 1974, pp.97–115.
7. *Matnot Ani'im*, 8, 1. It looks as if these statements go beyond the Talmudic sources and testify to the seriousness with which Rambam approached the subject, a seriousness reflected in his energetic action in redeeming captives in practice. It also emerges from the documents published by S.D. Goitein in 'P'ulato shel ha-Rambam Le Pidayon Shvui'im b'Eretz Yisrael,' in *Yishuv be-Eretz Israel bereshit ha-Islam u'betkufat ha-tsalbanim*, Jerusalem, 1980, pp.312–20. It seems that Maimonides' general concern for this Mitsvah constitutes a more palatable explanation for his activities than that recently offered by Goitein: '... making each and every member of the community acquainted with Maimonides' name ... a first-rate publicity stunt.' S.D. Goitein, 'Maimonides, Man of Action,' in *Hommage à Georges Vajda*, Louvain, 1980, p.162.
8. Mishnah Gittin, 4, 6.
9. Bavli Gittin 44, a, but see H. Albek, *Researches in Bra'ita and Tosefta and their relationship to the Talmud* [Hebrew] (Jerusalem, 1944), p.145, note 1.
10. This is the line taken in the Gittin sugyah, *loc. cit.*, though it does not bring the topic to a conclusion; it is clearly to be heard in the stand of R. Simeon b. Gsmliel in Gittin 52, a-b, as is noted by many of the medievals.
11. Gittin, *loc.cit.*, 58a. If Sternberg's supposition (see note 3 above) that the Bavli text meant to give preference to redeeming a sage is correct, then the critical tone I stress is found in the Yerushalmi and the Tosefta version of the story of Rabbi Yehoshua.
12. Gittin, *loc. cit.*, and see Rashi's commentary in its continuation after the sugyah that follows later. Besides the practical consequences flowing from these attitudes, we can also consider the theoretical aspect: does one legislate to limit the individual even on the ground of the predicted damage to the public in the future, or only on the ground of the present public situation? It should be noted, incidentally, that it is difficult to explain the Mishnah – 'books, t'fillin and m'zuzot are not to be had from non-Jews at more than their worth for the sake of the welfare of the world' – in order that 'the non-Jew should not become accustomed to stealing' as the commentators have it, since even if the nominal value is paid, this too encourages the thief (who made no investment in writing the Sefer-Torah!), and here we see that the main

## INTRODUCTION 2: THE REDEMPTION OF CAPTIVES

contention is that concern for the public purse serves 'the welfare of the world.'
13. See for example, Rabbi Asher Gittin, Ch.4, section 34, and R. Yoel Sirkis, *Ba'it Hadash (Bah) Tur; Yoreh De'ah*, section 242, s.v., 'one does not redeem.'
14. Gittin, 35a, s.v. *op.cit*, 58a, s.v. *kal*.
15. It is usually thought that a school exists which differs from this view and which is of the opinion that the enactment must be sustained even at the cost of loss of life, and with Rambam and Ramban as the foremost exponents of this attitude. I am not sure that it is correct to present this issue so unequivocally. Rambam does not deal explicitly with this possibility and it is only possible to infer his position by citing his statement that the captive 'is in danger to life' (*Matanot Ani'im*, 8,6) and from the fact that only someone sold to non-Jews, someone 'whom they wanted to kill, he is to be redeemed from their hands, even after several times' (*loc.cit.*, Halakha, 13). But this is the language of the Talmud, and – more important – a man 'in danger to life' is not yet a case of certain loss of life, and it may be that in such a case our rabbi would identify our captive with the man sold to a non-Jew (as Rabbi Menahem Hame'iri did, indeed). Ramban's words also call for second thoughts, for he differs (Gittin, *loc. cit.*) from those who would annul the enactment 'when there is fear of danger to life' but it is not clear how he would deal with a case of *certain* loss of life. Did the sages in fact demand observance of the Mishnah enactment in a place of death? Compare Shaviv, *op.cit*.
16. Mishnah Horayot, 3,7, where a distinction is drawn between 'to restore [the man] to life' and 'to get [him] out of captivity'. On the other hand, the impression is that the sages tended to see captivity in their day as a state of 'danger to life' and supported redemption at all costs. As regards the status of a woman captive who is redeemed, on the other hand, they assumed that she had not been endangered and they accordingly laid down that she could be married; see also what I wrote in *Shnaton ha-mishpat ha-ivri* 3/4, 1976, pp.40–55. Similar phenomena are known in the history of the Halakha, according to the recent researches of Katz and Soloveitchik. True, we must also remember that the marriage ban on a woman captive in general is based on doubt, and so the stricter assumption need not be made.
17. See Sternberg, *op. cit.*, pp.256–60.
18. The story of Rabbi Yehoshua seems a very slight problem compared with the various solutions put forward by the Tosafists in order to reconcile it with the Mishnah, all the more so since it was always possible to answer that this story (which happened at the time of the destruction of the Temple) took place before the enactment had been made. At all events, there is no sign anywhere of any proof that the enactment not to redeem captives for more than their worth did in fact influence the course of events, and we are definitely of the impression that Jews paid whatever they could. See Sternberg, *op. cit.*, and Goitein (*A Mediterranean Society*, 1, pp.329–30; *idem*, 'Social Services of the Jewish Community,' *J.S.S.*, 1964, No. 26, pp.79–80), who recounts how astonished the non-Jews were at the solidarity of the Jews and how they burst out in paeans of praise (Psalms 144, 15). And indeed the story told by Rabbi Shlomo Luria (*op. cit., Yam shel Shlomo*) – some 300 years after the event! – about the refusal of Rabbi Me'ir of Rotenberg to let the communities redeem him out of obedience to the enactment, is put forward as 'tradition,' but it is hard to know how trustworthy it is historically, all the more so as there are also other ways to explain both what happened and the fact itself of this contention being brought forward.
19. Responsa, Radbaz, Part I, Section 30. A certain difficulty in defining 'as much as their [the captives'] worth' is already manifest in Rabbi Menahem Hame'iri *cf*. Beit ha-b'hirah on Gittin 34a, K. Schlesinger (ed.), Jerusalem, 1955, 2, 197–198, with Beit ha-b'hirah to Ketubot 52a, 2nd ed., A. Sofer (ed.), Jerusalem, 1947, p.194. This problem is only exacerbated the further one moves away from times and places where people are sold as slaves.
20. See Shaviv, *op. cit.*, and also Bashan, *op. cit.*, pp.215–20.

21. All this, of course, is on the assumption that the Mishnah enactment was intended to prevent Jews from being taken captive in the future and did not stem from the need to protect the public purse, since this last is a matter of course (in all periods).

PART ONE

# From the Damascus Affair to the First World War

# 3

# The Crisis as a Factor in Modern Jewish Politics, 1840 and 1881–1882

## Jonathan Frankel

The crisis created by acts of Judeophobic, anti-Semitic aggression played a crucial role in the history of the Jewish people during the nineteenth century. A direct challenge to the security of the Jews in one country or another could not go unanswered, especially when, as was so often the case, it came in times of peace and relative tranquillity. The Jews had to respond in some way. But how to interpret the challenge? How best to react? These were questions of the highest complexity; and the answers varied radically according to time and place.

So long as they lived their lives in the Diaspora, scattered and essentially landless minorities, the Jews as a collectivity did not have to face the tests regularly imposed on sovereign nations by war and revolution. Of course, such all-engulfing eruptions caught up Jews and Jewish communities, often with far-reaching results, but only as parts within a greater whole. In contrast, events such as the Damascus blood libel of 1840, the Mortara case of 1858, the recurring anti-Jewish excesses in Rumania during the 1870s, the pogroms of 1881–82, the expulsion from Moscow ten years later, and the Dreyfus Affair involved the Jews, first and foremost, precisely as Jews, as a collective entity. It is this fact that lends these episodes their unique importance for the historian of modern Jewry. In studying them, he may hope to find his way to realities, forces, that in normal times remain hidden far beneath the surface of everyday existence. In this sense these crises in Jewish life were the nearest equivalent to war and revolution in the history of a state, a sovereign society. At such a juncture, every assumption, however time-honoured, may be called into question, and ideas normally too utopian to voice, can enter the discourse of the everyday. This is the extraordinary moment in the onward flow of time.

Crisis brought a number of interconnected issues into play. To what extent did the Jews act in accord with a sense of solidarity? How far did this impulse embrace Jewry across international frontiers – across Europe? Throughout the world? Had not acculturation, assimilation, allegiance to the host society, nation, nationalism undermined, in part or *in toto*, supraterritorial loyalties? With Judaism and Jewry under the most intense scrutiny, what positions were adopted by the public at large, by the various strata that in every country made up the majority society? And how, in turn, did these reactions influence the response of the Jews? Above all, was that response effective? And did it bring with it any lasting change in attitudes or institutions?

## I

Of all such episodes in the nineteenth century, by far the most significant was surely that involving the pogroms and the reaction to them in the years 1881–82. There are strong grounds for seeing here a decisive turning point. From then on can be dated the gradual but unbroken emergence of the new movements that in constant rivalry and interaction would transform the structure and content of Jewish politics – Jewish (Yiddish-speaking) socialism and populism, proto-Zionism (Hibbat Zion), and territorialism. On one side of the divide, according to this historiographical perception, was the era in which the Jews of Europe expected emancipation and worked for integration into the host societies; while, on the other, stretched the era in which the goal was increasingly proclaimed to be auto-emancipation, collective liberation, national self-determination.

Given that this thesis, however schematic and one-dimensional, is essentially correct (and there seems to be no adequate reason to doubt that it is), there still remain a number of related and fundamental questions facing the historian. In particular, it has to be asked in what relationship Jewish nationalism and socialism, increasingly important after 1881–82, stood to the politics that had previously predominated – to the 'emancipationist' system on the one hand, and to the 'traditional' on the other.[1]

## II

There are, of course, highly complex and emotive issues involved here. Indeed, to take just one important example, a reader turning for enlightenment on this subject to such a *locus classicus* as the essays (*Be-mifneh ha-dorot*) by the late Ben Zion Dinur will find it difficult, although perhaps not impossible, to reconcile the various strands of thought to be found there. Dinur saw the primary theme in modern Jewish history as the constant struggle within the collective organism between integrative and disintegrative, centripetal and centrifugal forces. Very much in the manner of Perez Smolenskin and Ahad Ha-Am, he described Westernization in Jewish life, the Berlin Haskalah, and the process of integration into the host societies during the nineteenth century in terms of self-denigration and, indeed, self-destruction.[2]

In the context of this struggle, Dinur discerned a number of disparate forces that nonetheless supplied Jewry with the vitality to survive. Most notably, he traced a new determination to resettle the Holy Land back to the late seventeenth century and saw there the beginnings of an unbroken process that would culminate eventually in Hibbat Zion and Herzlian Zionism. He dated the start of the modern period in Jewish history not from Baruch Spinoza or the Haskalah or the French Revolution but from about 1700, particularly from the aliyah in that year of Yehuda He-Hasid and his followers. Dinur discovered the modernity in this group of ultra-observant and, to all appearances, highly traditional Jews in their readiness to undertake the large-scale move to the Holy Land even before the coming of the Messiah.[3] In sum, he stressed the high degree of continuity that in his view fused the nationalism of post-1881–82 with the rabbinic, self-enclosed but nonetheless (as he saw it) modern world of piety.

To round out the picture, Dinur could simply have emphasized those facts that illustrated the ever-growing inroads made by assimilation and disintegration in Western Jewry. But he was far too sensitive a historian to do that. And he duly noted the Jewish solidarity that manifested itself in such affairs as the Damascus case, the proliferation of the new and extensive Jewish press, and establishment of such organizations as the Alliance Israélite Universelle.[4] What remains unclarified is how these examples of communal vitality in the West could be explained. Were they merely the exception that proves the rule, or perhaps a reassertion of the collective subconscious still fed subterraneously from the sources of age-old tradition, or, again, a premonition of later nationalism? Had Dinur pursued this line of questioning further he might have modified his tendency to describe modernization and Haskalah as simply standing in direct negation to forces of collective survival, to the continuum made up of traditional Judaism and Jewish nationalism.

As against Dinur's approach, it will be argued here that, in fact, the historian is best served by first conceptualizing the three categories under discussion – the traditional, the liberal or emancipationist, the postliberal or autoemancipationist – as strictly separate categories. Once they are initially held separate, as it were, the attempt can be made to trace the ways in which they interacted. Rather than Dinur's dichotomous analysis, the basic framework, then, becomes triadic, and the primary process, rather than linear, becomes dialectic – with a thesis (the traditional), an antithesis (emancipationism) and a synthesis (autoemancipationism).

But that can only be a beginning. To go a step further with Hegelian terminology, one stage is not only negated by the next but is also subsumed within it. A discontinuity, however sharp, can still encompass a high degree of continuity. Moreover, beyond this, it has to be remembered that the Jewish people during the nineteenth century increasingly took on the forms of voluntary association as the communities lost much of their autonomous (state-backed) power. Emergent movements, however popular or confident, did not have the means to crush or eliminate preexisting institutions and ways of thought. The old continued to exist side by side with the intermediate and the new. Internal revolution within the Jewish collectivity involved no bloodshed, no expropriation, not even in most cases any clear transfer of power, but rather the proliferation of rival power centres, movements, and ideologies. Such revolution is indeed very much more a historiographical construct than a clearly defined historical event.

### III

Crises such as those of 1881–82 and 1840 indeed cannot be fully understood except in terms of constant interaction among the highly disparate, often hostile, forces at work within, and on the periphery of, the Jewish world. True, in the period from April 1881 until the summer of 1882, the most conspicuous development was the emergence, almost overnight, of a politics radical in thought and action, in content and style, within the Russian-Jewish world. A new phenomenon with the most far-reaching consequences, autoemancipationism, has naturally riveted attention on itself.[5] The emigrationist ideas, whether centred on a territory in North America or on Palestine, were, of course, not entirely new; but the widespread support now given them, in the wake of the pogroms, undoubtedly was. So, too, was the startling analysis of M.L. Lilienblum in his article of October 1881 in *Razsvet* (Dawn), where he argued that the high point of European liberalism had been passed and that the rising waves of extreme nationalism were bound, eventually, to make life simply untenable for an awkward minority such as the Jews.[6]

In the name of *Palestinstvo* (a proto-Zionism) and *Amerikanstvo* (a proto-territorialism), the intelligentsia challenged the political leadership of the St. Petersburg oligarchy (the Ginsburgs, the Poliakovs) and the spiritual leadership of the inward-looking rabbinical circles. It sought to assume these roles for itself.[7] To mobilize public opinion, poets, writers, journalists, and students made remarkably effective, unprecedented use of the Jewish press, both in Hebrew and in Russian, as well as of mass petitions and synagogue demonstrations.[8]

The founding of the agricultural colonization parties or youth movements – Am Olam and the Bilu[9] – did more than anything else to demonstrate the intense atmosphere of the times and the depth of the commitment. The dramatic departure of many hundreds of young men and women determined to lay the foundations of a Jewish territory in the American West or in Palestine made a deep impression on Russian Jewry. Although the emigrants' grandiose schemes soon shattered on the rocks of harsh reality, the change in the nature of Russian-Jewish politics was to prove both permanent and profound.[10]

What took place in 1881–82, however, cannot be adequately described in these terms alone, even though the radically innovative developments surely represent the most important theme. The truth is that strands drawn from the traditional, premodern, strata of Russian Jewry were thickly interwoven into the fabric of events at this juncture. The most obvious example, perhaps, is the fact that the great majority of the Jews who went to settle the land in Palestine in the early 1880s were fully observant Jews, many from Rumania, eager to maintain the ordinances as laid down by rabbinic law and, it would seem, moved to become colonists as the result of religious impulse. Of course, this does not mean that they would have contemplated so drastic and dangerous a move if the Jewish people in Eastern Europe had not been put into a state of extreme turmoil by the emigration debate. They were moved by the great expectations then current, but how far their motives were political rather than religious, even perhaps messianically inspired, remains very much an open question. Of all the many colonies then founded, only Gederah and, to some extent, Rishon le-Zion were recognizably the work of the radical intelligentsia.[11]

Hardly less striking was the role played in key political ventures and innovations by a number of famous rabbis. The Hasidic movement, it is true, remained aloof, seeking to preserve its own way of life untouched by anything that smacked of secularism or modernization. (Only with the establishment of Agudat Israel in 1912 did the Hasidim adopt modern organizational means to attain that same ultraconservative end.) But among the Lithuanian *Mitnagdim*, the situation was different. There, cooperation with nonobservant or radical or even anticlerical Jews was not always automatically excluded. Thus, Rabbi Yitsak Elkhanan Spektor of Kovno, aided by his assistant Yaakov Halevi Lifshits, worked together with such prominent *maskilim* as the poet Yehuda Leb Levin to ensure that detailed reports of the pogroms reached the Jews in the West. The two highly influential articles published on the subject in *The Times* of London in January 1882 were based on material smuggled out of Russia disguised as a rabbinical legal opinion printed in Hebrew.[12]

During the 1880s Spektor was among those rabbis who identified themselves with the emergent Hibbat Zion movement even though its most prominent leaders, such as Lilienblum and Lev Pinsker, were *maskilim* by origin and still, in large degree, by outlook. Numbered among these rabbis, too, were Naftali Zvi Berlin (head of the Volozhin Yeshivah), Mordecai Eliasberg, and, of course, Shmuel Mohilever, who played a central role in the movement.

The nationalist intelligentsia and the more open strata within the traditional world strongly influenced each other.[13] The enormous stir caused by the youth triggered off highly emotional reactions in wide circles where the Exodus from Egypt, the River Sambation, the Ten Lost Tribes, and the Mountains of Darkness were very much part of a real world still saturated with messianic expectations.[14] A mass following – a *narod* – was thus there ready at hand for the new claimants to leadership. But there was a price to be paid. Many of the *maskilim*, now fully-fledged nationalists, had come out initially in favour of a territory in the New World where the Jews, in their view, would best be able to build a modern and liberal society free from theocratic or theological aspirations and clerical interference. But men such as Yehuda Leb Levin, Lev Levanda, Ludwig Zamenhof, and Lev Pinsker soon went over to the pro-Palestine camp, yielding to the power of popular sentiment.

However, a three-dimensional analysis of 1881–82 cannot ignore the decisive impact made likewise by the intervention and the image of Western Jewry. The great debate on organized emigration – its necessity, advisability, and destination – was sparked off in large part in the summer of 1881 by rumours of a decision supposedly taken by the Alliance Israélite Universelle to pay the passage of Russian Jews to America. This rumour contained only a small kernel of truth; the Alliance was thinking in terms of a strictly limited project.[15] Yet so great was the belief in the almost unlimited influence and power of the Jewish plutocracy in the West that the realities of the situation made little difference. The Russian-Jewish intelligentsia and, even more perhaps, the masses were convinced that, in the last resort, they could count on Western Jewry to underwrite their plans and projects.

Furthermore, in this relationship, too, the actions of each group fed those of the other. The Alliance was, in fact, stampeded by the massive flow of refugees across the frontier into paying for far more Jews to cross the Atlantic than it had planned. This action served to fuel the expectations of Russian Jewry still more. And hope was further stimulated, later in 1881, by the news that the Hebrew Emigrant Aid Society had been founded in New York and that Baron Maurice de Hirsch had apparently offered a million francs to advance Jewish agricultural settlement overseas.[16]

In turn, the reports smuggled out by Rabbi Yitshak Elkhanan Spektor and his group, once published in *The Times*, helped produce a major movement of public protest in England early in 1882. Its high point was the meeting at the Mansion House, presided over by the Lord Mayor of London and addressed by *inter alia* Cardinal Henry Edward Manning and the Earl of Shaftesbury, that resulted in the collection of large sums of money for aid to Russian Jewry.[17] Thus the pattern of 1881 was largely repeated in the spring of 1882. Once again, hopes of a grandiose emigration scheme soared; new parties and movements were founded; and the representatives of Anglo-Jewry found themselves arranging the transport and passage of thousands of Russian Jews, including the main Am Olam groups, to the United States.

Amid all this unprecedented flurry of activity, one episode perhaps stands out as exceptionally revealing. Among the emissaries chosen by the chief rabbi, Samuel Montagu, and other members of the Mansion House Committee, was Laurence Oliphant, an English gentleman and eccentric who, like so many Victorian men of letters, was irresistibly attracted to bizarre social experiments in utopian living, communalism, and free love. Oliphant came from an intensely evangelical family, and in 1880 he had published a detailed book that laid forth plans for the restoration of the Jews to Palestine.[18] His presence in Brody as an emissary of the Mansion House Committee, and later in Constantinople, was followed with intense interest by the Jews in Russia. It was confidently predicted that he would gain the Holy Land for the Jews by diplomatic means or even by personal purchase. Messianic longings were drawn to him as though to a magnet, and his mere presence at the centre of the stage helped sustain the confidence of the Bilu and other such groups into the summer of 1882.

Myths, focused primarily on Western Jewry – but also as in this case on Christians – played a crucial role in the formation of the new Jewish politics. Yet, like prophecies, myths are often self-fulfilling. A number of leading Jewish bankers were now inspired to devote large sums to Jewish colonization and agrarian efforts. Jacob Schiff financed settlements in America on a modest scale; Maurice de Hirsch would soon undertake his massive colonization effort in South America; Baron Edmund de Rothschild was induced, following meetings with Rabbi Shmuel Mohilever and with Yosef Feinberg from Rishon le-Zion, to underwrite the new colonies in Palestine. Without his support, they would have collapsed.[19] Thus, the nationalist movement was sustained not only by the radically new but, in essential ways, by forces drawn from both the traditional and the Western subworlds within Jewry.

## IV

While the crisis of 1881–82 has been the subject of intense historiographical interest almost throughout the twentieth century,[20] the Damascus case has attracted comparatively little close attention. The one overall account that goes into considerable detail remains Heinrich Graetz's very impressive chapter in his *History of the Jews* written more than one hundred years ago, although it should, perhaps, be added that J.M. Jost also gave considerable attention to the case.[21] A number of specialized articles illuminate limited aspects of the affair without making any attempt to discuss its overall significance;[22] and it is not assigned much space in the general histories.

Up to a point, this neglect by historians is justified. The Damascus case was surely more a landmark than a crossroads; it cannot compare in importance with the crisis in Russia some forty years later. Yet, when all is said and done, the events of 1840 absorbed the attention of world Jewry and riveted non-Jewish interest upon the Jews in ways probably without parallel between 1815 and the 1870s or 1880s. The space assigned to the case by Graetz and Jost reflected contemporary opinion. And the subsequent decline in interest has, surely, to be explained in part by the fact that modern Jewish history has increasingly been written in the twentieth century from the nationalist vantage point.

The degree of solidarity displayed by the organized Jewish communities in France, England, the United States, and, in more passive ways, in Germany, and the forces that they mobilized on behalf of their brethren in Damascus and Rhodes, do not easily fit into accounts that (like Dinur's) place the greatest emphasis on the assimilation and communal decline of Western Jewry. Thus an untypical statement by Abraham Geiger has received inordinate attention. In a private letter not published until 1896, Geiger declared that 'for me it is more important that Jews be able to work in Prussia as pharmacists or lawyers than that the entire Jewish population of Asia and Africa be saved, although as a human being I sympathize with them.'[23] There is a tendency to portray the action of the Jews in 1840 either as a throwback to traditional norms (Moses Montefiore, for example, being described as the last in a line of *shtadlanim*)[24] or else as a reaction against the prevailing norm. As S.M. Dubnov put it, the case brought with it a reassertion of

> Jewish self-consciousness at a time when West European Jewry had yielded to the charms of assimilation and disintegrated and split up into groups of Frenchmen, Englishmen, Germans of the Mosaic faith ... [It] was the beginning of later attempts to consolidate Jewry at first for philanthropical, cultural and political mutual aid, and later for a national ideal.[25]

But here, again, it is surely preferable not to merge the like with the unlike. The Damascus Affair offered the Jews of the West the opportunity, in coming to the aid of two distant communities in dire distress, to march under the standard of a liberalism triumphant. They were acting, as they saw it, in accord with, not in contradiction to, the spirit of the times. Even if Judaism were to be defined strictly in religious terms, stripped of national connotations – and very many Jews were in fact reluctant to make so clear a distinction – its adherents could still recognize a duty to assist their 'co-religionists' endangered by arbitrary tyranny and barbarism. Indeed, the

Damascus case is precisely of interest as the first full-scale example within the Jewish world of the emancipationist style of politics.

In the campaign, which was launched soon after the news of the blood libels, tortures, and terror in Damascus and Rhodes in April 1840, the arguments and the means employed had very little in common with those traditionally associated with the *shtadlan*. Adolphe Crémieux, Moses Montefiore, and the many other Jewish spokesmen chose to take their stand as members of European civilization, equally entitled with all other citizens (even if not fully emancipated in England) to appeal to the rights of man. They chose their methods accordingly. In large part, they acted out in the open, determined, as it was so often put at the time, to win their case before 'the court of public opinion.' A flow of letters to the editor was maintained. As documents came in from the Middle East, they were translated, distributed to the press, and published. Politicians and ministers were lobbied officially in London, Paris and Washington, and these efforts, too, were made public. It was arranged for questions to be asked in Parliament and in the Chambers of Deputies and Peers; the subsequent exchanges, too, were reported and became cause for comment in the press. On July 3, 1840, a protest meeting was held in the Mansion House, and the Lord Mayor followed it up by sending appeals to the various governments of Europe; again the correspondence was published.[26] Public subscriptions were launched to help finance the mission of Montefiore and Crémieux to the Middle East, and this undertaking in turn was given maximal publicity.[27]

The results of that expedition were also carefully packaged with an eye to effect. In its own terms, it was actually a failure in that it had gone out with the express purpose of arranging a full inquiry and fair trial, which it was unable to do. But Montefiore and Crémieux, making the best use of the firmans issued by Mehemet Ali and the sultan, did all they could – and quite effectively – to present the expedition as a triumphant success.

Of course, it was easier to conduct such a campaign in England, where the government, and especially Lord Palmerston, the foreign secretary, supported the Jewish cause, than in France, where the government of Adolphe Thiers, hostile and embarrassed by the case, sought to keep it out of the public eye.[28] That Crémieux, with the backing of the Consistoire Central, was ready to persist in the cause, even in defiance of his own government, demonstrates how little there was here of traditional *shtadlanut*. Crémieux – a brilliant advocate, vice-president of the Consistoire, well known for his persistent opposition to the use of the *more Judaico* (Jewish oath), a dedicated liberal who was named minister of justice after the February Revolution – was ready to defy Thiers in the name of French values, as he understood them.[29] Rather like Gabriel Riesser, who a few years before had brought out his journal *Der Jude* as a blow on behalf of a liberal Germany, Crémieux saw Jewish solidarity in the right cause as the highest expression of French patriotism.[30]

This argument is by no means meant to imply that the Western Jewish leaders were acting solely out of motives of abstract ideology or pure altruism. On the contrary, they themselves were often ready to admit that the accusations levelled against the Jewish communities of Damascus and Rhodes, if only because they were so widely credited in Europe, constituted a direct threat to their own interests and security.[31] As they saw it, the struggle of enlightened reason against medieval reaction and Judeophobia, which they tended, overschematically, to identify in large measure with forces within the Roman Catholic church, was one and indivisible.

Still, the story of the Jews in 1840, like that of 1881–82, incorporated not only a major but also minor themes. The principal actors may not have acted as *shtadlanim*, but it is well to remember how close many in that generation of Western Jewry were to a traditional way of life. A decisive role in the Damascus Affair was played by the Rothschild family, whose connections with the European governments in London, Paris, Naples, and, above all perhaps, Vienna were invaluable. Without its moral and financial backing, provided largely but not always behind the scenes, the campaign could never have won such broad support or achieved such success. Indeed, the fact that Montefiore was a close relative made it something of a family affair.

But at that time the Rothschilds were almost literally still only one step out of the ghetto. Anselm, of course, was still in the family home in the Jewish quarter of Frankfurt am Main and strictly observant. Solomon, in Vienna, although enjoying the title of baron, usually lived in a hotel because Jews were denied the right of permanent residence within the city. James, in Paris, disowned his niece in London when in 1840 she entered into the first mixed marriage in family history. Much of the correspondence, including that of its younger members, was still conducted in Yiddish, replete with Hebraisms.[32] It is thus hardly surprising that their almost instinctive reaction to the Damascus Affair was little different from that which would have been expected of such Jews so exalted by wealth throughout the centuries. And, indeed, the same can be said of the community leaders in Constantinople and Alexandria, who responded at once to the calls for help and were able to achieve much for the hapless victims in Damascus and Rhodes long before intervention from Europe could make itself felt.

Again, in 1840 as in 1881–82, messianic expectations and impulses of the most varied kind came into play. First, there was the fact – pure coincidence, it would seem – that 5600 in the Jewish calendar (corresponding to 1839–40) had been awaited for decades by many rabbinic and kabbalistic authorities as the year of the messianic coming. Were the tragic events in Damascus and Rhodes, then, a sign of the times, or birthpangs?[33]

What the Jews, especially the most orthodox and observant, did and thought was, in turn, closely followed by the English Christian missionaries, particularly by the London Society for the Promotion of Christianity among the Jews, which had dozens of posts scattered across Europe and the Middle East. In these circles, too, millenarian hopes flourished and the restoration of the Jews to Palestine was often seen as the necessary prelude to the second advent of Christ. It was hoped that when the Jewish Messiah failed to come in 1840, conversions to Christianity would greatly increase. In March of that year one of the missionaries in Jerusalem, G.W. Pieritz, a convert from Judaism, went specially to Damascus to seek ways of aiding the Jews there, and his written reports published in Europe exerted great influence precisely because he was considered an unbiased source.[34]

Intervention by millenarian societies and leaders in London with the British government followed two directions. They called for the defence of the Jews in Damascus and Rhodes, here working along the same lines as the Anglo-Jewish community. But they also took the opportunity provided by the Jewish plight and the impending war against Egypt for the control of greater Syria (including Palestine) to urge restorationist policies on the British government. As Anthony Ashley Cooper, soon to become the seventh Earl of Shaftesbury, was not only the most prominent evangelical advocate of the Jewish restoration to Palestine but also Palmerston's stepson-in-law, such proposals were not dismissed out of hand.[35] On the contrary, in a well-known dispatch of August 1840 to the British ambassador to the Porte, Palmerston suggested that the Turkish Government should be encouraged to promote large-scale Jewish settlement in Palestine.

There exists at present among the Jews dispersed over Europe a strong notion that the Time is approaching when their nation is to return to Palestine; and ... their thoughts have been bent more upon the means of realizing that wish ... It would be of manifest importance to the Sultan to encourage the Jews to return to, and to settle in, Palestine: because the wealth which they would bring with them would increase the resources of the Sultan's Dominions.[36]

Given the fact that the vast majority of European Jews were then living either closed within the premodern world of Eastern Europe or had set their sights firmly on equal citizenship and integration, they could hardly be expected, in the main, to welcome the many precepts of this nature then being mooted and publicized in England.[37] Most Jews simply ignored them. Some rejected them in anger, as did Ludwig Philippson, for example.[38] But there were also those who welcomed them with great excitement. A man like Yehuda Alkalai, still thinking largely in kabbalistic terms, saw in them a sign of the oncoming messianic age.[39]

More remarkable was the reaction of significant groups within the younger generation of German and Austrian Jewry, particularly the students. Frustrated by the lack of progress toward emancipation, shocked to the marrow by the widespread abuse heaped on the Jews in the German press during the Damascus case, they saw in the Palestine projects a welcome ray of light. It was at this point that Moses Hess wrote his article on the return of the Jews to Palestine, which he then put aside for more than twenty years, only to publish it finally as part of *Rome and Jerusalem*.[40]

The group led by Abraham Benisch, Moritz Steinschneider, and Albert Lowy was, of course, far more determined and resolute. Following meetings with Crémieux and Montefiore, they managed to have a detailed memorandum submitted to the Foreign Office in London through the good offices of W.T. Young, the British vice-consul in Jerusalem.[41] What is more, one of the German-Jewish periodicals, *Der Orient*, edited by Dr. Julius Furst, published their ideas frequently and at length. Of course nothing concrete could come of such projects at that time; they were clearly premature. Nonetheless, it is certainly significant that what can only be categorized as autoemancipationist themes were taken up so readily among the German-Jewish intelligentsia of the 1840s – a startling reminder of how often radical ideas that first caught on in the

Germany of pre-1848 were to emerge again in the Russia of post-1881.

The Damascus case was by no means the high point of the emancipationist model of Jewish politics. Following the Mortara case of 1858, those politics took on permanent, institutional form with the establishment of the Alliance Israélite Universelle in 1860. Affiliated organizations, the Allianz in Berlin and in Vienna, and the Anglo-Jewish Association in London were set up in the following years. As Michael Graetz has demonstrated so convincingly, the Alliance was initially the work of a group of men who had been influenced by theories of radical change and perceived Judaism as essentially a universalist system of social ethics.[42] It was natural enough that Crémieux should have become its president and, likewise, that its differences with the Consistoire and the Rothschilds should have been quickly reconciled. Over the next two decades the Alliance was active in the establishment of modern Jewish schools in the Middle East, a project launched by Crémieux in Egypt in 1840; in diplomacy, particularly its action on behalf of Rumanian Jewry culminating in the settlement at the Congress of Berlin;[43] in Palestine, with the foundation of the Mikveh Yisrael agricultural school; and in the Russian Empire, with the aid for selected emigrants to the United States in 1869–70.

All these projects were seen as an expression of the liberal, the emancipationist creed of Western Jewry. When 1881–82 came, the leaders of the new Jewish nationalism in Russia turned to the West with quite other expectations. They were to be sorely disappointed – but not entirely.

NOTES

1. For some recent essays on Jewish political traditions, see D. Elazar, ed., *Kinship and Consent: The Jewish Political Tradition and Its Contemporary Uses* (Washington, D.C., 1983). I am grateful to Eli Lederhendler, who has allowed me to read his work in progress: 'From Autonomy to Autoemancipation: Russian Jewish Political Development in the 19th Century and Its Roots in Public Life of Traditional Communities,' a Ph.D. dissertation to be submitted to the Jewish Theological Seminary of America.
2. Ben Zion Dinur, *Be-mifneh ha-dorot: Mehkarim ve-iyunim be-Reshitam shel ha-zmanim he-hadishim be-toldot yisrael* (Jerusalem, 1972), pp.9–18.
3. Ibid., pp.26–9.
4. Ibid., pp.36–46.
5. On the crisis of 1881–82, see, for example, Samuel Leib Zitron, *Toldot Hibat Zion, vol 1: me-reshit Yeme ha-tnuah ad she-nitasher vaad hoveve-Zion be-Odessah* (Odessa, 1914); Yisrael Klausner, *Be-hitorer am: ha-aliyah ha-rishonah me-*

*Rusyah* (Jerusalem, 1962); David Vital, *The Origins of Zionism* (Oxford, 1975); Shmuel Yavnieli, ed., *Sefer ha-Zionut, vol. 2: Tkufat Hibat Zion* (Tel Aviv, 1942).

6. M. L. Lilienblum, 'Obshcheevreiskii vopros i Palestina,' *Razsvet*, nos. 41-42 (Oct. 1881): 1598–1600, 1638–41.
7. For a broader survey of this development, see Jonathan Frankel, *Prophecy and Politics: Socialism, Nationalism and the Russian Jews, 1862–1917* (Cambridge, 1981), pp.57–64, 74–90.
8. See, e.g., Yehuda Slutsky, *Ha-itonut ha-yehudit-Rusit ba-meah ha-tsha-sreh* (Jerusalem, 1970), pp.121–41; M. Ben Hillel Ha-Cohen, *Olami*, Vol. 1 (Jerusalem, 1927): 164–6.
9. On Am Olam, see Avrom Menes, 'The Am Oylom Movement,' *YIVO Annual of Jewish Social Science*, 4 (1949): 9–33; and Hasiyah Turtel, 'Tnuat'am olam,' *He-avar*, 10 (1963): 124–43. On the Bilu, see Shulamit Laskov, *Ha-biliuim* (Tel Aviv, 1979).
10. For an analysis of the part played by members (later ex-members) of the Am Olam in America, see Ezra Mendelsohn, 'The Russian Roots of the American Jewish Labor Movement,' *YIVO Annual of Jewish Social Science*, 16 (1976): 150–77.
11. On the development of the First Aliyah, see Mordekhay Eliav and Yemima Rosenthal, *Sefer ha-aliyah ha-rishonah* (Jerusalem, 1981); and Yehoshua Kaniel, *Hemshekh u-tmurah: Ha-yishuv ha-yashan ve-hayishuv he-hadash bi-tkufat ha-aliyah ha-rishonah ve-hashniyah* (Jerusalem, 1981).
12. On this episode, see Yaakov Halevi Lifshits, *Zikhron Yaakov* (Frankfurt A.M., 1924), 3:20–89.
13. For a valuable insight into this interaction, see the massive correspondence reproduced in A.A. Drouyanov, ed., *Ktavim le-toldot Hibat Zion ve-yishuv eretz yisrael* (Odessa, 1919; Tel Aviv, 1932).
14. See, e.g., Shmarya Levin, *Youth in Revolt* (London, 1939), pp.30–5.
15. On the initial plans of the Alliance in the summer of 1881, see Alliance Israélite Universelle, *Bulletin Mensuel*, no. 10 (Oct. 1881): p.161; *American Hebrew*, 8 Sept. 1881, p.33; *Jewish Chronicle*, 7 Oct. 1881, p.7.
16. *Jewish Chronicle*, 7 Oct. 1881, p.7.
17. 'The Mansion House Meeting,' *Jewish Chronicle*, 3 Feb. 1882, pp.1–4, and 17 Feb. 1882, p.3.
18. Laurence Oliphant, *Land of Gilead, with Excursions in the Lebanon* (Edinburgh, 1880).
19. See, for example, Dan Giladi, 'Ha-baron, ha-pkidut ve-hamoshavot ha-rishonot be-eretz yisrael: Haarakhah me-hadash,' *Cathedra* 2 (1976): pp.59–68; and Simon Schama, *Two Rothschilds and the Land of Israel* (New York, 1978).
20. Suffice it to mention Drouyanov, Zitron, Yavnieli, Breiman, and Klausner. See, in addition to the works listed in fn. 5 and 13, Shlomo Breiman, 'Ha-mifne be-mahshvah ha-tsiburit ha-yehudit be-reshit shnot ha-shmonim,' *Shivat Zion*, 2–3 (1951–52): 83–227.
21. Heinrich Graetz, *Geschichte der Juden*, Vol. 11 (Leipzig, 1900), pp.464–500, published in English as *History of the Jews* (Philadelphia, 1895; reprint, 1956), 6: 632–66; J. M. Jost, *Neuere Geschichte der Israeliten von 1815 bis 1845*, Vol. 2 (Berlin, 1847), pp.345–84.
22. Albert M. Hyamson, 'The Damascus Affair, 1840,' *Transactions of the Jewish Historical Society of England*, 16 (1952): 47–71; N.M. Gelber, 'Österreich und die Damaskusaffaire im Jahre 1840,' *Jahrbuch der Judisch-Literarischen Gesellschaft* 18 (1927): 217–64; S.W. Baron, 'Abraham Benisch's Project for Jewish Colonization in Palestine (1842),' in *Jewish Studies in Memory of George A. Kohut*, ed. S.W. Baron and Alexander Marx (New York, 1935), pp.72–85. See also two new studies: U.R.Q. Henriques, 'Who Killed Father Thomas?' in *Sir Moses Montefiore: A Symposium*, ed. V.D. Lipman (Oxford, 1982), pp.50–75; Tudor Parfitt, ' "The Year of the Pride of Israel": Montefiore and the Blood Libel of 1840,' in *The Century of*

*Moses Montefiore*, ed. S.L. and V.D. Lipman (Oxford, 1985), pp.131–48.
23. 'Abraham Geigers Briefe an J. Derenbourg [22 November 1840],' *Allgemeine Zeitung des Judenthums*, 60, no. 24 (12 June 1896): p.284.
24. See, e.g., Howard Sachar, *The Course of Modern Jewish History* (New York, 1958), pp.133–6.
25. S.M. Dubnov, *Noveishaia istoriia evreiskogo naroda ot frantsuzskoi revoliutsii do nashikh dnew*, Vol. 2 (Riga, 1938), p.241, published in English as *The History of the Jews*, Vol. 5 (London, 1973), p.250.
26. 'Persecution of the Jews in Damascus: Great Meeting in the Mansion House,' *The Times* (London), 4 July 1840; 'The Jews of the East,' ibid., 24 July 1840.
27. On the mission, see *Diaries of Sir Moses and Lady Montefiore*, ed. Louis Loewe (London, 1890); and *The Damascus Affair: Diary of Louis Loewe, July–November, 1840* (Ramsgate, 1940).
28. See the official statements by Adolphe Thiers, 'Chambre des Députés,' *Journal des Débats*, 3 June 1840, and 'Chambre des Pairs,' ibid., 11 July 1840.
29. See Solomon Posener, *Adolphe Crémieux: A Biography* (Philadelphia, 1940).
30. See, for example, Moshe Rinott, 'Gabriel Riesser: Fighter for Jewish Emancipation,' *Leo Baeck Institute Year Book*, 7 (1962): 11–38.
31. See, e.g., the speech of Bernard Van Oven at the meeting in the Great Synagogue on 23 June 1840: 'We must put an end to the persecution in Asia, and if possible punish the persecutors, lest their success should encourage similar attempts nearer home, where there is enough, and more than enough, to stimulate bigotry and to tempt avarice.' *Morning Herald* (London), 25 June 1840.
32. Two recent additions to the large number of historical works on the Rothschild family are Anka Muhlstein, *Baron James: The Rise of the French Rothschilds* (New York, 1982); and R.W. Davis, *The English Rothschilds* (Chapel Hill, N.C., 1983). I wish to take this opportunity to thank N.M. Rothschild and Sons, London, for kindly permitting me to consult the archive of the bank, and Mrs Yvonne Moss, the archivist, for her great help in locating much relevant material.
33. On the year 5600 as a messianic year, see A.G. Duker, 'The Tarniks,' in *The Joshua Starr Memorial Volume* (New York, 1953), pp.191–202; and Aryeh Morgenshtern, *Meshihiut ve-yishuv eretz yisrael ba-mahazit ha-rishonah shel ha-meah ha-19* (Jerusalem, 1985).
34. See, 'Extract of Letters from Mr. Pieritz, a Christian Missionary Living at Jerusalem, to the Jews of Alexandria,' *The Times* (London), 6 July 1840, supp.; and a further report from Pieritz, ibid., 13 Aug. 1840.
35. See Edwin Hodder, *The Life and Work of the Seventh Earl of Shaftesbury, K. G.* (London, 1887); and the diary of Lord Ashley deposited at the Royal Commission on Historical Manuscripts, Chancery Lane, London.
36. Quoted in Albert M. Hyamson, *The British Consulate in Jerusalem in Relation to the Jews of Palestine, 1838–1914*, Vol.1 (London, 1939), pp.33–4.
37. Two recent books on the nature of Anglo-Jewish society and politics are Todd M. Endelman, *The Jews of Georgian England, 1714–1830: Tradition and Change in a Liberal Society* (Philadelphia, 1979); and M.C.N. Salbstein, *The Emancipation of the Jews in Britain: The Question of the Admission of the Jews to Parliament, 1828–1860* (Rutherford, N.J., 1982).
38. [Ludwig Philippson], 'Tages-Controle,' *Allgemeine Zeitung des Judenthums*, 4, no. 37 (12 Sept. 1840): 544. Philippson wrote of proto-Zionist plans: 'And what would a pitiful [Jewish] Free State be able to create in an empty corner except a trivial questionable existence amidst Muslims and Egyptians? What would a colony of homeless Jews be able to do? It would exist only by the grace of distant Powers ... without purpose or direction.'
39. E.g., Jacob Katz, 'The Jewish National Movement: A Sociological Analysis,' in his *Emancipation and Assimilation Studies in Modern Jewish History* (Farnborough, England, 1972), pp.129–45, esp. 133–4.

40. See Moses Hess, *Rom und Jerusalem: Die letzte Nationalitätsfrage* (Leipzig, 1862), pp.26–8.
41. Baron, 'Abraham Benisch's Project,' pp.77–82; Hyamson, *British Consulate in Jerusalem*, 1:41.
42. Michael Graetz, *Ha-periferyah haytah le-merkaz: Prakim be-toldot yahadut Zarfat be-meah ha-19* (Jerusalem, 1982).
43. See, e.g., L.P. Gartner, 'Roumania, America and World Jewry: Consul Peixotta in Bucharest 1870–1876,' *American Jewish Historical Quarterly* 58 (1968–69): 25–117; and F.R. Stern, *Gold and Iron: Bismarck, Bleichroder and the Building of the German Empire* (New York, 1977).

# 4

# Ethnicity and Jewish Solidarity in Nineteenth-Century France

## Phyllis Cohen Albert

Although nineteenth-century French Jews were under pressure to preserve the gains of the Emancipation through integration into French social, cultural, political, and economic life, they displayed a remarkable sense of ethnic identification and Jewish solidarity. Yet this aspect of their social life has been neglected and often denied as a result of the common argument that gives undue weight to their assimilatory tendencies.

It is a well-known fact that in 1791 France became the first modern nation to grant full civil and political emancipation to its Jewish population, and thereby to raise the Jews to full and equal citizenship. The story of the Napoleonic 'Sanhedrin' has often been told: the government's carefully chosen representatives of the Jews made the historic declaration that French Jews are, first and foremost, citizens of France who recognize France as their *patrie* and Frenchmen as their brothers. There were to be no religious obstacles to their full identification with, and integration into the French community; even intermarriage was possible, although it was not blessed by the rabbinate.[1]

The Emancipation spurred the political, social, cultural, and economic advancement of the Jewish population at a rate that had been impossible previously, and that would be achieved by European Jews outside of France only at a later date. Because the Emancipation was ultimately responsible for geographic and demographic changes in the Jewish population, and because it brought about a significant slackening in religious observance, scholars have claimed that the French Jews of the post-Revolutionary period were assimilationists, displaying optimism and confidence in France, and identifying more with France and Frenchmen than with Judaism and Jews. Such theorists claim that French Jews eschewed all notions of transnational Jewish solidarity and identity.[2]

The reality, however, was otherwise. Jews, in fact, *failed* to merge with the French population at any time in the history of French Jewry, until and including the present time. This reality became obvious to everyone only during and after the Second World War and the Six Day War, but it was equally true during times when it was not so brutally brought to the attention of the public.[3] Jews failed to merge politically, geographically, occupationally, ethnically, with the French population.[4] Antisemitism, although not in its most virulent or political form until the end of the century, was a constant factor that maintained the Jews' sense of insecurity and their fear that the gains of the Emancipation could easily, and almost without warning, be revoked. Each change of regime during the politically unstable century, brought the question: 'What will this mean to the Jews?' Deputations were sent offering felicitations to the new government, and not incidentally, to receive reassurances that the Emancipation would not be abrogated. This need for reassurance was not the result of Jewish paranoia. Rather, it was a realistic appraisal of the political situation. After all, the Emancipation had been granted, not because of French philo-Semitism, but because of logical imperatives implicit in the political meaning of the Revolution.[5] Anti-Jewish sentiment had been maintained institutionally in the post-Revolutionary period during the three generations following the Emancipation.[6] Social prejudices remained strong, and translated themselves into economic and occupational inequalities.

Insecurity and fear, then, rather than optimism and confidence in the France of 1789, determined the mood of nineteenth-century French Jewry. This insecurity, combined with past habits and associations, family ties and the religious needs of the always significant number of traditionally observant Jews, was responsible for the retention of ethnic institutions and ties (even 'ethnic politics') and Jewish solidarity. This is not to deny the acculturation of Jews that took place in France, but to deny the supposed equation between acculturation and all forms of assimilation.

The difference between the concepts of acculturation and assimilation has been stated by modern sociologists in varying ways.[7] For our purposes we use Milton Gordon's behavioral assimilation – that state in which the ethnic group has acquired the language, social ritual, and cultural pattern of the host community. It takes place at the level of secondary group associations.[8] This definition of assimilation is not incompatible with Jewish nationalism, cultural pluralism, ethnicity, or solidarity. According to it, Herzl, Weizmann, and every Zionist leader and member was assimilated, because it implies only the taking on of the language and values, and identifying with the history of the host country, without the loss of separate identity.[9] The second kind of assimilation, structural assimilation, takes place at the primary group level, and involves large-scale entry into cliques, clubs, and other institutions of the host society. It implies the ultimate disappearance of all particularism.[10]

Integration is a corollary of acculturation. With the taking on of the values and culture of the dominant society, the ethnic group finds a place for itself in the structure of the society. Such acculturated individuals are, however, still closely associated with the subgroup culture.

Prior to Gordon's distinction between behavioral and structural assimilation, sociologists wavered between the two meanings of assimilation,[11] and it is no surprise, then, that when historians speak of assimilation in regard to the Jews they do not always take the trouble to define the kind of assimilation they mean. At its most extreme, assimilation would mean the complete disappearance of the Jews, or the process leading toward that state. It could, however, also mean simple acculturation and integration. Although the term does not consistently imply a single attitude toward group survival and ethnic identity, it is generally used to indicate a state which is indifferent, or even antagonistic, to ethnicity and solidarity. When the French Jews are labeled 'assimilationist,' it is usually with such connotations that the term is used.[12]

Yet indications of ethnicity and examples of solidarity can be clearly enumerated for the entire period of the nineteenth century. There are three kinds of solidarity: local, national, and international. Local solidarity is evidenced by Jews' readiness to help other Jews and to act in concert with them at the local community level. National solidarity is demonstrated by the nationwide institutional and political ties within French Jewry. Finally, we can point to international connections and a sense of mutual responsibility that transcends national limits. At the end of the century the French Jewish historian Theodore Reinach felt constrained to explain the obvious solidarity of the Jews as legitimate and even morally necessary. Members of all religious groups, he argued, feel a special kinship for their coreligionists. But in the case of the Jews there is not only identity of belief; there are also common origins and historical experiences ('le souvenir de maux glorieusement soufferts en commun'). These factors reinforce fraternal sentiments and impose even greater mutual obligations than are felt by members of other religious groupings. Admitting that Israel constitutes a family, Reinach predicted that it will cease to be one only when all humanity becomes one large family.[13] He was, in short, hinting at the concept of ethnicity.

Like assimilation, the term ethnicity has been used in various ways. In order to define it, Gordon reminds us that the Greek word 'ethnos' means 'people' or 'nation.' The modern concept of an ethnic group is, therefore, a 'group with a shared feeling of peoplehood,' and this sense of peoplehood is called 'ethnicity.' The elements in such peoplehood are racial, historical, territorial, religious, and cultural, or any combination of these categories.[14] Clearly the ethnicity of the nineteenth-century French Jews drew on such elements. Jews were those whose ancestors had not been considered French, but Jewish. They had enjoyed a well-developed life in France throughout the Middle Ages, and were distinguished by civil, political, social, and religious factors. After their partial expulsions, enacted between the end of the fourteenth century and the beginning of the sixteenth century, two very different groups began arriving in France. During the sixteenth century, Marranos, or New Christians, arrived in the south, and Jews appeared in the east as a consequence of the annexation of Germanic lands. Until the Revolution this Jewry in Alsace-Lorraine and southwest France (and some made its way to Paris) had a clearly defined separate national existence. Even after the Emancipation and throughout the nineteenth century, French Jews frequently used the term 'race' in regard to ther own common origins and continued sense of kinship.[15]

A good indication of ethnicity is resistance to intermarriage. When Napoleon sought to effect structural assimilation through the requirement that a certain percentage of Jewish marriages be intermarriages, the Jews, although fearful for the security of the Emancipation, rejected the suggestion. Subsequently, when Napoleon requested that the Sanhedrin at least proclaim the religious legitimacy of intermarriages, that generally docile and acquiescent body adamantly refused. Through the nineteenth century, French Jews displayed a very low incidence of intermarriage.[16]

The vast majority of the Jews retained their own primary group associations. Persistence of ethnicity was not caused by discrimination alone, but was due to the preferences of the members of the groups for such ethnic ties as special schools, charitable institutions, and neighborhoods which served their special needs.

Recently scholars have been revising the earlier notion that there was a tendency within multinational states for the disappearance of ethnic identity. This is now considered *not* to be the case in diverse instances, both in repressive and in democratic regimes, such as Russia, France, and America.[17] Writing about America, Gordon says:

> My essential thesis here is that the sense of ethnicity has proved to be hardy. As though with a wily cunning of its own, as though there were some essential element in man's nature that demanded it – something that compelled him to merge his lonely individual identity in some ancestral troup of fellows smaller by far than the whole human race, smaller often than the nation – the sense of ethnic belonging has survived. It has survived in various forms and with various names, but it has not perished, and twentieth-century urban man is closer to his stone-age ancestors than he knows.[18]

A reappraisal of Jewish ethnic identification during the nineteenth century is called for in light of current perceptions of the ethnic reality of the twentieth. My hypothesis is that previous generations either failed to perceive ethnicity or consciously denied it for political purposes.

## II

The social and institutional history of nineteenth-century French Jewry demonstrates a sense of ethnicity and solidarity. Jewish geographical distribution was not the same as that of the general French population, and Jews tended to live in areas of Jewish density many times greater than the 0.26 percent that the Jews comprised in the 1861 general French population. In Toul (Meurthe), for example, 8 percent of the 1861 population were Jews. In three other cities in the east they comprised more than 5 percent of the population. In another three cities they comprised close to, or more than, 3 percent.[19] Thus, they were numerous enough to maintain their own communities and neighborhoods. A historian of the Dreyfus period who believes that the Jewish community was in a state of dissolution at the end of the nineteenth century admits, nonetheless, that there existed a sense of community.[20]

## ETHNICITY AND JEWISH SOLIDARITY

The 1860 *Manifesto* of the Alliance Israélite Universelle seems to address itself to a class of Jews who were neither religious nor completely assimilated. Today we would say that they exhibited feelings of ethnicity, but the word did not exist at the time and the concept was described with some difficulty. Thus, the document appeals to the Jews who 'remain attached to the ancient religion of their ancestors, regardless of how weak is this attachment.'[21] This wording suggests the existence of Jews who found expression for their sense of peoplehood, for their attachment to the Jewish community, in the only terms that were available, those of religion.

There is a curious parallel between our findings in this regard and those of Will Herberg, who studied the growth spurt of religious institutions in post-World War II America. Although Americans were becoming increasingly secular in outlook, the only forms available for expressing group identity and a feeling of belonging were religious institutions. But the categories into which men were classified were 'based less on theological than on social distinctions.' This was accentuated in the case of the Jews by the overlapping of religion and ethnicity for that group.[22]

The analogous phenomenon in nineteenth-century French Jewry is manifested by the advocates of Reform. Extreme reformers, such as Orly Terquem, proposed ritual changes of a far-reaching nature, including the transfer of the Sabbath to Sunday in order to bring Jewish behavior into line with general French behavior. His underlying religious assumptions were deistic, and designed to be identical with enlightened Christianity. When Terquem talks, therefore, of the need to reform Judaism in order to retain the Jewish elite and to bring it back to a Jewish existence, we may legitimately ask what is Jewish about the existence he envisages? Certainly not the religion; it would seem that Terquem's religious language hides an ethnic reality.[23]

Additional aspects of the religious behavior of French Jews indicate communal cohesion. We know that there were individuals whose attachment to their Jewish historical origins found expression only through the traditional ritual observance in which they no longer believed.[24] The notably low rates of conversion and intermarriage in nineteenth-century France are further testimony to the sense of peoplehood.[25]

The use of religious terminology and religious institutional expression delayed awareness of the ethnic reality that underlay these phenomena. But the use of the concept of religious union and of assisting one's coreligionists was, of course, useful in a nineteenth-century France that was actively claiming the right to protect Catholic and Christian holy places in the East. The same year that the Alliance Israélite Universelle announced its organization and aims, France landed an expeditionary force in Syria to protect the Christian population.

Jewish historians of the period evince a pride in what is clearly for them a national-religious heritage. L.M. Lambert, in his 1840 publication, *Précis de l'histoire des Hébreux, depuis le Patriarche Abraham, jusqu'en 1840*, wrote that Jewish history is not like ordinary history, because it teaches peace and virtue. In it we can point to great heroes, 'noble and sublime characters,' such as Judah Maccabee, who fought 'for religion and the fatherland.' In both Lambert's work and in *Histoire des Israélites depuis l'époque de leur dispersion jusqu'à nos jours* by Theodore Reinach (published in 1884), there is concern about Jewish status abroad and the battle for emancipation. Lambert writes of the ongoing struggle and reports the successes country by country. Reinach writes all of his modern Jewish history as a history of the Emancipation. The Jewish periodical press, which developed after 1840, was always full of news about Jewish status elsewhere and the struggles, successes, and difficulties of the Jews abroad.

III

The impression that Jews felt a sense of ethnicity is further supported by a linguistic analysis of contemporary documents. For example, in 1858 the Strasbourg consistory sent a letter of thanks to Lionel de Rothschild of England for his efforts to have Jews admitted into the Chamber of Deputies. That they chose to *thank* him, rather than congratulate him, reveals their ethnic identification. Similarly, the wording of the 1860 *Manifesto* of the fledgling Alliance Israélite Universelle also shows that the writers identified with suffering Jews abroad. In proposing a program of aid and assistance, it speaks of the 'prejudice which *we* still suffer' (emphasis mine). The Manifesto refers to the long-felt need for creating an organization of 'union.'[26] In fact, many voices had been raised during the previous fifteen years, calling for an organization to give expression to existent Jewish solidarity.[27]

Ethnic identity is expressed by nineteenth-century French Jews in the repeated use of certain words and expressions. For example, the Jews often used the word 'race' to describe their sense of peoplehood. 'Only the biological terminology of race provided a semantic framework within which all Jews could express their feelings of Jewish identity,' says one recent student of French Jewry.[28] However, there were in fact additional terms which served the same function. Thus we repeatedly encounter *nation, people, our brothers, family, Israel,* and even *solidarity*.

Throughout the nineteenth century the French Jews continued to use the pre-Revolutionary concept *nation* in referring to themselves. Often the term is used in referring to the past, but with the implicit, or even explicit, extension to the present. Thus, in his 1801 *Appel à la justice des nations et des rois*, Michel Berr regrets the fall of the 'Jewish nation.' If the Emancipation should fail to obtain for all of European Jewry the benefits the French Jews have been granted, Berr suggests that the Jews should arm themselves and reconquer their ancient homeland. Within the framework of the Emancipation, he imagines the Jews learning both the local language and their ancient Hebrew language. He suggests that the Jews will then regard the two languages 'as being almost equally national for them.'[29]

Forty years later, in 1840, Grand Rabbi L.M. Lambert, chief rabbi of Metz, wrote that he expected the Jews to one day reestablish their national existence. He objected to the notion that they, more than the Poles, Italians, or Greeks in exile in France, should be expected to promise never to intend to return to their old homeland. The Jews, he declared, 'merit nationality as much as the Greeks and the Poles.'[30]

Sometimes the idea that there is a national aspect to Jewry was expressed without actually using the term *nation*. For example, the word *Israel* was also used to refer to the totality of the Jews, understood in a tribal sense – a clearly ethnic notion.[31] Occasionally writers noted the lack of institutional expression for the national element in Judaism and proposed ways of filling the gap. Thus the Alliance Israélite Universelle, in its 1860 *Manifesto*, suggests that it will substitute for the nonexistent Jewish nation, by defending the interests of the Jews, as existing nations defend the interests of their nationals or of religious minorities whose protection they assure.[32]

It is clear that had the Jews been understood as a religious grouping, rather than a national one, there would have been more histories of Judaism and fewer of 'the Jewish people' or the 'Israelites.' In fact, the repeated use of these terms, and similar ones, amply demonstrates the widespread conception that the Jews were a national group. One of the earliest examples is the title proposed in 1813 for a journal which never appeared: *Annales*

*Historiques et Littéraires du Peuple Juif* (Historical and Literary Annals of the Jewish People).[33] Toward the middle of the century, Eugène Manuel, professor of literature and language in Paris, employed a similar notion when he claimed that he had been influenced by three classical sources: Greece, Rome, and 'mon peuple hébreu' (my Hebrew people).[34] During the period of severe political antisemitism at the end of the century, Hippolyte Prague, reviewing a book entitled *La Désolation du peuple juif*, by Abbé Soullier, condemned the religious antisemitism of the book, but also did not choose to dispute the author's use of the term *peuple juif*.[35]

The term *Israélite français* (French Israelite), in use from the very early days of the Emancipation,[36] and also the title of the earliest French Jewish periodical (1817–18), emphasizes Jewish identity, modified by the qualification 'French.' Later in the century it was suggested that the order of this familiar phrase be reversed to 'Français israélite' (Jewish Frenchman), thereby emphasizing the French nationality.

*Our brothers* ('nos frères') is often used to refer to other Jews, whether in France, Europe, Asia, or Africa. Examples of such usage include the 1844 call of Samuel Cahen to help the Jews in the East: 'It is urgent that Western Israelites raise up their Eastern brothers.'[37] Similarly, an 1860 article by S. Bloch recommends the establishment of an Alliance Israélite Universelle to protect the 'interests, the social position, often the life of our brothers.' It points out the need to be strong 'in view of the persecutions of which our brothers in many countries are still the victims.'[38] In 1865 the officers of the Alliance called upon their 'dear brothers' of Europe, America, and Australia, to contribute financially to the Alliance schools which were helping to 'regenerate' their 'brothers in Asia and Africa.'[39]

Underlying the usage of the term *brothers* is the concept of family, frequently used to explain and to justify Jewish ethnicity. It was often argued that coreligionists have a tight natural bond that unites them, analogous to that found among members of a single family. Although this observation was considered true of all religious groups, it is clear that the factor of descent – the ethnic factor – was assumed to characterize Jewish unity, far beyond any possible analogy in Christianity. The sense of family is evident, for example, in the title of a Jewish periodical published in Avignon from 1859 to 1891, *La Famille de Jacob* (The Family of Jacob).

Even the term *solidarity* was used and the concept openly acknowledged. The Alliance may have been the first Jewish organization to advocate such solidarity and to claim that free regimes had nothing to fear from it. In the *Manifesto*, which launched the Alliance, this is expressed unequivocally: '... a bond must be created, a solidarity established from country to country ...'[40]

## IV

Several factors were responsible for the retention of ethnicity among the French Jews. The international aspect of Jewish existence sharply clashed with attempts to deny any conflicts with local loyalties. In the face of this reality all arguments concerning Jewish patriotism had an unavoidable tone of apologetics. Related to this was the continual migration of the Jewish population during the nineteenth century. Not only did large numbers of Jews switch countries, and therefore loyalties, but they constituted a noticeable poor and nonacculturated mass, at least in the early years of their arrival in new places. The continual arrival in France of Jews from the East, as well as the internal migrations from areas of higher Jewish density in Alsace-Lorraine to the center of the country, contributed to the maintenance of a distinctly Jewish subgroup.[41]

Judaism itself, as a religion, in any of its denominational forms, is not easily differentiable from Jewish ethnicity, as has been well demonstrated by Will Herberg in his classic study, *Protestant–Catholic–Jew*.[42] Speaking of post-World War II American Jewry's 'return' to the form and institutions of Judaism, Herberg notes: 'The dual meaning of "Jewishness" as covering both ethnic group and religion made the "return" movement of the third generation into a source of renewed strength and vigor for the American Jewish community.'[43]

In addition to the difficulty of sharply differentiating between ethnic and religious aspects, the same third generation effect is to be observed in France. The third generation, as third generation Americans were to do later, wanted to remember what its parents wanted to forget.[44] This was the generation born between 1820 and 1840, and which became adult between 1840 and 1860. It is the generation, understandably, which established the French Jewish press, and which founded the Alliance Israélite Universelle.

Observant Jews realized there was a national component to their religion, and refused to give it up. They refused to deny the traditional hope for ultimate national restoration. They refused to do without traditional communal institutions, especially the *minyanim* (prayer meetings) and mutual aid societies, which predated the official consistory, had no legal status under the new regime, and were as much socio-ethnic societies as they were religious ones.[45]

The conservative leader, S. Bloch, editor of the *Univers Israélite*, pleaded for the continued observance of Jewish ritual law. The civil laws, he argued, 'do not separate us from the Jewish community' ('ne nous séparent point de la communauté israélite').[46] Further indication that Bloch was conscious of the social-national aspect of Judaism is to be found in the choice of words he used to denounce the Frankfurt Reformers, who sought, he said, a Judaism without Jews ('judaïsme idéal, spirituel, qui n'aurait ni révélation, ni histoire, ni tradition, ni fêtes, ni cérémonies, ... un judaïsme sans Juifs.')[47] The word *Juif*, used here by Bloch, was the word used by the nineteenth-century French Jews to indicate the old national type of unemancipated, ethnic Jew, as opposed to the modern 'Israelite,' the Jew by 'faith' alone.

Another reason that religion tended to foster the retention of communal consciousness and identity is that the truly secular state did not exist. The government was not blind to religion; rather, it recognized the major religious groupings and gave them certain legal status and financial assistance in their religious as well as social activities. The consistory's recognized charitable and administrative work thus betrayed an acceptance by all parties of a de facto and not unimportant vestige of the pre-Revolutionary corporate organization.[48]

The official Jewish institutions were involved in various 'regeneration' projects for the improvement of the educational and socio-economic level of the Jewish population. Such activities existed primarily on a national and local level, but to some extent also on the international level. With the founding of the Alliance Israélite Universelle in 1860, international solidarity increased. Ben Halpern has aptly noted that 'the actual nature of the work done – political intercession, aid to emigrants, vocational retraining, colonization – did not fall short of the scope of activities later undertaken by secular Zionists as an open program of ethnic politics.'[49]

The civil-ethnic quality of the consistorial institutions was not lost on contemporaries, both Jewish and non-Jewish, who discussed the nature of the institutions and the division of powers between the consistory and the rabbinate. It was often stated that the rabbinate was in charge of religious affairs, and the consistory was responsible for 'civil' affairs.[50]

The consistorial institutions served the function of retaining the Jewish elite by providing them with leadership positions within the Jewish community, positions that were grounded ultimately in the French governmental authority. Thus, ethnicity in France was served by the very institutions that were designed to promote assimilation. Had they not existed, it is possible that assimilation would have been more rapid.

Post-Emancipation France provided acceptable, and even official, outlets for talents that were related to the backgrounds of Jews, thus creating no need among the intellectual classes for denial of their origins. Jews became librarians and professors, specializing in Oriental languages, and especially in Hebrew and ancient and medieval Hebrew studies.[51]

Antisemitism is a pressure that has sometimes led towards renewed efforts at assimilation, and sometimes to an acceptance of, and even an assertion of, ethnic identity. Antisemitism was a constant factor during the nineteenth century, and social and even legal prejudice had to be recognized as part of the Jew's world. Although it is true that antisemitism became most virulent only in the post-1880 period with the European-wide development of political antisemitism, the assumption that pre-Third Republic France, and especially the Second Empire, was relatively free of anti-Jewish prejudice, is incorrect.[52]

Full documentation of the antisemitism of the period would itself constitute the material for an essay, and here we can only make brief reference to representative instances: Jewish status experienced its 'ups and downs' with the various regimes. It made the most tangible gains during the July Monarchy, achieving public funding in 1831, and permission to send chaplains to the military hospitals in 1839, but even this beneficent government was not uniform in its attitude. An 1832 court decision required Jewish 'usurers' to prove that the debts they tried to collect were legal according to the law of March 17, 1808 (which was supposed to have expired in 1818). In 1840 the press reported the accusations against the Jews of Damascus, without any reservations. The French Jewish population was shocked by this act of hostility of many of the leading newspapers.[53] In 1845 the French Jews had been complaining that their rights of trade and domicile in Switzerland, according to the French–Swiss trade agreement, were not being honored because of Swiss anti-Jewish regulations. The Orleanist government replied that it could do nothing about this situation because it had been agreed upon by a secret 1820 clause between the two countries.

A worsening of the Jewish position took place after the ascension of Louis Napoléon to power. In 1849, I. Weill, a Jewish teacher of mathematics, was refused a post in the public 'college' (secondary school) of Haguenau.[54] Later in the same year Isidore Cahen wrote to the central consistory, asking its assistance in his own case. Cahen had achieved third place in the competitive examination (*concours*) in philosophy, and had been named to a chair in the Lycée de Napoléon in Luçon (Vendée). The Bishop of Luçon had refused to allow Cahen's appeals, had not offered him another post at the appropriate level, but, rather, had insulted him by offering him a lower position. Cahen urged the consistory to act in the interest of all Jews to prevent the establishment of a precedent whereby being an 'Israelite' would be incompatible with the holding of a post as a professor of philosophy in the public secondary schools.[55] Despite consistory efforts, however, Cahen was never reinstated in his post, nor did he receive an appropriate alternative one. This experience launched him in a career in Jewish journalism and with the Alliance Israélite Universelle, of which he was one of the founders. Antisemitism had led to a reassertion of ethnicity and Jewish solidarity.

The campaign against Jews in the public schools continued. In 1850 Jérome Aron, a history teacher at the *Lycée* in Strasbourg, was fired.[56] The following year Jews (and Protestants) were barred from the competitive entrance examination for the prestigious teacher-training school, the École Normale.[57]

In 1851 there occurred several instances in which the government slighted the official representatives of the Jews by excluding them from public ceremonies. At least three occasions arose during 1851 and 1852, at which Jewish representatives were not invited to celebrations attended by representatives of other faiths. The central consistory complained about the discrimination, citing the 'great principles of equality.'[58] To the anxious inquiry of the chief rabbi of Bordeaux, Prince Louis Napoléon promised to maintain the principles of 1789 in regard to the Jewish population.[59] But antisemitism was deeply ingrained in France. In 1853 the Strasbourg consistory was advised by the central consistory that it was useless to expect governmental assistance in regard to the repeated threats menacing the Jews of Alsace.[60]

The campaign against Jews in the lycées took new turns. In 1853 two Jewish children of Macon were refused admission to the *Lycée*. After the central consistory complained to the government, the children were admitted, but for a while they were forced to participate in Christian religious worship.[61]

The problem spread to the courts. In 1853, a certain Weill, a Jewish lawyer of Colmar, was refused the right to practice at the bar of Colmar because of his religion.[62] In 1856 a Jew was refused a judgeship in Alsace on the grounds that the local population was prejudiced against Jews.[63]

The 1860 anti-Christian riots in Damascus threatened a repetition of the 1840 Damascus Affair. The French press printed unfounded charges against the Syrian Jews, claiming that they had participated in the massacres of Christians; French Jews took up pens in defense of their maligned brethren. But French anti-Jewish sentiment was prevalent. Throughout the 1950s journals all over the country had printed false accusations against the Jewish population and anti-Jewish pamphlets had appeared. The Jews had discovered that the law did not protect them.[64] Afraid of defeat in a court battle against such publications, the consistory had abstained from any public action. But a young rabbi, Elie-Aristide Astruc, was bolder. In 1859 he published a reply to one of the persistent antisemitic writers, Louis Veuillot, *Les Juifs et Louis Veuillot*. The following year Astruc was one of the founders of the Alliance Israélite Universelle. Again, antisemitism had led to ethnicity and Jewish solidarity. In addition to Cahen and Astruc, at least one other founder of the Alliance, Jules Carvallo, had personally experienced anti-Jewish prejudice.[65]

Antisemitic feelings and expressions continued to be manifested after the Alliance took up the battle against them. In 1862 Protestants in Nancy complained that a military service had been held in a Catholic church. Writing about the complainants, in order to dismiss their charge, the Marquis de la Rochejaquelin wrote, 'Ce sont des juifs!'

V

Solidarity among French Jews is demonstrated by the many examples of concerted action undertaken to solve Jewish material and physical problems, both within France and on an international level. Initiatives in this direction were taken by individuals, local community institutions, and consistories. The consistory was the official administrative unit of the French Jewish community. There were seven to nine branches located throughout metropolitan France, and they were hierarchically administered by a central consistory located in Paris. Each consistory was responsible for the entire region it governed, and for the local affairs of all the communities included in that region.

## THE DAMASCUS AFFAIR TO THE FIRST WORLD WAR

Because of a tendency to conservative political action at the central consistory level, the battles for Jewish rights and for protection against antisemitism and discriminatory practices were often waged at the regional level. For example, the attempt of courts in Alsace-Lorraine to enforce the special Jewish oath (moré judaïco) was a problem that the central consistory defined as a regional one. Ceding the initiative in the battle for the elimination of the oath to the eastern consistories, the central consistory nevertheless announced that it viewed the problem with sympathetic interest. The traditional solidarity of the Eastern communities was strong; the battle against the Jewish oath was fought at their initiative, and won.[66] Another example of the strength of traditional group loyalties is the maintenance of the old Sephardi–Ashkenazi distinctions. The failure of the central and Paris consistories to achieve a *rite français* through the fusion of Sephardi and Ashkenazi ceremonies, is testimony to the deep ethnic loyalties of the separate groups, more than to their religious difference of opinion.

Charitable institutions at a local community level are indications of spontaneous Jewish solidarity. One historian has noted

> ... the critical role which charity played in providing cohesion for a Jewish community divided by both class and interests. Jews of whatever background, of whatever Jewish consciousness, had sufficient memory of the time of persecutions to take pity on those who suffer ... This benevolence, commonly referred to as 'Jewish solidarity,' flowed from all elements of the Jewish community. Charitable associations, particularly in Paris, were the meeting-places for Frenchmen who had nothing in common but their Jewishness.[67]

It was a practice in the larger communities to build a Jewish hospital where, it was said, Jewish patients could be fed kosher food and would not have to fear the visits of Christian clergymen. But these two problems could have been solved in less drastic ways, within the institutional framework of the public hospitals. The Jewish hospitals were a historical outgrowth of the functions of traditional mutual aid societies, which assured sick-care as part of their services to members. Other charitable activities included the running of orphanages; charitable grants for maintenance of poor families; grants for special needs, such as clothing, weddings, childbirth, 'religious initiation;' loans to businessmen; vocational training; general education; even the bringing of Oriental Jews to

Paris for a French education to prepare them for leadership and educational roles in their home communities.

Not all charity was a product of official institutions. Traditional Jewish solidarity, expressed in the form of private personal charity, was a firmly entrenched custom in the Eastern communities, and even under the threat of consistorial reprisals for allegedly interfering with regeneration attempts, personal charity continued. During the 1850s three Parisian Jews, Manuel and Narcisse Leven and Eugène Manuel, took the initiative in organizing evening classes for young Jewish apprentices of the capital. These men had been inspired by the principles of 1848, but it is notable that they chose to express their liberal ideals through activity within their own ethnic group. The same three men were later among the founders of the Alliance Israélite Universelle.

At all levels (regional, national, and international) consistories spontaneously began to take initiatives – not required by law – to protect Jews and Jewish interests. It should not be assumed, however, that all of the instances which involved foreign Jewries were indeed examples of international solidarity. In many cases the real issue was ultimately French Jewish status within France and vis-à-vis the French authorities. Thus, the Damascus Affair of 1840, the accusations against Damascus Jews in 1860, the problem of Jewish rights in Switzerland, Jewish rights in Russia – all may appear at first glance to be indications of French Jewish mobilization for the assistance of foreign Jews. But there is a pattern in these cases. In all of them the French government and/or the press and public opinion in France had been aroused against Jewry, and French Jews had reason to fear a worsening of their position *within* France. It became extremely important to establish Jewish rights to equal consular and passport protection as French citizens abroad, and to see that the French government did not take any active public position – as it did in the 1840 Damascus Affair – which was openly hostile to Jewish interests. While the governments of England and Austria were actively intervening to obtain the release of the Damascus prisoners, France's consul was encouraging their persecution as part of the French Middle East policy of supporting Mehmet Ali against the Ottoman regime.

Similarly, at least part of the French Jewish concern for Russian and Swiss policies regarding Jews was provoked by the fact that the French government was not affording equal protection to its Jewish citizens in regard to the honoring abroad of the French passport and the rights granted to French citizens by international treaties. Thus, the main thrust of the complaints in these countries concerned the rights refused to *French Jews*, not to the local Jewish population, although a secondary benefit of the campaign in Switzerland was the eventual emancipation of the Swiss Jews. From the 1830s, for more than thirty years, French Jewish citizens and official representatives repeatedly appealed for French government assistance in obtaining equality for the French Alsatian Jews who had traditionally done business in Switzerland. The initiative was divided among the local consistories, the central consistory, and an especially active and devoted local leader, Rabbi Nordmann of Hegenheim.[68]

As an instrument for the expression of Jewish solidarity, the periodical press also operated on several levels. Some Jewish journals were concerned with local issues; others had a broader circulation and were engaged in exchanges with the foreign Jewish press. All of them were by Jews, about Jews, for Jews. The Jewish press is an ethnic institution *par excellence*; it was used to encourage Jewish achievement and socioeconomic advance, to maintain Jewish solidarity by informing French Jews of the status and problems of their coreligionists abroad. Thus, it became an instrument for combatting anti-Jewish prejudice by adopting the developing nineteenth-century liberal view that knowledge creates freedom. It was this growing liberal outlook, grounded ultimately in faith in public opinion, that spawned the Alliance Israélite Universelle. The founders of the Alliance were not unaware of this, and in their *Manifesto* made reference to the salutary effect the press had had in 'overturning mountains of prejudice ...' They added that 'at every moment there are facts to reveal, accusations to refute, truths to disseminate.'[69]

During the two decades preceding the founding of the Alliance, the press was, in fact, the instrument most responsible for spreading the idea of uniting to give practical expression to Jewish solidarity and to achieve material gains for Jews living under oppressive conditions. Thus, in 1844, at a time when the Jews of Russia and Poland experienced a worsening of their condition, Samuel Cahen, editor of the *Archives Israélites*, proposed the creation of a European committee for Jewish Colonization (comité européen de colonisation israélite) to improve the condition of persecuted Jewry by giving them land to work.[70] The following year another journalist recommended the creation of a world society for the defense of Jewish rights,[71] and in 1846 Jean Jacques Altaras of Marseille proposed colonizing Russian Jews in Algeria. In 1851 and 1853 Jules Carvallo used the medium of the press to suggest the convening of a

Jewish Congress (un congrès israélite).[72] In 1858, in the columns of the *Archives Israélites*, Isidore Cahen suggested that the Jews imitate the model of the Protestant organization, the Alliance Évangélique Universelle.[73] Early in 1860, Simon Bloch, in the *Univers Israélite*, endorsed the idea and even proposed the name that was subsequently used: Alliance Israélite Universelle.[74]

Even before the establishment of the Jewish press in 1840 there had been attempts by French Jews to use international diplomacy for the benefit of nonemancipated Jewry. The first French Jew to attempt to implement this idea was the eccentric lawyer Michel Berr. In 1801, on the eve of the anticipated international peace conference in Luneville, Berr published an appeal to the statesmen who were to participate in the conference. He urged them to support the cause of Jewish emancipation in their own countries.[75]

In 1833 James de Rothschild and Adolphe Crémieux secretly worked with 'The Philanthropic Society for the Acceleration of Jewish Emancipation throughout the World' (known as the Lafayette Committee). This committee had been organized by Polish non-Jewish émigrés in Paris, whose political motivations had interested them in the Jews of Poland and the Middle East. The Jewish members of the committee were involved purely because of their concern for Jews abroad, although they preferred not to release news of the society's establishment until a later date because 'at present it will be considered by the despotic government as merely political propaganda and thus might make worse the situation of the Jews who are scattered throughout the world instead of aiding them.'[76]

In 1936 a converted French Jew and former adherent of the Saint-Simon movement (until its demise in 1832), Gustave d'Eichthal, undertook a private project to obtain the emancipation of the Austrian Jews. Eichthal envisaged the emancipation of world Jewry as a necessary step in the eventual achievement of the Saint-Simonian ideal of the unity of mankind through the union of East and West. Deriving his thought largely from the writings of the French Jewish scholar, Joseph Salvador, Eichthal displayed a strong appreciation of the continual significance of the Jewish people's contribution to world civilization. Furthermore, his conception of Judaism was not a narrow 'confessional' view, but a larger racial view, which embodied biological and cultural elements. He spoke of the 'indelible character' of one's Jewish origins. He himself, although converted, associated mainly with Jews. Eichthal traveled to Vienna where he obtained an interview with Metternich, but failed to convince the chancellor of the need and value of emancipating the Jews. Although his mission failed, it is of historic note that Eichthal 'extended the battle for emancipation beyond the frontiers of a single country and thereby solicited Jewish solidarity.'[77]

Consistorial activity on behalf of Jewry in other parts of the world was entangled with, and not always well distinguished from, the history of the Rothschild family initiative. It frequently happened that the Rothschilds preferred to work through the consistory or its charity committee, in order to make their private activities appear to be official acts of the French Jewish community. For a long time Albert Cohn was the link between the Rothschilds and the Paris consistory's charity board, working in the employ of both. In 1854, when the Rothschilds sent Cohn to Jerusalem to create charitable institutions, they suggested that he be officially named to survey the status of Jerusalem Jewry on behalf of the central consistory. The Rothschilds provided the money to found a school for which the consistory agreed to raise maintenance funds.[78]

The Rothschilds frequently undertook to represent Jewish interests to the government, although they were not always given a sympathetic ear. Sometimes the consistory asked them to bring a case to the attention of the government; sometimes the Rothschilds took the initiative before the consistory even met to consider what action to take.

By around 1840 the third generation effect that we have described above began to be manifested by an increased interest in Jewish affairs abroad. In 1841 the Paris consistory asked the central consistory to organize financial aid for Smyrna Jews. In 1843 a private individual, Eugène de Dalmeyda, acting independently, published an appeal to the Pope, in which he argued that the edict of inquisition that had just been promulgated would ruin the Jews of the papal lands. In 1846 the consistory itself was involved in obtaining from the Pope a statement of benevolence regarding the Jews in the papal lands, as we know from an 1847 consistory letter thanking the Pope for his reassurances. Official influence in this case was possible because it coincided with French foreign policy; France was supporting the Pope against nationalist revolutionary forces. In 1849, when France sent an expeditionary army to suppress the Revolution and the 1848 constitution, the central consistory asked the government to maintain the Jewish liberties accorded by the Pope.

French governmental interests continued to coincide with Jewish interests in Poland. France had long been supporting the Polish national struggle against Russia (as part of her Middle East policy and her competition with Russia over the anticipated succession to the Ottoman Empire). Just as this kind of consideration had explained the policy of the Lafayette Committee, it also underlay France's policy in 1844, when Russia increased its persecution of Polish Jewry and the French government spoke out, earning the praise of both the Paris and central consistories.

For twenty years before the establishment of the Alliance and its widespread network of schools for Oriental Jews, French Jewry had a tradition of building schools in the Middle East. Crémieux had opened schools in Egypt, on his way home from Damascus in 1840. The Rothschild family built schools in Jerusalem, Smyrna, Alexandria, and Constantinople. They influenced the development of additional schools in Trieste, Cairo, and Damascus.[79] In 1856 Salonican Jewry asked the central consistory to supply them with a teacher. The consistory endorsed the proposal made by Ludwig Philippson in 1854 that young Jews from the Ottoman Empire be brought to Europe to study and prepare themselves for leadership and educational activities at home.[80] Arrangements were made – but did not materialize – for the students to live and study at the Strasbourg consistory's École de Travail. (The same idea later found expression in the Alliance's École Normale Israélite Orientale, opened in Paris in 1867.)[81]

French Jewry's interest in Oriental Jews was not confined to pedagogy. In 1854 the central consistory asked the emperor to try to obtain the same rights for the Ottoman Jews as were enjoyed by the Christians under the capitulations agreements with the Ottoman Empire. But French Jewry went further than requesting the assistance of their own government. In the same year Albert Cohn, on behalf of both the Rothschilds and the central consistory, obtained the following statement from the sultan in Constantinople: 'All the rights, privileges and immunities which have been or will be accorded to any Christian group will be accorded automatically to the Jews, because His Imperial Majesty's heart will never permit the establishment of the slightest difference among the non-Muslim subjects (*raias*) of his Empire.'[82]

In 1859 the central consistory, through the intermediary of James de Rothschild, influenced the French government to intervene on behalf of two Rumanian Jews imprisoned in Galantz. The two were released. In 1860 the central consistory appealed to French Jews for financial contributions to aid Moroccan Jews who had escaped to Oran in Algeria.

The consistory's consistent policy of aiding Ottoman Jewry fitted well into France's Middle East policy; not all suggestions to help foreign Jews were embraced by the consistory, if the French government could not be expected to exert a salutary influence. The choice of causes was thus based entirely on the practical evaluation of the likelihood of obtaining results by working through the French government. The central consistory considered that it did not have the right of freedom to act independently of the government.[83]

This constituted an essential difference between the consistory and the Alliance Israélite Universelle. The new organization, under the leadership of younger and less cautious men, was more solidly committed to the active public defense of Jewish interests, regardless of French government policy. Thus, in addition to continuing the tradition of support for Ottoman Jewry, one of the early acts of the Alliance was to intervene directly with Cavour in regard to the Mortara Affair, whereas the consistory had refused to take such bold action. The Alliance took up the battle of the Algerian Jews who were being discriminated against in taxation matters by the French military government and it raised a public cry against the missionary activities of Notre Dame de Sion – both unpopular causes with the consistory. This kind of vigorous approach earned the Alliance Israélite Universelle the suspicion and hostility of some consistory members – especially those in Paris.[84] However, within a few years of its establishment the Alliance had the support of – and in some cases even shared leaders with – the consistories, and by the end of the century it was more cautious to harmonize its activities with French public policy.[85]

## VI

It has long been the consensus of Jewish historians that nineteenth-century French Jewry was assimilationist in ideology and assimilated in practice. Historians, writing of the Jews of France, tend to present the single schema: Sanhedrin – assimilation – Dreyfus.[86] Scholars continue to repeat previous conclusions to the effect that nineteenth-century French Jews 'were totally absorbed in their non-Jewish surroundings;' that 'Judaism for this generation was no longer a religious, social, or political concept;' that Jewish history and tradition had no meaning for many French Jews.[87]

The latest to argue this point is Michael Marrus, whose *Politics of*

*Assimilation* contends that until the Dreyfus Affair, there was a single view within Judaism which saw Jewish loyalty as primarily directed toward France.[88] In my view this monolithic view of an assimilationist pre-Zionist French Jewry ignores the many shades of opinion that existed within the community and ignores the numerous examples of language and action which contradict the theory.

One of the reasons that the error has been made and repeated so often is that statements by nineteenth-century writers urging 'fusion' have been exaggerated, misinterpreted, and taken out of context. For example, L.M. Lambert wrote in 1840 of the need for civil, and even religious, fusion of Jews with the French population. The only differences that need remain, he said, are 'the obligations to our creator according to the Bible and the tradition.'[89] This is an impressive statement which could appear to be very strong evidence of assimilationism, if the reader is not familiar with the full range of Lambert's thought. Lambert, in fact, argued in the very same publication that the Jews deserve nationality as much as the Poles, the Greeks, and the Italians.[90]

If by 'assimilated' one refers to behavioral assimilation, or acculturation, then French Jews of the nineteenth century were assimilated.[91] But since this would be a trivial statement, encompassing even Jewish nationalists and Zionists, it is clear that the charge of assimilation generally made in regard to French Jewry implies a moving in the direction of total disappearance of all differences, and an eventual merging with the French population.

However, this claim is contradicted by much of the evidence: the low incidence of intermarriage, the low rate of conversion, the numerous ethnic institutions, the tendency among Jews to maintain primary group associations among other Jews, the many examples of language use which betray ethnic feeling, the repeated instances of international Jewish solidarity, and the attempts to use international diplomacy to improve the status of Jews abroad. Recognition of the ethnicity and solidarity of nineteenth-century French Jewry helps to explain the genesis of the twentieth-century ethnic reality.

NOTES

1. The Sanhedrin has been discussed in detail by R. Anchel in his *Napoléon et les Juifs*, Paris, 1928. Several editions of the minutes exist. For a list of them see Z. Szajkowski, 'Judaica Napoleonica: A Bibliography of Books, Pamphlets and

Printed Documents, 1810–1815,' *Studies in Bibliography and Booklore*, II (1956), pp.107–152; reprinted in his *Jews and the French Revolutions of 1789, 1830, and 1848* (New York, 1970).
2. This is the case, most notably, in Michael Marrus, *The Politics of Assimilation: A Study of the French Jewish Community at the Time of the Dreyfus Affair* (Oxford, 1971).
3. Although Zionism was late in implanting itself in France, it became obvious in the wake of the Six Day War that it had succeeded in commanding the loyalty of most French Jews. Since then, French Jewish students have been particularly active in the combatting of anti-Zionist campus activity. The once very inward-looking *consistoire* now devotes considerable space to the news from Israel in its community journal.
4. In my book, *The Modernization of French Jewry: Consistory and Community in the Nineteenth Century* (Hanover, N.H., 1977) these points are developed individually. For example, the geographic spread of the Jewish population, long anticipated as a beneficial result of the Emancipation, was of very minor significance. The 38 departments of France which held no Jews in 1808 had a total Jewish population of only 1034 (or 1.08 percent of the total French Jewish population) in 1861. Of this small number, most were concentrated in only 15 of the departments. Urbanization of the French Jewish population occurred at a rate far higher than that of the general population. Although there was an increasing diversification of Jewish occupations, throughout the nineteenth century, trade remained the dominant Jewish occupation, while some careers such as agricultural and military ones were chosen by Jews much less frequently than by the general population.
5. On September 27, 1791, Duport, deputy of Paris, observed that the constitution which had just been adopted guaranteed equality of rights for all, and that therefore all discrimination had to be abolished. Consequently the assembly revoked all exceptional provisions referring to the Jews; see François Delpech, 'La Révolution et l'Empire,' in Bernhard Blumenkranz (ed.), *Histoire des Juifs en France* (Toulouse, 1972), p.281.
6. Government funding of the Christian churches was instituted by Napoleon, but Judaism was not a beneficiary of such funding until after the July Revolution and the Institution of the Orleanist monarchy in 1830. The discriminatory special Jewish oath was abolished by the courts only in 1846, and after that year there were some provincial courts which sought to reinstitute it. The Jews were obligated to pay off their pre-Revolutionary communal debts, which unlike those of other religious communities had not been nationalized by the Revolution. This state continued in Alsace until the loss of that region in 1871 as a consequence of the Franco-Prussian War.
7. Arnold Rose, in his *Sociology; The Study of Human Relations* (New York, 1956), pp.557–58, defines them this way. Acculturation is 'the adoption by a person or group of the culture of another social group. Or, the process leading to this adoption.' Assimilation is 'the adoption by a person or group of the culture of another social group to such a complete extent that the person or group no longer has any particular loyalties to his former culture. Or, the process leading to this adoption.'
8. Milton Gordon, *Assimilation in American Life: The Role of Race, Religion, and National Origins* (New York, 1964), pp.65–71.
9. Marcus Hansen has spoken of the third generation effect: that the third generation wants to remember what the second generation wanted to forget; see his *The Problem of the Third Generation Immigrant* (Rock Island, Ill., 1938), pp.9–10.
10. Ibid., pp.62–67 and passim.
11. Park and Burgess, in 1921, defined assimilation in a way that corresponds to Gordon's structural assimilation, while a few years later, in 1930, Park's definition of assimilation was modified by a behavioral perspective to read more like Gordon's

definition of behavioral assimilation. For him an immigrant to America is 'considered assimilated as soon as he has acquired the language and the social ritual of the native community and can participate, without encountering prejudice, in the common life, economic and political' (ibid., pp.62–64).

12. Thus Marrus says that the Emancipation, in conferring citizenship, demanded assimilation. 'Jewishness might be preserved, but only in a sphere which did not affect the Jew's relationship with the nation' (Marrus, *Politics*, p.87). But Marrus does not analyze fully the type of assimilation that would be required to fulfill this demand. Clearly, structural assimilation would fulfill it, and, indeed, many Frenchmen, in the words of one contemporary, 'confuse[d] assimilation and uniformity' (Yves Guot, quoted by Marrus, *Politics*, p.86). But would behavioral assimilation (acculturation) also fulfill the requirement that the retention of Jewishness not affect the Jew's relationship with the nation? In fact, within the French Jewish community, as within France in general, there was a range of opinion as to what constituted a threat to the Jew's relationship with the nation, and therefore there existed a range of opinion as to what kind of assimilation was sought.
13. Theodore Reinach, *Histoire des israélites depuis l'époque de leur dispersion jusqu'à nos jours* (Paris, 1884), pp.388–90.
14. Milton Gordon (basing himself on Robert Redfield and E. K. Francis), *Assimilation*, pp.23–27. Cf. Nathan Glazer's definition of an ethnic group: 'A social group which consciously shares some aspects of a common culture and is defined primarily by descent.' (The Universality of Ethnicity,' *Encounter*, XLIV, no. 2, February 1975, p.8.)
15. Marrus, *Politics*, pp.10–27. For the earlier part of the century, I observed both this usage and the use of the word *nation* consistently in the Jewish periodical press and in the books of the period.
16. Ibid., p.63.
17. The literature on this topic is abundant and growing. Some trace the beginning of the awareness to the second edition of Nathan Glazer and Daniel P. Moynihan, *Beyond the Melting Pot; The Negroes, Puerto Ricans, Jews, Italians and Irish of New York City* (Cambridge, Mass., 1970).
18. Gordon, *Assimilation*, pp.24–25.
19. Albert, *Modernization*, p.25.
20. Marrus, *Politics*, p.83: '... it is apparent that at the end of the nineteenth century Jews in France were not so closely identified with French society that they had broken entirely with an older pattern of identification. This pattern persisted, though in a weakened form; it was a reality ...' Cf. ibid., p.3.
21. *Manifeste de juillet 1860*, reprinted in André Couragqui, *L'Alliance Israélite Universelle et la renaissance juive contemporaine* (Paris, 1965), pp.407–12.
22. Hansen, *Third Generation Immigrant*; and Will Herberg, *Protestant–Catholic–Jew* rev. ed. (New York, 1960), pp.31, 257.
23. Writing under the pen-name Tsarphati ('a Frenchman'), Orly Terquem published nine numbered 'Letter[s] from a French Israelite to his Coreligionists' between 1821 and 1837. He also wrote articles in the Jewish press, and after the deathbed conversion of his brother by the Jewish convert, Ratisbone, in 1845 Terquem published a pamphlet protesting against missionary activity.
24. Marrus, *Politics*, pp.62–63.
25. Ibid., pp.60–64.
26. *Manifeste*, pp.407–12.
27. For example, Simon Bloch, editor of the *Univers Israélite*, had written: Tous les esprits sérieux dans le judaïsme, tous les vrais et sincères israélites, ont depuis longtemps reconnu la nécessité d'un rapprochement, d'une union plus étroite entre nos coreligionnaires habitant les diverses contrées de la terre' (*Univers Israélite*, February 1860; reprinted in Chouraqui, *Alliance*, p.406).
28. Marrus, *Politics*, p.26.

29. Michael Berr, *Appel à la justice des nations et des rois* (Strasbourg, 1801), passim, esp. pp.54–55, 66–67.
30. L. M. Lambert, *Précis de l'histoire des Hébreux, depuis le patriarche Abraham, jusqu'en 1840* (Paris, 1840), p.414: '... ceux, qui ont répandu la morale et la civilisation sur toute la terre, méritent sans doute la nationalité aussi bien que les grecs et les polonais.' If we are tempted to speculate about Lambert's proto-Zionism, we are especially startled by his observation that there was a serious threat to the physical existence of world Jewry in 1840. Referring to the many false accusations of the period, he concludes: '... il ne s'agissait de rien moins que d'exterminer tous les Hébreux de la surface du globe' (ibid., p.421).
31. For example, S. Bloch wrote: '... quand Israël et son culte seront admis partout, et mieux connus des peuples, la lumière, la vérité, la conscience du monde fera le reste' (quoted in Chouraqui, *Alliance*, p.407).
32. *Manifeste*, p.411.
33. L. Setier, Paris, November 1813, 12 pp. The journal itself never appeared.
34. Chouraqui, *Alliance*, p.33.
35. *Archives Israélites*, March 12, 1891.
36. The earliest known use of this term occurs (in the Hebrew language) in a prospectus for a prayer book that was to be published in Paris about 1798 or 1799. My thanks to Dr. Simon Schwarzfuchs of Jerusalem who called my attention to this observation.
37. Quoted in Chouraqui, *Alliance*, p.22.
38. *Univers Israélite*, February 1860; quoted in Chouraqui, *Alliance*, pp.406–7.
39. *Appel de 1ᵉʳ mars 1865*, reprinted in Chouraqui, *Alliance*, p.247.
40. *Manifeste*, p.411.
41. Jews from eastern Europe began immigrating into France in the 1850s, and arrived in large numbers after 1880. Throughout the entire nineteenth century an internal migration, especially from Alsace-Lorraine to Paris, took place, such that the relative percentages of Jewish population in Alsace-Lorraine and Paris, respectively, were 79 percent and 6 percent in 1808, and 56.5 percent and 26 percent in 1861 (Albert, *Modernization*, p.19). Poverty levels were high. In 1870, 60 percent of the Parisian Jewish burials were at public expense. The poor shied away from official (consistorial) weddings, because of the expense, and tended to retain old communal customs which had a strong ethnic aspect (ibid., p.304).
42. Herberg, *Protestant–Catholic–Jew*.
43. Ibid., p.187.
44. Ibid., p.267.
45. In *Modernization*, pp.197–221, I develop fully the story of the stubborn maintenance of these nonconsistorial institutions in the face of continuous legal prosecution.
46. *Univers Israélite*, I (1844).
47. Ibid.
48. Separate schools and hospitals were maintained. Financial aid was provided for separate social welfare organizations. The various clergy were represented on certain public committees such as the education committee. Chaplaincies were maintained in the army, schools, and hospitals. Furthermore, the consistory was responsible, until 1870, for the collection of the outstanding pre-Revolutionary Jewish community debts. Early in their existence, during the Napoleonic regime, the consistories also registered Jews, provided lists of conscripts, and denounced those without a living (Albert, *Modernization*, p.308).
49. Ben Halpern, *Jews and Blacks: The Classic American Minorities* (New York, 1971), p.110.
50. Albert, *Modernization*, p.436 n.3; and p.309. In a personal letter to the German orthodox leader Rabbi Ezriel Hildesheimer, Grand Rabbi S. Klein wrote (5623, 1862–63) that the consistory had no interest in religion. Speaking of the degradation of Judaism at the hands of the consistory, he says, 'Ses pieds sont entravés, ses mains liées, et elle est livrée comme prisonnière aux mains du Consistoire.' Speaking of

the central consistory members, he says that less than three of the nine men observed Kashrut and Shabbat. Some did not even have their sons circumcised (Simon Schwarzfuchs, *Les Juifs de France* (Paris, 1975), p.256).
51. A few examples are Salomon Munk, Arsène and James Darmesteter, Hartwig and Joseph Derennbourg, Adolphe Franck, and Joseph Salvador.
52. For example, Michael Marrus argues that before 1880 antisemitism had 'little mass following' (*Politics*, p.124).
53. A particularly strong example of this kind of reporting appeared in *La Gazette du Languedoc*, June 14, 1840.
54. Archives, central consistory, 1B5, October 22, 1849.
55. Isidore Cahen to the central consistory, December 11, 1849.
56. Archives, central consistory, 1B5, November 10, 1850.
57. Ibid., July 29, 1852. Cf. Archives, Paris consistory, AA4, August 11, 1852.
58. Archives, central consistory, 1B5, January 27, 1851; January 11, 1852; May 3, 1852.
59. Archives, Bordeaux consistory, 2A6, October 20, 1852; archives, central consistory, 1B5, October 5, November 10, November 19, 1953.
60. Archives, Strasbourg consistory, Minutes, March 14, 1853.
61. Archives, central consistory, 1B5, October 5, November 10, November 19, 1853.
62. Ibid., May 17, July 11, 1853.
63. Archives, Strasbourg consistory, Minutes, December 18, 1856; and March 25, 1857.
64. Albert, *Modernization*, pp.160–65.
65. Chouraqui, *Alliance*, p.23.
66. The Supreme Court, in 1846, ruled that imposition of the moré judaïco oath was illegal.
67. Marrus, *Politics*, pp.77–78.
68. Nordmann deserves credit for keeping the issue alive and achieving ultimate victory.
69. *Manifeste*, p.409.
70. Chouraqui, *Alliance*, p.22.
71. Ibid., p.20.
72. *Manifeste*, p.408.
73. *Archives Israélites* XIX (1859), pp.623 ff.
74. Quoted in Chouraqui, *Alliance*, p.406.
75. Michel Berr, *Appel*, p.52.
76. Abraham Duker, 'The Lafayette Committee for Jewish Emancipation,' *Essays in Jewish Life and Thought, Presented in Honor of Salo Baron*, New York, 1959, pp.169–76.
77. Michael Graetz, 'Une Initiative Saint-Simonienne pour l'émancipation des Juifs,' *REJ*, CXXIX (1970), 167–84. Graetz errs in assuming that the Eichthal mission was the first example of enlarging the Emancipation struggle beyond the borders of a single country.
78. The Rothschilds carried out philanthropic activities in Jerusalem because they believed in the special role of Jerusalem in Jewish history. This is clear from an 1854 discussion in the central consistory during which two opposite views emerged – that of Adolphe Franck, who favored extending financial and educational aid to all the Jews of the Ottoman Empire, and Rothschild, who insisted that Jerusalem was a special case. It is worth remembering in this context that Rabbi Zvi Hirsch Kalischer had contacted Albert Cohn around 1836 with his views that settlement in Palestine would be the first step toward the messianic era.
79. Isidore Loeb, *Biographie d'Albert Cohn*, Paris, 1878, pp.67, 75, 77, 80, 82, 90, 108.
80. Ibid., pp.52–55. On this occasion the central consistory designated Cohn to survey the needs of the Turkish Jews and Loeb reports the incident without mentioning that Cohn was really sent by the Rothschilds.
81. On the École Normale Israélite, see Chouraqui, *Alliance*, pp.177–81.

82. Loeb, *Albert Cohn*, p.80.
83. Thus, the consistory turned down Montefiore's 1854 proposal that French Jews join British Jews in asking the Spanish Cortes, then about to meet, to revoke the expulsion of the Jews from Spain. The reason is that the central consistory was willing to act only when it could have the support of the French government in assuring a successful intervention. In the case of Spain, France was supporting the conservative monarchist interests; the queen had just fled to exile in Paris; and it would be dangerous for the consistory to intervene with the Spanish liberal revolutionaries who were in a position to legalize the status of the Jews in Spain.
84. A member of the central consistory declared at the meeting of October 18, 1860: 'Cette société agit avec peu de prudence et pourrait quelque fois, par ses démarches inconsidérées, nuire au véritable intérêt du judaïsme' (quoted in Chouraqui, *Alliance*, p.42). Cf. the reaction of even Ludwig Philippson, who was always active in organizing international Jewish pressure: 'La fondation de l'Alliance Israélite Universelle vaudra aux juifs un surcroît de discrédit, en renforçant la légende de la solidarité juive, du complot maçonnique dirigé secrètement par le judaïsme international ...' (quoted in ibid., p.43).
85. Marrus, *Politics*, pp.238–39. In 1861 the Strasbourg, Nancy, Bayonne, Bordeaux, and Marseille consistories offered their support to the Alliance. The journals *Archives Israélites, Univers Israélite,* and *Le Lien d'Israël* quickly offered the Alliance an enthusiastic welcome.
86. See, for example, Cecil Roth, *A History of the Jews from Earliest Times through the Six-Day War*, rev. ed., New York, 1970, p.323. Speaking of the Sanhedrin, Roth says: '... it is frequently regarded with good reason as having set the footsteps of French Jewry upon the pathway of assimilation ...' Roth's next statements on French Jewry are the reporting of the founding of the Alliance (p.346) and the Dreyfus Affair (p.349). The same program is followed by Howard Morley Sachar in his *The Course of Modern Jewish History*, New York, 1958. On pp.62–65 Sachar discusses the Sanhedrin; on pp.98–99 he describes the increasing assimilation of the French Jews into such institutions as the army, the universities, and politics; on p.227 he begins a discussion of the rise of antisemitism in France. An exception to the general pattern is Simon Dubnov, whose discussion of French Jewry during the Second Republic and the Second Empire is more sensitive to the reality, especially the problem of continual antisemitism in France. He too, however, judges that 'the process of assimilation with the surrounding milieu ... went on apace' (Simon Dubnov, *History of the Jews*, 5 vols. (London, 1967–73), V, 362–63).
87. Walter Laqueur, *A History of Zionism*, New York, 1972, pp.34–35.
88. Marrus, *Politics*, pp.120–21.
89. Lambert, *Précis*, p.413.
90. Ibid., pp.413–14.
91. The Jewish leadership was 'mildly liberal in regard to religion and integrationist socially and economically ... generally non-observant, although not assimilated' (Albert, *Modernization*, pp.305–6).

# 5

# The *Alliance Israélite Universelle* and French Jewish Leadership vis-à-vis North African Jewry, 1860–1914

## Simon Schwarzfuchs

The first body to display any interest in the Jewry of Algeria after the French conquest was the *Consistoire central des Israélites de France*. As early as 1833, three years after the landing of the French forces in Algeria, the *Consistoire* addressed its remarks to the French Government on the subject of 'the establishment of a Jewish Consistory in Algeria.' There is no way of knowing whether this had any effect, but the interesting thing is that as early as this the French Jews affirmed that it would be to the good if the Jews of Algeria were to adopt the pattern of organization and leadership in use by French Jewry. They were already certain that the French model was the desirable one for the Algerian communities. They had no doubts or hesitations in this regard. The process did not increase in momentum until the 1840s (the Central Consistory handed the matter over to the Marseille Consistory, which showed more interest in the problem and was nearer to the Algerian arena geographically) when a delegation of French Jewry came to Algeria and visited the big towns there. This delegation was headed by Jacob Isaac Altaras, an interesting personality from many points of view, seconded by Advocate Joseph Cohen. They travelled in Algeria, talked to the people, and penned a long, detailed report, which was presented to the French authorities for study at the beginning of 1843. A committee was set up, another report was put together, and on 5 November 1845 a decree was issued that laid down arrangements for directing the affairs of the Jewish communities of Algeria practically according to the French system. The situation developed fairly soon into a functional unification of French and Algerian Jewry. As early as 1862 a decree provided for supervision and control of the Jewish religion in Algeria by the Central Consistory in Paris, which would become the necessary link connecting the Algerian communities and the French Ministry of Religions. It was only a short step to the acquisition of French citizenship: the Jews of Algeria were granted French citizenship in 1870.[1]

The development of Algerian Jewry was the Consistory's affair and it is not surprising that it was removed, although not permanently, from the responsibility that had been assumed by the *Alliance Israélite Universelle*, the new body set up in 1860. The question at once arises as to who the founders of this body were and what their ideology was. According to its foundation charter,[2] this new organization was to act everywhere for the emancipation and moral advancement of the Jewish people; this meant that it would not function in France but only in countries where the Jews had not been granted rights, that is to say in Eastern Europe and the Islamic countries. There was thus a division of labour between the Central Consistory and the *Alliance*. It must be remembered that at that time the ideology of the Jews of France was consciously assimilationist, but this was according to the definition of the idea in that period and not according to its modern interpretation. Assimilation for them was the search for a way which would enable French Jews to identify themselves with their country and become an integral part of it without relinquishing their religion. In the eyes of the Jews of that generation, assimilation was a convenient way of being able to remain Jewish and even to strengthen their loyalty to Judaism. According to this definition, there was no contradiction between a secular way of life and religion: each had its own specific domain and co-existence was not only possible, but also desirable. The *Alliance* leadership was therefore an assimilatory, lay institution, faithful to Judaism and entirely devoted to the idea of improving the situation of the Jews in backward countries where they were not granted basic rights. This definition is *prima facie* a tissue of contradictions, but it should be clearly stated that the *Alliance* leaders were not aware of these contradictions and were not troubled by them. All they wanted was to help the Jews of North Africa who attracted their special attention because of their geographical proximity and because of their inclusion in the French Empire. There is no doubt at all that the *Alliance*, who enjoyed much less help from the French authorities than generally estimated, found in the mere fact of the presence of the French armed forces an encouraging and convenient factor for expanding its activities. Its representatives also shared a common language with the French officials. These representatives, who will be examined later, were first and foremost the principals of the *Alliance* schools. They did what the *Alliance* told them and sent reports of their activities to the *Alliance* Central Committee.[3]

The *Alliance Israélite Universelle* asked these representatives for descriptions and appraisals of the existing situation in the communities they were sent to and the replies they returned constitute a very important source on the entrance of these communities into the modern era. At times the letters report on shocking conditions. For example, this is how in 1909 the principal of the boys' school described the Casablanca community in its beginnings:

> There is the *Mellah* of the Jewish aristocracy, dirty enough but with fairly spacious houses, and beside it is the *Bhira*,[4] which looks like a Duar on the outskirts of the town, where there is a degenerated population of small peasants and paupers, whose whole possessions are a milch-cow or two. No stables. The alleyways disappear under thick layers of rotting dung. Hundreds of our wretched co-religionists are born, waste away and die here in this murderous filth, in this stench-filled atmosphere.

Already at this stage the Jews were no longer obliged to live in the *Mellah*, but the rich who could have helped had no feeling for the situation of these miserable people. The same school principal stated that the local community was divided into three parts: the *shillos* (he was referring to the *chleus*, Jews speaking the Berber language and living according to Berber customs), the *forasteros* (Arabic-speaking Jews with Arab customs, apparently *mustarat*) and the *roumi* (Spanish-speaking Jews).[5]

The *Alliance Universelle*, certainly influenced by the atmosphere of France rather than of central Europe, laid down that the way to improvement lay through schooling and artisanship. The school should be half secular and half religious with double and different staffs of teachers, one based on the French model and the other based on local Jewish manpower, that is to say on rabbis and Hebrew teachers. This organization facilitated co-existence between the lay school and what could perhaps be called the 'reformed *heder*.'[6]

At this point it should be noted that in most places the schools were not favourably accepted immediately. It is well known that the rabbis and learned men wanted to preserve their monopoly of the colleges and the *Kutabs*, which were a source of income for them, perhaps not particularly large but certain. It is a fact that the *Alliance* school principals wrote a great deal about the difficulties that they came up against from the parents and many community leaders, who did not have much use for these schools. They were only convinced finally once the French presence was a *fait accompli*. They then realized the great economic value of knowing the French language.[7]

It should be stressed that the *Alliance* had to fight not only traditional Jewish schools but also the French schools, even when the latter were intended specially for the Jewish population. In Mazagan, for example, a 'Franco-Israélite' school existed which threatened the development of the *Alliance* school: tuition there was free, while in the *Alliance* school well-off parents were asked to pay part of the tuition fees! The *Alliance* school feared, therefore, that the pupils from 'good' well-off families would escape to the State schools, where they would be exempt from all payment! The danger did not exist among the poor, who in any case did not pay anything at all.[8]

In 1912, Sagues, the *Alliance* director in Casablanca, faced a serious problem: he wrote to the *Alliance* leadership that the French Governor, General Lyautey, had issued an instruction ordering 'immediate construction of a school building that would be able to take up to about 600 pupils.' The building would be ready in about six months' time and would constitute a threat to the *Alliance* schools. Given the general 'enthusiasm for French institutions,' the French-speaking population would stream into the new schools and, as a result, the Jewish parents would also want to send their sons there. The director emphasized: 'The only obstacle that might prevent members of our faith from sending their children to French schools is their religious consciousness, and from that point of view the evolution of the well-off classes in the Jewish population is more rapid than we imagined. For them the problem of the Sabbath and the problem of religious education no longer represent an insuperable obstacle.' He therefore recommended improvements or changes in the *Alliance* school building and changes in teaching in order to meet the challenge. For all that, he was aware of the sort of contradiction in the *Alliance* platform: why bring the West to the Jews of Morocco, when the West was arriving on its own in the embrace of the French Government? He affirmed that 'in spite of the Protectorate the Jews still need the *Alliance*', and he added: 'General Lyautey is prepared to see *Alliance* representatives as effective and vital go-betweens between the authorities and the Jewish population. He desires, even demands their cooperation in the undertaking of reorganization that he has embarked on.'[9] Nevertheless, competition between *Alliance* and 'Franco-Israélite' schools continued until 1924, when they all joined the *Alliance* network and became part of it.[10]

The *Alliance* was not only concerned with education, however, but also with fostering useful trades by establishing vocational training schools, which were unsuccessful on the whole except in Jerusalem, and by a training method that came up against a difficult problem – there were no expert Jewish craftsmen to whom to entrust the apprentices. In the first stage, the *Alliance* encouraged acquisition of a trade in order to build a basis – or, in more modern parlance, normalize Jewish life – within the existing community. Fairly soon, however, we witness a different phenomenon: the acquisition of a trade facilitated emigration from the country that was not ready to grant Jews an acceptable *lebensraum*. There was a sort of abandonment of the idea of success locally and a turn to some other country for this purpose. This emigration was on a much larger scale and began much earlier than we usually think. We shall rest content with one example. In 1910 the principal of the boys' school in Mazagan wrote: 'Only 9 of the 96 pupils who completed their schooling in the local *Alliance* school emigrated, because of the good local conditions.'[11] That is to say emigration in the ratio of only 10 per cent was seen as something unusual. As we shall see later, it was not only the younger generation that emigrated. At all events fostering emigration by means of vocational training was somewhat discouraging for the prospects of local progress and it had to be recognized that no Jew in the East had a secure future in the East.

Problems of health and hygiene were made part of the teaching in *Alliance* schools, as is testified to by the inclusion of a chapter on the state of health and hygiene in the school population in the annual reports of the schools. The stress on this obligation will not surprise anyone who has read about the situation in the various *Mellah*s. In October 1906, Moïse Lévi, principal of the boys' school in Marrakesh, wrote that in less than three months since the beginning of the year, 300 children had died in the local *Mellah* as a result of an epidemic in the city.[12] In such circumstances, the school was not satisfied with just teaching – it wanted to change the conditions of the community.[13]

This trend appears in even greater clarity in a more sensitive sphere: girls' education. All the *Alliance* representatives protested indignantly at the phenomenon of child marriage as an iniquity that had to be done away with. The principals of the girls' schools were very active in this matter. (In accordance with the settled tradition in France – and in other countries too – only a woman could be the principal of a girls' school.) The wives of the principals of *Alliance* boys' schools who arrived then in North Africa were European born or European educated; they proclaimed themselves faithful Jewesses and they took an important position in local society. They were well aware that their functioning independently within a masculine society was in itself a break-through on the eastern anti-feminist front and, perhaps, not only a break-through but also a model. Some of them would also go on to declare themselves feminists and would fight to improve the status of women.[14] They fought on two fronts: (a) to get the girls into the schools; and (b) to keep them there, and more than once this called for interference in the pupils' family affairs. In all the *Alliance* schools, the families had to be taught that proper education called for regular attendance by the pupils. There were difficulties with the boys and far greater ones with the girls. One woman teacher wrote that after close study of the problem she was obliged to agree that the source of child marriage for girls was the parents' desire to be rid of their daughters as soon as possible.[15] In Marrakesh, one principal wrote, the parents took girls out of school even at the age of nine or ten in order to marry them off, and a principal of a girls' school had to bring her influence to bear to prevent these marriages.[16] In 1916 the woman principal of a school in Meknes reported proudly: 'I had the satisfaction of seeing some of *mes fillettes* [my girl pupils], even though they were already affianced, opposing their parents who were pressing them to get married from fear that the match would be called off.'[17] Without question, in this sphere the *Alliance* representatives acted with the full support of the Central Committee.

The very presence of French-speaking *Alliance* representatives, imbued with deep regard for the values of French culture, turned them into sought-after intermediaries between the French authorities and the Jewish population. Here, however, it is necessary to distinguish between the situation that prevailed in Tunis and the one existing in Morocco. Tunis was part of the Ottoman Empire until the French conquest (which was not recognized by Turkey, incidentally), and it remained subject to the regime of capitulations, so there was no very great problem for the *Alliance* representatives when they needed the support and protection of the French Consul. When Tunisia was made a French Protectorate in 1881, the *Alliance* representatives continued their activity even more energetically with the help and encouragement of the French authorities.[18] The first *Alliance* school was opened in Tunis in July 1878 and so it had functioned for less than three years under Tunisian rule![19] The *Alliance* people had close contact with the French representatives. There were frequent consultations between them, and we know from the *Alliance* reports that the French authorities consulted them over the appointment of a representative of the Jews of Tunis to the Advisory Council that was to deal with reform of the system of government.[20]

This was not the way things were in Morocco. A school was opened in Tetouan as early as 1882.[21] *Alliance* representatives did receive a certain backing from the French consular representatives and sometimes succeeded in acting through them, but there was a good stretch of the way to go before the French Army formally took over in Morocco. Towards the end of the first decade of the twentieth century, the French authorities in Morocco were concerned with organizing community life and *inter alia* that of the Jewish communities. Thus attention must be paid to an interesting phenomenon: the French tendency was to organize the life of the *Mellah* as if it constituted a city within the city itself. They would set up a *Majlis* for it, with representatives of the people of the *Mellah* and representatives of the authorities. There is evidence that the authorities wanted to hand over a highly important task to the *Alliance* school principals in each *Mellah*-city: that of Secretary-Treasurer responsible for administrative and financial affairs. This happened in Fez and it would also be the case in Marrakesh. The *Alliance* representative in that city reported: 'You know of the proposal to create a *Majlis* in this city – an exact copy of what has been done in Fez.'[22] The big difference was that the *Alliance* representative in Fez took the task upon himself as a full member of the committee, while the representative in Marrakesh hesitated and contented himself with the task of implementation without being a real member of the committee. It is clear, therefore, that the example of Fez was important. It is also clear that the French authorities imposed these tasks on *Alliance* representatives because they were acceptable to the local community and also close to the idea of modernization. From both viewpoints, they had a decisive part not so much in making changes – for which the initiative remained for the most part, if not entirely, in the hands of the French Army – as in carrying them out and securing the agreement of the Jewish community to their being put into practice.

In July 1913, Elmaleh, Principal of the boys' school in Fez, sent a letter to the *Alliance* in Paris, which gives a detailed, instructive description of all the changes that the local Jewish community had undergone, and his part in them as well. This document is of unequalled importance and deserves special attention. He noted, for example, the following:

> At the end of 1912, a *Mellah* city council was set up, composed of 6 elected members and 3 officials appointed to the post. The election took place in September, and the electors were the 50 notables who had previously been members of the national community 'board' (*Maamad*). The judges of the religious tribunal were disqualified from election, exactly as had occurred with the *Kadis* in the Muslim city. The Europeans were not given representation due to their being so few in the *Mellah*, a situation that was liable to change soon owing to their rapid increase in number. The Pasha served officially as Council Chairman, but was in fact represented by his Khalif.[23]

Elmaleh, by virtue of his *Alliance* position, was appointed Secretary-Treasurer with advisory rights. A third official was appointed, entrusted with tasks that had previously been in the hands of the local 'Sheikh-al-Yahud.' This third man was the son of an *Alliance* school teacher and was given the responsibility for having the Council's decisions put into effect. A French administration officer, of course, took part in the sessions of the *Mellah* Council. (There were no less than 29 sessions in the first year.) The writer later registered the decisions reached (he had copied them from the Council's minutes):

7.10.1912: Lighting installed in the *Mellah* by means of about 100 petrol lamps.

14.10.1912: Reorganization of the *Habus* – in other words: the *Wakf* – or Jewish religious endowment. According to Elmaleh, the Jews had followed the Arab custom on religious foundations. They were all set up by contributors in their wills. The property they bequeathed to the community could not be sold or mortgaged and all the revenues were dedicated to the poor. This was not always the way it was done, however, since the community had sometimes allowed individuals to take control of different land parcels, on condition that they build houses there and give a third of the built-up area to the *Habus*. As a result, a large part of the *Mellah* turned into *Habus*. Elmaleh valued this property at 400,000 to 500,000 pesetas, producing a yearly revenue

## THE 'ALLIANCE ISRAÉLITE UNIVERSELLE'

of 27,000 pesetas. In the course of time, these arrangements had been disregarded: houses had been sold not according to the rules, and it was felt that the whole matter needed to be reexamined. Two Council members took this upon themselves and the *Alliance* Director was made responsible for the financial side. In one year they succeeded in drawing up a full list of the endowment property, paying off debts and restoring a number of buildings. Towards the end of the financial year (in this case, Nissan 30), the endowment accounts were published in all the synagogues in the city. The *Habus* fund continued to pay salaries to judges as in the past (to a total of from 3,500 to 4,000 pesetas).

28.10.1912: Establishment of the *Tendif*, the *Mellah* health service. Throwing rubbish into the streets was prohibited and it was decided to have carts collect the rubbish, and to have the streets swept and sprinkled with water.

28.10.1912: (the same day): A municipal clinic was set up. The *Alliance* contributed a sum of 40,000 francs to build a permanent structure for the clinic, the expenses of which were to be covered by the Jewish Council and the Protectorate authorities.

4.11.1912: Instruction and regulations on stray dogs and rabies prevention.

11.11.1912: Repair of the sewage system of the *Mellah*, and arrangements for payment from the sale of land that the Council had received in the past as compensation for the area of the Old Cemetery.

18.11.1912: Building a new municipal abattoir.

20.11.1912: Organization of a population register (births, deaths, marriages).

20.11.1912: Establishment of a full-time police force of 8 men, all Algerian and Moroccan Moslems under the command of a Jewish *Naib*.

25.11.1912: Imposition of a tax on alcohol and prohibition of all gaming for money. Adoption of a regulation for supervision and prevention of contagious diseases.

2.12.1912: Measures against loitering by children and young people who should be in school.

23.12.1912: Preparation of a register of survey of lands in the *Mellah*.

30.12.1912: Construction of a new classroom for the *Alliance* school.
6.1.1913: Widening the *Mellah* main street by expropriating specific houses for public purposes. The work went on for four months and the compensation paid reached 150,000 pesetas, which the municipality had to borrow at 7 per cent interest.
5.3.1913: Adoption of a regulation providing for expenses for guardians of orphans.
19.3.1913: Obligation to plaster and whitewash the *Mellah* houses at least once a year.
19.5.1913: Construction of a wall around the Jewish cemetery, which had become a rubbish dump and the site of dubious rendezvous.
2.6.1913: Adoption of a regulation concerning riders and saddle-packed animals in the *Mellah*.

It is certain that in this period – the beginning of the consolidation of French rule in Morocco – the *Alliance* representatives, with the consent of the Central Committee of the organization, served in public posts that enabled them to put their ideas into practice for changing this Jewry's backward aspect. The *Alliance* did not limit itself to educational and cultural tasks and did not ask its people to deal with these matters alone. The organization was involved in every side of Jewish life.

As we have stated Algeria was supposedly outside the sphere of the *Alliance*. Was this really so? It is true that the *Alliance* did not intervene in what went on in the Jewish communities in Algeria, since these or at least the Jews of Algeria had received equal rights. In the spirit of the French Revolution it was expected that Jews of Algeria, French in every respect, would defend their rights with their own forces. As sons of the Emancipation, they would progress along a path from which there was no turning back. This was their state of mind until 1898. In that year disturbances broke out that threatened the property and the lives of Algerian Jews and the community entered a period of anxiety and instability. It is obvious that anti-Semitic circles in Algeria exploited the Dreyfus affair in order to inflame the mood of the public and to succeed where they had failed in 1871, that is to say, in cancelling the French citizenship of the Jews of the colony.[24]

According to the *Alliance* conception – and not to it alone – Jewish history had ended with the Emancipation: the moment a Jew secures equality of rights he stops being just a Jew and becomes a Frenchman, Englishman or American of the Mosaic faith. His destiny is swallowed up in that of the people he dwells among. According to this view, emancipation is part of progress and so there should be no appeal against it and there should be even less any attempt to annul it. The *Alliance* learned in 1898 that in reality things were different. This system had collapsed in Algeria and the Jews of Algeria turned to the *Alliance* to help them. Moshe Nahon wrote from Algiers in his report to the *Alliance* Central Committee of 27 September 1901:[25]

> The source of the *Alliance* undertaking in Algeria was the agitation caused by the violent anti-Semitic acts of 1898. Since the *Alliance* was engaged in the east and in other centres in North Africa, it held the view that Algeria did not belong to its sphere of activity. Is the country not French soil? Did not the members of our faith receive the status of citizens of the Republic in 1870?

He affirmed that cultural influence was supposed to lead to the evolution of an independent Algerian Jewry, which would rejuvenate itself under the protection of the law and with the encouragement of French institutions. 'The fearful explosion of 1898 was needed in order to set matters in their true light. Algeria was revealed as the last country where Jews could hope for orderly development.' The Jews were deprived of nearly all their civic rights. They were slandered and humiliated cynically and persistently in a way never seen there or anywhere else before, they were pushed out of society, at times persecuted, beaten like animals, and when the authorities defended them, they did not exert themselves unduly. The Jews were sometimes harassed by a weak judicial system and they feared for their right to work and their right to live. In school they had begun to learn of the genius of France which was all refinement and generosity, and had become attached to it. They had heard about the liberal achievements of the Revolution and of the nineteenth century and had been enthralled. Now they were witnessing the collapse of their ideal. The impossible had happened and now their alternative was to reject civilization, or at least its moral aspect, or to reject Judaism and curse the Jewish name and religion as the cause of all their suffering.

Nahon also testified that in fact Algerian Jewry was already neglecting Jewish religious education and attending good schools suited to Europe but not to the new countries, and as a result of this situation 'religion has disappeared under the impact of snobbery, leaving behind a skeleton of superstition and mechanical habits.' The heads of the Algerian communities turned to the *Alliance* to help them. Even though this meant having to provide services to French citizens, the *Alliance* agreed. It understood at once that for the Jews of Algeria it would have to find different methods of action from those customary in the other North African countries. The result was the establishment of modern *Talmud Torahs* that functioned in the big cities (in Algiers from 22 July 1900 and in Constantine from January 1903, and later in Oran and perhaps in other towns as well). The teaching was organized as follows: mornings and evenings on Sundays and Thursdays, and from 4.30 to 6.00 p.m. on the other days of the week (Monday, Tuesday, Wednesday). During the long vacation, the pupils learnt for two hours in the morning and two hours in the afternoon every day for seven to eight weeks. These *Talmud Torahs* were in fact what were called *Alliance* schools in Algeria. They were not intended to compete with the existing French schools, but for all that the fact of their establishment undoubtedly represented a revolution in general *Alliance* activities, not only because they were intended for French citizens, but also because they were concerned solely with imparting Jewish religious values. The mere fact that they were set up and were kept functioning provides a clear indication regarding the real plans of the *Alliance*.[26]

We may add that in Algeria the *Alliance* established an apprentice training system and – more important – it was also active in the political sphere. The same Nahon reported on 10 September 1905 that as soon as he arrived in Algiers, he realized 'there was no organization safeguarding their [the Jews'] overall interests and their common dignity or paying proper attention to events and their effects on the future of the communities.' He held back for a while until the *Alliance* undertaking was well established. When a government decree was issued arranging for the distribution of State lands and laying down that only 'Frenchmen of European origin and naturalized Europeans' could benefit from it, a condition clearly aimed at discriminating against the local Jews, only then was he convinced that action must be taken and he decided to set up a body to deal with problems of this kind. He sent out a circular which was well received and resulted towards the end of 1904 in the establishment of a voluntary body called 'Le Comité d'études sociales' (Council for Social Studies). He convened meetings where subjects were discussed such as the edict concerning settlement, return to the land among Jews, the regime of consular elections, the distribution of Jews in the liberal professions and in administrative posts, the Jews in Algerian statistics (where they appeared as a separate body and not as part of the French population), the Jewish proletariat, etc.[27] This body took firm root in Algeria and in fact held on until 1962, when it was still trying to defend the Jews on the eve of the proclamation of Algerian independence.

There is no doubt that research into the ideology of the *Alliance* people is faced with numerous problems. The researcher has to do a great deal of detailed work before he can get a complete picture. One fact emerges very clearly, however: the leadership of French Jewry and the leadership of the *Alliance* in particular – whatever each member's individual position in the leadership – certainly wanted to preserve the Jewishness of the Jews of North Africa and indeed to strengthen it. They themselves felt all right in France and preferred the model of Jewish existence in France to any other model. They wanted assimilation *à la française* and were repelled by the idea of being swallowed up and disappearing altogether. They were assimilated Jews and were convinced that only assimilation could ensure the continued survival of Jewry. Taking this stand, they opposed other trends in modern Jewry and they were also subjected to sharp criticism from them. It can nevertheless be said that they were prepared to learn and to adjust their policy to what happened in the field – and a great deal happened – but it is clear that the *Alliance*, and the Consistory as well, never treated Judaism, as they understood it, lightly. The ideological content of their Jewishness is certainly open to different evaluations, but there is no justification for denying or minimizing it. Even when it evoked energetic opposition, the message was there.

NOTES

1. On the development of these events see S. Schwarzfuchs, *Ha-yehudim ve-ha-shilton ha-tsarfati be-algeria (1830–1855)* (Les juifs d'Algérie et de la France 1830–1855), Jerusalem, 1981, pp.25–50 (Hebrew). For descriptions of the activity of the *Alliance Israélite Universelle* in North Africa, see in particular: N. Leven, *Cinquante ans d'histoire: L'Alliance Israélite Universelle (1860–1910)*, Paris, I, 1911, II, 1920; M. M. Laskier, *The Alliance Israélite Universelle and the Jewish Communities of Morocco, 1862–1962*, State University of New York, Albany, 1963.
2. See Leven, *op. cit.*, II, pp.79, 148–9.
3. These reports are found in the archives of the *Alliance Israélite Universelle* in Paris

(Series France) and on micro-film in the Central Archives of the History of the Jewish People in Jerusalem, which enabled me to study them. (Hereinafter A.I.U. Archive.)
4. According to Dr. Haim Ben-Tov: watermelon field.
5. A.I.U. Archive XIV, 25, France (microfilm Central Archives HM2/5904a).
6. See Leven, *op. cit.*, II, pp.18–20.
7. See Laskier, *Yehudei Maroko ve-kiah* (The Jews of Morocco and the A.I.U.), Mimizrah u- m'arav, III Ramat-Gan, 1981, pp.7–23, (Hebrew).
8. Letter from Josué Cohen of 15 Sept. 1918, A.I.U. Archive, *loc. cit.*
9. Letter of 25 Oct. 1912, A.I.U. Archive, *loc. cit.*
10. See letter from Graziani, principal of the Larache School, of 30 Sept. 1924, A.I.U. Archive, *loc. cit., cf.* Laskier, p.160.
11. Letter from Danon of 6 Nov. 1910, A.I.U. Archive, *loc. cit.*
12. Letter of 13 Aug. 1906, A.I.U. Archive, *loc. cit.*
13. A.I.U. schools were in fact both teaching centres and community centres of a kind that dealt with all the pupils' needs, but this is not the place to go into this in detail.
14. See Laskier, *op. cit.*, p.119. Letter from Fez of 1 Sept. 1903, A.I.U. Archive, *loc. cit.*
15. This theme appears in many reports. See e.g. letter from Danon of 15 Sept. 1910 (ibid.).
16. Letter from Danon of 15 Sept. 1910, A.I.U. Archive, *loc. cit.* See n.5 above.
17. Letter from Moyal of 1916, A.I.U. Archive, *loc. cit.*
18. See Leven, *op. cit.*, II, pp.119–22.
19. See Leven, *op. cit.*, II, pp.110–12.
20. See A.I.U. Archive, France, IV, F. 13–14 (microfilm Central Archive, HM2/5848b).
21. See Leven, *op. cit.*, II, pp.13–15, 48.
22. Letter from Danon of 15 Sept. 1910, A.I.U. Archive, France, XIV, 25 (microfilm Central Archive, HM2/5904a).
23. Letter from Elmaleh, 1913, A.I.U. Archive, *loc. cit.* (microfilm HM2/5904G).
24. See H.Z. Hirschberg, *Toldot ha-yehudim be-afrika ha-tsfonit* (History of the Jews of North Africa), II, Jerusalem 1965, pp.86–8 (Hebrew).
25. A.I.U. Archive, France VII, F. 13–14 (microfilm HM2/5848a), Report on activities from 1900 to 1901.
26. See Leven, *op. cit.* II, pp.143–9.
27. A.I.U. Archive, *loc. cit.*

# 6

# The Kovno Circle of Rabbi Yitzhak Elhanan Spektor: Organizing Western Public Opinion Over Pogroms in the 1880s

## Israel Oppenheim

### FOREWORD

On 11 and 13 January 1882 the London *Times* published two long and detailed articles describing the state of the Jews during the pogroms in Russia. The author[1] also dwelt on the share of the Russian authorities in organizing the pogroms and in passing anti-Jewish legislation at the time and afterwards as well. The articles reported on the hostile spirit animating the Regional Commissions set up by the Russian Minister of the Interior, Ignatyev, which began their work in September 1881. They were supposed to investigate the 'harmful influence of Jewish economic activity on the majority population and to recommend measures for remedying the situation.'[2] In these *Times* articles on the dire straits of the Jews the suspicion was voiced that these Commissions had been set up precisely in order to provide a pretext for expelling masses of Jews to the recently conquered region of Turkestan in Asiatic Russia. The readers of the articles must have realized that they were based on sources well-informed about what was happening in Russia.

These articles were destined to have a great effect. The Rabbi of Memel, Dr Ruelf, who played an important part in transmitting news from Russia to the West and in mobilizing public opinion on behalf of the Jews, affirmed that 'it was these articles which aroused the so sensitive humane feelings of the noble English people.'[3] The articles were reprinted in the *Jewish Chronicle*[4] and other English papers and also in a special pamphlet, *The Persecution of the Jews in Russia*.[5]

The press all over Europe followed in the footsteps of the English papers and began to print news about what was happening in Russia, reports based partly on the *Times* articles and partly on additional sources.[6]

In England the articles evoked a wide public response, the first manifestation of which was the Mansion House meeting on 1 February 1882,[7] as always an impressive assembly of representatives of the Church, the Universities, politics and other influential circles in the official residence of the Mayor of London. The wave of protest spread from England to other countries in Europe and further afield to the United States and South Africa.[8] Influential personalities from all over the non-Jewish world, together with part of the Jewish public, hastened to the aid of the victims. A specific characteristic of this activity was that it was not a one-off effort but was sustained over a lengthy period and was kept going notably by trustworthy information that regularly reached the circles concerned from Russia. It would not be accurate to say that what was happening in Russia was completely unknown before the appearance of the *Times* articles or that nothing had been done previously for the Jews. Previously, however, (a) the news had been sporadic and fragmentary in character and based mainly on chance sources such as private letters smuggled out and items copied from the Russian and Jewish press; and (b) these partial and vague sources had indeed awakened Jewish concern, but the activity undertaken by English Jews on behalf of the sufferers had not gone beyond the Jewish sphere – that is to say, the non-Jewish public had had no share in it.[9]

The lack of reliable and continuous reporting was due to the burdens that the authorities imposed on foreign correspondents, who were in any case few in number. Most represented conservative papers, which supported the existing regime and sympathized with its attitude to the Jews; they were not eager to send reports liable to affect Russia's good name. Those who were prepared to do so were kept under close surveillance, which was even stricter for the Russian press, not to speak of the Jewish papers which were obliged to obey endless orders and regulations as to reporting current affairs. When the pogroms were in progress, the Jewish press was forbidden to tell its readers about them.[10] Thus, for example, the first pogrom in Elisavetgrad was reported in *Hamelits* only on 3 May, that is to say 18 to 19 days later, and even then only briefly and in moderate terms. There was also a ban on giving information about the Regional Commissions and their deliberations, on the grounds that such information was liable to provoke criticism of the government.[11]

Private individuals were also deterred from sending news abroad for fear of heavy penalties, even though, as we have said, Russia was not completely cut off from the outside world. Anti-Semitic papers like *Novoye Vremya* (New Times) and others rejoiced openly, if not at length, over the pogroms and incendiarism and the harsh decrees, but even these items did not always get abroad past the strict censorship. The *Times* articles thus marked a significant about-turn. From then on activity on behalf of Russian Jewry was on an altogether higher level, relying on a flow of solidly based information that succeeded in interesting wide non-Jewish circles in the fate of Russian Jewry and getting them to act on its behalf. Moreover it countered the disinformation and blurring over the truth on the part of the Russian authorities, who were more than a little apprehensive over the repercussions of the news that was beginning to get out of their country at frequent intervals.

Who, then, was behind this success in outwitting the gigantic Russian Government apparatus? What was this enterprise that would have done credit to any clandestine revolutionary organization? Jewish historiography has indeed dealt at length with the public and Jewish campaign in Western Europe and America on behalf of Russian Jewry – questions in Parliament in Britain, aid to emigrants, and the like – but has hardly examined the source of all the information. Until the 1930s very little was known about the people behind this initiative, the scope of the group's activity, the way it was organized, how it got news out to the West, and what its place was in the Jewish community. A change came only in 1930 with the publication of the third volume of Ya'akov Lifschitz's *Zikhron Ya'akov*, which shed light on the Kovno circle. It was headed by the Rabbi of Kovno, Yitzhak Elhanan Spektor, along with his son and successor in the Rabbinate, Zvi Hirsch Rabinowitz, preacher (*magid*) in Vilna, and the above-named Ya'akov Lifschitz, principal of the Talmud-Torah school in Kovno and the moving spirit of the enterprise.[12] Even after this book appeared, however, the situation did not change much.[13]

Research on this question could be of significance for the history of Russian Jewry in general and specifically of relations between the ultra-Orthodox and the *maskilim*. The first person to lay the basis for systematic study of this subject was the late Professor Israel Heilperin, but he did not manage to develop the subject beyond two short articles about activity on behalf of the Jews of Russia at the

Courts of Denmark and Hessen-Darmstadt.[14] He succeeded in garnering a notable amount of material on the subject, and this serves as the basis of the present article.[15]

## THE KOVNO CIRCLE[16]

The Kovno circle of ultra-Orthodox activists headed by Rabbi Yitzhak Elhanan Spektor was active for a score of years from 1881 until the end of the 1890s. It did not leave off when the wave of pogroms ebbed and it busied itself with interceding on all sorts of issues concerning the Jewish community. Since there was no lack of repressive decrees, its hands were full,[17] but these matters, unlike the pogroms, were not used to mobilize public opinion, Jewish and non-Jewish, until 1890, that is to say in the period before the expulsion of Jews from Moscow.[18] That chapter however calls for separate study.[19]

As we have said, the circle's activity was formally headed by Rabbi Yitzhak Elhanan Spektor (1817–96). He served as Rabbi of Kovno in the years 1864 to 1896, and was highly appreciated by the Jews of Russia at the time and not only by the ultra-Orthodox camp. While the latter did not regard him as a great spiritual luminary, it nevertheless recognized him as a religious authority and accepted his rulings.[20] From one point of view Rabbi Spektor was an exceptional figure in the rabbinical world, which in that period generally refrained from intervening in secular affairs. Spektor, on the contrary, maintained close contact with Baron Horatio Ginzbourg, one of the most eminent and wealthy leaders of Russian Jewry, who resided in St. Petersburg, and he also found 'a common language with Jewish *maskilim*, and thus Kovno became a centre of general Jewish affairs,'[21] and all this without stepping an inch out of line to the left or the right from the prescriptions of the Law (*halakha*).

Rabbi Spektor acquired his great reputation in the general Jewish community by devoting himself to the problem of releasing deserted wives from their legal ties to missing husbands, a particularly delicate matter in the period under review, the beginning of the great Jewish migrations, when the Jewish population in Russia was in the process of transition from its traditional, static way of life to a dynamic, unsettled life as a result of processes of social and economic modernization in Russia. In dealing with these issues, Rabbi Spektor displayed great courage.[22] It was as a public figure involved in the life of the people and not only the life of his congregation that he made his contacts with Jewish personalities in

Russia and also Western and Eastern Europe, among them Dr Ruelf, with whom he was in contact before the 1880s.[23]

Ya'akov Lifschitz was a very different manner of man, the direct opposite of the tolerant rabbi with his talent for making friends with people even very distant from him and his outlook on the world. Lifschitz was the moving spirit of the enterprise for transmitting information to the West. He initiated, organized, arranged things; he talked with people throughout the length and breadth of Russia. He found ways to smuggle material out of the country and even drafted the great majority of the missives that were sent.[24] It is safe to assert that but for him the whole enterprise would not have come into being, and it was even said that but for him Rabbi Spektor would not have become a leader.[25] Despite his many qualities, his erudition and his grasp of human nature, Lifschitz was a controversial figure, because of his difficult character and his zealotry, and disliked even in his own camp and all the more so among the *maskilim*. He was absolutely intolerant of all ideas not in tune with his extreme ultra-Orthodox outlook. Some people contended that Lifschitz succeeded in completely dominating his rabbi, due to the latter's weak character, to the point where he did not dare stand by his opinions. For example, Lifschitz was hostile to the Zionist movement, 'Lovers of Zion,' which Spektor was inclined to favour, and succeeded in preventing Spektor from identifying himself with it publicly.[26] However, even his rivals acknowledged that he was wise enough not to impose his views on the rabbi in other matters, so that the two of them worked together in harmony for some 30 years.[27] The third member of the group was the Rabbi's son, Zvi Hirsch Rabinowitz, who carried things out but did not initiate them.[28]

## THE BEGINNINGS

The idea of appealing to the outside world took form in Lifschitz's mind six months after the pogrom in Elisavetgrad (28 April 1881), after the failure of a Jewish delegation to the Tsar (25 May), the publication of the instruction to set up Regional Commissions to investigate the damage inflicted on the economy by the Jews, and mainly after the failure of the first convention of Jewish activists in St. Petersburg, held from 30 August to 7 September 1881.

Lifschitz described the turn of events: At the end of the summer, he travelled to Vilna to meet Rabbi Spektor, who was staying over in that city on his way back from St. Petersburg. On their journey back to Kovno together, Lifschitz put forward the idea to the rabbi and his son that they should appeal to Nathaniel Rothschild in London through Asher Acher, a doctor and the secretary of the Ashkenazi Orthodox Great Synagogue in that city and a central figure in English Jewry.[29] Lord Rothschild should persuade leading personalities in the British Government to intervene with the authorities in Russia on behalf of the Jews in that country. Lifschitz decided to proceed in this fashion because he had reached the conclusion that the pogroms had not been organized by the Socialists, as claimed by some leaders of the Russian regime,[30] but in fact by these leaders themselves, acting from plainly anti-Semitic motives. Lifschitz's idea was accepted in principle by Rabbi Spektor and his son, but they were of the opinion that there should first be consultation for authorization from Jewish public figures – Baron Ginzbourg and Polyakov in the first instance. Lifschitz, however, with his acute political sense, knew that these personalities would not back a proceeding that would be liable to anger the authorities and give rise to doubt as to their loyal, patriotic posture. He therefore made a tactical move and argued that they – just the three of them – should begin after the event, as it were, 'quietly.' If they succeeded, he said, 'We shall be the clever ones and entitled to reveal that it is given to qualified, honest and humble people to be useful,' and if they failed, they would bear the sole responsibility,[31] in line with the general view that nothing succeeds like success but failure is its own penalty.

Lifschitz did not succeed easily in overcoming the hesitations of the rabbi and his son. They may have felt that Lifschitz was going beyond the traditional limits of Jewish activity and becoming a partner after the event to the radicalism of the Jewish intelligentsia which was so obnoxious to him, and that the actions he proposed were liable to help undermine the standing of the traditional leadership (and especially of Baron Ginzbourg), whom the rabbi had had dealings with for many years on public matters. It should also be remembered that at this time the traditional leadership was under attack by the radical *maskilim* for its position on a number of issues of concern to the Jewish community and especially on the question of emigration. The radicals considered that the opposition to emigration on the part of Ginzbourg and his circle showed their alienation from the Jewish masses, indifference to their sufferings, and their putting their own narrow selfish class interests before the common welfare of the community.[32]

It would appear, however, that the worsening situation of the Jews in Russia finally persuaded the rabbi to agree to Lifschitz's proposals, and on 2 October 1881 the first missive was sent to Dr Acher. The text was brief and it is given here in full:

> With the second post tomorrow there will be sent you pages of the Question of the Answer [Responsum] at length, called *Nahal Yitzhak*, by way of the unfortunate abandoned wife, and as heading will be written, 'Be Thou with the mouths of those whom Thy people Israel have deputed,' and when you receive it, do well to study it thoroughly to endeavour for the sake of the abandoned wife as fitting, in order to furnish her with release from the bonds of abandonment, and may the Lord assist those helping in this.[33]

The language employed in this missive calls for a brief explanation. The exchange of letters between the Kovno circle and Jewish personalities in Western Europe was conducted partly in a camouflage of rabbinical language and secret terms, because these quasi-conspiratorial means were the only way the writers could protect themselves from the censorship. This initial missive was entitled *Nahal Yitzhak*, because this was the title of Rabbi Spektor's first written work after his appointment as rabbi of Kovno.[34] The 'unfortunate abandoned wife' designated Russian Jewry, and the use of this expression was natural, since, as we have said, the matter of abandoned wives was one of the most important questions that Rabbi Spektor had to deal with in his Rabbinical Responsa. A considerable part of all his Responsa were concerned with this subject and it was these Responsa that earned him wide repute outside the borders of Russia as well.[35] The watchword, 'Be Thou with the mouths,' was taken from a prayer for the well-being of the congregation composed by an ancient poet, which is recited in the *Musaph* (additional liturgy) before the Ark of the Law in the synagogue on Rosh Hashana (the New Year) and in the *Mosuaph* preceding the service on the Day of Atonement:

> Our God and the God of our fathers, be Thou with the mouths of those whom Thy people Israel have deputed to stand in Thy presence today to pray and supplicate for Thy people, the house of Israel. Teach them what they shall say, instruct them what they shall speak and answer their request. May they not falter with their tongue nor be entangled in their speech so that their congregation who confide in them should through them be ashamed; suffer not their mouths to utter a word that is contrary to Thy will.[36]

Rabbi Spektor was the author of this first missive and he wrote it out in his own hand. The following one, which was more detailed and included a number of matters which will be gone into below, was written by Lifschitz, as were many more after that. When the Rav had authorized the contents, the missive was copied out in handwritten calligraphy by his nephew/son-in-law. The addressee in England was Dr Acher, who was supposed to pass it on to Nathaniel Rothschild. So that Acher could identify the writings and establish the connection between the first missive and the following ones, which were written in a different handwriting from the first one and were without a signature, the following ones bore the watchword, 'Be Thou with the mouths.'[37]

The second and third missives indicated the main lines of the Kovno circle's effort: they contained the news that served as the basis for the *Times* articles and the rest that followed. It is therefore desirable to describe their contents fully.[38] The second anonymous missive began by comparing the situation of Russian Jewry with that of the Jews in Persia, Rumania and Morocco: though the suffering of the Jews in these countries was well known, that of Russian Jewry was even worse, according to the writers, since they had no possibility of raising their voice in protest to induce different governments to intervene on their behalf.[39] They were condemned to remain silent in face of the pogroms.[40] In these missives the Kovno circle disclosed its specific theses on the origins of the pogroms: they were not a spontaneous popular reaction to Jewish exploitation, nor were they organized by revolutionaries – two claims frequently put out by the authorities – but it was the Russian Government itself and Ignatyev in person, the Slavophile Minister of the Interior, that organized the pogroms and fomented them.[41] Jews in the West were being asked to rebut the authorities' arguments and reveal the real truth of the matter.

The missive described the hostile attitude to the Jews that pervaded the Regional Commissions,[42] and expressed the fear that they had only been set up to provide a pretext for expelling the Jews to Asiatic Turkestan.[43] The Jews of Western Europe were asked to do everything possible to frustrate this evil design. The missive also dwelt on the various economic decrees aimed at harassment of the Jews in their different occupations.[44]

Lifschitz explained in his writings that he decided it was necessary to appeal to the outside world when the failure of the first Jewish activists' convention proved that in the existing situation the Jewish community was in no position to take action. This was not meant as criticism of the traditional plutocratic leadership. In his opinion, its inability to act stemmed directly from the government's policy of cruel harassment that condemned it to helplessness and with it the entire Jewish community. The Kovno circle suggested two ways in which the Jews in the West could act to change things: Firstly, 'the counsel of our patriarch Ya'akov always suited our people in Ya'akov's time of trouble.'[45] This alluded to an attempt to influence the course of events by means of bribery.[46] It is known from a number of sources that Ignatyev himself hinted at his willingness to receive a large sum of money from the Jews in return for a promise to alleviate their situation, and that he even spoke to Baron Ginzbourg on the matter.[47] Secondly, the press in the whole of Europe should be roused to protest against the ill doing and evil intentions of the Russian Government and 'cry out, "Pillage and oppression," over its abominations and wickedness;' the publishers of the great and famous European periodicals – the *Times*, the *Standard* and the like – and their most eminent reporters should constantly speak out and 'cry out against the evil regime for its acts of injustice and oppression.'[48] They must speak in their own names, Lifschitz stressed, and not as emissaries of the Jews.[49]

The first of these means fitted in with the traditional system of suing and interceding with superior authorities, the method that Lifschitz defended so heatedly in his book against the attacks of the radical *maskilim*, who saw the system as an anachronistic survival that was not only ineffectual but even damaging to Jewish self-respect. Lifschitz viewed their attitude as a serious deviation from legitimate Jewish tradition and as opportunistic aping of foreign values.[50] He therefore appealed through Dr Acher to Nathaniel Rothschild, Rabbi Sh. R. Hirsch and the Chief Rabbi of France, Cohen Zadok, urging them to intercede with statesmen and non-Jewish public figures who enjoyed connections with Russia and her Court to alleviate Jewish distress in that country.

The call to mobilize public opinion testified, however, to the Kovno circle's going outside the traditional framework and adopting methods belonging to the modern world. The circle was indeed aware of the tension involved in the use of two different systems. Lifschitz explained that these methods were necessitated by the difference in the conditions prevailing in Russia as against the situation in the West. In an autocratic regime like Russia's, public opinion had no weight at all with the government in making its decisions. There was no constitution based on universal principles. Decisions about the fate of the Jews were taken by individuals in an arbitrary fashion. Lifschitz was consistent, therefore, in spite of cooperating with the *maskilim* in the use of modern methods,[51] when he continued to attack them for rejecting intercession with the authorities. He believed this to be the most suitable method in the conditions prevailing in Russia, where pressure from public opinion in the name of universal principles was impossible. 'If leading Jewish figures came to solicit in the name of right and justice, could they have the slightest hope of finding anyone to listen to them?'[52] The situation was different in the West, where it was not necessary to have recourse to bribery and to sue for favours, but open action by public opinion was legitimate and had a prospect of influencing the leaders and getting them to bring pressure to bear on Russia to change her policy.

The Kovno circle was also well aware of the possible dangers involved in open protest activity, which might in fact lead to a hardening of the anti-Jewish line. They nevertheless decided to take the risk, for they felt that the situation of Russian Jewry was worsening steadily and there was little or nothing to lose. This feeling was reinforced by the deliberations of the Central Commission on Jewish Affairs under Gotovtsev, Deputy Minister in the Interior Ministry and acting at Ignatyev's behest. The Commission was charged with elaborating a general Jewish policy based on the summations of the Regional Commissions. The qualms of the Kovno circle over the dangers involved in public activity were expressed in a letter to Acher from Dr Ruelf of Memel of 26 February 1882 after the Kovno emissaries' visit to him there. 'We do not wish and we are not authorized to ignore the fact that all the agitation in the press, the public meetings, and so forth[53] have angered the ruler of Russia still more and filled him with wrath against the Jews,'[54] and that he was the only one capable of bringing Ignatyev and his crowd to a stop. Nevertheless, Ruelf affirmed – and presumably this was also the Kovno circle's view – that 'the agitation was necessary in order to awaken the sense of pity in the heart of the world, and in part also to show Mr. Ignatyev that he and his evil designs are notorious, and that if he is looking forward to the post of Secretary of State, he had better watch out not to fall from favour altogether, appearing as a robber and murderer in the eyes of the political world.'[55] In order to hold the man in check, Ruelf suggested finding a way to get to the Tsar directly, either through the heir to the English throne, or by means of the Duke and Duchess of Edinburgh, who should travel to Russia for the purpose.[56] Thus the Kovno circle had far-reaching projects, the main one being to bring about the dismissal of Ignatyev, considered the main architect of the increasingly harsh anti-Semitic policies. When Ignatyev was in fact dismissed, Ruelf hinted that he had had a hand in his downfall; he admitted however that this was due not to Western European protests on the Jewish issue but rather Court circles close to the Tsar who opposed Ignatyev's anti-German political line and brought about his dismissal.[57]

Lifschitz's political grasp is also testified to by his advice that the press should emphasize that the Russian Government's anti-Jewish policy was liable to rebound and harm its own interests. If the government went on permitting unrestrained action by the mob, the mob might end by directing its anger against its real exploiter, the regime itself, the cause of its downtrodden situation:

> If they get the mob used to pillage and violence and breaking the laws of the government and the customs of the country, the end will finally be that the arrows will pierce the heart of the government itself. If they give the mob the right to discuss and judge whether and with whom to act and what it is that is striking at its rights and damaging the economic situation this will finally let the masses judge directly who is at the root of their terrible wrongs and they will hereafter rise up against the government itself as well as throw the acts of the government into the crucible of criticism from the beginning to the end.[58]

Lifschitz understood an autocratic regime such as existed in Russia could not let itself put political initiative in the hands of the masses because of the danger of anarchy and of a radicalization that could shake the foundations of the existing political structure. The hope that this would happen was in fact behind the revolutionaries' support for the pogroms.[59]

The Kovno missives asked English Jewry to act in general through the Board of Deputies[60] and through the 'Fraternal League' (the Anglo-Jewish Association) as well.[61] They also requested these two bodies to turn to the *Alliance Israélite Universelle* in Vienna (the branch that was known to have intervened on behalf of the Jews of Rumania) and also to the branches in Berlin and Rome. (The *Alliance* was established in France in 1860 and in Vienna in 1873.[62]) The Kovno circle also asked them to mobilize the widest possible press and publishing circles for protests against the Russian Government, on the justified assumption that such protests would be more effective than Jewish action alone.[63]

In his secret missive of 6 November 1881, Dr Acher acknowledged receipt of the first two missives, namely the first, short 'secret language' missive of Rabbi Yitzhak Elhanan Spektor and the long, unsigned missive written in his name by Lifschitz; Acher stated that he would pass these missives on to Rothschild, who would without question act as requested.[64]

Lifschitz took this answer from Acher as the first confirmation of his project and his methods. Accordingly the circle decided to step up their clandestine operation, but not to reveal anything about it to anyone else until Ruelf's efforts bore fruit. They also decided to send another detailed missive in the series, 'Be Thou with the mouths.' This new missive partly repeated matters from the earlier ones and partly reported on new decrees enacted against Russian Jewry.[65] These decrees supported Lifschitz's earlier assumption that it was the Russian Government that organized the pogroms and was behind them. This missive recounted how the Kiev pogromists had been defended by the Defence Attorney Shalnikov; it reported on the broadsheets widely distributed calling the Jews 'foreigners,' on the new pogroms that had occurred since the dispatch of the previous missive, and on harassment of Jews in the economic realm, such as their being turned out of the distillery trade on the grounds that they were spreading drunkenness in the population, a step liable to ruin some 300,000 householders. Finally the writers reiterated that they were not petitioning the government in the name of universal principles of equality and emancipation but were laying their pleas before the government as loyal subjects:

> We do not come as petitioners in a law court, but ever as living in the way of the Law [Torah], ways of loving grace and mercy, our hearts seeking grace and favour from the government, in whose shade we live protected; we fulfil all our duties as citizens of the country properly and in every particular, in peace and in good-neighbourly feeling. We therefore request and seek from the government that it spread the wings of its grace over us and also over our holy religion, and then when we are privileged to find favour in the eyes of our government, the light will also shine on us as faithful children of the government and the monarch.[66]

It would be a mistake to take this declaration too literally. The writers of the missive were fully aware of the real nature of the Russian Government, a regime of evil and oppression that did not deserve unreserved loyalty on the part of the Jews. The considerations that impelled the writers of these declarations were apparently the following: in this autocratic regime there were no effective, Western, democratic methods, let alone effective radical ones. They therefore opposed the radical trends that were winning support among young Jewish *maskilim* and desired not to identify the radicals with the majority of the Jewish community, which the writers of the declaration believed they represented.

Finally, even this declaration was not of absolute loyalty. The last phrase of this missive implied that the Jews' loyalty depended on a change in the attitude of the government to the Jews and specifically to their religion, and there was something like a hidden threat that if the government did not change its posture, it could not count on their loyalty.

It is surprising that these two detailed missives do not mention the question of emigration since this was the main focus of public debate at that time.[67] On 16 January 1882 Interior Minister Ignatyev wrote a letter to L. Orshansky, an editor of the Russian Jewish paper, *Razsviet*, in which he stated *inter alia* that the Western frontier was open to the Jews, and that they were authorized to set up a committee to make arrangements for emigration. He added that the emigrants would not be allowed to return to Russia. Regarding the situation of the Jews inside the country, he said that the government had no intention of abolishing the Pale of Settlement and allowing Jews to settle in the inner districts, because this was liable to exacerbate the antagonism of the majority populations towards them.[68] This report was a shock to the Jewish community and intensified the debate between those who advocated emigration and those who opposed it. The rich of St. Petersburg were furious at the publication of the news and at Orshansky's claiming to speak for the Jewish community without being deputed to do so. In his article, 'They will recognize and know ...,'[69] the Jewish poet Yehuda Leib Levin – 'Yahalal' – defended Orshansky, attacking the Jewish aristocracy for its estrangement from the Jewish people and the realities of its life, in contrast to Orshansky who was actively involved in its life and had every right to speak in its name.

This affair was the main issue dealt with at the second convention of Jewish activists in St. Petersburg in April 1882.[70] It was not that the Kovno circle did not take a position on this vital issue (and this was indeed clarified in later missives[71]) but the two first missives centred on the main objective – immediate alleviation of the situation of the Jews where they were, then and there, in Russia.

The attitude of the circle to emigration, both to Palestine and to

America, stemmed from the assumption that emigration could not solve the problem of Russian Jewry as a whole. The members of the circle rejected the view that emigration was 'the only way out, the gateway, the sole salvation and the most honourable one for the people of Israel in their distress and their struggle.'[72] Lifschitz even hinted that emigration served the insidious designs of Ignatyev, that is to say, that the circles of the *maskilim* who were campaigning to set up a central committee to make arrangements for emigration were doing Ignatyev's work for him, even if against their will, since mass emigration would make it easier for him to brand the Jews as aliens and traitors to their motherland.[73] Spektor supported the view of the aristocratic leadership, which opposed emigration on grounds of principle,[74] but for different reasons. He spoke against emigration during the convention itself, moderately as was his way, saying, 'It is also necessary to mention emigration, but we must consider the whole people and seek all the means to heal its ills.'[75] It was also his opinion that emigration was an internal Jewish matter – 'there's no need to ask or to speak about it'[76] with the authorities.

A basic assumption of the Kovno circle was that emigration could not constitute an overall solution for Russian Jewry but only for individuals, for 'there is no way available to assist even one in a thousand to leave the country, and there is no reliably safe place for more than just a few people to get a foothold, and what would hundreds of thousands of people who left do – without a craft or knowing how to work the land and without ready money also – and how can we ourselves oblige them to go into exile without their knowing where they are going and what kind of life they will have there?'[77] The mass emigration project was a Utopia, at most an individual solution of sorts. At the convention, Spektor argued that they must concentrate on material aid to the sufferers and call on the authorities to enable the aid to be organized in an orderly public fashion.[78] This statement reflected the aspect of his circle's work that was known to the public. The participants at the convention of course knew nothing about the circle's clandestine activity. Thus, while on the surface there was apparent agreement between Spektor and the aristocracy, this agreement was in fact limited; unlike them, Spektor did not see the overall solution as the Jews' 'fitting in' into the surrounding society and their emancipation. He counselled limited action of interceding and petitioning for the abolition of the discriminatory legislation that was being planned, to prevent the enactment of 'the unfortunate six clauses, which will strike a death blow at commerce ... We merit equal rights, but it is not for us to put forward very large plans for ourselves. Right now, let them just put an end to dealing us blows.'[79]

As for the high hopes entertained by so many people regarding mass emigration, Lifschitz could affirm that he had been right not to believe that emigration would solve the problem of the Jews of Russia, when he ascertained that 'more children had been born than the people who left.'[80]

The two long, detailed missives reached London and the members of the Kovno circle learned from Dr. Acher's replies of the efforts made by the leaders of the Jewish community in England with Rothschild at their head, and of the slight prospect that he would persuade the British Government to intervene on behalf of Russian Jewry.[81] The greater part of these two missives had been written before the articles appeared in the *Times* and before any practical action had been taken. In the meantime, between the dispatch of the missives and the receipt of the answers to them, the Kovno circle decided to make contact with more Jewish public figures in Western Europe and turned to Dr. Yitzhak Ruelf of Memel as an intermediary.[82]

Dr. Ruelf was chosen because he was an exception among German rabbis in having close links with the Jews of Russia and in his work on their behalf. His first connections with them had been established in 1868–69, when he formed a committee to assist Jewish victims of the famine that raged in those years in Lithuania and Zamut. The connection with Ruelf was renewed in 1876 following the conflagration of Vilikomir. At that time Lifschitz appealed to Ruelf, with Spektor's consent, to organize aid for the victims. Ruelf was also involved in many other good works, to such an extent that the Jews of Lithuania called him 'Dr. Hilf' (Help).[83] In the articles that he published about Russian Jewry, Ruelf did not cease to emphasize that activity on their behalf must not be purely in the nature of philanthropy, but must embody the mutual solidarity of the members of one people.[84] This attitude earned him no little animosity on the part of certain circles of German Jewry, who complained that he wanted to 'burden [them] with all the "schnorrers" in Russia.'[85] He worked tirelessly to change Western Jewry's perception of Russian Jewry. In his book, *Three Days in Jewish Russia*,[86] he wanted, he said, to show

> people everywhere – and particularly Jews in other countries – the great worth of the Jews of Russia and to illuminate aspects of their lives in their homes and outside them which many fine

and good persons had not the slightest idea of and which would serve to open their eyes. And I shall prove to them, in my view, that they were maligning our brethren dwelling in Russia by imputing to them all manner of defects ... while the truth is that they are excellent in (their) essential qualities and attributes and in all their deeds faithful and honest.[87]

Having completed his activities on behalf of victims of the famine in 1869 he journeyed to Kovno and there established his first close ties with the community leaders of that city.[88]

Ruelf reached new heights in his work for Russian Jewry from 1881 onwards. Shortly after the outbreak of the disturbances of 22 May 1881 he penned the first manifesto that was published by the Committee for Aid to Victims of the Pogroms.[89] As in 1869, he now saw first and foremost to constructive assistance for the victims and those who fled to the West.[90] No wonder, then, that when the Kovno circle decided to extend its activity beyond Great Britain, it turned first to Ruelf. About his part in the enterprise Ruelf later wrote:

Then I made a covenant of love with my brother members of my faith, the sole chosen one, in the lands of Russia, Ashkenaz and England, a few humble men of this generation, who were not in the seats of the mighty, out of dire need they set themselves heart and soul to rescue the congregation of Israel drowning in a sea of sorrows ... and the work of these my beloved comrades and my work ... did not prove in vain, for people were to be found open to compassion, and our words as if beside streams of water bore fruit and inclined the hearts of king and pope and prime minister in the different realms to divert the rivers of their grace towards all the thousands of the exiled and outcast.[91]

For all that, they did not succeed in getting effective action taken on behalf of Russian Jewry because of the principle of non-intervention in the internal affairs of a foreign State.

The first contacts with Rabbi Ruelf for the new project were made by Rabbi Hirsch Rabinowitz, the son of Rabbi Spektor. He was sent to Memel for the purpose, bringing with him a letter from his father to Ruelf, explaining the aim of his visit.[92] Without hesitation Ruelf agreed to cooperate with the Kovno circle and asked to be provided with the factual material on which to base his work. This request was agreed to and he was sent the first two missives of 'Be Thou with the mouths.' He was much impressed by their content and he set to work at once.

> When Dr. Ruelf saw them, his eyes were opened to the light. He feasted on them like first fruits early in summer and hastened to copy them in the language of Ashkenaz [Germany]. With additions and clarifications from the 'Memel Committee,' he printed them in thousands of copies and sent them to Germany, France, Italy and America, where, as learnt afterwards, they made a remarkable impression.[93]

Thus the network began to spread over the whole world.[94]

Connections with Memel also had a clear geographical advantage, due to the city's proximity to the Russian frontier and the fact that as a port it was an important export centre for Russian merchandise. A good number of Jewish merchants came there from Lithuania, mainly timber exporters who went there to receive their rafts that had been sent down the river. Jewish businessmen of Lithuanian origin also lived in Memel permanently. Some of them knew Hebrew and German, and they helped translate the material as it arrived from nearby Kovno. Information could be disseminated from Memel in orderly fashion to the whole of Europe and the city thus became the main channel for the transfer of the material.[95]

The basis was laid at these meetings for the work of intercession in those royal courts whose monarchs had ties of family or friendship with Tsar Alexander III. At the suggestion of the Kovno circle, Dr. Ruelf was asked to recruit Rabbi Wolf, President of the Rabbinical Court of the Copenhagen community, and his deputy, Rabbi Simonsen, to help in approaching the Danish royal family. The two rabbis were close to the King, whose daughter, Dagmar, was the wife of Alexander III; she had considerable influence over policy, both in her husband's time and in the rule of her son, Nikolai II.[96] Ruelf was even asked to go to Copenhagen himself but he refused, believing that the missives were sufficient. He was prepared to act wherever it was necessary, but when Rabbi Zvi Hirsch asked him to go to Berlin to mobilize the rich Jews there and get them to intercede in German circles and with the German rulers, he refused for he was 'doubtful whether they would cooperate.'[97] Finally, however, Ruelf and his associates of the Memel Aid Committee overcame their hesitations and succeeded in penetrating into Jewish circles which until then had been far removed from Jewish affairs in general and even got them involved in the problems of Russian Jewry, turning them into activists on their behalf.[98]

In the third and last letter which Rabbi Zvi Rabinowitz sent from Memel to his father and Lifschitz, he reported on the process of translating and printing the missives and on discussions regarding financial matters. He also suggested bringing in additional people who could intercede at the royal courts and on a public level, and he repeated Ruelf's promise to take energetic measures to this end.[99] Indeed the network went on spreading wider and wider throughout Europe. The number of letters being sent to various personages increased.[100] In Germany among those recruited were Rabbi Sh. R. Hirsch, Rabbi Ezre'el Hildesheimer,[101] and Rav Asher Lemel Marks of Darmstadt, who stated that he was prepared to approach the ruler of Darmstadt in the matter.[102] Rav Bamberg of Wuerzberg stated that he was prepared to approach the King of Bavaria.[103] In France, Ruelf turned to Chief Rabbi Zadok Hacohen and Secretary of the *Alliance Israélite Universelle*, Isidore Loeb.[104] Where he had no direct contacts as in Holland, Ruelf took round-about measures and was able to spur the heads of the Jewish community into action.

It was only a short while before the intercessions and protests embraced a large number of countries.[105] The secrecy of the activity had been complete so far in the small Kovno circle, but the widening scope of the activity now obliged them to let more people into the secret. In Kovno a number of the well-off and the *maskilim* were told about it when one of them, Bernard Manishewitz, read a report in a Russian paper, *Golos* (The Voice), describing the Mansion House protest meeting in London; he read the report out to Spektor and Lifschitz and they told him that it was their circle behind the news furnished to London. He said, 'I would never have believed that an enormous diplomatic campaign like this could be worked out in the office of an Orthodox Rabbi, without publicity and without noise and giving the alert. If I hadn't seen it, I wouldn't have believed it any way whatsoever.'[106] So the circle secured the support, if only passive, of Manishewitz and the *maskilim* and other businessmen in their city who were told about their activity.

One group of people who were let into the secret were that of the Rabbi and other Jewish public figures in the city of Vilna: mainly Rabbi Eliahu Grozensky, the son-in-law of Rav Israel Salanter, and Rabbi Eliahu Strashun. They informed Lifschitz that they intended to recruit Rav Eliahu Meisels of Lodz to join and help them, and to send him to Western Europe to mobilize Jewish community leaders and chiefly the Rothschilds in order to promote the cause of Russian Jewry. When Lifschitz told them of the circle's activity, they gave up their own scheme, which had not progressed beyond the stage of vague, unclarified ideas.[107]

As their correspondence grew more extensive, the Kovno people decided not to rely on the post any longer because of the dangers involved and to spin a clandestine net such as was customary in Russian revolutionary movements at the time. Two brothers were found, living near the frontier, one on the Russian side and one on the German. They were dispatchers, whose business it was to transfer goods between the two countries. They agreed to take on the transmission of the missives, and sent them through for some ten years without the authorities discovering a single one, and this because 'we did everything quietly, intelligently and with common sense,'[108] as Lifschitz recorded with pride.

The channel to Ruelf may have been the principal one but it was not the only one. When it seemed to the Kovno people that activity to arouse public opinion was not as sustained in France as in England and Germany – not that there were no protests to be noted, but they were weaker and sporadic and not based on reliable sources and so had only a limited effect – they decided to turn to the Chief Rabbi Zadok Hacohen and the heads of the *Alliance Israélite Universelle*. Since dispatching missives through the post seemed dangerous, they took advantage of visits to Paris by two Jewish businessmen for transmitting their missives. These were marked with the old watchword, 'Be Thou with the mouths,' and an additional motto beside it, another versicle from the same prayer, 'and hearken to their request.'[109] These missives urged the Jews of France to exploit the special status their country enjoyed in Russia, particularly its great influence in every sphere on the ruling classes. They proposed that as in other countries, activity should be led by eminent Christian public figures and that Russian dignitaries visiting France should be approached. Alongside this traditional manner of interceding with eminent personages, it was also suggested that authors and journalists be used to mobilize the widest possible spectrum of public opinion. It was important that these should stress that the anti-Semitic disturbances in Russia were not an expression of the anger of the Russian people over Jewish exploitation, but were initiated as official policy. The French Jews were also told that more material would reach them through Dr. Ruelf.[110]

## COOPERATION WITH THE 'MASKILIM'

The Kovno group had a unique success in bringing in different circles of the public to help in their enterprise, circles often very distant from each other in the Jewish community and which acted under their leadership. In particular this was reflected in cooperation with the *maskilim* in various cities in Russia, which arose out of the need to provide the West with first-hand material and quantities of the most accurate data available on the situation of the Jews in Russia. The public campaign in Western Europe in general and in England in particular, following the appearance of the articles in the *Times*, caused the Russian Government concern and apprehension (unfounded as it appeared later) over possible political intervention on the part of Western countries. In order to counter the unfavourable impression made on public opinion by the news of pogroms, burnings and anti-Jewish legislation, the Russian Government started a counter-propaganda campaign. A lady-in-waiting to the Tsarina, a certain Mme. Novikov, was sent to England, where she had connections with the aristocracy, for the purpose of rebutting the accusations against the Russians. The most damaging reports had concerned (a) the part of the Russian authorities in instigating the pogroms, and (b) news of the rape of women and girls. Regarding the first accusation, the blame was put on the Jews themselves; the pogroms were described as the spontaneous uprising of the masses against Jewish exploitation. Russian propaganda admitted that some people had been killed but reduced the scale of the incidents to isolated cases and stressed that the worst of the damage was done to Jewish property, claiming that this matter too had been exaggerated by the Jews and their helpers.

Special revulsion had been caused by the stories of rape. In interviews in the press, Mme. Novikov cited the French-language official organ of the Russian Foreign Ministry, *Le Journal de St. Petersbourg*, in contending that these reports were a libellous Jewish invention aimed at blackening the name of Russia.[111] It would appear that at least part of the propaganda claims took hold in English public opinion and somewhat weakened support for Russian Jewry.[112] The Government of Russia also tried to bring pressure to bear on Russian Jews not to raise an outcry, since it was apprehensive of external political intervention, as we have seen. As it turned out, there was no prospect of this: the US Government was indeed inclined to make a move but on condition that it be part of joint action with a number of states and England in particular. At the time the latter was conducting a policy of political *rapprochement* with Russia, and Prime Minister Gladstone not only rejected intervention but even refused to transmit the petition of Anglo-Jewry addressed to the Tsar. The *Manchester Guardian*, in fact, published a letter signed by the Ginzbourg brothers with a denial concerning cases of rape. Yahalal, one of the *maskilim* most active in cooperation with the Kovno circle,[113] warned Ruelf not to believe the Ginzbourgs, who were not speaking in the name of the people and whose declarations were made under pressure from the authorities.[114]

Western European activists in the cause of Russian Jewry were concerned over the influence of the counter-propaganda campaign and they turned to the Kovno circle to provide them with trustworthy and exact information, especially on cases of rape, to enable them to rebut Mme. Novikov's falsehoods.[115] The circle decided to ask people in different places where there had been pogroms and raping to secure direct testimony from relatives of those murdered and especially from women who had been raped. They were assisted in this by the *maskilim* in various towns, outstanding among them the radical Jewish *maskil* already referred to, Yahalal (Yehuda Leib Levin), with whom Lifschitz had for long been in contact over literary matters.[116] Furthermore, Rabbi Zvi Hirsch Rabinowitz was sent to Kiev and other places to organize the collection of evidence. In his memoirs, Yahalal quotes a letter from Rabbi Spektor asking him to help his son, a letter written in the 'secret' language for fear of its falling into the wrong hands. It stated that his son's journey was in connection with purchases of sugar for Passover, and Yahalal was asked to help the son with the transaction in question.[117] Yahalal responded with the utmost willingness to Spektor's and Lifschitz's request, and over a period of time he played an important part in refuting the Russian Government's propaganda.

The controversy over the reports of murders and rape led the British Government to instruct their Consuls in the different Russian cities to investigate the charges and obtain testimony from victims and their relatives, especially from women victims. Yahalal was involved in this matter when he accompanied the English Consul Wagstaff on his inquiries regarding instances of rape in the Kiev suburb of Deneyevka.[118] It was then that Yahalal realised the harm done by these inquiries, since women who had been raped generally refused to admit it before strangers, whether from shame or for other reasons: the young women among them feared that their testimony would prevent their getting married in the future, and the married women feared that their husbands would disown them. The main harm, however, stemmed in Yahalal's view from the hostile attitude of the English officials themselves towards the Jews, and in fact their reports disproved the Jews' contentions and served as ammunition of the highest importance for Russian counter-propaganda. These reports may well have reinforced the British Government's reluctance to intervene on behalf of Russian Jewry.

Yahalal undertook to rebut Russian propaganda and prove the veracity of the accusations that had appeared in the press. We have 14 missives from 1882, some of them long and detailed, that were transmitted by him to Kovno and thence to Dr. Ruelf; some contained testimony in Yiddish, signed in their own handwriting by the women victims themselves, confirming charges of rape, and others from relatives of people who were murdered. There were documents attached from doctors who attended some of the victims of rape. Yahalal cautioned in these missives against giving credence to the reports of the British Consuls. The witnesses who had been questioned had been aware of the Consuls' superficiality and hostility and had not trusted them.[119] Yahalal and his companions also built up a network of persons who collected evidence in other places, and they secured factual material in large quantities on the pogroms in general and particular instances of rape and murder.[120] Without question this material buttressed the credibility of the data sent to Western Europe by the Kovno circle and played a significant part in weakening the effect of the Russian Government propaganda.

An essentially different role was filled by Shefer (Shaul Pinhas Rabinowitz), a well-known publicist, who had translated Graetz into Hebrew. Lifschitz brought him into their group through his brother, who lived in Warsaw.[121] Lifschitz asked Shefer to collect, edit and translate scattered news items in the Russian press on pogroms, burnings and anti-Jewish decrees. This material too was transmitted to Kovno and thence to Memel. Lifschitz had a high opinion of Shefer's work; he said it 'made a tremendous impression,' and affirmed further, 'Shefer (may he rest in peace) was a great help to us with his voluntary work over several months.'[122]

The idyll between the two men did not last long, however, and when Shefer went with Rabbi Mohilever to meet emigrants from Russia in Galicia at the time of the visits there of Montagu and Acher their pact broke up.[123] Lifschitz averred that this visit of Shefer's and a later one to St. Petersburg (for which he also received material benefits) stimulated his desire to become a public figure: 'Shefer saw that it was better for him to be a helper in work for the collectivity than to be a teacher or helper in the main battle of the era.'[124] Two things about Shefer angered Lifschitz particularly. First, in consequence of his acquaintance with Rabbi Mohilever he made a career for himself, so to speak, and obtained a post for himself in the Hovevei Zion office, a movement detested by Lifschitz, and devoted himself wholly to nationalist activity, entirely ignoring other needs of the Jews of Russia. Secondly, Lifschitz was no less angered by the fact that in his autobiography Shefer 'did not mention even by so much as a hint that the Lifschitz brothers made him an intimate of theirs and took him under their wing for service to the general community.'[125]

\* \* \*

Besides the Kovno circle's activity, although at a later stage, a number of the *maskilim* worked on similar lines on their own, and made direct contact with the West through the post. In his memoirs, M.Y. Freid related that Shefer used to go out at night to put memoranda into different post-boxes addressed to various journalists and statesmen abroad, 'so that they (the memoranda) shouldn't all pile up in one place and arouse the suspicion of the Tsarist secret police lying in wait for any protesting voice or any smallest sound about its evil deeds.'[126] Part of the material was posted to the USA, where it was translated into English and passed on to the authorities in Washington 'so that the US Government may address the Russian Government forcefully.' The results were sparse, but there was a favourable response from public opinion when the *New York Herald* published part of the material.[127]

At times the *maskilim* expressed views in their missives not precisely in conformity with those of the Kovno circle. Yahalal, for example, told Spektor that he had sent a missive to Rabbi Adler[128] in London through the intermediary of emigrants, in which he suggested directing the emigration to Palestine.[129] In their letters to the West, Yahalal and other *maskilim* criticized the stand of the 'plutocracy.' In his own name and that of the renowned eye-specialist and public figure from Kiev, E. Mandelstam,[130] Yahalal urged that moneys collected in the West for Russian Jewry should not be sent to St. Petersburg – that is, to the leadership of wealthy men, who might well just take control of it and use it according to their own sweet will – but should be turned over to the emigration organization. In these missives Yahalal condemned these rich men's indifference to the sufferings of the masses. He blamed them for their estrangement from the needs of the poor and those deprived of rights. The rich, he charged, acted out of narrow class interests in servile fawning before the authorities, thereby abetting the latter's campaign to shake off responsibility for the pogroms and acts of pillage and murder.

This was how Yahalal depicted the undermining of the people's faith in the traditional leadership of the wealthy and their associates.[131] This attitude was diametrically opposed to that of the Kovno circle and in particular of Lifschitz, whose book *Zikhron Ya'akov* praised the traditional leadership's methods based on cooperation between men of wealth and men of learning and was, in essence, a powerful brief defending against the accusations levelled by the young radical intelligentsia and especially by the Zionists among them.[132]

## LATER VIEWS ON THE KOVNO CIRCLE

In 1917 the author E. Frank published a series of articles in the Hebrew paper *Ha-tsfirah* (The Epoch) affirming that it was the *maskilim* who first mobilized public opinion in Europe.[133] They began this activity because they wanted to uncover the elements that instigated the pogroms. To this end there was an exchange of letters between a number of *maskilim* (Friedberg, Shefer, Dulitzky, Yahalal). When the Hebrew writers realized that the rich men of St. Petersburg had failed to intercede effectively because they were afraid of undermining their own standing in the eyes of the authorities, they began 'firstly to dispatch letters to all the Jews abroad and lay before them the tale of Jewish affliction.' In particular they asked the Jews of Vienna to intercede with the Emperor Franz Josef, 'known for his love of the Jews,' and beg him 'to incline the heart of the Tsar of Russia to spare the Jews and be compassionate towards them. The Jews of England were also requested to have Queen Victoria bring to the attention of the Tsar the shame that Minister Ignatyev was bringing on Russia.'[134] The complete text creates the impression that the author ascribed the initiative to the *maskilim*. He did in fact mention the Kovno circle but only as a minor factor, as a mere intermediary between the *maskilim* and the outside world, as though the writers who initiated the appeal abroad simply asked Rabbis Spektor and Mohilever to confirm the personal reliability of the writers and the credibility of their missives in transferring them to the West.[135] In the same issue of

*Ha-tsfirah*, however, a few paragraphs further on, he affirms the contrary, saying that all the same the initiative came from Kovno: 'among those working in the Jewish community then was Rav R. Yitzhak Elhanan of Kovno, who had *encouraged the Hebrew authors even earlier, when the pogroms broke out* [my emphasis – I.O.], to get accurate news about the dread deeds wreaked on the Jews and spread the reports in the world.'[136] Nevertheless, it appears that Frank was correct regarding the independent initiative of the Hebrew writers and this apart from their activity undertaken on the initiative of the Kovno circle, an example of which was the appeal to Vienna. Frank relates that no answer was received from Vienna and so they turned this time to Dr. Yellinek and Peretz Smolenskin and asked them to approach wealthy Jews and community leaders and get them to intercede with the authorities on behalf of the Jews of Russia. Yellinek did not even answer and Smolenskin in his reply tried to instruct them on international affairs and make it clear that it was not customary for one country to interfere in another's internal affairs and accordingly their intercession would have no chance at all of succeeding.[137]

Another attempt made independently of the Kovno circle was that recounted by Sokolow in 1935 in an article in Yiddish, 'The *Hajnt* and the pogroms in Russia.'[138] According to this article, a group of Warsaw lawyers and editors that included himself organized[139] and carried on correspondence with people abroad. He passed on news to the *Times* based mainly on what had appeared in *Ha-tsfirah* and more especially on the mass of reports from various provincial towns. The question remained as to how contact was made with the *Times*. Sokolow related that an Orientalist of repute on the *Times* staff approached the editor of *Ha-tsfirah*, Haim Zelig Slonimski, for help in translating into English some words from the Bible in the *makomas* of Al-Kahiri (1054–1122). When his questions had been answered, he also asked for news on the situation of the Jews in Russia. Sokolow answered him and this was the way a correspondence began that lasted for two years, till the death of the Englishman in 1884. Accurate news on the situation of Russian Jewry was sent to England in these letters and published in the *Times*.

Sokolow confessed that he wrote this article in order to correct the historical distortion created by the appearance of the three volumes of Lifschitz's *Zikhron Ya'akov*. In these memoirs and particularly in the third volume, the Kovno circle alone was given all the credit for the widespread activity of mobilizing public opinion in the West.

Sokolow wrote: 'Apart from us, the office in Kovno worked very well, headed by the Gaon Rav Yitzhak Elhanan,' but he complained that the Kovno group built up wide public relations for itself, while the Warsaw office, which had operated carefully in accordance with precise rules of clandestinity, was not commemorated in the historical record at all. At the same time he could not but admit, 'Kovno did useful and important work, and Rav Ya'akov Lifschitz was a great force in the matter of transmitting information,' and Kovno indeed preceded Warsaw. As regards the importance and value of their activity, however, he put the two groups on the same level: 'Two little groups in Warsaw and Kovno launched a campaign against Alexander III.'[140] He also recalled the activities of other people, Yahalal among them, but not in connection with the Kovno circle. It is hard to evaluate the accuracy of Sokolow's affirmations, which were made some 54 years after the events occurred and with a limited purpose, but it seems worth quoting them, even though they were not supported by any sources, as one fragment in the mosaic of the story of the public awakening in the early 1880s.

## CONCLUSION

The activity of the Kovno circle around Rabbi Yitzhak Elhanan Spektor presents a number of problems, which we shall deal with briefly:

(1) Why did an initiative of this kind come precisely from an ultra-Orthodox group and not from any other element in Russian Jewry? How did it happen that a group embedded in its entirety in the closed-in world of tradition managed to display so bold an initiative and succeed in rallying round itself heterogeneous circles of the Jewish community to help in an enterprise that aroused Jews and non-Jews in the whole world against the Russian Government's treatment of its Jews?

(2) How successful were they actually? That is to say, did they manage to change the situation of the Jews in Russia?

(3) Is there any historical significance in the cooperation between the Kovno circle and the *maskilim*?

We shall I think find it easier to answer these questions if we try even briefly to delineate the period under discussion. Dinur defined 1881 as the first year of a new epoch in the history of the people of Israel characterized by three distinctive features: political confrontation, people's defence and strengthened nationalism.[141] Does the Kovno circle's activity fit into this definition? At first sight it seems not, since their whole outook was encompassed by the ultra-Orthodox world, where extremist circles, for whom Lifschitz was an extreme but not a unique spokesman, utterly repudiated the first stirrings of nationalism and the radical, socialistic thinking that was spreading in the Jewish community and especially among the younger generation. The ultra-Orthodox circles utterly rejected the *maskilim*'s pretensions to serve as the legitimate representatives of the Jewish people in their fight for civil and political rights, and the ideologies and modern methods of organization that were meant to supplant the traditional means of defence – mainly intercession with the powers that be – which the *maskilim* considered anarchistic. Lifschitz's memoirs, *Zikhron Ya'akov*, and particularly the third volume, as we have already indicated more than once, largely constituted an apologia for the traditional leadership and its actions. Lifschitz wanted to prove that its methods, rather than political confrontations, not only were legitimate due to the historical experience they embodied but were also infinitely more effective than the political and party struggles that had only led to a worsening of the position of the Jews in Russia, given the political realities in that country.

When we scrutinize the Kovno circle's *modus operandi*, however, we find that they worked on two levels. On one level they followed the well-worn traditional path of attempting to reach ruling circles through the intercession of personalities they associated with, using bribery when this seemed likely to be effective. On another level, they adopted modern conceptions of employing mass communications to mobilize public opinion in the West in order to bring public pressure to bear on the Russian Government. On both levels the Kovno circle was remarkably effective. Their talent and sophistication in carrying out their work were exceptional, even by today's standards, even as they remained steadfast in their dedication to traditional views. This created a tension which, I believe, testifies to the fact that, as with German Jewish Orthodoxy, Eastern European ultra-Orthodoxy was not indifferent to the challenges of modernization, but responded to them in its own special way. This very complex subject calls for further study.

We can now answer the questions formulated above.

(1) In his article, 'New Material on the History of the Pogroms in Russia,'[142] Tcherikover tried to answer the first question by a process of elimination. He established that besides the ultra-

Orthodox there were two other groups in Russian Jewry capable of taking action to mobilize public opinion in Western Europe – the wealthy oligarchy in St. Petersburg and the young Jewish intelligentsia. The former did have connections with the West but was deterred from exploiting them by its posture of patriotic loyalty, which precluded any foreign interference in Russian affairs, and by its particularist class interests. The latter, the intelligentsia, had no connections at all with the outside world, Tcherikover contended, and so it never occurred to them to seek help from the West, while the ultra-Orthodox, as we have seen, in Kovno were maintaining contacts with the West through Dr. Ruelf as early as the 1860s.

We must amend Tcherikover's thesis, it seems to me, since the cooperation of the Kovno group with Ruelf in the 1860s was clearly a case of plain philanthropy permitted by the authorities, whereas the enterprise, 'Be Thou with the mouths,' far exceeded the bounds of a legal-philanthropic undertaking. Bringing public opinion in Western Europe to bear was more than just another practice of the same quality as the traditional ones, and for all Lifschitz's denials it substantially constituted a material turning-point. The ultra-Orthodox were in fact better fitted than the *maskilim* to take a step like this since, from the outset, they did not share the faith of the older generation of *maskilim* in the good intentions of the government towards the Jews nor the faith of the radical young *maskilim* in a revolutionary solution. When all these hopes were disappointed, both sets of *maskilim* were initially helpless in the face of the new problems. On the other hand, despite their protestations of loyalty, the ultra-Orthodox attitude to the regime was free of illusions from the beginning. They saw it as an evil regime and a hostile power from which the Jews could expect little. Perhaps they did not even want to get very much from it, and when they came to the conclusion that they had reached the end of the road and that the Jews were not assured of even a minimal existence, they did not hesitate to mobilize Western opinion to bring pressure to bear on the Russian Government. They were aware of the dangers involved, but they had no difficulty in overcoming the inhibitions they may have had. The *maskilim* joined them later, having overcome their disenchantment and discarded their illusions.

(2) As regards the degree of success of the enterprise, public opinion was indeed aroused and this caused the Russian Government no little concern, but public opinion was not powerful enough to get the Western governments to take action; they flatly refused

from calculations both of political tactics and of principle, which we have already touched on. Attempts to intercede with powerful personalities did not succeed either for the same reasons and the situation of Russian Jewry remained unchanged.

This was not the case in the internal Jewish sphere. The Kovno circle and others succeeded in awakening interest and concern among Jews in many countries. Their widespread activity served simultaneously as another link to strengthen the heritage of Jewish solidarity and as a factor that helped create modern Jewish national consciousness. From this viewpoint, the outcome of the Kovno circle's activity was another expression of the dialectic characterizing the history of the Jewish people in the modern period: adapting to the host society on the one hand and reinforcing a supra-national Jewish solidarity on the other.

(3) As regards the historic significance of the collaboration between the Kovno circle and the *maskilim*, this is a more complex matter. The picture that emerges from deliberations on the history of Russian Jewry in the nineteenth century highlights the prolonged schism between the *maskilim* and considerable sections of the Jewish community, in no small measure because the former were seen as agents of the hostile regime;[143] yet the enterprise described here created a complete harmony between the rival forces. The *maskilim* accepted the leadership of Rabbi Yitzhak Elhanan Spektor and Lifschitz unreservedly and acted according to their instructions in other matters besides 'Be Thou with the mouths.' For instance, they turned to Spektor to give legitimacy for all the Jews to the 'General Fast' that was proclaimed on the initiative of one group of Hebrew writers.[144] Can we conclude that the gulf between the *maskilim* and the ultra-Orthodox community was not as deep as we have usually believed? Beneath the cloak of controversy and contradiction, were not organic ties preserved, hidden ones it is true but strong enough to be revealed in the hour of need and to produce cooperation between the two 'camps' if only in limited areas? Finally, did not this cooperation in the hour of need bring in its wake a more tolerant relation between the two sides? It seems to me that the answer to these questions is, Yes. From the period of the Kovno circle the war waged by the *maskilim* against religion stopped almost completely and their attitude to it became more tolerant. This complicated issue still awaits a more thoroughgoing investigation than is possible in the limited format of this paper.

## THE DAMASCUS AFFAIR TO THE FIRST WORLD WAR

### NOTES

1. According to S. Dubnow, the author of the articles was Joseph Jacobs. See, *History of the Jews in Russia and Poland*, Vol. 2, Philadelphia, 1918, p.287.
2. See Z. Dinur, 'Tokhniotav shel Ignatyev le-pitaron she'elat ha-yehudim u-vidot netsigei ha-kehillot vepetersburg beshnot hrma-hrmb,' *He-avar*, No. 10, 1963, pp.5–81 (hereinafter, Tokhniotav), Hebrew; A. Linden, 'Prototyp des Pogroms in den Achziger Jahren,' in *Die Judenpogrome in Russland*, Köln 1909, pp.12–96 (ed. L. Motzkin). German.
3. See A. Levinson (ed.), *Doktor Yitzhak Ruelf, Mivhar Ma'amarav, b'tsiruf m'vo shel ha'orekh* (Dr. Yitzhak Ruelf, Selected Articles, with a Preface by the editor), Tel Aviv 1946, p.147 (hereinafter, Levinson ...). Hebrew. On the role of Ruelf, see further in the present chapter.
4. On 13 and 21 Jan. 1882.
5. London 1882. The pamphlet ends with a list of 167 places where pogroms took place, with a short account of each pogrom. The pamphlet was translated into German with the title, *Die Judenverfolgungen in Russland*, Berlin 1882. See too, *Russische Greuele*, Berlin 1882. German.
6. See, for example, Ita Szedlecki, 'Ha-itonut ha-y'hudit b'germania b'shanim 1819–1882. t'guvoteiha l-praot b'y'hudei russia ul'reshit ha-l'eumiut ha-y'hudit al reka hitorrerut ha-antishemiut b'germania.' (The Jewish Press in Germany in the years 1819–1882, its reactions to the pogroms among the Jews of Russia and to the beginnings of Jewish nationalism, against the background of awakening anti-Semitism in Germany.) Final thesis for M.A., unpublished, Hebrew University of Jerusalem, 1976. Hebrew.
7. For the record of the meeting see 'The City of London: Public Meetings against the Persecution of the Jews in Russia,' in *Kuntras l'talmidim – mekorot u'mehkarim* (Brochures for Students: Sources and Research), Study Circle on the History of the People of Israel, Hebrew University of Jerusalem, 1964.
8. See, for example, S.W. Baron, *The Russian Jews under Tsars and Soviets*, New York 1964. L. Greenberg, *The Jews in Russia*, Vol. 1, New York 1961. Lifschitz, 'De Amerikaner interventsen wegen de pogromen in Russland in de 80er yuren' (American intervention against the pogroms in Russia in the '80s) in E. Tchernikover (ed.), *YIVO Historishe shriften*, Vol. 2, Vilna 1937, pp.497–516. Yiddish.
9. From May 1881 increasingly numerous references appear in the London *Jewish Chronicle* to the situation of the Jews in Russia: accounts of pogroms and fire-setting and anti-Jewish legislation and also of the anti-Jewish hostile atosphere in the general population. Later on the paper also reported on the masses fleeing from Russia. In fact the emigrants who reached England on their way to the USA served as a most reliable prime source of information on what was going on in Russia; see, e.g., the issues of 20 May, 10 June, 5 Aug., 23 Sept., 11 Nov., 25 Nov. 1881. The paper sent a special correspondent of its own to St. Petersburg, and he complained of the difficulties he met with in obtaining reliable news on the pogroms and then in transmitting it when he had it. See issue of 5 Aug. 1881.
10. 'Newspapers were under obligation to observe numerous orders issued with regard to the handling of current events. During the Jewish persecutions in 1881 and 1882, for example, the papers were forbidden to mention them.' De Witt, 'Development of the Press in the Nineteenth Century,' in *Journalism Quarterly*, March 1944, Vol. 21, No. 1, p.54.
11. See E. Tcherikover (ed.), 'Homer hadash b'toldot hafraot b'russia ba-t'hilat shnot ha-shmonim,' in *Y'hudim b'itot mahapaha* ('New Material on the History of the Pogroms in Russia in the '80s,' in *Jews in Revolutionary Times*), Tel Aviv 1955,

p.385. Hebrew. (Hereafter, Tcherikover ...) See too, Letter from Shefer (Shaul Pinhas Rabinowitz) to Ruelf on the increasing severity of newspaper censorship. Letter No. 5, April 1882, Ruelf Collection, Central Zionist Archives in Jerusalem (hereafter, CZA).

12. *Zikhron Ya'akov*, Kovno 1928–30. The references are to the photogravure edition of 1948. This is perhaps the place for a few words on the nature of this work, which was intended, it must be stressed, as an apologia. The author's guide-line was that the methods of the traditional leadership of 'Torah and Eminence' – that is to say, men learned in the Law and men of wealth – had proved themselves over the generations and that therefore their repudiation by the *maskilim* and Zionists in the name of national honour was completely baseless. The three volumes contain extremely valuable historical material despite their hagiographic character, the controversies pursued therein, and the things ignored or misrepresented.

13. Except for Tcherikover's brief notes, *op. cit.* pp.358–62, Greenberg (*op. cit.* note 8 above), p.59 and more recently, J. Frankel, *Prophecy and Politics*, Cambridge, 1981, pp.61, 74–5.

14. See Israel Heilperin, 'Beit ha-melukha ha-dani ve-r'difot ha-y'hudim b'russia ha-tsarit' and 'Krovav shel ha-tsar aleksander ha-shlishi b'hesendarmstadt ve-r'difot ha-y'hudim b'russia' in *Yehudim ve-yahadut ba-mizrah europa* ('Relations of Tsar Alexander III in Hessen-Darmstadt and the persecution of the Jews in Russia' and 'The Danish Royal Court and the persecution of the Jews in Russia' in *Jews and Judaism in Eastern Europe*), Jerusalem 1964, pp.357–66 and 367–70. Hebrew.

15. The main source is the Ruelf Archive, CZA.

16. Jewish historiography has dealt fully with the history of Russian Jewry in the 1880s and we shall therefore not treat this aspect here. See Dubnow, *Divrei y'mei 'am olam* (History of the Eternal People), Tel Aviv, Vol. 10, Ch. 3. Hebrew. Baron, *op. cit.* note 8 above. Dinur, 'Plans ...' Greenberg, *op. cit.*, note 8 above, Tcherikover and others.

17. See *Zikhron Ya'akov*, Vol 3, pp.80, 93, 108, 111, 161, 202, and *passim*.

18. *Ibid.*, p.166 *et seq.*

19. For the years 1881–82 we have nearly 90 missives at our disposal. There were even more, and Lifschitz intended to publish them but did not do so.

20. See Y. Malk, *Gedolim fun unser tseit* (Great men of our time), New York 1927, pp.105–23. Yiddish. See too Ben-Zion Katz, *Zikhronot, Hamishim Shanah ba-histioriah shel y'hudei rusia* (Memoirs, Fifty Years' History of the Jews of Russia), Tel Aviv 1953, pp.44–54. Hebrew. E. Shimof, *Rabbi Isaac Elchanan Spektor, Life and Letters*, New York, 1959.

21. H. Shliosberg, *Baron Horatsi Gintsburg* (Baron Horatio Ginzbourg), Paris 1933, p.106. Yiddish. In his *Memoirs* (note 20 above) Katz stated, 'He was almost the first rabbi in Lithuania who was not a zealot; the *maskilim* in the whole country held him in high respect.' M.Y. Fried confirms this when he writes, 'Even the Jewish intelligentsia, which is not at all well inclined towards rabbis and clergy, has an entirely different attitude towards Rabbi Yitzhak Elhanan Spektor, one of exceptional recognition as a result of his great love of Israel.' M. Fried, *Yamim ve-shanim* (Days and Years), Tel Aviv 1938, Part I, p.98. Hebrew.

22. Y. Lifschitz, *Toldot Yitzhak* (Yitzhak's Story), Warsaw 1897, pp.39–41. Hebrew. Katz, *Memoirs* (note 20 above), Malek, *op. cit.* (note 20 above), p.110.

23. See below, and Katz, *op. cit.* (note 20), p.123 *et seq.*; *Yitzhak's Story* (note 22), p.24.

24. Shimof, *op. cit.*, p.115, and see below.

25. 'Dos iz a fakt as ven nit Lifschitz wolt R'Yitzhak Elhanan nit gekumen zu de madreigah un wen der alweltliher frur fun dor' (It is a fact that if it had not been for Lifschitz, Rav Yitzhak Elhanan would not have reached the level of a worldwide leader of his generation), Malek, *op. cit.* p.115. Yiddish.

26. See Fried, *op. cit.* (note 21), pp.96–7.

27. *Ibid.*
28. For his activity see below, and also *Yitzhak's Story*, pp.50–1.
29. *Some notes and articles by the late Dr. Asher Acher, M.D., 1837–1899, with reprints of his newspaper Obituaries, etc.*, London 1916.
30. See Dinur, 'Plans ...,' pp.15–16.
31. *Zikhron Ya'akov*, Vol. 3, p.21.
32. See Dinur, 'Plans ...,' p.29 *et seq.* See too Mordekhai Ben Hillel Hacohen, 'Natnah roshah' (Gave up the lead) in *Hamelitz*, Issue Nos. 1–3, 18 April 1882. In this article he cast doubt on the legitimacy of the traditional leadership and called for the setting up of an alternative leadership to represent the people and its interests. This is only one example among many in the Jewish Hebrew-language and Russian-language press along these lines, and the subject is treated at length by Dinur, Tcherikover, etc.
33. *Zikhron Ya'akov*, Vol. 3, p.21.
34. Part 1 of the book was published in Vilna in 1872 and Part 2, also in Vilna in 1882.
35. See Shimof, *op. cit.*, p.93.
36. On the different versions of this prayer and the customs with regard to it in the different congregations, see D. Goldschmitt, *Mahzor le-yamim nora'im* (Prayer book for the Day of Atonement), Vol A, Jerusalem 1970, pp.44–5, 230–1.
37. *Zikhron Ya'akov*, Vol. 3, p.22 *et seq.*
38. What follows is based on the contents of the missives as they appear in *Zikhron Ya'akov*, Vol. 3, pp.22–9. The first missive was written on 27 Oct. 1881, the second on the next day, and the third, a detailed one, on 13 Nov. 1881.
39. The governments of France and Austria intervened in 1886 on behalf of the Jews of Russia. In 1882 the *Alliance Israélite Universelle* (hereinafter *Alliance*) took steps for diplomatic intervention in Rumania in the wake of pogroms and deportations. In 1868 and 1870 to 1873, the *Alliance* once more regained importance when pogroms recurred repeatedly. As a consequence of the memorandum that the *Alliance* addressed to the Berlin Congress in 1878, the Congress's decisions included a clause on the matter of equal rights for Jews in the Balkan countries. The *Alliance* also intervened on behalf of Russian Jewry several times from the 1860s on. This holds good for the Jews of Morocco as well. See Sh. Dubnow, *Divre'i ...* (note 16 above), Vol. 9, Part 2, Ch. 4. Sh. Ettinger, *Toldot yisrael ba'et ha-hadasha* (History of Israel in the modern era), Tel Aviv 1969, pp.134–5. Hebrew.
40. *Zikhron Ya'akov*, Vol. 3, p.22.
41. *Ibid.*, pp.23–4, 32, 33, 40, 84.
42. For their activity, see Dinur, 'Plans ...,' p.9 *et seq.*
43. For these rumours, see the article by Erez-Tsederbaum, editor of *Hamelitz*, 'Bein ha-davar uvein hamarah' ('The difference between the thing itself and how it looks'), Issue No. 20, 1881. Hebrew. See too, Letter from Shefer to Ruelf of 22 February 1882, CZA, HiVi.
44. *Zikhron Ya'akov*, Vol. 3, pp.23–4.
45. *Ibid.*, p.26.
46. *Ibid.*, p.25. See also, Genesis Ch. 30, v.22: 'and God hearkened to her.'
47. *Zikhron Ya'akov*, pp.114–15. Dinur, 'Plans ...,' p.11 and note 14.
48. *Zikhron Ya'akov*, p.25.
49. *Ibid.*, pp.26–7.
50. *Ibid.*, pp.81, 89, 108–9. This whole matter deserves fuller treatment, but it is outside the scope of this chapter.
51. See below.
52. *Zikhron Ya'akov*, p.102, and see also, p.121.
53. See notes 3 to 8 above.
54. See Letter from Ruelf to Acher. See Levinson ... (note 3 above), pp.186–8.
55. *Ibid.* Similar apprehensions over possibly unfavourable results from protest activities were voiced by Rabbi Ezre'el Hildesheimer after his son returned from a

visit to Odessa and wrote to him to say that calling in Jews from abroad was liable to do harm and so was action through the press. See Letter of Rabbi Hildesheimer to Rabbi Sh. R. Hirsch, 8 December 1881. CZA, Hirsch Collection, B 213.
56. See Letter Ruelf to Acher. CZA.
57. J. Ruelf, *Die Russischen Juden* (The Russian Jews), Memel 1892, p.3. German.
58. *Zikhron Ya'akov*, p.25.
59. See e.g. I. Ma'or, 'Ha-kruz ha-anti-shemi shel narodnayah volya' (The anti-Semitic manifesto in *Narodnaya volya*) in *Tsion* (Zion), Jerusalem 1951, Issue No 14, pp.150–5. Hebrew.
60. The Board of Deputies of British Jews developed from a joint intersynagogal committee formed after the accession of George III in 1760.
61. The Anglo-Jewish Association was formed in England in 1871. The two institutions set up a 'Foreign Commission' in 1878, which was active on behalf of general Jewish causes outside Britain.
62. Founded in 1873.
63. *Zikhron Ya'akov*, pp.26–7.
64. 'Mikhtavav higiuni ba-itam, gam ha-m'amar 'nahal yitzhak' na-maleh torah v-hokhmah k-ya'eh ve-na'eh l-mhabrah. Esa mi'dvarav ha-n'imim al shulhan malakhim lifnei dodi tsah iadim, magen hu al kol ha-husim b'tsilo uve-haskamato afik mayanotav hahitsah ve-davar ehad ehad lo yipol artsah.' ('His letters reached me in due time as did the article 'Nahal Yitzhak' full of law and wisdom as befitted its author. I took his fine words and placed them on the tables of kings and before my pure red dearly-beloved [i.e. Rothschild – I.O.], a shield that defends all who shelter in his shade, and with his consent I shall pour forth fountains and not a single word shall fall to the ground.' *Ibid.*, p.29.
65. *Ibid.*, pp.29–36. What follows is based on this source.
66. *Ibid.*, p.36.
67. See below, *Hamelitz*, and also the Russian-language Jewish press from 1881 on. See, too, Greenberg, *op. cit.* (note 8 above), pp.55–75; Dubnow, *Divre'i*, Vol. 10, pp.60–116; also Y. Slutzky, *Ha-itonut ha-y'hudit-russit ba-meah ha-tsha-esreh* (The Russian Jewish Press in the 19th Century), Jerusalem 1970, Ch. 7. Hebrew.
68. *Razsviet*, Issue No. 4, 1882, pp.125–6. Sh. Briman, 'Ha-mifneh ba-mahshavah ha-tsiburit ha-y'hudit b'reshit shnot ha-shmonim,' in *Shivat tsion* ('The turning point in thinking on Jewish public affairs at the beginning of the eighties,' in Return to Zion), Nos. 2–3, Jerusalem 1951-2, p.72. Hebrew.
69. *Hamelitz*, Issue No. 10, 1882, pp.171–3. See also, *Yahalal, Zikhronot v'hegionot he-hadir v'tsiref mavo v'he'erot* (Yahalal – Memories and reflections with a preface and notes) by Y. Slutzki, Jerusalem 1968, pp.103–10. (Hereinafter, 'Yahalal, Memories...'). Hebrew.
70. See Dinur, 'Plans...,' pp.61–82.
71. And see below.
72. *Zikhron Ya'akov*, p.89.
73. 'Bakashat rishaion kazeh t'hashev k'hoda't ba-finu ki zarim anu ba'arets gam b'aine'inu' ('A request for permission of this kind – i.e. to set up an emigration committee – will be interpreted as an affirmation on our part that we are foreigners in the land in our own eyes as well.') Lifschitz, *Yitzhak's Story*, p. 97. Or: If they insist on setting up Emigration Committees, 'she-aza'i yitnu herev pifiot l'sotnei yisrael she-ha-y'hudim ainam hoveve'i moledetam ki im m'natsle'i ha-medinah u'ba-et she-ainam mots'im teref l'to'elet atsmam n'khonim hem l'asov et ha'arets' ('then they will be giving haters of Israel a double-edged sword [sharp weapon to prove] that the Jews do not love their fatherland but are exploiters of the State, and the moment they cannot find a prey to their purpose, they are prepared to leave the country'). *Zikhron Ya'akov*, p.91.
74. See Dinur, 'Plans...,' p.81.
75. *Ibid.*, p.53.

76. *Ibid.*, p.58.
77. *Yitzhak's Story*. See too what Lifschitz had to say on emigration in *Zikhron Ya'akov*, p.87: 'Im y'natslu eizeh yehudim bodedim nimlatim lo b'eileh yush'u erekh shishah milion napesh' ('If some isolated Jews flee and are saved, some six million souls will not thereby be rescued'). See too *loc. cit.*, p.90.
78. Dinur, 'Plans ...,' p.81.
79. *Ibid.*, *loc. cit.*
80. See Missive No. 14 in the series, 'Be Thou with the mouths,' *Zikhron Ya'akov*, p.182 *et seq*. The annual rate of natural increase among Russian Jews was 11%. Some 1,022,000 souls emigrated from Russia to the USA from 1881 to 1914. See L. Hirsch, *N'dude'i ha-yehudim ba-me'ah ha-shanim ha-ahronim* ('Wanderings of the Jews in the last hundred years'), as cited by Dinur. Hebrew. A. Tartakover, Y. Leczinsky (eds.), *Klal yisrael, prakim ba-sotziologiah shel ha'am ha'yehudi* (The community of Israel, chapters in the sociology of the Jewish people). Jerusalem 1954, pp.198–204. Hebrew. See Leczinsky on the scale of Jewish migration and its direction in the last century, *loc. cit*, p.186 *et seq*. See also, M. Wischnitzer, *To dwell in safety. The story of Jewish migration since 1860*, Philadelphia 1948.
81. See the brief letters of Dr. Acher to Spektor from late 1881 to early 1882. *Zikhron Ya'akov*, pp.36–8.
82. *Ibid.*, pp.16–17.
83. See Levinson (note 3 above), pp.6–7.
84. *Ibid.*, p.8. See also, 'Toldot y'me'i hai'ia' ('The story of my life'), passages from his autobiography. *Ibid.*, pp.50–1. Hebrew.
85. See Ruelf's letter to London, 10 April 1882. Levinson, p.142.
86. J. Ruelf, *Drei Tage in juedischen Russland*, Frankfurt-am-Main 1882. German.
87. Levinson, *loc. cit.*, p.52.
88. Ruelf, *Meine Reise nach Kowno*, Memel 1869. German.
89. See Levinson, p.52.
90. On his attitude to emigration, see his letter to H. Guelda, London, 19 April 1882. Levinson, pp.147–50. See also *ibid.*, p.10.
91. 'The story of my life' (Levinson ...), pp.52–3.
92. See Letter of Rabbi Yitzhak Elhanan Spektor of 13 Nov. 1881. Ruelf Collection, CZA. *Zikhron Ya'akov*, p.38.
93. *Zikhron Ya'akov*, *ibid*.
94. A detailed account of the discussions between Ruelf and the Rabbi's son and of the way activities were planned is to be found in the letters the latter sent to his father, the first on 11 Nov. 1881, *loc. cit.*, pp.58–9, the second, undated, pp. 59–61, and the third, 25 Nov., pp.61–2.
95. For the methods employed to transmit the material from Lithuania to Memel see below.
96. For details, see Heilperin, *op. cit.*, pp.357–66, and *Zikhron Ya'akov*, p.59.
97. *Zikhron Ya'akov*, p.60.
98. On this, Lifschitz writes: 'By means of the Memel Committee, the best sons of our people in Ashkenaz were aroused to pay heed to the disaster of our brethren in Russia. Up to now our brethren abroad regarded what was happening to our brethren in Russia with equanimity as a rumour from afar, but the writings [of the Committee – I.O.] and the voice crying out from Memel that described the fate of our brethren in Russia in vivid colours affected our brethren greatly. Besides the many contributions that reached us from Ashkenaz for the sufferers from the pogroms, we also received spiritual assistance. Many helpers and spiritual supporters were found for us among our brethren in Ashkenaz, thanks to the Memel Committee.' *Loc. cit.*, p.63.
99. *Ibid.*, pp.61–2.
100. Ruelf recounted that he passed on a total of 17 long and short missives in large numbers of copies all over Europe. See Ruelf, *Die russischen Juden*, Memel 1892,

p.32. German.
101. *Ibid.*, pp.39–43, 54–5.
102. See his letter of 26 Jan. 1882, Ruelf Collection, CZA. *Zikhron Ya'akov*, p.67. Heilperin, *op. cit.*, pp.367–70.
103. Letter of 23 Jan. 1882. Ruelf Collection, CZA.
104. *Zikhron Ya'akov*, p.82.
105. An account of these activities is outside the scope of this article. They have been fully described in the historical literature. See above, notes 3 to 11.
106. See *Zikhron Ya'akov*, pp.55–6.
107. *Ibid.*, p.56.
108. *Ibid.*, p.39.
109. They were Rabbi Elinka Kretinger from Lithuania and David Zablotowsky from Bialystok, who lived in Paris for a time. See this series of missives, *loc. cit.*, pp.82–9.
110. *Ibid.*, p.84.
111. Frankel, *op. cit.* (note 13 above), p.75.
112. *Zikhron Ya'akov*, p.57.
113. See below.
114. See his letter to Ruelf of 21 March 1882. Ruelf Collection, CZA.
115. See *Zikhron Ya'akov*, p.57.
116. *Ibid.*, pp.57–8.
117. See Yahalal, 'Memories . . .' *loc. cit* (note 69 above), p.71. In his preface to the work, Slutzky wrote, 'Yahalal lakah helek ba-fualatah shel kvutsat ha-sofrim ha- 'ivriim she-he'evirah ba'emtsa'ut d'r rilf Raba shel memel yedi'ot ne'emanot al mahalah hapra'ot le'yahadut m'arav eiropah' ('Yahalal took part in the activities of the group of Hebrew writers who transmitted reliable reports to the Jewry of Western Europe on the course of the pogroms through the intermediary of Dr. Ruelf, Rabbi of Memel.') *Loc. cit.*, pp.20–1. That is to say, the writer did not mention at all that the initiative came from Lifschitz; and at the same time Yahalal himself wrote that Kovno was the initiator and that the activity was led by Rabbi Yitzhak Elhanan Spektor.
118. *Ibid.*
119. See, e.g., the missives of 5, 14, 15, 19, 24 Feb. and 3, 21 March 1882 etc. Ruelf Collection, CZA.
120. See, e.g., letter to Ruelf of 3 March 1882, or the letter of 31 March 1882, where Yahalal reports on the terrible pogrom at Balata. *Ibid.*
121. *Zikhron Ya'akov*, p.64.
122. *Ibid.*, and see too, e.g., the missives from Shefer to Ruelf of 24 Feb., 30 March, 5 April, etc. Ruelf Collection CZA.
123. See Nussbaum, *Ha-dat ve-ha-t'hiyah ha-le'umit* (Religion and the national revival), Warsaw, pp.98–9. Hebrew. See too letter of 24 April 1882 from Rabbi Spektor to Ruelf on the preparations for the journey to Lemberg of Shefer and the Mohilever circle. Ruelf Collection, CZA.
124. *Zikhron Ya'akov*, p.95.
125. *Ibid.*
126. M. I. Fried, *Yamim ve-shanim* (Days and Years), Part II, pp.34–5, Tel Aviv 1939. Hebrew.
127. Y.Z. Eisenstein writes in his memoirs that he used to receive 'packets of letters from the writer Shefer and from Ben Ami [Moshe Leib Lilienblum – Malal – I.O.] about the abominations being done to the Jews in Russia.' He handed over the translations to Judge Meir S. Isaacs, who passed them on to government circles in Washington. See Y.D. Eisenstein, *Otsar zikhronotai* (Treasure-house of my memories), p.50. New York, 1930.
128. Adler Nathan Marcus (1803–1890), Rabbi of the English community (*kolel*).
129. See missive of 19 April 1882, Ruelf Collection, CZA, and missive of Yahalal to

Acher of 26 April 1882 on the same question, *ibid.*
130. Max Emanuel Mandelstam (1838–1912), a leader of the Zionist movement in Russia, noted for his public activity on behalf of the victims of the pogroms, headed the Committee of Assistance to the Victims of the Pogroms in Kiev.
131. See missives of Yahalal to Ruelf of 22 Feb. and 14 April 1882. Ruelf Collection, CZA.
132. See above, note 12.
133. See Frank ('ha-nidah'), 'Ha-sofrim ha-ivri'im ve-p'uloteihem b'y'me'i ha-pogromim ha-rishonim ba-russiah' ('Hebrew writers and their activities in the first days of the pogroms in Russia'), *Ha-tsfirah*, Issues 25–26, 30–32, 34, 37, 38 (1917). The following account is based on these articles.
134. *Ibid.*, Issues No. 25, 26.
135. *Ibid.*, Issue No. 32.
136. In Issue No. 34 Frank cites a letter from Shefer to Ginzbourg confirming that the initiative came from the Kovno circle and that the circle was both initiator and organizer, while the *maskilim* unquestioningly accepted the leadership of Rabbi Spektor. 'Then a power from on high descended upon us, a special unique power, the Talmud eagle [eminent scholar] of Torah in this orphaned generation, the spirit[ual power] of the great Rabbi Ga'on Yitzhak Elhanan Spektor, may he be blessed with long and good life, shepherd of the congregation in Kovno metropolis of Israel. And he told us to lift up stones of gloom and the shadow of death, and to incline our hearts [to hear] of acts of oppression done to the helpless flock ... to put their light like precious stones in the archives of history. We obeyed the teacher of righteousness, collected things buried deep from out of the darkness to tear the veil off the face of evil-doing.' And see Yahala, 'Memories ...,' p.70.
137. *Ha-tsfirah*, Issue no. 26.
138. *Haint* (Today), No. 11, 15 Jan. 1935, that is to say some 54 years after the outbreak of the first pogrom.
139. Mentions a number of names such as the lawyers Yanoshavsky, Forla and others.
140. All the quotations are from this article.
141. See his article, 'The new era in the history of Israel, its distinct quality, essence and image' in *Ba-mafneh ha-dorot* ('At the turning-point of the generations'), Jerusalem, 1955, pp.65–8.
142. See *Revolutionary Times* (note 11 above), pp.358–9.
143. See e.g. Ettinger, *op. cit.*, pp.128–9, Dubnow, *Divre'i*, Vol. 9, Part 2, Ch. 3.
144. Frank, 'Ha-sofrim...' (note 133 above), *Ha-tsfirah*, Issue No. 30, 1917.

# 7

# German Jews and the Jewish Emigration from Russia
## Moshe Zimmerman

This article analyses the reactions of German Jewry to the stream of migrants from Russia that flooded into the West in 1891. That was the year that marked a turning-point in everything to do with Russian-Jewish immigration into Germany, both from the German historical point of view and that of German-Jewish self-awareness. It was a crossroads in German history that also marked a change in the patterns of German-Jewish life. This was the start of a 'new era' (*neue Era*) when Germany had a new Kaiser (from 1888), Wilhelm II, and a new Chancellor, Caprivi (from 1890), who replaced Bismarck. In the year Bismarck was dismissed, the socialists' laws were annulled; in the elections held that year, the socialists received almost a fifth of the votes, and the left-wing liberals almost the same amount. Simultaneously the conservatives and the anti-Semites set out on the attack. In 1891 an anti-Semitic clause was inserted in the programme of the Conservative Party and the anti-Semites tried to pull themselves together and emerge from the crisis, when Stoecker, Boeckel and Ahlwardt took centre stage. For Jews in Germany this state of affairs presaged new possibilities and dangers. Caprivi launched a new economic policy, directed mainly to encouraging industry, and concluded new 'most favoured' customs agreements with Austria and Russia, which allowed *inter alia* for almost free immigration into Germany from those countries. Confronting this new economic policy of Caprivi's, pressure groups of landowners and peasants organized themselves. A new type of organizing began throughout Germany of political groupings such as the Peasants' League, or the 'Pan-German League.' The Jews also took part in creating new organizations: the League for the Defence against anti-Semitism, led by Heinrich Rickert of the left-wing Liberals, was an example of the new cooperation between Jews and non-Jews in the face of the new wave of anti-Semitism, of which the Xanten affair in that same year,

1891, was the most frightening episode. The new wave of Jewish immigration from the East was part of this picture, which helps to throw the Jewish reaction into relief.

Germany had known previous waves of Jewish immigration from the East – in 1868 as a result of the cholera epidemic, at a time when the Jews of the North-German Alliance were about to benefit from the Law of General Emancipation; and in 1881, when there was another wave of migration from Russia into Germany and through Germany as a result of the pogroms and the Czarist Government's decrees (the Regulations of May 1881). In both instances there was an overall combination of the desire to help persecuted brethren and to ward off being swamped inside Germany by the flood from Eastern Europe. The unfavourable image of the *Ostjuden* was accepted by the German Jews themselves and was a weapon in the hands of the anti-Semites, even without any mass immigration – the remark by von Treitschke in 1879 parodying Jews from the East selling trousers was a striking example. The mixed Jewish reaction to these migrations was therefore to be expected, as it was the same with every new mass influx from the East.[1] At the same time, the precise combination of events of 1891 produced special results: German Jews seeking new self-definition were shortly to create the important *Centralverein*, and the immigration from the East was an important element in this search for identity between stress on the unity of the Jewish group and stress on the unity of German Jews and the general German destiny. It is not surprising that we find here the beginning of Zionism organizing in Germany and of Jewish national activity. As we have said, this represents an interesting historical crossroads, where it is possible to isolate the variables and evaluate their relative weight precisely because of the change that was taking place. Here we may find out what the motives were that impelled one group of Jews – German Jewry – in the hour of confrontation and even persecution of their brethren, when the renewed wave of edicts and expulsions began early in 1891. Russian Jews (of Rabbi Spektor's circle, it seems) appealed to 'the greatest Jews' through the pages of the *Allgemeine Zeitung des Judenthums* to help their brethren of faith and race with the call, 'Help and Save!'[2] In the text of the appeal there was an affirmation of importance to the Russian readers and to the German ones as well that there were no Jewish 'rebels against the nations,' meaning that the Jews were not nihilists or revolutionaries. There was certainly room for this affirmation in Germany, given the background of the fierce campaign against

*Umsturz* (social democracy) and of German police suspicions precisely concerning socialist and revolutionary elements among the immigrants.

The immigrants' Jewish brethren in Germany described them as an 'influx of proletarians,'[3] and even if this was not an accurate designation, it is instructive as to the link it signified between this immigration and revolutionary socialism. In this year and later as well, there is no doubt that apprehensions weighed on the minds of German Jews not only regarding the uncultivated Eastern Jewish 'schnorrer,' but also regarding the Jewish revolutionary. This apprehension adequately explains the caution exercised in dealings with the Jews from the East over and beyond what was already called for on the strength of these Jews' foreignness and their backwardness as perceived by the Jews of Germany and the West.

Why did the Jews of Germany feel bound to do something? First of all, as they stressed repeatedly, the governments were not prepared to bring pressure to bear on Russia, since this was 'inopportune' from the international point of view.[4] Even 'decent people' advised against making an unnecessary fuss. Expressions of sympathy did not help either, that is to say, regarding the plight of the Jews in Russia itself (as was argued, for example, even by the German Christian Conservative organ[5] which condemned the persecution of the Jews in Russia, apparently because the Germans there were persecuted also).

The Russian Government was not going to change its anti-Jewish policy, as witness the Moscow expulsion after the panic-stricken emigration had already begun, so there was this problem. German and Western Jews could not be expected to show total indifference in the face of the persecutions and certainly not in the face of their bothersome practical outcome – the mass migration. When the stream of migration swelled into a flood, German Jewry living near the border with Russia in the region of westward transit had to take measures, all the more so given the apprehensions already referred to. Furthermore, bad experiences had recurred since 1882: too many migrants had returned to Europe.[6]

If it was impossible to prevent immigration, and if the infiltration into Germany itself was a cause for apprehension, and if there was well-founded fear of the migrants' returning, then as a matter of course there had to be some systematic way of dealing with the immigrants. German Jewry accordingly laid down its order of priorities. What with the stiff fight going on in the Reichstag under the auspices of the anti-Semites[7] over the right of Jews to hold government posts in Germany, and when the Xanten blood libel was actually happening,[8] it became clear that the problem of the immigrants was of primary importance for German Jewry, perhaps because it was necessarily connected with specifically German anti-Semitic expressions. Only then, not at the beginning of the year and not even immediately after the Moscow expulsion, did organized activity actually start.

A special body was set up on 28 May 1891 (*Zentralkomitee für den russischen Juden*) to deal with immigration, and in June 1891 the first meeting was held of representatives from all over Germany. From the organizational point of view dealing with immigration was an extremely difficult matter. Sub-committees of the Central Committee were supposed to supervise what was already being done in the frontier area, mainly on the borders of Silesia and Eastern Prussia, which were open for migration (unlike the Polish border). It was necessary to direct matters at the points of transit so as to arouse the least possible attention and disturbance, and it had to be done quickly without any possibility of controlling the numbers of those intending to leave Russia. The organizers' motives are testified to by the debate over the transit at Charlottenburg. In July 1891, this railway junction close to Berlin became a magnet for immigrants, or at least that was what the figures showed. The Central Committee for Russian Jews sought an explanation and found that the local committee responsible for this transit point was giving economic assistance to the Jews arriving there. According to the report of a head of the Berlin Committee, *Kommerzienrat* Goldberger,[9] 35,000 Jews arrived at this station from July to September.[10] News of the generous aid had spread abroad quickly in Russia, it was thought, hence the growth in the stream of immigrants. This was precisely what the Central Committee wanted to prevent.

The matter became the subject of public discussion, and the Central Committee's assumption was questioned in the press: the reason for the flood of immigrants, it was contended, was simpler – Charlottenburg was close to Berlin, which was why Berlin Jews were so concerned over it, and it was also a rail junction for Hamburg. It did not seem reasonable either to conclude that the news had spread so fast in the depths of Russia. Either way, the local committee was instructed to stop assisting the immigrants, and their number did indeed drop, but there is no way of knowing whether this was the result of the steps taken.[11] There was also a rumour that increased immigration was connected with the Baron Hirsch

Argentine land purchase. In order to stop the spread of this rumour, the Central Committee turned to the rabbis and congregations in Russia and asked them to prevent immigration on this account.[12]

The way in which the organizers complimented themselves over the years also bears witness to what their objectives were. Every now and again they affirmed that migration and transit through the German ports of Stettin, Hamburg and Bremen was 'smooth.'[13] Both in the first plenary session of the meeting of representatives and in the second, the same phrases are repeated – 'we channelled the flow along orderly routes' – 'in *geordnete Bahnen.*'[14] The definite declared intention (*zielbewusst*) was to send the Jews on further, far from Germany's borders. This intention would later be stated by Bodenheimer in a detailed memorandum to the German Government that perfectly reflected the positions of the Jews of Germany and Western Europe.[15]

There were two aspects to this policy. One was a policy of selection among the Jews at the Russian frontier, and the other was the choice of country of destination (*Endziel*). As to the first aspect, it was clear that anyone who had actually been expelled needed to be taken care of, but migrants who simply referred to persecution and pressure were not thought of as automatically deserving assistance to migrate, but were asked to go back where they came from. This was the government policy though not directed officially against Jews alone,[16] and it was also the policy of the Jewish committees. Over and over again the organizers repeated the rule that was the logical outcome and moral of the earlier migrations – to handle only the young, and people with a trade and heads of small families. The old and ill were 'of course' asked to return to where they came from and so were heads of families with more than six children. Isolated children and isolated women were taken care of only if there was a relative to receive them. It was greatly feared that young women would take to prostitution, and in this matter the Jewish community took action so as to deprive the anti-Semites of ammunition resulting from Jewish crime. Indeed, Hamburg police documents, for example, show that the percentage of Jews among both procurers and prostitutes was higher than their percentage in the general population in the last decade of the nineteenth century, and the names testified to their origin in Eastern Europe. At the second general meeting of German community representatives devoted to the matter of assistance to Russian Jewry it was openly stated, 'In Memel and on the Austrian border, with a heavy heart but with a firm hand we sent back all the entirely unsuitable elements' (*volkommen nicht geeigneten Elemente repatriiert!*)[17]

Deep anger was directed at migrants who slipped through the organizers' fingers. Sneered at as 'Schnorrers,' they were not only considered unworthy of aid but seen as actual saboteurs. The Hamburg representative at this meeting was apparently defending himself against the many attacks on his committee for helping lots of 'Schnorrers': he demanded that the complainants always insist on seeing the documents issued by the Hamburg Committee and not rely on the mere statements of the said 'Schnorrers' that they had indeed been referred to them by the Hamburg Committee. Even Gustav Cohen, who was a real supporter of the immigrants (and whose conclusions we shall deal with fully later), was highly critical of the migrants:

> We too have had some bitter experiences. Lies and the most cunning deception. People who sewed their money into a small packet and made themselves out to be penniless. Trading in passports and in addresses in America. Theft of the spoons at meals given free in the reception centres. Cheating children who had set out alone, or other inexperienced people, and instances (rare, it is true) of a husband who left his wife, or parents who left their children in distress.[18]

Sholom Aleichem too described in 'Motti-ben-Peisi' similar scenes – husband and wife fighting in the street and the police having to intervene, or a youngster stealing a bread-roll in the market.

Against this whole background it is also possible to comprehend the way the problem of Jewish migration, including that from Germany itself, was tackled forty years later, in the 1930s. What I have said is not intended as criticism of the organizers of migration of the Jews. Their policy was justified in terms of long-run considerations. It was not generally a question of life or death. Uncontrolled migration would have created difficulties both with the German government and with the countries receiving the migrants. Of course, over and beyond all of this there was another consideration – the confrontation with anti-Semitic arguments while emancipation was hanging in the balance in Germany and the other countries of Europe.

As regards the other aspect of the policy – Where to? – with no way of barring entry into the 'chosen land' of Germany, it was necessary to try out the possibilities of transit. One thing was agreed on without question and repeated over and over again: Germany and other countries of Europe would be beyond the pale. True, in spite of this policy of not taking in migrants from the East, some 70,000 of them settled in Germany in the generation before the First World War.[19] The policy was clear, however: *Europa bleibt als Endziel ausgeschlossen*.[20] The English immigration authorities were harsh, and it was only with great difficulty that migrants could be sent to English ports as transit stages on the way to America. As for the other countries of Europe, there were difficulties in controlling migration. Not only the 'Schnorrers' who got away from the Jewish committees but others too, who were clever, sent their belongings ahead to France before they received permission to enter the country. Outside Europe, there was not too large a choice, of course – there were three possibilities: South America with Baron Hirsch's undertaking, North America, and Palestine. Baron Hirsch's colonies were intended for defined, limited immigrant groups and did not represent a real choice for mass migration. There remained only two real alternatives, then. In the first stage, up to mid-1891, the Palestine alternative was not considered either, so that out of the three what was spoken of the whole time as the route for migration was that to the United States. There were people in Russia itself who thought that German Jewry was supporting the migration of Jews from Russia to America, while the Jews of France and England preferred the Palestine alternative, but it emerged that this was not so, as was stated by Emil Franzos, the Secretary (*Schriftfuehrer*) of the Central Committee.[21] At the same time, the German committee also laid down as matters developed that Palestine was not suitable because there was no Firman (Decree), land was dear, and in this type of migration there was a kind of declaration of Jewish nationality. It is certain that the rules and regulations and the directives regarding the policy selection at the Russian frontier were based on the knowledge of the *Endziel*, that is to say, the United States. If they had been weighing up sending Jews to Palestine, their criteria were not the important ones.

The question – Where to? – was accompanied by the question How? and an interesting idea was 'colonization.' This referred not only to the migration and dispersion of the Jews in their wanderings in various places but also to concentrating them and rendering the process more efficient. What was spoken of, then, was different alternatives of colonization at this time. As Franzos reported: 'There is no need to say why colonies are not wanted in Germany, Austria, France, and England.' This was in accordance with the principle that Jews should be sent only to places where there was no anti-Semitism.[22] A number of forlorn ideas were put forward, including Spain, Campagna in Italy, Cyprus, Australia, the Congo and Brazil,[23] but in the end the main persons making recommendations all reverted to migration to the United States by means of presenting the drawbacks of the Palestine alternative. It can therefore be said that the German Jews' help to their brethren in the East was summed up in their channelling the most promising migrants from Russia to the United States through the German ports, and as quickly as possible. Naturally, one should not overlook the material assistance rendered at the same time – food, lodging, clothing (Henrichsen reports that clothing was provided for 3,000 children, 2,000 women and 1,000 men in less than four months). Moreover, if we accept the testimony of Shmaryahu Levin, the reaction of German Jews to the distress of Eastern European Jews was 'splendid' and not merely given under pressure.[24]

Yet the Palestine alternative, even if not practical nor especially popular, was the one most discussed, not only because of the new experiments in colonization that had already been started in the previous decade, but because this *Endziel* was connected with a change in the German Jews' awareness of themselves precisely in these years. It was connected with the search for self-understanding and finding it in Jewish nationalism. Shmaryahu Levin went so far as to affirm: 'If Palestine had been a possible centre for immigration in those days, we could easily have persuaded the Committee of German Jewry to divert part of the stream of migration in that direction.'[25] He was saying that for a Jew not only seeking a way out of trouble but also wanting to contribute to Jewish national recovery, Palestine was the real opportunity that was not being exploited only because of international circumstances.

The question, *Was soll aus den russischen Juden werden?* (What's going to happen with the Russian Jews?) was already being asked at the start of 1891 by an anti-Semite who published a pamphlet with that title.[26] The pamphlets by Max Bodenheimer, a herald of German Zionism, and by P. Dimidov later in the same year, were better known and were widely discussed in the press.[27] The idea was not generated as a result of the immigration, but already existed previously. In February 1891 Gustav Cohen, an eminent Hamburg merchant and community leader, had already written a pamphlet called 'The Jewish Question and the Future,' with immigration serving him only as a handle for the main idea that in order to raise up the Jews from their lowly condition, in order to give them self-respect (*Selbstachtung*), it was necessary to adopt the national approach, which would find itself a centre in Palestine.[28] From one angle, this heralded a practical approach of linking the idea of straightening the bowed Jewish back in Germany with the migration of Jews from the East – not from Germany – to the national centre in Palestine. Gustav Cohen argued with his opponents: the Powers will not be against the idea, and the small size of Palestine need not worry us since in the past too Jewry was divided between Palestine and the Exile! This was the stand he took at the beginning when immigration speeded up, and he was reinforced in his ideas by the end of the year, after he experienced the influx of immigration through Hamburg itself. He had now discovered the Jews who would found a colony in Palestine and strengthen the Jewish backbone. In getting to know Eastern Jews he found that precisely this persecuted Jewry was proud and self-assured – qualities so lacking in German Jews. They had an aim – Jewish existence – lacking for Jews living under the sign of reform. Thus in Gustav Cohen's eyes, colonization in Palestine was not exactly a humanitarian solution for his brethren but rather a means for strengthening the Jewish consciousness of the Jews of Germany, who did not need to emigrate but only to help others to do so.

Most of the people who discussed the question were more practical: they wanted to know if there was a real prospect of immigration into Palestine, if the immigrants would not come back to Europe. Bernard Traubenberg reiterated his warning again and again in the *Allgemeine Zeitung des Judenthums* against illusions over Palestine, against the absolutist government there under which the Jewish community could not live and develop any differently from in Russia.[29] Emil Franzos, as we have said, enumerated the drawbacks of Palestine; even though he accepted the idea, he reminded Bodenheimer that Syria was in no way free of anti-Semitism, at least not for anyone who recalled the year 1840.[30] Against this contention, in Willy Bambus's view, was the compelling argument that there was no fear of Russia's conquering Turkey and nullifying the efforts invested in Palestine. Willy Bambus did not stress the Jewish value of Palestine, however, but its practical and tactical value, and he sharpened his argument by asking: 'Can our leading men face the danger of a return migration as in 1882, only bigger, since the migration is bigger now?'[31] That is to say, the United States was not a solution because the Jews would leave and return to Europe, to Germany. Even Bodenheimer, in sallying out to the defence of the proposal in his pamphlet, said that he did not aim to get people intending to migrate to America to change their plans and induce them to go to Palestine, but only to increase German Jewry's interest in the Palestine enterprise.

Thus the spiritual and material problem of German Jewry is thrown into sharp relief as motivating the Palestine solution. Palestine would take in Jewish immigrants without spewing them out again, and German Jewry would have an object for the practical realization of Jewish consciousness. Gustav Cohen, as we have noted, reaffirmed his opinion on the need for colonization in Palestine, and he stated flatly: 'Look how Germany itself gets excited over the visit of a chief of an African tribe, fearing harm but hoping for profit from the visit. The role of independent Jewry in the East will be crucial.' Independent settlement, a Jewish State such as he hoped for, would turn the Jews into a different living experience, which would naturally radiate back over Jews everywhere.[32] (How right he was is borne out by the behaviour of American Jews today.) This solution was of course preferable in his and other people's eyes to migration that would only export anti-Semitism to places that had not yet been infected by it, such as the United States. At all events, Motzkin was right at the time when he argued in his review of the rescue committee meeting in Berlin, that the entire rescue policy was directed to distributing the Jews throughout the world in small numbers in each place so as to prevent anti-Semitism being awakened. The fear of creating any large Jewish agglomeration anywhere as a breeder of anti-Semitism was the most basic explanation in Motzkin's opinion of the whole migration activity, and the Palestine solution had to be understood from this orientation.[33]

In brief, the use of Palestine was instrumental for an insecure Jewry rather than 'Zionism from compassion.'[34] Not all German Jews or most of them were insecure. Those who were more secure, or did not believe that they would draw security from Palestine or the immigrants there, proposed what *Justizrat* Makover suggested to his brethren in Russia – that they learn the customs of the modern Jew or the modern man, abolish early marriages, abolish the *Heder*, and help themselves.[35] If it had been possible to rest content with giving this kind of advice, German Jewry could of course have been saved the trouble of dealing with the unwanted migrants.

# GERMAN JEWS AND THE EMIGRATION FROM RUSSIA

## NOTES

1. Cf. J. Wertheimer, *German Policy and Jewish Politics. The Absorption of East European Jews in Germany (1868–1914)*, New York. Columbia University dissertation, 1978, Chaps. 1 and 2.
2. *Allgemeine Zeitung des Judenthums*, 1891, No. 1, 'Unsere Lage.'
3. Gustav Cohen, *Die Judenfrage und die Zukunft*, Hamburg, 1896, p.5.
4. *AZJ*, 15 May 1891, 'Eine Erinnerung.'
5. *Kreuzzeitung*, 25 May 1891.
6. *AZJ*, 3 July 1891, 'Die Auswanderung der russischen Juden.'
7. See note 4.
8. Xanten Blood Libel, 29 June 1891.
9. *AZJ*, 21 Oct. 1891, 'Die Delegierten-Versammlung.'
10. *Selbstemancipation*, 17 June 1891, p.6, reported 55,000 Jews up to 10 June 1891, 1,500 of them through Charlottenburg.
11. *AZJ*, 21 Aug. 1891, 'Zur russischen Auswanderung.'
12. See note 9. 6 Nov. 1891, Goldberger's report.
13. 'Gemeindebote,' Report from Berlin, 26 July 1891.
14. *AZJ*, 10 July 1891, 'Gemeindebote,' Report from Berlin, 4 July 1891.
15. *AZJ*, 28 Aug. 1891, 'Die russische Frage.' *Cf.*, Denkschrift Bodenheimer (s.d.) in *Central Zionist Archives* A 13/I/4, pp.2–4.
16. *Selbstemancipation*, 1 June 1891, 'Zurücktransportiert.' The call to help is based on the assumption that it is in the interest of the German Jews 'sie (the emigrants) ferne zu halten.'
17. See note 12. Also *Israelitisches Gemeinde-Blatt* (Muelheim zu Koeln), 31 July 1891 – 'ungeeignete Elemente.'
18. Cohen, *op. cit.*, pp.32 ff.
19. Wertheimer, *op. cit.*, pp.43 ff.
20. *AZJ*, 23 Oct. 1891, 'Gemeindebote,' Report from Berlin, 21 Oct. 1891.
21. *AZJ*, 20 Nov. 1891, E. Franzos, 'Die Kolonisationsfrage.'
22. *Ibid., Cf. Selbstemancipation*, 2 Nov. 1891, Motzkin's opinion.
23. *AZJ*, 3 July 1891, 'Die Auswanderung der russischen Juden.' *Cf.* CZA, A/15/II/6 (Toch–Bodenheimer).
24. S. Levine, *Forward from Exile*, Philadelphia, 1967, p.279.
25. *Ibid.*, p.280.
26. *Was soll aus den russischen Juden werden*, Berlin, 1891.
27. M. Bodenheimer, *Wohin mit den russischen Juden*, Hamburg, 1891; P. Dimidov (Israel Turoff), *Wohinaus*, 1891, *AZJ*, 24 July, 31 July 1891. *Selbstemancipation*, 18 Aug., 19 Sept. 1891.
28. Cohen, *op. cit.*, pp.9, 18, 21 ff.
29. *AZJ*, 4 Sept. 1891.
30. *Ibid.*, p.350.
31. *Ibid.*, 31 July 1891, 'Wo hinaus.'
32. Cohen, *op. cit.*, p.38.
33. *Selbstemancipation*, 2 Nov. 1891.
34. Cf. J. Reinharz, 'East European Jews in the *Weltanschauung* of German Zionists, 1882–1914,' *Studies in Contemporary Jewry*, 1984, Vol. 1, p.58.
35. *AZJ*, Sept. 1891, p.458, 'Die russischen Juden.'

PART TWO

# World Wars and the Shadow of the Holocaust

# 8

# Dr. Nahum Goldmann and the Policy of International Jewish Organizations

## Monty Penkower

There is a word in the English language for that figure of speech which, to make a point, combines contradictory or incongruous terms. That word is 'oxymoron,' rooted in the Greek *oxys* (sharp) and *moros* (foolish, dull). 'Sweet sorrow' can serve as one illustration. In my volume on free world diplomacy during the Holocaust, *The Jews Were Expendable*, I characterized the Allies' overall response with another oxymoron: 'thunderous silence.'[1] Moving closer to our own time, 'Lebanese government' suggests itself. For our conference, particularly those sessions which focus on the years before the establishment of the State of Israel, permit me to coin an additional example: 'Jewish statesmanship.'

If the statesman is one skilled in conducting state affairs, as in the expression *homme d'état*, and the diplomat represents his government professionally in relations between nations, then world Jewry could lay no claim to statesmanship for two millennia. Lacking the ground of an autonomous commonwealth under its feet, this people suffered the scourge of powerlessness that accounted for its repeated persecution and martyrdom at the hands of Gentile hosts. Successful intervention to aid fellow Jews, whether an individual or communal effort, proved to be transitory; justice, morality, and reason counted for little in the foreign world of *realpolitik*. Jews tried to survive as best they could, making no plans and hoping for Divine redemption. Put succinctly: 'During two thousand years of the Diaspora, the sole Jewish statesman was the Messiah.'[2]

It is fitting that the source of this last phrase should be the subject of our attention. Any analysis of modern Jewish survival and solidarity must perforce include Nahum Goldmann, called at various times the quintessential Diaspora man, Jewish ambassador-at-large, wandering Jew. While a political maverick who possessed nine passports, Goldmann achieved much as president of both the World Jewish Congress and the World Zionist Organization, as the initiator of German reparations to Israel, as President of the Claims Conference, of the Conference of Jewish Organizations, and of the Conference of Presidents of Major Jewish Organizations, among others. It is his earlier activities on behalf of Diaspora rights and Zionism in the period between the two world wars, however, which interest us here. For those decades, ominous antecedents to the Holocaust, perhaps most poignantly reflect the helplessness that came with the loss of Jewish sovereignty after Roman legions crushed Bar Kochba's revolt in 135 C.E.

Most poignantly, I suggest, since Jews had understandable cause at the beginning of the 1920s for harbouring great expectations. The Balfour Declaration, followed by League of Nations' sanction of a British mandate over Palestine and the establishment of a Jewish Agency to aid in creating a Jewish National Home there, signalled Great Britain's open support for Zionist dreams. In an unprecedented step, Lenin's new Soviet regime declared anti-Semitism to be a capital crime. The Weimar Constitution assured Jews full integration in Germany as first-class citizens; in 1924, more than one million people attended Walter Rathenau's funeral in condemnation of the Jewish foreign minister's assassination by anti-Semitic nationalists. Especially significant, the Versailles Treaty brought the process of Jewish emancipation to completion, promising as it did to Jews (and other minority groups) full civil rights.

Inserted by the victorious Allies in 'minority treaties' with new and enlarged states, these international guarantees owed much to the *Comité des Délégations Juives*. Spurred by the World Zionist Organization and the American Jewish Congress, Jewish delegations from 14 different countries had joined at the Peace Conference to form the Comité *ad hoc*. A memorandum, based on general secretary Leo Motzkin's 1919 statement of principles, called on the Conference to protect the individual rights, as well as collective national rights, of Jews and other minorities. Rejecting the concept 'national minority,' the more conservative *Alliance Israélite Universelle* and the Joint Foreign Committee (representing the Board of Deputies of British Jews and the Anglo-Jewish Association) independently sought the League's general recognition of minority rights. Such recognition was indeed acknowledged in the peace treaties, with Jews accorded specific rights relating to education, language, and Sabbath observance. The Comité's chief executives, Julian Mack, Louis Marshall, and Nahum Sokolow, hailed the final outcome, claiming that it 'will forever end the grave abuse of the past.'[3]

The following decade proved this optimism misplaced. In 1920, Hungary officially introduced a *numerus clausus* for Jewish attendance at universities. Virulent baiting and riots continued unchecked in Rumania against Jews, whose cultural and religious sensibilities were violated. The Latvian Government limited autonomy to schools; Lithuania's Jewish National Council and ministry of Jewish affairs were abolished in 1924, local Jewish community organizations disappeared the next year. Rampant economic anti-Semitism, diminished subsidies to Jewish schools, and a *numerus clausus* at state universities revealed Poland's attitude. Turkey renounced its minority obligations in 1926. Not included in the Peace Conference and hence in the minority treaties, the new Soviet Government proclaimed Birobidjan a Jewish autonomous region, but persecuted Zionists and employed Yiddish-language courts and schools to eradicate all vestiges of Jewish identity. Disunited and afraid to antagonize their respective governments, Jews in these countries did not, unlike other minorities, petition Geneva for redress.[4]

It remained to the Comité, under Motzkin's dynamic leadership, to defend Jewish rights in the public arena. An early proponent of *Gegenwartsarbeit* (immediate Zionist activity in the Diaspora), Motzkin had already written an extensive study of the early twentieth-century pogroms in Russia, moved public figures to protest the Beilis trial, and, as head of the World Zionist Organization's Copenhagen office, dispensed aid to Jewish communities in war-torn Europe. On his initiative, the Comité organized the World Jewish Aid Conference to coordinate relief efforts, sought to safeguard the Jewish cause in such forums as the International Congress of National Minorities and the International Union of League of Nations' Associations, and assisted in Shalom Schwarzbard's successful defence after the latter had murdered pogromist Petliura in 1927 to avenge the murder of Ukrainian Jews. Given the rising tide of European anti-Semitism, Motzkin, with strong support from Stephen Wise, president of the American Jewish Congress, also convened that same year the Zurich Conference on the Rights of Minorities. Sixty-five leading Jews, including Sejm member Isaac Gruenbaum, Sokolow, Austrian Chief Rabbi Zvi Chayes, and the historian Simon Dubnow, established a coordinating council, to be headquartered in Geneva.

In 1931, as the Nazi menace began to materialize, a provisional committee, meeting under Wise's chairmanship after the Zionist Congress, resolved to create a stronger organization for Jewish solidarity. To this end, the American Jewish Congress some months later approved the convening of an international conference of Jews, to be held in Geneva on 14 August 1934, where a World Jewish Congress would be considered. That May, the American Jewish Congress announced its choice to organize the preparatory conference: Dr. Nahum Goldmann.[5]

A propitious selection, indeed. At only 37 years old, this Lithuanian-born German Jew had published a book about his first visit to Palestine (1913); had sought, as a staff member during World War I of the *Wilhelmstrasse*, German appreciation of Zionism; had published a Zionist periodical for two years with Jacob Klatzkin; and together with him had initiated a Jewish encyclopaedia, which ultimately came to ten German and two Hebrew volumes. Representing the 'radical' faction on the Zionist Actions Committee, Goldmann charged World Zionist Organization president Chaim Weizmann with diverting the movement's attention from 'spiritual factors' and liberal renaissance to the cause of constructive political-economic settlement. Hence his related attack on Weizmann's plan to co-opt well-to-do non-Zionists like Marshall and Felix Warburg to the enlarged Jewish Agency on an equal basis with Zionists, a critical stance which won Stephen Wise's ringing approbation. Both Goldmann and Wise also thought the Zionist leadership remiss in responding to mounting crises in the Diaspora. As chairman of the political committee at the 1931 Zionist Congress, Goldmann played a decisive role in the majority vote against Weizmann's reelection to the presidency when the latter publicly downplayed the demand for Jewish sovereignty in Palestine. Varied experience and the sum of Goldmann's convictions, vigorously conveyed with fluency in several languages, seemed to augur well for the world conference this iconoclast was now to establish.[6]

The 94 delegates, from 74 countries, who met in Geneva for the First World Jewish Conference between 14 and 17 August 1932, agreed with Goldmann that the projected congress should 'establish the permanent address' of the Jewish people. Motzkin, who had suggested a 'World Jewish Congress' in his 1919 Comité memorandum, warned that Jewry in Germany and elsewhere faced an unparalleled war of 'cruel destruction' unless it mobilized collectively for Zionism and Jewish rights in general. Rebuking the perspective of the American Jewish Committee and its elitist counterparts in England, France, and Germany, which feared that any international organization would engender more anti-Semitism, Wise called for complete and open discussion of Jewish concerns. The conference elected an executive, and decided that a World Jewish Congress, based on the concept of Jewish national identity, should meet two years later.[7]

Methodical procedural preparation could not check the immediate assault against German Jewry once Hitler came to power, an emergency to which the Comité responded as energetically as possible. Relying on the German–Polish 1922 Convention, under which Germany undertook to guarantee for 15 years the rights of all minorities in Upper Silesia, the Comité instigated two petitions to the League of Nations on 17 May 1933. The first, signed by a store clerk in Upper Silesia named Franz Bernheim who had been dismissed under the new anti-Jewish legislation, was placed on the League Council's agenda. In two public sessions, many speakers denounced the Nazi persecution of Jews and curtailment of their minimum human rights. Faced with this first League censure of Third Reich policy, the German government pledged to honour the 1922 convention until the expiration date of 15 July 1937. Remarkably, this promise would be kept.[8]

Continued anti-Semitic excesses in Germany proper failed, however, to generate unity among existing Jewish organizations. B'nai Brith and the American Jewish Committee, thinking that the mass demonstrations advocated by the American Jewish Congress would both foment domestic anti-Semitism and endanger German Jewry, preferred the path of quiet diplomacy in Washington. A public boycott of German goods, spearheaded in their respective countries by Samuel Untermyer, Lord Melchett, and Vladimir Jabotinsky, struck a responsive chord with many. This spontaneous action ran counter to the 1933 *Ha'avara* agreement between the Jewish Agency and Berlin, which would ultimately facilitate the immigration of 60,000 Jews to Palestine before the Second World War by allowing the transfer of their capital there in the form of German export goods. Opposed to a boycott and wanting to 'destroy the World Congress idea,' as Board of Deputies chairman Neville Laski wrote to Cyrus Adler, president of the American Jewish Committee, the Joint Foreign Committee invited Jewish organizations to a private business conference for that October.[9]

The projected Joint conference did not deter World Jewish Congress leaders, who, anxious over escalating violence in the Third Reich, advanced their second preparatory conference from the summer of 1933 to September 1934. After the 'most tragic six months in Jewish history,' Wise declaimed, world Jewry here assembled had to mount an organized boycott against Germany. Only a World Jewish Congress, Goldmann added, could authoritatively defend Jewish rights everywhere, with Palestine the purview of the Zionist Organization and the Jewish Agency. Unanimously, the conference resolved to support the boycott worldwide, to ask the League of Nations to intervene for German Jews, particularly in regard to their emigration to Palestine, and to call for another gathering the next year.[10]

Few in the free world accepted the conference's warning that National Socialism's racist war against the Jewish people threatened the values and the very security of civilization as a whole. That same month, the League did appoint James G. McDonald as High Commissioner to protect the refugees and to investigate possibilities for their emigration. Yet this independent agency, removed from League jurisdiction and financing, was virtually powerless. McDonald's tireless investigation, assisted by Norman Bentwich and the financial support of Felix Warburg, would yield havens of no consequence for the oppressed Jews. A letter of resignation two years later, expressing candidly McDonald's frustration, captured morning headlines – nothing more.[11]

Other difficulties beset World Jewish Congress activists, but their movement gathered momentum. Motzkin's death, one week after he had attended an inconclusive Joint Foreign Committee conference in London, left a void in the Comité until Goldmann's election to the presidency that December. Zionist leaders focused on rapidly accelerating Jewish emigration to Palestine, Agency executive chairman David Ben-Gurion wrote Justice Louis Brandeis, in case of 'another world war' and to meet 'the Arab difficulty'; in February 1934, Weizmannites in the Zionist Organization of America quashed an endorsement of the world congress. Yet the third and final preparatory conference did convene in Geneva that August, delegates from 20 countries hearing Goldmann insist on 'unrestricted equality of rights' for German Jewry, and Wise deplore the fact that 'day by day tinkering has taken the place of long-view Jewish statesmanship.' Resolutions endorsed the continued boycott of Germany, criticized the League's 'narrow' treatment of the Jewish refugee question, and elected an executive committee (Goldmann its chairman) to prepare for a permanent World Jewish Congress.[12]

Until the Congress's genesis two years later, as Goldmann

subsequently reminisced, he and associates could only 'administer a few pinpricks' in the struggle against Nazism. With the assistance of Neville Laski, Goldmann helped obtain Western intervention in September 1934 against Poland's threat to abolish minority rights protection, but there could be no question thereafter of real enforcement of Jewish rights in that country. After receiving Goldmann, Austrian Chancellor Schuschnigg issued a communiqué accepting the principle of absolute equality for all citizens; anti-Semitic administrative practice did not disappear, however. A rare triumph followed Goldmann's personal interviews with Mussolini and French Foreign Minister Louis Barthou, among others, which contributed to a Franco-German agreement whereby Jews in the Saar had a year's grace to emigrate with all their assets despite that territory's reversion by plebiscite to Germany. His talks with Ambassadors Litvinov and Potemkine thawed the diplomatic ice surrounding the Stalinist regime, but signalled no change for Soviet Jewry at the time.

Success in obtaining censure of the Nuremberg Laws by the League of Nations' Union resulted in little of substance except the Third Reich's resignation from the Union and the revocation of Goldmann's German citizenship. Detailed memoranda and intercessions protesting additional manifestations of anti-Semitism carried scant weight in Rumania and Latvia. Representations throughout 1936 against an overt policy of Nazi *Gleichschaltung* by the Senate of the Free City of Danzig merely led the League to recall its High Commissioner, whereupon a new wave of terror struck the 10,000 Jews living there.[13]

Amidst these darkening shadows, the constituent session of the World Jewish Congress finally took place in Geneva from 8 to 15 August 1936. Such a voluntary, democratically elected association had to be organized across the globe, Wise stressed in the opening address, because 'Hitlerism's real war is against World Jewry.' Goldmann, aggressive, warned that totalitarian states currently oppressing Jews were a direct challenge to the democracies, yet the latter powers and world opinion remained apathetic. The historic gathering, whose 291 delegates claimed to represent almost one-third of the world's 16 million Jews, elected Wise to head the executive committee, with Goldmann (Jewish Agency representative to the League of Nations as of the previous September) chairman of the administrative body. Resolutions called for equality of Jewish rights, undisturbed development of the Jewish National Home in Palestine, facilitation of Jewish emigration overseas, solidarity with such groups as the Joint Labour Committee, and a concerted attack against all forms of anti-Semitism.[14]

Valiantly, the new world body tried to stem the onrushing tide of European Jew-hatred. With Goldmann centred in Geneva, offices were opened under Marc Jarblum in Paris and Maurice Perlzweig in London; 34 affiliates in 27 countries on five continents joined the Congress within a year. Mobilization of public opinion took place worldwide, even as the Congress explored with the Quai d'Orsay the possibility of Jewish emigration to France's colonies, especially from Poland. Representations to protect the 'vested rights' of Jews in Upper Silesia and establish a transitory regime designed to facilitate their emigration proved of no avail. Publicity and intercession at the League staved off introduction of the Nuremberg Laws by the Danzig Senate in 1937. Rallies in New York, London and Paris, as well as manifestos signed by eminent personalities, vainly protested the anti-Jewish campaign of pogrom, economic war, and university 'ghetto benches' in Poland.

A steady barrage of telegrams, press releases, and diplomatic conferences (including Wise's meeting with President Roosevelt) contributed significantly to Rumanian Prime Minister Octavian Goga's resignation in February 1938, followed by a new constitution professing equality for all that country's citizens. The same month, seven governments signed a Geneva Convention, initiated by Goldmann with the aid of colleagues Paul Guggenheim and Gerhart Riegner, which included stateless persons within the term 'German refugees,' banned the deportation of refugees to Germany, and provided League intervention to obtain work permits and other benefits for refugees.[15]

Yet, as former Berlin rabbi Joachim Prinz told a twentieth anniversary dinner of the American Jewish Congress in June 1938: 'only political counter-movements possess the strength to fight other political movements.' Jewish unity could not be had when the American Jewish Committee, B'nai Brith, the Board of Deputies, the Alliance, the Bund and Agudas Israel opposed the Congress's international campaign against persecution. Even the Congress's appeal, one month later, at the Evian Conference on Refugees, for a single delegation and joint memorandum of major Jewish organizations fell on deaf ears. With the British Council for German Jews especially fearful that the appearance there of so-called 'international Jewry' would strengthen anti-Semitic propaganda, 21 bodies appeared separately, each for three minutes. They 'swarmed like bees,' Goldmann accurately wrote Wise; it was 'a ridiculous performance.'[16]

More fundamentally, however, Evian symbolized the free world's default in the battle against barbarism. The governments represented adhered to stringent immigrant admission policies, while masking the unique Jewish catastrophe under rubrics like 'political refugees' and 'involuntary emigrants.' The leadership of a newly formed Intergovernmental Committee would consist of the same Evian personalities who had already washed their hands of the Jewish crisis. Subsequent suggestions for havens in Madagascar, New Caledonia, Angola, Mindanao, Abyssinia, Northern Rhodesia, and British Guiana went unheeded. Only the Dominican Republic expressed a willingness to admit up to 100,000 Jews if adequate financing were assured. Arrangements began in 1939 among Jewish circles to establish an international corporation providing up to $300 million, this going beyond a Nazi 'trust fund' proposal which governments and Jewish groups alike condemned as ransom.[17]

The press of events, the Congress fully realized, did not allow for protracted negotiation. Its petitions and *démarches* against the terror and expulsion of Jews which quickly succeeded Hitler's annexation of Austria sparked no League action. Demonstrations by affiliates buttressed Congress executive protests against the Zbaszyn deportations, *Kristallnacht*, and the wholesale denationalization of Rumanian Jewry – to identical effect. Only in the case of Danzig's Jews and those (after Munich) of the Sudetenland did the Congress, by steady legal intercession, gain valuable time for many there to escape the Nazi avalanche. Confronted by Hitler's January 1939 Reichstag warning that global conflict would also see the 'annihilation of European Jewry,' what more could Goldmann and the executive committee do than to publicly condemn 'a man who in his notorious *Mein Kampf* vindicated the necessity of war which alone, according to him, is capable of realizing the aim of his policy'?[18]

And, at that very moment, His Majesty's Government in London aimed at closing the most obvious haven – Palestine. Aware that only in that country could Jews be 'masters of their own fate,' especially in this most hazardous time, Goldmann had, with Weizmann, Ben-Gurion, and Moshe Sharett, been among the most ardent supporters of the Peel Commission's 1937 partition plan leading to Jewish and Arab states there. Rather than Britain implementing that recommendation, however, Goldmann and other Jewish Agency leaders heard Colonial Secretary Malcolm McDonald declare at the St. James Conference that imperial strategy dictated concessions to the stronger Arab position in the event of war. The May 1939 White Paper bore the stamp of this argument, even as the British authorities took energetic diplomatic steps to check the unsanctioned traffic of Jewish refugees to the Promised Land.[19]

With the world closed as never before to the Jewish people, as Goldmann now pointed out to his audiences, Jews everywhere had to fight anti-Semitism forthrightly 'before they face complete moral and physical destruction.' So the Congress intervened on behalf of foreign Jews threatened with expulsion in Bulgaria, sent Perlzweig to Rumania, Yugoslavia, and Poland to protect Jews, sought to ease the plight of Czech Jewry, and attacked the League's refusal to recall its High Commissioner when Danzig expelled the Jewish citizenry. Congress supporters established Jewish Economic Committees in Poland, and contacts were developed with the Hungarian Jewish National Committee.[20]

Opposing all government-coerced attempts at 'evacuation,' Jabotinsky's 1931 term for a necessary mass exodus of Jews voluntarily from Europe to Palestine, the Congress's administrative committee insisted on equality of Jewish rights while seeking to establish a central Jewish agency to deal with large-scale emigration, particularly from Eastern Europe. Jewish organizations, convening in May 1939 at Goldmann's request, thought a conference to this end 'inadvisable,' however, since opportunities simply did not exist. A follow-up meeting in late August concluded that the emigration, 'in a humane and orderly way,' of 400,000 Jews 'from Germany alone' would take four years; it called on the democracies to open their doors and to 'undertake substantial financial responsibilities,' given the inadequate means of private philanthropies to cope with 'this immense and ever-growing task.'[21]

Yet the free world's continuing mute response to Jewry's plight projected scant hope from that quarter. Western hemisphere countries had just denied temporary shelter to 937 German Jewish refugees aboard the liner *St. Louis*, and a bill to admit 20,000 Jewish children into the United States beyond the German quotas for 1939 and 1940 failed to muster Congressional passage. While hoped-for large sanctuaries still did not materialize, Intergovernmental Committee directors abruptly dismissed a last appeal in May from two German Jewish representatives (sent with Gestapo approval) for concrete action. Simon Dubnow's proposal for an international league to protect the stateless Jewish people, urging the World Jewish Congress to encourage its formation, got relegated to archive files.[22]

'We are approaching the critical hour in the world of Jewish history,' Goldmann privately concluded, and traditional recourse to migration, assimilation, or waiting for miracles could not meet the tragic emergency. The past two decades, he exhorted the 21st World Zionist Congress that August, witness to both unparalleled 'tendencies of so brutally revolutionary a nature' and the transience of liberal regimes, simplified unequivocally the choice for Jewry's survival: 'What we need is a final solution, the regularization of our national existence' in Palestine. Historic necessity, he ended his address, demanded the realization of Zionism, which alone would provide a haven for 'all eventualities' and sustain the menaced Diaspora with moral strength.[23]

Alas, before that achievement, a different 'final solution' would engulf European Jewry, one far more catastrophic than even the astute Goldmann could foresee. Against the greatest of odds, he, Motzkin, Wise, and like-minded colleagues had championed their people's rights with courageous persistence in the period between the two world wars. Certain Jewish organizations moved too circumspectly in not supporting this lead. Yet all remained victims of one harsh political fact: British Foreign Under-secretary R.A. Butler put it exactly, if very politely, when answering Goldmann's detailed defence of Zionist claims under the Palestine mandate: 'I readily admit that all the logic is on your side, but we have the Empire, and had we obeyed your logic we would never have had that Empire!'[24]

Without this reality of sovereign power, would-be Jewish statesmen like Goldmann, however gifted, could not ultimately resist the ruthless anti-Semitism of dictators and the callous indifference of democracies. Now the Second World War was about to be unleashed by Hitler's *Wehrmacht*. And ahead, for Jewry, loomed the blackest darkness.

NOTES

1. Monty N. Penkower, *The Jews Were Expendable: Free World Diplomacy and the Holocaust*, Urbana, 1983, p.97.
2. Nahum Goldmann, *The Jewish Paradox*, Steve Cox. trans., New York, 1978, p.61.
3. Alex Bein, ed. *Sefer Motzkin*, Jerusalem, 1939, pp.91-7 and 188-97 (Hebrew);

*Unity in Dispersion. A History of the World Jewish Congress*, New York, 1948, pp.22–7; *American Jewish Year Book 1920*, Vol. 22, pp.101–29; Oscar Janowsky, *Jews and Minority Rights, 1898–1919*, New York, 1933, part III; quoted by Bernard Richards, in *Universal Jewish Encyclopedia*, 1942, Vol. 8, p.313.
4. Jacob Robinson et al., *Were the Minority Treaties a Failure?*, New York, 1943; Ezra Mendelsohn, *The Jews of Central Eastern Europe Between the World Wars*, Bloomington, 1983.
5. Bein, *Sefer Motzkin*, pp.69–91, 97–106 (Hebrew); Natan Feinberg, *Ha-agudot ha-yehudiot le-ma'an hever ha-leumim*, Jerusalem, 1958; *Unity in Dispersion*, pp.27–31.
6. *The Autobiography of Nahum Goldmann, 60 Years of Jewish Life*, Helen Saba, trans., New York, 1969, pp.1–130; Nahum Goldmann, *Community of Fate, Jews in the Modern World, Essays, Speeches and Articles*, Jerusalem, 1977, pp.3–8; Weizmann to Weltsch, 15 Jan. 1924, and Weizmann to Feiwel, same date, Weizmann Archives, Rehovot, Israel; Carl H. Voss, ed., *Stephen S. Wise: Servant of the People*, Philadelphia, 1970, pp.156, 173.
7. *Unity in Dispersion*, pp.31–4; Bein, *Sefer Motzkin*, pp.196, 266–75.
8. Natan Feinberg, *Ha-ma-aracha ha-yehudit neged hitler al bimat hever ha-leumim (ha-petitsia shel bernheim)*. Jerusalem, 1957.
9. Adler to Lazaron, 13 April 1933, Adler-Germany, *American Jewish Committee Archives*, New York (hereafter AJC); Wise to Gotthell, 17 April 1933. Box 947, *American Jewish Archives*, Cincinnati, Ohio; Emergency Session, 20 May 1933, *American Jewish Congress Archives*, New York; Laski to Adler, 19 June 1933, Joint Foreign Committee, *AJC Archives*; Shaul Esh, *Studies in the Holocaust and Contemporary Jewry*, Jerusalem, 1973, pp.33–106; Edwin Black, *The Transfer Agreement*, New York, 1984; Moshe Gottlieb, *American Anti-Nazi Resistance, 1933–1941*, New York, 1982, Part II.
10. Wise to Goldmann, 12 June 1933, 214A, *World Jewish Congress Archives*, New York (hereafter *WJC*) (currently transferred to the American Jewish Archives, Cincinnati); Wise to American Jewish Congress, 28 July 1933, *WJC Archives*, 211A; *New York Times*, 6–9 Sept. 1933; *New York Times*, 23 Sept. 1933; Administrative Committee of the American Jewish Congress, *WJC Archives*, 211A and 217A/31.
11. *League High Commissioner files*, James G. McDonald MSS., School of International Affairs, Columbia University, New York; McDonald's letter was accompanied by a comprehensive memorandum, prepared by Melvin Fagen and Oscar Janowsky through AJC subvention, which detailed Germany's official policy of discrimination against Jews.
12. 1933 London Conference. *AJC Archives*; Laski to Adler, 4 Dec. 1933, Joint Foreign Committee, *ibid.*; Ben-Gurion to Brandeis, 5 Jan. 1934, file 20, Julian Mack MSS., *Zionist Archives and Library*, New York; Wise to Goldmann, 29 May 1934, file 403, Horace Kallen MSS., YIVO, New York; *Unity in Dispersion*, pp.37–9; 217A/35, *WJC Archives*. As late as mid-1936, Weizmann favoured delaying the Congress's formation. Weizmann to Warburg, 18 June 1936, *Weizmann Archives*.
13. Goldmann to Laski, 11 July 1934, Joint Foreign Committee, *AJC Archives*; Report on activities, Sept. 1934–Aug. 1935, 215A, *WJC*; Laski September 1934 report, file 76, Mowshowitz MSS., YIVO; Goldmann to Wise, 3 Jan. 1936, 76A, *WJC Archives*; Executive Committee, 28 Jan. 1936, 7A/128, *WJC Archives*; Executive Committee, 22 Feb. 1936, 210A/24, *WJC Archives*; Goldmann to Wise, 13 March 1936, 76A, *WJC Archives*; Goldmann, *Autobiography*, pp.150–67.
14. *Unity in Dispersion*, pp.45–73; Wise and Goldmann addresses, 8 Aug. 1936, Box 1038, *American Jewish Archives*; file 409, Kallen MSS., YIVO.
15. Report on Political Work, Aug. 1936–July 1937, 216A/3, *WJC*; Goldmann to Wise, 10 Nov. 1936, 76A, *WJC Archives*; Memorandum, c. December 1939, file 414, Kallen MSS., YIVO; Executive meetings, 216A/23, *WJC Archives*; 15 Aug. 1938

report, 17A/53, *WJC*; Wise to WJC Geneva, 24 Jan. 1938, 214A, *WJC Archives*; Executive Committee, 10 Feb. 1938, 216A/21, *WJC Archives*; Riegner report, 14 Feb. 1938, 14A/10, *WJC Archives*.
16. *New York Times*, 13 June 1938; Goldmann to Wise, 16 July 1938, file 10/21, Kallen MSS., *American Jewish Archives*; Goldmann report, 20 July 1938, S 25/3778, *Central Zionist Archives*, Jerusalem.
17. A.J. Sherman, *Island Refuge; Britain and Refugees from the Third Reich, 1933–1939*, London, 1973, pp.112–222; Henry L. Feingold, *The Politics of Rescue, The Roosevelt Administration and the Holocaust, 1938–1945*, New Brunswick, 1970, pp.22–113.
18. Memorandum, 10 Aug. 1938, 208A, *WJC Archives*; meetings, 8 Sept. 1938, 216A/21, *WJC Archives*; Sept.–Oct. 1938 report, 216A/2, *WJC Archives*; *Unity in Dispersion*, pp.87, 90–4, 101, 116.
19. Goldmann address, November 1938 convention speeches, *Hadassah Archives*, New York; Goldmann, *Community of Fate*, pp.11–13; Sherman, *Island Refuge*, pp.223–58.
20. *New York Times*, 27 and 31 Oct. 1938, 12 Dec. 1938; Goldmann report, 27 Feb. 1939, 208A *WJC Archives*; Sept. 1938–July 1939 report, 216A/1 *WJC Archives*; 22 June 1939 Executive Committee, 216A/16, *WJC Archives*; Perlzweig memorandum, 17 July 1939, 210A, *WJC Archives*.
21. Goldmann remarks, 13 Nov. 1938 meeting, Jewish Agency Executive Jerusalem, *Central Zionist Archives*; *New York Times*, 17 Jan. 1939; Administrative Committee, 19 Jan. 1939, 14A/11, *WJC Archives*; Executive Committee, 27 March 1939, 216A/21, *WJC Archives*; meeting, 7 May 1939, Joint Foreign Committee minutes, *Board of Deputies of British Jews Archives*, London; 22–23 Aug. 1939 conference, Myron Taylor MSS., Franklin D. Roosevelt Library, Hyde Park, NY. While an early awareness of the menace threatening European Jewry led Jabotinsky and his Revisionist Zionist associates to support unlimited 'aliyah bet' to Palestine, the World Zionist Organization's insistence on selective immigration only shifted after *Kristallnacht*.
22. Gordon Thomas and Max M. Witts, *Voyage of the Damned*, New York, 1974; David S. Wyman, *Paper Walls, America and the Refugee Crisis, 1938–1941*, Amherst, 1968, pp.67–89; Naomi Shepherd, *A Refuge From Darkness, Wilfred Israel and the Rescue of the Jews*, New York, 1984, pp.160–3; Dubnow proposal, 14 June 1939, 17A/76, *WJC Archives*.
23. Goldmann to Wise, 30 May 1939, 17A/76, *WJC Archives*; Goldmann address, 16 Aug. 1939, World Zionist Congress files, *Hadassah Archives*.
24. Goldmann, *Jewish Paradox*, pp.62–3.

# 9

# Rescue and the Secular Perception: American Jewry and the Holocaust

## Henry L. Feingold

The ineffectiveness of American Jewry during the Holocaust represents something of a paradox for the historian. Like other Diaspora communities in the West, American Jewry has a good track record in nurturing beleaguered Jewish communities abroad. During the Colonial period 'Messengers' who collected *chaluka* found American Jews generous.[1] As early as 1840 the small Jewish community requested diplomatic intercession from the Van Buren administration to help the libelled Jews of Damascus. In 1858 their protest over the kidnapping of Edgar Mortara was so vehement that it earned the antagonism of the American-Irish who felt that Mortara's baptism was a good thing. After the Civil War Jews requested and received from the State Department 'statements of concern' for the hard-pressed Jews of Morocco, the Swiss cantons, Russia and Rumania. Similarly, one Jewish historian recently found that the Dreyfus affair created almost as much stir among American Jews as it did in Europe. The State Department archives are full of anxious letters from American Jewish communities and congregations written after news of pogroms in Tsarist Russia reached them.[2] The Kischinev pogrom triggered such a hysterical reaction, and such a plethora of new relief organizations, that the establishment of the American Jewish Committee, its major defence agency, was founded to channel the unrest in what the patricianate called 'the congested quarter.' Its charter grandiloquently charged it with preventing 'the infraction of civil and religious rights of Jews *in any part of the world.*'[3] Between 1908 and 1914 Louis Marshall, the President of the AJC, tried to fulfil that charge by orchestrating a campaign to abrogate the Commercial Treaty of 1832 with Russia in the hope of wringing better treatment for the Jews of that benighted country. So skilful were his strategies that the abrogation campaign still stands as a model of how to project influence on American foreign policy.[4] There may be some alive today who recall the outpouring of American Jewish philanthropy to the *Yishuv* and Eastern Jewries during and after the First World War. That hardly exhausts the list and does not include the much heralded advocacy role of American Jewry without which the Jewish state could not have been established in 1948.[5] Moreover, the financial aid given freely to Israel thereafter is nothing short of remarkable since it was frequently given at the expense of its own institutions and infrastructure. In short, American Jewry may know little of the intricacies of *pidyon shevuyim* or *pikuach nefesh*, but it does know a great deal about political advocacy and philanthropy which might be considered their secular equivalents.

Then what happened during the Holocaust? Is it possible to imagine that precisely at that crucial historical juncture American Jewry abandoned the nurturing posture towards its brethren by which it virtually defined itself? I would like in the next few pages to examine one unheralded aspect of that lapse which centres on the impact of the twin forces of secularization and acculturation on its ability to respond to the crisis. Clearly the decades of the twenties and thirties witnessed such an intensification of these twin processes that what emerged was a community, if one could call it that, whose organization and leadership structure were altered beyond recognition, whose cohesiveness was weakened and whose perception of itself in relationship to other Jews was changed. We must hasten to add that this is only one aspect to explain American Jewry's failure during these critical years, not even the most important one. But the problem this paper probes may turn out to be a crucial one: Can Jewries in the process of modernization in a particularly benevolent and absorbent culture respond adequately to crisis in the world Jewish enterprise? For obvious reasons our colleagues in Israel ought to be particularly interested in this case.

Let me begin with a remarkable datum rarely confronted by those self-flagellators which American Jewry produces in such unseemly numbers. The American Jews recruited for the Lincoln Brigade, the military unit organized to fight Franco during the Civil War in Spain, came to approximately 30 per cent of all American volunteers. (Jews were 3.7 per cent of the population in 1935.) When combined with Jews in the contingents from other European states and Palestine, the Jews in that International Brigade might have gone down in history as the first sizable Jewish Army since Bar Kochba's time.⁶ Yet they fought and bled in a country that had four centuries earlier expelled its Jews and for a cause which could only be viewed as part of a Jewish interest by a stretch of the ideological imagination. Yet in 1940, half a decade later, when Jabotinsky made his appeal for the formation of a Jewish army to be composed of Palestinian and stateless Jews, a call taken up by the Bergson group, the response among American Jews was almost nil. Moreover, British reluctance to form such a contingent was matched by American Jewish leaders who were aware that American Jewry could no longer understand the reason for such a formation.⁷

That strange juxtaposition tells us at a glance something about the attitude of an important part of American Jewry. The case of the Lincoln Brigade could be supplemented by the disproportionate number of young Jews in the Peace movements of the thirties or the high percentages whose enthusiasm for the labour movement of the New Deal welfare state programme far outweighed their support of specifically Jewish causes or their apprehension about a specific danger facing European Jewry.

Theirs was a universalist perception in which Jews were only one of several victimized groups. That perception was abandoned only with great reluctance when it became clear that a very specific, ultimately murderous, intent was aimed at the Jews. Stephen Wise, whose interest in the Jewish dilemma was often overshadowed by such preoccupations as the Sacco and Vanzetti case or the corruption in the 'Jimmy' Walker administration of New York City during the New Deal period, or the progress of the newly formed C.I.O., was fairly late in accepting the idea that the Jews were to be singled out among all Hitler's enemies for a special fate. ⁸ In 1940 he rejected the idea that a special case had to be made for the rescue of European Jewry. His letters tell of his embarrassment at speaking in the Oval Office of the special crucible of the Jews when the entire world was in flames. He was exasperated that some Jews did not understand the dilemma in pleading such a special case before the power holders.⁹ It was his secular universalist outlook which made Wise an activist and he did not abandon it lightly. It was for the reverse reason that groups like the Agudath and the Bergson group, the latter composed primarily of Palestinian Jews, were so much better able to imagine the disaster and propose solutions more appropriate for the specific Jewish need. Both groups were not locked into the prevailing secular universalist perception. They wanted simply to save Jews *qua* Jews. The new more secular, more American perception had a disarming impact in other areas as well.

We now have five studies on the relationship of the Roosevelt administration and the Jews of America.[10] They differ considerably in their estimates of the possibility of rescue. But all agree on the forlorn posture of American Jewry which remained conflicted over issues which, given the desperation of the situation, appear today to be appallingly irrelevant. It might go too far to say that American Jewry fiddled while European Jewry burned, as I have said in my younger days. But there can be little doubt that they squandered the opportunities for speaking to power-holders with one voice. They were unable to put aside their differences to build a unity based on the desperate need of European Jewry.

Those divisions are well known and need not occupy much of our time. They were structural, cultural and above all ideological, and superimposed on all was the fragmentation of the religious community which in some aspects was as bitter in the thirties as it is today. No single group was ultimately able to impose its will on the whole. The Zionist consensus which had developed by 1939 was itself too weak and the movement locked in internecine strife to persuade other agencies to surrender their organizational sovereignty for the good of the whole. Rather than unifying American Jewry, the crisis seemed to exacerbate the things which divided it. The relationship between Jewish agencies lacked the basic civility which might have permitted them to act together even for limited objectives.

Virtually every issue became the subject of acrimony. Even their perception of the nature of the threat posed by the advent of the National Socialist regime in Germany differed markedly. The more established sections of the community at first shared the conventional assumptions that power would somehow mature and tame Hitler.[11] The powerful left-wing elements knew better. But what to do? In 1933 and 1934 the boycott movement triggered endless debate and ultimately fragmented the Zionist camp when it came into conflict with the transfer agreement. Should Jews press for a less stringent administration of the immigration laws which the Hoover administration had imposed at the outset of the Depression? The cognoscenti who knew popular and congressional sentiment and had become alarmed at the rise of restriction and anti-Semitic sentiment, argued against it. Refugee advocates who wanted the 'golden doors' opened a little more widely could not even be sure that they had the support of the Jewish grass roots, who were as concerned about the effects of immigration on the unemployment situation as other Americans.[12] Jewish leaders preferred to let non-Jewish rescue advocates argue for the admission of 10,000 Jewish children outside the quota system in 1939 and 1940. After the war began the question of mass resettlement of Jews outside of Palestine, favoured for obvious reasons in Washington and London, tore American Jewry apart. Most American Zionists could not conceive that resettlement in British Guiana or the Dominican Republic, advocated by Joseph Rosen of Agro-Joint, could replace Palestine, which they saw as the only clear answer to the refugee plight. If Palestine was being denied by political fiat then they would fight it politically. They would struggle against Nazis as if there were no White Paper and against the British as if there were no Nazis. But in truth they could barely hold their own on one front. In late 1943, the resettlement alternative, which paradoxically never approached reality, was accepted by the Bergson group which proposed separating the homeland goal of the Biltmore platform from the immediate need to rescue Jews.[13] Soon the bitter conflict between the Revisionist Bergson group and the mainline Zionists was waged in the public press and all this while thousands were being led to their death every day. If one reads David Wyman's *The Abandonment of the Jews* carefully one can still hear echoes of the conflict today.

Yet in the traditional field of philanthropy, used by wealthy secularized Jewry to maintain a connection with the community, a fragile coming together did occur. The United Jewish Appeal began again in 1939 and this time survived the rocky road to organized professional fund-raising.[14] It was one of the things that American Jewry could see eye to eye on. Paradoxically, the only other thing one could point to was the almost universal Jewish adoration of Roosevelt. The highly secularized Jewish patricians, notwithstanding Joseph Proskauer and Abba Hillel Silver, were for him.[15] And so were left-wingers who formed the American Labour Party in New York State in 1936, which they soon dubbed 'the party of the permanent New Deal.'[16]

How can one explain such disunity which in the case of American Jewry seemed to go far beyond the normal diversity of post-emancipation Jewish communities? When the Eastern migration began the German Jews held their noses, but they helped. Now the children of these same Eastern European Jews did not seem to be able to muster the interest and energy to repay in kind. It was partly the triple layers of immigration that formed the community which meant they lacked the requisites for unity – common experience, common language, and a common vision. American Jewry was more than simply disunited. In 1943 after the breakup of the

American Jewish Conference and the establishment of the Council for American Judaism it looked very much as if American Jewry was more anxious to tear itself apart than to help their brethren in Europe.

I would suggest that the impending crisis caught American Jewry in a dilemma. The inability to react collectively was part of the process of modernization with its intense individualization and voluntarism. They were in the midst of the dissolution of the old form of communalism and the new had not yet taken shape. There was no longer anyone who could order them to their Judaism. Leaders could not lead because followers would not follow. Superimposed on that process was the accelerated acculturation of the thirties which occurred at different rates among different strata of the Jewish population. And if that were not sufficient there were the intensely privatizing effects of the Depression. Most Jews in the thirties were pre-occupied with problems of *parnossah* – making a living. When the Depression did activate people politically it was over the question of domestic economic policy, the welfare state. That policy had after all been incubated in the Jewish Labour movement and had a special appeal for many Jews. There was then a Jewish kind of isolationism in the thirties which was related directly to the privatizing effects of the Depression.[17] The news reports about the depredations against their European brethren had first to work their way through a layer of consciousness about their own plight.[18] Moreover, until September 1939, the news they heard was largely stories about German Jewry which some still believed, like their parents before them, was competent enough to take care of itself. Most important, the free secular atmosphere of America had over two decades led to a process of fragmentation; it tended to act as a solvent on Jewish corporateness. Increasingly secular-achieving Jews, lawyers, professors, doctors, were committed to professional advancement. If they related to Jewishness at all it was merely one of several loyalties; and not necessarily the most important one. When the crisis called them back they were becoming less Jewish and more self-involved.

Nowhere is that fragmentation and resultant loss of coherence more apparent than in the development of a dual leadership rather than the single stratum of leadership which customarily made the Jewish agenda known in the American political arena. There had always been a small group of Jewish office-holders and achievers who had political influence. But in the early decades of the century they served only as a supplementary representation of the Jewish community. 'Silver dollar Smith,' a Jewish barkeeper who represented his district in Congress under the auspices of corrupt Tammany Hall, was not considered by Jews to represent their interests generally, although even he could be called upon to help, as was Representative Goldfogle during the abrogation struggle.[19] Primary issues such as immigration policy or the depredations in Russia were represented by Jews like Jacob Schiff, Louis Marshall, Oscar Straus or Sulzberger, who by dint of personal fortune and belonging to the same 'crowd' were recognized by Theodore Roosevelt and William Taft as Jewish spokesmen. Their role went beyond mere *shtadlanut* since the American system permitted, and even encouraged, the projection of influence directly on the electorate. Indeed, the American Jewish Committee spared little to influence American public opinion on the Russian depredations. The struggle to abrogate the Commercial Treaty of 1832 with Russia, or the way Jacob Schiff, by means of financial leverage available to him, tried to influence the outcome of the Russo-Japanese war, still serve today as models of how special interests can influence American public policy.[20] Once recognized and legitimated by the administration in power, the 'Jewish masses' went along, albeit increasingly reluctantly. The result was a measure of coherence. Everyone knew who spoke for the Jewish community, and through whom to speak to it.

By 1933 two things had happened to alter that simple workable system. The class that produced such leadership types, people willing to place fame and fortune at the service of the community, had experienced enormous attrition. It lost much influence after the death of Louis Marshall. The cry for democratization in Jewish life, first sounded by the 'illustrious obscure' who proposed a congress movement, made the interior political life of the American Jewish community far more raucous and ultimately far more universalist. Democracy, which is itself a secular/modern concept, rarely encourages blind submission to authority. Despite the two internal elections by the American Jewish Congress, the community structure had in fact become more amorphous and in that sense less effective, that is less able to project a coherent voice in the political arena. Franklin Roosevelt, we shall see, was not slow to capitalize on the altered situation, but he often had occasion to envy the simple situation faced by his uncle. He sometimes wished that the divided Jewish community would have a Pope like the Catholics.[21]

During the New Deal period American Jewry no longer transmitted its agenda through a leadership cohort recognized by both sides. There were now secular Jews who had risen to the top through various different power centres: the university (Felix Frankfurter), organized labour (Sidney Hilman), the law establishment (Ben Cohen, Isador Lubin, Sam Rosenman), the business community (Bernard Baruch, Herbert Lehman), who were located near political power and often were coopted into politics as advisors and managers. They did not see themselves as merely Jews, much less as spokesmen for Jewish causes, although some had a tenuous connection with Jewish organizations, especially the American Jewish Committee.[22] As a shorthand we can refer to them as the 'Jew Deal,' the pejorative used by anti-Semites at the time to express their hostility to the proliferation of Jews in the top echelons of the Roosevelt administration. (In fact their perception was not quite accurate, since in the federal judiciary and the highest echelons of the federal civil service, other ethnics, especially Italian-Americans, were granted more positions.) For the most part the 'Jew Deal' was composed of 'new' men whose loyalty was to career. They were not Jews incubated in a holistic Jewish environment who turned to the east-wall three times daily as if by Pavlovian conditioning. Such totally Jewish environments were, with the exception of a few insular communities, no longer influential in generating the Jewish outlook. For these men, when a Judaic influence played a role at all, it was merely one of several influences. They were in fact Americans who happened to be Jewish, in some cases unhappily so. Nor were they scions of the uptown 'crowd.' Felix Frankfurter was a descendant of Viennese *galitzianer* Sol Bloom, who played the 'shabbas goy' role at the ill-fated Bermuda conference. Isador Lubin, Ben Cohen, Sidney Hilman and David Niles were of Eastern European Jewish descent, and Bernard Baruch, for whom Roosevelt found little use, stemmed from Sephardic Jews.[23]

Not only did these 'new' men not inherit the tradition of service of the older Jewish patricianate, but their Jewish identity formation was so confined or hemmed in by other influences that if they perceived the Jewish interest at all it was through a universalist or an American prism. They were either out to improve the world or, American versions of Walter Rathenau, patriotic and utterly loyal to the nation they served. That explains the disproportionate Jewish recruitment for the Lincoln Brigade, or Frankfurter, Lubin and Cohen's brilliant legislative engineering of the New Deal domestic programme. The question of rescue for such men, when it was perceived at all, served as a disturbing counterpoint to the public business with which they were involved. Their assumption was naturally that the Jewish fate was linked to the fate of America. The Jews would be saved if America won the war. Therefore nothing could be done to impede that victory. That was the same argument used by the power holders in Washington. For many Jews it had a compelling logic even though it meant, in effect, that their brethren would not survive the war. They never remotely understood that it was being used as a ploy to avoid the rescue question. After 1943, bombing concentration camps would not have changed wartime priorities, just as sending food to Greece throughout the war did not alter them.[24] It was only when one of the members of the 'Jew Deal' saw through the ploy that serious rescue activity could be mounted. But even in the exceptional case of Henry Morgenthau, the risk to his political career caused by his activities in the rescue cause occurred only after it was clear that the light of victory could be seen at the end of the tunnel. Only then did it become possible to tamper with virtually sacred war priorities which were ordered on the assumption of victory before everything else.[25]

The 'Jew Deal' held one of the crucial keys to rescue. It was through it that leaders like Stephen Wise and others had to act. The route to the Oval Office was through the conduit that these marginally Jewish men offered. No effective advocacy could be conceived without them. The tragedy was that unlike their predecessors they were *of* the Jewish community but no longer exclusively *for* it. One can argue, as David Wyman does, that the best road to rescue was through an aroused public opinion.[26] But in the context of the availability of the 'Jew Deal' that seems a far less possible course of action. Most feel that it would have been impossible for an organized Jewish community to mobilize general American public opinion in the interest of Jewish rescue in 1943 and 1944. Some feel it would have been dangerous to do so. Most important, whether even such a mobilized public opinion would have led a preoccupied and inured Roosevelt to change his mind about the Jews is a highly dubious proposition. Even if that were possible an effective advocacy role would still have required the mobilization of these highly placed Jews who could no longer recognize, much less act in, a specific Jewish interest. The interesting fact for us is that the Holocaust itself served to mobilize most of these same Jews in the cause of establishing the Jewish state barely three years later, and it is such Jews who play a leading role in the United Jewish Appeal and the federation today. The transition to a new form of communalism has been made.

Lest we imagine that the failure to rescue European Jewry was the fault of American Jewry who failed to exercise their power, let us imagine the following: The burden of its historical development had been magically lifted from American Jewish shoulders; that rather than variation and pluralism which everywhere follows upon freeness, there was instead coherence and unity; that rather than projecting a cacophony of sound they were able to speak to power with one voice; that their Jewishness somehow remained intact and allowed for a better perception of the impending disaster; that Jewish leaders could be assured that free autonomous Jews would follow – in a word, that the myriad factors and conditions of modernity which interfered with a more effective response could be magically cancelled. Would it have made an appreciable difference?

After many years of working with this problem my conclusion is that what American Jewry did and did not do is perhaps 5 per cent of the problem. It is simply not true that the U.S. Government, acting under Jewish pressure, would have allowed the Second World War to become a war to save the Jews. Those who imagine otherwise assign American Jewry an influence on events which views it in the same power terms as the anti-Semitic imagination. There is in the first place an inherent structural and ideological limitation on how far a special interest group can pull foreign policy in its own direction. In the second place there is an even greater unwillingness on the part of governments who seek to persecute Jews to allow themselves to be persuaded by moral pressure. During the case of the depredations of Tsarist Russia or Rumania, a better organized, more coherent Jewry did not wring better treatment of its religious brethren even when the American Government was willing to act on its behalf. The Hitler regime gave the destruction of European Jewry a comparatively high priority and probably could not have been dissuaded merely by more exhortations. Regimes who murder in the name of progress, whether the victims are the kulaks or the Jews, are peculiarly immune from moral suasion. If they were moral, in our sense of the word, they would not conceive of such policies in the first place. How determined they were is clearly illustrated by the fate of Hungarian and Slovakian Jewry. Here murder was commited when Berlin knew the war was lost and within full view of an alerted world.

The secular outlook which, as we have noted, played such havoc with American Jewry's ability to perceive and respond to the crisis, was no less a factor among officials in Berlin, Washington or

London who implemented policy. It was as difficult to enlist them in the cause of rescue in the Allied camp as it had been easy earlier to enlist them in the cause of genocide in Nazi-occupied Europe. Subject to a *raison d'état* which viewed Jews as inimical, American officialdom matched that of Germany in being coolly inured to loss of life. It would seem that the role of a self-initiating bureaucracy which is so central to totalitarian regimes is also present in latent form in the governments of democratic nations.[27] They too produce a bureaucratic objectification which blocks the human agony from entering their consciousness. By their nature bureaucracies are interested in programmes, not people.[28] Philips, Reams, Moffat, Long in America; Law, Emerson, Winterton in Britain, the officials who managed the crisis, were, in their pervasive anti-Semitism and their replacement of feeling by a need to get the job done, the match for an Eichmann or a Heydrich. Against such odds and such power what little influence American Jewry had, came almost to nought.

\* \* \*

Examined here are two of the internal reasons for American Jewry's ineffectiveness during the Holocaust years. Stated briefly it comes to this: The historical development of American Jewry, especially the more recent process of secularization and acculturation in a free and open society, significantly altered its internal governing threshold so that the requisite coherence and will to play its advocacy role was diminished. By the 1940s American Jewry had virtually lost its corporate communal character and the new coherence based on voluntarism and managed by professionals had not yet taken its place. Yet historians will hardly need to mention that change because it made little difference in the larger picture. Even a more powerful American Jewry would not appreciably have changed the picture. The same process of modernization inured non-Jewish bureaucrats from sympathizing with the Jewish plight. In Washington and London the Jewish death toll was seen as numbers as much as it was in Berlin. Bureaucratic objectification is after all universal.

Finally those who argue that American Jewry was indifferent to the plight of their European brethren need to read American Jewish history. A concern for Jewries abroad virtually defines the American Jewish persona. They may have been ineffective but that is a far cry from being indifferent. Those who draw up the indictment against American Jewry, and the number grows yearly, are really unhappy with what American Jewry had become through an inexorable historical development. They would have liked it to be something else. It is like arguing with the direction of the wind. The real historical question is whether American Jewry did what it could within the parameters of what it had become and what was possible. I suspect that the answer to such a question will yield a more balanced, less polemical, history.

NOTES

1. Jacob R. Marcus, *Early American Jewry* (Philadelphia, 1953), Vol. II, pp.1,041–4.
2. Cyrus Adler & Aaron Margalith, *With Firmness in the Right: American Diplomatic Action Affecting Jews, 1840–1945* (New York, 1977), pp.261–98.
3. Naomi Cohen, *Not Free to Desist: The American Jewish Committee, 1906–1966* (Philadelphia, 1972?), pp.3–18.
4. *Ibid.*, pp.54–80.
5. John Snetsinger, *Truman, the Jewish Vote and the Creation of Israel* (Stanford, 1974). For another opinion see Zvi Ganin, *Truman, American Jewry and Israel, 1945–1948* (New York, 1979), pp.170–89.
6. Estimates vary considerably on the number of Jews in the International Brigade, since volunteers were listed under their nationalities. Thus Cecil Ely, *Between the Bullet and the Lie, Volunteers in the Spanish Civil War* (New York, 1969), does not make an estimate. C.V. Lipschitz, *Franco's Spain, the Jews and the Holocaust* (New York, 1984), p.15, observes only that the percentage of Jews was 'disproportionately high.' On the other hand Haim Avni, *Spain, the Jews and Franco* (Philadelphia, 1982), p.50, estimates that 10 per cent or 3,000 to 5,000 of the International Brigade, which consisted of approximately 40,000 volunteers, were Jewish. The most confidently stated figures come from Albert Prago, 'Fifty Long Years Later, Commemorating the Spanish Civil War,' *Jewish Currents*, March 1987, pp.4–7. He estimates that 18 per cent of the total Brigade, approximately 7,000 volunteers, were Jewish and about 30 per cent of the Lincoln Brigade were Jewish. But the highest percentage belonged to Palestine which sent 300 volunteers, a few of whom were Arabs. High percentages were also to be observed in the Italian and Polish detachments. The latter sent 5,000 volunteers, fully 40 per cent of whom were Jewish. It contained a segregated Jewish company (Dombrowski) composed almost entirely of Jews.
7. See Monty Penkower, 'In Dramatic Dissent: The Bergson Boys,' *American Jewish History*, Vol. LXX/3, March 1981, pp.281–309. An emotional account of the attempt to create the army is contained in Yitshaq Ben Ami, *Years of Wrath, Days of Glory: Memoirs from the Irgun* (New York, 1982), pp.248–52.
8. Melvin Urofsky, *A Voice That Spoke For Justice: The Life and Times of Stephen S. Wise* (Albany, New York, 1982).
9. Carl Voss, *Rabbi and Minister: The Friendship of Stephen S. Wise and John Haynes Holmes* (Cleveland, Ohio, 1964), p.39.
10. Arthur Morse, *While Six Million Died* (New York, 1967); David Wyman, *Paper Walls* (Amherst, Mass., 1968); Henry L. Feingold, *The Politics of Rescue* (New Brunswick, New Jersey, 1970); Saul Friedman, *No Haven For The Oppressed* (Detroit, Michigan, 1973); David Wyman, *The Abandonment of the Jews* (New York, 1985). In addition there are two new books in the pipeline and innumerable articles have been published in the journals.
11. See for example Frederick A. Lazin, 'The Response of the American Jewish Committee to the Crisis of German Jewry, 1933–1939,' *American Jewish History*,

Vol. LVIII/3, March 1979, pp.283–304.
12. David Brody, 'American Jewry, the Refugees and Immigration Restriction, 1932–1942,' *Publications of the American Jewish Historical Society*, Vol. XLV, June 1956, pp.219–84.
13. Henry Feingold, *Politics*, pp.237–39, 300–1. See also Aaron Berman, 'American Zionism and the Rescue of European Jewry: An Ideological Perspective,' *American Jewish History*, Vol. LXX/3, March 1983, pp.320–30.
14. Marc Raphael, *A History of the United Jewish Appeal, 1939–1982* (Providence, Rhode Island, 1982), pp.5–11.
15. Lawrence Fuchs, *The Political Behavior of American Jews* (Glencoe, 1965), pp.97–107, 177–87.
16. Deborah Moore, *At Home In America: Second Generation New York Jews* (New York, 1981), p.23.
17. Alfred Hero, *American Religious Groups View Foreign Policy; Trends in Rank and File Opinion, 1937–1969* (Durham, North Carolina, 1973), pp.279–84.
18. Deborah Lipstadt, *Beyond Belief: The American Press and the Coming of the Holocaust, 1939–1945* (New York, 1986), pp.240–278.
19. Naomi Cohen, *Not Free*, pp.69–70. See also Irving Howe, *World of Our Fathers* (New York, 1976), pp.377–8.
20. Henry Feingold, *A Midrash On American Jewish History* (Albany, 1982), pp.46–8. Also Gary Best, *American Jewish Leaders and the Jewish Problem in Eastern Europe, 1890–1914* (New York, 1982).
21. Selig Adler, 'Franklin Roosevelt and Zionism, The Wartime Record,' *Judaism*, Vol. XXI (Summer 1972), pp.256–76.
22. This observation and those which follow are fully developed in Henry Feingold, '"Courage First and Intelligence Second:" The American Jewish Secular Elite, Roosevelt and the failure to Rescue,' *American Jewish History*, Vol. LXXII/4 (June 1983), pp.424–60. See also Peter Lowenburg, 'Walter Rathenau and Henry Kissinger: The Jew As a Modern Statesman in Two Political Cultures,' *Leo Baeck Memorial Lecture*, No. 14 (New York, 1980).
23. Morgenthau, Lehman and Brandeis are interesting exceptions. They were Jews of Central European descent. Brandeis was a third generation descendant of a Prague family; Lehman and Morgenthau were second generation German Jews. All were fully Americanized.
24. Bernard Wasserstein, *Britain and the Jews of Europe, 1937–1945* (Oxford, 1979), pp.353–4.
25. Henry Feingold, 'Courage First ...,' pp.443–8.
26. 'American Jews and the Holocaust,' *New York Times Magazine*, 8 May 1982, p.94.
27. On the role of bureaucracy generally during the Holocaust see Raul Hilberg, *The Destruction of the European Jews* (New York, 1985), Vol. III, pp.993–1,029. For the self-initiating process of the bureaucracy in Vichy France see Michael R. Marrus, 'The Theory and Practice of Anti-Semitism,' *Commentary* (August 1982), pp.39ff.
28. Henry Feingold, 'The Bureaucrat As Mass Killer: Arendt on Eichmann,' *Response*, No. 39 (Summer 1980), pp.45–51. Also Feingold, 'The Government Response,' in *The Holocaust: Ideology, Bureaucracy and Genocide*, eds. Henry Friedlander and Sybil Milton (New York, 1980), pp.245–59.

# 10

# German Jewish Refugees in Palestine: The Early Years, 1932–1939*

## Jehuda Reinharz

### INTRODUCTION

Before the independence of Israel, Zionist land policy relied primarily upon the acquisitions made and held as a permanent, public, Jewish trust by the Jewish National Fund (JNF). As the JNF was an agency of the World Zionist Organization, its landholdings were, of course, uniquely important for Zionist policy, since the Organization alone determined how they were to be used.

Zionists had hoped, at times, that they could advance the interests of the Jewish national home by settling Jews on state lands. However, in spite of Britain's commitment under Article 6 of the Palestine Mandate to 'encourage, in cooperation with the Jewish Agency', close settlement by Jews on the land, including 'state lands and waste lands not required for public purposes,' no significant areas of state or waste lands were made available for Zionist colonization.[1] The Palestine administration proceeded slowly and cautiously in settling land titles and defining the boundaries of state lands; and it used the available state lands to maintain the 'rights and position' of Arab cultivators (including future generations) as well as to settle Jews. The Zionist eagerness to explore and develop these areas could not be satisfied under the Mandate as administered.

The Zionists also placed little reliance on lands held by private Jewish owners or by Jewish non-Zionist philanthropic organizations as a resource for the 'close settlement of Jews.' Yet such purchasers were earlier in the field than the Zionist Organization and, up to the outbreak of the Second World War, held almost two

---

* I would like to acknowledge with thanks the comments on an earlier draft which were made by Ben Halpern. Some of the ideas in this article are based on a larger work as yet unpublished that we are co-authoring.

acres for every acre in the possession of the Jewish National Fund.[2] Purchases by Baron Edmond de Rothschild and by groups of small investors and settlers had begun in the 1880s, while JNF acquisitions did not begin until the early 1900s, and even then remained minor until the First World War. In September 1939, after two decades of JNF activity, Jewish-owned land not in the possession of the JNF still stood at 885,100 dunams* to the 471,000 dunams directly controlled by the Zionist policy makers (concession lands excluded). Moreover, much of private Jewish farm land was concentrated in Palestine's orange-growing belt, where the population density was highest. The total population, the Jewish population, and even the number of Jewish farm workers supported by an acre of such plantation land were substantially greater than the comparable numbers supported by mixed farming in the heavy soil areas where much JNF land was concentrated.[3] It might seem, therefore, that the best way to achieve the Zionist aim of close settlement on the land would be to foster just such private land purchase. But the history of private Jewish land dealings in Palestine since the 1880s provided the Zionist movement with a store of bad examples sufficient to destroy their reliance on this method of colonizing the Jewish national home, even if the situation they faced in regard to land purchase had not forbidden it.

The Zionists, in the light of experience as well as ideology, developed the firm belief that the difficult task of turning urban Jewish middlemen into farm workers, permanently established, depended above all on questions of morale, of motivation; and these in turn depended on matters of social and economic organization.[4] They were convinced that the social and economic organization resulting from exclusively private land purchase and land holding, inevitably produced a climate of morale and motivations which would doom the Zionist programme to failure. The early private settlers, usually inexperienced in farm practices and, in any case, unfamiliar with Palestine's special conditions, had regularly lost their initial investments. They were rescued only by the timely intervention of Baron Edmond de Rothschild and other benefactors, so that some colonists were able to remain on the soil. But the Baron's philanthropy brought with it a paternalistic administration that stifled the initiative and destroyed the independence of the settlers, reducing them to a position not very different from the charity pensioners of the Old Yishuv; a position

---

* 1 dunam=1,000 square metres, or 1/10 hectare.

against which the whole spirit of the Zionist movement was in revolt. Dependency in the old colonies, the Zionists observed, also undermined the Zionist enthusiasm of the settlers, with results disastrous to the programme: they began to despair of success in Palestine, so that alternative proposals, such as the Uganda scheme, found strong support in the colonies of the First Aliya; their sons sought to complete in France the French-oriented education they received under the sponsorship of Rothschild or of the *Alliance Israélite Universelle*, and ended, in many cases, by seeking a career in other countries.[5]

The damage was compounded, in the Zionists' view, by the fact that the Baron, upon taking over the colonies, converted them from general farming to plantations. He felt that the light, skilled work involved in horticulture was better suited to the background and temperament of the Jewish settlers than the heavy labour required for peasant-style cereal farming; it was also a form of farming for which French expertise seemed available and which promised a higher cash return. But vineyards and other plantations involved years of growth before any crop could be harvested; and in that period the settlers had to depend entirely on the stipend advanced by Rothschild. Thus not only the paternalistic system, but an economy both mercantile and monocultural was forced upon the colonies by the conversion to horticulture. Even after the settlers had freed themselves from total dependence on the Baron's charity, they would have had to depend on the vagaries of a one-crop market. Instead of a well-rooted farmer-worker class, largely supported by its own produce, the Rothschild system would have produced a class of merchants dependent, precisely like the Jews in the Diaspora, on the chance of commerce.

The paternalistic approach was given up by Rothschild himself in the late 1890s, and he transferred to the colonists the lands they worked, as well as control of communal affairs and of the cooperative enterprises jointly conducted by the settlements. Moreover, the new colonies then established with Rothschild's aid were based on general farming, not on horticultural specialities. However, another aspect of private colonization that seemed quite as dangerous to Zionist hopes still persisted. The private colonists continued to occupy the same positions as farm managers or planters they had assumed under the Rothschild system, and they worked their lands with hired labour or through tenant-farmers, in either case mainly Arab. This reproduced a situation which – from the point of view of a Zionist, and especially of the Labour Zionist groups that became increasingly influential in the movement – was the central source of the Jewish problem in the Diaspora. The Jews remained concentrated in middle class positions even in their own land; moreover, they supervised the labour of a native population, thus compounding the potentialities of national with class conflict. Even more than the critics of private colonization feared the rise of a compounded anti-Jewish and anti-colonist feeling among the Arabs, they abhorred the prospect of a Jewish nationality of capitalists and employers in Palestine, for they regarded this as the ultimate defeat of their Zionist vision. Only if the land were worked by Jewish labourers would it be truly Jewish. This was true, they held, first of all in a moral sense. It was also true in a very practical political and social sense. If the private Jewish colonies became the home of more Arabs than Jews or served merely to increase the population density of Arab villages in their vicinity by offering new sources of livelihood, then the Jewish national cause was not at all advanced.

The private real estate 'boom and bust' cycles during the First and especially the Fourth Aliya reinforced these conclusions from another angle.[6] Private land purchase easily degenerated into private real estate speculation, the Zionists observed. In the upswing of the land boom, prices for land were driven to fantastic heights, burdening Zionist colonization with impossible costs. In its collapse, bankruptcies, unemployment, and even the sale of land out of Jewish hands presented still greater threats to the growth of a Jewish national home.

The Jewish National Fund, accumulated from the contributions of Jews throughout the Diaspora and devoted to the purchase of land in Zion as the inalienable possession of the Jewish people, was as old as the Zionist movement.[7] At the fifth Zionist Congress (Basle, 1901), the Fund was established, with instructions not to begin purchasing land in Palestine and Syria until a capital of £200,000 had been accumulated. At the next Congress (Basle, 1903) this restriction was removed and land acquisition by the JNF in Palestine began, with an initial annual budget of £600. In 1908, after years of debate between political Zionists (who wished to obtain a charter for settlement before beginning colonization) and practical Zionists (who felt that political titles could only be obtained and be meaningful if based on prior success in actual colonization), the Zionist Organization established a Palestine Office in Jaffa under the direction of Dr. Arthur Ruppin (1876–1943). In the programme for Zionist colonization he was to carry out, JNF land was a major asset. The total landholdings of the JNF in Palestine at the time were only about 4,000 acres scattered in four different regions of Palestine. But with these small areas, still for the most part unoccupied, and with the meagre capital and annual income of the Zionist funds, the practical Zionists undertook to initiate a programme intended to remedy some major defects of previous Jewish settlement policy at once, and others as fiscal resources and other necessary conditions made it possible.

The JNF landholdings and resources, at that time, were, of course, totally inadequate to approach the Zionist task of resettling Palestine on a scale adequate for establishing Jewish sovereignty. But they were sufficient, nevertheless, to achieve an aim symbolically essential for that larger goal. On those lands, by the coordinated policies of the Palestine Office in Jaffa and the labour settlers, it was demonstrated that a farmer-worker class recruited from Jews of the ghetto could be settled on the soil of Palestine. The methods adopted for this purpose by both partners were direct reactions to the defects, from a Zionist point of view, of the Rothschild-supported colonization of the First Aliya.

Firstly, they introduced the principle that the autonomy of the settlers must be respected. Dr. Ruppin, as director of Zionist colonization in Palestine, upheld this principle in conscious opposition to Rothschild paternalism, but did not suppose to preclude the use of trained agronomists as directors and supervisors of settlements of JNF land.[8] He proposed that the existing small JNF holdings be used primarily as a school for Jewish farm workers, and be cultivated under the direction of expert administrators with the immigrant apprentices serving as hired labourers. However, the hired farmer apprentices should be dealt with as organized cooperative groups and be completely free of the authority of the administrator, in all or most of their communal functions (including, for example, their medical care, kitchen and, above all, their cultural activities). These cooperative activities were to foster the *esprit* of the settlers as a dedicated band of nationalist enthusiasts. In this respect alone would the Zionist procedure differ from those of an agency such as the Jewish Colonization Association (JCA), which had been entrusted with the administration of the Rothschild lands in Palestine. Like the JCA settlers the hired apprentices on the Zionist farms were to become settlers on leasehold JNF farms, or to acquire their own land from the general Zionist land purchasing agency, the Palestine Land Development Company (PLDC), after completing their training. The Zionist

Palestine Organization, having encouraged the cooperative organization and communal initiative of the settlers while still in training, also favoured their permanent settlement in cooperative groups (as well as on private homesteads, of course) in what might be called the post-graduate stage of settlement.

But the plan did not go far enough to satisfy the labour Zionist groups, particularly those in Palestine. During the Second Aliya, a series of disputes broke out between the worker-settlers and the administrators of the Zionist Organization's farms which equalled in intensity the 'rebellions' on the Rothschild-sponsored settlements during the First Aliya. However, in this case, the outcome was not the complete defeat and cowing of the settlers. The farm workers won the right to contract directly with the Zionist Organization as a cooperative group and to take over the entire responsibility for the management of their farm, without an administrator. Beginning with an experimental annual contract, this system took hold in a broader, more permanent form which became predominant in all settlements on JNF land.

Whether as a *moshav* – that is, a 'small-holders' cooperative settlement' – or as a *kibbutz* or *kvutza* – that is, a 'communal settlement' – the organized workers' group contracted collectively both for employment on lands held by others and for settlement on land which they held themselves on a collective lease from the JNF. Their position *vis-à-vis* the Zionist Organization was one of such strong independence that experts familiar with the systems employed in parallel cases described it as a veritable dictatorship of the settlers over the colonizing agency, which had to relinquish effective control over settlement policy. For the removal of administrators, through whom a central policy of the Zionist Organization could be exercised, was only the first step in this development. The labour settlers, after 1921, were organized in the *Histadrut*, a national federation of urban as well as rural workers; and when they entered into contracts with the Zionist colonizing agencies, they enjoyed the full support in bargaining as well as the financial guarantee of the national labour organization.

In addition, the labour settlers developed, in the course of time, strong federations of their own (one organizing the *moshav* movement, three organizing distinct ideological varieties of the *kibbutz* movement). Final responsibility for the fate of the settlement group together with authority to determine its fundamental policies – that is to say, the recruitment of its membership, the nomination of the group for settlement, the negotiations for land to be leased, the concern for the current solvency of the group, as well as for its communal services, vocational competence, and even its political, ideological complexion – were as much, if not more, the concern of the federation in question than of the particular group. This was especially the case with respect to the more politically-minded and ideologically-oriented of the communal federations, less so with regard to the central organization of the *moshavim*. It was more markedly the case in the early stages of group organization, less so as a settlement became established. But, in any event, the direct involvement of the particular federation in the affairs of its settlements was greater than that of the *Histadrut* as a general sponsor of labour settlement. The direct responsibility and authority of the *Histadrut*, in turn, was greater than that of the Zionist colonizing agencies.

It was a system that fostered not only the initiative but the *esprit de corps* of the settlers. It achieved with eminent success, though in unforeseen and unplanned manner, the first aim of the policy-makers of Zionist colonization: to create (in conscious reaction against the condition of the Rothschild colonies) a Jewish farmer-worker-settler class that should retain the independence, initiative, and nationalist enthusiasm that were central values of the Zionist myth.

Secondly, the Palestine Office (and later central agencies of Zionist Organization), jointly with the labour settlers themselves, developed mixed farming instead of plantation or general (grain) farming, as the pattern of Zionist settlements on JNF land. At the very beginning of his work, Dr. Ruppin foresaw that certain crucial advantages could be secured if the Jewish settlers combined both plantations and cereal crops, and added to these farms branches, such as a dairy, poultry run, and vegetable growing which were hardly represented in the First Aliya settlements.[9] Such 'mixed farms' would provide work for the settlers themselves, as well as for hired labourers, throughout the year. Steady employment would make possible the settlement of Jewish workers in the villages, and make it unnecessary to depend on the casual or irregular employment of Arabs, for whom such work was no more than a supplement to their other sources of subsistence. It would also solve the cardinal problem of drawing women into agricultural work, and the new crops would both enrich the diet and raise the cash income of the settlers.

## ADJUSTMENT OF REFUGEES

Perhaps the greatest test of the methods and techniques developed in Palestine in order to retrain and resettle Jewish immigrants was their application to the problem of refugees, particularly German refugees after 1932.[10] The absorption of massive groups of involuntary migrants, their social readjustment[11] to a new country, new cultural surroundings,[12] new political conditions,[13] and new occupations, was accomplished successfully, and most successfully in the agricultural field.[14]

From 1933 to March 1939 German refugees numbering more than 60,000, or about 26 per cent of the total Jewish immigration, came to Palestine.[15] Not counting those trained by Hechalutz, the proportion of farmers among the German immigrants was put at 0.7 per cent.[16] If we include the young people who were trained by Hechalutz,[17] the proportion trained in farming was about 1.7 per cent. The number who settled on the land was at different times estimated at about a quarter, or more, of the number of immigrants.[18] Their retraining was certainly a severe test of the methods and facilities of Palestine resettlement.

Their distribution was as follows:

*In towns*: 34,000, of whom 16,000 in Tel Aviv, 11,000 in Haifa, 6,000 in Jerusalem and 1,000 in other towns;

*On the land*: 16,000, made up of 7,000 in Youth Aliya groups and settlers in communes, 3,500 middle-class farmer-settlers, 1,000 settlers with small plots ('auxiliary holdings'), 3,000 farm labourers in the plantation colonies and 1,500 non-farmers in rural areas.[19]

Among the above-mentioned groups which settled on the land, Youth Aliya was unique in that its members were integrated upon arrival in *kibbutzim* which had made arrangements to receive them properly, house, school and train them in agriculture. During the early phase of Youth Aliya (1932–35), these youths (15–17 years old) were accompanied by their counsellors (*madrichim*) from Germany. Some 5,000 youngsters came on Youth Aliya between 1934 and 1939. Of these 70 per cent came from Germany, 20 per cent from Austria and the rest from Czechoslovakia and Italy. The first group of twelve children came to Palestine in October 1932 at the initiative of Recha Freier of Berlin. The following year, under the overall leadership of Henrietta Szold, and the official support of the

Zionist Congress, the project expanded with great success. The children who arrived were trained and educated in *kibbutzim*, special institutions (like the Mossad Hinuhi of Mishmar Haemek) and in workshops in the cities.[20]

## ABSORPTION IN AGRICULTURE

Of those who settled on the land, the largest number were absorbed into existing communes or smallholders' cooperatives (*moshavim*).[21] Others, after a period of training in the existing communes and cooperatives, participated in the formation of new communes built on the same lines. A considerable number of the immigrants, especially those who had a sum of money to invest, established themselves in 'middle-class' mixed farming or specialized farm settlements, where new methods of agricultural resettlement were followed.

A survey made on 31 March 1939 established that by then 3,525 German settlers (not counting Youth Aliya groups) had been trained by Hechalutz before coming to Palestine and thereby brought into contact with delegates of the federations of communes they later joined. In some cases, as for instance in Kibbutz Givat Brenner, the new German settlers outnumbered other groups.[22]

German immigrants, trained in the existing communes and the plantation settlements, formed independent units. In the period of unrest after 1936, these units, particularly those formed by graduates of the Youth Aliya movement, served as pioneer outpost settlements.

In both the established and the new settlements, the basic capital equipment was supplied by the official Jewish (Zionist) colonizing agencies and financial institutions, and/or the capital import of the settlers. The absorption of the new German immigration was assisted, however, by loans from the Central Bureau for the Settlement of German Jews, which it made out of contributions set aside for such purposes. The main purpose of the loans was to provide for the buildings to meet the needs of increasing numbers of immigrants. In addition, loans were made (especially to groups preparing for eventual settlement, but also to existing *kibbutzim* or *moshavim*) for machinery, livestock, or other investment needs of the villages that would make possible the productive employment of new hands. A total of £P253,716 was loaned, to the above-mentioned 88 communal organized groups, that absorbed German immigrants at an average of about £P73 per immigrant absorbed. In addition, the

Central Bureau contributed £P30,000 towards the settlement of 1,200 persons in smallholders' cooperatives.

## NEW PATHS

The immigrants from Germany broke new paths, while utilizing all the agricultural experience previously accumulated in Palestine, in establishing 'middle-class' settlements. The middle-class German settlers were diverse, their status defined solely by the settler's ability to invest a capital sum of £P500 of his own in his farm.[23] At the disposal of these settlers were the following amounts of capital:[24]

| CAPITAL | % OF SETTLERS |
|---|---|
| Less than £P600 | 13.6% |
| 600 – 1,000 | 23.9% |
| 1,000 – 1,300 | 13.9% |
| 1,300 – 1,700 | 13.1% |
| 1,700 – 2,000 | 12.6% |
| 2,000 – 2,500 | 12.3% |
| over 2,500 | 10.6% |
| | 100.0% |

The average investment was about £P1,500. That sum was smaller than the amounts usually invested by capitalist settlers in citriculture, but sufficient to equip the small irrigated vegetable, dairy and poultry farms the German settlers founded.

In a typical German middle-class settlement the average age ranged between 37 and 43 at the time of establishment.[25] Many of the settlers had children who were later able to take over from their parents. The occupational distribution in their country of origin of the immigrant settlers from Germany had been:

- 56% merchants and white collar workers
- 34% academics and professionals
- 7% farmers and gardeners (including those who combined trade and farming)
- 3% artisans.

The earliest settlers from Germany immigrated to Palestine in 1933 and 1934, but their rural settlements (with the exception of Ramot Hashavim in 1933) were established between 1934 and 1939. After that time it became very difficult to import capital to Palestine, and this, among other reasons, slowed down the tempo of middle-class settlement.

The movement of middle-class German settlers back to the land was quite spontaneous. It originated among immigrants too old to become farm labourers in the 'colonies' or to enter the communal settlements with their rough living conditions, and yet without sufficient capital or knowledge of local conditions to feel confident of successful adjustment in industry, commerce, or citriculture. For those practical reasons, and for some, because of Zionist sentiments, it seemed best for them to turn their capital to the form of mixed farming already successfully developed in Palestine by the Zionists and PICA. For this their capital was adequate, even sufficient to give them housing and living conditions much better than other mixed farming settlers, and they could expect to live on their income from the first year; assuming, of course, they did most of the work themselves.

Some of the settlers at first carried out their own settlement under the guidance of experienced members of their groups, and with the advice of the German Immigrants' Association of Palestine (*Hitahdut Olej Germania*).[26] Others availed themselves of the services of JCA and EMICA, and finally of special companies founded by the Jewish Agency's 'Central Bureau for the Settlement of German Jews' and financed by the investments for German Jews through the *Haavara* Agency.[27] The *Haavara* continued to function until the Second World War. The total transfer amounted to £P8,100,000 (then $40,419,000). At least the same amount came to Palestine through parallel German commercial and banking transactions. With these funds major industrial enterprises were founded such as Mekorot, the national water works and Rassco, a major land and real estate developer. The *Haavara* transfer was a major factor in making possible the emigration of some 60,000 German Jews to Palestine in the years 1933–1939, and together with the money invested by the emigrants themselves, in providing an incentive for the expansion of agricultural settlement and for general economic development. Many of these settlements could be established only thanks to *Haavara*-related funds, and because the immigrant quota itself could be expanded.[28]

In settlements founded by the Jewish Agency, the groups of settlers were spared the expense of land purchase by being given lease-holdings on JNF land. The agricultural inexperience of the settlers was compensated for by several factors: the presence in the new settlements of members with earlier settling experience in the country, who for a number of years were available for individual guidance and instruction; the preparation of an agricultural plan for the whole settlement; and, in many cases, the founding of a cooperative organization for the purchase and sale of farm products.

The settlements were basically planned on the model of small-area, irrigated, mixed farming groups. They developed, however, in the direction of specialized vegetable and poultry farms, slowly expanding their dairies and fodder cultivation, commensurate with their ability to assimilate the techniques in those fields and to centralize production and marketing. In 1937, 46 per cent of all eggs marketed by Jews came from the German-Jewish settlements, 25 per cent of the vegetables, and somewhat less than 7 per cent of the milk.[29]

The new forms of agricultural settlement developed for the immigrants from Germany were clear evidence of the progress Jewish farming had made by then. Without the lessons of early experiments in mixed farming, and without the growth of an urban market preferring to buy Jewish agricultural produce, instead of Arab, the 'middle-class' settlements could not have succeeded as fast as they did.

## CONTRIBUTIONS IN THE CITY

In the city, too, the immigrants from Germany found the time ripe for introducing Western methods and resources. Earlier settlers had built up the foundations and framework of modern city life. The German immigrants added a modern façade, and gave the city new, modern business practices and housing conditions. The changes introduced by the German immigrants were immediately evident. One had only to walk from an old quarter of Tel Aviv to a new German section to find out. One of the more striking examples of the influence of the German settlers was the neighbourhood of Hadar Hakarmel in Haifa. By 1936 it had some 25,000 inhabitants, at least half of whom came from Germany. It had its own council and was marked by well-built, wide streets, large houses with stores on the ground floor, good water supply, a large public garden and many centres of culture.[30]

The German sections were built in the modern, functionalist architecture imported from Europe. Many Palestinian architects had adopted functionalist designs before the Germans arrived, but in the German sections it was dominant. The German immigrants brought with them many architects schooled in the new theories of le Corbussier, Gropius and the Bauhaus. These new arrivals put an end to eclectic architecture. Skilled and well-trained and having the self-assurance of those coming from the mainstream of the modern movement, these newcomers had no difficulty in winning over the local architects of the new functionalist movement into their camp. As a result, most of the buildings of that period reflected the Bauhaus philosophy as accepted by a spartan and puritanical generation. They were mostly flat-roofed, monochromatic monoliths of stuccoed concrete, with monotonous surfaces broken only by cubistic protrusions or slotted recesses of balconies and there was hardly any articulation of structure or materials, not to mention a complete lack of texture, ornamentation or relief work. This kind of architecture had made a deep impact on the direction that Israeli architecture was to take, an impact that is felt even in present-day Israeli architecture.[31]

The 'German' shops had large windows with goods attractively displayed, and small cards announcing the name of the window dresser. The techniques of German Jewish merchandising, including the establishment of large department stores, were applied in Palestine. German Jews also introduced attractive modern cafés and *pensions*, beauty shops, cosmetics shops, shops manufacturing silver and olive-wood art objects and utensils, Western bookshops, and lending libraries.

In the wake of German immigration came the growth of certain professional functions previously underdeveloped or non-existent. A symphony orchestra,[32] conservatories of music, clinics and an economic research institute in the Jewish Agency all owed their existence to, and were staffed in large part by, German-Jewish immigrants. This was also largely true of the Hebrew University, the Technical High School in Haifa (Reali School) and other academic institutions. The example of the Hebrew University is probably best known. A list of faculty members who taught at the Hebrew University prior to 1933, indicates that 24, more than half of the staff of 45, were either born or educated in Central Europe.[33] Forty-nine additional faculty members of Central European extraction were added to the staff of the University between 1933 and 1938.[34] Cadres of social workers, housing experts, famous medical researchers, and chemists for the laboratories of the agricultural stations were also German-Jewish contributors to the professional and scientific resources of Palestine. Their employment was often facilitated by special grants made through the Jewish Agency.[35]

The evidence is overwhelming in support of the statement by a prominent Israeli sociologist that

It is a noteworthy fact that scarcely any of the various *Landsmannschaften* managed to become a focus for organized cultural patterns of life ... The *Landsmannschaften* of the German immigrants alone assumed somewhat more significance during the late thirties and forties, serving not only as agencies of instrumental help, but also as centres for semi-communal activities ... . Only among these was the maintenance of such a tradition of more than purely private significance.[36]

The effect of German immigration on methods of banking, finance and business in Palestine was very important. Before the German immigration, Palestine had been developed mainly by the investment of capital brought into the country by individual immigrants in enterprises they themselves founded; publicly contributed capital also played a role in investment, of course. After more than a decade, the assets these investments had accumulated represented a substantial basis for securing loans. In addition to British insurance companies, the public agencies seeking loans for expansion found their best money market among the German immigrants, at first while they were still in Germany and later as an investing clientele in Palestine. From November 1933 until 30 June 1939, £P890,000 was invested *in Germany* in the stocks and bonds of several agencies in mandatory Palestine engaged in land purchase, resettlement, water supply and colonizing activities. £P910,000 was invested in industrial and commercial enterprises and in second mortgages.[37] One of the great economic problems of Palestine had always been the scarcity of credit and the high interest rates. The expansion of the money market and the development of trading in Palestine securities, for which the German immigrants were responsible, did not end all Jewish Palestine's financial worries, to be sure, but they certainly alleviated them considerably.

German Jews contributed in significant measure to the very noticeable development of industry during the years after 1932. In 1934–35, it is estimated, about 25 per cent of the new investment in industry was made by German immigrant businessmen. A partial list of the new industrial commodities and services they introduced to Palestine includes: cigars, canned vegetables, insulating materials for building, electric batteries, electric light bulbs, files, screws, steel furniture, carbon paper, typewriter ribbons, medicines, paints, dyeing, baths and pipes, earthenware and ceramics, piano-building.[38]

In part, the new enterprises founded by German Jews in Palestine drew upon skills acquired in Germany; the files of the American Economic Committee for Palestine, for instance, contain details of several projects advanced by experienced German producers for setting up electric light bulb factories. To a very large extent, however, the new industrial enterprises demanded a readjustment by the German immigrant investors to fields they did not know previously. The Jewish Agency Statistical Department's 1936 'Report on the Establishment and Progress of Industrial Undertakings by Immigrants from Germany,' covering 100 firms and 177 entrepreneurs of whom 88 per cent were Germans, showed the following facts regarding the occupations before the arrival of the founders of the new industrial enterprises:[39]

OCCUPATION AND SOCIAL STATUS ABROAD OF FOUNDERS OF INDUSTRIES AMONG IMMIGRANTS FROM GERMANY

| Occupation | Abroad | Status Abroad | | | |
|---|---|---|---|---|---|
| | | Owners | Managers | Workers | Unknown |
| Industry (in an identical branch abroad as in Palestine) | 65 | | | | |
| (in a different branch) | 16 | | | | |
| Total | 81 | 59 | 2 | 18 | 2 |
| Commerce | 55 | 32 | 4 | 16 | 3 |
| Free Occupations | 22 | 16 | | 6 | |
| Clerks | 3 | | | | |
| Unknown | 16 | | | | 16 |
| Total | 177 | 107 | 6 | 43 | 21 |
| % | 100 | 60 | 4 | 24 | 12 |

Of interest are the following facts: more than half of the new industrialists covered by the survey had not been industrialists abroad; only slightly more than one-third were continuing in the same branch of work as they had abroad; only two of all the 177 new industrialists had been plant managers abroad. Under previous conditions in Jewish Palestine, where the industrial workers had to be retrained for that kind of work, the industrialists who had the best chance of success were those with actual plant experience, capable of training their employees. Indeed, Palestine industry had to retrain most of its workers and owners, as the example of German industrialists shows.

## THE PROCESS OF READJUSTMENT

According to a census of Jewish workers taken on 2 March 1937 there were 12,322 workers among the German Jewish settlers in town and city.[40] Together with their dependants, those workers constituted a very large proportion of all the German Jewish immigrants, of whom about 36,500 in all lived in Palestine at the beginning of 1937.[41] The number of workers of German origin in the cities was 6,670. For many German Jews, becoming workers involved readjustment of both occupation and economic and social status.

This process is illuminated by a study of 487 male cases and 169 female cases of 'restratified' and readjusted workers made between September 1935 and January 1936.[42]

For these individuals the period before being put to work was exceptionally short, even considering the prosperous conditions of the time. Of 572 cases covered directly by the inquiry, 170 went immediately to rural settlements or private jobs in agriculture, later turning to urban occupations. Of the remaining 402, 212 or 52 per cent found work immediately; 77 had to wait the following periods of time before they found work:

| Period of Waiting | No. of Persons |
| --- | --- |
| up to 2 weeks | 18 |
| between 2 and 4 weeks | 26 |
| between 4 and 6 weeks | 13 |
| between 6 and 8 weeks | 10 |
| between 2 and 3 months | 5 |
| over 3 months | 4 |

The remainder, 69 persons, waited from one to six months before choosing their work.[43]

The reasons given for delay in accepting or seeking work, as well as for the choice of work and the changing from one occupation to another, suggest some of the problems involved in the process of adjustment. There was among the German immigrants, perhaps more than for others who came to Palestine, a conflict of motives affecting their occupational readjustment. For many, even among the non-Zionists, their treatment in Germany had so shattered their aspirations as to make them wish to recast their lives in totally new ways. It is probable that the extremely high proportion of German

Jews who went into agriculture included most immigrants of that sort, but the same motives no doubt drove some into non-agricultural trades.

A considerable number of urban craftsmen originally planned to settle in agriculture, and many were still working towards that end while in the city.[44] For others, their new-found trades were a welcome release from the academic and mercantile professions in which they had felt out of place in Germany. That seems particularly to have been the case among those who chose cabinet-making, metal-work and skilled construction crafts as their new occupations.[45] Similar cases were fewer among women, most of whom appear to have become maids and laundresses out of necessity and were doing their work with courage, but naturally without real inclination.

On the other hand, economic and other motives made it hard for a number of immigrants to remain in the agricultural and building trades to which they at first went. In this they were no different from other immigrants; but it appears that the German immigrants did not share the attitude of many Eastern European Jewish labourers, who believed that all labour was of equal value and attraction. Among the Germans, particularly among the adults, there seems to have been a greater value placed on skill and professional specialization even in the trades to which readjustment was made. The respect for special skills appears prominently in those first years among the motives for choosing or changing occupations in Palestine.

Thus, some selected entirely new occupations, because there were few opportunities for their old occupations in Palestine or because they wished to start their lives anew on a radically different basis. They became farmers, policemen, or metal and wood-workers. Others, who found no opportunity to go on with their old trades or professions, chose trades as close as possible to their former ones, hoping later to reestablish themselves in their original professions. Alternatively, they tried to get into easily learned, or relatively well and securely paid trades, or trades they had once practised in their student days.[46] Still others, who in Palestine moved from agricultural to urban trades, did so because wages were too low or too seasonal, or because they needed more money for their parents, or because of sickness, or because the work was too hard, or, in some cases, because adjustment to rural life or the life in collective communities proved too difficult.[47] Among those who in Palestine changed their occupations in the cities, the same reasons, insofar as they were applicable to both town and country, were given, and in addition some added that their firms or their employers' firms had gone out of business, either because of insufficient capital or other reasons. Of all the cases studied, *64 per cent had not had to change* their new occupations in Palestine, and of the 36 per cent who changed their new occupations, 149 out of 190 cases changed only once, 28 twice, and only 13 more than twice.[48]

Since the statistical basis of the study cited is not clearly stated, it cannot be used as an indication of occupational distribution. Of all the new trades learned, the study showed the building industry to be most important for men: 26.7 per cent of all cases of occupational changes were found to have occurred in the building trades, divided about equally between skilled and unskilled workers. There were 130 such cases, of whom 80 had been in mercantile trades in Germany, 15 in academic or professional occupations, and 26 in industries or crafts other than building. Next in order of importance were metal-workers, and taxi, truck, and bus drivers, the first with 13.1 per cent of all cases of occupational readjustment, the second with 10.5 per cent, constituting, together with the builders, slightly more than 50 per cent of all cases. The other new occupations, listed in order of importance, were wood and furniture, commercial and technical, hotel and restaurant, tile and brick, electrical, chemical, transport servicing, street and window cleaning, clothing, and miscellaneous other trades. In Germany this 50 per cent had worked in commerce (54 per cent), in academic and professional positions (27.4 per cent – including students) and in industry and crafts (12.6 per cent – chiefly in the metal-working, food, and clothing industries).[49]

A similar radical change in occupational and living habits was made by German Jewish women. The chief non-agricultural occupation for German women was domestic service, with 58 of 169 cases. Domestic service performed somewhat the same function for women as the building trades for men: it was the receiving centre for new, untried workers, and the refuge to which they turned when they could not find work in other fields. Next in importance were hotel and restaurant or café jobs (39 cases), clothing and clerkships (30 cases), commercial (20 cases) and retail store positions (11 cases).

Smaller numbers transferred to metal-working, food and drink, textiles, wood and furniture, paper, photography, transport service, road building, and book and periodical selling. In Germany the largest number of these women had not worked; of those who had been employed, 54 were in commercial occupations, 46 in academic or professional careers, ten were seamstresses, modistes, window dressers, and photography workers, and two were gardeners.[50]

## ORGANIZATION FOR REFUGEE AID IN THE CITIES

In their adjustment, the German immigrants to the cities had the assistance of various organizations, in greater measure and in a more effective manner as the years passed. But compared with the farm settlers, the assistance was improvised and amateurish.

The very first aid these immigrants got was the advice and instruction received in Germany from the Hechalutz Organization and the bureaus for prospective emigrants set up by the Jewish communities. In addition to assistance in arranging emigration, the organizations aided the refugees in acquiring new trades. Hechalutz, of course, concentrated on agricultural training; of the 170 cases in Dr. Britschgi-Schimmer's study who went into agriculture and later transferred to urban trades, only 72 had farm training in the Diaspora. In addition to the 72 trained in farming, 62 others had training in crafts, about half by individual apprenticeship and many others in courses organized by Jewish communities in Germany and France. Altogether, therefore, only about ¼ of the cases studied had occupational retraining already in the Diaspora. But very few had more than a year or a year and a half of training. In addition to the short duration of the course, it frequently turned out that what had been learned was not suited to the conditions of the trade in Palestine. As a result, for instance, about half of those with Diaspora training as carpenters and metal workers found themselves compelled to take unskilled work in Palestine.[51]

The deficiencies in training necessitated further retraining in Palestine. Considerable efforts were made to teach the immigrants Hebrew, as a necessary prerequisite to adjustment. In addition, the Jewish Agency's 'Central Bureau for German Jews' arranged formal vocational courses in cooperation with the General Federation of Labour and the Organization of German Jews in Palestine, the 'Hitachdut Olej Germania,' founded in 1932. In Tel Aviv those courses, mainly in the building trades, were offered by the Max Pine Trade School of the *Histadrut*, and in Haifa at the Technical High School, a Jewish Agency institution; in Jerusalem a course was also arranged for training stonemasons.[52] The immigrants in training received loans and assistance in getting part-time work during their courses. For women the Women's Council of the *Histadrut* and the WIZO (Women's International Zionist Organization) arranged similar courses in suitable trades.

The efforts at vocational retraining at first showed certain inadequacies, that in later years had to be corrected: the courses were found to be too short; the trade teachers were not trained in pedagogical methods; the students in classes were not homogeneous, nor sufficiently selected.

Another form of retraining, to which 47 of the men covered by Dr. Britschgi-Schimmer's study were admitted, was apprenticeship, mainly in the building trades, arranged through the *Histadrut*. The workers were hired on two arrangements: their low pay for apprentices was raised either after fixed periods or after production tests had been passed. For the immigrants, the apprenticeship form of retraining had the advantage of bringing in income and of acquainting the worker with actual trade conditions. Many of the workers in training, however, felt the need of systematic theoretical instruction, and in some cases that was arranged.[53]

During their readjustment, many of the new immigrants were in need of financial support. Of the cases studied, 106 had taken loans from various institutions. The chief reasons given for borrowing money included the necessity to take vocational training, to cover deficits in the current budget, to invest in a business, and to cover medical expenses. The largest individual loans were taken in order to enter transport cooperatives. The chief sources of loans were personal friends, the Organization of German Jews in Palestine, and the *Histadrut* Savings and Loan Societies. They were divided as follows: (a) Private sources: 13 loans amounting to £P2,327; (b) Organization of German Jews in Palestine: 45 loans amounting to £P1,175; (c) *Histadrut* Savings and Loan Societies: 22 loans amounting to £P445. The *Hitachdut Olej Germania* as well as other savings and loan societies received funds from the Jewish Agency's Central Bureau for the Settlement of German Jews to facilitate loans to the refugees.[54]

The material rewards the immigrants obtained after the rapid readjustment were minimal and for many, perhaps most of the cases, a long hard road stretched ahead before the immigrants could find their situation entirely satisfactory. But what had already been achieved in a short time was certainly an outstanding example of adjustment.

## SOME CONCLUSIONS

The adjustment of German Jews to new occupations took place in non-agricultural as well as in agricultural trades in Palestine. During the years of mass immigration and prosperity, the adjustment of those who were able to change their trades was accomplished with a remarkable degree of speed and success.[55] In the early years there was little institutional guidance available for the immigrant wishing to adjust in a non-agricultural trade, and the makeshift arrangements rapidly devised became effective only later. Nevertheless, the readjustment and retraining programme achieved a great deal. The primary elements favouring readjustment were the general acceptance of occupational change as a continuous requirement of the whole community, not only of the refugees, the prestige of the manual trades into which transfer was made, and, above all, the assistance of the already established and experienced Jewish community.

For certain classes of German Jews, however, and particularly after 1936 when times were harder, readjustment was difficult.[56] Lawyers had little chance of adjusting in their own trades, and physicians who tried to practise, if they obtained one of the restricted number of licences, had a hard row to hoe.[57] Actors became streethawkers while trying to adjust, and writers often continued to write in German. There was no social case work available for social workers; and many of them were, perforce, added to the overcrowded ranks of small retail shopkeepers in the Palestine cities.

Many of the German immigrants who went directly into agriculture in those first years became an immediate success. Well over a quarter of the German immigrants became farmers or farm hands, a proportion much greater than in earlier immigrant groups from other countries. The immigrants from Germany proved themselves exemplary in organized rural settlements and methodical agricultural planning in areas entirely new in Palestinian Jewish land-development.

### NOTES

1. Palestine Government, *A Survey of Palestine (1946)*, I, pp.233–7, 255–60; *Supplement to Survey of Palestine* (Jerusalem 1947), pp.31–2.
2. A. Granovsky, *Land Policy in Palestine* (New York 1940), pp.90 ff.
   See text table 10 in David Gurevich and A. Gertz, *Ha-Hityashvut ha-haklait ha-Ivrit*

be-Eretz Israel (1938), p.18.
4. See, e.g., Dr. Arthur Ruppin's Report to the Eleventh Zionist Congress of 1913, reprinted in his *Three Decades of Palestine* (Jerusalem 1936), pp.35–65.
5. Israel Margalith, *Le Baron Edmond de Rothschild et la colonisation juive en Palestine, 1882–1899* (Paris 1957), pp.136–45.
6. See Granovsky, *Land Policy*, pp.17–85.
7. A. Bein, *The Return to the Soil* (1952), pp.15–25, 44ff.
8. Ruppin, *Three Decades*, pp.13 ff., 20–25, 26 ff., 39 ff.
9. Ruppin, *Three Decades*, pp.12 ff. and Arthur Ruppin, *Hahityashvut Hahaklait shel Hahistadrut Hazionit be-Eretz Yisrael* (Tel Aviv 1925).
10. A brief general survey on the issue of settling middle-class Jews in Palestine prior to the Fifth Aliya is contained in Oren Amiram, 'Ha-hityashvut ha-haklait shel olei Germania bnei ha-maamad ha-benoni bishnot ha-shloshim: nizanim shel zurat hityashvut hadashah,' unpublished M.A. thesis, the Hebrew University, 1985, pp.1–11. For a brief recent overview see Mordechai Eliav, 'German Jews' Share in the Building of the National Home in Palestine and the State of Israel,' *LBIYB*, XXX (1985), pp.255–63. For a much more comprehensive overview see Margarete Turnowsky-Pinner, *Die Zweite Generation Mitteleuropaeischer Siedler in Israel* (Tuebingen 1962). See also Miriam Getter, 'Ha-aliyah mi-Germania Ba-Shanim 1933–1939,' *Cathedra*, No. 12 (July 1979), pp.125–47.
11. See Eva Belling, *Die Gesellschaftliche Eingliederung der deutschen Einwanderer in Israel* (Frankfurt 1967).
12. On this subject see Nusi Sznaider, 'Between Past and No Future. A Study of German Jews in Palestine,' unpublished M.A. Thesis, Tel Aviv University, 1984 and Curt Wormann, 'German Jews in Israel: The Cultural Situation', *Leo Baeck Institute Year Book*, XV (1970), pp.73–103.
13. See Miriam Getter, 'ha-hitargenut ha-politit ha-nifredet shel olei Germania,' *Hazionut*, VII (1981), pp.240–91.
14. Information about settlement possibilities for German Jews on the land was made available in Germany. See e.g. 'Vereinigten Komitee fuer die Ansiedlung deutscher Juden in Palaestina, Landwirtschaftliche Ansiedlung von deutschen Juden in Palaestina. Bericht ueber den Stand im Sommer 1933' (September 1933). This was a pamphlet published by the 'Palaestina-Amt der Jewish Agency for Palestine' which was housed in Meinekestrasse 10, the headquarters of the Zionistische Vereinigung fuer Deutschland. See also Arthur Ruppin, 'Die Ansiedlung von Juden aus Deutschland in Palaestina,' Referat auf dem XVIII. Zionisten-Kongress in Prag (1933) in *Dreissig Jahre Aufbau in Palaestina* (Berlin 1937), pp.331–41.
15. According to a Jewish Telegraphic Agency dispatch dated 12 April 1940, the Jewish Agency's Central Bureau for Settlement of German Jews estimated at that time that the number of Palestine residents coming from Nazi-occupied countries was 63,500. Total immigration between 1933 and 1948 was 265,000. See Shmuel N. Eisenstadt, *Israeli Society* (London 1967), p.11.
16. Keren Hayesod, *Palestine and Jewish Emigration from Germany*, p.14.
17. Jewish Agency Central Bureau for Settlement of German Jews, *Report to XXIst Zionist Congress*, pp.74, 76–7.
18. Central Bureau, *Report to XIXth Congress*, p.31; Ludwig Pinner, *Ansiedlung von 675 Familien aus Deutschland*, p.126.
19. Keren Hayesod, *Palestine and Jewish Emigration from Germany*, p.19.
20. See *Aliyat Hanoar, Korot Hamifal* (Jerusalem 1968), pp.10–24 and Recha Freier, *Let the Children Come. The Early History of Youth Aliyah* (London 1961), pp.17–21.
21. Immigrants from Germany established: Kfar Yedidyah, Ramat Hadar, Bet Yitzhak, Gan Hashomron, Kfar Shmaryahu, Kfar Bialik, Meged (partly German), Shavei Zion, Moledet, Sde Warburg, Ramot Hashavim. The town of Nahariya also

began in 1935 as a *moshava* of German Jews. See Amiram, 'Ha-hityashvut ha-haklait shel olei Germania,' pp.27ff. Amiram deals with the various settlements mentioned here except Moledet and Meged.
22. Central Bureau, *Report to the XXIst Congress*, pp.34ff.
23. Pinner, *Ansiedlung von 675 Familien*, p.14. Some 23,000 German Jewish immigrants belonged to the group of 'capitalists' or the group classified by the Mandate authorities in category AI – those immigrants possessing at least £P1,000. The 'capitalists' brought £P23 million to Palestine. See Nadav Halevi, *Ha-Hitpathut ha-kalkalit shel ha-yishuv ha-yehudi be-Eretz Israel 1917–1947* (Jerusalem 1967), p.37.
24. Pinner, *Ansiedlung von 675 Familien*, p.97.
25. *Ibid.*, pp.85ff.
26. (HOG) Founded in 1932, and later changing its name to Irgun olej Merkaz Europa (IOME), to reflect the fact that not only German Jews, but Jews from Central Europe were serviced by this organization as well. In 1942 German Jews founded a political party – 'Aliyah Hadashah' which was unsuccessful and disbanded in 1948. See Miriam Getter, 'Ha-hitargenut ha-politit ha-nifredet shel olei Germania,' *Hazionut*, VII (1981), pp.240–91 and Yael Yishai, "Aliyah Hadashah, 'u-beayat ha-haverut ha-kfulah be-Mapai,' *Zionism*, VI (1980), pp.241–73.
27. See *Juedische Rundschau*, 23 May 1933 and Werner Feilchenfeld, Dolf Michaelis and Ludwig Pinner, *Haavara-Transfer nach Palaestina und Einwanderung deutscher Juden, 1933–1939* (Tuebingen 1972).
28. Ludwig Pinner, 'Vermoegenstransfer nach Palaestina 1933–1939,' *In Zwei Welten* (Tel Aviv 1962), pp.133–66.
29. Pinner, *Ansiedlung von 675 Familien*, pp.109, 116, 117.
30. Zeev Vilnay, *Haifa beavar uva-hoveh* (Tel Aviv 1936), pp.113–14. See also Abraham Granovsky, *Land Policy in Palestine*, pp.162–81.
31. Amiram Harlap, *New Israeli Architecture* (East Brunswick and London 1982), pp.46–7.
32. When Bronislav Huberman founded the Philharmonic Orchestra in Palestine in 1936, he informed Ben-Gurion that 53 musicians came from abroad: 30 from Germany, four from Austria, 12 from Poland, three from Holland and four from Hungary. See Shlomo Erel, *Hayekim-Hamishim Shnot Aliyah* (Herzliyah 1985), p.27.
33. See *Die Hebraeische Universitaet Jerusalem, Entwicklung und Bestand* (Jerusalem 1938).
34. For the list and biographical data on the staff see S. Erel, *Neue Wurzeln* (Gerlingen 1983). For the list of teachers from Germany in the Reali School in Haifa during the 1930s see Sh. Halprin, *Doctor A. Biram u'beit Hasefer Hareali* (Jerusalem 1970), pp.220–21.
35. Jewish Agency, Central Bureau for the Settlement of German Jews, *Report to XIXth Zionist Congress* (1935), pp.51ff. *Report to XXth Zionist Congress* (1937), pp.53ff. See also Curt Wormann, 'Kulturelle Probleme und Aufgaben der Juden aus Deutschland in Israel seit 1933,' in Hans Tramer (ed.), *In Zwei Welten* (Tel Aviv 1962), pp.280–329.
36. Shmuel N. Eisenstadt, *The Absorption of Immigrants* (London 1954), p.55.
37. *Report to XXIst Zionist Congress* (1939), p.45.
38. Keren Hayesod, *Palestine and Jewish Emigration from Germany*, pp.26ff.
39. *Ibid.*, pp.25–6.
40. *Census of Jewish Labour in Pinkas*, No. 8, supplement to *Davar*, 1938, p.22.
41. cf. Central Bureau, *Report to XXth Zionist Congress*, pp.17 and 109.
42. Dr. Ira Britschgi-Schimmer, *Die Umschichtung der juedischen Einwanderer aus Deutschland zu Staedtischen Berufen in Palaestina* (Jerusalem 1936). Published in mimeographed form by the Central Bureau for the Settlement of German Jews.
43. *Ibid.*, pp.27ff.

44. *Ibid.*, pp.34ff.
45. *Ibid.*, pp.24ff.
46. *Ibid.*, pp.19ff., 23ff.
47. *Ibid.*, pp.31ff.
48. *Ibid.*, pp.36ff.
49. *Ibid.*, Appendix, Tables I and II.
50. *Ibid.*, Appendix, Table III.
51. *Ibid.*, pp.41ff.
52. *Ibid.*, pp.44ff.
53. *Ibid.*, pp.47ff.
54. *Ibid.*, pp.68ff. Central Bureau, *Report to XXIst Zionist Congress*, pp.42ff.
55. See Eva Beling, *Die gesellschaftliche Eingliederung der deutschen Einwanderer in Israel. Eine soziologische Untersuchung der Einwanderer aus Deutschland zwischen 1933 und 1945* (Frankfurt am Main 1967).
56. See Gerda Luft, *Heimkehr ins Unbekannte, Eine Darstellung der Einwanderung aus Deutschland nach Palaestina 1933–1939* (Wuppertal 1977).
57. Nevertheless the German Jewish physicians had an important impact on the practice of medicine in Palestine. See Doron Niederland, 'Hashpaat ha-rofim ha-olim mi-Germania al hitpathut ha-refua be-Eretz Israel,' *Cathedra*, No. 30 (December 1983), pp.111–60.

# 11

## The Emotional Elements in Ben-Gurion's Relation to the Diaspora during the Holocaust*

### Tuvia Friling

Early in the summer of 1936, Ben-Gurion flew from Rome to London. On his arrival he described the flight in his diary:

> Ten in the morning in Rome – ten at night in London, and that after we stopped in Milan, Frankfurt, Cologne, Amsterdam, Rotterdam – a journey 1,928 kilometres long. Of all the times I have flown, this journey was the most interesting, especially the hour-and-a-half crossing over Switzerland. About halfway between Rome and Milan, the earth was hidden in clouds, and it looked as if it had been well soaped and was wrapped in waves of white foam – so small, a green island glimpsed underneath which vanished at once. This was how we passed over Florence without seeing it, but as we neared the Po basin the skies cleared – not the sky, the earth – and northern Italy was revealed spread out in all its greenness. The hills, the slopes, the plains and valleys – all wrapped in green grass, wheat, orchards, not one inch left bare, uncultivated. The streams of the Po divide up the whole countryside and give the landscape variety. But this is only the prologue to what is to come after Milan, the overflowing splendour of the high snow-mountains, the shining blue-green lakes, the forests inset among the rocky ribs of the mountains, the dark gulfs stretching between the towering rock-ridges, the flashing ribbons of the waterfalls twisting and turning and vanishing on the steep

---

* This paper draws on my Ph.D dissertation which is now being completed at The Hebrew University of Jerusalem, under the supervision of Professor Yehuda Bauer.

slopes, and tiny towns and villages like children's toys set deep in wooded terrain that looks like one continuous green roof stretched over the distances and the depths, and again lakes and the crests of cliffs and the white of snow and the green of forests and the rejoicing wheat fields and vineyards, and here and there clouds, pile on pile outspread on the valley and on the mountain of rock at its head, and all this underneath you, while above you fan out the blue-green mists of the high heavens' wide horizons, and you are flying over the tops of the mountains spread out there, and not a single moment resembles the one before and you haven't yet taken in one wonderful picture when there is another hurrying towards you and gone in one glimpse, for a new lake is laid out below and new mountains crown it and the whiteness of the snow shines in their crevices, the forests turn green, mountain pursues mountain and behind a valley hides another valley, and the eye is not sated with this great sight that flees and escapes and returns new and different and hides at once and re-appears in the flicker of an eyelid in renewed garb of mountains and snow and green of leaves and blue of lakes and the darkness of the gulfs – you are breathless, as if there isn't air to breathe, because the plane soars over the heads of the mountain-tops to a height of 3,000 metres and more, and though the throb of the engines is deafening it seems to you that this awesome majesty pouring out beneath you is anointed in the silence of eternity like the unheard sounds of an enchanted song singing joyfully in your heart ... Here is Locarno at the end of the 'Big Lake' and soon Lucerne and immediately thereafter Zurich and at once Constance, and the mountains are shut off and the humpbacked plain of Germany unrolls before you – no more snow, nor the blue of lakes, only green fields and villages and rivers and the thin strip of railwaylines till you near Frankfurt. The enchantment has vanished and you only think of Hitler and you grieve over the rejoicing, bountiful fields contaminated by the swastika, and only after you leave behind you the Bear rearing up on his hind legs on the banks of the Rhine as it flows through Cologne and you approach the lowlands of the Dutch canals do you breathe freely, and it is with a lighter feeling that you get out at Amsterdam and Rotterdam and not at Frankfurt or Cologne ...[1]

This lyrical description, possibly influenced by Bialik, does not fit in with one's perception of Ben-Gurion. Although there are quite a few descriptions like the one above in his diary in different contexts and in his letters, mainly to members of his family, they are not a striking feature of his writings and are not characteristic of him. All the same one should not ignore their existence.

This particular example may serve as a convenient prologue to a discussion on the question of how 'human' Ben-Gurion was in the period of the Holocaust. A rather strange question, one need hardly point out, since it means our wondering whether Ben-Gurion experienced the Holocaust period just like other people, a question that stems from Ben-Gurion's image as a 'dry' and matter-of-fact leader capable of taking hard and even very cruel decisions in the hour of trial.

This question fans out into others, such as: What, if anything, did he know about the catastrophe at all? Did he perhaps try to avoid knowing the magnitude of the disaster and seal himself off from it? If he did know, did he relate to the knowledge? What, if anything, did he say and write about the Holocaust and the Jews of the Golah who were being wiped out there? What terms did he use, what sort of language, what words? If he did speak and write about it, in what setting was this? – in intimacy, within himself, or with people close to him, or in large, declaratory public settings as well? Did the nature of the setting dictate the nature of his words? What did he think about it – not just as a politician but as the leader who was bound to keep a cool head in the face of even a disaster like this, bound to carry on as the leader and to dig out from under the rubble whatever was still to be retrieved, even 'small' things? What did Ben-Gurion think as a private person, as an ordinary human being? Did he suffer with fraternal pain? And if so, how did he express his suffering and his anger? His frustration, perhaps?

Most if not all of these questions seek a Ben-Gurion who is not 'dry,' impassive, hard and cold, but a human Ben-Gurion with tears in his eyes. We shall direct our comments towards isolating this aspect of the man, even if we do not seek to draw any world-startling conclusions.

The question of 'knowing' is extremely complicated and needs further discussion that lies outside the bounds of this essay. So here we shall present the first link only in this matter, the danger in store for the Jewish people as Ben-Gurion envisaged it. The description of the aeroplane flight serves as an excellent example, for we can discover to what extent certain expressions stealthily crept into Ben-Gurion's way of speaking – both in public and in private –

expressions that showed his harsh forebodings of approaching disaster.

To what extent was Ben-Gurion, to whom a unique political intuition and an extraordinary capacity for prediction were attributed, sensitive to the ominous signs emanating from Europe? How did he interpret and analyze international developments and their impact on Jewish affairs since the rise of Hitler to power?

Scrutiny of the very extensive documentation that Ben-Gurion left behind him brings to light his intensive preoccupation with the international situation along with Hitler's rise to power and the consequences he foresaw for the fate of the Jewish people and the Zionist movement. This preoccupation of his is revealed in an analysis covering a number of motifs extensively documented and referred to in a variety of ways: (1) an inevitable world war; (2) a disaster of enormous dimensions in store for the Jewish people; (3) the Jewish people, caught in a terrible trap, bound to be abandoned; (4) the only basic Jewish solution is the Zionist one and the Yishuv has the historic duty and mission to carry it out.

In the course of a visit to Poland in April 1933, only a short time after Hitler took power, Ben-Gurion already described the danger in store for the Jewish people, which would be the first victim of oppression, loss of freedom and dictatorship. He averred that a world war was to be expected that would bring world-wide destruction and the massacring of Jews.[2] Some time later, early in 1934 after reading *Mein Kampf*, Ben-Gurion dwelt on the dangers embodied in the Hitler regime and affirmed, 'The disaster that has befallen German Jewry is not confined within the bounds of Germany alone. Hitler's rule endangers the entire Jewish people ...: Judaism is quintessentially different from Nazi teachings, and so the war Hitler has declared on the Jews of Germany is not specific to them alone, it has been declared on all the Jews in the world.' The Jewish people, the bearer of the ideas of justice, peace and freedom, stands on the ideological plane – as an obstacle to 'Satan [Hitler] in his ambition to have the German race rule the world. War is at the basis of the Nazi regime, which cannot exist without it. Hitler will start a war the moment he is ready, and it will cost more in victims and frightfulness than anything known before.' Ben-Gurion also fixed a time-table: 'between us and that awful Doomsday there lie perhaps no more than four or five years (if not less).' There are many more examples to illustrate this.[3]

Ben-Gurion was a *'homo politicus' par excellence*, not only on account of his character, but also by virtue of his role and the sense of his mission that was always with him as the one bringing the people to its Land and its State. Keeping track of international events and analysing them, he drew his forebodings of approaching disaster from the reactions of the democratic world to the increasing number of breaches of the Versailles Treaty's various provisions and from the series of critical events which in his view embodied a rearguard action against Nazism and Fascism on the part of the democratic world.[4] Among these he counted the Abyssinian Crisis (1935), the Spanish Civil War (1936), and the Sudeten Crisis and the Munich Agreement in its wake (1938-39). All these combined for him into a whole historical structure with its own internal even if crazed logic, with its end war and momentous disaster for the Jewish people.[5]

Ben-Gurion wrote with great bitterness about the surrender of the two great democracies to the German dictates; after the Sudeten crisis he affirmed that the handing over of the Czechs to the Nazis must undermine faith in alliances and undertakings and glorify the prestige of Hitler and the totalitarian system, and he noted: 'A new and fearful disaster will befall the Jews of Europe.' In all these crises – Ethiopia, Spain, China, and Czechoslovakia – the democratic world was 'consistent,' he said, in giving way to the aggressor and it would be so with regard to the Jewish question, too. Help for the Jews was not 'current coin in wide circulation these days. Hitler has broken the strength of the Jews and the handing over of Czechoslovakia finished the job ... Hitler will rule over Europe ... European Jewry no longer has anything to rely on ...'

In this intolerable forecast of his, Ben-Gurion described the powerlessness of the Jewish communities and the vice they were caught in: on the one hand the direct and indirect Nazi threat and the unfounded belief – the 'illusion' – that there was a Power friendly to them that would not abandon them, and on the other hand absence of any capacity to act. What could they do? Would they protest? And if so, how would the protest get through the various channels? And if it reached the [British] Government, would Malcolm [Macdonald] or Neville [Chamberlain] read the article in *Haint* or hear a protest presented in Pinsk? He ended with these words: 'In my mind's eye I see world cataclysms that will overturn the whole world ...'[6]

The Czech precedent, Ben-Gurion summed up, showed that in this 'realistic' period of ours, neither 'uprightness, nor justice, nor law nor solemn undertakings decide things – only physical power ..."[7] He noted that 'this is the age of "Power Politics".' He added that in this period 'moral values are invalidated, the claims of equity and justice are bereft of force. The ears of the rulers are closed – they can hear nothing but the voice of the guns. The Jews in the Golah don't have guns.'⁸ In this situation he viewed the Jewish people as 'stripped of assets.'⁹

The lesson that Ben-Gurion learnt from the Czech affair and the successive crises and the way they were 'settled' exacerbated his sense of a general disaster at the gates. Even if one could not foresee exactly the details and the extent of the disaster, Ben-Gurion felt that all the conditions for it had been 'created,'¹⁰ and he spoke explicitly again and again of the extermination of the Jewish people:

> No-one knows what is in store for the world in the years ahead, what changes are possible not only in relations between the peoples but also in their internal regimes. The outbreak of world war – which the Arabs are praying for so hard – will again face us with the danger of being handed over and utterly abandoned ... Hitler is not only the enemy and destroyer of German Jewry. What his envious, sadistic soul desires is the extermination of the Jews in the whole world.¹¹

The *Kristallnacht* was another brick laid in the structure of Ben-Gurion's analysis of the situation. At an assembly that convened in Jerusalem on 12 December 1938, Ben-Gurion gave his listeners an overall description of the situation and he pointed out a significant chronological link between *Kristallnacht* and the international situation, the general 'folding up' of the Powers:

> From time to time a historical date is renewed for us. We thought that 1933 was a new date in the history of torture and persecution of the Jews. We Zionists certainly did not underestimate the kind of disaster that befell German Jewry and Jewry in the world in 1933 with Hitler's rise to power. But even the pessimists among us could not have imagined what was in store for us from this evil, murderous regime. The month of November 1938 provides us with a new date or a new chapter without precedent in Jewish martyrology. This is not persecution, not deportation – it is organized extermination, the physical extermination along with sadistic outrages of a whole Jewish collectivity, the 600,000 Jews of Germany and Austria. But it is more than that. The Nazi pogrom of November is a signal for the extermination of the Jewish people in the whole world. May I be proved wrong. Up to now even Satan himself dare not commit atrocities like these. Now the rein has been unloosed. Our lives, our dignity, our possessions are given over, and there are no limits to the wrong it is possible to do to the Jews.

He reverted to the prophecy of extermination in different forms. 'There may be a war that will bring a holocaust upon us. ... Hitler's there and he can be relied on for this ... If there is a world war, he will carry it out; first of all he will exterminate the Jews of Europe.'[12]

What then was the nature of this prophecy, these feelings and forebodings of evil that Ben-Gurion built up systematically, laying brick upon brick, as he linked the complicated international situation with the growing strength of anti-Semitism as one of the murderous features of this situation? What was the nature of this prophecy, on the basis of which he appealed again and again – and even remained more than once in the minority – for a large-scale Zionist 'catastrophe policy,' for energetic and urgent practical action, for a fight for a 'militant Zionism?'[13]

What was the nature of this abundant use of expressions of disaster, catastrophe, ruination, destruction, physical extermination of the Jewish people – expressions that Ben-Gurion made use of more than any other Zionist leader – and what was the content he poured into them? Did they really signify the same thing as they did after the Holocaust? Was there any development in the course of the war and after it in the content filling these ideas? Did Ben-Gurion prophesy the Holocaust?

As already stated, this question calls for separate discussion and a review of the war period in all its complexity. We shall rest content therefore with the affirmation that Ben-Gurion did foresee many fundamentals of the situation in store for the Jews, and others not at all. He was right in 'prophesying war' and in foreseeing the democratic world's turning away from the Jews, and he was also right in his description of the Jewish people's helplessness, both in Europe and in the free world, and in his description of the trap into which it fell. He was right in his description of the place of the Yishuv and the mission that would be incumbent on it in the long run. He mistook the force of the prospective disaster. He did not see – perhaps he could not have foreseen – the way in which the murderous ideology would be translated in action into planned, systematic, collective extermination.

To return to the example we started with and to the matter of emotion, to the expression of the sense of solidarity, to those tears that we are on the track of. That first example can also serve as a convenient prologue to this particular theme, because it is a striking display of a side of Ben-Gurion 'not like Ben-Gurion' at all, and also because it exemplifies his capacity for unconventional expression. In the example in question we find a definite political message even among the very personal and very private expressions there, and this is a common enough phenomenon in his letters to members of his family, some of which he used to have passed on to be read by people in the 'national institutions' like Moshe Sharett, Berl Katznelson and others. How he recorded entries in his diary was no routine matter either: at the most dramatic moments he would note down laconically one or two lines in the middle of the 'dry' sequence of data, brief summations of a complex situation and of his own stormy emotions. Nor did he restrain his personal feelings, even stressing them in front of large audiences in very public settings.

From here on we shall deal with the questions that we have raised in the perspective of the settings in which Ben-Gurion said or wrote the things that illustrated his feelings towards the Jews of the Golah in the Holocaust period. For this purpose we shall divide these settings into three main types:

(A) Large public forums: what was said there was also meant to serve declaratory ends. Among these were big public meetings, elected Yishuv assemblies, and the committees and councils of the different parties.
(B) Restricted settings: their main characteristic was their constituting a forum for making reports and planning action, for analyses and drawing conclusions afterwards. These settings were mainly implementing, executive bodies or bodies that were convened for a defined purpose connected with carrying out a given programme. Among them were the Jewish Agency Executive, limited bodies of MAPAI and the Histadrut, committees and *ad hoc* sessions for such purposes as fund-raising.
(C) Intimate settings: among these we shall include Ben-Gurion's diary entries, letters to members of his family, private meetings and personal answers to people asking for his help.

Before we proceed with our examination in this framework we have proposed, we must devote a little space to the basic questions whether Ben-Gurion knew and in what detail he knew of the events in Europe. The answers will emerge clearly from the examples in each of three settings that will be presented below, but before we begin we have to make it clear that Ben-Gurion was the centre of attraction for a constant flow of very varied information, certainly also in connection with what was happening in Europe – before the war, in its first stages and later on as well. For this there are at least two explanations:

The first explanation is institutional, executive, and bound up with the customary methods of work in the Jewish Agency and other offices; a copy of all incoming material that was deemed important was also sent to the Agency chairman's office. Moreover, because of the institutional bureaucratic thicket characterizing the Jewish Agency Executive and its branches in that period and also because of unclear delineation of functions, duplication and so forth, the same incoming information was received from numerous offices.[14]

The second explanation is a personal one connected with Ben-Gurion himself. He was the type of executive who wants to know every aspect, scrutinizing, learning, curious even about things that seemed marginal and outside the defined sphere of concern of the person heading the hierarchy. This was especially true of topics that were central to the Zionist movement and fulfilling his responsibilities as its leader. He wanted to know what was happening to the human 'reservoir' of the Zionist movement, and it is not by chance that I selected this cynical definition 'reservoir.' For even if his attitude to people was instrumental, as some maintain, he had to know what was happening to the 'human infrastructure' on which he based his political programmes, including the Biltmore Programme. Further, as to the question of detailed, exact information, Ben-Gurion was not content with the institutional channels of information, not on this subject and not in general, and this too was characteristic of his line of action. On his own initiative he would get hold of people in every sphere, would question them about whatever he considered vital.[15] It must also be remembered that Ben-Gurion was notably addicted to newspapers of all kinds, both at home and when he was abroad.

Finally, it must be remembered that during his stay in the USA, Ben-Gurion met people who had information on the extermination. As early as July 1942 he himself took part in at least one public protest against the extermination.[16]

From what we have said so far, it is clear that all the information on what was happening in Europe had reached him, and the question of whether he knew receives a clear affirmative answer well before the official publication in the Yishuv.[17]

Let us pass on then to the questions we raised in accordance with the different settings:

## A. LARGE PUBLIC SETTINGS

These settings call for the use of rhetoric which will strike home to the listeners in accord with the degree of sincerity behind the spoken words. This clearly applies to Ben-Gurion and also to his approach to the Jews of the Golah in the Holocaust period.

On 20 November 1942, a week after the Jewish Agency Executive published its declaration on the extermination in Europe, an emergency meeting of the council of the Yishuv representatives was called with Ben-Gurion as the main speaker. He said *inter alia*:

> The emissaries of the Jewish people in its Homeland are assembled here today to cry out from Mount Zion to the people of the whole world against the spilling of Jewish blood for no reason, against the danger of extermination that awaits the entire Jewish people in Poland and in the other countries of the Nazi conquest and against the abasement of our Jewish dignity all over the world.
>
> We do not know precisely what abominations are being perpetrated in the Nazi vale of slaughter, how many Jews have already been butchered, murdered, burnt to death, buried alive, and how many are still there with the sword of extermination hanging over them. The Nazi place of execution is hemmed in by a rampart of machine-guns and specialist hangmen, none enters and none leaves. Only from time to time do atrocious deeds and frightfulness break through to us. Only from time to time does the cry of Jewish blood reach us, the cry of women and children, broken to bits and trampled underfoot. But we do know what Hitler is conspiring against our people, we know what he wrote in his book, *Mein Kampf*, and what evil he wreaked upon us in Germany even before the war and is wreaking upon us now in the course of the war in every country he has conquered.
>
> The whole world is going up in flames, a world war such as there has never been is breaking into fire in the length and breadth of the earth, on sea and land, in the air and under the waters. And we know with certainty that the regime of Hitler and his allies, the regime of slavery and murder and blood, will be wiped out and razed to its foundations. But we do not know whether the victory of democracy and freedom and justice will not find a great graveyard of the Jews in Europe, where the bones are scattered of our people in Europe – its men and its women, its old and its young. Trodden down in its blood, our people demands a judgment at the seat of History, a judgment from the conscience of humanity.
>
> We have learnt: Nazi oppression and injustice, murder and

pillage and violence have swept over all the conquered peoples – from Poland to Norway, from Holland to Greece and Yugoslavia – and there is no remedy for this disaster except the complete and absolute wiping out of the Nazi regime, the utter extirpation of Hitler and his allies. But what has happened to our people is not like the disaster that befell all the enslaved people. Germany set the Jews apart.

This setting apart, Ben-Gurion went on, began the moment that Hitler took power. Already while 'so-called peace' prevailed in the world,[18] already then Hitler declared a war of extermination on the Jewish people. Before a single bomb was dropped on the soil of Poland, Norway and other countries, Jewish synagogues were already being set on fire, the people of Israel were already spoil for the taking before the pillage began among other peoples. Ben-Gurion ascribed the setting of the Jews aside in this way to the essential difference in values between the ethics of the Jewish people and the Nazi teachings. The Jewish people bequeathed to the world the ideas of the sanctity of human life and the preciousness of the human being, the idea that man was created in the image of God, the commandment, 'Thou shalt not kill,' the rule that there is one and the same law for the stranger in the gates and for the citizen, and the precept, 'Love thy neighbour as thyself.' The Nazis preached abroad their creed of the superior race and the inferior race, war and bloodshed as an ideal, hatred of your neighbour and all other faiths or ways of life.

Though there were other peoples whose values were opposed to the Nazi teachings, the Nazis set the Jews apart. 'Only our children, ours, our women, ours, our sisters and old people they set aside for "special treatment," to be buried in graves they had dug with their own hands, to be burnt in furnaces, to be trampled to death by suffocation, murdered by machine-guns – without trial, without a reason, without any cause, without any sin even according to the Nazi book of sins, on account of only one sin – that these children were Jewish children.'[19]

And Ben-Gurion went on:

> The emissaries of the Jewish people in its Homeland have accordingly convened here to call on you, rulers of the great nations fighting against Hitler, the Prime Minister of England [sic], the President of the United States of America, the head of the Government of the Soviet Union, to stand in the

> breach with all the means in your power and not to allow the extermination of a people bound and held prisoner, the old and the infants, unarmed and defenceless. We know – you can't do everything. But there are German nationals in the USA, England and Russia and other countries: demand that they be exchanged for the Jews of Poland and Lithuania and the other countries of the Nazi gallows. Let all the Jews that can leave the Nazi hell get out, and do not close the door in their face! First and foremost let the children out, the maltreated babes and sucklings of Israel that perhaps do not even know as yet that they are Jews and that they are condemned to die because of this sin. Bring them out of the vale of slaughter, let them into neutral countries! Take them into your countries! Bring them in here, to their Homeland! Five hundred thousand Palestine Jews will gladly adopt the children of the Ghetto and devote themselves to them. Annul the death sentence that you have pronounced here, the edict that Jews from enemy countries cannot return to their Homeland. As long as this shameful edict exists, as long as the gates of our country are closed to the remnant of Israel – your hands too will be stained with the Jewish blood spilt in the Nazi hell. All who can only manage somehow to flee from the prison and the gallows – let them escape to any country not under Nazi rule and also, if they want to and if they only can, let them return to their Homeland!

This dramatic appeal, as can be seen, covered practical suggestions for rescuing Jews. Among the things that Ben-Gurion suggested was also this: 'Warn the heads of the German Army and the German people that they will be held responsible for the blood that is spilt, and say to the murderers: "Stop! The blood spilt will be on the heads not only of the Nazi hangmen, but of all those who are able to rescue and do not, who can prevent and do not, who could save and do not save!"'

Ben-Gurion also called on the Jewish people themselves with imperative words of command:

> We are also assembled here today to voice an appeal to the Jewish people themselves, the people here with us in the Homeland and also the one dispersed in the Golah. On us too, on every single Jew in the world, lies the responsibility for the blood that is spilt, the dignity violated, the danger of extermination – not for the first time in our people's history and who knows if it will be the last. All of us, every single Jew wherever he may be, must

vow not to be silent and not to rest until the Hitler regime is wiped out, until the blood of the guiltless is avenged and a new rule is established in the world, a rule of uprightness and justice and freedom, until there is full, faithful and real reparation made for the historic distortion inflicted on the people of Israel, until Israel's wanderers and exiles everywhere return to their Land, and the independence promised to every people and nation in the world is secured for the Jewish people in its Homeland.

And Ben-Gurion concluded his address with a vow of sorts:

> One last word – let us say to our tortured and martyred brethren in the Nazi ghettos: Your disaster is ours, your blood – our blood. We shall do all in our power to avenge you and we shall not be still until we redeem you both from the Nazi hell and the degenerate Golah; and we shall bring you up, all of you, to us and to our Land being built up and redeemed.[20]

This speech of Ben-Gurion's made at this assembly was addressed to the Yishuv and to the Jewish people, but mainly to the Powers. It need hardly be said that his purpose was declaratory, but the speech was not demagogic and did not include any inaccurate information or exaggerated evaluation. The viewpoint he reverted to again later, that the basic solution for the Golah and the Holocaust was immigration and a State, did not affect the aid and rescue actions he proposed, and alongside this were the sense of responsibility, the real pain, fear and anger – and the tears – needing no further illustration.[21] Ben-Gurion repeated things like this all through the war in different ways. For example, he said to the Pioneering Youth Movement:

> For me there is one question that comes before everything else: how to save the remnant of Israel from slaughter. I think that every youngster who is Jewish has to face this burning question. This is the mission assigned to the entire youth. There can be no going on to something else on the agenda until we have spoken of this burning question. In everything that depends on us, we shall try not to have to bear the shame of standing aside while this blood is spilt and not doing anything. No task is greater than this – I have nothing but scorn for the Jewish socialist for whom there is anything more important than this ...

And again:

> The entire youth must be mobilized for this purpose, the entire Yishuv, and even then it may not be enough ... a young

man who does not live for this purpose does not live for anything whatsoever. What is he working for, if not for this? Is there a way to mobilize the whole youth – the whole Yishuv – for the maximum effort? That's the question I'm asking you. That's the main thing.[22]

In his speeches in 1944 too, a notable amount of space is devoted to the question of the aid that the Yishuv ought to be giving the Jews in the Golah, and in these speeches too, Ben-Gurion is seen to be involved as an emotional human being, voicing his pain aloud. In January 1944, for example, Ben-Gurion said:

> The emissaries who are occupied in the sacred work of rescue and aid to the Golah on the threshold of Nazi Europe tell us of horrors but also from time to time of possibilities of rescue. The constant fear, the nightmare sense of calamity must be kept alive in our hearts and souls. Constantly before our eyes we have to see the bloodied Nazi axe hanging over the heads of millions of Jews, children and the old, men and women, so as not to give ourselves any peace here – or the Jews of England and America – not to desist from crying out, not quieten our conscience, not weary of bitter protest, and not weaken in the effort and in rescue – just as long as the nightmare of the murder of half of our people darkens our world ...[23]

'It is not my intention', Ben-Gurion went on, 'to review all the events of the recent period, but to concentrate on the tasks incumbent on the movement in Zionist, *Histradrut* and Party affairs. Nevertheless, there is one matter for which I shall make an exception: This year something happened that we must not lose sight of even for a single day. History has not been kind to the Jewish people even when it abides in its own Land, but never has it been as cruel to us as this year. ... The sword of extermination still hangs over the head of Jewish communities in all the countries of Nazi Europe.'

In 1944, Ben-Gurion repeated the evaluation he had presented in September 1943: 'The fact that the end of the war was visible on the horizon did not lessen the force of the threat. Hitler's death throes were all the more dangerous.' 'The Powers,' Ben-Gurion continued, are 'standing aloof, almost indifferent to our dead. But we shall be in danger if we put the blame on the indifference of others. The great danger is not only that the might in this world, Roosevelt, Churchill and Stalin, will ignore the murder of our nation. The danger is that we ourselves will tire, our senses will be blunted, we shall get used to the

Holocaust, and in our helplessness we shall acquiesce in the pretext of hopelessness.'[24]

In another setting, also at the beginning of 1944, Ben-Gurion again made use of the same far from 'dry' language in the same expressions of protest and pain:

> Now the question of rescue has been brought before us in all its extreme gravity. It is a good thing that we should gather together from time to time to be at one with those who were taken to the death trains and those who died singing 'Hatikva'. ... I believe that when one says 'rescue,' it isn't just speechifying – just as I believe that when one says brotherhood, it is true. And I do not think that there is anything more profoundly true here among us than the will to rescue – and not just among the workers in Palestine – among all the Jews of Palestine and in Zionism.
>
> The Yishuv has a central role as the bearer of the solution, and the moral and practical responsibility incumbent on it is a historic one. It is not possible to bring back the dead, but there are people alive in Palestine and in the Golah for whom the Yishuv bears the responsibility that the same thing should not happen to them as happened to the millions who have been killed. ... Many of us ... must ask ourselves if we are not in some measure responsible, that is to say, not for the six million ... but for many tens of thousands, perhaps hundreds of thousands, perhaps some tens of hundreds of thousands who were slaughtered – had we made a greater effort, perhaps they would have been with us here. And I do not know who among us can say with a quiet conscience that he had no share in this responsibility.[25]

In everything we have cited here, there runs a connecting thread of all the elements we wished to investigate: Ben-Gurion's suffering, his identification and his apprehension over the fate of the Jews in the Golah – strong expressions of solidarity clearly recognizable, and which Ben-Gurion did not hide in the least but presented openly and explicitly and in the most central forums, a fact that points up still more the question of why then his image was something altogether different.

All these same characteristics, far from 'dry' elements in Ben-Gurion's speeches, were at their peak in his address to the meeting held to commemorate 40 years after the death of Herzl. Ben-Gurion linked together the special marking of this day and Herzl's birthplace

(Hungary) with the suffering of the Jews there – the subject then in the forefront – and he cried out in protest:

> Herzl came to us from the Jewish community in Hungary. This community, now being strung up by the Nazi hangman and being led to the slaughter in death-cars day in and day out, ... gave us two great luminaries of political Zionism – Herzl and Nordau. If Herzl were alive today, he would see that even his worst forebodings of 48 years ago about the situation of Israel in the Golah were charming and cosy compared to the appalling reality that even a Satanic imagination could not have pre-figured. 'What then will be the end of the Jews?' asked Herzl some fifty years ago. 'Liking them all is impossible ...' Would he say that today?

At this time of the abominable murder of a third of the Jewish people, while the extermination was still continuing – Ben-Gurion went on – Herzl's spirit enjoins us

> to cry out to the world with a great and bitter cry: What have you done to us? Not those ravening beasts in human form, the scum of the human race called Nazis. We have no common language with them and nothing to discuss with them – they are beyond the pale of humanity. But what did you do to us, you the liberty and justice-loving peoples, fighting for democracy, for freedom, equality, socialism? What have you done to the Jewish people by standing aside as our blood was poured out endlessly without pause or hindrance – without your lifting a finger, without your offering help, without your saying to the slaughterer, Stop!
> Why do you profane our suffering and our anger with unsavoury words of sympathy that are nothing but bitter mockery of the millions burnt and buried alive day after day in the Nazi hell-holes? Why won't you even give arms to our rebels, or to the Jewish partisans confined in the Nazi prison? Why don't you let us go to them and make contact with them just as you allow contacts with the partisans in Greece and Yugoslavia and behind the fronts in Russia and in other countries? Would you have acted like this if day by day they had been burning alive thousands of Americans, English and Russian old men and women? Would you have kept so cool if they had been smashing the babes and sucklings of the Allied nations onto the paving stones?[26]

## B. RESTRICTED SETTINGS

In this kind of setting the speaker can say what he has to say with greater freedom. He can neglect rhetoric and the flowers of speech that are thought vital for influencing public opinion, internal or external. He can also assume that what he is saying will not be spread abroad. In this setting he can also find a refuge consciously or unconsciously from the need to 'present' an image not his own.

Things said in such a setting can therefore be considered as more 'balanced,' and as such they also display the natural distance between speech – however dramatic – and its translation into action according to which it is possible to gauge the strength of purpose behind the speeches and declarations. One may ask to what extent if at all these restricted bodies offered Ben-Gurion a 'refuge' from emotions and sensibilities, or whether emotional elements and expressions of solidarity were also evident in his guidelines for implementation.

Immediately after the official publication in the Yishuv of the report on extermination and after a series of sessions of various Yishuv bodies that met to discuss the subject of rescue, Ben-Gurion sent missives to Jewish Agency emissaries in the USA and England with his guidelines for action. In a letter to the US Supreme Court Justice Frankfurter, for example, then one of the heads of US Jewry and an adviser of Roosevelt's, Ben-Gurion urged him to make it clear to the heads of the US administration that the murder of the Jews of Poland was only the first step towards the extermination of all the Jews in the occupied countries. He called on President Roosevelt to take two immediate steps: (a) to warn the heads of the German Army and the heads of the puppet States and their citizens that they would be held personally responsible for the atrocities; and (b) to extend exchange programmes.

This was an important missive and attention should also be paid to the words struck out in the original draft document, which stressed how important it was to observe secrecy in these matters, and this may have been one of the reasons for the feeling – of people close to the affair as well – that nothing was being done or at least not enough was being done, that Ben-Gurion had turned a deaf ear and so forth. Ben-Gurion closed this missive with an anguished appeal: 'In the name of every Jew in Palestine, I must urge you to do everything in your power to save the life and retrieve the dignity of our people.'[27]

Another example of the merging of an open-eyed practical

approach with a cry of protest was Ben-Gurion's address to the MAPAI Secretariat (24 February 1943), when the Party's emissary, Yehieli, made a long and richly detailed report on the extermination in Europe, on the whole range of aid and rescue problems and on possible action. Ben-Gurion spoke immediately after and he too dealt with the various aspects of the rescue work and its difficulties. He spoke about how to get MAPAI bodies and the Jewish Agency to carry out the resolutions and conclusions reached in discussions held some ten days to a fortnight earlier, and he referred to the special session on aid and rescue convened with the MAPAI members on the Agency Executive, people concerned in immigra tion, members of the secretariat of the *Histadrut* Executive Com mittee, and people from the Agriculture Centre, who were working in secret on a whole range of rescue projects. Ben-Gurion spoke of the importance of the two Palestine offices – in Geneva – and their contacts with practically all the occupied countries. He also outlined the possibilities of 'small rescue,' saying,

> In some places there is hunger but help is also necessary for more vital matters. There are places where it is possible to help, but money is needed, money has to be handed over for this. There are countries where the 'goyim' [non-Jews] are prepared to help, and there are places where this is impossible without money. It is possible to pass from a more dangerous country to a less dangerous one, but not in large numbers. ... It is simply necessary to bribe officials in order to prevent massacres, slaughter, expulsions.

Ben-Gurion also stressed the secrecy needed in this sensitive matter. He told those present that the people actually working in the rescue actions had themselves stressed to him the need for secrecy, and he demanded energetically that everyone in the hall, 'whether they have been sent by the press or whether they have not been sent by the press,' should not let out and not publish anything at all on the various matters dealt with at the meeting. Any publication would be liable to lead to unnecessary difficulties endangering the aid projects.

Ben-Gurion stressed the urgency of providing help: 'There is no knowing how long is still left us to help, how long there will still be people in need of help ...' It was the duty of the Yishuv to live henceforth 'feeling, realizing and accepting that we – these few – are the spearhead of the Jewish people, a small vanguard numbering half-a-million souls.' These imperatives of his reached their high point in his designating the Yishuv as responsible for 'the blood that will be spilt, for more degradation and insult.'[28]

With Ben-Gurion, emotional personal tones could be heard even in his handling of the fierce difference of opinion that developed in the Yishuv over the 'Teheran children.' Ben-Gurion was called on to go into this affair mainly as an intermediary between the two sides, as someone trying to reach an agreement. The vital thing in his view was to secure a breathing-space and prevent differences of opinion which would hamper the rescuing of children. This was a complicated business, and in its course at a meeting with those involved in the difference of opinion, the Chief Rabbis Isaac Halevy Herzog and Meir Hai Uziel (Jerusalem, 24 June 1943), Ben-Gurion said:

> There may perhaps be a dispute one day when the people of Israel is not in danger of being slaughtered and having the land of Israel stolen from it; one day when the people of Israel is settled securely in its own country, perhaps then they will have disputes. But now, how to rescue the people of Israel comes before everything else, because without Jews there will be no Judaism. For me this comes first of all. When the people of Israel are in danger, that is the first thing, in my opinion. If the entire Jewish people were religious as Rabbi Herzog would like to have it, I should give everything in order to rescue the people of Israel. ...

This note was heard again at Ben-Gurion's meeting with representatives from the other end of the spectrum like those who spoke on behalf of the Agriculture Centre (13 July 1943).[29] The personal, emotional expressions – the pain unconcealed – are also found at a special meeting in September 1943 of people in commerce and industry convened to mobilize funds for rescue, and which was held in the context of the days dedicated to solidarity and togetherness with the Golah, from 25 September 1943 to the close of the Day of Atonement on 9 October 1943. Ben-Gurion again referred to a whole series of rescue actions of different kinds, both 'big' and 'small.' He reviewed the international situation and the about-turn that could be discerned, he thought, in the English attitude to the Zionist Movement, but he also warned against 'superficial optimism.' He analysed the dialectical interaction between the liberation of Europe from the Nazis, a liberation redeeming the surviving remnant on the one hand, and on the other the danger involved in the death-throes of Nazism, since there was no knowing, he said, what the Nazis might do in their retreat – one victim is at their disposal 'on whom they can wreak all the anger of their hatred and their revenge – the Jews.'

## THE SHADOW OF THE HOLOCAUST

Ben-Gurion emphasized the fight against time as a central factor in rescue and the ability of the Yishuv and its emissaries to bring about delay:

> I have no words – I am not speaking of the disaster, the language for it has not yet come into being, I think – but I have no words to stress the tragic and fatal importance of the one single factor called time. The situation is such that if by any means whatsoever we can succeed in putting off disaster for one day or two days, that can mean the difference between life and death for thousands and tens of thousands ... You will hear at first hand from the comrades who were recently closer to the site of the Holocaust and you will be told more details. I only want to say to you that if in some town, in some province, one succeeds by various means, means that will be no use without money, in putting off the evil edict – if it's an edict regarding money or something else – this putting off signifies just one pace between life and death ...

These things may come suddenly, even disaster may result from invasion, and retreat can happen suddenly. Ben-Gurion's imperative and his conclusion were these:

> Every possibility that will exist for those on the watch – in the small measure that we are standing on the watch – in the small measure that it is *possible* for us to stand on the watch – if they succeed in putting off the factor concerned for some space of time – this can mean rescue.

He closed on a personal note:

> To save the life of Jews on the gallows, Jews with the knife at their throats, to save them is possible by postponement of a week or a month. ... We are told one thing: to do everything humanly possible, whatever is given to flesh and blood to do, in order to extend material help to those standing on the watch of rescue, to put off the disaster as far as it is possible to put it off, to do this right away with our best will and capacity. Because this is so serious, I am afraid to say that we should do the maximum: we are flesh and blood and we cannot do the maximum, but we shall do something.

At the end of this meeting, a sum of 30,300 Palestine pounds was raised.[30]

Another example of how Ben-Gurion drew a distinction between an emotional outburst and action that in his opinion had some chance of success is seen in the meetings he had with delegates of the Rescue Committees of the *Landsmannschaften*. A delegation of Bulgarian Jews told him *inter alia* that they had even weighed up the possibility of a sit-down strike in the Jewish Agency offices in Jerusalem. He said to them:

> If I thought that a sit-down strike in the Agency building might save the Jews of Bulgaria, I myself would have suggested it. But if this is for the purpose of pressure on us, then they're mistaken [in thinking] that this will put more pressure on us than the fact itself of the danger in store for Bulgarian Jewry in Bulgaria.

This summed up the distinction between an action that has some prospect and something else that may perhaps offer an outlet for people's feelings. Ben-Gurion said it made him sorry that not all of them felt that apprehension (for the fate of Bulgarian Jewry) was shared by everyone concerned, and he told them of the efforts that were being made to get a thousand Jews out of Bulgaria.[31]

Replying to the contentions of another delegation, he let out a hint on the project for ransom – 'Goods for blood' – and said:

> ... the hangman will not make any distinction between the Jewry of Warsaw and the Jews of Salonika. The thing isn't over yet, the sword still hangs over our heads. We are still occupied with this – this is the main thing we are occupied with. Mr. Shertok is flying specially to London about this; Kaplan has also left for Constantinople on this matter. We are holding negotiations with governments, we are negotiating with Satan himself on this. ...[32]

Examination of what Ben-Gurion said in these restricted settings, if we consider even the few examples given here, shows that he was well informed concerning all the types of rescue, both 'big' and 'small,' both on the level of guiding principles and on that of practical action. As regards Ben-Gurion, this is not surprising, for by nature he wanted to know all about matters of current importance, sometimes to the point of pedantry. Not only in this respect, but also in the restricted settings where Ben-Gurion might have taken 'refuge' and felt freer to revert to his 'drier' matter-of-fact unemotional self, here too were present not a few expressions of his emotion, his pain and his identification with the Golah.

## C. INTIMATE SETTINGS

It will remain an open question, it seems, whether any setting existed where Ben-Gurion talked in all simplicity. His diary was a work-tool where he collected data for the time when he would need them; it was a means for improving communication between him and his comrades in the leadership through the passages he passed on for his colleagues to read about his actions, his analyses, his evaluations, his plans. We know that it was said that every entry was calculated, written 'for history,' but even if this were correct, one should not draw final conclusions about the diary. There are in fact many places, including entries on the subjects we are concerned with, where in my estimation he put down his thought without any ulterior calculation, without any 'practical aim' – expressions of feeling, emotion, intimate thinking – unburdening himself, calming down, as it were, or letting go, one more 'un-Ben-Gurion' thing about him, as was shown in the example from his diary that we opened with. Precisely the diaries from the Second World War period are missing in part, and what is to hand is largely fragmentary: just where it would have been natural to find his secret, heartfelt wishes, his thoughts and feelings – free of frills – about the Jews of the Golah and the Holocaust, precisely these we are deprived of, though there are some examples in what remains.

A remarkable expression of such feelings is to be found in Ben-Gurion's letter of September 1938 to his 13-year-old daughter, Renana. Though this is a document from before the war, there is an interesting combination of personal, family matters and pre-eminently political issues, apprehension for the fate of the Jews of Europe, a heavy sense of evil foreboding, all against the background of the Sudeten crisis and the Munich Conference:

> Dear Renana,
> Mother left this evening by train and she is crossing from England to France by sea. ... I am now back in my hotel – and not for a long time have I felt so sad and lonely. The room is emptied – as if everything is empty, and I myself feel as if I'm forlorn, sad, with nothing to lean on. And it's strange – I'm used to being alone, both in Palestine and in the Golah.
> And I like being alone and cut off. I don't know why this time my loneliness is so trying and depressing. Alone, on-one. Empty. Anguished, weighed down. If I were a child, I should cry – perhaps it would make things easier to bear. I'm not crying, I

> feel choked. It's hard. But why should I make you sorry – you, the mischievous girl who loves nonsensical chatter and talk and being happy and getting up to mischief! If you were here – perhaps you'd ease my sadness. But there is no-one here. Silence and oppression. Yes, I'm in the same room, with the same table, the same books and the same furniture – but something has blown away, disappeared – and it's emptied, narrow, difficult and sad.
>
> And I feel afraid – Mother is also sad – she's lonely and things are difficult for her – and now she's getting further off by train ... soon she'll be at the coast and then tossed about on the waves and reach dry land again – far, far from here, and I am here alone.

As was his way, Ben-Gurion also looked for rational, external explanations – political ones, too – for what he was living through and for his depressed state of mind, and he went on to write:

> And perhaps it is because these are woeful, sad days, because a bitter drama full of suffering has been acted out before your eyes, the shadow of war hovered above our heads, an abyss of blood and fire opened up and the peoples of Europe glimpsed the maw of the terrible crater – and the danger has passed, supposedly – but at what a price! A small people, but decent and enlightened, was dealt a cruel, malignant blow, and not only at the hands of a foreign enemy but also from so-called friends, from allies, France and England, who were supposed to be ready to go to war to protect the existence of the Czech people and who lent a hand to the ruffian and tyrant ruling Germany and settled her fate – to be cut to pieces.
>
> True, peace was saved, and peace is a great thing. Who knows how many thousands, tens of thousands and millions of men, women, children and the old, would have lost their lives in the war, whole countries too would have been destroyed. How great would have been the ruin of humanity if a new world war had broken out. And it's good that there's peace. But what a peace! And for how long? Isn't this peace just a short breathing-space for the German robber to expand his armament, reinforce his soldiery and one of these days fall upon his victim with added force like a beast of prey? Sad days ... .

And from this dark, depressing spectacle, he returned to his young daughter:

And in Palestine it's also sad. The disturbances continue with new victims day after day. And who knows how long it's going to go on. But why do I sadden you with things you know all about! Life is suffering, hard to bear – but it's good that you forget it . . .[33]

In the previous section we gave further examples from the period after the Yishuv publication, from the entries in his diary where Ben-Gurion noted down for himself the details of meetings he took part in. A meeting like this, which we have not mentioned so far, was one at which Menahem Bader of *HaShomer HaTsa'ir* asked Ben-Gurion to help him to break through what seemed to him the superfluous bureaucratic difficulties put in his way when he was trying to get to Constantinople for rescue purposes. Then there were also Ben-Gurion's meetings with Agudat Yisrael people or Revisionists on matters of rescue, which we shall not detail here, but they help to illustrate Ben-Gurion's method of entering things in his diary, places where the record is 'clean,' unadorned, and without any sidelong look at history.[34]

In January 1943 a new group of exchanged persons arrived. One woman in the group, Helena (Helinka) Goldblum, came as an unofficial emissary of the Jewish Fighters' Organization in Warsaw and in Zaglmavia, with the mission of bearing witness and raising a cry of protest. When she reached Palestine, she met Ben-Gurion as well. This encounter – both according to Helinka's testimony and to the letter Ben-Gurion wrote afterwards – also throws light on the subject we are concerned with and from another additional angle. This is her account: 'I told him everything . . . informed him of every detail . . . Ben-Gurion asked for details . . . When I had finished, I saw tears in his eyes. . . . Ben-Gurion sat and wept . . .'[35]

Ben-Gurion described this meeting some days later in a letter to Miriam Cohen-Taub, who had been his secretary when he was in Washington, and told her of the feelings hidden in his heart and his pain:

> I am unable to free myself from the nightmare brought before us once again last week by fifteen people who arrived from Poland, among them a young woman, member of *Hehalutz* in Sosnovitz. . . . The day before yesterday I went to Haifa to see her, and for three hours I listened to a tale of atrocities and travail that no Dante or Poe could have imagined – you feel absolutely helpless, and you can't even go out of your mind – the sun rises in all its power and glory, and you too have to carry on with your usual work – and it isn't easy, please believe me.[36]

## BEN-GURION'S RELATION TO THE DIASPORA

This is how it was too at the end of November 1944, when Ben-Gurion visited Bulgaria and could not enter Rumania because of Soviet and British opposition. This was a very crowded visit, his first and moving encounter with the surviving remnant. In his diary he recorded his emotion over what he saw and over the reception he had. In expressing the storm in his heart, he cited a verse from a poem with special significance in the circumstances of that time, a poem by Hannah Szenes:

> Blessed is the match that is burnt and lighted flames
> Blessed is the flame that burned in the secret places of the heart
> Blessed is the flame that could burn itself out worthily
> Blessed is the match that was burnt and set the hearts on fire.

In other places, too, Ben-Gurion wrote outspoken entries laden with emotions, as well as outspoken comments. After a welcome reception given him, he recorded, 'Oh good Lord, who knows what's waiting for me in Sofia ...' or, 'The welcome at Plodivo was also shattering,' and after a meeting with the wives and mothers of soldiers and hearing from them of the horrors on the Bulgarian front, he expressed his feeling of real helplessness: 'For five years their husbands have been doing hard labour in the camps and now they have been sent to the front. They want me to get their husbands back. What am I to answer them?' And after a visit to a poverty-stricken Jewish quarter: 'Atrocious, the end, the abyss ... frightful.'[37]

More examples in this context can be found in his diary in his dramatic descriptions of his two visits to Germany after the war. Amongst other things, he again copied out poems there, the Song of the Partisans and Gewirtig's poem, 'The Town is Burning,' and in another place he copied out a long list of inscriptions on the stones of the common graves he saw in Bergen-Belsen. In these entries the strength of his emotion and his pain is plain for everyone to see.[38]

Ben-Gurion was also a figure people turned to even in the early stages with all kinds of appeals for help, a wide range of private individuals, Zionist activists who had stayed in the Golah or others who had managed to get out in time, and members of various committees that were organized, mainly *Landsmannschaften*. In some of the answers that he sent to these appeals, Ben-Gurion went beyond dry, down-to-earth factual statement and revealed his personal feelings besides commenting on the operative suggestions in the appeals or on the prospects of assistance:

> I have received your missive and I thank you most cordially for

writing to me and for what you say. You do not have to make any apology at all – it is your right and duty. Who doesn't have a relative or acquaintance in the Nazi hell? Is there any Jew whose heart isn't touched by this matter? Your suggestions are good and correct for the most part and the Zionist Executive is already dealing with them. People have already been sent to neutral countries, and we are also trying to send people to the Ghetto itself. May your volunteering bear blessed fruit! I shall pass on your proposals to the people dealing with the matter, and they will get in touch with you.[39]

In his answer there was more than a hint of the plan for parachuting and other plans for sending Jews from Palestine to the conquered territories.

Ben-Gurion's emotional side can also be seen in this context – if only by way of anecdote – in the sort of names he called Hitler and the Nazis. Here too, was he cool and restrained or did he particularize them and call them names just like other people? An examination shows that Ben-Gurion called Hitler a long list of names, among them the Bear rearing up, ruffian, head of a band of ruffians, Satan, gangster, 'motorized Attila,' terms he heard used and adopted.[40] In this too, then, he was human just like everyone else.

## CONCLUSION

It emerges that in following on the track of something that might seem precisely secondary, those 'hidden tears,' in seeking to discern the human being behind the leader, the apprehension behind the strength, the pain behind the apparent coldness, we have made manifest in a systematic and orderly fashion of Ben-Gurion's involvement in rescue activities on the level of guiding principles and that of implementation, the activities which are the main thing in determining the issue of Ben-Gurion and the Golah in the Holocaust period.

As we have already mentioned, we did not intend to draw world-shaking conclusions from this examination of the emotional element in Ben-Gurion and from his verbal expressions of solidarity, but just to bring into focus the conclusions regarding the problems we raised.

Having regard to the three types of setting we enumerated, we can now affirm that Ben-Gurion's attitude to the Holocaust and the Golah is seen in retrospect to have been perfectly explicit – he related to the Golah not as a far-off, estranged, abstract notion, but as a description for collections of brothers and sisters, parents and other relatives, people in danger of being put to death.

In all three settings and all through the war, Ben-Gurion expressed his personal feelings, even if in varying doses. Alongside his generally cool and sensible-minded aspects, there also appeared his warm, live, suffering side. The Holocaust, then, did not pass him by, he did not avoid learning about it and deliberating on it and its various phases. All this is to be seen in the expression he gave to his fears, his pain and even his open outcry.

From this examination of ours, we can learn at least one more lesson on the value of the quantitative method as applied to the subject of Ben-Gurion and the Holocaust.

Much has been expended on this question of quantitative testing – to the question of *how much* if anything at all Ben-Gurion said about the Holocaust,' as compared with how much he said on other subjects. This quantitative testing, it must be said, has not been absolutely thorough, for technical reasons connected with the vast amount of documentation Ben-Gurion left behind him and perhaps also for other reasons that we cannot discuss in the present context. On the basis of the system of 'quantitative testing,' far-reaching ethical and educational conclusions have been drawn about Ben-Gurion's share in the aid and rescue activities in the Holocaust period, conclusions that in our estimate also oblige even someone who rejects this test on principle to give them consideration commensurate with the system's vulnerability.

What then can we conclude and what may we assert on the basis of the examination we have carried out, with regard to the quantitative test?

(a) Ben-Gurion all along related extensively to the Holocaust and its various implications. Even before the war broke out he related extensively to the approaching disaster.

(b) Ben-Gurion related to the Holocaust and its implications in a lengthy series of settings and bodies – both formal ruling bodies like the Jewish Agency Executive and the Zionist Action Committee and also various Jewish Agency and Party political committees, of MAPAI and other parties he appeared before.

(c) Ben-Gurion related to the Holocaust in large, declaratory forums, councils, mass meetings and assemblies, as well as in restricted forums of experts.

(d) Ben-Gurion related to the Holocaust in speeches and in his writings: in long letters, in telegrams and articles, in his diary and in guidelines for policy implementation.

On the subject of quantity, it should also be remembered that many links in aid and rescue activity in the Holocaust were secret. The weight of a superfluous word about them could be measured in lives. Ben-Gurion himself repeatedly referred to the importance of secrecy and not seldom complained that 'this people of ours has not yet learnt the importance of keeping a secret.' It seems that there is no need to explain the connection between this and the matter of quantity.[41]

Ben-Gurion's part must also be remembered in 'little' rescue and in 'big' rescue. We cannot deal with this question here, but we can state that Ben-Gurion was involved in both.[42] We must also recall that censorship left its mark on 'quantity' as well, and every researcher of the period knows how sensitive the British were to reports that could set off unrest in the Yishuv.

Finally, a good way both to sum up what has been said here on the matter of quantity and to look at Ben-Gurion again as the strong leader, cool-headed and practical but also with an emotional side, is to use the words of Ben-Gurion himself. He could make speeches that went on for hours and hours and he could go on writing at great length, but he could also describe an event, however dramatic it might be, in a line or two. On 7 and 8 May 1945 when the war was seen to be ending and Germany was surrendering, Ben-Gurion was in London. From his window he could watch the English rejoicing in the streets. All his feelings, all his emotion over the importance of this historic moment and what it meant for the world and the Jewish people he summed up in his diary: 'Victory Day – sad, sad indeed.' Elsewhere he copied down for himself a verse from Hosea (Ch. 9, v.1):[43]

Rejoice not, O Israel, for joy, as other people.

With regard to the Holocaust, too, Ben-Gurion is to be seen as a human being just like everyone else.

### NOTES

1. Ben-Gurion Research Centre and Archives (hereafter BGA), Ben-Gurion Diary, 14 July 1936, London. For a further analysis of recent literature on the role of Ben-Gurion in rescue attempts, see 'Ben-Gurion and the Holocaust of European Jewry 1939–1945: A Stereotype Reexamined,' *Yad Vashem Studies*, Vol. XVIII, 1987.
2. *Ibid.*, 14 April 33, Memel.
3. At the second session of the Fourth Histadrut Congress, 10 Jan. 1934, D. Ben-Gurion, *Me-Maamad Le-Am* [From Class to Nation], Tel Aviv, 1956, pp.474–5. On 1933 as a critical turning-point and the new dangers, see Ben-Gurion at the MAPAI Council, 22 March 1934: 'Last year, 1933, serves as a turning-point, at all events the beginning of an about-turn in the history of the Zionist movement: (a) because of the exacerbation of the Jewish question in the world, both internally and externally. This is expressed in the great impoverishment of the masses of Israel in Eastern Europe, the reinforcement of

anti-Semitism in every country and medieval persecution, which began in Germany, with no-one's knowing when it will end. ...' Ben-Gurion bought *Mein Kampf* in Aug. 1933. See Sh. Teveth, *Ha-Derekh l'Iyar* [The Road to Iyar – May 1948], Tel Aviv, 1986 (hereafter, Teveth, *Ha-Derekh*), p.213.
4. Ben-Gurion Diary, 21 June 1935, London, in a talk with Lord Melchett; *ibid.*, 3 Jan. 1929, New York; *ibid.*, 15 March 1939, London; *ibid.*, 24 March 1939, Paris; *ibid.*, 28 April 1939, Tel Aviv. On the breaches of the Versailles Treaty, on Hitler's promises and on the historical background to all these events, see William L. Shirer, *Aliyato U-Nfilato Shel Ha-Reikh Ha-Shlishi* [The Rise and Fall of the Third Reich], Tel Aviv, 1963, pp.299–368.
5. On the Abyssinian crisis, see, e.g., Ben-Gurion Diary, 7 Sept. 1935, Lucerne; letter to Geulah and Amos, *ibid.*, 16 Sept. 1935; and also *ibid.*, 22 Sept. 1935, Paris; *ibid.*, 25 Sept. 1935, London; and also *ibid.*, Sept., Oct., letters to 'Comrades in Warsaw' (Anshel Reiss), to Moshe Sharett and Feinstein. On the Spanish crisis, see Ben-Gurion Diary, 21 Aug. 1936, Ben-Gurion letter to Moshe Shertok, and also *ibid.*, 5 Dec. 1936.
6. Ben-Gurion Diary, 20 Sept. 1938, London, Ben-Gurion to Shertok. For an updating of the situation, see, too, another Ben-Gurion letter to Shertok, *ibid.*, 21 Sept. 1938, in which he presents the isolationist trend in the USA and the need to secure US help. See, too, *ibid.*, 21 Sept. 1938, Ben-Gurion, London, to Geulah; and also *ibid.*, 22 Sept. 1938; *ibid.*, Ben-Gurion letter to Ussishkin, secret and personal; *ibid.*, 26 Sept. 1938, 27 Sept. 1938, Ben-Gurion's letters to Geulah and Dr. Schwarzbart; and there too, 28 Sept. 1938 and 29 Sept. 1938.
7. Ben-Gurion Diary, 1 Oct. 1938, after a working meal in the home of Weizmann.
8. *Ibid.*, 2 Oct. 1938; see *ibid.*, 18 Oct. 1938, Ben-Gurion to Joseph [Dov Joseph], an additional definition of the policy of Chamberlain: 'This attempt fits in with the general line of Chamberlain's "appeasement" [sic] – this "peace-making" had meant acquiescence in the past – acquiescence with the aggressor ...'
9. 'No one will stand beside the Jews, not isolationist America nor the League of Nations.' For this see at length: Ben-Gurion Diary, 2 Oct. 1938. A copy of this passage was also sent to Reiss, 3 Oct. 1938, and Ben-Gurion added: 'Show the letter to Kleinbaum too;' and see also *ibid.*, 7 Oct. 1938, Ben-Gurion, London, to Geulah, Amos and Renana.
10. *Ibid.*, 10 Dec. 1938.
11. *Ibid.*, 20 Oct. 1938.
12. Central Zionist Archives, Jerusalem (hereinafter CZA), Ben-Gurion, Vaad Le'umi, 12 Dec. 1938: the same things under the heading: Ben-Gurion, Yishuv Assembly, Jerusalem, 12 Dec. 1938, Zionist Archives, New York; see too: Jewish Agency Executive, 3 Oct. 1938. On the *Kristallnacht* see too: Ben-Gurion Diary, 21 Dec. 1938, Ben-Gurion, London, to Eliezer Kaplan; *ibid.*, meeting with Silver. On the forecasts and fears foreboding evil of other eminent Zionist leaders, see e.g.: Jabotinsky to the Peel Commission, 11 Feb. 1937, on 'disaster' in store for the Jews of Europe if a Jewish State was not set up in Palestine; Weizmann to the Peel Commission on the 'superfluous six million' that must be got out of Europe in time. Y. Heller, 'Weizmann, Jabotinsky and the Arab Question – the Peel Affair,' in *Zmanim*, 11 (1983), pp.78–91 [Hebrew].
13. For example, CZA, Agency Executive, 11 Dec. 1938, Ben-Gurion: 'This is a catastrophic period, and catastrophic measures are called for;' and again, at length: M. Bar-Zohar, *Ben-Gurion*, Tel Aviv 1975, Vol 1, Part 3 [Hebrew]; and Meir Avizohar, *Tsionut Lohemut* [Militant Zionism], Kiryat Sede Boker, 1985.
14. On the material flowing to Ben-Gurion from the different departments of the Jewish Agency see: CZA, 'Ben-Gurion Office', S44, masses of examples. On material reaching Ben-Gurion in various meetings he had, see, e.g., Ben-Gurion Diary, 23 Nov. 1939; and too *ibid.*, 10 Nov. 1939, on the worsening situation of the Czech Jews immediately after the arrival of Eichmann in Prague; see too, *ibid.*, on the same date a similar meeting with a delegation of *Poale Zion Smol*.
15. On Ben-Gurion's instrumental attitude, see, e.g., Sh. B. Beit-Zvi, *Ha-Tsionut Ha-Post-Ugandit Be-Mashber Ha-Sho'ah* [Post-Uganda Zionism and the Holocaust Crisis],

Tel Aviv; also, Hava Wagman-Eskholi, 'Emdat ha-manhigut ha-yehudit be-eretz yisrael le-hatsalat yehudei europa' [The position of the Jewish leadership in Palestine with regard to rescue of the Jews of Europe] in *Yalkut Moreshet*, 24, 1978, pp.87–116 [Hebrew].

16. The meeting in Madison Square Garden, New York, 21 July 1942. On Ben-Gurion's participation in the meeting see interview with Miriam Cohen-Taub, 17 Jan. 1977, interviewed by Y. Donyetz, New York, BGA, Oral Documentation Section; also Teveth *Ha-Derekh*, pp.207–8.
17. Ben-Gurion heard about the *Bund* Report, e.g. at the latest on 30 July 1942, at a meeting with Francis Katani. Ben-Gurion Diary, list of meetings at the end of the Diary for 1942; and also CZA, Agency Executive, 6 Oct. 1942.
18. Ben-Gurion was referring to the peace reached as a result of the British policy of appeasement, which he called a short-term peace. We have dealt with this above, and see his letter to Renana further on in this connection. And on the human-emotional element, see too BGA, Speeches, Ben-Gurion at the Yishuv Assembly, 12 Dec. 1938: 'Gentlemen, I do not bring good tidings today. I shall not relate the sorrows of Israel. As far as is humanly possible, I shall try to free myself from the terrible pain, and I shall try to address you on the situation from the political point of view alone.'
19. The idea of the people of Israel's being 'set apart' in Nazi 'teaching' is a recurrent theme in Ben-Gurion's speeches. It appeared first at a very early stage, in 1934. See Ben-Gurion's address to the second session of the fourth *Histadrut* Congress, 10 Jan. 1943, and he reverted to it again after the *Kristallnacht*, CZA, Vaad Leumi, 12 Dec. 1938.
20. BGA, Speeches, 30 Nov. 1942, Ben-Gurion at the Assembly of Elected Representatives.
21. The question whether there was a contradiction between the rescue activities and Zionist political aims in the Second World War period is a central question. In our estimation there was no contradiction between working for a Hebrew state and a Hebrew army and rescue activities, neither as regards Zionist ideology, since 'negating the Golah' did not mean 'abandoning the Golah' as some people contended, nor as regards practical action. On Ben-Gurion's position on this issue and his stressing the importance of the Yishuv's taking part in rescue activity, see e.g. BGA, Articles and Speeches, 17 Jan. 1943, at the Yishuv Assembly of Elected Representatives, *ibid.*, 2–3 April 1943, Ben-Gurion's address at the Secretariat of Immigrants' Camps [*machonot ha-holim*]; *ibid.*, Ben-Gurion at the *Ha-Kibbutz ha-meuhad* Congress, session of 19 Jan. 1944, and others, part of which is given below. This is so, in our evaluation, also regarding the practical manpower. On the actions of the Yishuv in the sphere of aid and rescue in the Holocaust period, see the important research of D. Porat, *Hanhaga be-Malkodet* [The Leadership Caught in a Trap], Tel Aviv, 1986.
22. BGA, Speeches, Ben-Gurion at the Secretariat of Immigrant Camps, 2–3 April 1943.
23. Labour Party (MAPAI) Archives (hereafter: LPA), Beit Berl, MAPAI Council, 15 Jan. 1944.
24. *Ibid.*
25. BGA, Speeches, Ben-Gurion at the *Kibbutz ha-meuhad* Congress, 19 Jan. 1944.
26. *Ibid.*, Ben-Gurion, 'Herzl Day,' 10 July 1944; see too *Ha'aretz*, 11 July 1944; parts of this speech were also published in an article of Ben-Gurion's in *Zionist Review*, 22 Sept. 1944.
27. *Ibid.*, correspondence, 8 Dec. 1942, Ben-Gurion to Arthur Lourie for F.F. [Felix Frankfurter]; and also his letter of that day to Nahum Goldmann and Berl Locker.
28. LPA, MAPAI Centre, 23 Feb. 1942.
29. BGA, Minutes of meetings 24 June 1943, 13 July 1943.
30. *Ibid.*, 23 Sept. 1943, meeting of industrialists and businessmen.
31. As part of the affair of the 29,000 and parallel with it. On this affair, see Tuvia Friling, 'Ben-Gurion's position on the Rescue of children affair, November 1942 to May 1945,' in *Yalkut Moreshet*, 41, 1986, pp.119–37 [Hebrew]. The meeting with Bulgarian Jews: BGA, Ben-Gurion Diary, Jerusalem, 14 Sept. 1943.

32. *Ibid.*, Ben-Gurion Diary, and minutes of meeting, 6 July 1944.
33. *Ibid.*, Ben-Gurion Diary, London, 30 Sept. 1938, Ben-Gurion to Renana.
34. Meeting of Ben-Gurion and Bader, see: Ben-Gurion Diary, 21 Dec. 1942, M. Bader, *Shlihuiot atsuvot* [Sad Missions], Merhavia, 1948, p.43. Agudat Israel members–Ben-Gurion, e.g., Ben-Gurion Diary, 14 Dec. 1942, 20 Dec. 1942. Revisionists–Ben-Gurion, e.g. *ibid.*, 11 Nov. 1942, 17 Jan. 1943.
35. Cited in A. Ronen, 'Shlihuta shel Halinka' [Halinka's Mission] in *Yalkut Moreshet*, 42, 1986, pp.55–80 [Hebrew]. See the description there of the meeting and details of Halinka's mission.
36. Cited in Teveth, *Ha-Derekh*, p.217.
37. BGA, Ben-Gurion Diary, Nov.–Dec. 1944, detailed description of the visit to Bulgaria.
38. *Ibid.*, Oct. 1945, Jan. 1946, detailed description of the visits to the camps.
39. BGA, Correspondence, 18 Jan. 1943, Ben-Gurion to A. Yerushalmi. See too, *ibid.*, 25 Jan. 1943, Ben-Gurion to Dr. Leo Kolinski.
40. Ben-Gurion Diary, 14 July 1936; *ibid.*, 12 Feb. 1938, Ben-Gurion, London, to Geulah; Ben-Gurion Diary, 27 Sept. 1938, minutes of meetings 7 June 1944; Ben-Gurion Diary, 8 Sept. 1940, Ben-Gurion, London, to Pola; Ben-Gurion Diary, 7 June 1940, Ben-Gurion, London, to Pola.
41. On stressing the importance of secrecy, see: Ben-Gurion Diary, 29 Jan. 1940: 'Our people don't yet know how to confer secretly and keep the secret;' see too the 'erasures' in the draft of the letter to Lourie, 8 Dec. 1942.
42. On his involvement in the Rescue of Children Affair see note 31.
43. BGA, Ben-Gurion Diary, 7–8 May 1945.

# 12

# Activity of the Yishuv on Behalf of Iraqi Jewry, 1941–1948

## Daphne Tsimhoni

The emigration to Israel of 120,000 Iraqi Jews, almost the entire Iraqi Jewish community, was the culmination of a revival of interest in Iraqi Jewry by the Jewish community in Palestine (hereinafter: the Yishuv) and represented the pinnacle of Yishuv activity on behalf of that community since 1941. After a protracted period of detachment between Iraqi Jewry and the Yishuv, the former once again began to assume an important place in the consciousness of the Yishuv from 1941 on, for three reasons:

(a) The riots against the Jews of Baghdad on 1–2 June 1941 (*Farhud*) alerted the Yishuv to the deteriorating position of the Iraqi Jews in the light of the upsurge of Arab nationalism and Nazi propaganda, and the growing scale of the Jewish–Arab confrontation in Palestine.

(b) Thousands of Yishuv members had gone through the war in Iraq in either military or civilian capacities (mainly as drivers and Solel Boneh construction workers). Thus, their ties with the Iraqi Jewish community strengthened, and they became more aware of its plight and of the prospects for the Zionist enterprise offered by these ties.

(c) The halting of European immigration and the blockade of the Mediterranean during the war resulted in a search for alternative immigration routes and sources, and focused attention on neighbouring states accessible by land. This became an increasingly important consideration as news about persecution began to arrive, and particularly so when reports of the annihilation of European Jewry began to reach Palestine in late 1942.

## ACTIVITY OF THE YISHUV

## THE 1941 RIOTS AS A TURNING POINT IN THE YISHUV'S ATTITUDE TOWARDS IRAQI JEWRY

On Shavuot, 1–2 June 1941, after Rashid Ali al-Kaylani and leaders of his pro-Nazi regime had fled from Baghdad and before British forces entered the city, anti-Jewish riots erupted in Baghdad on a scale unknown by the Jewish community there or elsewhere in the Middle East in modern times. For two days, a rabble including Iraqi soldiers and policemen ran amok, while the British army stationed on the outskirts of Baghdad refrained from entering the city and intervening so as to avoid confrontation with the nationalistic masses.

The Jews were powerless, except for a few instances in which they defended themselves and managed to repel their attackers. Casualties included 150 dead and more than 450 wounded. Most of the damage was to property; 1,500 houses and shops were looted. All in all, some 3,000 families suffered, and the total damage was an estimated £800,000 sterling.[1]

Rumours and reports of the riots began to reach Palestine later in June of that year, either through letters and first-hand accounts by returning soldiers or workers, or through Iraqi Jews who managed to escape to Palestine. Official sources attempted to play down the reports of the riots and their dimensions.[2]

After years of dissociation and indifference, news of the riots reawakened the Yishuv's interest in Iraqi Jewry and its problems. True, there had been earlier attempts in the 1920s to establish a Zionist presence in Iraq, and Zionist associations had been set up there. But the Zionist idea in its modern form took root only among a small group of intellectuals, and held no sway among the masses – although these constituted the largest immigrant potential in Iraq and other countries of the Middle East. During the 1920s and 1930s there was a trickle of immigration, inspired mostly by religious motives. The Iraqi immigrants, like Oriental immigrants in general, usually adopted the ways of the Old Yishuv, and did not integrate into the organized New Yishuv. The Iraqi Jews did not share the motivation of the European Jews who reached the country after the First World War. Unlike the Europeans, they were not swept away by the tremendous Zionist revival; the post-war years were marked by economic prosperity for the Jews of Iraq, and the British Mandatory authorities provided Western-educated Jews with new opportunities in the civil service and the white-collar professions.

Economic prosperity and relative social calm were not the right milieu for promoting emigration to Palestine.

It is therefore no wonder that Yishuv institutions in Palestine took no interest in the Jews of Iraq. These institutions refrained from sending emissaries or instructors, and Iraq itself lacked a local Zionist organizational infrastructure institutionally linked to Palestine. The only Zionist enterprises active in Iraq in the 1920s and early 1930s were the Zionist funds that attempted to canvass the well-to-do, and a few teachers who were sent to teach Hebrew in Jewish schools and attempted to expand their activities in Zionist directions. The Yishuv leaders displayed little interest in the Jews of Iraq and of the Orient in general, with a few exceptions, notably Yitzhak Ben-Zvi, Chairman of the National Committee of Jews of Palestine (Va'ad Leumi), who visited Iraq on several occasions and was interested in the cultural roots of its Jewish community. When immigration control was toughened and quotas were set in concert with the Jewish Agency, Iraqi Jewry did not figure high on the Yishuv's list of priorities. Thus Zionism in Iraq suffered from a dual handicap: minimal interest on the part of the Yishuv, and severe restrictions on Zionist activity. The latter drawback developed into an outright ban, and the last of the Hebrew teachers were expelled in 1935. This date marked the effective cessation of ties between Yishuv institutions and Iraqi Jewry.

It is important to stress that the situation of the Jews in Iraq deteriorated in the 1930s for three main reasons:

1. An upsurge of Arab nationalism, including attempts to oust the British from Iraq. On the whole, the Jews did not enter this struggle, except for isolated cases of identification with and support for Arab nationalism. Their ties with the West, however, made them suspect in the eyes of the Arab nationalists, who thought of them as seeking European protection and consequently tried to make life difficult for them.

2. Iraq's growing involvement in Palestine following the 1936 Arab uprising also meant greater identification on the part of Iraqi nationalists of the Jews with the Arab–Jewish problem in Palestine, although they were not yet suspected of Zionism. The presence of Palestinian exiles in Iraq, headed by the Mufti, in the late 1930s also contributed to increased awareness of the Arab–Jewish conflict and support for the Palestinian Arabs, and exacerbated the hostility of the Muslim majority in Iraq toward local Jews.

3. Nazi propaganda undermined the British presence in Iraq and

took on anti-Jewish undertones. From 1934 on, the Nazi-Fascist influence began making itself felt in assaults on Jews in Iraq, and the Arab nationalists' anti-Zionist struggle became an anti-Jewish one. Many senior civil servants were dismissed, others were denied promotion, and an unofficial *numerus clausus* against Jews was instituted in government schools. The Arab nationalist press began to incite the population against the Jews. Violence against Jews broke out in 1936 and continued thereafter, aggravated by the unstable conditions that developed in Iraq. The worsening plight of the Jews reached a peak with Rashid Ali al-Kaylani's pro-Nazi anti-British coup of April 1941. Under his regime, Jews in Baghdad, Basra and other cities were routinely robbed and assaulted. Jews were accused of collaborating with the British, although there were Jews who supported Rashid Ali and contributed financially to his cause.

News of the attacks against the Jews of Baghdad shocked the Yishuv leaders and aroused a feeling of solidarity with them. Although these reports bore no proportion to those of the suffering and persecution of European Jews at the same time, the Yishuv was shocked and outraged by the very fact that for the first time in modern history organized violence was being perpetrated against Iraq's established and affluent Jewish community. The sense of outrage was heightened by the fact that the mass presence of British forces on the outskirts of Baghdad had not prevented the *Farhud*, and by evidence that it had been planned during the final days of Rashid Ali al-Kaylani's rule, with the knowledge and assistance of his men.[3]

There was not much the Yishuv and its institutions could do in response to the events in Baghdad and the need to act on behalf of the Jews there. Organizations of Iraqi Jews in Palestine were the first to sound the alarm and demand action for their brethren. On 1 and 3 July 1941, a delegation of *Va'ad 'Adat Ha-Bavlim* (Council of the Iraqi Jewish Community) met with Yitzhaq Ben-Zvi, Chairman of the National Committee, and informed him that 600 Jews had been massacred and that many others were missing, that there were 2,500 refugees, that Jewish property was being systematically looted, and that no Jewish home had been spared. The delegates expressed their fear that these disturbances merely augured a far more serious wave of violence. They informed Ben-Zvi that the Iraqi Jews were exceedingly anxious to leave the country – most of the businessmen for India, and the rest for Palestine. The

Committee pressured Ben-Zvi to ask the British to intervene with the Iraqi Government for the lives and property of the Iraqi Jews; to raise funds from American Jews for victims of the assaults; and to obtain thousands of immigration certificates for much of the embattled Iraqi community.[4] The number of victims, it later transpired, had been overstated at this meeting.

After the meeting, Ben-Zvi wrote to the Chief Secretary of the Mandatory government in Palestine, Mr. John MacPherson, and described the riots against the Jews of Baghdad according to the accounts he had heard. He mentioned the thousands of refugees left destitute, the fear of many Iraqi Jews that the slaughter was merely an augury of far worse to come, and the wish of many victims to emigrate to Palestine. In the name of the National Committee, Ben-Zvi requested that MacPherson ask the British consul in Baghdad to intercede with the government of Iraq on behalf of the Jews there by guaranteeing their lives and property, searching for all missing Jews, and inflicting harsh penalties on all those who helped organize or participated in the riots: especially members of the army and police. He also demanded that the Iraqi Government compensate the victims of the onslaught, help them return to normal life, and facilitate the emigration of refugees to Israel by granting certificates to this end. Finally, Ben-Zvi asked MacPherson to meet with him to discuss the facts of the case and the practical proposals he had made in his letter.[5]

During the meeting, which took place on 10 July 1941, Ben-Zvi provided MacPherson with yet more details on the extent of the Baghdadi Jews' losses in lives and property. The Jewish community had been decimated, he said; many had been left without shelter and food. Although an action committee had been set up in Baghdad to raise money for the victims, its resources were limited. Although order had been restored, the plight of the Jews had not improved. Although a number of people had been arrested, many of the policemen who had participated in the attacks remained free. Rumour had it that Jews were still being assailed, particularly in the form of kidnapping for ransom. Policemen were telling Jews that the previous harassment had been nothing compared with what was about to take place. All these factors heightened their wish to emigrate to Palestine at all costs, but they were afraid of being branded as Zionists and subjected to even greater abuse. Ben-Zvi repeated the requests he had made in his memorandum, and added a new one: that a National Committee representative be allowed to visit Baghdad in order to assess the situation, confirm it, and organize aid. In reply, MacPherson promised to present the requests to the High Commissioner and inform the National Committee of the answer.[6]

In early July 1941 the problem of the Iraqi Jews became a focal point of deliberations in the Yishuv institutions. It was first discussed in a Mapai (*Mifleget Poalei Eretz Yisrael* – Eretz Yisrael Workers' Party) meeting on 9 July 1941, where aid options focused on four areas:

(a) Financial aid.
(b) Political assistance through appeals to the United States and Britain, and contacts with Iraqi politicians.
(c) Assistance in emigration to Palestine.
(d) Assistance in setting up an organization for self-defence.

Moshe Shertok (Sharett), head of the Jewish Agency's Political Department, quoted reports of 500 slain, many wounded, and rampant attacks on property. While acknowledging that the number of victims claimed appeared to be exaggerated, he argued that this did not detract from the horror of the massacre as such, which was all the more blatant for its having been directed against the Jews as a community, and for the apathy of the British, who had not raised a finger to help or save the Jews. Had the attacks continued another day or two, the entire community might have been wiped out. Iraq's record in treating minorities was nothing to boast of, but the massacre of Assyrians, which the Jewish Agency had denounced to the British Government at the time, was nothing compared to the slaughter of the Jews. The Baghdad massacre proved that the Jews were in danger wherever they were, and that in Iraq they were staring death in the face.

Berl Katznelson cautioned that the Yishuv knew nothing about the massacre. He himself had learned about it only from chronicles of a meeting of mourning held by members of the Iraqi Jewish community in Jerusalem. He said that the massacre must on no account remain a matter for the Iraqi sect alone, while the Yishuv at large remained ignorant of it. If censorship had kept the affair out of plain sight, the public must be informed by other means. Eliyahu Golomb pointed out that the reports were far more serious than Shertok had reported, and compared the wholesale massacre and attacks on Baghdadi Jews to a poem by the poet Haim Nahman Bialik, 'City of Slaughter.' Evidence had it that the situation of the Iraqi Jews had not much improved; they were now victims of extortion and kidnappings. Because the Iraqi Jews did not consider it possible to travel to Palestine, it was the Yishuv's duty to help them organize in self-defence. Such organizations had proved effective in the few cases where Jews had successfully defended themselves against their attackers. Finally, Katznelson stressed the importance of keeping the problem of the Iraqi Jews on the agenda in negotiations with the authorities in Palestine and Egypt.

A. Liechtenstein compared the events in Baghdad to the sufferings of Jews in Hitler's Germany, and called for demonstrating solidarity and concern among the public in Palestine. He said the matter should be brought up in London and America, and that the Yishuv's reaction to events in Iraq should not be limited to the dispatch of memoranda to high officials. The Jews in Baghdad must be made to feel that their Palestinian compatriots were concerned about them. Even if the Iraqi Jewish community had its share of affluent members who could provide assistance, it should be made to feel that the Yishuv was sharing its troubles and was ready to help financially, even if merely symbolically. Finally, he mentioned the necessity of organizing emigration from Iraq to Palestine by all possible routes, in order to meet the needs of the emerging Palestinian Jewish community, and to take advantage of the events of Baghdad to build the Yishuv. 'The Jews of Iraq are now ready to do audacious things, and their Zionist feelings will undoubtedly grow. We have to organize immigration quickly, while the ordeal is fresh in their minds and the lessons of the war have not yet faded.' Berl Raptor also mentioned emigration as a priority item in order to consolidate the Yishuv:

> We have almost solved the problem of unemployment in Palestine. In the event of a call-up for war, there will be new jobs and not enough workers ... Therefore we must do everything to promote immigration and promote extensive political activity in Palestine and London. We have to seek out new sources of immigration. Perhaps we can begin promoting immigration from the Middle East ... We must work rapidly to encourage immigration from neighbouring countries such as Syria and Iraq.

Eliyahu Dobkin, deputy head of the Jewish Agency Immigration Department, also stressed Iraqi Jewry's grave plight following the riots, and said that the Yishuv's help must include practical aid to the victims. He mentioned Ben-Zvi's approach to Chief Secretary MacPherson, and asserted that the Jewish Agency too should appeal to the authorities on behalf of Iraqi Jewry. He mentioned how, after years of apathy, the Iraqi Jews were strongly motivated to emigrate to Palestine in any feasible way and had requested 10,000 immigration certificates. It was the Jewish Agency's job to demand special certificates for them. Furthermore, he declared, the Yishuv should send an emissary who, subordinate to and together with the British ambassador, would help organize aid for the victims and arrange their emigration to Palestine. These functions could not be handled by an Iraqi citizen.

Golda Meyerson (Meir) suggested that the Yishuv demand that the British Government permit it to send a delegation bearing financial aid, among other things, for the Jews of Iraq. Yisrael Galili backed her proposal, arguing that the best way to publicize events was through a financial appeal. Eliezer Kaplan concluded the meeting by asking all members of the Secretariat who belonged to other Yishuv institutions to help Iraqi Jewry in every possible way.[7]

Several days later, on 13 July 1941, the Jewish Agency Executive met to discuss the onslaught against Iraqi Jewry and ways of helping the community. Ben-Zvi reported on details of the riots, relief schemes, and the beginning of contacts with the British authorities on this matter. Dr. Bernard (Dov) Joseph of the Jewish Agency's Political Department said that news of the massacre had been forwarded to London and New York, and that the Jewish Agency intended to request 2,000 immigration certificates for Iraqi Jews. Y. Gruenbaum suggested that a certain sum, at least £P100, be allocated for the victims of the riots. Ben-Gurion described the Baghdad uprising as a Kishinev massacre Arab-style, and said efforts were being made to forward the reports to Britain and the United States for mass dissemination. Jewish organizations in the United States were also called on to ask the United States Government to demand an explanation of the riots from Baghdad's envoys there. In conclusion, Kaplan said that he favoured the National Committee's proposal to send a Yishuv delegation to Baghdad and to promote emigration from there to Palestine.[8]

Meanwhile, the first reliable information on the Baghdad riots came in. The source was Moshe Ittah, a native of Haifa who had settled in Baghdad 20 years previously, had been involved in community life and in ruling circles there, and was visiting Palestine. Ittah met with Ben-Zvi and A. Almaliah of the National Committee, and with Dr. B. Joseph of the Jewish Agency's Political Department. The reports he presented proved that previous information on the scale of the onslaught, which had been circulated by the National Committee, had been exaggerated. The Baghdad community council reported 120 dead and missing, and 500–700 wounded; most of the damage had been done to property and was estimated at £P800,000. The riots were financed by Nazis in Baghdad and organized by agitators from Syria and Palestine headed by the Mufti. The number of participants in the rioting was estimated at 3,000, of whom 2,000 had been arrested. The new regime, eager to preserve Iraq's reputation, punished the rioters severely via a military court set up for this purpose. Eight of the rioters – including officers and policemen – were sentenced to death and others to 15 years hard labour.

The community's affluent members had contributed toward rehabilitating the victims, and an action committee had been set up to collect a target sum of £P50,000. The donors included Prime Minister Jamil Midfai, who gave £P200 from his own funds, and the Iraqi Regent, who contributed £P1,000. Ittah reported that the Jews of Iraq were no longer in danger, and that one could hope for peaceful days ahead since the new Iraqi Government was not anti-Jewish. It was trying to purge the bureaucracy and police of pro-Nazi officials, and if British forces remained in Iraq the future of Iraqi Jewry would be secure. The Jews' morale and the attitude of the government and the Muslims toward them had improved. Nevertheless, many Jews still spoke of leaving Iraq. The rich wanted to emigrate to America, India, and Iran, but visas were hard to obtain. The less affluent were willing to emigrate to Palestine. Ittah believed the Iraqi Government would not deny the Jews exit permits, and would allow the Yishuv to assume responsibility for aiding the victims of the riots.[9]

Ittah's report on the state of Iraqi Jewry after the riots placed things in perspective: the Jews of Iraq faced neither imminent extermination nor extinction of their community due to mass emigration to Palestine. The community was attempting to rehabilitate itself, but needed help. Thus, in another session of the Jewish Agency Executive, on 20 July 1941, the focus turned to the provision of financial aid to the Jewish community in Iraq in the aftermath of the massacre. Members of the Executive were divided into two camps: those favouring symbolic aid (Y. Gruenbaum) and those who insisted on something more substantial (Y. Ben-Zvi). Ben-Zvi also spoke of contacts, via Dr. J. Magnes, with the Joint Distribution Committee for an allocation toward rehabilitating the Jewish community in Iraq. He stressed how important it was – for the Zionist cause – that financial and other assistance come via Palestine, and that a delegation from Palestine visit Baghdad to assess the true state of affairs. The debate concluded with the adoption of a proposal by M. Ussishkin that the Jewish Agency decide on the size of its allocation after the Jewish National Committee had made its own allocation public.[10] A week later, the National Committee decided to allocate £P1,000 for the casualties of the rioting in Iraq, and continued its contacts with the JDC, via Dr. Magnes, for aid to the victims. Finally, it asked the government for permission to dispatch a delegation to clarify matters and organize aid; the latter request was turned down.[11]

News of the Baghdad rioting reverberated through the Yishuv and aroused feelings of solidarity. S. Yanovski of the Council of Non-Partisan Organizations (*Mo'etset ha-irgunim ha-bilti miflagtiyim*) suggested to Moshe Shertok, head of the Jewish Agency's Political Department, that fish imports from Iraq be boycotted in protest against Iraq's treatment of Jews, but the proposal was rejected on the grounds that it would be useless; the Yishuv would suffer more than anyone else from such an action and would probably not abide by it; if they did, the Arabs would take over the local commerce in fish.[12]

Various Yishuv organizations sent contributions to the National Committee for the Baghdad victims: the Eqron Guards' Organization donated £P2,000, and the Organization of Guards of the Internment Camps contributed £P2,735.[13] According to reports from America, the JDC had collected $60,000 for the victims of the riots. This would be used as a revolving loan fund monitored by the JDC's representative.[14] In sum, the Yishuv institutions sent £P4000 to the victims of the Baghdad rioting.[15]

Meanwhile, Jewish Agency officials followed the efforts of the Iraqi community to rehabilitate the victims, with particular attention paid to government compensation. On discovering that the £P20,000 allocated for compensation by the Iraqi Government had not yet been handed out, they informed Jewish Agency representatives in London in expectation that they would exert pressure through Britain to have the money released.[16] In late May, 1942, tempers cooled when Moshe Ittah, who had meanwhile resettled in Haifa, reported that the Iraqi Government had indeed distributed £20,000 sterling to the victims of the pogrom. A special committee of three community dignitaries headed by attorney Yusuf Alkabir had been set up to process the compensation. Allocation of government compensation was facilitated, if indirectly, by Dr. Magnes's appeal to the JDC, proposing a loan of £P20,000 to the leaders of the Jewish community via the US Embassy in Iraq.

Simultaneously, the Iraqi Government sought to keep Iraqi Jews from seeking help from world Jewry by providing compensation itself. Deliberations about this compensation began two months after the massacre, but the government, fearing attack by the opposition and a re-awakening of anti-Jewish sentiments, hesitated to bring the matter to a decision. The negotiations with Dr. Magnes, although conducted in secret, became known to the government and catalysed the government into passing a resolution in Parliament to allocate 120,000 Iraqi dinars as compensation for damage to property of British and Iraqi subjects during the disturbances of May–June 1941. Of this sum, the cabinet later allocated 20,000 dinars to the Jewish victims of the disturbances. By this device the government was able to avoid bringing up the subject of financial aid to the Jews in Parliament, thereby averting the antagonism of some members of Parliament. In addition, some affluent community members, most of whom dwelled in Iran or Bombay, contributed another 20,000 dinars.[17]

Ben-Gurion and other Yishuv leaders were in favour of publicizing the massacre in the West, for two reasons: to pressure the Iraqi Government into improving its treatment of the Jews and preventing a recurrence of the assaults, and to wield the issue as a lever by which the Zionist enterprise in Palestine would be recognized as the solution to the Jewish problem. Visiting London in early August 1941, Ben-Gurion met with the manager of the *Manchester Guardian*'s London office and discussed events in Baghdad, the situation in the Middle East in general, and the Yishuv's contribution to the war effort. This meeting resulted in the publication the next day of an article that discussed *inter alia* the Baghdad pogrom, which had been passed over up to that time in England. The following conclusion was presented at the article's end: 'We ought to establish a Jewish Palestine that can survive, defend itself and return its people to their homeland, be they free or persecuted, from any part of the world. Without such a state, which it is our duty to assure, there can be no lasting settlement.'[18]

The same goal spurred the Yishuv leaders to raise the problem of the Iraqi Jews in talks with Arab leaders. Thus, Ben-Gurion took up the issue in talks with Nuri Said, Iraq's most conspicuous pro-British leader, in July 1941. Not only did Said refrain from glossing over the riots and the Iraqi Government's responsibility for them, but his estimate of the number of dead was higher than that currently held by the Jewish Agency. He even admitted police complicity in the riots, but insisted that the reason for the riots and Rashid Ali al-Kaylani's rise to power was the Palestine problem, which was also the bone of contention in Iraqi–British relations. Nuri Said rejected emigration to Palestine as a solution to the Jewish problem, insisting that the basis for any agreement had to be the assumption that Palestine had to remain Arab. While admitting that there was a Jewish problem, Said did not see Palestine as the solution and even suggested that Iraq absorb Jewish refugees.[19]

Moshe Shertok, in his meeting with Nuri Said in mid-July 1941, also brought up the issue of the Iraqi Jews. Again, Said did not deny assaults on the Jews had taken place. He assured Shertok that the government, after having put down the riots, was now working energetically to punish those responsible.[20] On 27 July 1941 Eliyahu Sasson of the Jewish Agency's Political Department met with the newly appointed Iraqi Consul in Jerusalem, Jamil al-Rawi, who was reputed to be pro-British and sympathetic to the Iraqi Jews. Al-Rawi expressed a favourable view of the Zionist enterprise in Palestine, and in the name of the Iraqi people deplored the attacks on the Jews. These, he stated, were not only against Arab tradition and Muslim faith, but did nothing to enhance Iraq's reputation as an independent country that undertook to protect its minorities; rather, they attested to the strength of Nazi propaganda in Iraq and to the nation's own weakness. On the brighter side, he pointed out that the disturbances had not spread beyond Baghdad, that the Jews had incurred no great loss of life or property, and that their Muslim friends had defended them and sincerely commiserated with them in their disaster. The current government, he said, had taken harsh measures against the rioters. Almost all plundered property had been retrieved, and committees had been set up to restore this property to its owners and to aid the victims. The Consul acceded to Sasson's request to dispatch a Yishuv delegation to Iraq, expressing the hope that he would be able to arrange its admission into Iraq soon, and promising to provide its members with letters of introduction to his friends and members of the government, who would help it with its work. Finally, he expressed his wish to stay in touch with the Jewish Agency.[21]

Using officials of its Political Department, who had been sent to Iraq by the British on a specific assignment, the Jewish Agency followed the situation of Iraqi Jews and attempted to gauge the intensity of their wish to emigrate. In May 1941, Eliyahu Epstein (Eylat) of the Political Department of the Jewish Agency was asked by the Chargé of Special Affairs of the British Embassy in Istanbul to visit Basra and Aden in order to investigate the situation of the Jews there and to establish links between the community leaders and the

British, which would be used to enlist members of the Jewish communities in the British war effort. With the Jewish Agency's approval, Epstein left in June for Iran, where the new pro-British Iraqi ambassador set up a meeting with a group of wealthy Jews who had fled to Teheran from Rashid Ali al-Kaylani's regime. Epstein tried to persuade them to emigrate to Palestine and invest their money there, but met with refusal. Several said they had 'had enough' of life in the Orient and wished to emigrate to Britain or the United States, where they could live quietly; others did not believe in Zionism and did not consider emigration to Palestine a solution to the Jewish problem. However, all asked the Jewish Agency to help them obtain entrance visas to the countries to which they wished to emigrate. Epstein tried to persuade them to contribute to an immigration and education fund for children orphaned by the Baghdad riots, or to help establish a settlement in memory of massacre victims. Again, he was turned down. Before he left Teheran, the Jewish refugees there organized a party in his honour, during which the Iraqi ambassador spoke sympathetically of the Zionist enterprise in Palestine. His viewpoint was far more favourable than that of the Jewish refugees themselves.

Epstein's next stop was Basra, where he made contact with the leaders of the Jewish community. He found that, although no Jews had been killed during the riots, property had been damaged and the Jews were highly apprehensive about their future in Iraq if the British should fail to impose their authority on the Iraqis. Epstein tried to persuade the Jews to emigrate to Palestine, but here, too, he found that the affluent wished to head for India or the West since they had no intention of exchanging Iraqi Arabs for Palestinian ones. The only likely candidates for emigration to Palestine were the poor, the riot victims, and those people with relatives there. To arrange their emigration, organization and financial aid were essential. The community requested that this operation be handled clandestinely, lest they attract the attention of their enemies in Iraq. Epstein's major success was in persuading the Jews to cooperate with the British despite their distrust of them.[22]

By July 1941, the Jewish Agency Executive was fully aware, in view of first-hand accounts and reports received, that there would be no massive influx of Iraqi Jews. Nevertheless, immigration work became the focus of activity on their behalf, in keeping with the central tenet of Zionism: that the fundamental solution to the problem of Jews anywhere in the Diaspora was emigration to Palestine and the ultimate establishment of Jewish sovereignty in

Palestine as a centre for world Jewry. Cognizant of conditions in Iraq and Palestine, however, the Yishuv did not immediately map out a comprehensive plan of action for the mass immigration of Iraqi Jews; talk was confined to increasing the possibilities for refugee immigration. In July, the National Committee and the Jewish Agency asked the Mandatory Government to persuade the British Government to intervene with the Iraqi Government on behalf of the Jews, and to obtain 2,000 special immigration certificates for the victims of the riots. Urgent telegrams were sent to the World Jewish Congress and the Zionist Office in London, calling on them to alert Parliament and British public opinion to the plight of Iraqi Jews, and to pressure the British Government to grant them the requisite thousands of immigration certificates.[23] The Jewish Agency's representatives in London applied to the Colonial Office, but after the Office consulted with the High Commissioner for Palestine, the request was turned down on the grounds that the economic situation in Palestine did not warrant special dispensation for the admission of Iraqi Jews; furthermore, the 2,000 certificates requested by the Jewish Agency would hardly solve the problem of the 100,000 Jews in Iraq.[24]

Because the Mandatory Government refused to grant special immigration certificates, the Jewish Agency had to allocate them to the Iraqi Jews by drawing on its regular quota. In a Jewish Agency Executive meeting in August 1941 on this topic, Dobkin expressed disappointment in the non-creative nature of the Iraqi immigrants, whom he considered 'unproductive.' His disappointment stemmed mainly from the disparity between the 'working Zionism' envisioned by the Yishuv leadership and the nature of Iraqi Jews. Thus, most of the certificates allocated for Iraqis were earmarked for manual and skilled labourers, although the Jewish Agency had 100 certificates for wealthy people which were of doubtful value. The immigration potential of Iraqi Jewry lay within the urban lower-middle classes, who lacked Zionist pioneering indoctrination and who had been brought up, in the Oriental spirit, to consider manual labour degrading. Therefore, Dobkin proposed the allocation of only 90 permits for Iraqi Jews, as against 100 for the Yemenite Jews. The latter, in his opinion, were a productive, useful group, whereas the Iraqis were mainly peddlers drawn to city life. Dobkin was also motivated by the absence of a Jewish Agency representation in Iraq, which encumbered certificate allocation. His proposal for a reduced immigration quota for Iraqi Jews met with opposition. Kaplan feared that unless the current certificate quota was used up in the short interval remaining until the next list was presented, it would very probably be curtailed, and that top priority should therefore be given to immigration from neighbouring countries. Ussishkin brought up the Yishuv's moral obligation toward Iraqi Jews – to deliver them from their living hell – and was supported by other members of the Executive. In the end, Gruenbaum's proposal to allocate 110 of the 500 certificates for July–September 1941 to Iraqi Jews, an unprecedentedly large proportion, was accepted.[25]

Immediately after the 1941 riots, there was a revival of emigration to Palestine on the part of Iraqi Jews. Since legal immigration was impossible due to the shortage of certificates, the summer of 1941 saw a wave of spontaneous clandestine immigration. Hundreds of Jews left Iraq for Palestine, travelling through the desert as stowaways on Egged (Yishuv transport) or British Army convoys, aided either by Jewish drivers from the Yishuv or by Arab smugglers. Others arrived as tourists with temporary permits issued for reasons of health, study, etc., and stayed in Palestine once these expired. Many of these immigrants were apprehended and sentenced to imprisonment or deportation. The Jewish Agency Executive appealed to the Mandatory authorities in Palestine and the Colonial Office in London to override immigration laws and allow these illegal immigrants to remain in Palestine as refugees for humanitarian reasons in the category of war refugees.[26] The Mandatory Government refused to place these immigrants in a separate category, agreeing to grant individual permits in exceptional cases only. Thus, deportation orders to Iraq were not rescinded, on the grounds that the deportees' lives were not in danger there.[27] The Jewish Agency Executive and the Zionist Organization in London continued to press, and Dr. Chaim Weizmann's intervention with Lord Moyne led to the withdrawal of deportation orders against Jews who had fled to Palestine following the June 1941 riots. The Mandatory Government's attitude toward these illegal immigrants also softened somewhat: many were released from jail, and bail bonds deposited for them with the police were returned to their guarantors.[28]

Youth Aliyah played an important part in the immigration enterprise. Yitzhaq Ben-Zvi introduced youth groups in Iraq to train for agricultural pioneer work in Palestine based on the rescue programmes for Jewish youth in Nazi-occupied Europe. Ben-Zvi met with Youth Aliyah heads Henrietta Szold, Dr. Landauer, and H. Beit, informed them of the anti-Jewish riots in Iraq and of the relief programmes instigated by the National Committee, and requested that they take immediate action to bring Jewish youth from Baghdad to Palestine. 'We must take advantage of the ferment within Iraqi Jewry to bring the youth over and train them for productive work in Palestine; they will be the vanguard of the Iraqi Jewish community.' He went on to warn that, unless these steps were taken, these youngsters might fall into the clutches of Christian missionary schools. Henrietta Szold was not overly enthusiastic about the idea. She agreed in principle to organize a group of Baghdadi youth for training in Palestine, and even suggested that the minimum age of this group's members be reduced from 23 to 15. She stipulated, however, that the Department would participate in this venture only if a representative of her choice joined the Yishuv delegation – if it travelled to Iraq – in order to assess the people involved and handle the finances, since 'In Baghdad, a considerable participation in the expenses [by the local community] can be expected.' She said that once a report on the visit was received, an emissary would be sent to Baghdad for several months because 'with no youth organizations there, it will be hard to operate.'[29]

Insufficient thought was given to the nature of the population and to the fact that living conditions in Iraq were unlike those in Europe; nor was enough consideration given to the nature of the young immigrants, who, lacking the educational infrastructure of a pioneer movement, in no way resembled their counterparts in Nazi-occupied Europe. Appeals by families wishing to send their 16-year-olds to Palestine to study at the Hebrew University of Jerusalem were rebuffed on the grounds that the children were too young, while Szold refused to deal with these cases, claiming that they were unsuited to Youth Aliyah. With no appropriate institution to care for these youngsters in Palestine, the Immigration Department of the Jewish Agency turned down these requests.[30] The dean of the Technion asked the Jewish Agency Executive to negotiate with the Iraqi Government regarding the departure from Iraq of students admitted into the Technion and equipped with immigration certificates; his appeals were ignored, and no students came.[31]

## THE YISHUV DELEGATION LEAVES FOR IRAQ

Because the Iraqi Government would not let an official Yishuv delegation enter the country, emissaries were sent in disguise and by clandestine routes. The first emissary sent to Iraq on behalf of the Jewish community there was sponsored by the leaders of the Iraqi community in Palestine. Shortly after the riots, Yitzhaq Azarya, chairman of *Hitahdut Olei Aram Naharayim be-Eretz Yisrael* (Association of Iraqi Immigrants in Palestine) and former head of the Zionist association 'Ahiever' in Iraq, met with Ben-Zvi and demanded that substantive action be taken on behalf of Iraqi Jewry. Ben-Zvi arranged a meeting between Azarya and the head of the Jewish Agency Immigration Department, Hagana representatives, and activists in the *Mossad La-'Aliya Bet* (Institute for Illegal Immigration), including Shaul Meirov (Avigur). Azarya presented his proposal for the immigration and absorption of Iraqi Jews in Palestine and offered his services as an emissary. In a subsequent meeting with Meirov, the latter encouraged him to organize the emigration of Jews from Iraq, mainly by illegal means, and promised him as much help as possible in funds and in arms.

Azarya left for Iraq in late June 1941, as an emissary of the Jewish Agency Immigration Department. Using his Iraqi passport and the pretext of a family visit, he stayed there until September. He found the Iraqi Jews very eager to emigrate to Palestine, and tried to establish an organizational infrastructure for clandestine emigration. Thus, he formed a four-man committee to coordinate emigration and establish initial ties with drivers and with police officials in Baghdad and Ramadi who would aid emigration. During his stay, he arranged for the emigration of hundreds of people – the vast majority illegally, since the number of certificates he had been granted was negligible.[32]

In early November 1941, Azarya returned to Iraq for about a month. This time, he reported that the Iraqi Jews' economic situation had improved substantially, as had the Muslim population's attitude toward them. For this reason, and because it was hard to obtain passports in Iraq, they were much less eager to emigrate. Would-be immigrants were asking for certificates before applying for passports. Azarya sought to make the selection and processing of immigration candidates the exclusive province of the immigration committee he had set up in Iraq, in concert with the Committee of Aram Naharayim (Iraqi) Immigrants in Palestine. The Immigration Department rejected his request, and the organizational immigration infrastructure that Azarya had attempted to establish in Iraq disintegrated after he returned to Palestine.[33]

In February 1942, the Immigration and Youth Aliyah Departments sent Mazal Museri to Iraq. Museri, a member of a respected Jewish family in Egypt with relatives in Iraq, travelled in the guise of a wealthy Egyptian tourist, using her connections to mask her true mission. The decision by the Yishuv institutions to send her reflected their wish to help the Jews of Iraq on the one hand, and their reservations about them, rooted in feelings of alienation, on the other. Museri was to assess the Iraqi Jews' situation, evaluate their willingness to emigrate, and select candidates for Youth Aliyah. She reached Iraq with 40 youth immigration certificates, and during her stay the Immigration Department sent her 100 permits for manual labourers. Youth Aliyah, however, did not accede to the Immigration Department's request that it, too, increase its allocation of youth immigration certificates, preferring to wait until the first 40 youngsters had arrived. This refusal came at a time when the war and the sealing of points of exit from Europe had caused a grave downturn in youth immigration.[34] Museri reported that the Jews in Iraq lived in great fear for their future and were being threatened by their Muslim neighbours. The presence of the British forces gave them a modicum of security, although the British dissociated themselves from the Jews and offered no help. Although most of the Jews wished to emigrate to India, the West, or Palestine, entry permits to these lands were difficult to obtain, as were passports and exit permits from the Iraqi Government. Museri made special mention of the British Consul's reluctance to arrange entry visas to India and Palestine so as to avoid friction with the Iraqi Government. Under such conditions, Jews seeking to emigrate to Palestine were objects of exploitation, and a black market in passports and exit permits was developed by some Jews. Museri saw no way of preventing this situation.

Museri found candidates for Youth Aliyah primarily within the community's poorer segments, who had suffered in the riots – particularly girls for whose safety they were concerned. These young people could pay travel and clothing expenses, but could not afford tuition. Museri reported that the youth had awakened to the need for self-defence, against their parents' opposition, and were increasingly willing to emigrate to Palestine, primarily for the continuation of their studies. Museri herself succeeded in issuing 54 certificates, according to given criteria, to young people, manual labourers, and a few community dignitaries. She handed the remaining certificates over to reliable people for distribution after her departure. She also set up a permanent liaison between Iraq and the Yishuv institutions through a Jewish driver. At the same time she alerted the Yishuv institutions to other categories of potential immigrants, particularly the affluent. She provided them with a list of wealthy people who wanted to emigrate, and recommended an investigation into ways of absorbing them and investing their capital in Palestine. Finally, Museri reported that her visit had altered the community members' attitude toward agricultural occupations, which they now viewed as a respectable profession; thus, a great service to the Zionist cause was accomplished. The community, she said, greatly admired the Yishuv's efforts to save indigent children and orphans. Thanks to Museri, a group of boys and girls from Iraq immigrated to Palestine and were absorbed by Youth Aliyah institutions there. Nevertheless, Museri was not asked to continue her work, although she expressed willingness to do so.[35]

The first emissary to leave for Iraq with the express purpose of laying the foundations for a pioneer movement, a defence organization, and a continuous organized immigration activity was Shaul Meirov (Avigur), a Hagana activist and one of the heads of Aliya Bet. After months of unsuccessful attempts to obtain an entry permit to Iraq, Meirov left for Baghdad in March 1942 in a Jewish transport unit, disguised as a British soldier and aided by one of the unit's drivers, Yaakov Trachtenberg.[36]

Meirov's main aim was to contact the Youth Rescue Organization ('Shabab al-Inqadh'), which had formed in Baghdad during and as a result of the riots. News of this group was based on declarations signed by the organization, which called on the Jews of Iraq, especially the youth, to arm and organize against the rioters. During his visit, Meirov met with these youngsters, formed initial ties with several community members who were sympathetic to the Zionist idea, visited community institutions, and met with some of their leaders.[37] Meirov was one of the first members of the Yishuv establishment to consider the emigration to Palestine of most if not all Iraqi Jews as the correct solution to their problem. By his own account, his visit left him firmly convinced that 'the only hope for the Baghdad community and the Iraqi Diaspora was a rapid uprooting from Iraq and settlement in the Land of the Patriarchs, Eretz Israel.' He predicted that the Yishuv's growing strength would increase the Arabs' hostility toward the Jewish communities in their midst, and that the Jews' lives would be in growing jeopardy.

In this he agreed with Ben-Zion Yisraeli, who had visited Iraq in 1934 under Jewish Agency auspices and even then stressed the importance of the resettlement of Iraqi Jews in Palestine. 'Apart from suffering the bitterness of exile, they could be the first victims to pay for our enterprise in Palestine .... The aim is to eradicate this Diaspora, nothing less ... and the first step is to set up a pioneer movement to prepare for immigration, teach Hebrew, Jewish history, defence, and promote immigration in all possible ways.'[38]

## ACTIVITY OF THE YISHUV

Upon his return Meirov met with Berl Katznelson, leaders of Aliya Bet, and the Histadrut Executive Committee. He reported on the Iraqi Jews' situation and declared it necessary to dispatch top-level emissaries at once, for two reasons: the dangers to the Jewish community posed by the possible collapse of Nuri Said's shaky regime, which relied on British artillery; and the existence of the Iraqi Jewish youth, who could be saved and who would be useful in realizing the Zionist idea and developing the country.[39]

### THE ENCOUNTER BETWEEN YISHUV EMISSARIES AND IRAQI JEWS

Meirov's visit augured the first dispatch of emissaries to Baghdad. In early April, Enzo Sereni of Kibbutz Givat Brenner reached the country disguised as a Solel Boneh agent, in order to organize the activities of Aliya Bet emissaries in Iraq. A fortnight later Shemarya Gutman of Kibbutz Na'an was sent to promote emigration, and Iraqi-born Ezra Kadouri of Kibbutz Maoz Hayyim arrived to organize Jewish defence. Neither had legal papers; they arrived as stowaways in an Egged (the Palestine Jewish Transportation Cooperative) military convoy.

Sereni made contact with several local Jews whom Meirov had met a month earlier. With their aid, he began to establish relations with the Youth Rescue (self-defence) Organization in Baghdad. Relative to the information received in Palestine, Sereni's encounter with this group was a disappointment. 'In fact there was no real organization. It was a movement begun by children. Weapons were acquired randomly ... There was no training.' Sereni persuaded the group's members to join the defence organization that he had established. Virtually overnight, the emissaries set up two groups, in which 25 participants commenced weapons instruction so that they could later train others. Similarly, the city was mapped in preparation for any catastrophe. The turnout was massive: 'Unlike Zionism and immigration, the idea of defence caught on at once. Arms acquisition commenced on a large scale. They saw us as their saviours.'[40]

The emissaries' initial meetings with the Jewish community in Iraq demonstrated their inability to relate to or understand the community and its customs. This major factor delayed their operations and those of the Yishuv institutions in Palestine on behalf of Iraqi Jewry. The emissaries arrived full of zeal to promote emigration to Palestine and create pioneers who would help build the country, but there were numerous setbacks, and they were hard put to find common ground with members of the community. Visiting Palestine briefly in 1942, Sereni lectured the *Histadrut*'s Immigration Committee on the emissaries' activity in Iraq. His remarks reflected his disappointment at the disparity between the ideal – to effect the immigration of as many people as possible, as quickly as possible – and the reality – prosaic activities focusing on Hebrew language instruction and general conversation. 'So far little has been accomplished on the ideological plane, but many people are showing an interest in the "kibbooss" (kibbutz), although I'm not saying they know what it entails.'

His impressions of the local Jewish community typified the prevailing sense of alienation:

> The Iraqi Jews' world is an Arab world ... Their mother tongue is Arabic ... Their culture is Arabic ... It's hard to speak of their having a religious world; rather, it's a traditional one ... Their religious culture is poor. There are no important rabbis ... and tradition is disintegrating without a fight ... There is absolutely no interest in religion, no profound religious feeling.

He described the Iraqi Jews' community institutions and extensive philanthropic activities as follows:

> There are no charitable institutions in Iraq. The hospitals and synagogues were built by the good graces of one individual ... [and yet] despite the assimilation of the Jewish world and culture, the Jews consider themselves Jewish ... They know they are Jewish and not Arab. They would find it hard to pinpoint the difference ... and yet there is a difference ... This primitive and yet very deep-rooted feeling provides a foothold for our Zionist and educational activities. The main problem now is how to translate this feeling into an awareness.

Sereni listed the difficulties the emissaries faced in their Zionist endeavour:

1. The Jews were adjusting to the situation in Iraq in the hope that things would straighten out. There was no Zionist political consciousness, even among the young people who had organized for Jewish defence. 'They feel national and human dignity but they have no Zionist thinking, or even a Zionist instinct ...' Almost no one had any Zionist political consciousness.

2. The intelligentsia and the young adults were sympathetic to communism, although their knowledge of socialism was rudimentary.

3. The venture was underfunded. About 300 people, mostly from the community's poorer strata, could not afford more than half the cost of the trip. Therefore, the Yishuv institutions had to cover the difference, and they lacked the finances to do so.

4. There was a considerable gap between the socialist pioneer ideology of Sereni and the emissaries, products of the Labour Movement, and the traditional Oriental life experience of the Iraqi Jews. Sereni saw the emissaries' task as not only to promote emigration to Palestine, but also, and no less so, to promote social mobility – by converting them to the ideal of productive labour:

> Our task is to organize the Iraqi community's immigration to and absorption into the Yishuv. We must ensure that the Baghdad immigrants become labourers, not merchants ... Since they do not understand the Zionist and moral value of labour – and actually hold physical labour in contempt – the major problem facing us in educating Iraqi Jews is labour-oriented education.

Nevertheless, Sereni acknowledged that most of the Iraqi Jewish immigrants would gravitate toward the cities, and suggested that a teachers' seminary be founded for them along the lines of that established by the Association of German Immigrants. His impression of Jewish Iraqi youth was mixed: 'There is "deep water" – youth who could be pioneers just like you or me ... but there is also the "foam" – youth of the Levantine-Arab type, who are not good material.' The major aim, he asserted, was to promote the immigration of 15- and 16-year-olds: 'We can make them into decent human beings if we resettle them in an environment that will mould them into decent human beings.' With this in mind, he spoke to Henrietta Szold of the Youth Aliyah Department, which had surplus certificates because the immigration of European youth had been halted. But the Department would not cover the travel expenses of the Iraqi youth. There was another problem: how to find suitable instructors for them.

Because Sereni's main activity in Iraq was educational, he requested Arabic translations of ideological-informational publications for dissemination among the Iraqi Jews: anthologies such as *Sefer He-Halutz*, articles from *Devar Ha-Po'elet*, etc. – material unpublishable in Iraq. All in all, Sereni was optimistic about the willingness of the Iraqi Jewish population to emigrate if only they were given the chance. The proof was that despite the fear of Egypt's collapse after the fall of Tobruk, and notwithstanding the uncertainty in Palestine, many Iraqi Jews remained interested in Palestine. 'We won't have to canvass for candidates; on the contrary, we'll be able to select the most suitable from the hundreds and thousands who will come forward.'[41]

The emissaries focused on the common people in the belief that they had learned the lesson of the riots – that there was no future for them in Iraq – more clearly than anyone else, and because, unlike the affluent people who set their sights on America and India, the poorer strata held Palestine as their only hope.[42]

The emissaries, of whom there were never enough, operated on a very tight budget. They would have been far less effective but for the help of Jewish soldiers and Solel Boneh workers, who functioned as instructors and Hebrew teachers, carried mail to Palestine, and established a wireless connection with the Hagana office in Palestine. Their activity was especially significant in northern Iraq, where, on their own initiative, they made contact with the Jewish community and laid the groundwork for Hebrew instruction and Zionist activity. Sereni, visiting Kirkuk, outlined a plan of action for the activists: to set up vanguard cells that would organize emigration to Palestine by all possible routes, and to instil the principles of the socialist Zionist Labour Movement. A nucleus of 25 youths was quickly set up, all of whom planned to emigrate to Palestine. A similar attempt was made in Mosul, but it failed. In their reports, the emissaries stressed the growing involvement of soldiers and Solel Boneh workers in Zionist activities. They suggested appointing 'political commissars' to instruct the soldiers and workers regarding both the clandestine nature of their assignment, and suitable informational literature.[43]

Initially, Sereni attempted to arrange legal emigration to Palestine, using the certificates that had been allocated for the Iraqi Jews. However, problems soon arose: in addition to the shortage of certificates, their delivery and classification was delayed by communication difficulties and the British consul's unwillingness to cooperate. The Iraqi Government made it increasingly difficult to obtain exit permits, especially for men of army service age. Consequently, certificates were not utilized and were wasted. This situation quickly gave rise to a black market in permits run by Jewish middlemen; as the pressure grew, the black market price rose. The emissaries, lacking an official Zionist office in Iraq, had no option but to turn a blind eye to what was going on.[44]

Sereni sought ways to expand legal immigration; one was by having students admitted into courses at Palestine educational institutions unaffiliated with the Jewish Agency. Although letters of admission to such institutions were often delayed, the venture was partially successful. Girls were accepted into institutions run by *Mo'etzet Ha-Po'alot* (General Council of Women Workers).[45] Another technique proposed by Sereni was the enlistment of Iraqi Jewish youth into army service in Palestine. This idea was eagerly embraced by the Yishuv institutions in Palestine, but an appeal by Shertok to army headquarters in Cairo was rejected.[46]

At approximately the same time (July 1942) the first attempts at illegal immigration were being made. A test group led by a guide left via Syria, and Shemarya Gutman, helped by the Solel Boneh people in Mosul, organized a second group to follow. When the first group was arrested in Aleppo, however, the departure of the second group was put on hold. The immigrants' families protested, and Gutman and Kadouri, who were in Iraq illegally, had to go underground. As a result of this setback, Sereni decided that a distinction had to be drawn between 'educational activities' and 'clandestine immigration.' Following the failed attempt at the latter in Mosul, a group of illegal immigrants was organized in Baghdad, but they were apprehended and forced to return. The local community reacted with such bitterness and anger toward the emissaries that they despaired of this activity.

These setbacks led Sereni to reassess the Iraqi Jewish community's actual willingness to emigrate to Palestine. He concluded that a change in the emissaries' operational tactics was in order. In September 1942, Sereni reported a change in the mood of the local Jewish community, which was moving 'toward an end to the Eretz Israel awakening that had been spawned by the persecutions of recent years and last year's riots.' Factors in this volte-face were: (a) the characteristic Jewish ability to forget and adjust; (b) economic prosperity produced by the war; (c) an improvement in the Iraqi authorities' attitude toward the Jews; (d) the intensification of communist propaganda, in particular among Jewish intellectuals, which turned the public against Zionism by accusing Zionists of collusion with the British; (e) the failure of the spontaneous immigration that followed the 1941 riots according to testimony in letters written by immigrants as well as first-hand reports which spoke of the harsh conditions, lack of commercial opportunities, and compulsory army service that characterized life in Palestine.

This led Sereni to the following conclusion:

> If we originally believed our main task to be the organization and promotion of immigration, today we must admit that these are pointless ... Let us not forget that we have missed the right time for fast action by not being here immediately after the riots, and even before then, by failing to prepare the necessary mechanism for exploiting this moment ... We are now reaping the bitter fruit of years of neglect. Our sin of omission can no longer be rectified through propaganda and stirring up fleeting enthusiasm ... We must beware of going against the current, by trying – despite reality – to pave the way for a mass immigration that will not happen. Rather, we must be sure not to neglect the present imperative of preparing for the future and taking advantage of all the opportunities for action available today.

His major duty, he now saw, was twofold: to train a core group of local youth to continue the work of the emissaries in Iraq; and to form a local infrastructure for a Zionist organization for fund-raising and the dissemination of informational literature. The emissaries were to focus on youth, through whom the entire Jewish community would be won over. Information material in Hebrew, English, French, and Arabic was essential. Its dissemination did not call for a large investment on the part of the Yishuv institutions. In sum, despite the difficulties, Sereni still believed it possible to attain the long-term goal of '[effecting] the immigration of Iraqi Jews in the pioneer spirit and retraining them for a life of manual labour.' In spite of everything, the 1941 riots had undermined the Jews' self-confidence and led to a spiritual reassessment that would, in all probability, be directed toward pioneering channels. If the emissaries were to abandon their posts, however, they might choose a totally different course.[47]

Following Sereni's assessment, Munya Marder (Mardor) – a Hagana member 'on loan' to Aliya Bet for the planning of illegal immigration routes via Syria – was sent to Iraq to study the emissaries' methods and coordinate escape routes for Aliya Bet by way of Syria. His visit angered Sereni, since it had not been coordinated with him and the informational material he had requested had not been sent with him. Marder's report largely corroborated those of the emissaries with respect to the Iraqi Jewish community's waning enthusiasm for emigration, and the reasons for this change: the 1941 riots and the resulting wave of spontaneous emigration had not been properly exploited by the appropriate institutions at the time. And once the immigration apparatus had been installed, conditions in Iraq had changed. With the added risk involved in illegal immigration, it was not surprising that 'Hardly anyone was willing to immigrate under Aliya Bet.' This paradoxical situation, Marder claimed, was the result of the Yishuv institutions' long-term disregard for Iraqi Jews' education. Like Sereni, Marder felt the emissaries should concentrate on educating youth, but questioned the Aliya Bet personnel's obligation to undertake this job. Marder challenged Sereni's conclusion that illegal immigration should be halted at least temporarily; instead, he proposed clandestine immigration, using the cooperatives' convoys, and the establishment of transit stations. In view of the poor response and the attendant risks and high expenses, however, he changed his mind: it would be best to make do with the existing routes via Syria without investing too much effort in developing them at least for the time being. But he felt that they must not settle for immigration – they should also create a 'transition period for education' in Palestine to ensure the immigrants' successful absorption.

Since large-scale immigration from Iraq was not imminent, Marder proposed that activities focus on the self-defence organization the Iraqi Jews had set up in the event of future attack. He visited Baghdad's Jewish quarters and drew up guidelines for defensive action, which included expanding the emissaries' training of a special force responsible for street combat, and providing this force with suitable literature, training, and weapons. Some arms and equipment, including a wireless, would be sent from Palestine and stored in three large warehouses, but local weapons purchases would have to be promoted as well. For security reasons, he proposed the dispatch of a special emissary responsible solely for organizing the defence.[48] Meirov and the Mossad's leaders accepted Marder's assessments. Returning to Palestine, he arranged for the transport of weapons and ammunition to Iraq via convoys organized by the bus cooperatives and via the British Army's Jewish transport units. The first radio set arrived in April 1943, complete with its operator, Malka Rofe. The emissaries were now able to expand basic defence training in Baghdad. Several dozen young men and women belonged to the defence organization at the time.[49]

Despite Sereni's pessimistic conclusions, some of the emissaries' work produced encouraging results. By the end of his first year in

Iraq, Sereni had managed to build up a nucleus of 500 Jewish youth and to establish ties with many others who were willing to participate. To create an educational infrastructure, however, he needed more emissaries and Arabic translations for dissemination among the local Jews. Because Sereni's activity was chiefly educational and went beyond that of Aliya Bet, he applied directly to the Jewish Agency's Organization and Political departments for financial aid, information, and more emissaries.[50] Until the latter arrived, he made do with soldiers and Solel Boneh workers from Palestine, who were becoming increasingly involved in vanguard activities.

As Zionist activity intensified, so did the pressure exerted by the British and Iraqi security services. In February 1943, Sereni reported that the Iraqi authorities were aware of the renewed Zionist effort and had begun trying to throttle it.[51] In letters, and while on leave in Palestine in March–April 1943, Sereni asked to return to Palestine, where he would train replacements for himself and his colleagues. Back in Baghdad in May, he found himself under even greater surveillance after communist newspapers had exposed the underground. Sereni was summoned for interrogation, his papers were confiscated, and several days later he was deported. With both Gutman and Kadouri on home leave at the time, the mission in Iraq was now leaderless.[52]

Two new emissaries (Uri She'ar-Yashuv and Yisrael Kopit) reached Iraq in the summer of 1943, but they were soon forced to return to Palestine because of the growing pressure of surveillance and intelligence activity. A Jewish deserter from Anders' army had informed on Aliya Bet activists in Iraq after gaining their confidence. As a result, Iraqi police arrested local Zionist activists' relatives as well as Jewish soldiers. The emissaries found themselves under ever-increasing surveillance, and had to be spirited out of the country. Zionist activity came to a near-standstill.[53] To fill the void, Aryeh Eshel (Schill) was sent to Iraq in October 1943 disguised as a Solel Boneh worker. His initial encounter with the Jewish community was as disappointing for him as it had been for his predecessors; he was discouraged by the lack of Zionist commitment and enthusiasm for emigration, which he attributed to Iraq's current prosperity. As he put it:

> They call themselves Zionists and say that their material and spiritual situation is hopeless, that the Rashid Ali affair can recur, and that they are ready to emigrate to Palestine ... yet

all this is not Zionism, a yearning for Eretz Israel, a desire to settle there ... rather, it is first-class hypocrisy and the height of Levantinism ... They consider the 'certificates' an insurance policy rather than something requiring them to emigrate ... Meanwhile, they are making money in Baghdad, and these are considered true Zionists.

Nevertheless, he reported that quite a few Jews with a small capital were willing to settle in Palestine if it offered investment opportunities in trade and industry. Eshel tried to contact economic organizations in Palestine for advice on such opportunities.[54]

It took Eshel several weeks to begin organizing Zionist activity, which had stagnated after the summer of 1943 crackdown. Under his leadership, Zionist efforts expanded in the provincial cities – particularly Basra, which was free of security-service monitoring largely due to the initiative and activity of Palestinian Jewish soldiers belonging to a company that had been entrusted with port traffic control and garrisoned in the city since the beginning of 1943.[55] By the end of that year the movement had 260 members, including 30 instructors, and more candidates than it could accommodate. The movement's organizational structure was formed in 1944: its major institutions were a council (central committee), a coordinating committee (representing the various branch groups), a central secretariat, branch secretariats, and miscellaneous committees. Heading the movement was the emissary, who participated in its institutions in an advisory and guiding capacity.[56] The movement expanded and consolidated despite a spate of arrests and searches in June 1944, after the Iraqi police seized a packet of incriminating letters.[57] In subsequent years the movement displayed its maturity by holding its own amid crises and in the absence of emissaries from Palestine.

## IRAQI JEWRY AND THE PLANNING OF EMIGRATION TO PALESTINE

Immediately following the 1941 riots, as stated, the Yishuv institutions became aware of the need to help Iraqi Jews emigrate and to set up emergency operations for the refugee victims of the massacre. Yet by June 1942, a year after the Baghdad disturbances, Iraqi Jewry no longer dominated the institutions' immigration discussions. Several factors account for this. First, the Yishuv leaders were disappointed in the 'human material' of the Iraqi immigrants who, in their opinion, were not sufficiently productive or pioneering. Second, the Iraqi authorities obstructed the exit of Palestine-bound Jews. Most important, however, were the emissaries' reports on the Jews' declining enthusiasm for immigration in view of Iraq's prosperity. Iraqi Jewry, despite fears for its future, was no longer perceived as a community in distress.

With these considerations in mind, the Jewish Agency decided in June 1942 not to increase Iraq's quota of immigration certificates, notwithstanding worries that some certificates would not be used because the war had sealed off the route from Europe. Thus, the Jewish Agency Political Department asked the Mandatory Government to reduce its quota for the next quarter-year from 10,000 certificates to only 5,000, because – the Immigration Department claimed – the country could absorb no more.[59] Neither did the Jewish Agency's attitude change even in November 1942, when reports of the annihilation of European Jews were confirmed. With increasing concern for the need to use surplus certificates, because of the substantial contraction in the number of potential immigrants from Europe and the disruption of transit routes from that continent, a decision was made to grant 600 out of the total quota of 3,000 certificates to Oriental Jews, including 100 to the Jews of Iraq.[60]

Iraqi Jewry regained its priority in Yishuv deliberations on immigration from 1943. The turnabout originated mainly from the needs of the Jewish sector in Palestine and from Ben-Gurion's plans to expand the Yishuv, seeing this as an essential step toward establishing a sovereign Jewish state in Palestine, and an awareness of the virtual halt of immigration from Europe as a result of the war. Immediately upon his return from the Biltmore Conference in November 1942, by which time details of the Holocaust had become known, Ben-Gurion spoke of the need to enlarge the Yishuv to three million or four million people by encouraging immigration from all countries, East and West alike.[61]

Another factor in this turning point was news in 1942–43 of attacks and incitement against Iraqi Jews, along with emissaries' reports of the thriving Jewish community's lack of interest in emigrating. In February 1942, there was apprehension in case of a German invasion of Turkey, and objective intelligence sources noted concern for the future of Iraqi Jewry.[62] Amin Zaki, the moderate Kurdish Iraqi leader who was sympathetic to the Jews and who had been a member of the Iraqi Government before the rise of Rashid Ali's regime in 1941, expressed fear of a massacre liable to obliterate the Jewish community if the British withdrew or the Germans invaded. Zaki argued that the only solution to the problem of Iraq's Jews was their organized evacuation by Jewish organizations in Palestine, Britain, and the United States.[63] Other reports spoke of Iraqi Jewry's growing identification with the Jewish–Arab conflict in Palestine, of pressure exerted on Jews to identify with the Arab cause, and of government incitement against Jews – symptoms of the political instability of Nuri Said's regime and of Iraq's burgeoning involvement in the Palestine problem.[64] In the summer of 1943, the threat of new attacks on Jews and government-inspired anti-Jewish incitement were such that by October the Jews were forced to request the protection of the American ambassador in Baghdad; only through his vigorous intervention was the menace averted.[65]

Because of this renewed concern for the fate of the Iraqi Jews, in addition to reports of the extermination of European Jewry, the problem of Iraqi Jewry cropped up again in the Yishuv institutions' discussions, but the European Jews still took precedence. In early March 1943, the Jewish Agency Executive discussed the Mandatory Government's decision to allot 29,000 certificates – the entire Jewish immigration quota according to the White Paper. Ben-Gurion ruled that although as many Jews as possible had to be saved from Nazi-occupied countries, such mass immigration was highly improbable because exit routes had been cut off. 'Meanwhile, however, there are Jews in the Oriental countries, too, and we have to save them.' The communities of Yemen, Iraq, and Syria were also in grave danger, and would probably be the first targets for destruction when the Jewish–Arab conflict in Palestine resumed after the war. Iraqi Jewry was especially vulnerable because its host country was already notorious for slaughtering minorities; news of the mass murder of Jews in the Holocaust would only make the extermination of the Jews in Iraq easier. Therefore, Ben-Gurion sought to allocate some certificates to the Jews of Yemen and Iraq. But Dobkin, who had the emissaries' latest reports in hand, explained reality to Ben-Gurion: Iraq was enjoying an economic boom, the Jews would not leave now, and only immigration-oriented education would change their minds. The only country with immigration potential was Yemen. Shapira seconded Dobkin's stance. Gruenbaum objected to the very idea of transferring certificates because this would give the Mandatory Government a pretext to argue that the Jewish Agency admits no need for so many certificates. Instead, he asserted, the government should be told that the quota of 25,000 certificates was a drop in the bucket; the reserve could be used for immigration from Yemen and Iraq. Summing up, Ben-Gurion announced that the 25,000 certificates were needed now, and stated that a regular quota would be proposed soon, but he noted that the Jewish Agency would not confine itself to the figures cited in the White Paper.⁶⁶

Dobkin described the 'rediscovery' of the Jews of Iraq and their significant immigration potential at a meeting of the Mapai Central Committee on 12 July 1943:

> Our task vis-à-vis this Jewish community can be defined in one phrase: Zionist conquest of these Diasporas and their relocation to Palestine ... The value of these Diasporas has grown in several respects:
>
> (a) We do not know how many Jews will survive the extermination campaign in Europe, and how many we shall be able to contact.
> (b) We all know the simple truth that the secret of our policies today is to reinforce our strength by bringing more Jews to Palestine; as we are well aware, this Jewish community will be the first to join us, in advance of Jewish communities in Europe.
> (c) They are more accessible to us, and we to them.

However, Dobkin also recognized the intrinsic problems of this kind of mission: 'although geographically they are so close to us, they are strange and distant, and the estrangement is mutual ... Thus far our interest in these countries has been comparable to the mere curiosity of tourists ... Until recently we did not consider it a primary function of Zionist policy to handle immigration from these countries.'

Therefore, he asserted, it was necessary to take thorough, basic action. Unlike European Jews, Iraqi Jews – and Oriental Jews in general – had to be alerted to the need to resettle in Palestine. 'We realize it will be no simple matter, even after the events in Baghdad, to launch an immigration movement among prosperous Iraqi Jews.' Dobkin insisted that the Yishuv take responsibility for the fate of the Iraqi Jews (and all Oriental Jews) since they would be the first to suffer, running the risk of slaughter and destruction, when the Jewish–Arab struggle in Palestine resumed following the war. Therefore it was imperative to act swiftly on their behalf, even if they themselves were unaware that they were in danger. However,

Dobkin felt that immigration in itself, although the prime goal, was not sufficient. A change in social-class orientation was also essential: 'We must teach them the cardinal value – that of labour, the need to adapt to a life of labour.' The Yishuv would have to uproot the Iraqis' contempt for manual labour. It was not enough to bring them to Palestine; they also had to be integrated into the *Histadrut* labour faction. The main debate centred on a proposal for action and education of the Oriental Jewish communities, including Iraq, drawn up by a 'Committee of Three' (B. Katznelson, A. Dobkin, and S. Meirov) appointed by the party bureau. The proposal called for the establishment of a uniform pioneer movement based on the values of the Zionist ideal, labour-oriented education, and defence.

Enzo Sereni, who attended the meeting, accepted this plan in principle, but in view of his intimate familiarity with the Iraqi Jewish community he proposed that an alternative framework be set up for the middle classes, who were not interested in physical labour. His proposal was rejected by the others, who viewed the immigration of Iraqi and Oriental Jews from the European perspective of *halutzim* (pioneers) rebelling against social conventions and the traditional family framework. As Labour Movement stalwarts, they considered work a supreme social, moral and national value – 'a Jewish human endeavour of prime importance,' as Hayyim Rokah said, supported by B. Eisenstat and Y. Kosoy. Pinhas Lubianker (Lavon) spoke of the need to unify the pioneering Zionist movement so as to deny the Revisionists a foothold and to counteract the growing influence of the Communist party in Iraq. Ben-Gurion summed up the debate by stressing the need to inculcate Labour Movement values as an integral part of the Zionist idea. It was decided to set up a unified Hehalutz Movement body as the basic formula for Zionist activity in the East.[67]

When Yishuv leaders began to discuss the situation that would arise after the war in a Jewish Agency Executive session on 20 June 1944, Ben-Gurion outlined his 'one million plan' for the immediate immigration of one million Jews. The Iraqi and Oriental communities figured prominently in this plan. Indeed, henceforth their political weight in such discussions increased, as counterweight against the Arab population in Palestine, as proposals for a population exchange began to surface as a possible solution to the Jewish–Arab conflict. In his scheme, Ben-Gurion dealt first with European Jewish refugees, and only afterward with 'bring[ing] over all the Jews from the Arab countries.' He estimated their numbers at

400,000 in the Orient and another 400,000 in North Africa; all, he argued, were at risk of annihilation and cultural and human atrophy.

Rabbi Fishman expressed reservations as to the feasibility of an immediate mass absorption of one million Jews. A. Kaplan had reservations about a mass transfer of all Oriental Jews to Palestine. He cited integration problems and the transferees' non-refugee status, which meant that – unlike the European refugees – funds could not be raised for them. Kaplan pointed to the low cultural level of the Yemenite immigrants (which was creating integration difficulties), treating it as typical of all Oriental Jews, including the Iraqis. By contrast, Immigration Department head M. Shapira favoured including the Oriental Jews in the 'one million plan' as Ben-Gurion proposed, because of the many dangers in their future and the distinct possibility that they would be victimized like European Jewry. He therefore considered the Yishuv duty-bound to work speedily for their deliverance, and stressed the importance of the Iraqi Jews as a counterweight to that year's Arab-population transfer plan.

M. Shertok expressed support in principle for integrating the Oriental Jews into the 'one million plan.' From a practical standpoint, however, he questioned both their willingness to emigrate and the Yishuv's willingness to accept them. 'If we were to poll [the Iraqi community] today regarding emigration to Palestine, I think we would find that no more than half would say "yes" ... This would be true of the entire Oriental Jewish community, including the 90,000 Jews of Baghdad.' Although Shertok also had reservations about the low cultural level of these communities, he did not see this as a reason to curtail their immigration. Rather, he said, the Yishuv should appeal to American Jewry as a 'real' immigration reserve.

Despite these misgivings, Ben-Gurion's summary of the debate emphasized the need to promote the immigration of Iraqi as well as all other Oriental Jews, both because of the dangers they faced in their countries of residence and because of the need for one million Jews to emigrate swiftly to Palestine, thereby making its Jewish population the majority:

> If we fail to take responsibility for this, we shall have to take responsibility for their massacre ... I foresee a worse fate for the Jews of Iraq than emigration to Palestine and a drop in their standard of living. Complaining Jews – let that be our smallest problem once they are here with us in Palestine. I envisage far

worse troubles for both them and us if they stay there and we stay here ... Large-scale immigration does not mean 30,000, it means one million, i.e., a Jewish majority in Palestine. But we must draw up a clear plan.[68]

Ben-Gurion consolidated his scheme during 1945, basing it on experts' reports about Jewish willingness to emigrate and opportunities to do so in various countries. These included 850,000 of the two million Jews who survived the war in Europe and Russia, 30,000 of the 100,000 Iraqi Jews, and 150,000 of the 855,000 Jews in other Muslim countries. Thus, an estimated 30 per cent of Iraqi Jews were likely to emigrate, slightly less than the percentage of European Jews. The estimate was culled from a comprehensive survey of potential immigration sources conducted by David Horowitz of the Jewish Agency's Economic Department.[69] Under this plan, as in the deliberations among Yishuv institutions, Ben-Gurion considered Oriental Jews, the Iraqis included, as destitute refugees in need of basic social and economic reform. They would be moulded into manual industrial labourers. On the other hand, no allowances were made for the immigration of the upper and middle classes.[70]

Ben-Gurion elaborated on the 'one million plan' several months later, stressing its importance for establishing a Jewish state in Palestine as the basis for the continued existence of the Jewish nation and for a peace treaty with the Arabs. In this context, he identified the most likely sources of Jewish immigration, calling for the immigration of all Jews from the Orient, most of those from Western Europe, as many as possible from Eastern Europe, and pioneer youth from the Anglo-Saxon countries.[71] His scheme was evidently influenced by statistician Roberto Bachi's assessment that even if a million Jews were to immigrate, the narrow Jewish majority in Palestine would be short-lived because of the Arabs' birthrate. This factor led Bachi to conclude that Palestine must be partitioned, that Arabs living in Jewish territory must be transferred to Arab territory, and that Jews from Arab countries – the only source of immigration that could be fully tapped – should be resettled in Palestine.[72]

Although in long-range plans and in the Yishuv leadership's consciousness, Iraqi Jewry was becoming more important, this was not reflected on the operational plane. Throughout the period, demand for immigration certificates for Iraqi Jews far outstripped supply. While this was mainly because most resources were channelled to European Jewry, there were other factors: most certificates allocated by the Immigration Department were for youth and manual labourers, whereas most of the would-be immigrants from Iraq belonged to the middle class or had relatives in Palestine. Thus, many applicants were refused even though they managed to obtain exit permits, and repeated appeals in this matter by Iraqi immigrant organizations were either rejected or ignored.[73] Another problem was wastage of certificates due to red tape and faulty communication. Sometimes by the time certificates arrived, exit visas had expired. In other cases, certificates were received but the Iraqi Government refused to grant exit visas. In addition, the certificates of immigrants who returned to Iraq shortly after immigration were revoked. Finally, the Yishuv institutions suspected that exit visas were being traded for immigration certificates granted by recommendation of the Iraqi immigrant organizations, although the latter categorically rejected the charge. All the above made the Immigration Department reluctant to issue certificates for immigration applicants in Iraq.[74]

Because Iraqi immigrants were not represented in the Jewish Agency institutions, the Iraqi immigrant organizations in Palestine functioned as a pressure group and lobby for immigration from Iraq. These organizations also considered themselves responsible for absorbing Iraqi immigrants in Palestine. Thus, they wanted a greater say in the selection of potential immigrants, and official recognition by the establishment. The Immigration Department rejected their request. There had been friction on this issue as early as the summer of 1941, which spurred members of the Council of the Iraqi Jewish Community to violence in the Jewish Agency's Jerusalem offices. Following this outburst, the Immigration Department promised maximum consideration of the Committee's recommendations and collaboration with its representatives.[75] Nonetheless, most of the Committee's applications for immigration certificates were turned down for the aforementioned reasons. Nor was the Committee consulted as to the arrangements made for the absorption of Iraqi immigrants, even though such consultation could have been helpful.[76]

In 1944 and thereafter, the number of certificates allocated to Iraqi Jewry was further curtailed, most resources now being used to absorb Holocaust refugees. At the same time, however, the Iraqi Jews – fearing for their future in view of Iraq's growing involvement in the escalating Jewish–Arab conflict in Palestine – exerted greater pressure to emigrate. The Association of Aram Naharayim Immigrants in Palestine again requested a minimal certificate allocation for Iraqi Jewry, stressing that it was not disregarding the grievous plight of the Holocaust refugees, it was simply concerned about the worsening predicament of Iraqi Jews and the dangers that awaited them, as Ben-Gurion had so frequently mentioned in his speeches, and it feared that Jews might soon be prohibited from leaving Iraq, the Association warned. But the request was rejected. The Committee of the Iraqi Jewish Community then sought to obtain certificates for Iraqi Jews who had reached Palestine as tourists and wished to settle there.[77] Amid the diminishing supply of and surging demand for certificates, the fact that Iraqi and Oriental Jewry was in general unrepresented in Jewish Agency institutions was significant. The Associations of Iraqi and Kurdish Immigrants appealed in desperation to public figures and sympathetic leaders for immigration certificates. Thanks to Ben-Zvi's intervention, their requests were partly met; in certain instances, however, even this did not help.[78] Another public figure, Ze'ev Leibowitz of the Jewish Agency's Immigration Department, took it upon himself to intervene on behalf of Iraq's Jews by approaching the Department head. Leibowitz repeatedly warned that the Department had approved a few certificates only for this community, and that many applications by would-be immigrants with exit permits were not being considered. He demanded more certificates for Iraqi Jews in view of their deteriorating situation and his apprehension that the Iraqi Government would treat them as scapegoats for events in Palestine. At the very least, he insisted, certificates should be reserved for Iraq's Jewish tourists who were already in Palestine and Iraqi Jewish deportees in Syria.[79] The combined pressure of immigrants' groups and public figures evidently led to a certain response in allocations – certificates were set aside for Jewish tourists who were already in Palestine. In sum, the number of certificates for Iraqi Jews was small. Only 70 certificates were issued to Iraqi Jews between the beginning of 1944 and mid-1945.[80]

With regard to Yishuv emissaries in Iraq, Ben-Gurion's vision of the immigration of Iraqi Jews, and Oriental Jews in general, was also highly unrealistic. Few emissaries were sent to Iraq – usually not more than three, sometimes only two, and occasionally none at all. There were few resources at their disposal, too. During the war years the manpower shortfall had been offset by the many helpful Palestinian Jewish soldiers posted in Iraq. But the emissary shortage was sorely felt once the war ended and the Jewish units were removed from Iraq, especially since the pioneer movement in Iraq had expanded to several branches and hundreds of members by then.

Two major factors behind the paucity of emissaries were the limited resources available to Aliya Bet, and the transfer of most of its activity to Europe at the end of the Second World War. Another influence was partisan and sectarian bickering within the Yishuv. Although efforts were made to keep word of these disputes from reaching Iraq, bits of information inevitably crossed the desert and infringed on the emissaries' work. Because of fears that a rival organization would gain a foothold among the Iraqi Jews, any activity other than that of the Labour-run Aliya Bet was throttled. Thus, the operations of Stern Group emissaries in Iraq were nipped in the bud in 1942, as was another attempt by them in 1944.[81] Similarly, all Hebrew-instruction activities by soldiers under YMCA auspices, so successful in 1944–45, were stopped, although the soldiers considered themselves non-partisan emissaries of the Yishuv at large.[82]

Even within the Labour camp, Mapai leaders worried that the United Kibbutz Movement was over-represented among the emissaries in Iraq. Thus they stopped sending UKM emissaries to the country, in spite of the upsurge of activity in Iraq. Lacking other suitable candidates, such an approach undermined efforts to increase the number of emissaries.[83] Emissaries in Iraq did everything they could to oust a would-be colleague affiliated to Ha-Shomer Hatzair, who reached Basra in early 1945, even though they were drastically shorthanded. After he was indeed ejected in July of that year, Basra was virtually leaderless and its Zionist activity paralysed, necessitating a later reconstruction of the entire Zionist apparatus.[84]

## POST-WAR YISHUV ACTIVITY ON BEHALF OF IRAQI JEWS

After the relative prosperity and calm of the war years (1942–45), the Iraqi Jews again became anxious about their fate. The departure from Iraq of most of the British forces and all the remaining Palestinian soldiers bred insecurity. As debates on the future of Palestine resumed, the Muslim authorities and population grew more hostile toward the Jews. Furthermore, the government promulgated regulations designed to remove Jews from key economic and commercial positions, and to reduce the number of Jewish civil servants. The Iraqi Government was holding the Jews hostage (in the words of Nuri Said), making it difficult for them to obtain visas to any country, and forcing those seeking to travel to Palestine to post a 2,000-dinar bond to ensure their return to Iraq.

The emissaries in Iraq asked the Jewish Agency to use the press and Jewish organizations in Palestine, Britain, and the United States to alert the public to the worsening plight of the Iraqi Jews. They also urged that a special department be set up within the Jewish Agency to coordinate, together with the relevant immigrant organizations, the handling of Iraqi and Oriental Jewry and to send instructors and spiritual leaders to these communities. And they recommended the establishment of a committee that, in concert with economic organizations in Palestine, would develop absorption programmes for Iraqi Jews and provide them with investment channels in Palestine.[85] As seen, however, the Yishuv institutions substantially expanded their post-war efforts in Europe, and the problem of the Iraqi and Oriental Jewish communities was shunted aside. Emissaries were always scarce and sometimes unavailable altogether. They repeatedly remonstrated with the institutions about their neglect of Iraqi Jewry, and pleaded with them – in vain – to appoint more emissaries and allocate more resources for their activities.[86]

The Zionist movement in Iraq matured and coalesced during the war years, and the infrastructure then established demonstrated its ability to stand alone. Membership grew from 400 in 1944 to 700 in May 1945 and over 1,000 in 1946. Local instructors took over from the soldiers, and the head office organized seminars for guides. The movement made inroads in the Jewish public, although it had to contend with the growing Communist influence on Jewish youth, particularly in the large cities. This factor led to a membership decline in late 1946 and early 1947, although in 1948 the ranks again swelled to 2,000 people, operating out of 16 branch offices.[87]

As the Zionist movement coalesced, the Hagana (Ha-shura) resumed operations in Iraq. Ezra Kadouri had laid the groundwork for this activity in 1942, but with his return to Palestine in 1943 the movement lost momentum and ground to a halt after its great crisis of 1944. Dan Ram, a Hagana emissary from Kibbutz Hanita posted to Baghdad, revived the movement in July 1945, providing the real impetus for expanded defensive action in Iraq and the Hagana's consolidation as an operational body. From scratch, he recruited members within and outside the movement, arranged instructor and officer courses, and stockpiled weapons from Palestinian and local sources. He organized training in the use of firearms and other weapons, and courses in first aid, and physical fitness. He ensured that all Jewish quarters in Baghdad were mapped and apportioned into regions, with an officer in charge of each. Ha-shura members were divided into platoons, and weapons were stored within easy reach.

After Ram's return to Palestine in April 1946, local defence activity flagged somewhat until Mordechai Binczewski (Ben-Tzur), a Palmah emissary, arrived in December. Binczewski restored the organization's momentum, expanded its ranks, and trained local commanders to take control after he left during the critical period of March 1948. He also set up defence branches in Basra and Kirkuk in 1947, but his focus was Baghdad, where most Iraqi Jews lived.[88] Throughout this period he kept in close touch with Palmah commander Yigal Allon, who instructed him in overall strategy while leaving the tactical details to him. The purpose of the movement was patently defensive: to defend Jewish neighbourhoods against mob attack until the Yishuv was able to mobilize international intervention on their behalf. Allon warned members of the defence group not to be the first to open fire, lest they provide the other side with a pretext for massacre.[89]

During the entire time of its existence, Ha-shura was never called upon to prove its strength and implement its plans. Its major functions were organization and maintaining a state of alert. On 2 November 1946, the anniversary of the Balfour Declaration (accompanied each year by tension and incitement), there were rumours of planned attacks against Jews. Ha-shura immediately placed its members on standby, staked out positions, and handed out weapons. The day passed uneventfully, and there was no need to deploy the defence forces. In January 1948, when the Portsmouth crisis erupted and demonstrations took place against the new British–Iraqi treaty, Ha-shura was again on alert. Again, there was no need for action. By far the largest Ha-shura undertaking was its preparation for a possible pogrom on 15 May 1948, when the State of Israel was to be declared. On 14 May, the organization's 350 members went on standby, including 100 liaisons and medics, with 150 weapons available. With the help of the community, the quarters were subdivided and roadblocks were set up. This day, too, ended without incident, and the defence forces were demobilized on 16 May.[90]

Pressure to emigrate from Iraq mounted as the Second World War ended. Because of the prevailing conditions, however, emigration activity decreased. Almost all possibilities of legal immigration had been blocked. All that remained was clandestine immigration using desert routes. A final attempt to spirit immigrants out of the country with the last Palestinian Jewish military convoys led to increased government vigilance on the northern borders, which shut down the Iraq–Syria border route.

Another futile underground immigration endeavour by four men who were stopped at the Iraq–Transjordan border, and the bombing of the Jordan River bridges in June 1946, brought illegal immigration to a halt. The Iraqi Zionist movement, which as an activist vanguard could not survive without ongoing emigration, felt the impact. Thus, once it clearly could not further the immigration cause, defections began. The emissaries did all they could to seek alternative routes, whilst Aliya Bet centred in Palestine restrained these attempts. This may have been due to circumspection, lack of resources, or doubts as to the Iraqi Jews' ability to endure the strain of the illegal immigration routes and life in Palestine itself. Jonathan Rabinowitz (Yonas), reaching Iraq in early 1946 to organize emigration, gave up in despair and returned to Palestine. After Yerahmiel Asa and Mordechai Binczewski came to Iraq in late 1946 and Yonas returned in January 1947, an attempt was made to smuggle 40 immigrants across the desert in a truck. The adventure ended when the truck overturned, leaving a number of dead and wounded. Illegal immigration missions continued between February and April 1947, usually in the form of small groups led through the desert by amply rewarded local tribesmen. These forays also ceased when local funds for the border-runners ran out and required funding was not supplied by Aliya Bet.[91]

By now, only a skeletal movement remained. When the immigration efforts fell through, the movement's educational activities, under Asa and Binczewski, began to intensify. Hebrew and socialism classes expanded, and in June 1947 the first instructional camp was organized in the Khanaqin area. Because of the restrictions, however, the only agricultural training was offered in the movement's Kirkuk branch. The movement tried to increase its influence on Jewish schools and community institutions – successfully in the country's north but less so in the large Jewish communities of Baghdad and Basra.[92]

The emissaries repeatedly demanded the resumption of immigration activities, which were the movement's life-blood and a vital concern for the Iraqi Jews, whose situation was deteriorating. Echoing this demand were Iraqi immigrants' associations in Palestine and the liaison office of the He-Halutz movement, which had co-opted Iraqi immigration activists who had settled in Palestine. They called for greater efforts on behalf of Iraqi Jewry (i.e., to effect the community's immigration), more emissaries, and action designed to alert the Western powers and the world to their plight.[93] In response, and with overland routes blocked, Aliya Bet decided to mount an airlift. Thus, in August 1947, Aliya Bet organized a clandestine flight in which two American pilots brought 50 illegal immigrants to Palestine (Operation Michaelberg). Following this successful operation, a second flight was launched in September 1947. These operations were among Aliya Bet's great triumphs, but they were not continued.[94]

The UN debates on the partitioning of Palestine and the establishment of a Jewish state imperilled the Iraqi and Oriental Jews, putting them back on the Yishuv institutions' agenda. On 9 December 1947, during the Mapai Secretariat's first meeting after the declaration of the partition plan, Aliya Bet head Meirov depicted the rescue of Oriental Jewry as a matter of the utmost urgency, regretting that too little had been done in this domain:

> We saw what was about to happen in the Oriental countries, but we did very little. We may have brought over 8,000–9,000 Jews ... Now we have to know what's happening this evening in Baghdad and elsewhere.

Meirov called for the establishment of a special department to deal exclusively with saving Oriental Jews. Most of the debate, however, concerned not Oriental Jewry but the Jews of Rumania, upon whom the Iron Curtain was liable to descend imminently. The Yishuv institutions considered this problem more urgent, and aimed to solve it before turning to the rescue of the Iraqi and Oriental Jews.[95]

Yishuv activity on behalf of Iraqi and Oriental Jewry diminished from the end of 1947 until May 1948. Emissaries were few, activity was fragmented among different bodies, and there was no overall plan or vision. Emissaries repeatedly warned about neglect and the need for a unified entity to serve Iraqi and Oriental Jewry in view of the growing danger as war clouds gathered in Palestine.[96] As stated, however, the lack of resources and the focus on Holocaust survivors precluded any radical change in dealing with the Iraqi Jews until the State of Israel was established.

In early 1948, several attempts were made at overland illegal immigration with the help of border-runners. These ended tragically in March (by which time battles were already raging in Palestine):

two teenagers had traversed the desert with the aid of a smuggler and were trying to cross the Jordan into Palestine when they were caught by Kaukji's men. Their fate remains unknown, although they were probably murdered. From then until Israel was declared, illegal immigration from Iraq ceased.[97] After the establishment of the State, Aliya Bet began concentrating on organizing new immigration methods. Immigration from Iraq, previously a partisan venture, became part of the State's overall immigration planning.

## CONCLUSION

Yishuv efforts on behalf of Iraqi Jewry from the 1941 riots until the declaration of the State of Israel in May 1948 can be divided into three stages:

1. An awakening and spontaneous activity in response to the 1941 riots;
2. The laying of the foundations for a Zionist movement and illegal immigration from Iraq during the Second World War (1942–45);
3. Consolidation of the Zionist movement in Iraq after the war, the search for new clandestine routes, and protection of the Iraqi Jews in preparation for the establishment of the State of Israel.

After years of detachment, Iraqi Jewry became a prime concern of the Yishuv institutions as a result of the 1941 riots. The Yishuv reacted spontaneously, displaying its eagerness to help on three levels: financial aid, alerting the world to the Iraqi Jews' plight, and promoting immigration. However, the Yishuv's possibilities for providing effective assistance were limited. Within a few months it became acknowledged that most activity had to take the form of a resumption of emissary work in Iraq, the main objective being the furtherance of emigration to Palestine as the solution to the problem of Iraqi Jewry.

After the first emissaries were sent to Iraq, it transpired that the Jews of Iraq could not be defined as a community in distress; in view of Iraq's wartime prosperity, it would take a long-term effort to educate the public in Zionism and immigration. The emissaries attempted this, but they lacked human and financial resources. Nevertheless, an underground Zionist core was established, which – despite a dearth of emissaries and funds – managed to extend its network and influence within the Jewish community at large. The emissaries also organized a local defence force to prevent recurrent anti-Jewish riots in Iraq. As a rule, Iraqi and Oriental Jews were of secondary importance in terms of the Yishuv institutions' activity in Palestine. When reports of the Holocaust reached Palestine and the Yishuv began planning a Jewish state there, their importance as a future immigration reserve grew. In reality, however, most resources were devoted to European Jewry, leaving few for the Iraqi and Oriental communities. The end of the war witnessed a further contraction of resources set aside for the Jews of Iraq. It was the emissaries who spurred and planned immigration from Iraq.

The Yishuv's major effort on behalf of the Jews of Iraq was its establishment of a Zionist movement there. Despite its crises and lack of resources, it was able to function independently, and was destined to play an important role in organizing mass emigration to Israel. The Yishuv also helped assemble a defence force that, although never tested, was meant to defend the Jews if riots against them ever recurred.

## NOTES

1. Glitzenstein-Meir, A., 'Ha-pera'ot bi-yehudei baghdad hag ha-shavu'ot tasha (1–2 June 1941)' ('Disturbances against the Jews of Baghdad on Shavuot 5701 (1–2 June 1941)'), *Pe'amim*, 8 (1981), pp.21–37.
2. Testimonies and reports collected from the Central Zionist Archives (hereinafter: CZA), S 25/5290.
3. E. Epstein to M. Shertok, 25 June 1941. For his talk with the new naval attaché in the American Embassy in Jerusalem, who had arrived several days previously from Baghdad, see CZA S 25/5290.
4. The meeting is described in '*Al ha-pera'ot bi-yehudei' Iraq* (The Riots against the Jews of Iraq), a publication of the National Council Press and Information Department, 4 July 1941, CZA S 25/5290.
5. Undated copy of the letter: *ibid* and CZA Z4/6062.
6. National Council Press and Information Department, '*Al ha-pera'ot bi-yehudei 'Iraq* (supplements), 14 July 1941, CZA S 25/5290.
7. Mapai Central Committee Minutes, meeting of 9 July 1941, Labour Party Archives (hereinafter: LPA).
8. Minutes of the Jewish Agency Executive meeting of 13 July 1941, CZA.
9. Report on Ittah's visit by Almaliah, 18 July 1941; Ittah's attestation to Dr. B. Joseph, 20 July 1941, CZA S 25/5290.
10. Minutes of the Jewish Agency Executive meeting of 20 July 1941, CZA.
11. Report on Ben-Zvi's meeting with H. Szold and Dr. G. Landauer on the emigration to Palestine of Iraqi Jewish youth, 27 July 1941, CZA S 6/3381; E. Sasson to M. Shertok, 6 July 1941, CZA S 25/9825.
12. Yanovski–Shertok correspondence on the topic, Aug. 1941, CZA S 25/5289.
13. Transfer of donation moneys, 10 Aug. 1941, CZA S 25/5289.
14. Keren Hayesod to Jewish Agency Political Department, 20 Feb. 1941, CZA S 25/5289.

## ACTIVITY OF THE YISHUV

15. M. Ittah to M. Shertok, 26 May 1942, CZA S 25/5289.
16. Y. Bechar, Jewish Agency Immigration Department, to Leo Cohen, 24 May 1942, CZA S 6/4575; Leo Cohen to J. Linton, 1 June 1942, CZA Z 4/3865.
17. Ben-Zvi to the Jewish Agency Political Department, 14. Oct. 1942, M. Ittah's report to Shertok, 26 May 1942, CZA S 25/5289.
18. *Ben-Gurion Diaries* (hereinafter: BGD), 9 Aug. 1941, Ben-Gurion Archives at Sde Boker (hereinafter: BGA).
19. Report by Ben-Gurion on the Mapai Central Committee meeting of 27 July 1941, minutes of meeting, CZA.
20. Shertok's report on the meeting, 21 July 1941, CZA Z 4/14.797.
21. E. Sasson to M. Shertok, 28 July 1941, talk with the new Iraqi consul in Palestine, CZA Z 4/14.797.
22. E. Epstein to M. Shertok, 'Shlihuti le-Iran u-le-'Iraq' ('My Missions to Iran and Iraq'), Top Secret, 28 Aug. 1941, CZA Z 4/14.797.
23. M. Shertok to B. Locker, 11 July 1941, CZA S 25/1555; report of Jewish Agency in Jerusalem to the World Jewish Congress, 19 July 1941, CZA Z 4/14.797; Bernard Joseph speaking for the Jewish Agency Executive to the Chief Secretary of the Government of Palestine, 16 July 1941, CZA S 25/2522; the Chief Secretary to the National Committee, 31 July 1941, CZA S 25/5289.
24. H. MacMichael to Lord W.G. Moyne, 5 Aug. 1941 (copy), FO 371/27128 E4474.
25. Jewish Agency Executive minutes, 24.8.1941, CZA; internal report of the Jewish Agency Information Bureau, 28 Sept. 1941, CZA S 25/2522.
26. Reports on many instances of border-running, some futile, CZA S 25/5290; L. Cohen for the Jewish Agency Executive to the Chief Secretary of the Government of Palestine, 10 Oct. 1941, CZA S 25/2522.
27. Chief Secretary to the Jewish Agency Executive in Jerusalem and the Jewish Agency branch office in London, 13 Nov. 1941, CZA S 25/2522.
28. Jewish Agency Immigration Department to Political Department, 6 May 1942, CZA S 25/2522; L. Cohen to J. Linton, 1 June 1941, CZA Z 1/14.797.
29. Report on Ben-Zvi's meeting with Henrietta Szold, 27 Feb. 1941, CZA S 6/3381.
30. See, for example, correspondence on the matter, Na'im and Murad Shaguri, the Hebrew University, Jewish Agency Youth Aliyah and Immigration Departments, Dec. 1941–Jan. 1942, CZA S 6/3381.
31. Technion Director S. Kaplanski to Jewish Agency Executive, 17 Sept. 1942, and Jewish Agency's reply to him, 30 Oct. 1942, CZA S6/3460.
32. Y. Meir (Yehoshaphat), *Me'ever la-midbar – ha-mahteret ha-halutzit be-'Iraq* (Across the Desert – the Pioneering Underground in Iraq), Tel Aviv, 1973 (hereinafter: Meir), pp.39–45; Shaul Avigur, *Im dor ha-hagana* (With the Hagana Generation), II., Tel Aviv, 1961 (hereinafter: Avigur), p.119.
33. Y. A. (Yitzhak Azarya) to E. Dobkin, Director of Jewish Agency Immigration Department, report on his mission to Iraq, 6 Nov.–11 Dec. 1941, 25 Dec. 1941, CZA S 25/5289.
34. Y. Bachar, Immigration Department, to Youth Aliyah Bureau, 24 March 1942, and H. Beit's response, 29 March 1942, CZA S 6/3381.
35. Mazal Museri to Y. Bechar, Jewish Agency, Jerusalem, 18 Feb. 1942, CZA S 25/5289; Mazal Museri's report on the situation of the Iraqi Jews (confidential, unsigned), 8 April 1942, CZA S 6/4575.
36. For a detailed description of his mission, see Avigur, II, pp.112–30.
37. Avigur, II, pp.120–4.
38. Avigur, II, p.125. A similar version of Ben-Zion Yisraeli's remarks appears in his letter to Enzo Sereni during his mission to Iraq, 30 Aug. 1942, CZA S 25/5290.
39. Avigur, II, p.131.
40. Sereni's lecture to the Histadrut Immigration Committee, 2 July 1942, CZA S 25/5290; Meir, pp.56ff.
41. Sereni's lecture to the Histadrut Immigration Committee, 2 July 1942, CZA S 25/5290.

42. Ibid.
43. S. R.'s (Shalom Rashba's) report on initial activities among the Jews of Kirkuk and Mosul, attached to Sereni's lecture, CZA S 25/5290; for a detailed description of the soldiers' activities see Y. Gelber, *Toldot ha-hitnadvut III: nosei ha-degel: shlihutam shel ha-mitnadvim la-'am ha-yehudi* (History of Volunteer Activity, III: The Standard-Bearers: The Role of Volunteers for the Jewish People), Jerusalem, 1983 (hereinafter Gelber), pp.28–9, 35.
44. Letters from Ehud (Sereni) on the subject, 9 June 1942, 17 June 1942, 31 June 1942, 9 Dec. 1942; Y. Bechar to Ehud, 15 Nov. 1942, 5 Feb. 1943, CZA S 6/3785.
45. Lengthy correspondence on this topic: Sereni–Immigration Department–Youth Department and Women's Labour Council, Sept.–Dec. 1942, CZA S 6/3785, S 6/3460, S 6/3781.
46. Letter from Ehud (Sereni), 6 Dec. 1942, CZA S 6/1960.
47. Letter from Ehud, 22 Sept. 1942, CZA S 25/5290.
48. Tsefoni (Mardor) to Nissim (Meirov), 'Review of My Visit to Iraq, 7 Oct. 1942–15 Oct. 1942' (Hebrew); Tsefoni, 'Summaries and Conclusions during My Last Visit to Iraq', 12 Dec. 1942, CZA S 6/1960 (Hebrew); M. Mardor, *Shlihut 'aluma* (Secretive Mission), Tel Aviv, 1957, pp.84–97.
49. Mardor, see note 48 above, pp.87–91; Gelber, p.37; Meir, pp.76–7.
50. Letter from Ehud, 3 Feb. 1943, CZA S 25/5289.
51. Letter from Ehud, No. 6, 22 Feb. 1943, CZA S 6/1960.
52. Ruth Bondi, *Ha-shaliah* (The Emissary), Tel Aviv, 1973, pp.355–66.
53. Gelber, pp.39–43.
54. Golani (Aryeh Eshel) to Yosifon (Dobkin), confidential, 31 Oct. 1943, CZA S 25/5289.
55. Gilbor, pp.44–5. Cf. H. Cohen, *Ha-pe'ilut ha-tzionit be- 'Iraq* (Zionist Activity in Iraq), Jerusalem, 1969 (hereinafter: Cohen), p.184.
56. Cohen, pp.186–9.
57. Letter from Golani (Aryeh Eshel), 29 July 1944, CZA S 6/3785; B. Habas, *Portsei ha-sha'arim mi-mizrah u-mi-yam* (Gatecrashers from East and West), Tel Aviv, 1960, pp.66–7.
58. Dobkin's review in meeting of Jewish Agency Executive, 22 Feb. 1942, minutes, CZA.
59. Shertok's speech before the Jewish Agency Executive, 14 June 1942, minutes, CZA.
60. Minutes of the Jewish Agency Executive meeting, 29 Nov. 1942. The remaining certificates were distributed as follows: 1,000 for French youth, 1,300 for labourers, 100 in reserve for the continued evacuation of Iran and North Africa.
61. Ben-Gurion's speech before the inner executive committee of the Mapai Central Committee, 15 Oct. 1942, LPA.
62. Leo Cohen to J. Linton, 23 Feb. 1942, CZA Z 4/14.797.
63. E. S.'s (Eliyahu Sasson's) report to Moshe Shertok, 5 March 1942, on his talk with the Kurdish politician Amin Zaki, CZA, S 25/5289.
64. N. Wilenski to Dr. B. Joseph, 26 Feb. 1942 (BGA, General Chronological Documentation) (hereinafter: GCD).
65. Reports from Iraq, 10 July 1942, Labour Movement Archives (hereinafter: LMA), 14/19; letter from a Jewish informer in Iraq, 10 Oct. 1943, CZA S 25/5289.
66. Jewish Agency Executive meeting, 7 March 1943, minutes, CZA.
67. Mapai Central Committee meeting, 12 July 1943, minutes, LPA.
68. Jewish Agency Executive meeting, 20 June 1944, minutes, CZA.
69. 'Plan to Settle One Million Jews,' BGA, BGD, 7 March 1945, p.38; *Le-heshbon ha-tzionut la-ahar ha-milhama* (Zionist Reckoning After the War), BGD, 30 July 1945; D. Horowitz, *Absorption of One Million of Jewish Immigrants in Palestine*, BGA, GCD, Oct. 1945.
70. 'One Million Plan,' BGA, BGD, pp.37–41.

ACTIVITY OF THE YISHUV

71. *Zionist Reckoning After the War*, BGA, BGD, 30 July 1945, pp.129–31.
72. Roberto Bachi to D. Ben-Gurion, 27 Oct. 1944, confidential memorandum, BGA, GCD.
73. Committee of the Iraqi Jewish Community in Jerusalem to Jewish Agency Immigration Department, 6 Aug. 1942; B. Yoffe, Tel Aviv Immigration Bureau, to Y. Bachar, Immigration Department in Jerusalem, 4 Aug. 1942; Ze'ev Leibowitz to Y. Bachar, 3 Aug. 1942; CZA S 6/3785.
74. Many cases are documented in CZA S 6/3785. For example: Y. Bachar to Ehud (Sereni), 27 July 1942, 12 Aug. 1942; Immigration Department to B. Yoffe, 19 Aug. 1943; letter from Ehud (Sereni), 31 Dec. 1943; Yehoshua Batat for the Committee of the Iraqi Jewish Community to Jewish Agency, 11 Jan. 1944.
75. Jewish Agency Information Bureau internal memorandum, 2 Sept. 1941, CZA S 25/2522.
76. Association of Aram Naharayim Immigrants to Jewish Agency Immigration Department, 13 Jan. 1942, CZA S 6/1430; repeated requests by A. Binyamin for the Committee of the Iraqi Jewish Community to Jewish Agency for approval of immigration certificates for candidates who received exit visas, and approval of a few of them: Binyamin to Jewish Agency, 22 Sept. 1943, reply to him, 11 Oct. 1942, and its response, 24 Oct. 1943; CZA S 6/37–85.
77. Numerous appeals in this matter: S 6/3785. For example: S. Sehayyeq for Association of Aram Naharayim Immigrants to Immigration Department, 15 May 1944, and Department's reply to him, 6 July 1944; Committee of Iraqi Jewish Community to Immigration Department, 17 Jan. 1945, and M. Shapira's reply, 28 Jan. 1945, CZA S 6/3785.
78. Meeting of Kurdish immigrant delegation with Ben-Zvi, representing Jewish Agency Immigration Department, 27 Oct. 1943; Immigration Department to Schill, 3 April 1944; correspondence between Ben-Zvi, Immigration Department, and Kurdish immigrants, Aug. 1944; memorandum of Kurdish community and Oriental immigrants in Haifa to Ben-Zvi, 3 July 1945, CZA S 6/3785.
79. Ze'ev Leibowitz to Immigration Department, 7 Dec. 1944, response to his letter, 12 Dec. 1944, and additional memorandum by him, 11 Jan. 1945, CZA S 6/3785.
80. Committee of Iraqi Jewish Community to Immigration Department, 22 March 1945, 22 April 1945, 22 May 1945, CZA S 6/3785; Immigration Department to Committee of Iraqi Jewish Community, 29 May 1945, CZA S 6/3785.
81. Gelber, pp.59–60; Shaul Avigur's comments in meeting of Histadrut Executive Committee, 19 April 1944, LMA.
82. Gelber, pp.65–7; Meir, p.101.
83. Cohen, p.190; Y. Braginski, *Im hoter el hof* (A People Striving for the Shore) Tel Aviv, 1965, pp.304–5.
84. Letters from Shammai (Shlomo Hillel), 2 July 1946, 29 Sept. 1946, 23 Oct. 1946, CZA S 6/1960; Cohen, p.191; Meir, pp.105–6.
85. Brief survey of Iraqi Jewry (by emissaries in Iraq), confidential, received 12 July 1946, CZA S 25/5289.
86. Letters from Shammai, 2 Sept. 1946, 29 Sept. 1946, CZA S 25/3972; 25 Oct. 1946, CZA S 6/1960.
87. Report of the Sixth Meeting of the National Secretariat, 6 March 1947, CZA S 6/1960; Cohen, pp.184–5; Meir, pp.106–7.
88. Meir, pp.142–7; A. Sharon, 'Ha-hagana be-'Iraq' ('The Hagana in Iraq'), in Z. Yehuda (ed.), *Mi-bavel li-yerushalayim: kovetz mehkarim u-te'udot 'al ha-tzionut ve-ha-'aliya me-'iraq* (From Babylon to Jerusalem: Collection of Studies and Documents on Zionism and Immigration from Iraq), Tel Aviv, 1981, pp.91–3.
89. Y. Allon, *The Making of Israel's Army*, London, 1970, pp.133–5.
90. Meir, pp.162–6; Cohen, pp.199–201.
91. Meir, pp.111–13, 131–42; S. Hillel, *Ruah kadim: bi-shelihut mahtartit le-artsot 'arav* (Operation Babylon: On an Underground Mission to the Arab Countries), Jerusalem, 1985, p. 120; Z. Tsahor and Y. Hadari, *Pleitim menatzhim imperia* (Refugees Vanquish

267

an Empire), Tel Aviv, 1985, pp.334–5.
92. Minutes of the Sixth Meeting of the National Secretariat, 6 March 1947; Yerah (Yerahmiel Asa) to Jewish Agency Hehalutz Department, 30 April 1947, CZA S 6/1960. Shammai (Shlomo Hillel) to Hehalutz Department, Histadrut Executive Committee, and Kibbutz Secretariat, 27 May 1947, CZA S 86/322.
93. Shammai to Jewish Agency Hehalutz Department, 27 May 1947, CZA 86/322; Council of Iraqi Jewish Community to Jewish Agency Political Department, 4 Nov. 1946, report on meeting with Iraqi youth, 30 May 1947, CZA S 25/5289; G. Golani for the Palestine Liaison Bureau of the Hehalutz Movement in Iraq to Jewish Agency, 15 May 1947, CZA S 6/1960.
94. Hillel, note 91 above, pp.18–54; Tzahor and Hadari, note 91 above, pp.335–8.
95. Mapai Secretariat minutes, 9 Dec. 1947, LPA.
96. Shlomo Hillel, memorandum to Aliya Bet, 'Problem of the Oriental Jews and Our Activity Among Them,' 3 March 1948, Hagana Archives, Bet 14/27.
97. Meir, pp.169–70, Hillel, note 91 above, p.122.

# 13

# The American Joint Distribution Committee and Polish Jewry 1944–1949

## Yosef Litvak

1944–45: THE RESUMPTION OF JDC ACTIVITY IN POLAND

Aid from the American Jewish Joint Distribution Committee (JDC) for Polish Jewry began during the First World War, even before Poland was reconstituted as an independent state. The JDC continued to support Polish Jewry, insofar as it could, during the Second World War. It supported Jews trapped in ghettos and incarcerated in concentration camps in the Nazi-occupied territories, and assisted the hundreds of thousands of refugees who fled Poland, most to the Soviet Union and a few to other countries. After the ghettos were liquidated, the JDC continued to act for the rescue and sustenance of Jews hiding on the Aryan side, channelling the money through the welfare agencies of the Polish Government-in-exile in London. At the same time, the JDC developed an extensive and variegated system in which parcels of food, clothing, shoes, drugs, and other essential commodities were shipped to the refugees in the Soviet Union. When the liberation of Poland began in the second half of 1944, the JDC moved quickly to offer its help to the few survivors in the liberated territories, and the thousands who began to stream into these territories from the Soviet Union and the liberated concentration camps in Germany and Austria.

In the last third of July 1944, Polish territory from the River Bug in the east to the Vistula in the west – about 73,000 square kilometres, with a population of some five million – was freed from Nazi occupation. In Lublin, the major city in this area, the Soviets set up a provisional government of sorts, known as the 'Polish Committee for National Liberation' (Polski Komitet Wyzwolenia Narodowego, hereinafter the PKWN). The PKWN's first manifesto to the Polish people was issued on 22 July 1944 in Lublin. Apart from announcing the fact of its establishment and communicating its political platform, it contained a paragraph devoted to the Jews: 'We promise the Jews, who were cruelly annihilated by the occupier, full rehabilitation and full equality *de jure* and *de facto*'.[1] Although time did not fulfil the hopes the Jews pinned on these laudable intentions, they appear to have been sincerely expressed at the time.

Immediately after the West became aware that the Lublin area had been liberated and the PKWN had come into being, Paul Baerwald, chairman of the JDC Executive, applied to Andrei Gromyko, the Soviet Ambassador to Washington at the time, for a meeting where the possibilities of obtaining urgent aid for the surviving Jews in the liberated territories of Poland might be explored.[2] The JDC Executive hoped for permission to send an emissary into liberated Poland to assess first-hand the survivors' needs, the help necessary for their rehabilitation, and the ways and means of its delivery. The PKWN still had little autonomy; it was essentially a symbolic and formal body. Since Soviets held the reins, the decision to allow any Western party to help residents of the liberated territories was theirs alone. In fact, the Soviets had previously denied the JDC the opportunity to help Jews who had fled Poland into the area conquered by the Soviets in 1939–40, i.e., the Ukraine and western Belorussia, the Baltic countries, Bessarabia, and northern Bukovina. The authorities permitted the shipment of relief parcels – food, drugs, and clothing – to Jewish refugees only after Hitler had attacked the Soviet Union. The Soviets acceded to this kind of aid in view of the severe famine and distress that had overtaken their country, and after their attempts to persuade the JDC to ship relief non-sectorially, through their Red Cross, had failed. The JDC sent its relief parcels from its warehouses and offices in Teheran, on the basis of the addresses of individual refugees which it had acquired indirectly and by chance.

In the second half of 1944, with the liberation of Poland underway, the problem of how to help the few Jewish survivors in the previously Nazi-occupied zone, and those who had begun to arrive from the Soviet interior, began to surface. The relief parcel campaign to individual Polish Jews in the Soviet Union reached its peak of momentum and volume at the time – about 10,000 packages per month, with some 40,000 refugee families on file as recipients.[3]

At that time, however, the new political constellation that had come about in the wake of military developments on the fronts presented the JDC with a new complication. The Soviet Army reached the outskirts of Warsaw in late July 1944, and liberated about one-fifth of Poland. Almost all Soviet territory had been liberated by then, and the the Soviets, sustaining their offensive, entered Rumania in August and Bulgaria and Yugoslavia in September.

Great Britain and the United States spurned the PKWN and the ZPP (the 'Society of Polish Patriots' or Zwiazek Patriotow Polskich), and refused to help them in any way. They still hoped to effectuate a compromise between the Soviets and the Polish Government-in-exile, and supported the latter body as long as such compromise was not at hand. The Western powers' stance was binding on British and American Jewish organizations as well. The Soviets, while holding the upper hand and showing no inclination to waive long-term political and strategic plans, still pursued the tactic of trying to attain their objectives gradually, outwitting their Western allies by displaying an ostensible willingness to compromise while going to great lengths to win the sympathy of Western public opinion. Thus they continued to let the JDC send relief to the Jewish refugees from Poland, although this was not to their liking.

The Soviets had an interest in keeping the JDC going, too, because they had no alternative to propose. They understood that shutting the JDC operation down would be severely detrimental to the refugees, and, therefore, to the refugees' perception of the Soviet regime. The Soviets sought the refugees' favour upon their return to Poland, in view of the stiff struggle they faced to improve their image in the eyes of the hostile Polish population. Since they attributed great value to the Jews' influence on Western – especially American – public opinion, they feared that any harm to the JDC would harm their cause. Thus they laboured to obtain the JDC's agreement to cooperate with the ZPP and the PKWN. One of the measures undertaken in this direction was the establishment of the Jewish Committee under the ZPP, which appealed to Western Jewry for help, and the installation of Dr. Sommerstein, a Zionist, as its chairman. This step was also clearly meant to further additional political goals in Poland itself.

A JDC emissary was sent into liberated Poland more than a year after these efforts by Sommerstein in Poland and JDC functionaries in the United States and Western Europe. Dr. Joseph J. Schwartz, the JDC director in Europe, reached Poland in October 1945, about three months after the Polish Government of National Unity had been established and recognized by the Western powers. By this time, it seems, this government no longer needed the Soviets' advance approval for decisions of this kind. Even then, however, Schwartz entered Poland not as a JDC representative but as a member of a team of advisors under Earl Harrison, sent by President Truman to examine the circumstances of the DPs (Displaced Persons). Harrison found him a place on the support team accompanying a group of wounded Polish POWs being repatriated via France in an American military aircraft. Only after he reached Poland was he given a *de facto* reception by the authorities. The welcoming committee was in fact quite honourable, including government ministers. With it Schwartz was able to reach agreements and arrangements that laid the foundations for extensive JDC relief activity on behalf of Polish Jewry.[4]

The JDC had in fact resumed its operations in Poland before Schwartz's journey. Both the JDC and the Jewish Agency for Palestine hastened to offer relief to the Jewish survivors in the Lublin area as soon as reports of its liberation had arrived. Soviet consent, too, was attained for the dispatch of relief supplies from the JDC warehouses in Teheran directly to Sommerstein, in his capacity as Chairman of the Central Committee of the Jews of Poland – first in Lublin and subsequently in Warsaw after its liberation. Neither did the intent to ship relief to the Jewish Committee in liberated Poland contradict State Department policy. The Foreign Economic Administration (the FEA) was even permitted to sell goods to the JDC for the purposes of relief in Poland.[5]

Once the political obstacles were cleared away, the EAC immediately allocated $100,000 for the first relief shipment to Lublin, and $250,000 for further shipments. The EAC also decided to place goods sought by the Jewish Agency Executive in Jerusalem for this purpose at that body's disposal.[6]

The relief material, however, still had a difficult route to ply before reaching its various destinations. Some of the difficulties were objective and technical, and others were political – the handiwork of the Soviet authorities. The technical problems were rooted in transportation constraints while the war still raged and in the lengthy route that had to be followed: from Teheran across the Soviet Union to Lublin (and, later, to Warsaw). Then, too, the relief operation had to contend with the sticky fingers of the various Soviet personnel who handled the shipments en route. Major consumer commodities, including food, were in grievously short supply in the Soviet Union at the time. Theft of such items, wherever they were kept, was a national plague. The perpetrators were not necessarily professional thieves but rather anyone who came into contact with the goods, including their ostensible guards – the regular and undercover police. It is therefore no wonder that the shipments meant for some Jewish committee in 'faraway' Lublin and Warsaw fell prey to thieves and arrived only in part. In some cases only scraps remained;[7] in others, large shipments disappeared altogether. Thus, in January 1946, the manager of the Odessa port rounded up twelve freight cars and attempted to spirit away a shipment of hundreds of tons sent to the CKZP in anticipation of the arrival of tens of thousands of Jewish repatriates from the Soviet Union. The attempt was foiled.[8]

Until the end of the war, there were no direct mail and telephone communications between the CKZP and the Jewish organizations in the West, except for those through Moscow, which were under Soviet supervision. Between November 1944 and February 1945, these, too, were completely severed by unknown factors. After the war, when maritime transportation between the West and the Polish ports of Gdansk and Gdynia resumed, the CKZP asked the Jewish organizations in the Free World to send aid via French ports and Stockholm.[9] This was a short cut and saved time and expense.

Because of delays on the American and, later, the Soviet side, as well as objective technical problems, the first shipments of relief supplies reached the CKZP only in early May 1945, although the first shipment of 50 tons from Teheran had been ready for dispatch in October 1944. Thus the starving, sick, and exhausted survivors who came out of hiding, or who were still alive after the liberation of the German death camps, were denied the urgent first aid they needed during those hard months of the winter of 1944–45, when the battles in Poland were still in full force and everything was in short supply.

In December 1944, the JDC announced a second relief shipment to Poland. Valued at $700,000, it included all the equipment to outfit three 100-bed hospitals.[10] The JDC announcement of 25 July 1945 illustrates how substantive and varied was the aid sent to the Jews of Poland over those months. The shipments since January 1945 (i.e., in addition to those sent in 1944) comprised 350 tons of supplies including 225 sewing machines, 20,000 pairs of underwear, and 20,000 new pairs of socks. In addition, the Canadian JDC sent 300,000 cans of fish, 10,000 pairs of army shoes, and 17,000 pieces of woollen clothing. Another 150 sewing machines were sent from Sweden, together with 870 machines for use in various trades and 25 tons of food.[11]

Until the end of 1945, relief came only in the form of goods; no money (dollars) was provided. There were several reasons for this. In view of the tremendous scarcity and poverty in devastated Poland, it was almost impossible to buy with cash the basic commodities required by everyone, especially the totally destitute Jewish survivors and refugees. The new Socialist regime impeded the organization of free commerce, and was dilatory in setting up governmental manufacturing, distribution and marketing systems. Only at the end of 1945 did the banks reopen, after which it was possible to import foreign currency and use it legally. The official exchange rate was ludicrous – 12 zloty to the dollar, against the real (black market) rate of 400 zloty. Importing dollars at the official rate meant in fact giving them to the state treasury, with neither a return nor a possibility of helping the needy Jews for whose benefit they had been donated.

During 1945, aid delivered by the CKZP and its branch organizations was sporadic. Although this was contrary to the JDC's principles and way of handling matters, there was no choice. As a rule, the JDC extended its aid only after thoroughly investigating the needs of the population and the specific local conditions wherever it operated. Thus it customarily provided its relief through a select, experienced staff of experts in the fields required: accounting, law, economics, health, education, culture, welfare, religion, etc. Almost all staff members were local residents and citizens of the states in which the activities were carried out. Only the head of staff, such as the JDC director in each country (Country Director), was appointed by the main office in New York. In most cases he was an American citizen, an *émigré*, or the son of immigrants from the country to which he was sent. He knew the national vernacular and the languages spoken by the local Jews. His foreign citizenship, usually American, was apparently meant to guarantee his loyalty and subordination to the JDC Executive and its policies, especially with respect to not allowing the host government to interfere in its work, insofar as this was possible. An additional advantage of being a foreign citizen was the absence of affiliation with any element of the local Jewish establishment, for these were usually rife with quarrels, and the absence of any particular obligation to anyone. Thus he could devote positive and unbiased attention to the Jewish public as a whole, including all strata and groupings, and would be accepted as a neutral, objective actor.

Running the office required cash as well, at a time when it was still illogical to bring in dollars legally at the official rate of exchange.

David Gozik, a senior JDC official who returned to Poland after the war, improvised an *ad hoc*, convoluted way to handle this – by engaging the help of the Zionist pioneer 'Brichah' ('Flight') movement, which had begun operating in Lublin as early as mid-1944. Its agents brought him dollars from the JDC office in Bucharest, which he could exchange for the Polish zloty at full value.[12] Eventually, the problem of the dollar exchange rate was partially solved when Dr. Schwartz visited Poland in October–November 1945. Schwartz managed to persuade the Polish Treasury to pay the JDC in Warsaw 100 zloty per dollar, 'subsidizing' each dollar by 88 zloty above the official rate, and to add another 40 zloty to each dollar spent by the JDC through the CKZP. Although in fact the real (unofficial) rate of exchange of the dollar now stood at 1:500, Schwartz had to settle for this accord, realizing that he could do no better under the conditions prevailing in Poland.[13] As a result, most JDC aid to the Jews in Poland had to be in kind, and not in cash. Only in January 1948 did the Polish Treasury raise the return for dollars imported as social welfare and gifts to 400 zloty. When government banks opened in November 1945, it became possible to implement the subsidy accord for the JDC's dollars. For the first time since its welfare work in Poland resumed after the war, the New York headquarters was able to send $250,000 in cash to the Warsaw office.[14]

An examination of local needs, the opening of a JDC office in Warsaw, and the possibility of transferring dollars to it provided Dr. Schwartz with the means to draw up an estimate for a provisional budget for the next few months. To that end, it was essential to obtain data on the Jewish population. In May 1945, at the end of the war, a CKZP census found 42,662 Jews in Poland, comprising 30,000 survivors of Nazi concentration camps, about 3,000 partisans, and approximately 9,000 survivors who had been in hiding, or had held forged Aryan identity cards.[15] This data served as a basis for setting up a welfare programme for the destitute Jewish population. The Jewish committees had to tend to the Jews' most elementary needs – housing, work, health services, education, cultural activities, and religious imperatives. The registry helped them to look for relatives, a cardinal and vital need for every survivor. As the postwar repatriation brought in a growing number of returnees from east and west, the data were constantly changing and had to be updated regularly.

At the end of 1945, the number of Jews swelled to 86,000,[16] including about 30,000 repatriates from the Soviet Union.[17] Of them, 67.3 per cent lived in three cities – Lodz (37.3 per cent), Warsaw (17 per cent), and Krakow (13 per cent); the rest were scattered in 232 towns and villages.[18]

Upon returning to the Polish 'homeland' after its liberation from Nazi occupation, the Polish survivors faced murderous hostility on the part of the local population, a large majority of whom would not accede to the reappearance of Jews on Polish soil, however few they were. Murder of Jews was a daily and routine phenomenon throughout the country. Hersh Smolar, a Jewish Communist leader close to government circles at the time, attested to this:

> Reports of the murders reached us from every part of Poland – Lublin, Krakow, Lodz and Danzig, Bialystok, Bielsk Podlaski, and Bytom ... In Nowogard, the patriotic murderers took out five Jews, all survivors of Hitler's death camps, and bestially tortured them to death ... In the trains to and from Bialystok, there was a savage daily hunt for Jews ... Reports were received that in a number of cities, terrible danger awaited every Jew. In Czestochowa there was an attempted blood libel ... Pogroms were attempted in Radom, Miechow, Chrzanow and Rabka ... In Krakow, on 11 August 1945, true to the 'classic' setup under the Czarist regime and pre-war Poland, uncontrolled, large mobs looted whatever remained of the Jewish survivors' property. Lone Jews were hunted down and murdered by large, wild mobs, including students and uniformed onlookers. According to the Secretary of the PPR Regional Committee, even policemen took part in beating Jews.[19]

Reports of executions of Jews and the tragic plight of the Polish Jewish Holocaust survivors quickly spread among the Jews in the Western world. As early as January 1945, the Jewish Agency in Jerusalem received an interim report on the situation from the Zionist Coordinating Delegation in Poland, which reached Bucharest together with the first 'Brichah' agents. The report described the extreme anti-Jewish hostility prevailing in Poland, and quoted verbatim the motto then rampant among the Poles: 'That Hitler – what he did he did, but may he live to 100 for having wiped out all the Jews' (Hitler was still alive at the time). The report also related that Jews were still concealing their identity due to fear of murderers, and Poles who had saved Jews were asking the survivors to keep this information secret lest disclosure imperil their lives. Not a week went by without the murder of a Jew. In a sign of the times, 12 Jews were murdered in the town of Yanw-Podlaski on the day Osolka Morawski, head of the Provisional Government, announced that Jews would be given equal rights. All the Jews wanted to get out, except for a group of Communists and Bundists who, under the circumstances and with government support, became the 'leaders' of the local Jews. They could do nothing to alleviate their constituency's plight, but they did have the power to disrupt Zionist activity and Jewish emigration.[20]

Government aid to the survivors was a negligible 120 zloty per month – enough for one pound of sugar. Only 2 per cent of the survivors actually received this aid. Dr. Klinghoffer, a Zionist activist from Krakow, called on the Jewish survivors to leave Poland at once, lest they be annihilated.[21] According to an official Polish study, 434 underground gangs operated in 1944–45, including about 300 that were organized in the spring of 1945. In that year alone 7,393 persons were murdered: 1,714 employees of the security forces, 359 'political activists' (active members of the ruling PPR–Y.L.) and 5,300 others.[22] It is reasonable to assume that the latter were in fact Jews, since the gangs did not harass Poles unless they were members of the security forces or ruling party activists. Only Jews were murdered for their nationality alone. Quite a few Jews among the murdered, of course, had also been security personnel or party activists.

Under these circumstances, it was only natural that the ever-present threat to the lives of the Jews in Poland made a powerful impact, though it was not the only reason the Jews sought to leave this land of bloodshed. Many of the Jews were emotionally unable to rebuild their lives in a land that had become the grave of their loved ones and their people. Many Jews repatriated from the Soviet Union were anxious to distance themselves from territory under direct or indirect Soviet rule, and to reach the Free World as soon as possible. Religious Jews feared staying on in a country where the Communist regime was taking over and digging in. Others wished to be reunited with relatives in the West. Zionists fervently wished to reach Palestine. However, the 'Free World,' including Palestine, was closed to Jewish immigrants. Jews could obtain legal exit permits only if they had entry visas to other countries, and these were very few in number. Without an entry visa, it was impossible to get an exit permit or a *laissez-passer* to cross the countries bordering Poland. Thus the Jews had no choice but to remain in Poland for the interim.

The first to respond to the Zionist organizations' call to leave

Poland were the young, who had courage and were not burdened with obligations and responsibilities. In their wake, thousands of other Jews of all ages, including heads of families, joined 'Brichah'. Some had not been Zionists previously, and some were former communists and Bundists. The Polish authorities, while not encouraging Jewish emigration, treated the exodus with benign neglect. Within a short time the 'Brichah' turned into a mass movement encompassing tens of thousands of Jews. A 'private' escape route for economic gain took shape alongside the Zionist route. In the latter half of 1945, over 30,000 Jews – about one-third of all Jews in Poland – left Poland by the two channels, heading for the refugee relief camps in Germany, Austria and Italy. About 10,000 left Poland in October alone.[23]

The JDC underwrote most of the expenses of 'Brichah,' covering the escapees' travel fare and upkeep en route to the refugee camps. The camps themselves were under the auspices of the Western liberation armies, the U.S., Britain, and France, each in its own sector. Camps in the American sector were the favoured destination. There the JDC continued to help support the refugees, supplementing the rations supplied by the American army, or later by the United Nations, and financing their health, education, culture, welfare, and religious needs.

On 7 January 1946, Dr. Schwartz testified about the conditions under which Polish Jewry was living and the 'Brichah' escape route, to the Anglo-American Committee of Inquiry, which investigated the problem of the Jewish refugees in Europe and explored possible diplomatic solutions to the Palestine problem.[24]

> ... I have no statistics, but in the five weeks I spent in Poland [his visit took place in October–November 1945], I visited the major cities. I held talks with senior government officials, British and American journalists, and the leaders of the Jewish communities. I believe that 80–90 per cent of all the Jews [in Poland] wish to leave.

As for the JDC's support of 'Brichah' operations, Schwartz said the following on a different occasion:

> We did not organize 'Brichah,' but we did help the escapees and did not deny it. We even freely disclosed our role in this work to the United States and other Western countries. We were guided by our principle that we must help Jews in distress and who need assistance, examining neither why nor whence

they are fleeing. We helped every Jewish organization that needed help, regardless of whether it was called 'Brichah' or 'the Central Committee of the Jews of Poland.'

During the Holocaust years, the JDC departed to some degree from its strict adherence to the principle of legality. The JDC Administration, especially its representatives and employees in the various countries, realized that adherence to the laws of those countries frequently clashed with the goal of saving Jewish lives. This held true especially for the embattled areas in Nazi-occupied Europe that were liberated afterwards by the Red Army. Because the latter quickly established Communist hegemony, it was no wonder that Dr. Schwartz, director of the European JDC before and after the liberation, was one of the first JDC senior officials to adopt a policy of overriding the principle of legality when this principle threatened Jewish lives. David Gozik, a Polish Jew and Holocaust survivor who reinstated JDC work in Poland after its liberation, behaved similarly. As mentioned, he coordinated his efforts with 'Brichah Route' personnel from its inception, to the benefit of both sides.

## 1946: REPATRIATION AND EMIGRATION

In 1945 the JDC went to considerable lengths in Poland, laying the foundation for extensive rehabilitation operations there. This notwithstanding, activity of this kind was of secondary importance in the larger context of relief to the Jews of Poland. Most Polish-Jewish survivors of the Holocaust were still in the Soviet interior, and the JDC continued to send them some 10,000 relief parcels every month. The mass repatriation of Polish-Jewish refugees from the Soviet Union began only in February 1946, and ended in greater part in August of that year. During these five months, 203 organized convoys brought 120,975 Jewish repatriates back from the Soviet Union.[25] Approximately another 6,000 Jews arrived on their own, and still another 10,000 arrived in July 1946.[26] To handle the monthly throng, the CKZP and the JDC had to mount an absorption and rehabilitation campaign of tremendous qualitative and quantitative dimensions – operating under the especially harsh conditions in Poland at the time. The mass repatriation to Poland permitted and even forced the JDC to halt the shipment of relief parcels to the refugees in the Soviet Union, and to pledge all these resources to the rehabilitation of the returning Jewish refugees in Poland.

The organizational infrastructure for the absorption and rehabilitation project had been established in the second half of 1945. The operations were implemented, particularly during those months, through the CKZP and its branches in Poland, which relied on financial and other resources supplied by the JDC. The JDC activated its office and procured the subsidies for its dollars as per Dr. Schwartz's arrangement with the Polish Government. Schwartz also designed the operative plans and drew up the estimated budget for their implementation.

Implementation of the plan to resettle and rehabilitate the Jewish refugees – both those who had gathered in Poland in 1944–45, and those expected to return upon repatriation from the USSR – became an evident objective necessity in early 1946. Although most Jewish leaders, including Schwartz, were convinced that the Jews' resettlement in Poland could only be temporary in nature – for there did not seem to be any future for the Jews in reconstituted Poland – the rehabilitation operations could not be postponed.

The JDC felt obliged not only to handle the needs of individuals but also to look after the interests of the community and the entire Jewish public. Thus it saw to the redemption of Jewish children who had been in the care of Christians; the search for relatives; commemoration of Holocaust victims, ghetto rebels, partisan fighters, and soldiers in the armies of liberation; establishment of a historical committee for Holocaust documentation and research; the publication of books and newspapers, etc. Support was provided to Jewish individuals and groups according to need. Because need was the point of departure, JDC support of institutions and children's homes run by the Communists, who had no interest in Jewish values, national or religious aims, was equal to that given to Hebrew schools, Talmud Torahs, and yeshivot. The JDC also gave generously to institutions and other bodies that made efforts to reintegrate the Jews and sink roots in the economy and social clime of Poland, and to the 'kibbutzim' run by the Zionist youth movements and political parties to prepare their followers and trainees for Brichah and subsequent emigration to Palestine.

The JDC's position and its activities in Poland in those years were based on its view of the surviving Jews in that country as particularly afflicted and downtrodden. In Western European countries as well as in Germany and Hungary, where the JDC also operated immediately after their liberation, there were entire Jewish population groups and localities where large numbers of Jews emerged from the war with only partial damage; thousands of

Jewish families survived intact. In Poland, by contrast, William Bein, head of the JDC in that country after David Gozik was killed in a plane accident in March 1946, defined the Jews' situation as follows: 'In effect, the Jews of Poland present a problem worthy of special attention. Many of them survived by a miracle. They are alone, bereft of family, and broken in spirit. They all need tenderness and constant care, and all this only the JDC can provide'.[27] Dr. Schwartz, testifying before the Anglo-American Commission of Inquiry, voiced a similar view.

Most JDC aid, in kind and in cash, was funnelled through CKZP channels, institutions, and local branches. Any attempt to circumvent the CKZP, which was dominated *de facto* by the Communists and their supporters – though these were a small minority among the survivors – would have endangered the JDC's very ability to operate in Poland. The CKZP was recognized as the official representative of the Jewish community and received the regime's backing and patronage, at least during the years under review. On the other hand, the Jewish Communists, too, had to make peace with concessions to their political and ideological opponents on the Jewish scene and acknowledge their right to exist and act, just as the heads of the regime were still rather tolerant of their domestic Polish rivals. Despite their reliance on Soviet bayonets, the Polish Communist leaders knew they were still too weak and few in number; therefore they had to spread the Sovietization of Poland over several years, implementing it gradually. Naturally, the Jewish communists adopted a similar tactic in the realm of Jewish affairs. Furthermore, the attempt to rehabilitate the Holocaust survivors – a materially, spiritually and psychologically destitute and spent community – and to rebuild a vibrant Jewish life from the ruins, depended entirely on help from Western Jewry. This total reliance on Western Jewish resources forced the Communist leadership, at least at the outset of its activity, to display willingness to cooperate with their former opponents in the Jewish community, i.e., Zionists of all shades (except for the Revisionists, who were labelled 'fascists' and not permitted to organize), the Bund, and Agudath Israel. Operative unity, based upon programmes embracing all parties within the CKZP, held together until 1949, when those parties and groups not affiliated to the Communists were swept out of Jewish public life by decree of the ruling party. This was in accordance with the official 'unification' policy that embraced the entire country and all spheres of life. In the accepted political jargon of the time, this wall-to-wall coalition, operating until then under the CKZP, was called the 'fan' (Wachlarz in Polish); it was composed of many and diverse functions operating in harmony.[28]

The JDC reserved the right to instruct the CKZP and other bodies it supported to use the funds granted them in accordance with JDC principles and guidelines. It also set up a supervisory and control system to monitor the proper use of funds as stipulated between the donor and the groups supported, and to prevent criminal corruption. The JDC strove to get the agencies it supported to streamline their work, trimming administration and its attendant expenditures while leaving the level and quality of services unscathed. One measure in this direction was the establishment of joint committees with the CKZP, the health organization TOZ [*Towarzystwo Ochrony Zdrowia*], and the Religious Communities Association [*Vaad HaKehilot*] (the latter two were the largest bodies supported directly by the JDC, i.e., not through the CKZP). Their task was to check and work out the budgets in detail.

The JDC representatives insisted that the needy pay to the limit of their ability for the services offered them, and that services would be offered gratis only to those who had no income whatsoever. Not only did the JDC attempt to entrench the principle of users' fees as abilities permitted, but they also expected the Jewish community as a whole to gradually increase its fund raising and collections from local (governmental and municipal) and independent sources. These funds were to be used to maintain JDC institutions and reduce dependence on donations from Jews abroad to the unavoidable minimum. As for the nature of the work of the Jewish committees, William Bein reported the following: 'The programme is carried out by the committees. We inspire, supervise, and monitor, [but] we participate directly only in counselling and instruction.'[29]

The strict JDC control over the use of funds was initially not well received by the CKZP functionaries, who originally thought the JDC would fund them with no strings attached. Only after much effort and lengthy discussion was Bein able to persuade the CKZP to acquiesce to the JDC's operating principles and methods.

Bein and his aides also had to contend with partisan groups and organizations. These often made demands which, in the JDC's opinion, were totally at variance with their field of activity. They displayed opposition and, at times, hostility to the JDC's supervision, and its refusal to finance activities which it considered to be outside its domain of responsibility and aims. The JDC took a vigorous stance against any involvement in inter-party struggles, and, in the end, found it necessary to declare in advance the nature of the activities it felt duty-bound to finance, and to reject demands for allocations outside the defined spheres of activity. Thus, for example, Bein informed the Zionist organizations at the beginning of 1947 that following the completion of the mass escape (see below) the Zionists would receive allocations for the following purposes only: care of children (including maintenance of children's homes), 'kibbutzim,' canteens, vocational training, and cash assistance for the indigent and the sick.[30]

In any event, beginning in early 1946, the JDC proffered massive aid in kind and in cash for the absorption and rehabilitation of Jews repatriated from the Soviet Union and survivors who had returned to Poland in 1944–45. The organizational infrastructure for the reborn Jewish community, and the welfare services that would use the funds for the needy, were ready for action. The JDC's budget for Poland in January 1946 alone, covering current expenditures and investments in the constructive rehabilitation infrastructure, was $1,220,000. A breakdown of this budget (enumerated in Polish zlotys) indicates the variety of JDC activities:

TABLE 1
THE JDC BUDGET IN POLAND (JANUARY, 1946)[31]

| | |
|---|---|
| Direct aid for food, housing and maintenance | 8,400,000 |
| Child care in closed institutions and care of their families (3,250 children) | 7,762,500 |
| Youth care: health, education and vocational training | 12,955,000 |
| Health, medical care, hospitals, and medical equipment | 5,500,000 |
| Religious communities and services | 980,000 |
| The Historical Committee and various publications | 500,000 |
| Administrative expenses | 308,000 |
| Subtotal: | 36,397,500 |
| Non-recurrent expenditures | |
| Constructive loans and economic rehabilitation | 50,000,000 |
| Repair of institutions, including orphanages | 33,000,000 |
| Total current and non-recurrent expenditures | 119,397,500 |

Tens of thousands of repatriated Jews were referred directly to the western territories annexed from Germany. Houses and factories there had been abandoned by their original inhabitants and German workers, and the Polish Government was interested in the immediate resettlement and productivization of these areas.

Large Jewish communities on the scale of those times settled in the cities of Szczecin [Stettin], Wroclaw and Walbrzych, and smaller communities gathered in scores of other towns and villages. There were some attempts at agricultural settlement in abandoned villages. The JDC also set up and equipped 38 absorption centres, ten in various cities in Silesia and six in Krakow. Repatriates were sent there for temporary stays until suitable permanent living quarters and jobs could be provided. The JDC imported all the equipment for two hospitals, one with 500 beds and the other with 100.[32]

These resettlement plans were not to proceed undisturbed. The arrival of tens of thousands of Jews in large convoys provided the anti-Semitic nationalist underground with a pretext to spread the libel that Poland was threatened with an 'inundation' of Jews whom the Soviets had sent to take over the country. Thus, for example, a leaflet was circulated in Lodz in the beginning of July, to the effect that the government was about to bring 60,000 Jews to the city as a first step in handing control of the entire country's economy to the Jews. The proclamation demanded the expulsion of all the Jews from Poland.[33] Anti-Semitic incitement was further aggravated by the important positions held by Jews in the government, and especially their standing in the security forces that laboured to repress and eradicate the underground. S. Mikolajczyk, the Deputy Prime Minister in the Government of National Unity, stated: 'Too many Jews are pushing their way into high positions in the regime and especially into the security forces [dominated by Communists] that the people detest.'[34]

On 30 April 1946, seven Jews repatriated from the Soviet Union – five women, a man of 30 and a youth of 14 – were murdered near Krakow. Only two days later, another 12 Jews were murdered in the vicinity.[35]

The wave of bloodshed reached a climax in the Kielce pogrom of 4 July 1946, when 42 Jews were massacred (of whom seven were not identified) and 70–80 were wounded. A blood libel to the effect that Jews had kidnapped a Christian child to make use of his blood was the pretext for the slaughter. The pogrom took place in broad daylight at the premises of the Jewish Committee, proceeding for five hours with no interference from the security forces. Not only did the latter refrain from defending the Jews, but the mob was led by uniformed police and soldiers.[36] Another 33 Jews were murdered elsewhere in Poland that month.[37]

The Catholic Church, the most influential factor in Polish national life, justified the attacks against the Jews. Cardinal August Hlond, head of the Church in Poland, declared on 11 July, a week after the Kielce pogrom, that the Jews themselves were responsible for their deteriorating circumstances, since they had usurped positions of leadership in the government and striven to impose on the Polish people a regime which it did not want.[38] Bishop Wyszinski of Lublin reacted even more harshly. He spurned a Jewish delegation that had asked him to denounce the pogrom on the grounds that the Beilis trial in no way proved, at that time, that the Jews did not make use of Christian blood.[39] The Vatican sided with the Church in Poland; its journal commended the Bishop of Kielce and the Archbishop of Krakow for refusing to denounce the Kielce rioters.[40]

The Brichah movement, in a momentum-gathering stage up to that point, now turned into a wild flight of tens of thousands of Jews. The Polish Government could no longer treat the phenomenon with benign neglect. Thus it granted the Brichah movement its informal sanction and supervision, so as to prevent the smuggling of foreign currency and of arms that could reach non-Jewish underground organizations hostile to the regime. An accord in this vein was reached, just a few days after the Kielce pogrom, between Yitzhak (Antek) Zuckerman and Dr. Adolf Berman – the Jewish representatives – and Stanislaw Radkiewcz, Minister of Public Security, and his aide, General Marian Spychalski, then serving also as Deputy COGS – representing the government.

The Jews found another avenue of exit from Poland to the DP camps when the Government of Czechoslovakia agreed for humanitarian reasons to let them cross its territory. The agreements with the Polish and Czechoslovak Governments could only have been made with the silent consent of the Soviets, the ultimate military and political rulers of the area. General Czerwinski, commander of the Polish border patrol and a Soviet officer of Polish extraction, was assigned on loan to the Polish Government. He ordered his subordinates to allow Jews to cross the Czechoslovak border and to monitor this traffic in conjunction with Brichah activists, commanded at that time by Zvi Netzer of the Brichah leadership.[41] The arrangement suited the interests of all the aforementioned actors. The Polish leaders seem to have hoped that the mass exit of the Jews would lessen popular resistance to the regime, just as the mass influx of Jews and the fear of a Jewish 'takeover' had played into the hands of those who opposed and incited against the regime. The Soviets were interested in hindering the British in their search for a solution to the Palestine problem, thus helping dislodge them from the Middle East. The Czechs, apart from their humanitarian consideration for the Jews, were interested in cooperating with their allies, the Poles and the Russians.

Because Brichah became a crucial matter after the Kielce pogrom, with the Jews fleeing a truly life-threatening menace that lurked throughout Poland, the JDC stepped up its aid to Brichah, providing its leaders with two large trucks for the transport of fleeing Jews. It also supplied food and clothing for the refugees. At the transit station of Klodzko on the Polish side of the border, the JDC set up a depot for food supplies and a soup kitchen to provide for the thousands of Jews passing through daily. The cooperation between Brichah leaders and JDC personnel in carrying out their urgent task of saving Jews brought them into close and warm relations.[42]

In July alone, immediately after the Kielce pogrom, about 19,000 Jews left Poland through the organized Brichah. In August 35,346 left, and another 12,379 followed in September. Thus about 67,000 Jews left Poland in the three months immediately following the pogrom.[43] The Brichah escape route led through Czechoslovakia and Austria to the American occupation zone in Germany, where the refugees were received in DP camps to await the possibility of emigration. The JDC supported and tended to these fugitives all the way, meeting their needs in the DP camps as well. The JDC's operations there are a story unto themselves, although they remain outside the domain of this chapter. It will only be mentioned that the JDC not only shouldered the expense of the refugees' health, education, and vocational training, culture, welfare, and religious needs, and emigration services, but also supplemented their rations. Daily rations in the American sector were 1,500 calories per person, which the JDC augmented by 1,000 calories. In the British sector, the refugees received only 800 calories a day, and the JDC added another 1,200.[44]

The flight of Chabad Jews, whose situation was particularly difficult – both materially and in view of the mortal peril they faced because of their complicated legal standing – aroused much interest. They were Soviet nationals who left the USSR as 'repatriates' to Poland, although they had never been citizens of the latter state. They had to be spirited away from Poland and the Soviet bloc as quickly as possible, lest their real identity be discovered. This operation involved much danger, valour, and toil – as well as the great expense of bribing Soviet officials of various kinds. Many of the hassidim were taken straight from prison and concentration camps and arrived in Poland in rags; because this alone could betray them, proper clothing became a matter of urgency. A total of about 3,000 Chabad hassidim passed through the hands of the Brichah.[45]

The Agudath Israel and ultra-Orthodox Jews of all stripes, too, received special care from the JDC. Their special requirements in the realm of dietary laws, Sabbath observance, and other imperatives, meant setting up separate arrangements especially for them. Most of them did not want to go to Palestine and waited for other emigration possibilities. The JDC set up a hostel and two separate transit camps for them in Czechoslovakia.[46]

The Brichah also embraced Jewish children, primarily orphans redeemed from monasteries and Christian families. They first had to be located, rescued from the Gentiles, and placed in Jewish children's homes; this was an exceptional, dramatic episode, fraught with peril and heroism, since the Polish Government refused to return these Jewish children to their people by legislation. At the beginning of 1946, an estimated 1,200 Jewish children were staying with Christian families, and another 1,500–2,000 were accommodated in monasteries. The Zionist parties and youth movements, factionalized entities that struggled for every Jewish soul, united to redeem the children from Gentile auspices and set up a single body called the 'Zionist Coordination for the Children.' They understood that only by uniting could they succeed in this dangerous and difficult task; they had enough to contend with in their struggles with the non-Zionist organizations and with the CKZP. Admittedly, the latter made no special effort to redeem Jewish children, but they did accept into their institutions children brought by Poles who demanded reimbursement for the cost of having maintained them up to the time of the liberation. The JDC set a sum of 5,000 zloty for the ransom of each child, but exceeded this when necessary.[47] Many children, neither orphans nor redeemed, were handed over to Brichah movement workers by their parents, who had decided provisionally to stay in Poland but wished to spare their children the dangers awaiting them; they hoped to join them at a later date.

The Communists and Bundists spurned the 'Exodus from Poland' and decried it vehemently in their verbal and written propaganda. One of the reasons, they explained, was that 'To help Jews leave Poland is to grant Hitler and zoological anti-Semitism a complete victory.'[48] They claimed that an 'ambience of panic' had been stirred up by Revisionist-Agudist elements, who were trying in this way to drive a wedge between 'progressive' and 'reactionary' Zionists. Yet another absurd claim they promoted was that the escapees were non-productive elements, while the 'proletariat,' the skilled and unskilled workers, were staying.[49] Nevertheless, they avoided any open confrontation with Brichah as long as the regime itself lent this movement its backing. They also realized that the conditions were not yet ripe for a struggle with the Zionists, and certainly not with the JDC, which was the CKZP's major bankroller. The regime was interested in preserving the CKZP at that stage, for this strategy conferred political advantages as well as dollars channelled through the CKZP into the State coffers.

In early 1947, crucial developments took place in the general political circumstances of Poland, and in their wake, in the status of the Jews. Ostensibly free elections for the Sejm (parliament) were held in January of that year. The 'democratic bloc' of the ruling PPR and its supporters took 80.1 per cent of the votes. The election returns proved that much if not most of the populace had resigned itself to the regime, realizing that any opposition would be futile.[50] The Government's resolve to put a stop to murderous terror, aimed chiefly at the Jews, encouraged several Jewish bodies to believe that Jewish settlement and life could be maintained in Poland. These hopes were further nourished when the regime continued to view the Jewish community favourably and to permit pluralism and political-ideological freedom, including Zionist activity, within it. Another factor that added to the Jews' sense of security was the permission granted to Jewish committees and other institutions, such as children's homes, old age homes, 'kibbutzim,' etc., to set up armed guards after the Kielce pogrom. To lend these forces legal authority, they were incorporated into the civilian police auxiliary (ORMO – Organizacja Milicji Obywatelskiej).

William Bein was among those in Polish-Jewish circles who were cautiously optimistic. In his June 1947 report to the JDC European administration in Paris, he wrote:

> ... Although there is still quite a measure of anti-Semitism here, there is no doubt that it has lost much of its momentum and that many anti-Semitic tendencies have been restrained. Since the election returns were made public, no violent outbursts against the Jews have been recorded. But the few Jewish survivors are very jittery, and hope that more tolerance will be displayed towards them. Although many Jews who previously awaited emigration certificates have settled down and taken on jobs, hoping to be able to live in a placid environment, there are still thousands who wish to emigrate to Palestine or else-

where. A change in the political climate in Poland has made it possible that some Jews who left for the occupied territories [in Germany] during the great flight will now return to Poland.[51]

Developments outside Poland also lessened Jews' desire to leave the country in 1947. The strife in Palestine worsened. The British stepped up their struggle against the Yishuv and the clandestine entry of Jews. Thousands of illegal immigrants were deported to detention camps in Cyprus. On the other side, the Irgun and the Stern Group stepped up their anti-British terrorism. The prospects of a solution in the near future, acceptable to the Zionists' aims and consistent with free immigration, seemed rather weak. Neither did the Jews enjoy unrestricted access to the other immigration countries. Life in the DP camps was no substitute for normal, permanent living conditions, although many of the inmates, especially the young, married and had children. Anti-Zionist circles agitated for a 'back-to-Poland' movement. Poland was flooded with rumours that the DPs were in dire straits, that suicide was rife among them, and that friction between them and the local German populace was escalating. It was reported in the name of an UNRRA director that 21 Jews had taken their lives in an eleven-week period, that three Jews had been murdered in one week, and that Jews had been thrown out of an electric tram in Munich.[52]

British agents in UNRRA and PCIRO (which assumed the care of the refugees after UNRRA was dissolved) also propagandized among the Jews in the DP camps, encouraging them to return to Poland. PCIRO Director John S. Widdicombe, reporting on a visit he had made to Lower Silesia in the summer of 1947, claimed that relations between the Jews and the Poles were excellent, as attested to even by Zionist leaders in the places he visited. The Jews were proud of having become a productive element in society; their institutions were doing very well, and many Jews were returning to Poland not only from the DP camps but from Palestine, no less. The British, of course, were interested in eliminating or at least alleviating the Jewish DP factor as a tool of pressure against the British policy restricting emigration to Palestine. The head of the PCIRO repatriation bureau suggested that this report be circulated to all inmates of the DP camps.[53]

The propaganda against the 'exodus from Poland' and in favour of Jews returning to that country from the DP camps did not prove very successful from the vantage point of its sponsors. Some 1,100 Jews did return to Poland in 1947, with UNRRA assistance. Several hundred more apparently returned on their own by various means. Still another 22 families who had handed their children over to Brichah operatives for transport to Palestine demanded their children back.[54] However, Jews continued to leave Poland in 1947, too, by the thousands, using every possible route – organized by Brichah and other, private means. When the Polish Government closed its borders to the unrestricted passage of Jews into Czechoslovakia in early 1947, Brichah continued along alternative routes. Thousands of entry visas were obtained from the Mexican consul; they were good for leaving Poland but did not confer the right to enter Mexico. Thousands of additional temporary permits were obtained for Belgium, Italy, France, and other countries. All these activities were aided, and largely financed, by the JDC emigration department.[55]

### 1947: REHABILITATION OPERATIONS

At the beginning of 1947, after the mass escape, 105,000 Jews were left in Poland. Of these, thousands continued to leave by means of Brichah, if at a slower pace, and thousands more waited for safer and easier ways to emigrate to Palestine or elsewhere. There were certainly many Jews, too, who hoped to settle in Poland itself, make a living there, and live without further fear for their physical wellbeing and their children's future. The JDC was completely and generously willing to help them fulfil their wishes, as it applied itself with the same generosity to helping those Jews who saw no future for themselves in Poland.

*Economic Rehabilitation: The Cooperatives and the Rehabilitation Banks*

The JDC regarded its economic rehabilitation programme as the most important of all its operations. Its basic policy was to invest great efforts and resources in this activity, and to promote and expedite the process by which the Jews they supported would be able to sustain themselves and their families. In this, JDC policy was consistent with the aspirations and programmes of the CKZP, which set 'productivization' as its prime goal. The Zionists favoured the same goal, but unlike the Communists and Bundists, who viewed it as a vehicle of integration into Polish society and economy, the Zionists believed in economic rehabilitation as a means of preparing and training Jews for eventual immigration to Palestine.

The organization of production and service cooperatives was the major route to employment and economic rehabilitation for the Jews, who had begun to resettle in the Polish urban centres, especially those in the annexed western parts of the country. The regime, too, promoted the establishment of cooperatives and viewed this as one of the building blocks of a socialist economy. Apart from this, Jews were now able to accept employment in new industrial plants and other enterprises that had been nationalized and were undergoing rehabilitation.

It was only natural that the Jews who tended to organize into cooperatives were those with no professional or white-collar training, who had to earn their living by manual labour. The cooperative enterprises still left some room for personal initiative and a feeling of sharing in ownership. Most important, new cooperatives set up by the Jewish workers offered Jews the company of compatriots and a Jewish atmosphere. Here they could work without the hostility they encountered in other workplaces, where they were a minority, if not a handful, among many gentiles.

As will be recalled, the JDC took care to pack items such as sewing machines and tailors' and shoemakers' tools in the very first relief shipments to the Lublin area after its liberation. When Poland was entirely liberated, thousands of Jews poured into Lodz, the country's second largest city, which was well suited to receive them. Unlike Warsaw, which had been partially levelled during the 1943 ghetto uprising and devastated in the general Polish uprising in the second half of 1944, the war hardly scarred Lodz. Furthermore, tens of thousands of Germans who had lived in Lodz before the Second World War, and additional tens of thousands who settled there after its annexation to the German Reich, all left after Poland's surrender. Thus, upon the liberation, Lodz had many empty buildings and apartments to offer. By mid-1945 the first Jewish settlers had set up six tailoring cooperatives with about 100 sewing machines, and other cooperatives for bakers, shoemakers, builders, and plasterers. Jews also opened up about 100 small private shops. In June 1945 there were 9,600 Jews in Lodz, of whom about 6,000 had lived there before the war.[56]

The Jewish cooperative movement took on great momentum when large-scale JDC aid began in 1946. An umbrella organization of Jewish cooperatives – 'the Economic Centre – Solidarnosc' – was founded in April of that year. The Centre helped the cooperatives obtain credit, raw materials, mechanical equipment and tools; coordinate their marketing; and implement technological advances in production, administration, and finance. In February 1947, Solidarnosc embraced 164 cooperatives with 3,955 members.

In December 1947, investment per worker approached 3,000 zloty in the cooperatives that produced machines, electricity and apparel, and approximately 6,500 zloty in cooperatives engaging in services and food. Wages were very modest and non-standardized; they varied according to each cooperative's income. The lowest wage recorded in 1947 was 4,300 zloty ($10.30) per month in the shoemaking cooperative, and the highest was 11,900 ($29.45) in the weaving cooperative. These wages were very low, especially considering the sharp inflation affecting all basic commodities that year. Moreover, food was rationed. Wage-earners were entitled to 30,000 calories a month on the basis of ration cards. Although prices were low and government-controlled, delivery was poorly handled and staples were not always easily obtained. In 1947, white-collar workers and students were declared ineligible for ration cards. Under these circumstances, even those who had steady work – including members of cooperatives – needed relief aid for food, clothing, and medicine. This was provided by the JDC.[57]

In July 1947, 22 per cent of the 778 cooperatives existing in Poland were Jewish. By the end of 1948, when this development peaked, there were 208 Jewish cooperatives. Of them, 173 (employing 9,044) belonged to Solidarnosc. The JDC estimated that the share of the Jews employed in the cooperatives in 1947–49 represented 18–20 per cent of the entire Jewish labour force in Poland. According to the same source, the cooperatives were supporting about 18,000 persons (workers and their families) in mid-1947.[58]

The JDC aided the cooperatives and their union, Solidarnosc, in cash and with the import of equipment and raw materials unobtainable in Poland. The Polish Government did its share by extending credit and allotting such factory buildings and equipment as were locally available. Raw materials and equipment imported by the JDC for the cooperatives, and other imported relief such as food, clothing, blankets, and medicine, were exempt from customs and rail transport charges. The Government also provided the JDC with warehouses in the port city of Gdynia, where the goods could be stored pending distribution around the country.[59] JDC aid to the cooperatives and Solidarnosc was officially extended as credit. The money, once repaid, was to be used by the JDC to further its relief programme, particularly with respect to social services: health, education, culture, and welfare.

After the cooperatives and Solidarnosc, the second instrument of rehabilitation – not necessarily in terms of importance – was the Jewish bank. It began as a modest loan fund that was founded in Lublin in January 1945, and moved to Warsaw in March, together with the CKZP after the capital was liberated. In October it was renamed the 'Cooperative Bank for the Productivization of the Jews' (Spoldzielczy Bank dia Produktywizacji Zydow). The bank's activity gained momentum at the beginning of 1946, when the JDC granted it an initial budget of 15,000,000 zloty. In September of that year the bank's capital reached 67,000,000 zloty, including 52,500,000 zloty in cash from the JDC and 1,261,000 zloty in machinery and equipment. The JDC provided both Solidarnosc and the bank with machinery and tools, because Solidarnosc could turn these over to the cooperatives only while the bank could distribute them among private artisans. Similarly, the bank lent both to cooperatives and to private enterprises (artisans, doctors, engineers, lawyers, storekeepers, etc.).[60] The Jewish bank supplied the Jewish cooperatives with about two-thirds of all their credit. The JDC lent the bank a total of 229,500,000 zloty between 1946 and 1948, augmenting this by 75,000,000 zloty in 1949.[61]

In addition to Solidarnosc and the Jewish bank, the JDC used local and other institutions as conduits for the supply of equipment – sewing machines and tools – to cooperatives and private Jewish artisans. In 1947 alone, for example, the JDC provided various institutions and individuals throughout Poland with another 728 sewing machines and 142 cases of tools without the intermediation of Solidarnosc and the bank.[62]

Just as Solidarnosc had begun repaying its debts to the JDC, the Jewish Bank was supposed to start doing the same in 1950. At the end of 1949, however, the bank was shut down and nationalized, resulting in the loss of the JDC's investment.

*Educational Rehabilitation*

One very important link in the network of economic rehabilitation institutions and activities were the vocational schools and courses. Initially, the CKZP handled them, with JDC assistance. Soon afterwards ORT took over. Other organizations, mainly Zionist 'kibbutzim,' were active in this work, backed largely if not entirely by the JDC. By the end of 1945, enrolment in these vocational programmes stood at about 4,000.[63] In 1946, ORT expanded its network and offered many half-year, one-, two-, and three-year courses. The Polish Government supported ORT: in 1948 it provided 7,000,000 zloty in cash and 10,000,000 zloty in machinery and equipment supplied by the Ministry of Commerce and Industry, and it furnished the organization with a building in Wroclaw valued at 35,000,000 zloty. That year, the government also permitted a one-off import of Swiss watches, financed by ORT's world headquarters in Geneva. These were then sold, enabling ORT to obtain a more realistic exchange rate for its foreign currency.[64]

Many vocational trainees had to be housed and their needs met. Canteens were set up not only for students but for teachers, counsellors, and ORT workers. Most of the funds for these canteens and for housing came from the JDC. The ORT institutions earned a good reputation in non-Jewish circles as well, and were often asked to accept non-Jewish students. In 1949, ORT's last year in Poland, non-Jews outnumbered Jews in many courses.[65] That year, ORT ran ten schools and training centres for 2,159 students, including institutes of radio technology (with 34 students) and montage photography (21 students).[66] In all, ORT organized over 100 courses in 1945–49, training thousands of skilled workers. Its diplomas were recognized by the authorities, and many graduates found work in the Jewish cooperatives. The JDC not only financed most of ORT's budget; it also granted ORT students full scholarships throughout their studies. At the beginning of 1950, the ORT institutions were nationalized and expropriated.[67]

From 1945, the beginning of its activity in Poland, until June 1948, the JDC provided approximately 6,000 men and women, young and old, with vocational training in the institutions it financed wholly or partly. By June 1948, the JDC was supporting 72 trade schools and one agricultural school, which had 30 students (besides 'Hachshara' training on the pioneering Zionist 'kibbutzim'). The JDC also maintained 14 residences for 700 students and apprentices.[68]

*Health Services*

Health and medical care were two of the most acute problems in rehabilitating Holocaust survivors. Many of the survivors of the Nazi concentration and death camps and the repatriates from the USSR – most of whom had also been liberated from camps or prisons and had endured epidemics and starvation – were ill, spent, or disabled. In liberated Poland there was severe distress, and food, clothing, and adequate housing were scarce. The most elementary medical conditions were lacking: hospitals, medical equipment, medicines, and a competent staff. It was only natural, then, that the first relief supplies sent by the JDC from Teheran to liberated

Lublin, at the end of 1944, included equipment for three 100-bed hospitals and a large quantity of drugs.

Dr. A. Rosenblitt, a head of the OSE (Society for the Protection of the Health of the Jews – Russian branch), was the first representative of the World Jewish Organization permitted, as early as February 1945, even before the end of the war, to visit Lublin and Warsaw in order to study the possibilities for resuming the work of TOZ (Polish branch of the OSE).[69] In 1946, the JDC began to fund TOZ generously toward the development of a large-scale network of medical facilities.

In the first quarter of 1947, the Jews' situation began to stabilize after the mass repatriation from the USSR and the large-scale Brichah. At this stage, TOZ had 65 district, sub-district, and local branches including a small hospital in Krakow with 16 beds, clinics, small infirmaries, a total of 20 operating theatres, six laboratories, 36 first-aid stations, and 15 pharmacies. Sixteen clinics had dental departments. Pre-natal counselling was available in 23 cities. Preventive-medicine facilities treated 136 children, and 24 infant-care centres handled 384. Three convalescent homes served 280 adults and children with tuberculosis, and a similar facility including workshops accommodated another 50. Thirteen public-health workers dealt with small communities that had no clinics. In sum, TOZ ran 208 medical institutions staffed by 474 Jewish doctors, 71 dentists, 168 medical students, and five dentistry students. There were 177 specialists in internal medicine, 50 paediatricians, 55 gynaecologists, and 40 dermatologists.[70]

TOZ's crowning achievement was the opening of a relatively large hospital, equipped with the best and most up-to-date equipment, in the city of Walbrzych, in Lower Silesia. Word of its high standards quickly spread, and the Jewish medical centre was overwhelmed with non-Jewish patients, whom it did not turn away. By 30 September 1948 the hospital had treated 518 people, of whom only 147 were Jews. In October 1949, the Municipality of Walbrzych expropriated the hospital. In July 1950, TOZ discontinued its activities nation-wide and its institutions were nationalized.[71]

*Education and Culture*

Educational and cultural activities began in the first months after the liberation from Nazi occupation, when the survivors began to form communities. But they gained tremendous momentum only in early 1946, with the return of tens of thousands of repatriates from the USSR and with the JDC's generous grant. Physically and psychologically devastated, the survivors nonetheless evinced a great vitality and will to live, and there was a broad spectrum of active participation in community life, especially in education and culture. But exaggerated ideological and political fragmentation soon developed, recreating the pattern of Jewish life in Poland prior to the Holocaust. It was as though nothing had happened in the interim. The only difference lay in numbers. It was simply their previous existence in Poland in microcosm.

Bein expressed amazement at the intense cultural awareness and interest, considering it a reaction to the sensory deadening and spiritual standstill of the Holocaust. Yet he criticized the numerous conventions and assemblies that the JDC was asked to finance. He also noted that until Poland's new Jewish community could fund these ventures, it would have to limit its activities.[72]

Very few concentration-camp survivors and people in hiding were children. Only among the repatriated Jews from the USSR were there several thousand children. The first Jewish day school was opened in Bialystok with a few pupils studying Yiddish, Hebrew, and arithmetic. At the beginning of the 1945–46 school year, Jewish day schools were established in Lodz, Lublin, Warsaw, Rykbach, and Chorzow. The Lodz facility was the largest, with eight grades, 350 students, and 15 teachers. Lower Silesia began that year with only one small school (in Rykbach), but by the end of 1946 it had 23, with 1,700 pupils and 116 teachers.

There were no curricula, books, or other equipment. The teachers, not all of whom were formally trained, improvised their lesson plans through sheer dedication. The CKZP Education Department sponsored a country-wide education congress on 1 November 1946, in Lodz. About 150 teachers, educators, and education functionaries attended, as did a representative of the Ministry of Education. Many arguments ensued, particularly between the Zionists and their opponents, over languages of instruction and curriculum. It was agreed *de jure* that children would begin learning Yiddish in first grade, and Hebrew and Polish in second grade. The Ministry representative demanded that Polish be taught in first grade, with Hebrew starting only in fourth grade. The congress rejected his demand and the state education authorities let the matter lie, but not for long. It was also decided to note Jewish holidays and teach Jewish history. Educational goals and curriculum content were agreed upon in confused and compromising terms open to interpretation by each faction: 'The goal of the Jewish school is to give the young Jewish generation a national, democratic, and secular education reflecting the progressive ideals of our times.' It was further resolved, with the Zionists abstaining, that the educational system should be uniform.[73] But the political fragmentation and the deep disagreements between the Zionists and the non-Zionists, and between ultra-Orthodox Jews (albeit a weak minority) and secularists, prevented the implementation of the congress's decisions; as long as the different parties enjoyed freedom of action, fragmentation inevitably spilled over into education.

While the congress deliberated, Lodz already had a seven-grade Hebrew school with 260 pupils and 10 teachers. Most schools remained within the CKZP network as long as it was allowed to exist, but the pioneer movements constructed no parallel chain of Hebrew schools. The ultra-Orthodox set up some Talmud Torahs and yeshivas. The JDC supported all these schools equally, on the basis of the number of pupils and teachers. At the end of 1946, the JDC reported 349 educational and cultural institutions that it recognized and supported. These served over 20,000 children, youths, and adults.[74]

In 1947–48, the Jewish schools began to merge with the national school system. This merger applied to the CKZP schools, which had to follow the state curriculum. Nevertheless, they were allowed to continue to teach Yiddish and Hebrew as a supplement, with financing by the Jewish authorities. In a sense, this eased the burden of maintaining the Jewish schools, which the Ministry of Education now shouldered. Yet the CKZP, and indirectly the JDC, continued to finance Jewish studies, including hiring a special teaching supervisor. They also had to pay their teachers the difference between the state teachers' salary, 7,000–8,000 zloty a month, and that paid by the Jewish schools before the merger, 18,000–19,000 zloty a month. This increment seemed essential, lest the good teachers abandon their posts for better-paid work.

The order to merge applied neither to the Hebrew schools, run by the Zionist pioneer movements, nor to the few Talmud Torahs (all financed by the JDC). Hebrew schools, with their 900 pupils, were designated for liquidation in any case, for in 1949 all Zionist organizations were disbanded. The few yeshivas were closed by the end of 1946, when almost all their students left during the mass Brichah. About 600 of them arrived in Paris, where the JDC looked after them until they could leave for Palestine or the United States.

In 1949, the Zionist Coordination for the Redemption of Children was liquidated by government order. (This organization had received particularly generous aid from the JDC.) Jewish children who had not been redeemed by that date were lost to their people forever. At the same time, yet another attempt was made to open a yeshiva – in which 20 students were to have been trained as community rabbis – but it failed after its initiator, Chief Rabbi David Kahane, hurried off to Palestine.[75]

The rehabilitation of Holocaust survivors in Poland also involved intensive social and cultural activity. Most of this activity – lectures, seminars, literary evenings, concerts of song and general and Jewish music – was engineered by political parties interested in attracting as many members and sympathizers as possible. Scores of intellectuals, authors, journalists, and artists contributed greatly to the cultural life in the cities. Almost all of them had been repatriated from the USSR. Every Sunday – the official day of rest – Jewish communities bustled with activity. Every local Jewish committee had a cultural sub-committee, which organized various shows, choirs, drama groups, libraries, etc.

In December 1946, 400 young people and 1,100 invitees – all cultural activists – convened in Wroclaw and resolved to set up a Jewish Society for Culture and Art. In the summer of 1947, a founding convention met to create a country-wide society for Jewish culture. In 1950, this society became the only organization representing the Jews of Poland after the liquidation of the CKZP and its branches, which in fact merged with the Cultural Society.[76]

The Jewish Authors' and Journalists' League was established in Lodz and given a large building housing a sizeable performance hall (mainly for 'literary evenings'), an office, and a members' canteen, where about 60 people ate every day. The League produced a literary monthly called Yiddishe Schriften ('Jewish Writings') and maintained a publishing house, 'Yiddishe Buch,' which published eight books in 1948, 10 in 1949, and 23 in 1951.[77]

Jewish periodicals and newspapers flourished, too – relatively speaking. The CKZP published a Yiddish-language newspaper *Dos Naje Lebn* (The New Life), which appeared thrice weekly, and the Jewish faction in the ruling party PPR published a weekly in Yiddish called *Volks Shtimme* (Call of the People). All the parties and youth movements together published dozens of weeklies and monthlies in Yiddish, Polish, and Hebrew.

Two central theatres were founded, in addition to dozens of local drama groups: in Lodz, actress Ida Kaminska directed what became the State Yiddish Theatre in 1950, while another Yiddish-language theatre was established in Wroclaw.

Immediately following the liberation of Lublin, the Central Jewish Historical Committee began gathering documents and other evidence of the Holocaust of Polish Jewry. A major impetus to expand its scope of activity came with the discovery of Emanuel Ringleblum's archive, offering a daily chronicle of life in the Warsaw Ghetto until its last day. Part of the archive was discovered in September 1946, with the rest unearthed in December 1950, after the Historical Committee had become the Jewish Historical Institute and part of the Polish Academy of Sciences in 1948. By mid-1947, the Committee had published 35 research studies and reports.

The rich social-cultural activity among the Holocaust survivors in Poland during these years was financed entirely by the JDC. Its representatives understood the survivors' physical and spiritual needs and did their utmost to fill them. In 1948, for example, the JDC spent 151,100,000 zloty on cultural programmes in Poland, or 21 per cent of its annual operational budget.[78]

*Welfare*

The Warsaw JDC estimated that in early 1947, over one-third of Poland's Jews were ill, handicapped, elderly, or women unable to work outside their homes.[79] They were not the only persons needing relief. All the Holocaust survivors were destitute and helpless in a ravaged land where shortages and distress gripped virtually the entire population. Many non-Jews also needed help. Therefore, the Council of Foreign Voluntary Agencies established 23 foreign philanthropic organizations (in addition to local ones) in the first years after Poland's liberation. By the end of 1946, the UNRRA had also set up operations in Poland.

The JDC distinguished between persons needing temporary aid – such as workers requiring income supplements, vocational trainees, students, pioneer 'kibbutz' members waiting to go to Palestine, legally or 'illegally,' etc. – and Jews who needed permanent assistance: the ill, the elderly, and the disabled. Top priority, however, was given to children. The few children who survived the Holocaust, and those who were born to survivors after the war, were cherished not only by their parents, but by the entire Jewish people, and they were given special care and provisions. Many were orphans, and with children of working parents were placed in children's homes. Such homes were set up by the CKZP, and by political parties seeking to influence these children. As stated, TOZ children's homes cared for sickly youth. As for the care given, Bein remarked:

> The children's facilities in Poland are as good as those in the United States. Some are exemplary. For instance, one home just outside Warsaw offers full facilities and a degree of self-government. The children do all their work under expert supervision ... and if you wonder whether they have enough time for their studies, I can tell you that the best students in all the government schools are these Jewish pupils from the children's homes.[80]

The JDC also gave special consideration to the few elderly Holocaust survivors. In early 1947, when the Jewish population became relatively settled, nine old-age homes were founded for 377 persons. Eight were run by the CKZP, and one, with 12 residents, by the Va'ad Hakehillot (Council of Religious Jewish Communities). The disabled and chronically ill were placed in homes with the elderly, but in 1948 – despite the extra maintenance costs – the JDC divided the three groups among separate institutions to improve the care, since each had special requirements. TOZ took care of the institutionalized cases.[81] In 1948, the JDC's welfare department spent 41,500,000 zloty on welfare payments to adults.

This aid, mostly goods rather than cash, benefited the entire Jewish population – institutions, organizations, and individuals. It began in 1944 and continued until 1949, when the JDC was forced to stop its operations in Poland. Goods shipments included foodstuffs (powdered milk and eggs, canned meat, fish, fruit and vegetables, flour, Passover matzo, sweets and chocolate, and tea and coffee), shoes and other apparel, sheets and blankets, drugs and medical equipment, raw materials, tools and equipment for cooperatives and self-employed artisans, instructional and other aids for schools and educational institutions, tableware and kitchen appliances, religious articles, and other materials required by institutions. In addition, the JDC provided vehicles for organizations. In 1946, the JDC imported 12 trucks: five for the CKZP, two for TOZ, two for Hechalutz, and three for itself.

In addition to material aid, the JDC answered the need for legal aid. A legal department in its Warsaw office dealt with the legal problems of the JDC's work and dispensed legal aid to Jews in need. Director-General Bein and Secretary-General Gitler-Barsky were both recognized by the regime as lawyers and were granted the attendant formal authority, which simplified their contact with the government. The JDC was asked to provide legal aid in two main areas: restitution claims and legal emigration documents.

The JDC legal department also provided important aid to Polish Jews in Poland, and to those abroad and in need of various documents affirming their origin. The major document required was the birth certificate, essential for emigration papers and other imperatives. Many survivors had been forced to adopt aliases and had been saved by forged documents, but had to document their true identities after the war. This was a tall order for the JDC, since witnesses had to be found in each case.[82]

Finally, the JDC in Warsaw had a missing-relatives department. In the early postwar years, this department worked with Jewish organizations throughout the world, and Jewish newspapers ran long lists of persons seeking relatives. Survivors and European Jews sought each other's relations. In 1947, the department employed 12 of the JDC's 127 employees in Poland. That year it sent the European administration 16 books listing all the survivors in Poland, to be distributed throughout the Jewish world.[83] The department traced 564 relatives and put them in touch with those seeking them. It also traced 60 lost children, returning six to their parents.[84] Late in 1948, the department and those of welfare and emigration were closed as the JDC cut back its operations, and were shut down altogether in Poland a year later.

## EMIGRATION

When the State of Israel came into being, there was no immediate, large-scale immigration from Poland. The entire Soviet bloc had not yet set a clear policy on such immigration and was highly inconsistent, apparently because of its accelerating Cold War with the West after Czechoslovakia was forced to become a 'people's democracy' in May–June 1948, and because of the emergence of deviationist Titoism. Thus, 2,500 young Jews were allowed to leave for Israel, having signed up with the Hagana and undergone military training in Poland, while other emigration was severely limited. Wladyslaw Wolski promised Israel's envoy, Yisrael Barzilai, that immigration would not be stopped altogether.[85]

On 4 December 1948, the JDC emigration department in Warsaw was closed. The UB (internal security service) confiscated the archives and arrested the JDC clerk in charge, ostensibly for trying to arrange emigration papers for two ineligible friends. Another office worker was arrested at a later date. Henceforth, the immigration department of the Israeli representation handled all emigration to Israel, while Jewish emigration to other countries was channelled through the CKZP.[86] The decision to close the JDC emigration department was political, agreed upon by the authorities and the CKZP.[87]

Even though the JDC emigration department was shut down, emigration to Israel did not come to a total halt, nor did the JDC discontinue its financial aid to all emigrants. Zionist activists were allowed to leave for Israel in 1948, and their emigration was speeded up in 1949 with intent to stamp out all local Zionist activity. In August 1949, the Polish Ministry of the Interior informed the Va'ad Hakehillot that all Jews could leave for Israel within 12–18 months. The CKZP attempted to abort this emigration by issuing Jewish-identity certificates just two hours a week. But the Polish Government kept its promise and dealt very liberally with the Jews, allowing the exit of Jewish soldiers and of mixed families.[88] By December 1950, Polish authorities had issued 32,416 transit certificates (Israel-bound emigrants did not receive passports, and were asked to renounce their Polish citizenship). Only 28,594 Jews reached Israel this way. The rest relinquished their rights due to a high-powered CKZP propaganda campaign based on accurate reports from Israel of immigrant-absorption difficulties. These were the years of mass immigration, with most immigrants placed in Jewish Agency-run tent cities and shanty towns. Some Jews seeking to leave for Israel were former active communists who feared that they would be turned away, fired from their jobs, and persecuted.[89] The JDC financed the transport of Polish Jews headed for Israel, as it funded all Israel-bound Jews during the mass aliyah. Hundreds of these Poles were TB victims, but Israel accepted them – along with the other infirm and handicapped – for fear that this was the last chance to rescue Jews from Poland. (Immigration resumed in 1956–58 and in 1968–69.) As we know, the JDC also took care of the ill, elderly, and handicapped immigrants after they settled in Israel.

## ZIONIST ORGANIZATIONS

Zionist activity in Poland resumed immediately after the Lublin area was liberated. The organizers included survivors of the Zionist underground – who had operated in partisan units in the forests, the last surviving ghetto fighters, and members of Zionist parties and youth movements, who had been among the first repatriated from the Soviet Union. Among these Zionists were soldiers from the Red Army and the pro-Soviet Polish army. The relative political freedom in Poland in those early years of liberation from Nazi occupation made Zionist activity possible. Zionist leader Sommerstein was elected chairman of the CKZP. In the first months after the liberation, it was widely thought in Zionist circles that the Holocaust and subsequent conditions had rendered many of their political and ideological rifts meaningless. They considered themselves united by one goal: emigration to Palestine for all Holocaust survivors. As the murder of Jews increasingly proliferated in restored Poland, the Zionists considered this emigration – and its Brichah alternative – a continuation of their efforts to save Jews from extermination, which demanded cooperation and organization. Thus, in December 1944, they formed the Zionist Coordinating Committee in Poland in Lublin, and Polish Brichah activists established the Eastern European Survivors' Division in Bucharest in April 1945.[90]

However, this unity was short-lived. As members of the various movements renewed ties with their Palestine headquarters – which retained their traditional, pre-Holocaust party rifts – the organizational and ideological patterns in Poland resurfaced among the survivors. Factions split and merged. The non-socialist parties set up one body known as 'Ichud,' which included General Zionists of all sorts, Mizrachi, the Revisionists (who were forbidden to set up their own organization), and Hitachdut (which paralleled Hapoel Hatza'ir in Israel and its youth movement, Gordonia). The Hechalutz, a pre-war umbrella organization of all pioneer movements, including Gordonia, was reinstated. WIZO, too, resumed activity. The JDC lent financial support to all these Zionist organizations, although Bein decried the exaggerated division among them, unable to understand it.

These organizations concentrated on their 'kibbutzim' and youth and children's homes. The former were necessary to maintain the Holocaust survivors in Poland, of whom many if not most were alone. In addition, young couples and new families, then forming in great numbers, found it hard to secure housing and even harder to run an independent household. There was also a grave security risk. The 'kibbutzim' – communal dwellings furnished with JDC equipment and supplies – provided relatively simple solutions to their residents' problems of daily survival and personal security. The shared ideal of each movement's 'kibbutz' fostered closeness, understanding, and mutual aid among its members, who organized cultural and intellectual activities and entertainment. These 'kibbutzim' offered an alternative to family homes destroyed in the Holocaust, and served as bases for organizing and consolidating groups escaping via the Brichah routes, and, after Israel was established, for the Jewish state.

Alongside the 'kibbutzim' were youth and children's homes. The movements competed to attract unaffiliated young people, adults, and children. The JDC maintained the 'kibbutzim' and homes, supplemented by many 'kibbutz' members with outside jobs. The Jewish Agency and movement headquarters in Palestine also provided aid. In the first quarter of 1947, for example, the Zionist organizations received about nine per cent of all JDC funds spent in Poland.[91]

Due to emigration to Palestine, membership in the pioneer movements and 'kibbutzim' fluctuated. In July 1946, before the Kielce pogrom and mass flight, they had numbered 11,800 members.[92] In June 1947, there were 114 'kibbutzim' with 6,755 members, compared with 87 and 3,903 respectively, in January 1948, and 71 and 2,225 in June 1948. In the second quarter of 1948, the population of the Zionist youth homes dropped from 1,020 to 694.[93]

The pioneer movements remained active as long as possible in 1949, so as not to surrender Polish Jews solely to communist influence. At the end of the year, the authorities disbanded both the JDC office and the Zionist movements. To protect the Zionist leaders in December 1949, their last month of activity, Bein sent them 11,000,000 zloty for expenses and debt repayment, thereby saving them from imprisonment.[94]

Historically, several of the Polish Zionist organizations' most important activities were the enlistment, training, and dispatch of volunteers to defend Israel in the War of Independence. The Polish Government promoted this effort. As part of the Russians' short-lived pro-Zionist policy, the Polish authorities received orders at the end of 1947 to allow young Jewish men to be drafted into the Hagana, and to establish a base where they could be trained by Hagana emissaries from Israel. General Waclaw Komar, a Pole of Jewish extraction, was appointed to command the operation. Ironically, CKZP Communist chairman Hersz Smolar was the liaison between the authorities and emissaries. The volunteers came from the pioneer youth movements, but Jewish communists, too, were permitted to volunteer. Some were recruited for espionage. The training base was set up in remote Bolkow, in Lower Silesia. Recruitment of volunteers began in April 1948, and ceased half a year later, when the USSR changed its policy toward Israel. About 2,500 young people went through basic training in Bolkow and were sent to Israel.[95] The JDC outfitted and fed the volunteers and, after their training, gave them $25 each to get from Warsaw to the port of Marseilles. It also paid for their medical examinations.[96]

## VA'AD HAKEHILLOT

The percentage of ultra-Orthodox Jews in Poland was far lower after the Holocaust than hitherto. The few ultra-Orthodox in Poland, and the first repatriates from the USSR, quickly organized themselves and set up the basic religious facilities so sorely lacking. They were encouraged by the new Polish regime's tolerance towards adherents of all religions, including Jews, which meant they would face no interference in resurrecting their religious life. As in any Jewish community, even the non-observant required such religious services as traditional weddings, circumcisions, burial in a Jewish cemetery, a prayer quorum for mourners' rites, etc. Thus there was considerable demand for rabbis, circumcisers, and ritual slaughterers, and cantors were especially sought after during the High Holidays, which drew many irreligious Jews to the synagogue. The demand for these religious functionaries far exceeded the supply.

The ultra-Orthodox set up their own religious community organizations, ignoring the CKZP and local Jewish committees which were dominated by Communists and Bundists. The JDC was particularly sympathetic to the Orthodox and their institutions. Lecturing to the JDC European administration staff in Paris on 28 February 1948, Bein explained the emotional motives behind his concern for the ultra-Orthodox:

> I want you to know that we are giving special attention to all the concerns of the religious groups because the fathers of at least 70 per cent of all the Jews in the world today came from Poland. The ultra-Orthodox lost their leadership in the Holocaust, and have received no support from any source. Thus, it is up to us to take concrete action in looking after them.[97]

After Poland was liberated and some Jewish communities reorganized, the ultra-Orthodox set up a national union known as the 'Religious Union of Members of the Mosaic Faith in Poland' (Zwiazek Religijny wyznania Mozeszowego w Polsce), or the *Va'ad Hakehillot* in Hebrew. The union had its headquarters in

Warsaw, in the CKZP and JDC offices. Mizrachi and Agudath Israel belonged to the union, as did (unofficially) the Zionist 'Ichud,' which was also represented within the CKZP.

The *Va'ad* and its activities were financed by the JDC. Sometimes donations for health, education, culture, and welfare institutions were received from the Rabbinical Council of America and from private donors, whereas the CKZP received about 20 per cent of its funding from the central and municipal authorities. There was no discrimination involved, since the authorities did not support the Catholic church either.

In 1946, with generous JDC help, the religious community organizations grew unwieldy and inefficient. In the first half of 1947, when the community stabilized, the JDC urged a reorganization of its administration. The resulting new administration included three full-time salaried positions. The Warsaw office also housed a chief rabbinate headed by Rabbi David Kahane. The union embraced 80 communities and maintained 18 local rabbinates, 38 synagogues, 68 cemeteries, 51 kosher kitchens supplying 2,875 meals daily, four guest houses with 100 beds, two children's homes with 52 residents, two old-age homes with 24 residents, four ritual bathhouses, and 36 Talmud Torahs with 1,100 pupils. In addition, the JDC distributed matza to all Polish Jews who so desired. On Passover of 1947, 100 tons of matza was distributed, together with 40,000 lb. of matza meal.[98]

The matza distribution operation, carried out by a joint committee of the CKZP and the *Va'ad Hakehillot*, had an important byproduct – an unofficial census of Poland's Jews. The JDC assumed that almost all Jews would want matza, which was distributed free of charge. The census recorded about 90,000 Jews in 158 communities, including 43,000 in Lower Silesia. The largest communities were in Lodz (13,860 Jews) and Wroclaw (9,102). It appears, however, that 10–15 per cent of the Jews were overlooked. We may therefore estimate the Jewish population in Poland at the time at almost 100,000 – about 44,000 men, 40,000 women, and 16,000 children under 16.[99]

In view of the successful matza operation, the JDC suggested that the *Va'ad Hakehillot* and the CKZP form committees to deal with projects important to both: burial of Holocaust victims in Jewish cemeteries, restoration of synagogues and cemeteries, recovery of religious articles held by non-Jews, and return of Jewish public property to Jewish ownership.[100]

After the establishment of Israel, the scope of operations undertaken by the *Va'ad Hakehillot* and the regional communities narrowed rapidly. The ultra-Orthodox left Poland any way they could. Among the first to go were rabbis and community leaders. The few left were poorer, occupied a low social stratum, and lacked functionaries with leadership ability. The number of community organizations dropped, and those that survived grew weaker. The joint committee projects were not carried out. In 1948, the government ordered the local authorities to return the gravestones that had been uprooted from Jewish cemeteries for paving sidewalks, but the communities no longer had the leadership or the money to press the matter.[101]

As the Jewish communities dwindled in number and activity, many Torah scrolls went unused. In the spring of 1949, the JDC financed 26 shipments of Torah scrolls from Poland to settlements being established in Israel.[102] Meanwhile, the *Va'ad Hakehillot* and the JDC prevented any shortage of religious articles among the ultra-Orthodox. In its last weeks in Poland, the JDC ordered 500 prayer shawls, 250 pairs of tefillin, and 500 kilogrammes of raisins for the production of Passover wine.[103]

When the JDC was forced to cease its operations in Poland, Bein went to great lengths to ensure a steady flow of meaningful aid to the *Va'ad Hakehillot*. He initiated an agreement whereby 20 per cent of the JDC's assets in Poland would pass to the *Va'ad*, 10 per cent would be used to maintain Jewish cemeteries and 10 per cent for interring Holocaust victims in Israel. Thus, 40 per cent of the JDC's assets in Poland were earmarked for religious needs.

Formally, at least, the *Va'ad Hakehillot* still exists. When the axe of 'unification' fell on almost all the Jewish institutions in 1949, and on the CKZP and its branches in 1950, the *Va'ad* was spared. The Polish authorities reasoned that a puppet religious union might benefit them and improve their image in the West, and among Jewish tourists, as a state where religious freedom is 'guaranteed.'

## LIQUIDATION AND EXPULSION

In 1948–49 Poland was in the midst of accelerated Sovietization and Stalinization, as were the other Soviet-bloc countries. Naturally, there was no longer room for Western organizations, especially American ones, which the Soviets viewed as espionage fronts. As previously noted, the JDC's emigration department was closed in December 1948. In February 1949, Interior Minister Wolski informed Bein that the JDC had to quit Poland on 31 December.

The Minister consented to allow four or five clerks to work another three or four weeks after that date, winding up accounts, repaying debts, and shutting down the office. It was also agreed that a Successor Committee would be set up to transfer assets and operations to other bodies, and that most of the JDC archives would be moved to the Jewish Historical Institute. Bein asked to take part of the archives, including a collection of photos of religious artefacts, and he asked to expedite the issue of exit visas to JDC workers emigrating to Israel, in order to spare them prolonged unemployment.[104]

The JDC's investments in Poland during its 5½ years of activity approached $21,000,000, or 7.6 per cent of its total expenditures (about $276,000,000) world-wide. The scale of its outlays varied each year with the scope of needs and objective possibilities.[105]

JDC INVESTMENT IN POLAND, 1944–1949 (THOUSANDS OF DOLLARS)

| Year | Amount |
|---|---|
| 1944 | 6,154.5 |
| 1945 | 1,684.5 |
| 1946 | 7,666.2 |
| 1947 | 5,603.1 |
| 1948 | 2,995.1 |
| 1949 | 2,357.2 |
| Total | 20,920.6 |

As evident in the table above, 1946 was the most bountiful year for operations and expenditures. That year 160,000 repatriated Jews returned from the USSR, and many of them, as well as tens of thousands of their predecessors, fled Poland frantically amid the slaughter of their co-religionists. The massacres peaked in the Kielce pogrom.

In 1947, after the nationalist underground laid down its arms and stopped butchering Jews, the situation stabilized somewhat, and the Jews envisioned a future for a renascent Jewish community in Poland. This fantasy led to massive JDC investment in the economic rehabilitation of the country's survivors. Simultaneously, the JDC generously aided Zionist and religious circles who saw no future in Poland and considered it a temporary refuge preceding emigration to Palestine or the United States.

Even if the hopes of a bright future for Holocaust survivors in Poland proved false, the JDC's efforts and investments were not in vain. They were not only vital but urgently needed. Many of the JDC's endeavours, especially in health and welfare, were a matter of life and death. The educational, cultural, and vocational-training activities also contributed crucially to the rejuvenation of the survivors in Poland and in their countries of refuge.

The collaboration between the JDC and the Bundist-Communist organizations was a necessary adjunct of the JDC's policy of helping all groups within the Jewish community, and of enabling them to live their way of life without discrimination. Moreover, without this collaboration, the JDC might not have been allowed to operate in Poland.

In addition to the JDC's contribution to the material and spiritual rehabilitation of the Jews in Poland, which was impressive in its scope and quality, the JDC should also be credited with a very important but less prominent achievement not reflected in statistical or budgetary terms: the strengthening of Jewish identity among Holocaust survivors of all ages. The JDC's educational work helped Jews, especially youth and children, to effectuate the unity of Jewish peoplehood and fate, love of fellow-Jews, and the sense of fraternity with Jews overseas whose unprecedented philanthropy funded activities beneficial to every survivor.

The JDC's contribution to the rehabilitation of the Jewish community of Poland – though it was cut down in its prime – transcended its time and place to become a lasting blessing to the Jews of Poland.

NOTES

1. *Dokumenty i materialy do historii stosunkow Polsko-Radzieckich*, Tom VIII, Styczein 1944–Grudzien 1945, Warsaw 1947, p.146.
2. AJDC Weekly Digest, 31 Aug. 1944.
3. JDC Archives (hereinafter: JDCA), 1945, Poland General File, Charles Passman's concluding report, 18 Feb. 1945.
4. The Institute for Contemporary Jewry, Hebrew University, Jerusalem, Department of Oral Testimony (hereinafter: DOT), No. (4)6, Testimony of Dr. Joseph Schwartz.
5. JDCA, Poland General File 1944, letter from M. Leavitt, JDC New York, to John P. Dawson of the FEA, in Washington, 10 Oct. 1944, and the latter's response, 20 Oct. 1944.
6. *Ibid.*, reports of the EAC, 10 and 17 Oct. 1944.
7. Central Zionist Archives (hereinafter: CZA). File 1579/S26, letter from the Central Committee of Polish Jews in Warsaw to the United Polish Jewry Relief Committee in Tel Aviv, 5 April 1946.
8. DOT (4), 153, Testimony of Moshe Bonko, member of the Jewish Organizing Committee of the ZPP, which was responsible for managing the Committee's financial affairs, including relief.
9. *Op. cit.*, note 7 above.
10. JTA *Daily News Bulletin* (hereinafter: JDNB), 12–18 Dec. 1944.

11. JDNB, 25 July 1945.
12. DOT, No. (4)53, Testimony of Yitzhak (Antek) Zuckerman, pp.34–5.
13. Report of the Secretary, Moses Leavitt, JDC Work Book, Thirty-First Annual Meeting, 9 Dec. 1945, pp.1–10.
14. JDCA, Poland General File, 1945. Urgent directive from the JDC administration in New York to the Amalgamated Bank of New York to transfer $250,000 to the JDC's Warsaw account, 29 Nov. 1945.
15. H. Smolar, *Auf der Letzter Positziemitt der Letzter Hoffnung*, Tel Aviv, 1984, p.402 (hereinafter: Smolar, 1982).
16. *Das Neue Leben* (Journal of the CKZP), 22 Jan. 1946.
17. JDCA, Poland General File, 1945, letter from J. Schwartz, JDC Rome, to Ch. Passman, JDC New York, 24 Dec. 1945.
18. Reuven Artzi, 'Yahadut Polin Le-Ahar Ha-Milhama' (Polish Jewry after the War), *Gesher*, 1978, No.1–2 (76–79), p.110.
19. Smolar, 1982, pp.50–2.
20. CZA, File 1210/S26, Interim Report of the Delegation of the Jewish Coordinating Committee from Poland in Bucharest, 20 Jan. 1945.
21. JDCA, Poland General File, 1945, Report on the Situation in Poland, 9 Sept. 1945.
22. I. Blum, *Z dziejow wojska Polskiego w latach 1945–1948*, Warsaw, 1960, pp.13–14.
23. Y.Bauer, *Ha-Brichah*, Tel Aviv, 1970 (hereinafter: Bauer, *Brichah*), p.118; CZA, File 1597/S26, report on a discussion at a convention of Brichah activists in Europe, held in Paris on 21 Dec. 1945.
24. DOT, No.(4) 6, Testimony of Dr. Joseph Schwartz, p.15.
25. *Tetikaits Baricht zun Zentral-Kommitat fun die Yidden in Poilin, fun 1 Januar bis dem dreisiktin Juni, 1946*, Warsaw, 1947, Table 2, p.22 (hereinafter: Operations Report).
26. *Ibid.*, p.12.
27. JDC Archives, Geneva–Jerusalem (hereinafter: JDCA-GJ), JDCA-GJ report 61.034, Box 12b, Folder c. of AJDC, II Quarter, 1947, p.18.
28. Smolar, 1982, pp.73–5.
29. Bein Report, March 1948, p.212.
30. Bein Report, June 1947, pp.3–4.
31. *AJDC Weekly Review*, 18 Jan. 1946, Vol II, No. 3.
32. Smolar, 1982, pp.73–5.
33. JTA, DNB, 10 July 1946.
34. Sh. Samett, *Bevoii lemocharat – mas'a be-Polin 1946*, Tel Aviv, 1970, p.175.
35. *Das Neue Leben*, 10 May 1946.
36. *Ibid.*, 12 July 1946.
37. M.J. Proudfoot, *European Refugees: 1939–52*, London, 1957, p.341.
38. *American Jewish Year Book*, 1947–1948, p.385.
39. *Das Neue Leben*, 2 Aug. 1946.
40. *Das Neue Leben*, 19 July 1946 (as reported in the Vatican Journal *Osservatore Romano*).
41. DOT, No. (4)53, Testimony of Yitzhak Zuckerman, pp.37–9; *ibid.*, No. (4)21, Testimony of Zvi Netzer, pp.12–22.
42. Smolar, 1982, p.64; Bauer, *Brichah*, p.221.
43. Bauer, *Brichah*, p.221.
44. JDC Digest, 11 Sept. 1946, Dr. J. Schwartz's Report.
45. JDCA-GJ, Box 12B, Folder C-61.061. Letter from the JDC, Lubavitcher Yeshiva, Warsaw, to Dr. J. Schwartz, JDC Paris; Bauer, *Brichah*, p.221.
46. Bauer, *Brichah*, p.222.
47. CZA, File 525/262, letter from M. Yishai in Warsaw to M. Shertok, Jewish Agency Executive in Jerusalem, 24 Dec. 1946.
48. *Das Neue Leben*, 19 Aug. 1946.
49. Smolar, 1982, p.60.

50. *Ibid.*, p.84.
51. Bein Report, June 1947, p.1.
52. Smolar, 1982, p.63.
53. JDCA-GJ, Folder C-61.024, Lower Silesia, 1947, Box 12B.
54. *Ibid.*, Folder C-612.034, letter from M. Bein, JDC Warsaw, to J. Schwartz, JDC Paris, 14 July 1947, Section 11; *ibid.*, Folder C-61.012, two reports from Amelia Eigel, child-care consultant at JDC Paris, 18 May 1948, and 7 July 1947.
55. Smolar, 1982, p.63: DOT No. (4)21, Testimony of Zvi Netzer, pp.12–22.
56. JTA DNB, Moscow, 28 June 1945.
57. JDCA, Box 12b, Folder C-61.034, 'Review of Economic Rehabilitation of Polish Jewry,' AJDC European Executive Council, Reconstruction Dept., 1949, p.12 (hereinafter: Review of Economic Rehabilitation 1945–1949); Bein Report, First Quarter 1947, p.2.
58. JDCA, Box 23a, Folder S 2104.9, Remarks of Dr. Nathan Reich on Poland, Extracts from Minutes of Staff Meeting in New York, 22 Sept. 1947.
59. First Quarter Report, 1947, p.4.
60. *AJDC Weekly Review*, 14 March 1947, Vol. III, No. 11.
61. 'Review of Economic Rehabilitation 1945–1949,' p.25.
62. JDCA, Box 320B, Folder Arch misc/29, Draft of Report of Reconstruction Session, Second JDC Conference, Document No. 49, p.9.
63. JDCA, Box 269B, Folder Nr. Med. 92, AJDC Aid for Vocational Training, Research Dept., Report No. 2, New York.
64. JDCA-GJ, Box 12B, Folder C-61.047, Letter from the JDC Executive in Warsaw to the JDC Administration in Paris, 31 Dec. 1947, and letter from the Directorate of ORT in Warsaw to the JDC Administration in Paris, 8 March 1949.
65. Smolar, 1982, p.175.
66. JDCA-GJ, Box 12B, Folder C-61.064, Cooperatives, Poland, Memorandum from the JDC Head Office Administration in New York to the ORT offices in New York, 18 March 1948.
67. Smolar, 1982, p.175.
68. Review of Rehabilitation 1945–1949, p.49.
69. JTA DNB, New York, 1 March 1945.
70. Bein Report, June 1947, p.11.
71. Smolar, 1982, pp.88–91.
72. JDCA-GJ, Box 12B, Folder C-61.034, Letter from JDC Warsaw, to the Research and Budgeting Department, JDC Administration, Paris, 30 April 1949.
73. Smolar, 1982, pp.88–91.
74. *AJDC Weekly Review*, 9 May 1947, Vol. 3, No. 17.
75. JDCA-GJ, Box 12B, Folder C-61.046.3.
76. Smolar, 1982, pp.93–4, 187–9.
77. Smolar, 1982, p.198.
78. Leib-Tropper Report, 1948, p.6.
79. Bein Report, June 1947, p.5.
80. Bein Report, March 1948, p.212.
81. Bein Report, June–Sept. 1948, pp.11–12.
82. Bein Report, March 1948, p.221.
83. Bein Report, June 1947, pp.61–71.
84. *Ibid.*
85. CZA, File S 6/5037, report from Y. Barzilai to the Foreign Minister, the Director-General of the Foreign Ministry, and the Director of the Eastern Europe Department, 1 June 1949.
86. Bein Report, First Quarter 1949.
87. DOT, No. (4)123, communicated by H. Smolar in a conversation with the author regarding the completion of his testimony.
88. CZA, File S 6/5037, exchange of telegrams and letters between the Israeli

Delegation in Warsaw and the Foreign Ministry in Jerusalem, and the Immigration Department of the Jewish Agency, Aug.–Sept. 1949.
89. *Ibid.*, Report on immigration from Poland, 6 Dec. 1949.
90. Yehuda Bauer, *Yalkut Moreshet* No. 2, 1965, pp.113–15 (Heb.); CZA, File S26/1210, Interim Report of the Delegation of the Zionist Coordinating Committee in Poland, Bucharest, 10 Jan. 1945.
91. Bein Report, June 1947, p.13.
92. CZA, File S6/1870, Report by the leadership of Gordonia – Maccabi Hazair in Lodz – to the Immigration Department of the Jewish Agency in Jerusalem, 28 July 1946.
93. JDCA, Box 12B, Folder C-61.061, Operations, Poland. Report on the JDC's operations in Poland in April–June 1948, p.2.
94. Bein's concluding report, 18 Jan. 1950, pp.4–5.
95. Smolar, 1982, pp.123–9; CZA, File S6/5037, Report on a conversation between Yitzhak Rafael, Director of the Immigration Department of the Jewish Agency, and Israel Koppit of the Immigration Department of the Israeli Representation in Warsaw, 25 April 1949.
96. JDCA, Box 12B, Folder C-61.016, letter of agreement between W. Bein and Dr. J. Schwartz concerning withdrawal of funds, Paris, 27 July 1948.
97. Bein Report, March 1948, pp.11–12.
98. Bein Report, June 1947, pp.11–12.
99. *Ibid.*, p.5.
100. *Ibid.*, p.12.
101. Bein Report, June–Sept. 1948.
102. JDCA, Box 12B, Folder C-61.034, Report from JDC Warsaw to the JDC European Administration in Paris, 9 July 1949.
103. *Ibid.*, Box 12B, Folder C-61.062: Passover Supplies to Poland, telegrams from JDC Warsaw to JDC Paris, 5 Dec.1949.
104. JDCA, Box 12B, Folder C-61.062, Liquidation of Warsaw Office, from JDC Warsaw to JDC Paris, 8 Feb. 1949.
105. Smolar, 1982, pp.173–4, Note 136.

# PART THREE
# The Contemporary Period

# 14

# Jewish Solidarity and 'Refuge Zionism': The Case of B'nai B'rith

## Allon Gal

### I

The declaration of principles of B'nai B'rith Constitution, drawn up when the order was founded in 1843, has remained substantially unchanged. The declaration reads:

> B'nai B'rith has taken on itself the mission of uniting Israelites in the work of promoting their highest interests and those of humanity; of developing and elevating the mental and moral character of the people of our faith; of inculcating the purest principles of philanthropy, honor and patriotism; of supporting science and art; alleviating the wants of the poor and the needy; visiting and attending the sick; coming to the rescue of victims of persecution; providing for, protecting and assisting the widow and orphan on the broadest principles of humanity.[1]

Over the course of the nineteenth century B'nai B'rith was mainly a fraternity order. At the same time, there was definitely a component of Jewish solidarity in its functioning – 'the rescue of victims of persecution', the penultimate principle listed in the above declaration. In the nineteenth century this was not a central element of the B'nai B'rith. The organization was supposed to care for its members and also respond to the needs of the local community. Concern for other Jews, who were not members of the order and not living in the US, was on the periphery of the responsibilities assumed by the organization. In 1913, the order created the Anti-Defamation League to combat anti-Semitism, though only within the United States.[2] All the same there were already in the nineteenth century B'nai B'rith characteristics that qualified the order to later evolve into an organization expressly dedicated to solidarity.

It should be emphasized that unlike other Jewish organizations in the US, the B'nai B'rith order developed in the last quarter of the century from an American-Jewish Fraternity into an *international* Jewish fraternity.

The first overseas lodge of the B'nai B'rith was founded in Germany in 1882. Before Hitler's take-over, there was a wide network of over a hundred B'nai B'rith lodges, tied in with a whole chain of institutions. In the second decade of this century, the organization became truly international, with lodges spread throughout most of Western Europe, some East European countries and the Near East as well, including Palestine.

In this non-Zionist organization the prevailing belief was that by developing noble qualities among the Jews and by drawing inspiration from the surrounding society, emancipation would finally succeed. This also explains the special success of the order in those European countries where it appeared that emancipation had taken root. The internationalization of the organization, by itself, did not transform solidarity into a solemn duty, but it did constitute an element of solidarity and contributed to the special character of the order.

Alongside internationalism was the humanitarian principle of the order. This refers in the first place to mutual aid and charity. Mutual aid operated mainly among the members of the order, and charity was generally expressed in the context of the Jewish community.

The humanitarian character of the order is an important key to the understanding of B'nai B'rith's later development. Towards the end of the nineteenth and the beginning of the twentieth century, B'nai B'rith concerned itself with a variety of humanitarian activities that called for a degree of professionalism. The organization was not properly qualified to administer orphanages, old age homes, hospitals and the like. To do so properly necessitated increases in management and operational costs. The scope narrowed for Jewish humanitarian activity in the traditional B'nai B'rith pattern, and the humanitarian impulse sought new outlets.

An additional factor contributing to the shift in the order toward solidarity was its relatively popular nature. This was not an elitist philanthropic organization like the American Jewish Committee but a fraternal order with its roots in the middle classes. As the organization strengthened its basis after the Civil War, it sometimes acted on the diplomatic level on behalf of Jewish victims of persecution in Russia and other countries; but the specific quality of B'nai B'rith activity was rather on popular-philanthropic lines. The organization provided assistance to the waves of immigrants arriving in the US. As a result, the B'nai B'rith concern for the fate of Jews abroad became stronger and more direct. Thus, the social base of the organization and its declared purposes in Jewish America prepared it to assume responsibility for the fate of Jews everywhere.

In sum, several factors – international Jewish fraternity, the deep humanitarian impulse and the (relatively) populist nature of the order – combined to reinforce the solidarity component in the B'nai B'rith and created a great potential for Jewish solidarity in the twentieth century.[3]

## II

An early manifestation of B'nai B'rith Jewish solidarity in this century was the opposition to the pogroms in Russia in 1905. The organization was also active during the First World War; but here circumstances came about that had an important influence on the nature of B'nai B'rith activity later on. The situation of the Jewish people in Europe and in Palestine during the First World War represented need on an unprecedented scale. The American Jewish Joint Distribution Committee was founded during the war and by 1918 it had given some fifteen million dollars for aid. The considerable sums collected by B'nai B'rith seemed small compared to those gathered by the main philanthropic bodies. Against this background, the order decided in the course of the war to act only within the limits of its financial capability. In 1920 the organization decided to concentrate on the adoption of orphans, victims of the crisis in Europe, as an expression of solidarity. This decision was an indication of the future brand of solidarity – the personal, direct involvement of the members of the organization on behalf of Jews in distress.[4]

This process that was generated in the years 1914 to 1920 was strengthened in the 1920s and 1930s. In 1920 it was still possible to turn to American Jews to become foster parents of the orphans of the Jewish people, but just a few years later Jewish humanitarian sentiments could no longer find an outlet in this way. First of all, the US was almost completely closed to immigrants, especially Jewish immigrants. Secondly, Jewish distress was gradually but steadily reaching new dimensions. A task such as adoption of orphans, for example, could not remain the responsibility of any single Jewish organization: it now needed a coordinated, comprehensive Jewish operation.

During this period, the President of the B'nai B'rith (1925–1938) was Alfred M. Cohen, of German Jewish origin. In those years there was a rising tide of anti-Semitism in the US, Nazism was installed in

Germany, increasingly large sections of European Jewry were reduced to dire straits and frightful danger loomed on the horizon. In Alfred M. Cohen's time, however, traditional B'nai B'rith fraternity had not yet been translated into a pattern of active solidarity. Even when the Nazis liquidated the order in Germany (in April 1937), the leadership in America retained a very low profile and mainly acted behind the scenes.[5]

The constraints on B'nai B'rith solidarity in the period before 1938 were also manifest in the attitudes and decisions adopted on refugees. The B'nai B'rith did not fight for a change in the US immigration laws and not even for filling the quotas possible under the limiting legislation. In 1938 the organization's fifteenth General Convention passed minor resolutions recommending that the B'nai B'rith executive devise modes of action in two matters: obtaining affidavits and support guarantees for men, women and children wishing to reach the US as immigrants fleeing persecution; and setting up machinery to help them settle in the US.[6]

At the same time, it is instructive to observe that in this period when the order had a definitely non-Zionist leader it was already beginning to take on a tinge of support for Zionism. It was now making up, albeit hesitantly, for its lack of active solidarity in preceding years by showing concern for one specific aspect of the Zionist idea – Palestine as a place of refuge for persecuted Jews.

In January 1935 Alfred M. Cohen took part in the National Conference for Palestine held in Washington DC at the initiative of the Zionist Organization of America and the United Palestine Appeal. At this conference, Cohen supported the building up of Palestine as the main way to alleviate Jewish distress. The text of his speech was printed in its entirety in the US Zionist periodical, *The New Palestine*, under the appropriate heading, 'The League [of Nations] has failed the refugees'.[7]

Cohen began by saying that he was happy to be sharing in the development of Palestine in order to make it a refuge, a hope and a reality for the Jews. He was speaking on behalf of the fifty thousand B'nai B'rith members in America and tens of thousands in twenty-nine other countries, including Palestine, where the order had members in Jerusalem, Tel-Aviv, Haifa, Safad, Rishon le'Tzion, Rehovot, Zikhron Ya'akov, Hadera and Tiberias. Today, he said, many 'Hamans' have arisen to put an end to us, and all the gates are closed, but Palestine has taken this care upon itself and is ready to go on taking responsibility for the fate of the threatened Jews. Fifteen months before, the League of Nations had set up a high commission for refugees but nothing had come of it, averred Cohen in deep disappointment. And behold, little Palestine is helping the refugees more than all the countries of Europe and perhaps more than all the other countries in the world together. Palestine should be given support so that it could continue to act on behalf of the refugees as it had been doing for the previous two years. Part of his speech, expressing the inchoate conception of 'Zionism as refuge' which would increasingly characterize the B'nai B'rith, ran as follows:

> To relieve this world wide dire situation in which the Jew is the victim, further upbuilding of Palestine is imperatively necessary. There seems to be no alternative under these circumstances. All Jews worthy of their heritage must join in giving whole hearted support to such plans as may be devised to advance as speedily as possible the economic development of Palestine.

The term 'Zionism' and even the term 'Yishuv' were not mentioned once in the speech. As against this, Cohen ended by citing the order's declaration of principles, stressing the B'nai B'rith commitment to serve the whole House of Israel and voicing his support for the building up of the country in this spirit of humanitarian service.[8]

A message was received at this Conference from Chaim Weizmann, President of the World Zionist Federation, in which he urged B'nai B'rith to contribute in a practical way to increasing the capacity of the land of Palestine to support refugees. The B'nai B'rith institutions responded favourably and entered into discussions with Israel Goldstein, head of the Jewish National Fund (JNF) in the US. The Zionist movement proposed that B'nai B'rith should contribute about $100,000 and the JNF would provide five thousand dunams for settlement. The order was accepted, almost as if under compulsion, on practical grounds, in the spirit voiced by Alfred M. Cohen: 'Whereas the situation of the refugees from Germany and other countries where in Jews are persecuted constitutes a condition of grave emergency,' and 'Whereas the flight of refugees from persecuted lands in large numbers to Palestine has created an emergency by reason of lack of funds and land for the settlement of these refugees ...'.

The resolution also stated that new settlement would be named for Alfred Cohen. (The *moshav* was founded in July 1937 in lower Galilee. It is called today 'Moledet B'nai B'rith' or 'Moledet' (homeland).)[9]

The B'nai B'rith representative at the February 1936 Conference on Palestine, Oscar Berman, like Cohen the year before, spoke about Palestine as the practical solution for the refugee problem. The Palestine programme, he stressed, did not mean relinquishing the civil rights of the Jews wherever they might be nor was it put forward in despair of emancipation; but to our great sorrow the Jew today is again a wanderer in the world, and thank the Lord, said Berman, there is a place for him to stop and rest in the course of wandering to and fro. There were hundreds of thousands looking for a resting place, and 'to help them enter this haven is our sacred duty,' affirmed the B'nai B'rith representative.[10]

In his farewell address as President in 1938, Cohen began by surveying the desperate situation of the Jews of Germany since Hitler took power. He confessed to his listeners that he (and they) had had illusions at the time of the previous B'nai B'rith Convention (1935): 'We could not bring ourselves to believe that such an order of affairs could continue much longer. But we were mistaken. Three more years have been added to the two [since Hitler came to power] and the end is not yet in sight.' He went on to criticize Arab opposition and British inflexibility as responsible for preventing Palestine from becoming a bigger and safer shelter for persecuted Jews. Superficially this criticism resembled that put forward at the time by the Zionist leaders against enemies of the Zionist enterprise, but Cohen's criticism began and ended with only one theme – Palestine as a haven for refugees: 'Many more of them would have gone to the ancient home of Israel if that land, which offered so much of promise, had not been sorely rent by Arab uprisings, resulting in the destruction of many of the fine improvements made by Jews and sacrifice of many Jewish lives. Changed conditions in Palestine constitute an added tragedy in Jewish life.' He amplified, asserting: 'We believed that there was at least one spot on earth to which our people could go and be welcome. Was that not assured by the Balfour Declaration and the British Mandate for Palestine under the League of Nations? Certainly we thought so. But here again the Jew was doomed to disappointment.'[11]

Thus despite its Zionist tone, his criticism did not go beyond the bounds of non-Zionism; rather, it could be called the 'refuge Zionism' version of the criticism. The reproach levelled at those who were harming Jewish Palestine – British appeasers and Arab chauvinists – was not accompanied by any attempt at a systematic analysis of the social and political causes of the Jewish situation. In this comprehensive farewell address, Cohen presented the Yishuv as a beacon of hope for the refugees from Europe, announced the establishment of a settlement in the country in the name of the order, but also concluded with an elegy for the past and a lament over the present day, and what had suddenly befallen the Jews. Thirteen years before, claimed Cohen in closing, the skies had been clear. Now there was an economic crisis, 'an adventurer – an Austrian, an agitator ...' who wanted to lift up the Germans through hatred of the Jews, 'and then the Jews of Germany fell.' Cohen said he was shaken by the situation of the Jews in Europe, but he was mainly concerned over the fate of B'nai B'rith members who had come to harm in the different European countries and especially in Germany. As has been noted, there was no analysis or even the smallest beginning of any mental clarification that might show the critical situation of European Jewry to be anything more then a purely chance disaster. The traditional clinging to emancipation, even regarding Europe, permeated Cohen's every word.[12]

The spirit of Alfred Cohen's summary was that of a humanitarian fraternal order rather than that of an organization manifestly dedicated to solidarity; its interest in Zionism was very narrow, sporadic and ambiguous. In 1938, however, this approach was typical of an era that was coming to an end. As early as 1925, when for the first time in the history of B'nai B'rith there had been an open contest for the Presidency, there was a candidate with a different approach – Henry Monsky, who sought to give the order's accepted idea of fraternity a new meaning – collective national responsibility, Jewish solidarity.

## III

It is highly instructive to study Henry Monsky's nomination address at the 15th B'nai B'rith National Convention. Beyond question he rose to this position largely if not decisively as one who symbolized the new Jewish solidarity that many leading members of B'nai B'rith sought and hoped for in those tragic years, as testified to in the speech of Sigmund Livingstone when he officially presented Monsky's candidacy on 11th May 1938. He began with an outline of the order itself as an organization whose *raison d'être* was Jewish solidarity:

> For almost a century this Order has been the champion of human rights and liberties, against tyranny and superstition. It has given 'succor to the starving; it has taken unto its bosom the fatherless;' it has always listened to the cry of despair and

> thrown a lifeline to those unfortunates battling against the terrors of persecution. It has, to the best of its power, tried to break the rusted fetters of intolerance. It has stood vigil in the darkest night of terror in Bucharest and Kishineff. It has been the watch of the night for almost a century wherever the need was greatest. In the jungles of life it has cut down the thorns which pierce the heart and burrs which cleave to the soul.

He turned to the qualities Monsky would have to display:

> To assume the leadership of such an Order means sacrifice; to such a leader no night can be peaceful, if he knows there is work not done which should have been done. There is no refuge for such a one from the cry of human misery, except the solace of having given the whole of one's self. Such a leader must be a man described by the prophet, 'whose loins are girded with righteousness and whose sides are armed with truth.' That one in the prime of life is willing to make this sacrifice can come only through the urge of Jewish consciousness. Endowed with a splendid mind, with a gift of perception, with a heart which feels the pangs of torture of his fellow men, with a soul linked to the spirit of Israel, he willingly surrenders material success and places upon the altar of service to our cause all that he has – his mind, his heart and his soul.[13]

As customary at B'nai B'rith conventions, the new president's response was brief and mainly a matter of formal courtesy, but it was clear to those present that Monsky was taking over the Presidency under the banner of dynamic Jewish solidarity mandated by the conditions of the late 1930s. Monsky held office from 1938 to 1947.

The *B'nai B'rith Magazine* published a special piece about Monsky when he was elected President, describing him as a man of feeling. Immediately after the electoral convention, Monsky visited the Washington offices of the organization's leadership. The article described how he stopped at a window and looked out, and then announced that he was proud to say that his first official act as President had been to preside at an executive meeting of the order which decided to allocate $10,000 to Youth Aliyah for the rescue of Jewish youth from the countries of oppression in Europe to enable them to begin a new life in Palestine. We recall B'nai B'rith's concern for Jewish orphans twenty years before. The Jewish solidarity of Monsky and the B'nai B'rith now found an expression, albeit restricted, in the Zionist enterprise.[14]

This development also characterizes Monsky's career; he came from an Orthodox family background in Eastern Europe; he had Zionist and liberal leanings. In his eyes, the main challenge to his organization was to develop Jewish unity and solidarity in order to enable the nation to survive. He viewed Palestine as the natural home (but not the only one) for the refugees from the European hell, one that could ensure their survival.[15]

After the publication of the White Paper decrees, he began devoting more and more of his time to bringing Jewish pressure to bear to have the gates of Palestine opened. This activity too was rooted in solidarity. Monsky was revolted by the British White Paper (May 1939) more because it represented an obstacle of arbitrariness and insensibility toward his tormented brethren seeking rest and less because it was an anti-Zionist policy.[16]

One of the first demonstrations of Monsky's feelings on Palestine was at the United Palestine Appeal conference in January 1941, conducted by Rabbi Abba Hillel Silver. The Conference passed a very sharply worded resolution on the White Paper policy, and another – the first by any important US Zionist body – in favour of establishing Palestine as a Jewish commonwealth after the war. Monsky spoke in the name of 150,000 B'nai B'rith members and stressed not the political aspect but the practical humanitarian one:

> The greatest catastrophe that has ever befallen the people of Israel has engulfed our fellow Jews in the lands of darkness and despair. Millions, veritably millions, have been economically devastated and have been rendered homeless and helpless. This very circumstance gives to the Palestine Conference a place of first importance. Many solutions have been suggested. This is but natural since the problem is one of great magnitude. The solutions quite generally have been unrealistic and impractical. ... Palestine, in the light of long term planning, presents the single most realistic opportunity for the resettlement of large numbers of the unfortunate and victimized of our people. ... It matters not whether you think of Palestine as a national home, as you do there, as a cultural center, as a haven of refuge – the instrumentalities for its upbuilding command the respect and are entitled to the support of every Jew interested in the problems of his people.[17]

The 16th B'nai B'rith convention in the spring of 1941 was an important landmark both for the organization's deepening solidarity and for the process of its 'Zionization.' At its opening

Monsky told the delegates: 'You are the messengers of mercy and sympathy to a stricken world, you have by your activity manifested your profound interest in the problems of our people ... We meet here to plan a positive, constructive program of rehabilitation and reconstruction, both materially and spiritually.' The ceremonial opening address by the former President, Alfred Cohen, was apparently made in the same spirit: the people who had come there represented positive good over against what Hitler represented.[18]

In the course of the convention, however, Monsky made his aim clear in his presidential address. He was going to raise the Jewish humanism of the order onto a new, higher level. What he wanted to do was to turn the B'nai B'rith from a fraternal order into a multi-functional service organization completely interwoven in the history of the Jewish people everywhere. He explained that this was what he had been working towards since he became President and he would continue to direct all the B'nai B'rith activities in the future in the light of this aim. Jewish solidarity thus became the pivot of this dynamic President's many-sided activities and his supreme aim. In the words of Monsky himself:

> I look upon the B'nai B'rith as essentially a great service organization, wholly apart from any of its fraternal aspects. It is a service organization whose history has been inseparably interwoven with the history of Israel throughout the past century ... It has been and is consecrated to the preservation of Jewish values, to the perpetuation of Jewish ideals; to the moral, mental and physical welfare of our people.

From this axiom of active, committed solidarity Monsky derived his programme centred on the building up of Palestine. He also differed from Alfred Cohen in that he left the matter of emancipation entirely alone and thereby bestowed a historic dimension on every debate concerning the role of Palestine in the given tragic circumstances. He allotted a large section of his presidential address to the Palestine theme. He began and ended this section with a sort of new 'credo' of the 'Zionism as refuge' version. First, he dwelt on the catastrophe that had befallen millions of sons of the Jewish people, declaring, 'In the light of long term planning, Palestine presents the most realistic opportunity for the resettlement of large numbers of the unfortunate and victimized of our people.' He closed his speech affirming: 'All the foregoing activities grew out of a profound conviction on the part of your President, wholly aside from his personal sympathy with the Palestine movement and without reference to any political considerations or nationalistic philosophy, that the present chaotic conditions which prevail on the European scene impose upon us the solemn and sacred responsibility of giving unreserved support to the program of the upbuilding of Palestine.'

Palestine figured as a refuge, but in Monsky's term it was referred to in the context of 'the Palestine movement' and the 'Palestine program'.[19] In the course of the convention, it was decided to establish another settlement in Palestine. This *moshav* was founded on the border of lower Galilee and Emek Jesreel in January 1942 on JNF land acquired by the order in the US and called Ramat Zvi in honour of Henry (Zvi) Monsky.

There was a basic similarity between the arguments in favour of establishing this settlement and those in favour of the previous one, named for Alfred Cohen. There were also, however, instructive differences. The first point in the arguments was this: 'Whereas millions of Jews, the victims of the Nazi terror, are homeless, and grave emergency has been created,' and the second was: 'Whereas more than 280,000 refugees have been settled in Palestine and the Jewish National Fund has made available large tracts of land for the settlement and rehabilitation of the refugees ...' There was no mention this time of the suffering mainly of German Jewry, but instead the grave emergency of millions of Jewish victims of the Nazi terror; Palestine did not figure purely as a refuge but as a dynamic centre including care for the refugees in the enterprise. Identifying the new settlement with the B'nai B'rith (as seen later in the resolution) was now stated in a broader context than in the previous instance.[20]

Warm congratulations on the founding of the new *moshav* and bitter criticism of past B'nai B'rith shortcomings were voiced by Aaron Teitelbaum, the Palestinian Zionist who attended the Convention. The Palestine office had all along pressed for more B'nai B'rith Zionist activity, he said. If the US B'nai B'rith members had responded in time by many-sided activity to strengthen the Yishuv, the suffering in the Jewish migration would now be less terrible, he said accusingly.[21]

The Palestinian Zionist was listened to most attentively. There is no doubt that in the 1940s the US order went through a process of Zionization, but this did not result from the influence of the Palestine lodge on the world order nor from the energetic propaganda of the US Zionist movement. The basic historic process in which the B'nai B'rith was involved, in face of the awful fate of the

Jews of Europe, the increasingly vital necessity for the Jewish centre in Palestine and the threat to it, was the growing power of Jewish solidarity. The partial adoption of Zionism served as the means for enhancing the solidarity component of the order.

The trend of increasingly strong solidarity in the B'nai B'rith was seen in the work done by the order in organizing the American Jewish Conference and shaping its aims. There was an unofficial preparatory meeting in May 1941 at the St. Regis, headed by Weizmann, aimed at securing unity under Zionist direction. Monsky was extremely cautious and began to move independently in order to secure a general framework that would not exclude non-Zionists. At the second St. Regis conference in December 1942 Weizmann met Monsky and the B'nai B'rith executive vice-president, Morris Bisgyer, for the same purpose.[22] Monsky for his part, however, went on working for American Jewish unity in his own way, and on 6 January 1943 on his own initiative he sent invitations to the leaders of 34 national organizations for a preparatory meeting in Pittsburgh on the 23rd and 24th of that month. The main subjects for this meeting were to be the situation of the Jewish people and the building up of Palestine after the war. All those invited came, except for the representatives of two organizations. Monsky delivered the opening address, speaking in the name of European Jewry in its hour of disaster. Already at this stage the proper aims for united action were the restoration of the lost position of European Jewry and the right to build up Palestine in order to alleviate if not to solve the Jewish problem. Monsky closed with a call for internal tolerance, unity and indomitable determination to survive and live as Jews. This preparatory meeting issued a long, sorrowful declaration of solidarity with martyred European Jewry and took a number of decisions in the spirit of Monsky's address.[23]

The American Jewish Conference convened in New York from 29 August to 2 September 1943, representing the decisive majority of the Jews of America. The opening address was delivered by Henry Monsky, and his opening sentence was in Hebrew: 'Behold, how good and pleasant it is for brethren to dwell together in unity.' The main drive in his speech was this spirit of unity and solidarity.[24]

The heart of Monsky's address was a description of the catastrophe of European Jewry and identification with its bitter fate. Monsky spoke forcefully on the theme of Jewish solidarity. He came out against those who clung to the old style of pleading with influential people for intervention and refraining from public expressions of concern over other Jews. He argued emphatically and with the utmost clarity that Jewish solidarity demanded open, courageous action. He also proposed a number of ways to act to rescue Jews.[25]

Monsky concluded his address by placing the question of Palestine within the context of the catastrophe of European Jewry. His answer was that Palestine had become and would go on being the refuge for persecuted Jews and for those rescued. Moreover, Jewish Palestine was now writing a chapter of creation and heroism that could be an inspiration to Jewish communities everywhere. With regard to the status of Palestine there were minimum and maximum programmes, Monsky noted, but this was not the main thing; and he refrained from taking a stand on the political issue – the Conference would decide on the desired degree of sovereignty, he said.[26]

It is well known that in the course of the Conference, Rabbi Silver delivered a fiery address on the need to establish Palestine as an independent Jewish commonwealth at the end of the war. Monsky supported the Resolution proposed by Silver, but this was not his original purpose in having the Conference, even though some months earlier he had already personally given his approval to this political aim. Like most of the others at the Conference, he was carried away by Silver's proposal. What political form Palestine would assume as it took in the refugees was not his main interest, as we have shown; certainly it was not for the sake of this specific resolution on the political plane that he had worked to have the Conference convened.

The Conference passed two main sorts of resolutions: on the rescue of European Jewry; and on the foundation of Palestine as a Jewish Commonwealth after the war.[27]

At the 17th B'nai B'rith Convention (New York, 6 to 10 May 1944) Monsky devoted a considerable part of his opening presidential address to the American Jewish Conference. In his opening sentence he stated that he had worked to get the Conference convened the year before 'in the B'nai B'rith spirit' in order 'to meet the plight of our people in this, the most tragic period in our history.' In the B'nai B'rith there could be no imposition of ideas by the majority on the minority, he said, but 'B'nai B'rith would cease to be worthy of its tradition if, under the guise of neutrality, it failed to adhere to and participate fully in a program of action calculated to meet the challenging problems and the stark realities of the gravest tragedy in the history of the Jewish people.'

Thus in his viiew participation in the American Jewish Conference was not in the main a matter of ideology but an expression of organized Jewish unity for the sake of carrying out the imperatives of Jewish solidarity. Concern for the victims of the terrible tragedy was what had led him to support the Conference Resolutions including those on the Palestine question. When it was a matter of mutual caring, urged Monsky, there was no room for appeasement – not in face of anti-Semitism at home nor of Arab threats to the country of refuge. Jewish leadership to be worthy of the name must identify itself with every section of the people, with the weaker sections as well. The enemies do not make distinctions between different Jews. In the Nazi forced labour camps were Zionists and non-Zionists, bankers and workers, assimilating Jews and religiously observant Jews – the simple fact was that they were all Jews.[28]

Monsky remained the central figure in the American Jewish Conference. At its second meeting (in December 1944), he continued weaving the same threads as at the earlier meeting: building up Palestine – against the background of the catastrophe – as a place for the Jews to live in a human, restorative home: 'It no longer serves any good purpose to discuss the ideological differences which have in the past, and which continue even in the sorrowful present, to plague the household of Israel. It is enough to appraise the unequal contribution to the cause by the United Nations and to the causes of relief, rescue, resettlement and rehabilitation of stricken Jews made by the Yishuv in Palestine.' He praised the Yishuv for its pioneering spirit and its dedication to democratic principles; but his words were aimed mainly at depicting the Yishuv as a refuge for martyred and persecuted Jews; it is worth quoting from the passage that interweaves his conception of Jewish solidarity, the aim of unity and the connection with Zionism as refuge:

> Who can be so indifferent, so callous to the suffering, the devastation, the misery, the destructive forces that have affected our people, as to be unaware of the complete 'homelessness' of millions of wandering, uprooted, terror-stricken, helpless Jews, and who would deny them the physical and spiritual sustenance which we in America, through the graciousness of a Divine Providence, have the ability to furnish? Where shall these tragic souls go? Even though, God willing, the day of victory be hastened, does anyone delude himself with the belief that Poland, Hungary and Rumania, or any of the many Nazi-philosophy-infected countries, will afford opportunity for the immediate resettlement or rehabilitation of the tens of thousands of the victims of the Nazi terror, or

that they will afford in the near future opportunity for reconstruction of Jewish life? Must we not face realistically the inexorable fact that the Nazi war of extermination has produced a psychological atmosphere that can be purged of its hatred only through a long and tedious process of education? Can we depend on the democracies to furnish a haven of refuge for more than a comparatively insignificant number of those who seek and require a new home? Where in the whole universe, except in Palestine, do we find a community with its arms outstretched to receive their brothers in ever-increasing numbers – yes, to receive them with enthusiasm and with a deep profound interest in their welfare?[29]

Brotherly aid and the development of the country founded for the sake of this assistance was the context in which Monsky supported the Resolution in favour of establishing Palestine as a Jewish Commonwealth accepted at the first meeting of the American Jewish Conference, as he told his listeners. In this spirit, he took care in the course of the second meeting of the Conference to direct its activity exclusively toward the needs of suffering Jewry abroad, resisting the attempts made to exploit the Conference for shaping the life of the Jewish community in America.[30]

The third meeting of the Conference took place in February 1946, after the end of the war, when the scale and the horror of the Holocaust were already common knowledge. This time, unlike his stand at the earlier meetings, Monsky brought to the fore the version of Zionism as the movement of national rebirth. All the same, the dominant motif in his argumentation was the version of Palestine as the land of refuge and the Yishuv as a home for unfortunate Jews and not exactly as the basis for a renewed national life. He reverted to what he had told the Anglo-American Commission in January 1946, that opening the gates of Palestine was an imperative of conscience and a humanitarian move. Palestine alone would give the Jewish refugees 'security, peace of mind, and opportunity for normal development as free men.' This was the last meeting of the American Jewish Conference that Monsky took part in. He closed it just as he had opened his historic first meeting of the Conference with the Hebrew sentence, 'Behold, how good and how pleasant it is for brethren to dwell in unity.'[31]

The 18th B'nai B'rith Convention (Washington, 11 to 14 May 1947) convened shortly after Monsky's sudden death (2 May). The new president was Frank Goldman, of Lowell, Massachusetts, who regarded himself rightly as Monsky's faithful follower. This was the first post-war B'nai B'rith Convention and it reached a detailed decision on the subject of the refugees and Palestine. As for the resolution on the refugees in the American context, the decision was a general one: it called on the U.S. Government to pass immigration laws that would enable the maximum number of people who had suffered in the war to be admitted and rehabilitated.

The long well-argued Resolution on the subject of Palestine revealed the process of Zionization of the order and at the same time the specific nature of B'nai B'rith's pro-Zionist conception. The order prided itself on its long history of partnership in the development of Palestine. The emphasis in this text soon came on the current refuge problem. A home or a national home had been created in Palestine for Jews. The various phrases used were mild reiterations of the Balfour Declaration, with the stress on the development of the Yishuv in Palestine as an address for refugees and the needy. The British Government White Paper policy was attacked as disrupting the natural and normal process of the influx of refugees into the country. The order deliberately refrained from addressing itself to the question of the regime desired for Palestine. The decision stated that this subject was burdened with political aspects (which were precisely what the B'nai B'rith wanted to sidestep). The approach adopted to the question was that it was a challenge and a test of Jewish solidarity: 'We nevertheless feel that we must give expression to our view concerning matters which affect the very lives and existence of our brethren.' After this came three demands, bound up with each other: cancellation of the White Paper; opening the gates of Palestine to Jewish immigration; cancellation of the restrictions on the purchase of land in Palestine by Jews.[32]

The closing Resolution called on all the peoples in the world to help 'in the establishment of a homeland for Jewish people in Palestine.' This closing sentence reflected the 'non-Zionist' dimension of B'nai B'rith. The text did not say 'a national home *for the Jewish people* (as in the Balfour Declaration) but *for Jewish people*: but this sentence itself in the text exhibited the kind of Zionism that had crystallized in the B'nai B'rith. This Zionism or pro-Zionism was as it were a practical translation of the basic B'nai B'rith Jewish solidarity approach. 'The longing of generations' to return to Palestine was mentioned in passing. The main thing in the document was the declaration of loyalty to suffering brethren and the commitment to creating a home for them so that 'the tens of thousands of homeless Jews, the remnants of the Jewish people of Europe, may at long last find a haven of permanent refuge, peace and security to which every normal human being is entitled.'[33]

The fourth and last meeting of the American Jewish Conference was held from 29 November to 1 December 1947. This came after the decision of the supreme lodge of the B'nai B'rith (September 1947) to give full support to the partition plan for Palestine and exactly at the same time as the U.N. decision in favour of the establishment of a Jewish state in part of Palestine. Frank Goldman delivered a lengthy address in memory of the founder of the Conference, Henry Monsky. He sketched out a portrait of his predecessor, and spoke of the spirit in which Monsky had founded and directed the Conference in identification with 'the beginning of the realization of Israel's ancient aspirations.' In emphasizing Monsky's humanism, his sense of solidarity and his dream of unity within the principles in whose light he wished to direct the Conference and contribute to the establishment of a Jewish State, Goldman was simultaneously expressing his own heartfelt inclinations. The clearly national motifs that had been perceptible in part of Monsky's last appearances emerged clearly from Goldman's remarks. He no longer had to be as cautious as his predecessor, recalling formally that in Zionist affairs he was not acting in the name of the order. The pro-Zionist president now stood on the firm ground of B'nai B'rith support for Jewish sovereignty in the Land of Israel.[34]

IV

For all the pro-Zionist change that had occurred, the order's original outlook manifested its great power of persistence and of adaptation at the same time; the B'nai B'rith periodical, *The National Jewish Monthly*, constantly and firmly reflected the pro-Zionist solidarity emphasis of the order in the years leading up to the establishment of the State. The magazine published articles by Horace Marston, who toured the Displaced Persons camps in Europe on behalf of the American Jewish Conference and the B'nai B'rith; he dwelt on the hard and humiliating conditions in these camps and the inmates' longing to immigrate to Palestine. That country appeared as a place of healing for the wounded soul and as the sole means for restoring the victims' human dignity. Articles like these (accompanied by dramatic photographs), a combination of authentic reporting and great moral power, had a strong influence in shaping the attitude of the B'nai B'rith mass membership of brothers in patterns of solidarity and humanitarianism.[35]

This basic solidarity-humanitarian approach was also expressed in the order's material assistance to the new born fighting State of Israel. At the beginning of June 1948 the B'nai B'rith set up an emergency project, 'B'nai B'rith Aid to the People of Israel;' all the B'nai B'rith lodges throughout the U.S.A. collected funds for ambulances, medication, mechanical equipment, food and clothing. In the State of Israel's first year of existence, the B'nai B'rith sent over materials and equipment to the value of $4 million. The material dispatched was intended not only for the fighting forces but also for the needs of the new immigrants. The head of the project, A.B. Kapplin, reporting to the organization's executive at the beginning of 1949, described the prevailing B'nai B'rith outlook: in his opinion, the project had practically no content of ideas at all. It is worth quoting his summing up, after he had detailed the equipment dispatched:

> It is of historic significance that the B'nai B'rith national emergency appeal united our own men and women in one great effort for human relief. All shades of opinion disappeared and no longer were there Zionists, non-Zionists and anti-Zionists among the ranks of the Order with respect to this effort. With the realization of a 2,000-year old dream and the hopes of modern Zionism for a state in Palestine, B'nai B'rith responded to the call for help as a strong single army, with the vanishing of all former differences. Always a common meeting ground for Jews everywhere, B'nai B'rith thus demonstrated once again its basic philosophy for unity in Israel.

In the same year, 1949, the women in the order took under their wing the institution in Israel for helping children harmed by the horrors of the Holocaust. Even more instructive from the point of view of principles, was the fact that the directorate of the Aid for Israel project recommended that the order work out a programme for the adoption of families in Israel and especially recent immigrants. The recommendation was that this adoption programme should be started precisely when the material aid project came to an end.[36]

In section II of this article we dealt with the B'nai B'rith programme after the First World War for adopting Jewish orphans devastated by the European maelstrom and for helping them to rebuild their lives in the U.S.A. We saw that B'nai B'rith solidarity could not provide the very large sums needed for all the services involved, and so direct humanitarian steps were taken instead. In 1934, a year after Hitler took power, the order opened a hostel for refugees in Jerusalem. Now after the Second World War, the same pattern of direct humanitarianism was repeated, but with a difference: this time the context was Israeli. In 1949 the aid was planned as a link in the systematic effort to strengthen the independent Jewish State.

B'nai B'rith leaders energetically supported the United Jewish Appeal in the U.S.A., and the sale of Israel Bonds became an inseparable part of the activity of the Order. B'nai B'rith became a partner in the activity of a considerable section of the social and the financial elite of American Jewry, a section also motivated for its part by the sense of Jewish solidarity. An interesting case is that of Henry Morgenthau Junior, whose family has belonged to B'nai B'rith in New York and Washington DC for three generations. From 1934 on Henry Morgenthau Junior served as U.S. Secretary of the Treasury. In 1943 he accused State Department officials of failing to utilize the budget allocations intended for the rescue of Jews from France and Rumania. Under pressure from Morgenthau, the War Refugees Board (comprising the Secretaries of State, Treasury and War) was formed in January 1944 to snatch Jews from the talons of the Nazis. After the war the B'nai B'rith honoured Morgenthau at a festive public banquet with the participation of Henry Monsky, President of the order. Morgenthau received the order's gold award, engraved on one face in Hebrew, 'lover of Israel,' and on the other in English, 'Presented to the Hon. Henry Morgenthau, Jr., by B'nai B'rith for his services to humanity.' Morgenthau served as General Chairman (1947 to 1950) and Honorary Chairman (1951 to 1953) of the United Jewish Appeal. He was one of the initiators of the Israel Bonds and served as Chairman of its Board of Directors from 1951 to 1955. There seems to have been a close tie between Morgenthau and Monsky. At all events, there was no difference in ideology between Morgenthau's attachment to Israel and the Zionist connection of the Monsky kind. Both men viewed the Palestine enterprise in the first place in terms of humanitarian solidarity, as a place of refuge and of restoring the dignity of persecuted Jews.[37]

Monsky, it will be remembered, did not live to see the establishment of the State of Israel. Frank Goldman, the B'nai B'rith President in the first years of the State, was in any case following in his footsteps, but instead of the Yishuv it was now the sovereign

State that was assuming the role of caring for the rejected and suffering people. So too there was no great difference between Frank Goldman and Henry Morgenthau with regard to Israel. At the first B'nai B'rith Convention after the establishment of the State (March 1950), Frank Goldman said in his presidential address that the establishment of the State of Israel had been the dominant theme of the previous three years in the Jewish world and in the activities of their order. For them, he elucidated, the establishment of the State of Israel was first and foremost an enterprise in taking in hundreds of thousands of martyred Jews, who had been robbed of their homes and goods. Even before the establishment of the State, the B'nai B'rith had taken upon itself the task of conscience, caring for Jews in desperate straits. The supreme Jewish ideal is aid to brethren in need, the *raison d'être* of the order; he summed up this theme in the most outspoken terms. Indeed, the version of Zionism as refuge metamorphosed imperceptibly into what at times is termed 'pro-Israelism.'[38]

A striking personification of this metamorphosis appears to have been Morris Bisgyer, Acting Vice President of the order for about thirty years. In a wide-ranging letter that he wrote some years after the establishment of the State to a B'nai B'rith leader (in the State of Illinois), who was worried about Zionism as ideology, Bisgyer explained clearly what had consistently been the stand of the order:

> The State of Israel is a reality and Zionism or 'Jewish nationalism' is not at all an issue. Approximately three quarters of a million refugees have been admitted to the State of Israel, and practically none of them could find a haven elsewhere because of restrictions in the admission of immigrants. Even in our beloved United States the McCarren-Walter act is an insurmountable barrier at present for our co-religionists who wish to enter this country. Where can these people go, if not to Israel? B'nai B'rith has a historic tradition of helping the poor, oppressed and homeless.[39]

Bisgyer wrote a semi-autobiography aptly entitled, *In the Struggle for Jewish Survival*, where he described his visits to Israel. For him the State represented solidarity, unity and survival. His first visit to the country was in 1948 after the State was established; it climaxed in his meeting with an Israeli woman who had been badly wounded in the War of Independence and had been flown to the U.S.A. for medical treatment.[40]

Bisgyer visited Israel again ten years later and again experienced to the full what he himself sought in the Jewish State, the sense of solidarity. This time he chose to write about the driver who was 'loaned' by the Government Tourist Office to him for his stay in the country; for Bisgyer, this driver's behaviour, and through it that of the whole country, symbolized the world-wide Jewish family: 'Yaacov, the driver like those in high places, symbolized Israel .... In him is a deep, even passionate love for our people. He actually bled for his brethren. This is the force that drives him with acceleration that beggars description. Even though the hot war is not on, he still retains the alert, watchful air of the frontier guard that was his job during the siege of Jerusalem.'

The Israeli driver, in his natural expressions of Jewish solidarity, provided the Bisgyer family with its profoundest experience and cemented its emotional ties with the State of Israel:

> Yaacov got my wife 'into the act' when he asked one day if we would mind if he picked up his mother to make a visit that was only about twenty miles out of the way. It was Forty! My wife, not knowing what she was in for, readily consented: being a grandmother of seven, any mention of motherhood immediately appeals to her. So they drove together to a kibbutz on the way to Haifa. There they met another woman, a friend of Yaakov's mother. It appeared that they were old friends, and her daughter was to marry Yaakov's brother. My wife was actually drawn into helping to make arrangements for the wedding. Her advice was eagerly sought, and Yaakov was very proud that he had brought along an American expert in these matters. Only in Israel could it happen! And only a personal visit can really disclose the uniqueness of the Israeli.[41]

Arnold Forster, the veteran leader of the B'nai B'rith Anti-Defamation League, visited Israel for the first time several years after the establishment of the State. His attachment to Israel was steeped in his devoted service over so many years to the victims of anti-Semitism and his concern for refugees. He was much surprised to find so much social and material creativity in the country. It emerged that his previous idea of the State had been that it was just one big Jewish refugee camp. With him as with other B'nai B'rith leaders, Israel's brilliant military victories buttressed another motif besides the impulse of solidarity. The State now appeared not only as a refuge for the oppressed but also as giving them self assurance, straightening their backs, crystallizing their personality. In general, this new motif did not replace the older one but was bound up with it;

this found expression, for example, in the resolution passed by the order in March 1950 to adopt Israel Independence Day as a holiday in the B'nai B'rith calendar of fixed holidays:

> Whereas, Israel's Declaration of Independence and statehood, supported by courageous military actions, marked the culmination of a 2,000-year-old dream for world Jewry, and
> Whereas, the achievements and accomplishments of Israel's heroes have not only given the persecuted Jews of the world a haven and revival of freedom, but have also added to the stature and dignity of the Jews the world over,
> THEREFORE BE IT RESOLVED, that the Supreme Lodge in Convention assembled this 20th day of March, 1950 in Washington DC, recommended an annual commemoration or observance of Israel Independence Day by its lodges, the form and manner of such celebration to be at the option of the individual lodges.[42]

When Frank Goldman visited Israel in the Spring of 1953 – he was the first B'nai B'rith President to visit Israel – he at once felt at home and was proud of every aspect of the State's achievements. The Jewish State was necessary, he said, 'because a large segment of our people needed it so desperately.' He marvelled at the look of the people, finding the traits of courage, the inner calm of free men determined to build a good life for the future.[43]

Adopting Independence Day and identifying completely with embattled Israel was also connected with the Palestine tradition of the order, that is to say Palestine had always been included in the sphere of B'nai B'rith fraternal and solidarity activities. This tradition dated from as early as 1865, when the organization sent a contribution of thousands of dollars to help the victims of the cholera epidemic in the country; in the following decades the order regularly allocated funds to the Alliance Israélite Universelle in France for distribution to institutions in Palestine. In June 1888, a B'nai B'rith lodge was established in Jerusalem, and additional lodges were created in other places in the country. From the 1920s on the B'nai B'rith leadership began to treat expansion in Palestine seriously, not as an ordinary affair but as deserving of special encouragement. Various B'nai B'rith initiatives in Palestine received increased backing from the world B'nai B'rith leadership.[44] Some of the relevant developments in the 1930s and the early 1940s have been expatiated on in previous sections of this chapter.

After the establishment of the State, within the conception

of 'Zionism as refuge,' the theme was strengthened of Israel as national rebirth. B'nai B'rith publications and part of the order's educational programmes in the 1950s and thereafter reflected growing interest in the cultural, religious and values image of the Jewish State. For example, Frank Goldman's interest in Israel from his visit had a certain cultural tone added to it in the course of time: he became a member of the Board of Governors of the Hebrew University in Jerusalem (Henry Morgenthau was its chairman from 1950 to 1952). There is no doubt that this status signified a great deal for Goldman (as for Morgenthau), expressing identification and symbolizing Jewish continuity. At the same time, service in this position reflected a growing interest in Israeli cultural and intellectual life.

The version of Zionism as refuge was also enriched over the years by the aspect of social ideas. The B'nai B'rith organization traditionally identified itself with the American ethos. With the establishment of the State, the B'nai B'rith stressed the values common to youthful Israel and the American republic. Endless speeches and articles went on and on about Israeli democracy as the twin sister of American democracy.[45]

Morris Bisgyer's book was typical, ending with a call to Jews to adopt the heritage of Brandeis, Morgenthau and Lehman (of the older generation) and of Arthur Goldberg, Javits, Klutznick and Ribicoff (of the contemporary period). For him these people represented loyalty to Jewish origin, responsibility to the dispersed of Israel wherever they might be and the hope for an enlightened, pluralist society. Bisgyer assumed that the Jewish State would continue to develop in the light of the liberal-humanist heritage he was so proud of.[46]

At times the young State was even extolled as near to realizing distant, longed-for American ideals. Achievement of these ideals would transform the Jewish State into an example and a model for the world at large. At Thanksgiving in November 1948, the *National Jewish Monthly* gave prominence to an editorial article entitled 'Palestine and the Plymouth Rock.' The editors found a direct connection between the ideas of the immigrants to America and those of the idealists who settled in Palestine. The immigrants who landed on Plymouth Rock laid the foundation for the greatness of enlightened America, and the Jewish settlers in Palestine would certainly in the course of time establish a noble society in the spirit of the prophets, a society that would be a sort of new edition model of the enterprise of the American pioneers.[47]

All these were, generally speaking, just nuances (prevailing among the leaders rather than among the mass membership) or aspects of the basic B'nai B'rith conception of solidarity. The *National Jewish Monthly* carried out a survey among its readers on their attitude to the Jewish State. Most of those who answered spoke warmly as if the Israelis were beloved close relatives who had to be treated properly, whose actions must be cherished and who must be helped as much as possible.[48]

## V

The savage anti-Semitism of Europe, Nazism and the Holocaust, the indifference of the Western Powers in the face of the Jewish catastrophe – all these led to intensified solidarity on the part of U.S. Jewry in all its various organizations. The Yishuv, as it rehabilitated the refugees, and then the State of Israel, taking in the surviving remnant and opening its gates to every Jew, became the symbol of Jewish solidarity. American Jewry's processes of solidarization and Zionization were not however entirely uniform. An important organization like the American Jewish Committee refrained from resolutions recognizing the emerging State of Israel until the State was recognized by the U.S. itself. This hesitancy was one of the reasons why the Committee remained unpopular among U.S. Jews for at least a decade after the establishment of the State of Israel.[49]

The American Jewish Congress was active at the other end of the spectrum. This organization had a historic Bill of Rights of radical actions of solidarity, and its trend was to merge its conception of Jewish solidarity with Zionist ideology. This organization did not have a central place in the life of U.S. Jewry either.[50]

As the historian Deborah Moore rightly pointed out, the B'nai B'rith more than once found itself in the middle, as it were, between the American Jewish Committee and the American Jewish Congress. It was the Monsky stance reaffirming the order's basis of solidarity that turned the B'nai B'rith, unlike these other two organizations, into a mass organization rooted in American Jewish life. In the years 1938 to 1946, the organization's membership rose from 60 to 190 thousand men and about half that number women members (before Monsky's time women were not full members of the order). All through the war years there was no national membership director of the B'nai B'rith; there was a joke current in the organization that the national membership director was – Adolf Hitler. Solidarity its hallmark, B'nai B'rith gave Hitlerism the spontaneous answer of the masses of the House of Israel in America

## JEWISH SOLIDARITY AND 'REFUGE ZIONISM'

– 'The people of Israel lives!', 'all of Israel is pledged to each other!' and 'long live the State of Israel!'[51]

The fact that there was no director of national membership in the B'nai B'rith in those decisive years is perhaps symbolic. The organization developed in numbers but it did not develop a new ideology (not to any striking extent, at all events). It will be remembered that the B'nai B'rith declarations of principles remained unchanged throughout. Monsky, the dynamic President, changed the order from a fraternal organization to one primarily of solidarity, but this, in any case, did not amount to general acceptance or development of any Zionist ideology.

The growing Zionist orientation of the B'nai B'rith lacked three basic characteristics, from the exemplary (or European) Zionist viewpoint: (1) a diagnosis of the problematic nature of Jewish existence in the Diaspora; (2) the proposed solution of bringing the Jews together in their independent homeland; and (3) systematic deployment of the means for achieving this end.[52]

The B'nai B'rith version of Zionism – building up Palestine as a refuge for the persecuted – seems incomplete even in comparison with American Zionism. The Zionist movement in the U.S., in its main currents at least, never regarded America as a Golah, but nevertheless saw Zionism as a movement of rebirth embracing every sphere of national life.[53]

The version of Zionism as refuge enabled the B'nai B'rith to raise the banner of Jewish solidarity without identifying itself with Zionist ideology. From this viewpoint, the order that supported the establishment of the State of Israel and contributed large means toward its strength and prosperity remained 'non-Zionist.'

Light is thrown on this 'non-Zionist' facet of B'nai B'rith in the period by the organization's efforts, since the founding of West Germany in 1949, to reestablish itself in Europe. Its efforts were crowned with success in 1955 and the European District (district 19) was established.

This also illustrates the vital energy of B'nai B'rith solidarity: Jewish collectivities have arisen even in Europe, the blood-soaked continent, and have fitted into the worldwide network of the organization. Its traditional basis of fraternity was of course prominent in this setting. In the very same year, however, when B'nai B'rith reconstruction began in Europe, the organization also joined in the setting of solidarity with the Jewish Board of Deputies in Britain and similar bodies in some other countries. One way or another, B'nai B'rith remains dedicated in the Monsky-Goldman spirit to the values of the unity of Israel and collective national responsibility.

As we have seen, the version of Zionism as refuge was gradually filled with a richer content, especially after the foundation of the State of Israel. At the same time, at least during the historical period surveyed here, Zionism-as-refuge was an instrument for formulating the process of B'nai B'rith's deepening solidarity; so too the conception of solidarity was basically what dictated the support for the State of Israel and the hopes for its welfare and prosperity. In B'nai B'rith's view, Israel was indeed a vital, precious link in the comprehensive effort to ensure the survival of the people of Israel everywhere and the realization of the values of Jewish solidarity.

NOTES

1. B'nai B'rith International Archives, Washington DC; I am grateful to Hanna R. Sinauer of these archives and to Lawrence Sternberg of the Center for Modern Jewish Studies, Brandeis University, for their assistance. The declaration remained unchanged except for the substitution in 1956 of the phrase 'persons of the Jewish Faith' for 'Israelites.'
2. E. E. Grusd, *B'nai B'rith: the Story of a Covenant* (New York, 1966), and D. Dash Moore, *B'nai B'rith and the Challenge of Ethnic Leadership* (Albany, 1981), have provided the historical background for this chapter.
3. For B'nai Brith during the 19th century, see Grusd, *B'nai B'rith*, chaps.1-9; Moore, *B'nai B'rith*, chaps. 1-3.
4. Cf., Moore, pp.96-101.
5. Moore, pp.176-8.
6. *Proceeding of the Fifteenth General Convention of the Supreme Lodge B'nai B'rith* (Washington DC, 8-11 May 1938), pp.336-9.
7. *New Palestine*, XXV, No. 4 (25 Jan. 1935), p.9. For a sketch of American Zionists' criticism of 'refugeeism' in the mid-1930s see Samuel Halperin, *The Political World Of American Zionism* (Detroit, 1961), pp.21-4.
8. Ibid.
9. *Proceeding of the Fifteenth Convention*, pp.39-42.
10. *New Palestine*, XXVI, no. 7 (14 Feb. 1936), p.3.
11. *Proceedings of the 15th General Convention*, pp.5-6.
12. Ibid., pp.64-5.
13. Ibid., p.421.
14. *B'nai B'rith Magazine*, June 1938, p.342.
15. Mrs. Henry Monsky and Maurice Bisgyer, *Henry Monsky: The Man and his Work* (New York, 1947), chapter 6.
16. *Proceedings of the 16th General Convention of the Supreme Lodge B'nai B'rith* (Chicago, 29 March-2 April 1941), pp.40-3.
17. *New Palestine*, XXXI, no.16 (31 Jan. 1941), p.15.
18. *Proceedings of the Sixteenth General Assembly*, pp.2-3, 21-2.
19. Ibid., pp.35-6, 40-3.
20. Ibid., pp.139-53.
21. Ibid., pp.183-6.
22. I. Neustadt-Noy, 'Toward Unity: Zionist and non-Zionist Cooperation, 1941-

1942,' in M. I. Urofsky, ed., *The Herzl Yearbook, vol. 8: Essays in American Zionism, 1917–1948* (New York, 1978), pp.149–65.
23. A. S. Kohansky, ed., *The American Jewish Conference: Its Organization and Proceedings of the First Session, August 29 to September 2, 1943, New York* (New York, 1944), pp.15–19, 33–4.
24. Ibid., pp.67–70.
25. For the full text see Monsky, 'A Common Basis for Action' (29 Aug. 1943), a typescript at B'nai B'rith Archives; see esp. pp.5–12.
26. Ibid., pp.12–15.
27. Kohansky, pp.127–30, 178–81.
28. *President's Message to the Supreme Lodge B'nai B'rith, Seventeenth Convention* (New York City, 6 May 1944), pp.3–17; for the order's support of Monsky's course regarding the American Jewish Conference see *Summary of the seventeenth Convention Supreme Lodge B'nai B'rith* (New York City, 6–10 May 1944), pp.31–5.
29. Alexander S. Kohansky, ed., *The American Jewish Conference. Proceedings of the Second Session, December 3–5, 1944, Pittsburgh, Pa.* (New York, 1945) pp.23–4.
30. Ibid., pp.178–82.
31. R. Hershman, ed., *The American Jewish Conference: Proceedings of the Third Session, February 17–19, 1946, Cleveland, Ohio* (New York, 1946), pp.32–3, 36.
32. *Summary of the Eighteenth General Convention of the Supreme Lodge B'nai B'rith* (Washington, D.C., 11–14 May 1947), pp.132–3.
33. Ibid., p.133.
34. R. Hershman, ed., *The American Jewish Conference: Proceedings of the Fourth Session, November 29–December 1, 1947, Chicago, Illinois* (New York, 1948), pp.14–25; for the growing support of B'nai B'rith for sovereignty see M. Kaufman, *Lo-tsionim be-Amerika ve-maavak al hamedina* (Non-Zionists in America and the Struggle for Jewish Statehood, 1939–1948) (Jerusalem, 1984) [Hebrew], pp.93 ff.
35. H. Martson, 'Vignettes of the Displaced,' *The National Jewish Monthly*, vol. 60, no. 9 (May 1946), pp.314–15, 334–5.
36. A.B. Kapplin, 'B'nai B'rith Aid to the people of Israel, Annual Report to Executive Committee, January 1, 1949,' B'nai B'rith Archives, pp.1, 9.
37. 'Morgenthau at dinner,' *The National Jewish Monthly*, vol. 60, no. 4 (Dec. 1945), pp.136–7; see H. Morgenthau, Jr., 'They Look To Us,' and '1948: UJA "Year of Destiny"', in ibid., vol. 61, no.8 (April 1947), pp.270–1, and vol. 62, no. 8 (April 1948), pp.276–7, resp.; Monsky & Bisgyer, *Henry Monsky*, pp.134–5.
38. For Morgenthau see note 37, supra; *Summary of the Nineteenth General Convention of the Supreme Lodge B'nai B'rith* (Washington, DC, 18–22 March 1950), pp.2, 3; Arye L. Dulzin, 'Maintaining Zionism in an Age of Pro-Israelism,' in Moshe Davis, ed., *Zionism In Transition* (New York, 1980), pp.275–84.
39. M. Bisgyer to Louis M. Goldman, Jr., 2 April 1954, B'nai B'rith Archives.
40. M. Bisgyer, *Challenge and Encounter: Behind the Scenes in the Struggle for Jewish Survival* (New York, 1967), pp.206–14.
41. Ibid., pp.215–16.
42. Arnold Forster interview by the author, NYC Sept. 1986. *Summary of the Nineteenth General Convention*, p.79.
43. *B'nai B'rith News*, vol. 67, no. 9 (May 1953), pp.327–8.
44. The section 'B'nai B'rith in Israel', in Y. Alfassi, ed., *B'nai B'rith*, pp.45–56.
45. Allon Gal, 'Israel in the Mind of B'nai B'rith, 1938–1958,' in *American Jewish History*, LXXVII, no. 4 (June 1988).
46. Bisgyer, *Challenge and Encounter*, pp.278–9.
47. *The National Jewish Monthly*, vol. 63, no. 3 (Nov. 1948), p.71.
48. 'Our Relation to Israel,' ibid., vol. 63, no. 4 (Dec. 1948), pp.118–22.
49. Kaufman, *Non-Zionists in America*, pp.176 ff; N. W. Cohen, *Not Free to Desist: The American Jewish Committee 1906–1966* (Philadelphia, 1972), pp.555 ff.
50. M. I. Urofsky, *A Voice That Spoke for Justice: The Life and Times of Stephen S. Wise*

(Albany, 1982), chaps. 9, 20, 24.
51. Moore, *B'nai B'rith*, chap. 7; Grusd, *B'nai B'rith*, pp.238–9.
52. Gideon Shimoni, 'Ideological Perspectives,' in Davis, ed., *Zionism In Transition*, esp. pp.7–9.
53. Allon Gal, 'American Zionism Between the Two World Wars: The Ideological Characteristics,' *Contemporary Jewry*, vol.5 (1988) [Hebrew], pp.79–90.

# 15

# Diplomacy Without Sovereignty: The World Jewish Congress Rescue Activities

## Avi Beker

> 'A man consists of a body, a soul and a passport'
> *(Russian proverb)*

It is hard to conceive of diplomacy and international influence in our time without the basic condition of sovereignty and political power. An analysis of the World Jewish Congress rescue activities during the Second World War can only highlight these limitations and examine how the WJC operated under these conditions. The absence of Jewish sovereignty gave the world states an excuse for not taking any stand on the extermination of the Jews and also explained the splintering and disunity in Jewish foreign policy. After the war, the WJC had a better strategic position in the fight for Jewish sovereignty than any other Jewish organization, combining as it did both the objectives of rescue and of Zionism. This combination would receive still more concrete expression after the establishment of the State in the diplomatic campaign conducted by the WJC for bringing the Jews of North Africa to Israel.

Any discussion of the development of international relations, more particularly in the twentieth century, must focus on two ideas: the nation-State and power. After the mid-seventeenth century and the end of the Wars of Religion (Peace of Westphalia, 1648), the nation-State became the focal point in international contacts and activities. 'State' and 'nation' are utilized as ideas that merge into each other, but it is important to distinguish between them: the State is a political unit defined in accordance with its population, territory and independent government. As against this, the nation is a historical idea based on the cultural identity of a people, not necessarily concentrated in a territory. Thus the 'State' creates the basis for political loyalty, which finds expression in citizenship, while the 'nation' endows the individual with a sense of identity and emotional identification.[1]

In international law, the 'State' is seen as comprising four basic conditions: nation, territory, government and independence.[2] In the period of the Second World War, the Jewish people had in fact only the first of these four: nation – without territory, without government and without independence. The idea of 'nation-State,' signifying the territorial concentration of each nation, received international sanction in President Woodrow Wilson's 'Fourteen Points' towards the end of the First World War in 1918, before the establishment of the League of Nations under the Versailles Peace Treaty in 1919.

The second key element, power, which governs the existing reality of relations between States, was also not at the disposal of the Jewish people at the time of the Holocaust, owing mainly to the absence of a sovereign state framework. The Second World War revealed the bankruptcy of the idealistic school of political thought, product of liberal pacifist-universalist circles, which envisioned and preached an end to the era of power dominance and *realpolitik* in international relations.[3] The rise of Nazi Germany, largely facilitated by the naïveté and indifference of the company of nations, swept aside pacifism and the idea of European disarmament; the policy of surrender to Hitler seemed as if intended to finally prove the basic axioms of the realistic school that saw international politics as a permanent struggle for power between nation-states.[4] Another power function that was also inserted into international conventions dealing with State rights and obligations, in addition to population, territory and government, was that the State as an international legal personality must possess 'the ability to establish relations with other States.'[5] That is to say, the independence of a State and in fact its power as well is expressed in its ability to conduct foreign policy relations with other States.

Any review of the WJC rescue in the Second World War period must therefore set out from the starting-point of the absence of these two decisive factors for activity in the international arena: a sovereign nation-State and political power in relation to other States. Before I am drawn into criticism and historical accusations in raising the legitimate question whether it would have been possible to do more, it is desirable to recognize the fact that Jewish rescue activity during the war turned into an attempt to develop a policy at the international level in spite of the absence of these primary data and customary basic conditions. World Jewish Congress representatives, such as Hillel Storch in Stockholm, Dr. Gerhard Riegner in Geneva or Dr. Morris Perlzweig in London, courageously and even with shameless 'chutzpah' tried to acquire for themselves 'the ability to maintain relations with other States' laid down in international law – without their having the necessary basic elements at their disposal.

In the archive of the late Hillel Storch, head of the WJC office in Stockholm, there are documents and testimonies in quantity, on which no research has yet been done, recording the widespread diplomatic activity in the field of rescue throughout the war. Storch maintained contact with the Red Cross and was directly involved in Folke Bernadotte's attempt to rescue those held in Ravensbrück Camp, and in Raoul Wallenberg's activity in rescuing the Jews of Budapest. He was the address for requests for aid in the field of rescue action by Jewish Agency representatives in Europe and families from Latvia, Lithuania, etc.[6] Storch's involvement is known through the memoirs of Himmler's physiotherapist, Felix Kersten, in connection with the supplying of food and medication to the camps and the evacuation of the Jews from the camps to Sweden at the end of the war in 1945, negotiations that ended with Himmler's meeting Norbert Mazov, replacing Storch, who could not leave Stockholm.[7] Until today, however, there has been no reference in the literature to what is revealed in the documents in the Storch archive, that as early as September 1942, the head of the legal department of the Swedish Foreign Ministry, Gosta Engzell, noted that two Germans had visited Hillel Storch of the World Jewish Congress to try to begin negotiations with the Jews.

In the absence of sovereignty and normal diplomatic channels, the WJC acted in complicated, roundabout ways in order to influence the Allied governments. At times the WJC was also obliged to make contact with the enemy and even with the Nazi 'Devil' in person in order to save Jews. In 1940 and 1941, the WJC network of representatives and contacts was already spread out everywhere in the world – in Europe, North America, Australia, Rhodesia, Japan, etc. Unlike other Jewish aid and rescue organizations, the WJC tried to develop a global strategy of diplomatic activity on behalf of Jews in Nazi-occupied or threatened areas. Nahum Goldmann and Dr. Aryeh Tartakower, head of the Assistance Department in New York, stressed political connections with the various governments in Europe and America; Dr. Riegner in Geneva, who reported in October 1941 on the expulsion of Jews from Germany and Czechoslovakia to Poland, called for active contacts with the governments-in-exile in London.[8] In 1941 the WJC tried to get the governments-in-exile to issue a declaration condemning the imposition of anti-Jewish laws by the occupying forces; in 1942, after a wearisome series of contacts, demonstrations and protests, when the news of the 'final solution' programme was already public knowledge, the United Nations saw fit, on 17 December, to put out a Declaration in the name of eleven governments, for the first time referring explicitly to Nazi crimes *against the Jews*. The importance of Dr. Riegner's reports from Geneva for the awakening of international opinion and the official reference in the text to extermination of the Jews is the bedrock of Holocaust historiography.[9] The declaration, made in response to the reports after months of delay, was read out, in the name of the British Government by the Foreign Minister, Sir Anthony Eden, in Parliament in answer to a question of M.P. Sidney Silverman, head of the British section of the World Jewish Congress.[10]

The book by Arthur D. Morse, *While Six Million Died* (the Hebrew version was published under the title, *And the World Was Silent*), gives a detailed account of why the declaration was delayed for so long and the problems Dr. Stephen Wise came up against when he tried to bring it before the British Cabinet and the White House in the USA.[11] The delays also stemmed from the non-sovereign status of the WJC, which had to fight from a position of inferiority against states which were exposed to an anti-Semitic atmosphere and did not see 'the Jewish question' as a first priority in the war effort against the Axis. The governments' representatives were often evasive, like General Sikorski, head of the Polish Government-in-Exile, and contended that anti-Jewish crimes should not be mentioned explicitly, since every Jew had to be considered as a citizen of his country of origin.[12] As Bernard Wasserstein explains, in the British Foreign Office there was unwillingness all along to pick out the Jews as victims of the Nazis in British information and propaganda policy, so as not to give colour to Goebbels' propaganda about the power of the Jews in Britain. So too, in 1941, the WJC proposal was rejected that the Latvian Ambassador in London should broadcast a warning to the Latvian people not to collaborate with the Nazis in their persecution of the Jews, so as not the harm the USSR.[13] In October 1943, Jan Masaryk, head of the Czech Government-in-Exile, told A.L. Easterman, the

WJC Political Secretary, that consultations had been held with the Foreign Ministers on the declaration regarding crimes against the Jews and they had recommended postponing it, since 'on no account should a line be drawn making a distinction between persecuted Jews and other inhabitants of the occupied territories.'[14]

Before the war, too, when the Nazi racial laws were already in force and Jews were being discriminated against, humiliated and expelled, there was a refusal on the part of governments to recognize the specificity of the Jewish factor as the Nazi objective; thus, for example, at the unsuccessful Evian Conference, which convened in July 1938 and where it became clear that not a single state was ready to open its doors to Jewish refugees, the plenary session refused to hear representatives of the World Jewish Congress and the Jewish Agency on dubious grounds of the absence of sovereignty, stating that there was no place in the plenary for representatives of 'private' organizations. The WJC therefore presented its memorandum to the conference sub-committee.[15] According to David Wyman, these problems of sovereignty explain why Dr. Stephen Wise was held up at the end of 1942 waiting for the US State Department confirmation of the Riegner report from Geneva. Government confirmation was vital in order to accord international credibility to a statement that had reached them from a Jewish source. It was clear to Dr. Wise that if he disregarded Under-Secretary of State Welles' request to hold up publication of the information, he would be harmed and thereby relations would be harmed with the institution in charge of US rescue policy.[16] In sum, the lack of Jewish sovereignty enabled many states and statesmen, including those of Britain and the US, to shrug the matter off and evade taking a position on the appalling crimes against the Jewish people. Instead of talking about Jews, various other expressions were utilized: persecuted peoples, a luckless people, political refugees, oppressed and persecuted minorities, etc.[17] The WJC recognized and understood this political-moral Achilles' heel and constantly called for explicit references that would specify the Jewish people's suffering and create an international commitment to rescue Jews from the Nazis.

## THE PROBLEM OF PASSPORTS AND RANSOM

Early in the history of the League of Nations when there were deliberations regarding refugees and their status, the question of passports for refugees already presented a complex problem in a world where sovereign states were the sole authorities for deciding policies of migration and naturalization. The first High Commissioner for Refugees, the Norwegian D. Fridtjof Nansen, appointed to the post on 1 September 1921, was confronted with the problem of the refugees from Russia after the Revolution and decided to have the League of Nations issue substitutes for national passports; these certificates were promptly dubbed 'Nansen passports,' which were inferior in status to any state passport and their validity and renewal depended on the goodwill of the host countries. All the same, the Nansen passport gave its holder a certain sense of identity and helped him to get visas and apply to representatives of the Commission for Refugees in the various cities.[18] Since decisions in the League of Nations needed the unanimous agreement of all the member states, the organization had difficulty in dealing with the refugee problem, because for every refugee group there was at least one hostile state.[19]

In December 1935, James G. McDonald, the League of Nations High Commissioner for Refugees (Jewish and others) coming from Germany, resigned from his post, submitting a letter of resignation warning of the approaching catastrophe. In view of the 'terrible human calamity' that already existed, he would be recreant if he remained silent, he said. 'When domestic policies threaten the demoralization and exile of hundreds of thousands of human beings, considerations of diplomatic correctness must yield to those of common humanity.'[20] The lessons for the WJC were clear. Since no state would give passports to the refugees, new techniques must be found and passports fabricated – documents and 'requests' giving cover of a sort to the refugees. In 1939 Jewish organizations in Eastern Poland were already acting on behalf of refugees who were not sent to Siberia by virtue of their possessing a passport or visa for Palestine or for some other country. In cooperation with the Jewish Agency, 'requests' on behalf of the refugees were also secured from Paraguay, Costa-Rica, Guatemala, etc. In this way refugees moved from Lithuania all the way to Japan and thence to America; some even obtained South American passports in Switzerland. From late 1943 the WJC headed the effort to rescue the holders of South American passports, mainly in the Vittel Camp, through the Swiss Foreign Ministry. After a diplomatic effort over several months, the Americans saw fit to help, but it was too late by then; the prisoners had already been sent to Auschwitz death camp. Only a few benefited from the diplomatic effort connected with these passports.[21]

In 1939 the WJC set up the Relief Committee for Jewish War Victims (RELICO) in Geneva to combine welfare activities with diplomatic-political negotiations.[22] This organization did a great deal to bring out Jewish refugees with the help of forged passports and to get thousands of letters out of the occupied territories, setting up children's homes and keeping constantly in touch with the Red Cross. By means of the contact with the Red Cross, food, clothing and medication were sent to Jews in occupied Poland and to Jews held prisoner in Yugoslavia and Greece.[23] The WJC's policy was guided throughout by James McDonald's dictum that diplomatic correctness must yield to considerations of common humanity.

German representatives' demands for ransom in return for releasing Jews raised problems of policy and in the end forced the WJC to surrender to the dictates of rescue and overcome policy considerations. Late in 1938 the President of the German State Bank, Hjalmar Schacht, established contact with George Rublee, head of the Intergovernmental Commission on Refugees set up by the Evian Conference, in order to work out a programme to allow Jewish émigrés to transfer abroad the German loan-bonds that they would receive in return for their confiscated property, and to do so by means of the export of German goods. The deal was supposed to permit the emigration of 40,000 Jews in five years. Agreement was reached between Rublee and Helmuth Wohlthat, who replaced Schacht, dismissed by Hitler; its provisions detailed the conditions of the offer of property and counterpart funds for Jewish émigrés. The Germans wanted to tie in the exodus of the Jews with a parallel growth in German exports, stressing dependence on world Jewry and the interested governments. A meeting of the WJC Executive in January 1939 decided to oppose the plan and affirmed, 'The Jewish people cannot lend a hand to a solution of the problem of the refugees from Germany if this involves granting the Nazi regime economic advantages in return for the policy of confiscation and expulsion that it is conducting against the Jews.'[24] Stephen Wise and Dorothy Thompson were among those who inclined to agree to the idea of ransom.[25] The Jewish opposition also rested on the refusal to give retrospective justification to Nazi propaganda about 'international Jewry,' all the more so since the USA and Great Britain were also dubious over Germany's intentions in the ransom initiative.[26] Representatives of the WJC were later found in fear and desperation over the extermination and ready to be more flexible and even take the initiative in the matter of ransom.

Dr. Riegner openly backed the idea of ransom in order to pay for the exodus of the Jews of Rumania in mid-1943. The supporters, headed by Dr. Wise, who met with President Roosevelt on this issue, argued that this was not in fact a question of ransom but of the transfer of funds needed to finance the exodus of some 7,000 Jews.[27] Henry Morgenthau, U.S. Secretary of the Treasury, tried to put through the programme and overcome the opposition of the State Department and of the British Foreign Office (which had been holding the operation up for ten months). The WJC was involved in the negotiations of Solly Mayer, the Joint representative in Switzerland, with S.S. Col. Becher in meetings on the frontier from August 1944 to April 1945 (sometimes in the presence of Kastner) for the release of Jews in return for money and trucks.[28] The WJC had to overcome all scruples of principle for the sake of these negotiations and also to contend with the US War Refugees Board, which opposed money transfers that would assist the Nazis.[29] According to one researcher on the Holocaust, it was finally clear to the WJC representatives at a given moment that ethical criteria took precedence over laws and regulations enacted by ordinary human beings. Unlike representatives of more institutionalized organizations such as the Joint and the Jewish communities of Switzerland and Sweden, Hillel Storch and people like him stood out in contrast for their inconceivable, desperate exertions to rescue the Jews of Europe by the use of bribery, forged certificates, the smuggling out of stateless refugees, sending in parcels and so on, and when necessary by contacting the Nazi Devil's representatives themselves in the attempt to save the lives of survivors who had escaped the Hitlerian furnaces.[30]

## DIVISIONS AND SCHISMS IN THE JEWISH CAMP

Division and schism is apparently a Jewish phenomenon with ancient roots – it emerges in the sovereign Jewish State as well. It is nevertheless clear that in the absence of sovereignty and of the usual exclusive political representation for the conduct of foreign affairs, Jewish divisions were exposed for the whole world to see, seriously damaging Jewish bargaining power and influence. Since its foundation the WJC had aimed to take all Jewish communities and organizations under its wing; so now it aimed to reach a united Jewish stand at the Evian Conference and present a jointly agreed-on memorandum to the states participating there, but it did not succeed. Instead, the Conference witnessed the ridiculous spectacle of separate appearances before the Conference of every Jewish organization – there were 21 of them – for three minutes each.[31] In his report on the Conference, Dr. Nahum Goldmann apportioned the blame: 'The Jewish organizations made an embarrassing and even ridiculous impression .... They are to blame. ... The Evian Conference must serve as a lesson to point to the need for united representation.'[32]

The British were alive to the effects of Jewish division and had the lowest possible opinion of the Jewish organizations. On occasion they might listen to the British wing of the WJC but they did not take much stock in its claim to serve as a 'permanent address for the Jewish people,' since the other Jewish organizations disagreed with this strongly.[33] The US Assistant Secretary of State for special problems, Breckinridge Long, who acted against bringing Jews into the USA, also 'discovered' the factors of division in the Jewish community and exploited them for his own purposes. He referred openly to the internal splits, rivalries and jealousies, the heavy competition and absence of cooperation among the Jewish organizations.[34] For example, in the course of the rescue of children in southern (Vichy-controlled) France and their clandestine transfer via the Pyrenees and Spain to Portugal by the WJC, aided by the Joint and the Jewish Agency, the 'wars of the Jews' still went on between the Joint and the WJC.[35]

Inside US Jewry there was constant in-fighting between Zionists and non-Zionists on whether to concentrate the diplomatic-political effort on the theme of rescue or on Palestine (see below). Among the Zionists themselves, there was fierce personal rivalry between Rabbi Stephen Wise and Rabbi Abba Hillel Silver, and when the Joint Emergency Conference to Save the Jews of Europe was set up in November 1942, it survived as a body representing a number of Jewish organizations for two weeks only.[36] All the same, the WJC did succeed in crystallizing and representing a united stand, which was at times adopted by the entire Jewish community, as happened, e.g., with the mass meeting at Madison Square Garden on 2 July 1942, which in fact adopted the WJC resolutions.[37]

## THE FIGHT TO ACHIEVE SOVEREIGNTY – ZIONISTS VERSUS NON-ZIONISTS

In the literature of rescue operations in the Holocaust, one repeatedly meets discussions and at times accusations against the Zionist leaders to the effect that by over-concentration on achieving the establishment of the Jewish State they neglected efforts to rescue the Jews of Europe. Included in these accusations against the Zionists – and the WJC leadership too – was the charge that they were deep in 'post-war planning' and paid little heed – and that only formally – to the tragedy of European Jewry, while their representatives in Constantinople and Geneva were voicing urgent appeals for immediate action.[38] David Wyman, an American Protestant researcher into the Holocaust, confirms that the Zionist effort to harness the Jewish communities to the issue of Palestine damaged rescue activity, which was rated second in the order of precedence. Wyman however refutes the accusations and explains that this policy was deliberately adopted when the Zionist leadership came to the conclusion that rescue was hopeless: Hitler had European Jewry by the throat and the Allies showed no interest in saving it. The feeling of hopelessness intensified especially after the failure of the Bermuda Conference, which crushed the last hope of getting an international move to organize a rescue effort for Jews. On the other hand the Zionists stressed that a great effort was needed to prepare public opinion for the fight over the shape of things to come *after* the war, in order to achieve the establishment of the Jewish State. The emphasis then was put on getting what seemed possible instead of what appeared to have no prospect at all. After the Bermuda Conference, Dr. Goldmann was convinced that the emphasis had to be shifted to Zionist objectives and that it had to be recognized that there were not enough people available to keep on organizing giant demonstrations for rescue and at the same time wage the fight for the Zionist programme.[39] Wyman rejects the charge of cynicism brought against the Zionists to the effect that they thought that the greater the number of Jewish victims in Europe, the better it would serve the cause of the Jewish State. There is absolutely no proof of this, Wyman says, and the feelings of guilt induced later among the states in the world are no proof that this was the result of Zionist planning. The Zionist leadership in Palestine, too, contrary to accusations of selfishness, did help rescue refugees and even appealed to the USA and other countries to open their gates.[40]

The WJC was in a key position in the middle of the apparent 'rushing to and fro' from aims of rescue to aims of Zionism. With its special structure and its political leadership, the WJC merged a Zionist movement with the Jewish organizations and communities represented by it. Its leaders held key posts in the Zionist movement and sometimes appeared in the name of both organizations. At Evian Dr. Goldmann, representing the WJC, and Dr. Ruppin from

Palestine presented a joint memorandum, from which it appears that they both represented the Jewish Agency for Palestine as well.[41] The WJC memorandum to the Evian Conference especially stressed the importance of the Jewish National Home in Palestine among the programmes for rescuing refugees. This stand was to be maintained by the WJC throughout the war and would be upheld at the climax of the post-war fight in the United Nations for the establishment of the State. In 1947 the WJC helped to crystallize the broadest Jewish consensus, as opposed to non-Zionist circles in the USA and outside it, in favour of the establishment of the Jewish State.

In the World Jewish Congress, therefore, we find the combination of the two objectives, rescue and Palestine. Together with the American Jewish Congress, it was the most active of all the representative organizations in the USA in the matter of rescuing Jews. It filled a central role on the executive that planned the campaign for public opinion and the diplomatic activity of contacts with the US Congress and the administration. On the 'Temporary Committee for Rescue' (this is what the Joint Emergency Conference to Save the Jews of Europe was called at the time; on this committee of US organizations besides the WJC were the American Jewish Congress, the Jewish Labour Committee, B'nai B'rith, the Council of Synagogues of America – Reform – and Agudat Israel) the WJC was the most Zionist in policy.[42] In the sub-committee on post-war reconstruction that convened in September 1943, the WJC displayed a clear pro-Zionist stance,[43] supporting the Biltmore Programme adopted by the Zionist movement in New York in May 1942 explicitly demanding the establishment of the Jewish National Home in Palestine. In sum it can be said that more than any other Jewish organization the WJC tried to develop a rescue policy that would manoeuvre as far as possible between Zionist aims and the urgent needs for rescue and finding asylum everywhere. It should be noted that it was easier to harness US Senators and members of the House of Representatives to support Zionist claims because these were directed at Britain and did not clash with US immigration problems that concerned US Congressmen. Thus in January 1944, the US Senate and House of Representatives adopted decisions calling for the opening of the gates of Palestine for free entry for Jews and the setting up of a Jewish State, and this despite the urgings of the War Department requesting a postponement of these decisions for fear of the Arab reaction.[44]

THE CONTEMPORARY PERIOD

## THE DIPLOMACY OF SOVEREIGNTY – THE RESCUE OF NORTH AFRICAN JEWRY

The story of the emigration to Palestine of the Jews of North Africa and other Arab countries is of course very different from the rescue of the surviving remnant in Europe during and after the Holocaust. In this matter the World Jewish Congress utilized its diplomatic connections in order to help rescue Jews, but in this instance it had the benefit of the existence of a sovereign state, an integral part of real, existing international power relations, a state capable of taking in Jewish immigrants and refugees with open arms by virtue of its objectives. No need for international conferences, for the search for an address for Jews to go to, or for immigration quotas that would never be put into effect. Interestingly enough, it is just this chapter in the story of WJC activities for rescuing Jews that is less known and has not yet had the research and documentation it deserves.

What characterized the World Jewish Congress diplomatic activity in the French-speaking countries of North Africa was the fact that its contacts and connections with the local political leadership were already developed during the period of French rule. The centre of WJC activity in North Africa was the regional office in Algiers headed by Jacques Lazare. The Jewish communities of Algeria, Morocco, Tunisia and Egypt too were among the founders of the WJC in 1936. They took part in WJC conferences, and the first conference of North African Jewish communities took place in Algiers in June 1952 under the auspices of the WJC (the link with the communities in Egypt, Libya, and the Sudan was not direct).[45] In all the contacts, maintained chiefly by Mr. Alex Easterman, head of the WJC Political Department, and Morris Perlzweig, as well as Dr. Gerhardt Riegner and Yosef Golan, the Congress sought to ensure the safety of the communities in face of the occasional outbreaks of anti-Semitism, and mainly to obtain the right to emigrate, with the destination Israel recalled sometimes openly and sometimes by oblique hints. A scrutiny of WJC reports reveals the 'constructively vague' approach adopted at times by the WJC representatives in their talks about Jewish emigration and emigration to Israel. Different formulas for the same thing were chosen in accordance with the situation and the specific political atmosphere. For example:

(a) the document presented to the leaders of the Neo-Destour (the

Tunisian independence movement) in January 1954 referred to ensuring rights for the Jews in every sphere, including 'freedom of movement with their property inside Tunisia and from there abroad.'[46]

(b) in July 1955, Easterman met the Neo-Destour leader, Habib Bourguiba, at the Château de la Ferte near Paris (where he was imprisoned by the French). The situation and the atmosphere enabled Bourguiba not only to promise equal rights but also to refer openly to the (unnameable) 'right of emigration to Israel.'[47]

(c) at a special conference with the leaders of the Moroccan independence party (the Istiklal) on 9 August 1955, as a result of the deteriorating political situation in Morocco before the liberation, WJC representatives demanded that full rights be given, without anti-Semitism or discrimination, after independence, and maintenance of the principles of the Universal Declaration of the Rights of Man (which includes the principle of the right to emigrate), by which they of course meant the right to emigrate to Israel.[48]

The rise of Arab nationalism in North Africa was closely followed by the WJC people, who developed connections with the liberation movement, although the local Jewish communities refrained from doing so, while taking care to notify the French about these contacts.[49] It can be seen that the WJC had prestige in the eyes of the liberation movement leaders. In January 1955 the Moroccans were asking to meet WJC representatives to complain to them that the local Jews were not giving them support and to promise full and equal rights in government posts after independence. WJC representatives met Sultan Mahmud be Yussuf in his exile in Madagascar, and he reiterated the promise of the right of the Jews to emigrate.[50] The success of the WJC representatives in obtaining a declaration on Jewish rights from the Istiklal Party Secretary, Ahmed Bella Farif (later Premier and Foreign Minister), before the decisive date of 20 August 1955 must be considered an important achievement; this date was presented as an ultimatum demand to the French for the granting of independence. This declaration, which reiterated equal rights and affirmed that Morocco was also the state of the Jews of Morocco, was published in the press in Morocco and France and broadcast to Morocco by radio as well as in a nationalist manifesto calling on the people not to harm the Jews; and indeed in the rioting on 20 August practically no harm was done to the Jews.[51]

At the Aix-les-Bains conference of the French and the Moroccans,

WJC representatives were present together with people from the Moroccan Jewish community, and they succeeded in getting guarantees of Jewish rights included in the proclamation of independence. WJC representatives met King Mahmud V when he returned from exile and Si Bukai, the leader of the liberation movement, as well as a Jewish Minister brought into the government as a symbol of equality.[52] Six months after independence, however, difficulties arose over the issue of emigration to Israel. (From 1949 until then there had been emigration to Israel at the rate of approximately 3,000 a month.) Emigration was suddenly stopped by the Moroccan Interior Ministry on the grounds that the 'Kadima' organization (which dealt with emigration to Israel) was a foreign organization for mobilizing Moroccan citizens for a foreign state and strengthening the military power of Israel, which was engaged in a conflict with Arab states with which Morocco had ties of religion and nationality. (Morocco joined the Arab League only in 1959.) The Interior Ministry also explained that Morocco could not permit herself the loss of her Jews, who constituted an important factor in her population and economy – the equality of rights granted them obliged them to assist in building up the state. In the face of this crisis, WJC representatives were mobilized for prolonged political negotiations, including visits to Morocco and the submission of memoranda to the Prime Minister. Easterman wrote a particularly pressing missive dated 31 May 1956, to Prime Minister Si Bokai. After recalling the meetings of the previous two years, Easterman asked Bukai to reappraise the question of Jewish emigration, and referred again to the principle of 'the right to emigrate' guaranteed by the Charter of Rights of Man. According to Easterman, the right to emigrate to the Holy Land was an immemorial one and should not be seen as implying disloyalty to Morocco. Easterman drew a special distinction emphasizing that those Jews who wanted to emigrate from Morocco did so on 'economic grounds,' as most of them were very poor pedlars and tradesmen, illiterate and uneducated. They needed an organized framework for arranging their emigration and this should be allowed them on humanitarian grounds. According to him, the number of those leaving was small. Because they were uneducated and lacking any special skills, their departure would not harm the economy of Morocco; those Jews who were active in the economy had not manifested any intention to emigrate.[53]

After several wearisome months of diplomatic negotiation, 8,000 Jews were permitted to emigrate, and they were brought to

Mazagen camp near Casablanca. The government of Morocco, for its part, made it clear that it supported the principles of the Charter of Human Rights, but interpreted the undertaking given thereunder as given to *private individuals* and not for *collective* emigration, organized by such bodies as 'Kadima.' By agreement with the WJC, the promise was given that the Jews in Mazagen would be allowed to leave collectively from 12 August to 26 September, and that thereafter there would be no limitations on the emigration of *private individuals*. In practice, however, administrative limitations were imposed and requests for passports were rejected. In October 1957, Nahum Goldmann visited Morocco for a meeting with the Minister of the Economy, Ibrahim Buabid, who agreed on a monthly quota of emigration to Israel to be settled on jointly. On 7 January 1958, Mr. Easterman returned to Morocco and as a result of his talks there it was decided that a way would be found for Jewish emigration to continue on an individual basis and that guidelines to that effect would be issued to the appropriate authorities. Easterman returned again on 7 April but the government fell on 14 April and all decisions were suspended. Nevertheless, contacts continued, even after Morocco joined the Arab League.

In the cadre of the WJC and its meetings, it can be seen how carefully the leaders preserved the margin needed for manoeuvre between loyalty to the State of Israel on the one hand and safeguarding their diplomatic connections and their leadership over the Jews of Morocco, on the other. Representatives of the Jewish communities of Morocco attended WJC deliberations and sometimes in expressing their loyalty to Morocco demanded that the WJC be free of pressures from foreign governments, including Israel. Nahum Goldmann rejected the assertions of some representatives (such as Anschel Reiss of Israel) that the situation was desperate and even comparable to that of the Jews in Germany under Nazi rule; he contended that they had not reached the point where 'there was nothing to lose.' He declared that they could not act like 'Elders of Zion' and dictate to the Jews of Morocco how to behave, and that there should be no demonstrations against the King of Morocco on his visits to New York. He said he was alive to the fact that there were restrictions and pressures on an observer on behalf of the Jewish community of Morocco (Marc Saba), but the very fact of his appearing there was important and useful. Dr. Goldmann was careful on the other hand to maintain Israeli superiority in the matter of emigration of Moroccan Jews, and rejected the idea of having an 'Arab desk' in the World Jewish Congress and calling on the State of Israel to be neutral on the issue.[54]

## SUMMING UP

Besides anti-Semitism and the silence maintained by the free world in the face of the programme of the 'final solution' and its execution, political science must study the absence of Jewish sovereignty and power in order to comprehend the helplessness of the Jews in the Holocaust period. Amid all the difficulties, the World Jewish Congress tried to overcome the lack of sovereignty and power and to evolve a diplomacy of rescue on the international level. The advantage of having a roof organization of Jewish communities and organizations was already evident in the course of the war, an organization representing them faithfully and at the same time concerned with promoting the Zionist interest. The story of rescue operations in the Holocaust runs counter to all the rules of international diplomacy in an era of sovereign states and the contest for power and influence in international relations.

The special standing of the WJC as an organization representing the whole Jewish people and not only the Zionist movement enabled it to act in Arab countries and get Jews out at a time when the Arabs were engaged in armed conflict with the State of Israel and harboured a deep enmity against it. This situation has been maintained up to the present, despite the fact that the Zionism of the WJC is an open secret expressed in its constitution, and that it holds all its plenary sessions in Jerusalem. At the same time, its institutional separateness from the Zionist movement enables it to act inside the East European communities and in Morocco and even to enter into diplomatic negotiations inside the walls of the Kremlin as recognized representatives of the Jewish people, and discuss the exodus of the Jews of the Soviet Union to the State of Israel.

## NOTES

1. Theodore A. Couloumbia and James H. Wolfe, *International relations: Power and Justice*, Englewood Cliffs, New Jersey, 1982, pp.43–4.
2. Yoram Dinstein, *HaMishpat ha-beinle'umi v-ha-medina*, Tel Aviv, 1971, p.97.
3. On the debate between the idealistic and the rationalistic schools in international relations, see Edward H. Carr, *The Twenty Years' Crisis 1919–1939: An Introduction to the Study of International Relations*, London, 1939.

4. An outstanding representative of the rationalist school: Hans J. Morgenthau, *Politics Among Nations: The Struggle for Power and Peace*, 5th edition, New York, 1973. For his disputation regarding Woodrow Wilson and other idealists: *Scientific Man vs. Power Politics*, Chicago, 1946.
5. The Montevideo Agreement of 1933: Convention on Rights and Duties of States, 1933, *American Journal of International Law*, 1934 (28) Supp., 75, 76.
6. For example, requests from Yizhak Grinbaum and Gelber to Storch on behalf of the Jewish Agency, asking him to take action for Schutzpassen (certificates of protection) for the Jewish Agency leadership in occupied Europe (1944). Storch Archive, Document 146 C4.
7. Monty Noam Penkower, *The Jews were Expendable – Free World Diplomacy and the Holocaust*, Chicago, 1983, Ch. 9.
8. Elizabeth Eppler, 'Te'ulot hatsalah v-ezra b-shanim 1933–1945 m-ta'am ha-kongress ha-y'hudi ha-olami,' *Gesher*, 16 Sept. 1970, p.196. Martin Gilbert, *Auschwitz and the Allies*, New York: Holt, 1981, p.17.
9. Yehuda Bauer, *HaShoah – Hebitim histori'im*, Tel Aviv, 1982. On p.63 he defined the Riegner cable of 8 Aug. 1942 to New York and London as 'the first reliable and authoritative news of the mass murder of the Jews of Europe.'
10. Bernard Wasserstein, *Britania v-yahadut europa, 1939–1945*, Tel Aviv, 1983.
11. Arthur D. Morse, *While Six Million Died – A Chronicle of American Apathy*, New York, 1968.
12. Elizabeth Eppler, 'Pe-ulot hatsalah she ha-kongress ha-y'hudi ha-olami b-t'kufat ha-shilton ha-natsi,' in *N'sionot v-pe'ulot hatsala b-t'kufat hashoah*, Second international conference of Holocaust researchers, April 1974, *Yad Vashem*, Jerusalem, 1976, p.47.
13. Wasserstein, *op. cit.*, pp.242–3.
14. Haim Barlas, *Hatsala b-y'mei ha-shoah*, Tel Aviv, 1975, p.144.
15. Eppler, *Gesher*, p.186.
16. David S. Wyman, *The Abandonment of the Jews – America and the Holocaust – 1941–1945*, New York, 1984, p.54.
17. *Ibid.*, p.418, Note 98.
18. J.G. Stoessinger, *The Refugee and the World Community*, Minneapolis, 1965, Chap. 2.
19. *Ibid.*, pp.32–3.
20. Eppler, 'Pe-ulot hatsalah ...', p.41.
21. Nathan Eck, *Shoat ha-'am ha-y'hudi b-europa*, Jerusalem, 1976, p.306.
22. *Unity in Dispersion – A History of the World Jewish Congress*, New York, 1948, pp.197–8.
23. Penkower, *op. cit.*, pp.224–5.
24. Eliahu ben Elishar, *Kesher ha-hashmada – m'dini'ut ha-hutz shel ha-raikh ha-shlishi v-ha-y'hudim, 1933–1939*, Jerusalem, 1978, pp.170–7.
25. Henry L. Feingold, *The Politics of Rescue – The Roosevelt Administration and the Holocaust, 1938–1945*, New Jersey, 1970, p.60.
26. Ben Elishar, *op. cit.*, p.177.
27. Wasserstein, *op. cit.*, pp.202–3.
28. Feingold, *op. cit.*, p.279.
29. Wyman, *op. cit.*, p.251.
30. Penkower, *op. cit.*, p.286.
31. *Unity in Dispersion, op. cit.*, p.115.
32. Eppler, 'Pe-ulot hatsalah ...', p.42.
33. Wasserstein, *op. cit.*, p.41.
34. Feingold, *op. cit.*, p.115.
35. *Ibid.*, p.284.
36. Wyman, *op. cit.*, p.73.
37. Barlas, *op. cit.*, p.138.

38. Bauer, *op. cit.*, p.65.
39. Wyman, *op. cit.*, pp.175–6.
40. *Ibid.*, p.177.
41. Eppler, *Gesher*, p.185.
42. Wyman, *op. cit.*, pp.68, 77.
43. *Ibid.*, p.167.
44. *Ibid.*, p.172.
45. Report of the Political and International Affairs Departments 1957/1958. Geneva, July 1958, World Executive Committee WJC.
46. Report of the Political and International Affairs Departments 1958/1959. Fourth Plenary Assembly, Stockholm, August 1959, p.13.
47. *Ibid.*, p.14.
48. *Ibid.*, p.17.
49. *Ibid.*, p.11.
50. *Ibid.*, p.16.
51. *Ibid.*, p.17.
52. *Ibid.*, p.21. On the reasons for emigration (the economic motive and the emigration of the lower strata of uneducated people to Israel, while others went to France and the West), see Haim Y. Cohen, *Ha-gormim l-aliya me-artsot asia v-africka b'me'ah ha-esrim*, Jerusalem, 1968, pp.21–4.
53. Minutes of Meeting of World Executive Committee, WJC, Geneva, 20–23 July 1961, pp.20, 34.
54. Report of Political Department, World Executive Committee, Geneva, July 1958, p.24.

# 16

# Jewish Solidarity in the Integration of North African Jews in France

## Doris Bensimon

### A. PRELIMINARY OBSERVATIONS

1. From 1950 to 1975 France was the foremost country of Jewish immigration after Israel. Its Jewish population rose from approximately 180,000 people in 1945 in the wake of the Second World War, to 535,000 in 1980. As a result, French Jewry today comes third in size, after the USA and the USSR, among the Jewish communities of the Diaspora.
2. Since the mid-1950s, Jewish immigration into France has come mainly from three North African countries, the former French colonies of Algeria, Tunisia and Morocco. Some 235,000 Jews from these countries settled in France between 1950 and 1980. Two-thirds of this immigration was from Algeria and the other third from Morocco and Tunisia. Thus, when one takes into account the first and second generations of North African immigrants, the majority of the Jewish population in France today is Sephardic, 54 per cent of the Jewish population in the Paris region and 60 per cent of that in the provinces.[1]
3. This migration was different from all other Jewish migratory currents. In the course of colonization from the nineteenth century on, French Jewry developed more or less close relations with the Jewries of North Africa, with the degree of French influence varying from one country to another.

   Algeria was conquered in 1830. The Jews of France, in particular the Consistoire, speedily exerted themselves in bringing French civilization to Algerian Jewry. They became concerned with schooling and particularly with reforming the organization of ritual and that of local leadership. French Ashkenazi Rabbis were put in charge of organizing the indigenous rabbinate. At the same time, French Jewish notables campaigned to have the Jews of Algeria made French citizens. The Crémieux Decree of 1870 extended French citizenship to the Jews of Algeria. Thereafter these Jews went through a rapid process of Frenchification, though they preserved their distinct cultural identity.

Tunisia was made a French Protectorate in 1881. The French cultural influence was particularly strong in urban Jewish milieux in Tunisia, especially in the city of Tunis. Some 17 per cent of the Jews of Tunisia acquired French citizenship individually.[2]

Morocco did not become a French Protectorate until 1912. As early as 1862, however, the *Alliance Israélite Universelle* opened its first school, in Tetouan. Under international treaties in effect since the end of the nineteenth century,[3] the Jews of Morocco owed allegiance to the Sultan and could not acquire French citizenship as long as they resided in Morocco.

Nevertheless, in Morocco as in Tunisia new Frenchified elites came into being. The French Jews' organizations were implanted in these countries, occupying themselves mainly with education and social work. Ties were created between metropolitan French Jewry and the new elites. Thus the process of Frenchification was on the way in both these countries, and when the two became independent, a considerable fraction of the Jews there chose France. Emigration to France was recruited mainly in Morocco and to a somewhat lesser extent among the more Frenchified Jewish populations in Tunisia. When these Moroccan and Tunisian Jews reached France, most of them would be speaking French and would feel themselves French, even if they had regrets for a more than 2,000-year-old past.

When these North African Jews reached France, were they refugees? At all events, the Jews of Algeria – and Tunisian Jews of French nationality as well – were 'repatriates,' like all those who returned to France in the aftermath of de-colonization.

## B. BRIEF HISTORICAL RECAPITULATION

Since the end of the nineteenth century, French Jewry took in numerous Jewish immigrants, mostly of Eastern European origin. In the 1930s, these were joined by Jews from Germany and other countries of Central Europe. On the eve of the Second World War, of approximately 300,000 Jews living in France, one-third were more or less of veteran French stock and the other two-thirds were recent immigrants. The Jews of East European origin spoke Yiddish. They belonged to the popular strata – workers, small craftsmen, small traders. They had a variety of different cultural patterns. The Jews of French stock were better educated. They were integrated in the mid-level strata and the bourgeoisie and they were assimilated.

Tension was rife between the two groups: indigenous French Jewry had little regard for the immigrants, and in the context of rising xenophobia in the 1930s even accused them of causing the rise in anti-Semitism. The immigrants reproached the veteran Jews with their having assimilated. French Jewry with its internal divisions on the eve of the Second World War was hardly ready to confront the persecution ahead.[4]

2. It was persecution and the resistance to the German occupiers that finally brought the two groups together. Their *rapprochement* was consolidated at the end of the war by the creation of the *Conseil Représentatif des Israélites de France* (CRIF), which regrouped representatives of the older French Jewish organization and those of the immigrants.

In 1950, Dr. Modiano, President of the CRIF, who was of Sephardi origin, cast a severe, critical look at this solidarity born of the war:

> The Jews living in France are perhaps no less numerous than before, no less prosperous or intelligent, but they are no longer jointly occupied and preoccupied as Jews. The latest phase of their solidarity in a common destiny was produced *from the outside* and was in some sort a *negative solidarity* imposed on them by the hostile outside world, not by the collectivity itself, conscious of its personality and its aims, intellectual or political.[5]

3. In effect, after 1945 French Jewry slowly revived, trying first of all to ensure its material existence and if possible to forget the Holocaust. It was however at a crisis on the religious, intellectual and political planes. A rapid review of the Jewish press of the period reveals multiple critical judgments analogous to that of Dr. Modiano quoted above.

The immigration of Jews of East European origin having virtually dried up, the leaders of French Jewry pondered over the community in crisis and asked themselves where to look for renewal. Some of them had already turned towards North Africa from the beginning of the 1950s, but even then they had their doubts. What shook them was the poverty of the Jewish masses, especially in Morocco. The author and activist W. Rabi returned heart-sick from a journey in North Africa. 'The Mellah is our sin,' he cried, 'It must be destroyed!'[6] At the same time he was deeply impressed by the wealth of human resources in Moroccan Jewry: 'A young generation is in the making, full of ardour, sound, proud – but the ground they walk on is slipping under their feet. There is already a rising elite to be seen, strong, courageous, conscious of its responsibilities – but it is still groping its way forward against an undecided destiny.'

The French Jews also admired the vitality of the Jews of North Africa, the strength of their attachment to Jewish traditions. Armand Lunel wrote, after a journey in Algeria,[7]

> A living Judaism that I observe thus – the family that has remained patriarchal; religion practised from the bottom of the heart, in the home and in the synagogue; pride at being a Jew who feels himself Jewish and holds his head up high, always ready to give the riposte to snubs; a large solidarity at work at every level of society ... He who is free dedicates himself to helping whoever is not yet free; note is taken of everything concerning Zionism and the State of Israel; finally there is the adherence, the loyalty to tradition, and the consciousness of the moral values of Judaism, the obligation not only to safeguard this treasure but to enrich still more its unity and universality ... Is it not conceivable that the Jewry of metropolitan France, enfeebled and brought down by the years of terror, given over to indifference if not to conversion, might do well to take example from North African Jewry, where it might find some chance of rejuvenation by symbiosis?

These were prophetic words from the pen of a historian of the Jewish communities of Provence, written in 1954 before the massive emigration of the Jews of North Africa to France had begun.

4. Nevertheless, despite the intellectual and moral crisis, the principal Jewish institutions of France were rebuilt after the Second World War. We shall cite only some of them:

   (a) The local consistories and the central Consistory, their creation going back to Napoleon I. Their function is to organize religious life for French Jewry.

(b) The CRIF (*Conseil Représentatif des Israélites de France*), founded clandestinely at the end of 1943 to regroup the main Jewish organizations. It would emerge as the political spokesman of French Jewry for the French Government and international organizations.

(c) The FSJU (*Fonds Social Juif Unifié*) set up in 1948 for social and cultural planning, in some sort modernizing the community's philanthropic activity. As the official correspondent of the Joint Distribution Committee, it benefited from considerable subventions provided by U.S. Jews in the 1950s and 1960s, which enabled it to play an essential role in the reconstruction of the Jewish community in France and later on in taking in the Jews of North Africa.

## C. THE POLITICAL EVOLUTION OF NORTH AFRICA AND OF THE JEWRIES OF FRANCE AND NORTH AFRICA IN THE EARLY 1950s

1. Arab nationalist sentiments began to awaken first in Tunisia and Morocco. Pierre Mendès-France, Prime Minister of France and a Jew, prepared the way for the independence of these two countries in 1953 and 1954. There were some outbreaks of rioting, but the accession to independence of Tunisia (1955) and Morocco (1956) was carried through under relatively good conditions; both countries maintained very amicable relations with France, at least at the beginning.

2. The Jews in France were of course alive to the development of the political situation in North Africa. Some of them were concerned mainly over the future of France in these colonies and the fate of the French minorities after independence. Others were particularly worried over the future of the Jewish communities, not yet imagining that the Jews of North Africa when faced with de-colonization would opt massively for departure, though the first refugees, mainly Tunisians, were arriving in France in 1955.

   Jewish opinion in France, like French opinion in general, was divided between those who were in favour of decolonization, believing that every people had the right to independence, and those who wanted to see the colonial regime maintained, perhaps with some amelioration, especially in Algeria.

3. Opinion was divided among the Jews of North Africa themselves. The leaders of Tunisian and Moroccan Jewry thought at first that the future would not be too threatening. Having secured

assurances from President Bourguiba and Sultan Mohammed V, they believed they would have a part to play in these new nations. Indeed in the first decade after independence, many Jews in Tunisia and Morocco, better educated than the Arabs, participated in the economic life of both countries, and there were many who took the place in the administrations of the French who left.

In Algeria, the situation of the Jews was clearer but more complicated. They were French citizens, and the Algerian Arabs' war was a war against France. There were nevertheless Jews who decided to support the demands of the F.L.N. (*Front de Libération National*). Others went to join the O.A.S. – the extremist organization of the French of Algeria – in the last months of the war, confronting not only the F.L.N. but above all the government and army of France.

The official organizations of Algerian Jewry, for their part, counselled the strictest neutrality and affirmed the 'Frenchness' of the Jews as French citizens – a neutrality difficult to sustain. Caught between the F.L.N. and the O.A.S., a hundred Jews were assassinated (among 10,000 dead), including a number of rabbis. Were they killed because they were Jews or because they were French? Or because they were politically committed?

The F.L.N. for its part declared several times that the Jews of Algeria were Algerians and that their future would be secure in independent Algeria.[8] The Jews of Algeria, however, *en masse* declared themselves French and withdrew to metropolitan France when the war ended.

### D. THE WAVES OF NORTH AFRICAN IMMIGRATION TO FRANCE

1. Emigration to France of Jews of North African origin was not entirely a new phenomenon. It went back to the end of the nineteenth century and was accelerated between the wars. At that period, about 75 per cent of the Jewish immigrants came from the Mahgreb, mainly Algeria. In the aftermath of the Second World War, from 1945 to 1949, 47 per cent of the immigrants into the Paris region were Jews from North Africa.[9]
2. For all that, the massive emigration of North African Jews to France was the consequence of decolonization. From 1954 to 1959, some 75,000 Jews reached France from North Africa. They

already represented 30 per cent of all Moroccan and especially Tunisian immigration and 17 per cent of Algerian immigration. From 1960 to 1975, some 160,000 North African Jews settled in France: 66 per cent of the Tunisians and Moroccans and 73.5 per cent of the Algerians arrived after 1960. Since 1975, however, this immigration has virtually dried up.

This wave of immigration was not, however, distributed equally over these 15 years. Jews left Tunisia and Morocco in bigger or smaller groups according to fluctuations in the relations between their countries and France: every deterioration in political relations provoked new departures. The same was true between 1967 and 1973, when the waves of immigrants were a function of the wars between Israel and her Arab neighbours.

Among the 800,000 French of Algeria who returned to France in 1961 and 1962 there were some 100,000 Jews. Like all the other French, they were 'repatriates,' entitled to government assistance in settling in the metropolis.

3. In effect, the Algerian immigration must be distinguished juridically and by its composition from the Tunisian and Moroccan immigrations. Between 1950 and 1962, the quasi-totality of Algerian Jewry was transplanted to France while only 15,000 emigrated to Israel. Every social stratum was represented in this wave of emigration. The Jews of Algeria were French citizens and as such entitled to government assistance. This 'repatriation' constitutes a unique case in the history of Jewish migrations in the Diaspora. It was as citizens and not as refugees that these Jews 'returned' to France, even if this transfer meant their being psychologically uprooted.

The Tunisian and particularly the Moroccan immigrations, on the other hand, were selective. The more 'Frenchified,' the better educated, especially among the Moroccan Jews, chose France. The Tunisian immigration was more varied in com-position and took in part of the popular strata of Tunisian Jewry. A fraction of the Tunisian Jews had French nationality, but the 'foreigners' among the Moroccan and Tunisian Jews faced difficulties in obtaining residence and labour permits. It was they who constituted the chief potential clients of the Jewish com-munity's special services.

THE CONTEMPORARY PERIOD

E. RECEPTION

1. No one in the French Government or the Jewish organizations had foreseen the massive arrival of the 'repatriates' in mid-1962. It was believed that the French population of Algeria would withdraw at a slow rate, like the French of Tunisia and Morocco – some 100,000 souls a year over a period of perhaps ten years. So the summer months of 1962 were marked by indescribable disorder. Every 'repatriate' has a harrowing tale to tell of that exodus.

   Nevertheless, the government and the private institutions organized themselves fairly rapidly. Jewish solidarity was mobilized in its entirety. The F.S.J.U. played a main role in immediate reception, sending representatives and volunteers to all the shipping ports and airfields. It developed social services, which moreover collaborated with the governmental organizations to help people obtain lodgings and work, and to help the social cases, especially persons alone, the elderly, and the sick. Above all, the F.S.J.U. set up an Information and Orientation Service, where the arrivals could get useful information and legal advice. The main task of this Service was to build up relations rapidly between the established Jewish community and the new arrivals.

   The philosophy behind the activity of the F.S.J.U. and the other Jewish organizations was clear – it was necessary to avoid the mistakes that had been made in receiving former waves of immigration and to avoid the birth of tensions between the established community and the newcomers, by listening to them and helping them to the greatest possible extent.

2. The government for its part drew up a plan for distributing the repatriated population over the whole territory of France. This plan had only partial success, but it did bring about an important change in Jewish settlement on French soil. Before 1939, the Jews lived mainly in Paris, in Alsace-Lorraine and a few big cities. In 1957 there were Jewish communities in 128 localities; by 1966 this figure had risen to 293. In the course of the next decade, however, a new regrouping could be seen. At the beginning of the 1980s, an estimated 50 per cent of the Jewish population of France was living in the Paris region (especially in the new towns constructed around Paris from 1960 to 1970), 25 per cent in the Midi (south), and 25 per cent spread over the rest of France. The

creation of these new communities and the considerable increase in the Jewish population of the older communities would oblige the Jewish institutions to review their entire policy of religious and cultural activity.

## F. CHANGES IN JEWISH LIFE IN FRANCE

1. The Jews of North Africa would bring in fresh blood to revitalize the life of French Jewry. In the 1960s, the community's leaders feared accelerated assimilation with the break-up of families that had preserved cohesion and observance of Jewish tradition in North Africa. Families were indeed dispersed, but family solidarity was mostly preserved. Above all, new communities were built up swiftly and new organizations were created by the North African Jews themselves.

The Jews of North Africa presented a number of requests to the established Jewish institutions. First, they asked for assistance from the religious councils for the building of synagogues or the opening of halls for meetings and prayers. In North Africa, the synagogue was not only a place for religious services and study but also a meeting place, a centre of community life. The synagogues they asked for were put up as part of the programme of 'Consistory works' ('chantiers du Consistoire'). Furthermore, the North African Jews wanted to continue with prayers according to their own traditions which often incorporated significant local variations. Solutions were found in the older communities to meet this need too.

In North Africa *kashrut* was still widely observed, and kosher butcher's shops increased in number many times over. In Paris alone, their number rose from five before 1955 to over 150 today. Other requests were presented to the cultural organizations, which responded by setting up numerous community centres as well as many full-time Jewish schools. The media were all developed too – first the Jewish press, later radio and then television. There was also a perceptible flowering of Jewish culture on the literary and artistic plane and in scientific research.

Assimilated French Jewry obviously did not possess the necessary cadres for all this development. The North African Jews, however, organized rapidly, producing their own cadres: rabbis, teachers, cultural organizers, social workers. From the 1960s, most of the technical staffs of Jewish organizations were from North Africa. From the 1970s, the Jews of North Africa

began to be charged with important community responsibilities. The present Chief Rabbi of France was born in Algeria.
2. The revival of Jewish life in France is not confined to the community of North African origin. True, the North African Jews created their own special organizations, but it was more usual to find them acting inside institutions such as community centres where Sephardis and Ashkenazis meet and work together.

TABLE I
THE SOCIO-PROFESSIONAL DISTRIBUTION OF THE ACTIVE JEWISH POPULATION OVER 15 YEARS OF AGE[10]

| Place of enquiry/Origin | Socio-professional categories | | | | |
|---|---|---|---|---|---|
| | Liberal professions High officials | Craftsmen Traders | Mid-level cadres | Workers Personal service | Total |
| *Paris region* | | | | | |
| Algerians | 14.4% | 19.5% | 55% | 11.1% | 100% |
| Moroccans, Tunisians | 22% | 12% | 49% | 17% | 100% |
| Entire J. population of the Paris region | 25% | 21% | 43% | 11% | 100% |
| *The Provinces* | | | | | |
| Algerians | 14% | 22% | 48% | 16% | 100% |
| Moroccans, Tunisians | 12% | 18% | 58% | 12% | 100% |
| Entire J. population in the Provinces | 15% | 22% | 53% | 10% | 100% |

## G. THE INTEGRATION OF NORTH AFRICAN JEWISH IMMIGRANTS IN FRENCH SOCIETY

Twenty to twenty-five years after the mass arrival in France, socio-economic integration in French society is a success. The active Jewish population has joined the middle-level strata of French urban society.

This overall enquiry approach testifies to good socio-economic integration. It also shows the selectivity of the Tunisian and Moroccan immigrations into France: the more popular strata of these two Jewries went mainly to Israel. As against this, the transfer of practically all the Jews of Algeria is expressed in the proportionately higher ratio of middle and even popular strata.

This overall picture, however, masks the successes of individuals:

numerous Jews from North Africa are now eminent in the sciences and research as well as in literary and artistic life. Some fill positions in the very first rank in French political life.

The generation if not born at least bred in France did not experience any difficulties in the schools. Over and beyond compulsory schooling up to the age of 15, the results achieved have been impressive (see Table II).

TABLE II
PROPORTION OF STUDENTS AGED OVER 15 ATTENDING SECONDARY AND HIGHER SCHOOLS[11]

| Origin | Age groups 15–19 | 20–24 |
|---|---|---|
| *Paris region* | | |
| Algeria | 73% | 57% |
| Morocco, Tunisia | 82% | 56% |
| Entire J. population of the Paris region | 80% | 55% |
| Entire J. population in the Provinces | 93% | 62% |

Secondary and university studies not only attracted the Jewish population of the Paris region but they do so at a rate higher than in the big provincial cities. In relation to the overall population, the Jewish population, including the fraction born in North Africa, shows a clear lead. Indeed, the most optimistic forecasts see 80 per cent of the French youth aged 17 to 18 taking advanced studies by the year 2000.

The immigration of the Jews of North Africa has diversified the socio-economic structure of French Jewry; it thereby plays an important role in French socio-economic and socio-cultural life. Above all, the North African immigration has not only helped French Jewry become numerically the largest in Western Europe but has also revitalized Jewish life in France. Proudly affirming their Jewish identity, the North Africans have transfused a new vitality into a community in crisis.

Jewish solidarity? In the French case, one may allow oneself to wonder, who saved whom? Did the Jews of metropolitan France save the Jews of North Africa, or was it not rather the Jews of North Africa who saved their fellow Jews in France?

## THE CONTEMPORARY PERIOD

### NOTES

1. D. Bensimon, S. della Pergola, *La population juive de France: socio-démographie et identité*, Institute of Contemporary Jewry, the Hebrew University, Jerusalem, and Paris, 1984.
2. D. Bensimon-Donath, *L'intégration des Juifs nord-africains en France*, Paris-LaHaye, 1971, p.16.
3. *Ibid.*, p.16.
4. P. Hyman, *De Dreyfus à Vichy. L'évolution de la communauté Juive en France, 1906–1939*, Paris, 1985.
5. Cf., 'Une enquête sur la situation du judaïsme français,' in *Evidences*, Dec. 1950, No. 15, p.15.
6. W. Rabi, 'Le Mellah est notre péché,' in *Evidences*, March 1955, No. 46, pp.28–34.
7. A. Lunel, 'Esquisses nord-africaines,' in *Evidences*, Jan. 1954, No. 37, pp.27–30.
8. H. Chemouilli, *Une diaspora méconnue: les Juifs d'Algérie*, Paris, 1976, pp.268–71.
9. D. Bensimon, S. della Pergola, *La population juive de France*. All the figures cited from here on have been taken from this enquiry, carried out in the 1970s.
10. *Ibid.*, pp.188–9.
11. *Ibid.*, pp. 174, 176.

# 17

# Israeli Activity on Behalf of Soviet Jewry

## Benjamin Pinkus

In the years 1969 to 1985, 266,000 Jews emigrated from the Soviet Union, of whom 164,000 went to Israel.[1] This was an impressive achievement – perhaps unexpected too – with few precedents in the modern history of the people of Israel. It had of course numerous *accoucheurs*. The activists of the Zionist movement in the Soviet Union credited it to their heroic, self-sacrificing struggle. People in Israel responsible for activity on behalf of Soviet Jewry prided themselves that only their prudent and many-sided policy over a long period could have brought this about. Their opponents contend that if only the policy that they proposed had been adopted, the achievement could have been secured ten years earlier and with still better results. The bystander may be astounded at the miracle occurring before his eyes and take it for the work of providence, but the historian cannot jump to conclusions and must examine this complex and sensitive subject in balanced fashion and base his findings on all the relevant material at his disposal.[2]

The question of State of Israel activity on behalf of Soviet Jewry has in the past provoked bitter controversy, political sensibilities and 'wars of the Jews,' and it continues to do so today, though with lessened intensity. It is one of the main existential problems in the life of the State and the Diaspora since the Holocaust. The sensitivity of the issue and the exaggerated secrecy around it for many years had made it difficult until now to carry out unprejudiced, objective research.[3]

All research on Israeli activity on behalf of Soviet Jewry must address itself to a certain number of basic questions.

First of all, the primary question arises whether throughout the period under review Soviet Jews were indeed in any need of activity on their behalf on the part of the State of Israel and world Jewry, and if so whether all or most of them were interested in it.

Second, was the State of Israel really bound to lead the fight on behalf of Soviet Jewry, and was there indeed full and absolute identity of interests between the State and the Jews of the Soviet Union?

Third, it is important to understand the basic conception that prevailed in Israel in this matter and how it affected determining short- and long-term aims.

Fourth, it is necessary to examine the means to be adopted and the optimal conditions for reaching these aims, or in other words, what the most propitious historical constellation is for achieving the best results.

Finally, it is important to consider the central question whether it is at all possible to influence the Soviet administration and get it to adopt the policy desired by Israel and part of Soviet Jewry, and if so, how.

In order to answer these basic questions, we shall deal in concentrated résumé with the following points: Soviet Jews and the State of Israel; the obligation of the State of Israel towards Soviet Jewry; the policy of the State of Israel on behalf of Soviet Jewry in practice; and the results secured, as a basis for reaching conclusions for the future.

## 1. SOVIET JEWS AND THE STATE OF ISRAEL

The short historical period of 1947 to 1948 was one of decisive importance for understanding Soviet policy regarding the Jewish question, in all its many internal Soviet, Israeli and global components. In that period an exceptional correlation came into being: a positive attitude to Israel was accompanied by a cessation of attacks on Zionism, this without any immediate worsening of the situation of the Soviet Jews, a correlation which signified strengthening their national awakening, as we shall see later; the Soviet reaction to this awakening produced a negative correlation – a change of attitude towards Soviet Jews and in consequence thereof to the State of Israel as well. At first glance, the development of a correlation of this kind seems strange and even paradoxical, since the initial positive Soviet attitude to the State of Israel should impose a similar attitude to the Jews in the Soviet Union, in the knowledge that their fate was important to the State of Israel and to the Jews of the Diaspora. This also holds good in the opposite direction, that is to say, a favourable attitude to the Jews in the Soviet Union does not go together with unlimited hostile attacks on the State of Israel. In the national policy of the Soviet Union, however, a correlation of this kind is precisely 'natural.'[4]

Clearly it is not possible to treat the Jews in the Soviet Union as an organic entity all of a kind, with common desires, fears and expectations. Actually, substantial differences came into being between various sectors of the Jewish population under the influence of geographical, demographic and socio-economic factors. These differences are manifest in the different Republics and in the different communities (for example, Ashkenazi Jews and others), observant Jews and the non-religious, Zionists and anti-Zionists, and so forth.

Nonetheless there is no doubt that the trauma of the Holocaust, the exploded myth of the Soviet fraternity of peoples and the continued policy of anti-Semitic discrimination during the war and after it brought many Soviet Jews to a reawakened sense of their nationality. Soviet support for the establishment of the State of Israel in the years 1947 to 1948 greatly helped to channel this awakening along Zionist lines, as was tangibly demonstrated when Jews from all ranks of the people issued calls for action to help the new State fighting for its existence; there was volunteering for army service and organizing of Zionist activity. The thousands who crowded into the Great Synagogue in Moscow were only an external sign of the most secret sentiments in the hearts of Soviet Jewry.

Mordekhai Namir, a leading member and later the Minister heading the Israeli Legation, relates in his memoirs:

> We of course expected to attract attention, but what happened was far beyond anything we could have imagined. When we reached the street of the synagogue, we found ... thousands of people blocking the approach, but when they became aware of our presence they burst into loud applause with cries of 'Shalom' and 'hedad' (hurrah!) that went on and on ... When prayers ended, Golda was among the first to go out into the street and until all of us managed to get outside she was already hemmed in by the huge crowd swarming round her and shouting hurrahs, 'Next Year in Jerusalem,' and all sorts of endearments.[5] ... Some people would say it aloud and some would whisper to us, 'You've no idea how much Jewish pride and joy you've brought us. For the love of God, take us to Israel too – don't desert us.'[6]

In 1951 a member of the Israeli Legation was given a note from an anonymous Soviet Jew, which said, 'Shall we be there one day with our own kind? Do you think of us at all? ... Why do you never broadcast to us?'[7] Another report recounted, 'I was already in the street, when a young man passed close to me and whispered, without turning his head, "*Moadim lesimha!* [Happy Holiday] – Aliya, aliya!" and hurried away.'[8]

At the end of 1955 a piece written by Barukh Weissman in Kiev reached Israel:

> With trembling breath I whisper this short address and in my heart I ask myself – Is this the right address? The State of Israel – is this really and truly the right address? And my brother? Who knows my brother in the State of Israel? Each and every builder and defender of the new State with its many enemies – he is my brother. My words are addressed to him.[9]

A broader, more general Zionist awakening with new Jewish circles entering the arena – including young Jews till then far away from any Jewish or Zionist interest – came about in 1956 and 1957 as a result of the 1956 Sinai campaign (Operation Kadesh) as in 1948; collections were made for a Defence Fund and there was a rising interest in the subject of Israel and possibilities of aliya. Many Jews were influenced and moved to begin Zionist activity and seek contact with the State of Israel by the International Youth Festival which was held in Moscow in July and August 1957. Notes and postcards handed to members of the Israel delegation of *Halutzim* ('Pioneer Youth') said things like, 'Do you know about us?' 'Do you know how we live here?' 'Tell them about us, tell about us ...' 'We have not forgotten the Land of our Fathers ... Israel, thou our motherland, our shield, be hard as rock of flint!'[10]

In the many meetings that members of the Israeli Embassy, Israeli delegations and many tourists had with Soviet Jews, they were repeatedly appealed to and urged to have the State of Israel and world Jewry take energetic action on their behalf.

The Six Day War had a tremendous impact on Soviet Jewry in its swift transition from deep fear for the fate of Israel to boundless joy over the brilliant victory. Numerous were those who pressed Israel and world Jewry to mobilize in the fight for Soviet Jewry, and the pressures and appeals were reinforced with the arrival in Israel of the first Zionist activists from the Soviet Union in the years 1969 to 1971.

It is important to stress that the State of Israel became a symbol immediately on its establishment, representing the Soviet Jews' hope of a speedy solution to their grave problems. The creation of the State and the fact of its existence were however outstandingly static elements, something in the nature of a beacon in the darkness by which to chart and guide hopes and dreams, its victories something to be proud of; but the only chance of success they could see in their unequal struggle with the powerful Soviet regime was real, practical activity by the State of Israel on their behalf in every sphere and with all the means at its disposal. Israel's fight on their behalf in the international arena imbued them with the feeling that they were not entirely cut off and isolated in the field, that they had weighty support and backing.

How many Soviet Jews nurse Zionist or pro-Israel sentiments today it is hard to estimate, but in the 1970s they represented from a quarter to a third of the two million Jews in the Soviet Union, that is, all those who wanted to get exit permits for Israel even if they did not intend to settle in Israel.

We have no data at all on the attitude to the State of Israel and to world Jewry of the greater part of the Jews living in the Soviet Union, the 'silent majority,' and it is therefore difficult to know how that majority regards Israel's activity on its behalf. In the first place, a Moscow activist in the Zionist movement, V. Meniker, thinks that there is no one who is indifferent to the State of Israel, 'and that for all sorts of reasons – even for the simple reason that everyone reads the newspapers.'[11] At all events, clear distinctions can be drawn between a number of groups with different attitudes to their national identity and therewith to the State of Israel. The broadest group quantitatively is that of assimilated Jews who have already gone through the process of linguistic and cultural adjustment and aspire to cut themselves off completely from Jewry, but who are still tied to it by their umbilical cord, both because of the existence of their registration in their identity certificates and because of the fact that the hostile environment does not recognize them as an integral part of itself. The assimilated Jew would certainly prefer to completely ignore the very existence of the State of Israel if it were only possible, but in the majority of cases he is not hostile to it; sometimes he is even proud of it and benefits from its struggle on his behalf. A clear expression of this attitude is to be found in Semyon Lipkin's poem, 'The Ally' (a play on the Russian 'y' and 'and', and 'ally' for 'conjunction' ), which the censorship allowed to appear, apparently by mistake, in the literary periodical, *Moskva*, in December 1968. It reads:

In it lies buried my fear, your fear/ It's our ally and support/ the 'yud'./ In the Asian Sea, I'm told, there's a people known by the letter 'yud'./ Without conjunction, the dictionary would be silenced,/ the world would go off the tracks,/ There'd no longer be humanity/ Without the people whose name reads – 'yud'.[12]

The 'national Communist' formed the next biggest Jewish group, and it had the most hostile attitude to Zionism and the State of Israel, but its strength declined sharply and it is doubtful whether it has much influence in the Jewish public in the Soviet Union today. The third group, the traditional-religious one, even if it is not Zionist in the sense of wanting or aspiring to emigrate to Israel, without a doubt welcomed Israeli and world Jewry's activity on its behalf, since it enjoys limited religious rights today thanks to this fight.

## 2. THE STATE OF ISRAEL'S OBLIGATION TO SOVIET JEWRY

The State of Israel's obligation towards the Jews of the Soviet Union – and especially to Jews in dire straits who are persecuted because of their being Jews – is something many-sided. It draws sustenance from a variety of sources and of levels of legitimization. It is first of all the product of a very long history of the sufferings of the Jewish people in their dispersion, which engendered a constant need to rescue Jews persecuted for their faith and for their belonging to the people of Israel. The Holocaust of the Jews of Europe and the trauma it has bequeathed to world Jewry, which failed to render the assistance so urgently needed, have reinforced the perception of this need since the end of the Second World War.

Next, the essence of Judaism from the earliest times, its deep-rooted traditions and consecrated laws governing personal conduct, all perpetuate the idea of the duty of rescue, aid to one's neighbour, redemption of prisoners, and enshrine the rule, 'Everyone of Israel stands surety for everyone else.'

Third, the Zionist ideology was built and exists purely and solely on the basis of the unity of the Jewish people, which can survive as a nation by the ingathering of the exiles in a Jewish State. Zionism, then, in essence is to find a speedy solution to the dichotomous existence of a Jewish State and a Jewish Diaspora, with a supreme common interest outweighing the particularist and temporary interests of each separate Diaspora.

Fourth, an explicit and binding legal commitment exists in constitutional enactments of the State of Israel in the years 1948 to 1952; the Declaration of Independence, the Law of the Return, and the Law on the Status of the Zionist Federation and the Jewish Agency for Palestine. In the debate on the Law on the Status of the Zionist Federation, David Ben-Gurion declared:

> The proposed law that is being submitted to you is no ordinary law, but one of the basic central laws making this State specifically a State with a mission to serve as an instrument and a forge for the redemption of Israel. The Law therefore contains directives of principle without the formal content of a law that lays down punishments and penalties for this or that breach or contravention of its provisions; but these directives express the special historic significance of the State of Israel and they establish the link between the State and the people of Israel. They also endow the World Zionist Federation with State rights within the State of Israel.[13]

Finally, there is a clear State obligation, affirmed in the programmes of the Zionist Parties in Israel and part of the basic line of all the successive governments, the obligation to assist persecuted Jews wherever they may be and bring them to Israel.

Israel sees itself, then, as responsible for the fate of Jews everywhere in the world and appears openly as the natural defender of Jews in distress and under duress. It is clear that there will always be a gap between the general obligation, even the most consecrated and confirmed in law, and current policy in practice on a specific issue. It is important, therefore, to go into how this obligation was conceived by the State of Israel's policy-makers.

In practice three central personalities laid down Israeli policy on Soviet Jewry in the years from 1948 to 1974: David Ben-Gurion, as leader of the largest political party, Prime Minister and Minister of Defence, in the years 1948 to 1963; Golda Meir, by virtue of her closeness to Ben-Gurion, as the first Israeli Minister to Moscow, Foreign Minister and Prime Minister at different periods; and Shaul Avigur in direct, sole charge of everything concerning Soviet Jewry, officially until 1969, but in practice after that date as well. As against this, other foreign ministers at different times – Abba Eban and Yigal Allon – had little influence in this matter; Moshe Sharett, Foreign Minister from 1948 to 1956, did have some influence, mainly when he served as Prime Minister from 1954 to 1955.

The basic approach of Ben-Gurion to the subject of Israel–Diaspora relations was already essentially functional in the period of the Mandate and even more strongly so after the establishment of the State. Declared Ben-Gurion:

> The restoration of the State of Israel is the greatest event in Jewish history in the last three thousand years. ... The advantage of the State over the [Zionist] Federation is not only its State power and its international status and in the profound influence of all parts of the Jewish people wherever they may be; its advantage is one of substance and it existed before the establishment of the State.[14]

He did not deny that the State of Israel was in fact the creation of the Jewish people and created for its sake, he even accepted the premise that the State is not the final aim of Zionism – according to him, the final aim is the ingathering of exiles. All the same, he contended that the State is superior to the Exile functionally in virtue of its being a sovereign body with instruments and means that were never ready to hand for Jews in the Exile. 'A State is the greatest asset the Jewish people as a whole now has, apart from its being the individual hope of thousands of Jews who aspire to build up the State and be built by it.'[15] Since the fate of the Jews in the Exile is closely bound up with the existence of Israel, they have to assist it financially, economically and politically, but only by personal fulfilment through *aliya* would they be acting as true Zionists. Ben-Gurion did not conceive of *aliya* as first and foremost a means of rescuing Jews but as a State of Israel enterprise for its own reinforcement, whence it followed that as long as the Exile continued to exist, it would have to serve as a reservoir of forces to meet the needs of the State.

From time to time in his public appearances and in articles, Ben-Gurion dealt specifically with the question of the Jews in the Soviet Union. Before the establishment of the State, he made various efforts to reach agreement with the Soviet leadership on creating ties with the Yishuv in Palestine and organizing *aliya*. For this purpose he went to the 1923 Agricultural Exhibition in Moscow, and in 1933 and 1934 he negotiated with Soviet representatives, all without result. He met the Soviet Ambassador to Britain, Ivan Maisky, in London and Palestine during the Second World War.

Ben-Gurion laid stress on the disturbing fact that only one national entity in the Soviet Union – the Jews – was 'sentenced to death nationally and spiritually, not because of any specially unfavourable attitude towards the Jews on the part of the Soviet regime, but because of the objective reality of a dispersed people without a mother-country, a people that the foreign ruler takes no account of.'[16] This is how he evaluated the situation in May 1951:

> At this time, it's as though there's no prospect for aliya of the Jews of Russia, but we have no firm reason to abandon the hope that it will yet be granted this Jewry to play its part in the life of the State and of the entire Jewish people; and if the gates are opened in Russia and the Jews are allowed to emigrate, we can expect to have a Yishuv of four million within ten years – and even if we do reach that, it will be a minority of the Jewish people.[17]

In the 1950s however, the prospects for this *aliya* seemed to him feeble in the extreme:

> We have not despaired and we do not despair of this tribe of Jews – let us hope that the day will come when Soviet Jews will be permitted to play their part in the restoration of their historic motherland, but at this day and hour – and there is no knowing how long this day and hour will last – it's as though Russian Jewry did not exist from the viewpoint of the State of Israel.[18]

Taking into account Ben-Gurion's pragmatic approach to politics, according to which one need not occupy oneself with something that is not yet ripe and therefore not on the cards, we can conclude that in the 1950s the question of Soviet Jewry was not yet on the order of the day in any immediate, clearly defined form. At the same time, Ben-Gurion felt for the Jews in the Soviet Union and saw their forced isolation from the State of Israel as the great tragedy of the Zionist movement. He encouraged the people who were occupied with the subject of Soviet Jewry, he decided on sending Golda Meir as Minister to the Soviet Union, and he was always on the alert in this matter.

Golda Meir was deeply affected by the unexpected and moving mass welcome that was accorded her by some 50,000 Jews at the Rosh HaShana High Holidays immediately after her arrival in Moscow.[19] Lou Kadar, who served with Golda Meir in the Legation at the time, relates: 'At the sight of these Jews, tears streamed from my eyes. Golda didn't cry, but I could easily feel what was going on in her heart. ... She was bound to this Jewry with every bone in her body and all the days of her life – this renewed encounter with this Jewry was an ineffable experience for her.'[20] However, Golda Meir confessed a score of years later: 'Since then and till today I blame myself for daring to think that from the Jewish point of view there were no longer any Jews in the Soviet Union.'[21] It appears then that the 'Moscow experience' did not directly influence Israel's policy and did not even lead to a revision of the usual conception of the matter.

Shaul Avigur, Russian in origin, like Ben-Gurion and Golda Meir, was already active in the affairs of Soviet Jewry in the early 1920s when he volunteered to go to the Soviet Union as a Zionist emissary. His initiative was rejected by Berl Katznelson. During the Second World War, Shaul Avigur was posted to Teheran: from his base there he was active in the affairs of Soviet Jewry, and after the war he was responsible for the organized undertaking of the *bricha* (escape) from Eastern Europe.

Avigur's views on the situation of the Soviet Jews after the war and his assessment of their national and Zionist identification did not differ basically from what Ben-Gurion said: 'The Soviets have already succeeded in getting the younger generation away from the Jewish people. But we have to do what we can. Whether anything will come of it or not, no one can foresee.' Avigur defined the policy to adopt regarding Soviet Jewry as one of 'Cast your bread upon the waters' and 'Keep the lamp burning.'[22] He noted that 'Even if there weren't any immediate results or any results at all, we couldn't stand aside – we had to use every means at our disposal to strengthen the national consciousness of the Soviet Jews.'[23] In 1977, in one of his rare interviews with the Press, Shaul Avigur said:

> People today are wise after the event. When we – my friends and I – began the fight on behalf of Soviet Jewry after the establishment of the State, we knew that the story did not begin with us, that there were others before us in the fight, but the circumstances were such that for a long time it seemed 'a lost battle.' We tackled the problems empirically, cautiously, and we don't have to be ashamed of this caution.[24]

Dr. Nahum Goldmann did not, it is true, have any official role in the State of Israel, but by virtue of his two positions, head of the Zionist movement and President of the World Jewish Congress, he was in close contact with the people in Israel who were concerned with the cause of Soviet Jewry. In the 1950s he was in entire harmony with them, but from the beginning of the 1960s there was increasingly wide disagreement between them, and it is therefore important to explain his stand.

Dr. Goldmann was already active in the early 1930s in making contact with the Soviet Union. In Geneva, where he lived, he met high-ranking Soviet diplomats and came away from these contacts in an optimistic frame of mind. Already then Dr. Goldmann favoured quiet diplomacy and he was not prepared to change this position of his later on. He wrote:

> Many Jewish extremists hold the view that there is no prospect of securing any alleviations for the Jews living in Russia. They conclude that we must renounce all efforts to maintain this community and concentrate on immigrants. I rebel against this analysis that signifies, after the Nazi tragedy, giving up at one go more than a fifth of the Jewish people. I have always believed that there can be Jewish life even under the communist regime.[25]

Dr. Goldmann aimed at reaching an agreement with the Soviet authorities under which Jews would be granted the same conditions as in a number of East European States: cultural and religious institutions and the possibility of representation on an international Jewish body like the World Jewish Congress. According to Goldmann, one had to beware of exerting pressures on the Soviet Union: 'There should be no use of these damaging political pressures – it is impossible to compel the Russians to do something, but mostly it is possible to persuade them. There has been a great deal of exaggeration in accusation of anti-Semitism against the Soviet Union. ... The Senator Jackson business was fine proof that the Russians mean to remain masters of the situation.'[26] We shall see later how this stand of Dr. Goldmann's affected his cooperation with the Israeli administration in activity on behalf of Soviet Jewry.

Right-wing opposition parties in Israel condemned this official conception and categorically called for a determined, energetic activist policy on behalf of Soviet Jewry, but when they took office in 1977 they in fact went on with the same old policy of the Alignment governments. Furthermore they left untouched the 'Liaison Office' headed by Nehemia Levanon, whom they had so vigorously attacked earlier on.

It appears that the change in the accepted conception has taken place only recently; it was expressed by Shimon Peres when he declared that if he had to choose between diplomatic relations with the Soviet Union or *aliya*, he would choose the latter. Moreover, he appears prepared to link a solution to the problems of Soviet Jewry with a general political Middle East settlement that would involve co-operation with the Soviet Union.

## 3. PRACTICAL POLICY IN STATE OF ISRAEL ACTIVITY ON BEHALF OF SOVIET JEWRY

The term 'State of Israel' is used here to indicate the central institutions of the regime, such as the Knesseth, the Government and the Presidency, the political parties and the public organizations acting in the matter of Soviet Jewry, as well as the mass media, whether public or private, with their importance in shaping public opinion.

We shall briefly review the various sub-periods in the State of Israel activity on behalf of Soviet Jewry and describe the changes that occurred in these periods.

### A. 1948 to 1952 – *the period of diplomatic activity*

In the years 1948 to 1952, when the '*aliya B*' operation ended and the organization stopped functioning, no other State institution was created in its place which could have organized activity for Soviet and East European Jewry. Such an institution was sorely needed, given the special situations of the Jews in these countries and the need to deal with the matter in special, unconventional ways and methods. The policy on Soviet Jewry was formed by the government on the strength of information and proposals brought from Moscow and elaborated in the Foreign Ministry in Jerusalem. The policy was a cautious one in the fullest sense. In the frequent contact that the Legation people had with high-ranking Soviet officials, including the Foreign Minister, the question of the Jews in the Soviet Union was never brought up openly or clearly. The central issue from Israel's point of view – the possibility of Jewish emigration from the Soviet Union – was generally on the lines, 'The State of Israel is in need of manpower and it would be fine if those who wanted to were enabled to emigrate to Israel from the countries of Eastern Europe as well.' The first time that the question of *aliya* was raised more openly was when Foreign Minister Moshe Sharett met Soviet Foreign Minister Andrei Vyshinsky at the UN Assembly in Paris in 1950.

Furthermore, a great deal was already known of the mass arrests in the Jewish population, the extreme anti-Semitic campaign waged on the pretext of combating nationalists and cosmopolitans, and the total liquidation of all the institutions of Jewish culture, but this shocking news was not published clearly and emphatically in Israel and the world. No action at all was taken against Stalin's anti-Jewish policy. Until November 1952 the desperate situation of Soviet Jewry was brought up only two or three times in the Knesseth. In April 1949, Knesseth Member Ben-Eliezer of 'Herut' asked the Finance Minister: 'Is it true that the Government has vetoed sending parcels to Russia?'[27] In August 1950, Knesseth Member Hillel Kook (also of 'Herut') asked for a debate for the first time on the subject of Soviet Jewry. He said:

> I want to bring up a very painful and tragic question for discussion – especially tragic because in our public reality it has been designated 'a sensitive question.' It is, in fact, very sensitive but a tragic question will not be solved by the traditional methods of going to eminent persons with solicitations, for in this area the government is conducting its business in the best traditional Galut lines of appeals etc. – and with the same results.[28]

The stormy debates on the question of accepting restitution payments from Germany also involved the subject of Soviet Jewry. Golda Meir, then Labour Minister, speaking in this debate, said:

> Every time Knesseth member Riftin or one of his fellow party members comes up to this dais to speak on a political issue, I wait for it. All the compliments and all the right and privileges go to the Soviet Union, but why is it forbidden, why do you restrain yourselves and refrain from saying a single word, one very weak and moderate word, about the millions of Jews who live there and who cannot say a single word on the matter before us? ... Perhaps in the middle of all they've got there, and all the heartache they've got there, perhaps there's one more thing they have – their belief that we have not forgotten.[29]

Zalman Aranne, Chairman of the Foreign Affairs and Defence Committee, replied to the debate:

> The aliya of Soviet Jewry is a large question, one bound up with the fate of Russian Jewry, and for over thirty years now, ever since the Revolution, this Jewry and its fate have been the crux of Hebrew history, not on account of any discrimination or anti-Semitic tendencies [sic!]. A few months ago, we heard 'Let my people go!' from the lips of the Prime Minister of Israel, when he spoke at Afikim and raised the demand for aliya of the Jews of the Soviet Union.[30]

In the Knesseth on 27 February 1952, David Ben-Gurion read out an important Government of Israel Note in response to a Soviet missive of 8 December 1951. Paragraph 8 of the Israeli Note stated, 'As is well-known to the Government of the Soviet Union, the Return of the Jews to their historic homeland represents the central objective of the State of Israel. ... In this connection, the Government of Israel calls on the Soviet Union to enable Jews of the Soviet Union who wish to do so to emigrate to Israel.'[31]

In the wake of this communication, there was a stormy debate in the Knesseth between the Minister for Education and Culture, Ben-Zion Dinaburg (Dinur) and Knesseth Member Arieh Altman of 'Herut.' Dinur said, 'I must express astonishment and stupefaction over Knesseth Member Altman's manner of speech, his irresponsibility and the abounding arrogance with which he permitted himself to speak of the Jews of the Soviet Union. This is no way to serve the cause of Soviet Jews' *aliya* to Israel and to promote the cause of the people of Israel.'[32] Altman answered:

> I did not say that the Government was not demanding aliya for Soviet Jewry. ... I know that people talk about it all the time – that was not what I complained about. What I said was that it was time we understood that all direct, polite appeals for decades have brought no results. ... The Jews there are surprised at the fact that we here in the free countries do not raise our voices frankly and constantly in order to raise the problem of their emigration ... I know this psychology of yours and this tradition that it is forbidden to speak out aloud because it can do harm. This damaging system has not borne fruit in this area nor in any other.[33]

In this period, three basic attitudes crystallized in the Knesseth and in the public sphere on what policy ought to be adopted regarding the Soviet Union. The attitude of the extreme left (at that date MAKI and MAPAM) was one of adamant opposition to all discussion of the subject of Soviet Jewry. The right wing, mainly the 'Herut' movement, insistently demanded debate and action. The midway approach was that of MAPAI and the religious parties, who remained content with the official policy that was being carried out.

It is important to note that in these years, 1948 to 1952, the question of the Jews of the Soviet Union was not even raised in the international arena, including the UN bodies. Nor was any special activity undertaken in these years by public organizations in Israel concerned with the affairs of Soviet Jewry. One such association had been in existence since 1929; this was *Magen*, a company headed by B. West and Sh. Aharonov set up to aid Jews persecuted on account of their being Jews or for their Zionism and to deal with everything pertaining to the Jews in Soviet Russia. Another was the Organization of Jews from Russia. One of the main activities of *Magen* was its appeal to the 1951 Zionist Congress to include a clause in its decisions calling for *aliya* from Russia and the release of 'prisoners of conscience.' *Magen* even published a news-sheet devoted to Soviet Jewry, poor in content and appearing only irregularly.

The main reasons for this lack of deeds lay in the objective circumstances of the State of Israel immediately on its foundation, when the main battle front was military and economic, and the active Soviet policy favourable to Israel and the Soviet support for Israel in the international arena rendered it difficult to tackle the matter of Soviet Jewry because of Soviet sensibilities on this issue. Finally the pessimistic conception entertained by Israeli leaders, which we have already described, set the pattern of activity. Thus we see that there was a clear contradiction in this period between the immediate interests of the State of Israel and those of Soviet Jewry, and what was decisive in the end was the need to 'maintain the State of Israel,' as Golda Meir put it.

## B. 1953–1959 – forging the tools and shaping policy

At the beginning of 1953 a special body was set up of people from the former organization for 'Aliya B' headed by Shaul Avigur, for the purpose of concentrating all the activities connected with *aliya* of Jews from Eastern Europe. Up to 1955 this body worked alongside the Prime Minister's Office. In 1954 Shaul Avigur was posted to Europe to be closer to the area concerned. He established two focal points for action on behalf of the Jews of the Soviet Union and East European countries, one in Zurich and the other in Vienna.[34]

Soviet foreign policy veered around sharply with regard to Israel in 1955 and it was as a result of this and not, it would seem, by chance that there was a significant turning-point in Israeli State organization with regard to Soviet Jewry. A new body named 'Bar' was established with a double aim: (a) to carry out a continuing information campaign in Israel and abroad to keep the world reminded of the existence of the problem of Soviet Jewry; and (b) to handle material coming from the Jews in the Soviet Union via the

Israeli Embassy in Moscow and otherwise.[35] This body operated jointly with the security forces, but after a year Shaul Avigur was appointed to head the body and made responsible solely to the Prime Minister. Information activity in the West was put in the charge of Dr. Binyamin Eliav. After much discussion, the body dealing with Soviet Jews was attached formally to the Foreign Ministry, with the title 'Liaison Office.' Because of the unnecessary and sometimes excessive secrecy around the activity of this office, it was called variously in the press: 'the nameless office,' 'Avigur's office,' 'Lebanon's office,' and the like. It is worth noting in this connection that West Germany, which also dealt with immigration of its nationals from the Soviet Union and Eastern Europe, put activities for this purpose in the hands of a public organization like the Red Cross and dealt with the matter officially in the Interior Ministry, without any veil of secrecy like that in Israel.

The top people working in this body had generally been connected with 'Aliya B' and the *Bricha* ('escape'); they included people who had been released from Soviet imprisonment and had emigrated to Israel, as well as Foreign Ministry officials. Jews from Israel, the USA, France and England – journalists, authors, scientists – were mobilized for information activity abroad, in full and close cooperation with Jewish institutions – the Zionist movement, the Jewish Agency, the World Jewish Congress and others.

The policy laid down for the information campaign covered the following points:

1. To make the problem of Soviet Jewry an international moral and legal problem by stressing the demands for cultural and religious rights for Soviet Jews and the right of family reunion. (The right to 'repatriation' was not brought up at all before the early 1980s.)
2. To separate the problem of Soviet Jewry from the 'cold war' between the Power blocs.
3. To maintain absolute secrecy on the connection between Israel and the people active on behalf of Soviet Jewry.
4. To supervise the material published so as not to leave an opening for accusations of falsification, unreliability or misleading propaganda.
5. To operate indirectly through leading Western figures, scientists, men of letters and statesmen.

The central aim was to get material on Soviet Jewry into the mass media by every possible means, through journalists and through independent newspapers and by publishing periodicals such as *News-Letter, Jews in Eastern Europe, The Jews and the Jewish People*. All three appeared in England from the end of the 1950s. Another method was to give material to journalists for them to publish in their own name. In order to keep the issue in the public eye, questions on Soviet Jewry were put to Soviet representatives all over the world and in UN bodies.

In February 1953 as soon as the Soviet accusations against Jewish doctors were published and relations were broken off between the Soviet Union and Israel, the Israeli Government made its first important open move. Berl Locker, Chairman of the World Zionist Movement, called a conference of leaders of the Israeli medical profession, members of the Medical Association executive, so as to start a series of protests from international medical organizations. Locker went to the US to get a conference of world Jewry convened in Switzerland in the first half of March to 'protest against the false accusations in Prague and Moscow' and to arouse world opinion on the grave dangers involved in these false charges. The conference was cancelled with the death of Stalin and the consequent hopes for a change in Soviet policy, but the very fact that there had been this idea of a conference of world Jewry and preparations had begun was of great importance.[36]

On 30 August 1953 a meeting was held in the home of Foreign Minister Moshe Sharett to discuss policy on Eastern Europe. It was decided that the major part of the activities connected with the Soviet Union should be carried on in the Western capitals and in the UN.[37] In spite of this, Israeli activity in the UN in the 1950s was limited. Special importance attached to the appearance of Golda Meir in 1953 at the debate on racial and religious discrimination, when she harshly criticized the policies of the Soviet Union and the East European countries towards the Jewish minorities in their midst.[38]

In the international arena the main activity undertaken was mobilizing intellectual circles in the West, including Communist Parties there, to bring their influence to bear on the Soviet Union. What can be seen as a striking success in this field was the concern displayed by the leaders of the French Socialist Party when they raised the subject of Soviet Jewry at length during their meeting with Soviet leaders in May 1956.[39] So too, the meeting between the heads of the American Jewish Committee and the Soviet Deputy Premier in New York in January 1959,[40] as we see, showed that policy in these important fields developed very slowly and was limited enough.

Without any mobilization of large financial means or any real, energetic drive, it was not possible to get better results.

The first full, proper Knesseth debate on Soviet Jewry took place only at the beginning of 1953 in the wake of the Slansky trial and the 'doctors' affair.' This time the majority of the House was in agreement, except for MAPAM, which was trapped in a very difficult and embarrassing situation, and MAKI, which simply stuck to the line of total defence of Soviet policy.[41] In May 1954, Moshe Sharett, both Prime Minister and Foreign Minister at the time, admitted, 'We are not prolix with declarations on *aliya* of Jews from the Soviet Union,'[42] but in November of the same year he was saying, 'The demand for *aliya* of Jews from the Soviet Union and its allies is on the order of the day all the time. For the moment we can only point to a small alleviation that has taken place this year regarding *aliya* of elderly parents of Israeli citizens.'[43]

No less significant than activity in Israel and in the international arena on behalf of Soviet Jewry was the direct assistance Israel extended to Jews in the Soviet Union. One of the important areas was providing information that Soviet Jews lacked about Israel and the Jewish people. Embassy activity in disseminating knowledge about Israel had been nil even in the 'finest hour' of Soviet–Israeli relations and it was certainly limited in the 1950s. It was clear then that ways and means had to be found to remedy this, such as utilizing Jewish delegations and tourists. One of the main means at Israel's disposal was radio broadcasting, but owing to the cautious official policy there were no foreign Russian-language broadcasts on the Voice of Israel. Early in 1957 Yosef Avidar, Israeli Ambassador to Moscow, proposed a one-off broadcast in Russian on Israel's Day of Independence. The policy was described in the following terms: 'You have to appear slowly, slowly, like a mouse poking its nose out of its hole slowly so as not to frighten people by appearing suddenly ... Israel must be especially cautious if it wants to reach the Jews in the Soviet Union.'[44] The primary aim was to impart knowledge about Israel and the Jewish people and certainly not to bring up questions touching the existence of Soviet Jewry or the internal affairs of the Soviet Union. Until the end of 1961 there were broadcasts only on the Sabbath Eve, on the Sabbath and the end of the Sabbath; only in the early 1960s was this expanded to four times a week. A periodical in Russian for distribution in the Soviet Union, *Israel Herald*, began to appear in May 1959.

In sum, the official Israeli activity on behalf of Soviet Jewry in this period can be described as preparatory organizing, without any wide echo or any spectacular success.

In the public field, the *Magen* association continued with its current activities. A new 'league' was founded in December 1958 called *Ma'oz* (Fortress) with the aim of alerting Jewish and world opinion to the tragic situation of Soviet Jewry. The organs of this association were a general conference, a national committee (representing the association publicly and conducting its affairs between conferences) and a national secretariat. Its first chairman was Shabtai Beit-Zvi. In 1959 the association published its first news sheet. In March of that year, *Ma'oz* organized its first mass meeting in Tel Aviv.

In the late 1950s and early 1960s, institutes for research and documentation on Soviet Jewry were set up on Shaul Avigur's initiative and with financial support from his office. The Israeli Historical Society, headed by Professor Ben-Zion Dinur and Israel Halpern, began to concern itself with this subject. An Association for Research on East European Jewry was founded to gather material, disseminate information and conduct research on Soviet Jewry; it was directed in the 1960s by Shmuel Ettinger, Mordekhai Altschuler and Benjamin Pinkus. Abroad, information centres were set up in the USA, Britain, Italy and the Argentine which distributed the material on Soviet Jewry sent to them from Israel.

*C. 1960–1968 – transition to organized international activity*

The turning-point for the policy of the State of Israel and some of the world Jewish organizations in the fight in the international arena on behalf of Soviet Jewry came in 1960, with the convening of an international conference on the situation of Soviet Jewry in Paris on 15 September of that year. Among the 40 personalities who took part in the conference were Daniel Mayer, a former French Government minister and President of the international League for the Defence of Human Rights, who was chosen chairman of the conference, Dr. Nahum Goldmann, André Blumel, Martin Buber, and others.[45] People who gave their support, though they did not take part in the conference, included Jean-Paul Sartre, Bertrand Russell and the Italian Communist Senator Umberto Teraccini. Preparations for this conference began early in 1960; there was close cooperation between Shaul Avigur's Office and Dr. Nahum Goldmann's World Jewish Congress, with assistance from André Blumel, one of the leaders of the French Zionist movement. While preparations were going on, the Soviet Union brought increasing pressure to bear both on the organizers and on the prospective participants in order to prevent its being held. This pressure, in the form of both promises and threats, had its effect on some leaders of American Jewish organizations who had even before then contended that Israel was creating an artificial problem about Jews in the Soviet Union in order to get increased *aliya* to Israel. Dr. Goldmann changed his mind and was ready to cancel the conference or postpone it, and it was only with the intervention of Israeli Prime Minister Ben-Gurion at a meeting in Sede-Boker with everyone concerned that the decision was made final to hold the conference on the date set.[46] Similar conferences, though with more limited representation and in national settings, were held in October 1963 in Italy, in October 1964 in France, and in 1965 in Sweden with the cooperation of men of learning from all the Scandinavian countries.[47] These conferences evoked a wide response, particularly in intellectual circles of the European left-wing parties.

An equally important field of action was the United States. The first attempt to influence the administration and get it involved in the issue of Soviet Jewry was made during the presidency of Kennedy. Israeli representatives were greatly assisted in this by American Jewish personalities like Supreme Court Justice Arthur Goldberg and Senators Jacob Javits and Abraham Ribicoff. Judge Goldberg was even an outstanding supporter of a change-over from quiet diplomacy to broad public activity properly controlled.[48] In October 1963 a conference of Jewish activists in the cause of Soviet Jewry met in New York, and in December the idea was born of creating an American League for Soviet Jewry. The activity of the general Jewish organizations and of those set up for the express purpose of handling assistance to Soviet Jewry received an impetus in 1964 and 1965, in spite of opposition from various quarters – the institutionalized Jewish organizations on the one hand and the circles of the Lubavitcher Rabbi on the other. Dispute focused mainly on the best tactics to adopt towards the Soviet Union – quiet diplomacy, controlled public activity or open mass action with all the means available to Israel and world Jewry. Differences between Shaul Avigur's Office and some Americans active in the cause of Soviet Jewry had already emerged in 1966 and they grew wider after the Six Day War. They concerned questions of tactics, of financing activities and American Jews' independence of action.

Official Israeli activity in the 1960s was on a number of levels and in general along the same lines as before. Important work was done in maintaining secret contacts with activists in the Zionist movement in the Soviet Union, both by direct links with the help of the Israeli Embassy up to 1967 and through Jewish delegations visiting the Soviet Union. Levi Eshkol's new policy of trying to improve relations with the Soviet Union did not immediately affect these contacts because of Shaul Avigur's increasingly strong position in the party in this period of the Eshkol/Ben-Gurion rivalry.

In 1968 a change was made in the Russian language broadcasts to the Soviet Union. This important additional step was decided on after the 1967 rupture of relations with the Soviet Union. Daily broadcasts at fixed times now gave programmes on specific themes such as Jewish history, life in Israel, and developments in the Diaspora. However, the request of Zionist activists in the Soviet Union that the broadcasts over the Voice of Israel serve as an instrument in the fight for *aliya* was not acceded to until 1969.

In the years 1960 to 1968 the Knesseth dealt with the subject of Soviet Jewry more intensively than in the previous period. The arrests and trials of Jewish community heads in Leningrad (Petchorsky, Dinkin and Kaganov) led Knesseth Member Menahem Begin to call for a debate in the Knesseth, 'now that leaders of the Jewish community have been arrested in Leningrad and accused of spying.'[49] Foreign Minister Golda Meir, as usual in such cases, had the Knesseth refer the discussion to its Foreign Affairs and Defence committee, which declared that the arrests 'increased the deep concern for the fate of the Jewish collectivity in that State and for their rights as a people. ... Israel calls on all States and the Soviet Union among them to ensure Jewish collectivities freedom of collective national life and to grant every Jew the right to leave if he wishes to do so in order to join his family and his people in the State of Israel.'[50]

Activity by Israeli representatives in UN bodies on behalf of Soviet Jewry (such as the appearances of Judge Haim Cohen and Moshe Avidor) was attacked in the Knesseth by communist members (MAKI).[51] Prime Minister Levi Eshkol defined the government's policy on the subject of Soviet Jewry in May 1965: 'I say right out and I'm not saying it just for the sake of controversy that "real steps of goodwill" towards the people of Israel means, first of all, allowing the Jews in the Soviet Union to live their lives as a national collectivity like the rest of the peoples of the Soviet Union, and enabling everyone who wants to to join us in building the Jewish State.'[52]

Among the public associations, *Ma'oz* was especially active: in December 1964 it published and distributed manifestos headed,

'Let My People Go,' sent memoranda on the situation of Soviet Jewry to international institutions and organizations, such as the one to the Socialist International (23 April 1960). From 1964 on, *Ma'oz* initiated the 'Empty Chair' at the Passover Seder, a project aimed at the public and at schools in Israel and Diaspora Jewish communities, to stimulate and signify identification with Soviet Jewry. This project was criticized by Israeli left-wing parties; on 4 April 1967 Knesseth Member M. Erem wrote to *Ma'oz*, 'I feel I owe it to myself as a duty to tell you with complete frankness – I do not like your activity, especially not this year. Indeed I see it as harmful and liable to sabotage the small quantity of aliya that has opened up from the Soviet Union.' At the beginning of 1965, *Ma'oz* succeeded in signing up 100,000 people on a petition to present to the Knesseth.[53] In 1968 the association put forward the proposal to establish a 'Higher Committee for the rescue of Soviet Jewry.'[54] As the government had so far contented itself with indirect representations and the use of personal contacts, a policy that had brought no results, the general feeling in 1968 was that even if this policy was not basically mistaken, it had lost its usefulness and that new activities and new ways of carrying on the fight must be devised.

### D. 1969–1985 – seeking a new policy

The turning-point in official Israeli policy on public activity for Soviet Jewry came late in 1969, when Golda Meir told the country in an address to the Knesseth about a petition from 18 Georgian families to the Human Rights Commission of the UN. The Israeli Ambassador to the UN, Yosef Tekoa, simultaneously published the contents of the petition at a press conference in New York.[55]

A number of factors led to this turning-point. In the first place, there was the effect of pressure from the Zionist activists in the Soviet Union and those of them who had emigrated to Israel – they were threatening the Liaison Office that unless there was an immediate change in the policy of Israeli officialdom they would start independent action. Second, there was disappointment over the unfulfilled Soviet promises to permit emigration under the programme for 'Reunion of Families.' Third, there was a general feeling that the policy of 'quiet diplomacy' had not produced the hoped-for results and was in fact bankrupt. Finally, there was a sort of 'tactical retreat' on the part of those responsible for activity on behalf of Soviet Jewry in order to calm things down and not lose control.

In 1969 the international conference on the situation of Soviet

Jewry held its third session in Paris under the presidency of Daniel Mayer and with the participation of men of letters, Jewish and non-Jewish, many of them from France. This activity in a framework of limited though influential circles no longer seemed adequate in the new situation that was coming into being in the Soviet Union itself and in the West with the change-over to wider public action. At the beginning of 1970 the idea took form of calling a world-wide conference for Soviet Jewry.[56] A decision to this effect was taken on 12 April by representatives of Jewish communities in Europe, and the preparations were speeded up when the news became known on 15 June of arrests of Jewish activists in the Soviet Union. The first Leningrad trial took place in 1970 and the death sentences that were passed came as a shock; it was decided to hold the conference forthwith. (The storm of public protest in the world led to the sentences being commuted to 15 years imprisonment.) Until then Shaul Avigur had opposed participation by official Israeli personalities in meetings with Soviet Jewry. As he put it, he wanted to give the movement 'the tone of a fight of the whole Jewish people and not only of the State of Israel.'[57] He now decided that a first rank personality must be brought in and settled on Ben-Gurion, though old and ill and out of office.

> I told my people, 'You have to see the difference between a conference that Ben-Gurion appears at and one where Ben-Gurion doesn't appear; everything possible must be done to have him take part in the Brussels Conference.' My people accepted my view and I went to see Ben-Gurion and appealed to him to go to Brussels, but he refused. He said he was with us wholeheartedly, but it was beyond his strength. So I forgot all the rivalry and tensions – and very hard things had passed between us over the Eshkol affair – and I said to him, 'Ben-Gurion, I think you have to go,' and he accepted my opinion and he went.[58]

The Soviet authorities launched unrestrained attacks on the organizers of the Brussels Conference, using every means available to persuade the Belgian Government to reverse its agreement to the holding of the Conference.[59] In the Soviet Union itself they drummed up widespread, frenzied propaganda against the Conference with active help from the 'Jewish public' – that is to say, from personalities like General David Dragunsky, Aharon Vergelis, the editor of *Sovietish Heimland*, and the like. All this activity undoubtedly produced the opposite result from what the

Soviet authorities wanted to achieve, for it aroused wide international interest in the Conference.

The Brussels Conference was held on 22 to 25 February 1971 with the participation of 760 delegates from 38 countries, representing all the main communities in the world that were active in the cause of Soviet Jewry. There were also 250 newsmen and broadcasters from all over the world. A message was read from Prime Minister Golda Meir, saying *inter alia*: 'Your Conference is the outcome of a widespread public volunteer effort. It takes place at a time when a great Jewish national revival is stirring throughout Soviet Jewry, particularly among the youth. Your Conference is a conference of Jewish unity.'[60] Testimony heard at the Conference from Zionist activists from the Soviet Union made a deep impression: Grisha Feigin, Vitaly Svechinsky, Mendel Gordin, and Kraine Shur (sister of Hillel Shur, prisoner of conscience). The Declaration of the Brussels Conference ended: 'We will not rest until the Jews of the Soviet Union are free to choose their own destiny. Let my people go!'[61] On his return from the Conference, Ben-Gurion recorded in his diary:

> This Conference of world Jewry that came together in the last days of February 1971 in Brussels (Belgium) was unique in Jewish history. It was not a conference of a party or organization or community or sect but a meeting of world Jewry from the whole Diaspora and the State of Israel, from every continent and country. The writer of these lines was also sent to this Conference, delegated by Israeli Jewry. My doctors permitted me to be present at this Conference for ten minutes only and to say a few parting words. It seems to me that never before has there been a coming together of world Jewry like this. I am not sure that the Conference will change Russia's policy towards her Jews but without doubt it will strengthen Russian Jewry and reinforce its Judaism and its aspiration for aliya to Israel.[62]

Repercussions of the Conference were strong, not only in the Western communications media, but also – and largely thanks to the Soviet campaign against it – among the Jews in the Soviet Union, to whom it brought the tidings that they were not alone in the battle. Conferences also took place in more limited circles of people dealing with special aspects of the situation of Soviet Jewry; two international Jurists' conferences were held, one in December 1972 in Rome and one in September 1974 in London.[63] The second World

Conference for Soviet Jewry (17 February 1976) was also convened in Brussels, with the participation of some 1,400 delegates and 400 newsmen from all over the world. The final Conference declaration stated:

> The delegates to the World Conference for Soviet Jewry in Brussels, representing Jewish communities from the four corners of the world, hereby affirm before our brethren in the Soviet Union: We are with you in your faith, we appreciate your courage, be assured that you are not alone in the battle ... We declare that the Jewish people, which draws strength from the State of Israel, the embodiment of its spirit, will stand fast and will overcome all those who want to stifle its aspirations.[64]

The third World Conference for Soviet Jewry was held in Jerusalem on 15 to 17 March 1983 in the presence of 1,500 delegates from 31 countries, at a time when there was practically a complete standstill of Jewish immigration from the Soviet Union.[65] There were differences of opinion over the choice of the site for the Conference, whether it would not have been wiser to hold it outside Israel so as to reach a wider public. The Conference called for reopening the gates for *aliya*, release of prisoners of conscience and an end to the persecution of Jews who wish to live according to the faith of their fathers, preserve their people's culture, and learn and teach the Hebrew language.

The Knesseth dealt repeatedly with the Jewish question in the Soviet Union in its debates in the years 1969 to 1985. We have already referred to the dramatic occasion when Golda Meir read the letter of the 18 families from Georgia to the Knesseth, an occasion which opened a new era in the official Israeli policy on action for Soviet Jewry. The Knesseth allocated time for energetic protests over arrests of Zionist activists and it discussed all the aspects of *aliya*, including 'drop-out' and the integration of Soviet Jews in Israel. The main initiators of all the discussion in the Knesseth on this subject were Likud Knesseth Members Menahem Begin, Geula Cohen and Shneur Zalman Abramov. It is of interest that Knesseth Member Geula Cohen kept up her attacks on the Foreign Ministry's 'Liaison Office' even when there was a Likud government. Thus, for example, in a debate on 11 July 1979 she declared, 'Minister Shostak, you are permitted to read the minutes – I can give you the minutes – you'll read what Nehemia Levanon said, representing the Office. I think all this secrecy around this ought to end for once. Read what was said to us at the Conference by that Foreign Office representative, and it's the same things he whispers in the Prime Minister's ears, and the Prime Minister accepts his testimony.'[66]

The public campaign for the cause of Soviet Jewry reached its peak in Israel in the 1970s. The *Ma'oz* movement had its ranks strengthened by Zionist activists from the Soviet Union and it criticized official Israeli policy. In December 1970 a new association, an 'Action Committee of Soviet Immigrants,' was founded on the initiative of Leah Slovina, a Zionist activist from Riga. In the same month the semi-official 'Public Council on behalf of Soviet Jewry' was founded on the initiative of Golda Meir and Shaul Avigur with government financial support; it was headed by Avraham Harman, Sh. Z. Abramov, Dov Yosefi and Ruth Bar-On. The Council has been extremely active in organizing and coordinating Israeli public moves on behalf of Soviet Jewry.

## 4. STATE OF ISRAEL ACTIVITY – RESULTS AND FUTURE PROSPECTS

To what extent State of Israel activity was effective on behalf of Soviet Jewry is very hard to assess. The State of Israel's obligation to act is certainly unequivocal, as we have shown, an obligation to manifest solidarity with the Jews of the Soviet Union, even if it seemed clear that it would not have any effective influence. We have seen, nevertheless, that even if the State of Israel's activity came late in the day and was not always very adequate, it did have an important effect on Zionist activists in the Soviet Union on the one hand and on organization and coordination of Western Jewish bodies on the other. Moreover, without Israel's involvement there is no certainty that the American administration would have been prepared to take action as it did on behalf of the Soviet Jewry. The real question remains, therefore, of how one can influence the government of the Soviet Union to change its policy regarding Soviet Jews in general and the question of Jewish emigration in particular. The Soviet Union has succeeded – and in fair measure with the help of various circles in the West and persons like Dr. Nahum Goldmann in creating an image for itself of being impervious to influence by any external factor regarding any issue it sees as vital. This image is not however supported by the facts. Pressures and influences that are brought to bear can produce favourable results if there is a constellation of favourable factors present together or at least in partial combination on both the internal and the external planes. On the *internal Soviet plane*, the best constellation for securing favourable results on the Jewish question is as follows:

(1) The existence of a transition period in the regime, as in the years 1953 to 1955, 1965 to 1966 and 1983 to 1984, when a struggle for power was going on and policy was not yet set finally.
(2) The existence of circles with their own interests and with influence in the Soviet administration that press for a solution of the Jewish problem by emigration.
(3) The existence of at least partial positive/positive correlation, that is to say, a favourable attitude to Israel accompanied by a favourable attitude to Soviet Jews, as was the case in the years 1947 to 1948, exceptional years in the history of the Soviet Union.
(4) The existence among Soviet Jews of an ardent aspiration to emigrate and readiness to fight to achieve this aim, as emerged clearly in the years 1969 to 1971.

The following circumstances are particularly important on the *external plane*:

(1) The existence of a policy of compromise or détente in international relations and a desire common to both super-Powers to reach agreement in various spheres.
(2) The desire of the US Administration to fit the problem of Soviet Jewry into its global policy.
(3) Jewish activity in the USA and elsewhere in the Diaspora, and the existence of a supportive general public opinion for Soviet Jewry.

The situation that came into being in the Soviet Union at the beginning of the 1980s was not conducive to a renewal of Jewish emigration. The period of transition for the regime in the years 1983 to 1984 ended without a new policy being settled on regarding Jewish emigration. The war was intensified on dissident movements in the Soviet Union, including the Zionist movement, which was already declining from the end of the 1970s on. A significant change also occurred in the tendencies current among Soviet Jews themselves under the influence of a number of factors that weakened the urge to emigrate. The serious worsening in international relations from 1979 on, as a result of the Afghanistan and Polish affairs, lessened the bargaining strength of the USA. Then, too, there was a certain measure of fatigue among Israeli and Jewish activists on behalf of Soviet Jewry, resulting from an accumulation of factors –

the slow pace of emigration with its high 'fall-out' rate and the tension this caused in Israel–US relations.

As for the future, the matter will depend largely on changes in the ensemble of factors described above.

### NOTES

1. See, B. Pinkus, 'National Identity and Emigration Patterns among Soviet Jewry,' *Soviet Jewish Affairs*, No. 3, 1985, p.20. On the subject of the emigration of national minorities, see, too, my article, 'The Emigration of National Minorities from the USSR in the post-Stalin Era,' *Soviet Jewish Affairs*, No. 1, 1983, pp.3–36.
2. These sources are: interviews with Zionist activists from the Soviet Union and with people in Israel and the Diaspora concerned with Soviet Jews; material published or issued for publication by institutions and organizations concerned with Soviet Jews in Israel; memoirs; Soviet and Western newspapers and literature, both publicistic and scientific. Surveys of great importance have been carried out in the Soviet Union, in Western countries and in Israel and these have also been utilized; see my article (Note 1 above), 'National Identity ...' pp.3–19.
3. No research at all has hitherto been published on the subject of Israeli activity on behalf of Soviet Jewry. The subject has been approached, usually very critically regarding the people in Israel concerned with the matter and based on one-sided material, in the following publications: L. Schroeter, *The Last Exodus*, Jerusalem, 1974; R. Rass, M. Brafman, *From Moscow to Jerusalem*, New York, 1976; G. Cohen, *Ehad she-Hefer et ha-Dmama – Eduto shel Yasha Kazakov* [One who Broke the Silence – the Testimony of Yasha Kazakov], Jerusalem, 1976. As against this, research has been published on the activity of American Jewish organizations on behalf of Soviet Jewry: W. Orbach, *The American Movement to Aid Soviet Jews*, Amherst, 1979. See too, D. Bland-Spitz, *Die Juden und die Jüdische Opposition in der Sowiet-Union*, Diessenhofen, 1980.
4. On this subject see my two works; *The Soviet Government and the Jews 1948–1967, A Documented Study*, Cambridge, 1984; *The Jews of the Soviet Union; the History of a National Minority*, Cambridge, 1988.
5. M. Namir, *Shlihut le-Moskva* [Mission to Moscow], Tel Aviv, 1971, p.65.
6. *Ibid.*, p.62.
7. State of Israel Archives, Foreign Ministry, letter to Ehud Avriel, Director-General of the Prime Minister's Office, 24 October 1951, to be handed to David Ben-Gurion.
8. State of Israel Archives, Foreign Ministry, News for Israeli representatives abroad, No. 182.
9. B. Weisman, *Yoman mahteret ivry* [Jewish Underground Diary], Ramat-Gan, 1973, p.40.
10. *Album tmunot ve-teudopt; ha-mishlahat ha-tsionit halutsit le-festival be-Moskva* [Album of Pictures and Documents of the Zionist Halutz Delegation to the Moscow Festival], Tel Aviv, 1957. See too, N. Shaham, *Pegishot be-Moskva* [Moscow Meeting], Merhavia, 1957.
11. M. Altshuler, V. Meniker, Y. Stern, *Maamada shel Medinat Israel be-Kerev Yehudei Brit ha-Moatsot* [The Standing of the State of Israel among the Jews of the Soviet Union], Jerusalem, 1983, p.12.
12. S. Lipkin, 'Brith' [Covenant], *B'hinot*, No. 1, 1970, p.96.
13. *Divrei ha-Knesset* [Knesseth Record], 1952, Vol. 13, p.24.
14. *Ibid.*, pp.60–1.
15. D. Ben-Gurion, *Hazon va-Derekh* [Vision and Path], Tel Aviv, Vol. 3, 1957, p.152.

16. D. Ben-Gurion, *Netsakh Yisrael* [The Exiles of Israel], Tel Aviv, 1974, p.19.
17. David Ben-Gurion, *Hazon va-Derekh*, p.155.
18. *Ibid.*, p.197.
19. See, too, G. Meir, *Hayai* [My Life], Tel Aviv, 1975.
20. *In Memory of Golda*, Tel Aviv, 1981, pp.75–6. See, too, M. Syrkin, *Golda Meir, Israel's Leader*, New York, 1969, pp.219–34.
21. Institute of Contemporary Jewry, Interview with Golda Meir, Film No. 1349, 22 April 1968 to 10 July 1968.
22. Interview of the author with Shaul Avigur, at kibbutz Kinneret, 28 June 1976.
23. *Ibid.*
24. H. Izik, 'Shaul Avigur neged Bitul Misrad ha-Klita' [Shaul Avigur opposes abolition of the Absorption Ministry], *Davar*, 11 Nov. 1977.
25. N. Goldmann, *Ha-Paradoks ha-Yehudi* [The Jewish Paradox], Jerusalem, 1971, p.138.
26. *Ibid.*, p.148.
27. *Divrei ha-Knesset*, Vol. 1, 1949, p.397. On the subject of the dispatch of parcels to the Soviet Union, see archive of *Magen*.
28. *Divrei ha-Knesset*, Vol. 6, 1949, p.2,423.
29. *Divrei ha-Knesset*, Vol. 10, 1951, p.298.
30. *Divrei ha-Knesset*, Vol. 6, 1950, pp.2,423–2,424.
31. *Divrei ha-Knesset*, Vol. 11, 1952, p.1,465.
32. *Ibid.*, p.1,826.
33. *Ibid.*, p.1,828.
34. Interview with Shaul Avigur (Note 22, above).
35. Interviews of the author with Binyamin Eliav, Jerusalem, Jan.–Feb. 1972.
36. *Ha-Tnuah ha-Tsionit ve-Hasokhnut ha-Yehudit Din-ve-Heshbon al ha-Piilut 1951–1956* [The Zionist Movement and the Jewish Agency, Report on Activity from 1951 to 1956], pp.13–14.
37. State of Israel Archives, Foreign Ministry, Summing up of meeting held at the home of the Foreign Minister, 2 Sept. 1953.
38. *United Nations Bulletin*, 1953, Vol. XIV, No. 6, p.319.
39. *Les Réalités*, 1957, No. 136, pp.64–7, 101–4.
40. See *Doh al ha-Pgisha bein Mar A. Mikoyan le-vein Roshei ha-Vaad ha-Yehudi ha-Amerikai* [Report on meeting of Mr. A. Mikoyan and heads of the American Jewish Committee], Tel Aviv, 1959.
41. Knesseth Member Moshe Sneh, who had not yet joined MAKI, appeared in the Knesseth as representing a left-wing faction and made a fierce attack on the idea of holding a world conference on Soviet Jewry. See *Divrei ha-Knesset*, Vol. 13, 1953, pp.820–1.
42. *Divrei ha-Knesset*, Vol. 16, 1954, p.1,597.
43. *Divrei ha-Knesset*, Vol. 17, 1954, p.67.
44. Interview with Binyamin Eliav (see Note 35, above).
45. See *Conférence internationale sur la situation des Juifs en Union Soviétique*, Paris, 1960; *Jews in Eastern Europe*, No. 6, 1960.
46. Dr. Goldmann presents himself as the organizer of the conference and its chairman and in his memoirs he does not mention the fact of his having opposed the idea of the conference. Interview with Binyamin Eliav.
47. Z. Alexander, *Mediniut ha-Aliyah shel Brit ha-moatsot (1968–1978)* [Policy on Soviet Aliya (1968–78)], *B'hinot*, Nos. 8–9, 1977–78, p.8.
48. Orbach, *op. cit.* (see Note 3, above), p.20.
49. *Divrei ha-Knesset*, Vol. 32, 1961, p.363.
50. *Divrei ha-Knesset*, Vol. 43, p.867.
51. *Divrei ha-Knesset*, Vol. 42, 1965, p.1,694.
52. *Divrei ha-Knesset*, Vol. 43, p.1,932.
53. *Divrei ha-Knesset*, Vol. 42, p.1,221.

54. *Ma'ariv*, 2 April 1968.
55. See article by Sh. Redlich, '*Ha-Atsumot shel Yehudei Brit ha-Moastost ke-Bitui le-Hitorerut Leumit*' [The Petitions of Soviet Jews as a Sign of National Awakening (1968–70)], *B'hinot*, 1974, No. 5, p.14.
56. See Orbach, *op. cit.*, p.57.
57. The Ben-Gurion Research Institute, Interview of Yigal Dunyets with Shaul Avigur, 15 Feb. 1978.
58. *Ibid.*
59. For the Conference, see R. Cohen (ed.), *Let My People Go*, New York, 1971, pp.119–227.
60. *Ibid.*, pp.126–7.
61. *Ibid.*, p.1,142.
62. D. Ben-Gurion, '*Ha-Neum Shelo Nisa be-Vidat Brisel; Ha-Emet ha-Komunisti al Medinat Yisrael*' [The speech he didn't make at the Brussels Conference/ the Communists' 'truth' about the State of Israel], *Ma'ariv*, 19 March 1971.
63. *Conférence internationale de juristes sur le status des Juifs soviétiques et la primauté du droit, Londres 21–22 Septembre 1974*, Paris, 1974.
64. *Ha-Intelligentsia ha-Yehudit be-Brit ha-Moastot* [The Jewish Intelligentsia in the Soviet Union], No. 6, 1982, p.26.
65. See J. Jacobs, 'The Third World Conference on Soviet Jewry,' *Soviet Jewish Affairs*, No. 2, 1983, pp.71–74.
66. *Divrei ha-Knesset*, 1979, p.3,475.

# 18

# Jewish Solidarity and the Jews of Ethiopia

## Ephraim Isaac

World Jewish solidarity, encompassing Jews living in Ethiopia, echoes back to antiquity. In spite of some scholarly disagreements, a strong case can be made that the names Cush (Genesis 2:13; 10:16ff; Is. 43:3), Sheba (Genesis 10:7, 28; Kings I 10:1ff; Ez. 27:22ff.), and Havilah (Genesis 2:11; 10:7, 29; 25:18) refer to parts of northern and western Ethiopia, and indicate ancient Jewish contacts with these lands. Ethiopian legends claim that Jews settled in Ethiopia in King Solomon's time. According to a midrash based on the intriguing Biblical reference to Moses' Ethiopian wife (Numbers 12:1) Moses found refuge in Ethiopia after he fled from Pharaoh's palace. According to Josephus, Moses fought for the Egyptians against the Ethiopians, but conspired with the king's daughter, whom he later married.

Whatever the veracity of these legends, Jews did migrate to Ethiopia from early times and lived within the borders of the Ethiopian Empire, which included pre-Islamic Yemen during much of the first six Christian centuries. The discovery in Ethiopia of such lost, important Jewish literary works as *The Book of Enoch* and *The Book of Jubilees*, the strong Jewish theological flavour of the Ge'ez language, and the overall Jewish moulding of Ethiopian culture attest, as the great German philologist August Dillman asserted already in the nineteenth century, to the unquestionably strong Jewish presence in Ethiopia by early Christian times.[1]

Although Jewish presence in Ethiopia began to be eclipsed in the sixth century with the suppression of the Jewish revolt in Yemen by King Kaleb (527–547 c.e.), and before the Talmud had reached all of Jewry, some contact did persist. Some time in the ninth century, a special sense of world Jewish spiritual solidarity emerged as a direct result of the activity of Eldad ha-Dani, a Jew from

Ethiopia. His reports on the whereabouts of the Ten Lost Tribes of Israel brought new hope and generated a new sense of Jewish solidarity which persisted throughout the ages in the desire to establish contact with the exiles 'beyond the rivers of Cush.' The stories of Benjamin of Tudela in the twelfth century; Elijah of Farrara and Obadiah of Bertinoro in the fifteenth century; and Rabbi David Ibn Zimra, the Kabbalist Abraham Levi, Elijah of Pesaro, Abraham Ferussol, Abraham Yagel in the sixteenth century; and Moses Edrei in the seventeenth century attest to this. In particular, Rabbi David Ibn Zimra affirmed the continuing Jewish solidarity in his responsa concerning an Ethiopian Jewish woman and her offspring. However, many years would pass before scholars would sift legend from history to describe the contacts between the Ethiopian community and the Jewish world.[2]

## THE AGE OF EXPLORATION TO THE NINETEENTH CENTURY

Reports brought by the Portuguese missionaries in the sixteenth and seventeenth centuries undoubtedly contributed to stimulating international curiosity about Ethiopia. These missionaries not only wrote about the prominent role of the Jewish religious practices in the Ethiopian Church, but also referred to 'the Jews of the mountains' whom Jesuit theologians like Jeronym Lobo clearly distinguished from the Judaizing Ethiopian Christians. Subsequently, late eighteenth century reports of James Bruce, who introduced the first Ethiopian manuscripts of the lost Jewish *Book of Enoch* to Europe, and of early nineteenth century visitors to Ethiopia – explorers like Henry Salt, Charles T. Beke, Antoine Thomson D'Abbadie and others – heightened the interest in Ethiopia and its Jews.

The earliest Jewish scholarly work on Ethiopian Jews, that of the linguist Filosseno Luzzato, goes back to this period. The son of the Jewish exegete Samuel D. Luzzato, of the famous Italo-German scholarly family, Filosseno read Antoine D'Abbadie's narratives of his travels to Ethiopia, and published his first article in 1851 in the *Archives Israélites* of Paris. The London *Jewish Chronicle* published some translated portions of these articles. His history of Ethiopian Jews, which was published posthumously in 1854, undoubtedly contributed to sustaining the thread of Jewish solidarity with Ethiopian Jewry.

It was not until after the ascendancy of Emperor Theodore II

(1855–68) that direct and permanent contact between world and Ethiopian Jewry was made. This was a consequence of a strong Jewish reaction to modern European Christian missionary activities. News of the success of Martin Flad and the convert Henry Aaron Stern in bringing some Ethiopian Jews to embrace Christianity was brought to the attention of European Jews by Jewish journalists and caused much concern.[3]

Very little was done immediately to aid Ethiopian Jews. Some writers hold the view that this was because of doubts concerning the Jewishness of Beta Israel or because the notion of a 'Jewish race' seemed to rule out the existence of black Jews. But this is reading a modern rationale into past history since the predominant view at that time was that European Jews, unlike the white Aryans, were descendants of dark complexioned 'primitive' Semites.[4]

In my view, the real cause of the lack of immediate aid to Ethiopian Jewry cannot be separated from Jewish and world social, political, and economic conditions. West European Jews, despite political emancipation, did not enjoy social equality and unlimited freedom, while East European Jews were themselves suffering from discrimination and poverty. A major intervention in far-away Ethiopia, beyond the borders of the Ottoman Empire, would not have been a realistic goal.

Nevertheless, the central committee of the French-based Alliance Israélite initiated and authorized a visit by Joseph Halévy (1827), the first European Jew to establish personal contact with Ethiopian Jews in modern times, and British Jews supported it. The trip, whose objective was chiefly to counteract the Christian missionary activities among Ethiopian Jews, cost about ten thousand francs – not a small sum of money then – and was a breakthrough for world Jewish solidarity.

Halévy reached the port of Massawa on the Red Sea in October 1867, coinciding with the 1867–68 British military offensive in Ethiopia. The trip was no mean undertaking, as the then prevailing atmosphere was hostile to Europeans, but Halévy successfully worked his way into the highland regions, and for three months visited Jewish villages in the Wolqayet, Armachoho, Djanfancara, and Qwara districts. He did not reach the town of Gondar. Upon his return, Halévy wrote on the history, religious practices, social and economic conditions of Ethiopian Jews.[5] He also edited Ethiopic Jewish texts and translated them into a European language for the first time.[6] Thus, Halévy opened the way for future contact with Ethiopian Jewry by bringing first hand information about the need to assist them and to counteract foreign Christian missionary propaganda.

## TWENTIETH CENTURY: FAITLOVITCH

There is no doubt that the foundation for modern Ethiopian and world Jewish solidarity was laid by Halévy, a Sephardic Jew brought up in Adrianopole. His plea for action to aid Ethiopian Jews was not acted upon expeditiously by the leaders of the Alliance, who doubted his reports. The building of the solidarity bridge was left to one of his intellectual heirs, a Polish Jew, Jacques Faitlovitch (1880–1955).

Faitlovitch was an early twentieth century Orthodox Jewish liberal whose dedication and personal zeal won over many European and American Jewish leaders for the cause of Ethiopian Jewry. Whereas Halévy (for whom a Chair of Ethiopian Studies was established at the Ecole des Hautes Etudes at the Sorbonne) came to be known as the 'Father' of Ethiopian Studies, Faitlovitch became world Jewry's 'Apostle' *par excellence* to Ethiopian Jews. Armed with the knowledge of modern Ethiopian languages, which he studied with Halévy at the Ecole, Faitlovitch made his first trip to Ethiopia in 1904. The trip was sponsored by the Alliance and subsidized by Baron Edmond de Rothschild. Altogether he made six successive trips between 1904 and 1955 (1904, 1908, 1913, 1920, 1924, and 1946). His missions received the support of many world Jewish leaders, including Chief Rabbi Zadok Kahn of Paris, Chief Rabbi Hertz of England, and Chief Rabbi Abraham Kook of Israel.

Faitlovitch's first trip took place in the time of Emperor Manalik II (1889–1913) and lasted about 18 months. He travelled from Asmara to Gondar via Axum and Adowa and made his first contact with Ethiopian Jews. Ethiopian Jews were initially suspicious of Faitlovitch, an outsider, calling himself a Jew, particularly since some European missionaries had used this as a ploy to convert them.[7] Despite this initial impediment, Faitlovitch gradually convinced the community that he was not an ordinary missionary. He did not question their Jewishness, but deplored what appeared to him as their isolation, poverty, and ignorance.

Going well beyond the mandate to counteract evangelization, Faitlovitch viewed education as the best way to strengthen the bridge of solidarity between world and Ethiopian Jewry and made this his central concern. He saw the importance of training abroad young Ethiopian Jews in Western Jewish education and returned to

Europe in 1905 with two Ethiopian young men, Gete Eremyas and Taamrat Emmanuel, whom he enrolled in the Ecole Normale of the Alliance in Paris. Through his influence, the Hilfsverein der Deutschen Juden decided to sponsor other young Ethiopian Jews to study in Europe and at its training school in Jerusalem.

In Europe, Faitlovitch launched an aggressive lecture tour to raise funds, primarily for educational purposes. As a first step he put forward a plan to build a school at Asmara where there was a Yemenite Jewish community, whose history is also deeply-rooted in Ethiopia. Moving his headquarters from Germany to Florence, he successfully recruited Samuel H. Margulies – Chief Rabbi of Florence, and well-known both as a scholar and an activist in charitable organizations – to head the movement.[8] Most importantly, Faitlovitch persuaded 45 leading Orthodox rabbis to sign a letter reaffirming Jewish kinship and common destiny, unity, and solidarity with Beta Israel.

In 1908, Faitlovitch returned to Ethiopia with a translation of the letter of the distinguished rabbis and a promise to provide books and other educational facilities. In Eritrea, in the north, which was then under Italian rule, he sought official approval for starting a school in the capital Asmara. He enrolled Gete Eremyas and Solomon Yishaq at the Hilfsverein der Deutschen Juden in Jerusalem for further education, and with Gete later established headquarters in Amba Gualit in the Seqelt district. He also established an aid centre in Frankfurt-am-Main in March 1914.

In spite of his successes, not the least of which was curtailing missionary activities, Faitlovitch's relationship with the Alliance suffered from a lack of mutual confidence. Perhaps because of that, in 1908, overlapping with Faitlovitch's second trip, the Alliance sent a two-man fact-finding mission to Ethiopia. Upon their return to Europe, one of these men, Rabbi Haim Nahoum, published a negative report in the *Bulletin* of the Alliance. He was opposed to the building of schools to help Beta Israel on the grounds that they were too few, too scattered, and too backward to benefit from modern education. Nahoum's report generated an energy-draining dispute. In spite of this, Faitlovitch successfully worked out a compromise with the Alliance concerning one disagreement with them: to offer a general education, including Hebrew, which he wanted, in combination with vocational training, which the Alliance wanted.

During the 1920s, Ethiopian and world Jewish solidarity appeared to grow stronger with Faitlovitch's success in recruiting spiritual and financial support from another corner of the world: the American pro-Falasha Committee. This organization became very prominent, and existed in the United States until the early 1970s. Among his American friends were distinguished rabbis and academics. In addition, in 1921 Chief Rabbi Abraham Isaac Kook of Palestine made an appeal to world Jewry to support Ethiopian Jewish *aliyah*.

During this time, then, Jewish solidarity seemed to bear fruit. Faitlovitch visited Ethiopia at least twice, and was finally able to achieve his goal of establishing schools. Gete Ermyas became a teacher and subsequently the director of the Hebrew school in Asmara. Taamrat Emmanuel became the director of the new Hebrew school in Addis Ababa, where another significant Yemenite Jewish community was already active. Faitlovitch also brought his sister to join in the administration of the Addis Ababa school. Somewhat later, other schools were also opened in the northwest, in the Wogara, Balasa, Qwara, and Wolqayet regions.

The Ethiopian clergy and nobility at this time were generally hostile to Western education, condemning it as a corrupting influence of foreign missionaries and culture. Hence it was not uncommon for teachers to be arrested or incarcerated and the operations were not easy as a whole. Nevertheless, the schools continued to function until 1936 when the Italians occupied Ethiopia.

The period 1935–45, the decade of the Holocaust, is one of the gloomiest in modern European Jewish history. It also affected Jews living in Ethiopia, both Yemenites and native born. (My own father was incarcerated three times by the Italians, and narrowly escaped death in a prison, thanks to the liberation of Ethiopia by patriotic and international forces in 1941.) The Italians confiscated books and evacuated the school in Addis Ababa. Faitlovitch left for Jerusalem under the orders that all foreigners leave the country. Taamrat temporarily moved the school to Gondar, but was forced to flee to Jerusalem. He subsequently joined Emperor Haile Selassie in exile in England – no doubt the reason for his appointment to high government posts after the liberation.

The post-war period opened a new chapter for Ethiopian Jews as it did for world Jewry. However, since the recovery from the Holocaust and the struggle for the independence of Israel initially consumed most of the energy of Western Jewry, little thought was directed toward distant Ethiopia. In 1948, with the birth of the State of Israel, hopes rose that the Ethiopians would soon join their fellow-Jews in their newly regained homeland. It goes without saying that Faitlovitch himself pressed for an Ethiopian *aliyah*. These hopes were dashed when Jews from other areas of the world were given a higher priority for immigration into Israel. Moreover, the policy of the Emperor of Ethiopia, whose friendship the Israeli Government sought, was hostile to emigration of Ethiopian citizens. Thus, the hopes for *aliyah* soon diminished. Ironically, the long historic romance of the Ten Tribes and the more recent Western Jewish solidarity with Beta Israel appeared to pass into oblivion just as the Jewish people regained their long-lost independence.

## THE FIFTIES AND SIXTIES: TOKENISM AND APATHY

In the period following the birth of Israel, the Jewish Agency decided to aid Ethiopian Jews primarily at home. It set up a token teacher-training boarding-school in Asmara and elementary schools in the Gondar region. The school in Asmara opened in January 1954 with 57 students, and in 1955–56, 27 of those students were sent to Israel to study in Kfar Batya, a Youth Aliyah village sponsored by the Mizrachi Women of America.

The Kfar Batya programme was a failure. As David Kessler puts it, 'The Jewish Agency pleaded lack of funds.'[9] In addition, the programme lacked any definable objective. The student group was never intended, as some Ethiopians thought, to spearhead *aliyah* to Israel. It was not preparatory to higher education. It was not a vocational training programme. It was not a formal or planned educational curriculum. It was not even an experimental programme to see how Ethiopians would adapt to Israel. According to a first-hand report from one of the participants, those who had the aptitude for college education were discouraged from seeking it. One of the students, the son of a prominent Ethiopian Jew, sought and received Ethiopian Government assistance to pursue a college degree in Israel and a doctorate in France after having been flatly denied any assistance by the Israeli Ministry of Education. Thus the programme ended when most of the Kfar Batya students returned to Ethiopia in 1957.

Unfortunately, at about the same time, Ethiopian Jewish education was shrinking rather than growing. The school in Asmara was closed and moved first to Wuzaba and then, after its facilities were vandalized by hostile villagers, to Ambobar. Though a few of the students from Kfar Batya initially found jobs as village teachers, because of poor economic circumstances they eventually took modest jobs in Israeli companies, in particular, the Incode meat-packing plant and the Solel Boneh building firm. A few continued to work as school teachers in the Ambobar School, for which the Jewish Agency continued to offer modest support.

In February 1960, Ethiopian Jews sent an open letter to world Jewish leaders expressing their disappointment over the lack of action on the part of their fellow Jews. In this letter they requested help for *aliyah* to Israel and medical and educational assistance at home. Perhaps as a response, in 1962 an Israeli doctor named Har-El and his wife were sent by the World Jewish Congress to serve in the Gondar region, providing some modest social services. With the assistance of an Ethiopian Jewish male nurse, Har-El administered free vaccinations, distributed UNICEF supplies, and developed a family health care programme which was available to all and free of charge, as required by the Ethiopian Government. He helped to set up several health stations in both Jewish and Christian villages and gave lectures on his field experiences at the Public Health College in Gondar. After two years he was succeeded by an Argentine-born Israeli doctor, Mario Felszer, who continued similar services.

The limitations of these modest if praiseworthy efforts met with some criticism abroad. In England, the late Professor Norman Bentwich, former Attorney General of Palestine, former Visiting Professor of Hebrew University, and a distinguished leader of the Anglo-Ethiopian Friendship Society became a powerful spokesman for Ethiopian Jews. Bentwich was openly and vehemently critical of the Jewish Agency and world Jewry for their neglect of Ethiopian Jews.

Due to Bentwich's efforts and under his leadership, the British Jewish community, in collaboration with the Jewish Agency, sponsored an Israeli doctor to set up three village health centres. In addition, the number of schools grew to about seven. However, the budget was too meagre to support this programme. I might add that these schools received additional support from the National Literacy Campaign Organization which was under my directorship at the time (1966–74).

Throughout this period, Ethiopian Jews continued to struggle for survival. Since in most areas they were not allowed to own land, they worked as sharecroppers, paying exorbitantly high rents to the landowners. In the late 1950s, their leaders appealed to Emperor Haile Selassie in a palace audience on at least three occasions, requesting protection from the high rents and taxes which were exacted from them. Additionally, they brought complaints against local people who falsely accused them of sorcery, which sometimes resulted in their being murdered and in attacks of arson. Even when the restrictions against their buying land were finally lifted, most owners were reluctant to sell land to Jews. Thus, they continued to be harassed and could be driven off the land at will.

Various other attempts were made by Ethiopian Jews to ameliorate their own situation. One such attempt was the participation in the Setit-Humera Development Project organized by the Ethiopian Government with the assistance of the United Nations (FAO) and the World Bank. The project involved clearing malaria-infested lowlands in western Begemeder, near the Sudanese border, and developing farms. Ethiopian Jews initially regarded this as an opportunity to acquire their own land and to grow cash crops. A group of people formed a commune, and for five years worked side by side to clear and cultivate some 5,000 acres of land. Unfortunately, the experiment turned sour. At first, they were feared and harassed by some Sudanese as Zionist agents. Then the general lack of safety in the area due to the various warring factions finally made life unbearable and forced them off the land.

Following the historic revolution of 1974, there was new hope for religious equality and land reform. On 3 March 1975 came the Land Reform Declaration of the Provisional Military Government: land was nationalized and cooperative farms were instituted, though farmers were allowed to own land up to 25 acres. But in fact, the economic and political conditions of Ethiopian Jews deteriorated. The government did not have firm enough control in the countryside to enable them to benefit from its declaration. If anything, the areas inhabited by Jews became veritable battlefields between the government and three of its staunchest enemies: the rival socialist Ethiopian People's Revolutionary Party in Woggera; the anti-Marxist, Moslem-backed Ethiopian Democratic Union in the Gondar area; and the nationalist Tigrai People's Liberation Movement in the north. It has been argued that the Jews were not 'specially selected for persecution,' but the fact is that many of them found themselves in the line of fire. Rebellious landlords also individually formed bandit gangs and increasingly harassed the farmers, kidnapping or killing many of them. To make matters worse, the government could not even control the hostile actions of its own administrative representative against the Jews in the province where most of them lived. Complete figures on casualties have never been made available.

In spite of these problems, Ethiopian Jewish emigration to Israel was not put on any official Jewish agenda. From the time that I came to the United States as a student in the late 1950s, I was invited to give numerous lectures in synagogues and Hillel Houses. In 1974–75, I was a Visiting Lecturer at the Hebrew University, and was interviewed on radio and television. I found world Jewry as a whole eager to learn about Ethiopian Jews. But concern for their rescue and *aliyah* did not develop until the late 1970s.

It has been alleged that powerful and vocal leaders who objected to Ethiopian Jews because of their colour and supposed primitiveness brought pressure to bear at a secret Israeli Government consultation meeting and successfully shelved the *aliyah* agenda. It should be noted, in this connection, that until the Yom Kippur War of 1973, Israel had strong and important diplomatic and economic ties with Ethiopia. The opponents of *aliyah* also held that raising the issue of mass immigration might jeopardize this relationship.

## THE REVIVAL OF ETHIOPIAN JEWISH *ALIYAH*

The 1970s, particularly the late 1970s, represent a happy about-turn in the history of Ethiopian and world Jewish relationship. The meagre effort of the British referred to above was continued with the establishment of more schools after the 1974 Ethiopian revolution. An English Jewish teacher, Julian Kay, took over the administration of these schools and was replaced by the Israeli agronomist, Gershon Levy. Levy expanded further the educational and communal projects. In cooperation with the government, he worked on a revolving credit fund for farmers. One of his undertakings was a census of Ethiopian Jews: he found a total population of 28,189 Jews, consisting of 6,092 families in 490 mixed villages. Although his census was private and unofficial and did not take into account the traditional Ethiopian suspicion of counting people, it has been regarded by non-Ethiopians as authoritative.

In the post-Faitlovitch era, the American Pro-Falasha Committee became dormant. But in the early 1970s, when it came under the leadership of Martin Wurmbrand, it evolved into the 'American Friends of Beta Israel [Falasha] Committee,' established by Jed Abraham, an Orthodox Jewish Peace-Corps volunteer who had been in Ethiopia in the late 1960s. It was absorbed, in turn, into the American Association for Ethiopian Jews (AAEJ), established by Graenum Berger, formerly of the New York Jewish Federation. AAEJ came to be known as an activist organization committed chiefly to *aliyah*; in fact, it had little interest in social or educational activities in Ethiopia. It has come to be regarded as a controversial organization and its important contribution to the history of Ethiopian Jews has not yet been fully recognized.

If AAEJ was not concerned with educational activities in Ethiopia, other American organizations were. The Joint Distribution Committee, in conjunction with the World Jewish Congress, retained contact with Ethiopian Jews. Beginning in July 1977, the Organization for Rehabilitation through Training (ORT) worked with the Joint in Gondar on a programme emphasizing technical education and community development. By 1979, ORT administered 19 village schools with about 1,600 pupils; in 1980 this number had grown to about 2,245 pupils. Clinics were also restored in Ambober and Tedda. A clean drinking water fountain and a flour mill were provided at Ambober. A road from Tedda to Wuzaba and a factory for manufacturing hollow-block bricks were also built. The community development programme of 'revolving credit fund' provided assistance to about 384 families. Religious institutions and programmes were also supported. Hebrew prayer books were donated through the help of Yemenite Jews in Addis Ababa. Fifteen synagogues, each having a Hebrew class, and about 26 priests were directly supported by ORT.

In the late 1970s, ORT came under criticism by an association of Ethiopian Jews in Israel and by the AAEJ in America; both groups advocated work toward *aliyah* as the best way of helping the Ethiopians. Ironically, ORT also came under Ethiopian Government criticism because some officials thought that it was encouraging *aliyah* via the Sudan. In October 1981, the government took over ORT's programmes except the medical clinics.

## THE DIFFICULT ROAD TO *ALIYAH*

In Israel, a committee was formed in the early 1970s to assist Ethiopian Jews. Chaired by Professor Arieh Tartakiwer, among its members were Ruth Dayan, and Ovadiah Hazzi, a retired career officer with a distinguished history of service in the Israeli army, who became the most active member of the committee.

Hazzi himself was an Ethiopian Jew of Yemenite origin. He had never lost contact with Ethiopia, and frequently visited the Jewish communities there. Dedicated to the cause of Ethiopian Jews, few did as much for them at a crucial period in their history. An ardent Zionist, he used his extensive connections in Israeli official circles to bring about recognition of Ethiopian Jews by the government.

## THE CONTEMPORARY PERIOD

When in 1973 the Sephardic Israeli Chief Rabbi Ovadiah Yosef made his historic affirmation of the Jewishness of Beta Israel and called for their emigration to Israel, it was in the form of a response to Ovadiah Hazzi. From his ruling ensued the affirmation two years later of the Ashkenazi Chief Rabbi Shlomo Goren and of the Israeli Ministry of the Interior that Ethiopian Jews were eligible for immigration under the Israeli Law of Return.

With the Rabbinic decision and international pressure – particularly American – the *aliyah* of Beta Israel was underway. But there were other obstacles to Jewish immigration. First, there were no official ties between Israel and Ethiopia. Second, the Ethiopian Government was opposed to mass emigration, fearing, among other things, general minority group unrest. Third, there were outside pressures on the Ethiopian Government to keep Israel at arm's length. Luckily, Ethiopia needed the support of Israel against its Arab-supported enemies. Thus 'unofficial' channels of communication were opened between the two, and the Ethiopian Government turned a 'blind eye' to the emigration of two groups of between 50 and 60 who arrived in Israel by air in 1977, in exchange for a small supply of arms. This ended, however, when Minister of Defence Moshe Dayan confirmed reports of the deal in an interview. In spite of this damage, a few Ethiopian Jews continued to reach Israel independently after 1977.

About this time, the criticism directed at the Israeli Government by the AAEJ and the American Jewish media began to grow. Stories and editorials about Israeli inaction appeared in Jewish newspapers. Lectures critical of Israel were given in American Jewish institutions from Yeshiva University to Hillel Houses. In local speeches, G. Berger, the founder of AAEJ, outlined the plight of Ethiopian Jews and accused the Israeli Government of being indifferent. His successors as AAEJ Chairpersons, Howard Lenhoff and Nate Shapiro, argued for pressure on the Israeli Government to increase immigration. The Israeli Government was accused not only of indifference but even of obstructing the efforts to help Ethiopian Jews immigrate since the 1950s.

The criticism of the Israeli Government by AAEJ escalated when, beginning in 1979, the Council for Ethiopian Jews, a group consisting primarily of the immigrants of the 1970s to Israel, protested over the slow rate of immigration. These immigrants held that the Israeli Government was stalling on the issue, hiding behind a concern for secrecy. They met with Prime Minister Begin, who promised to act. To ensure that things would begin moving forward they sent letters to American Jewish organizations asking them to increase pressure on Israel. This appeal to world Jewish solidarity further increased international attention. The climax was in October 1979 when Yona Bogale made a historic appearance at the annual meeting of the Jewish Federation in Montreal. By 1981, Ethiopian Jews were beginning to reach Israel by 'circuitous routes'.[10]

Arguments over whether Israel was right or wrong led to bitter exchanges among various Jewish groups. Israeli Government, Jewish Agency, World Zionist Organization, and American Jewish leadership meetings on the issue of immigration were characterized by heated debates concerning the rate of immigration and the division of responsibilities. While Israeli officials claimed to have the situation under control, Ethiopian Jews in Israel lamented the death of some 3,000 in refugee camps. A telegram signed by Begin and sent to the AAEJ asking all organizations to coordinate their rescue efforts with the Jewish Agency was branded a fraud. Israeli consuls abroad, trying to respond to criticisms of inaction, were met by even more criticism. There were innumerable letters and editorials exchanged on the pages of the *New York Times*, the *Washington Post* and the Jewish press between the detractors of Israeli immigration officials and those accusing American Jews of interfering with internal Israeli policies.[11]

Ethiopian policy towards Beta Israel itself became a bone of contention. Many Israeli and Jewish leaders regarded the policy as benign; others condemned it. The report of World Jewish Congress visitors to Ethiopia claiming that Jews were no worse off than other Ethiopians infuriated even some Knesseth members. Journalists who visited Ethiopia reported stories of persecution, the closing of synagogues, imprisonment, and torture. The threat was said by some to come from anti-government forces; others claimed the danger stemmed from the Ethiopian Government itself. There was one thing on which all seemed to agree: Jews were subjected to abuses by rebel forces and active government persecution originated from local rather than national authorities.[12]

## OPERATION MOSES

In America, Jewish solidarity with Ethiopian Jews and the determination to bring about their emigration to Israel led to various actions. Local communities declared 'Ethiopian Jewry Day' and expressed grave concern for the plight of the Ethiopians. On a federal level, in its 1982 report on human rights in Ethiopia, the State Department highlighted the plight of Ethiopian Jews and asserted that the Ethiopian Government was blocking their immigration. According to its additional report, 'Aid Efforts,' it even proposed accepting Ethiopian Jewish exiles in the United States in case Israel was not prepared to receive them. Several United States Senators and Congressmen either visited Ethiopia or issued statements on behalf of Ethiopian Jewry. In 1983, the House of Representatives introduced House Resolution 107 in support of Ethiopian Jews and sent a letter to the State Department which pressed Secretary of State Shultz concerning both the issue of Ethiopian Jewish emigration to Israel and Ethiopian famine relief. The Senate joined with its own Resolution 55 calling for Ethiopian Jewish emigration. The Ethiopian Government repudiated sharply the Senate resolution as an act of foreign interference and denied allegations of mistreatment of Jews.[13]

Emigration of Ethiopian Jews to Israel had to emerge as an urgent priority. No amount of apology could dim the popular world Jewish interest in and support for the rescue of Ethiopian Jews; and world Jewry would no longer accept the complacency of some of its leaders. By the beginning of the 1980s conflicting Jewish groups set aside their differences and united in traditional solidarity. The initial efforts of Rav Ovadiah Yosef and Rasar Hazzi bore fruit when Prime Minister Begin and members of the Knesseth came forward with concrete immigration plans. It should be remembered that it was during Begin's tenure that the first major contingent of Ethiopian immigrants entered Israel. It was also Begin who published, before his retirement, an outline of Israeli efforts to negotiate with the Ethiopian Government on Jewish emigration. In May 1982 the Knesseth considered the formation of a committee to assist Ethiopian Jewish absorption. Educational material on Ethiopian Jews outlining their history, immigration issues, and various aid alternatives began to be prepared. Final plans were completed under Prime Minister Peres.

By November 1984, 'Operation Moses,' the massive airlift of Ethiopian Jews to Israel, was underway in full force. In some ways it was reminiscent of the 'Magic Carpet,' the equally dramatic airlift of Yemenite Jews in 1948–49. It involved an extraordinary cooperation among many nations, not to mention unusual arrangements with ambivalent Ethiopia and hostile Sudan. Initially a secret operation, it was unwittingly revealed to the public by a member of the Jewish Agency before its completion. This caused its abrupt halt on 6 January 1985 and led to an international crisis. Sudan disavowed it; Ethiopia called it international piracy.

But the momentum could not be easily stopped. Prime Minister Peres, who confirmed the Jewish Agency announcement, vowed in a speech before the Knesseth on 8 January that the rescue would continue. Further secret negotiations ensued, with the American Government playing an active role. Tragically, in the meantime, many Jews died in the camps while others gave up hope and found their way to Europe or America or back to Ethiopia. In the end, Sudan had to let the Jews remaining in its territory leave, but not without the official stipulation that they could not go to Israel. In the second phase of the airlift, dubbed 'Operation Joshua' and 'Operation Miriam' by some, an estimated 1,100 Jews were brought to Israel in a circuitous way, beginning in March 1985. By the time the whole operation had been completed there were over 15,000 Ethiopian Jews, mostly young people under the age of 20, in Israel. By 1986 their number had grown to close to 16,000.

'Operation Moses' was a joint effort of many people and many organizations. World Jewry, particularly North American Jewry, including both the American and Canadian Jewish communities, responded generously. The United Jewish Appeal pledged sixty million dollars towards the effort of the Operation, and actually raised about seventy million by the time the campaign was concluded. The Government of Israel, the United States, and other nations, the Jewish Agency, Israeli and international airline personnel, international negotiators, and many people in every walk of life helped carry out the historic operation.[14]

## CONCLUSION

The *aliyah* of Ethiopian Jewry has been a striking example of solidarity in modern Jewish history. It has generated a new Jewish zeal and heightened the Zionist spirit. It has deflated the pernicious claim that Israel and Zionism are racist. Although there has been some criticism based on reports that Ethiopian Jews might be settled on the West Bank or that their culture was being destroyed or that they were induced to become dependent on the government, the predominant opinion has been favourable and great support for *aliyah* has been maintained inside Israel and throughout the world. A speech given by Marvin S. Arrington, President of the Atlanta City Council, which was reprinted in the *Atlanta Journal and Constitution* reflected sympathetic international reaction:

Television news revealed that the Israeli Government had airlifted thousands of starving black Jews from the Sudan and Ethiopia to a new home in the holy land ...

The Israelis have demonstrated to the world that there is brotherhood of man and that it is not bound to race. So many talk of love, but Israel has acted. It is relatively easy for the wealthy to send their money to feed the hungry of Africa for a few weeks. For Israel, that is not enough. Israel has seen through the immediate problem to its cause and has taken action to break the cycle of starvation by transporting these thousands into a new land where they can build new lives and become self-sufficient. That, in itself, would have been remarkable, but Israel has done more ...

As no group of people have ever done, the people of Israel have demonstrated that we are our brothers' keepers and that kinship transcends race. A tiny nation of approximately three million people has shown the world clearly that we can live by our loftiest ideals.

This *aliyah* is a remarkable event in modern Jewish history. Among the specific exiled communities of Jews mentioned in more than one place in our Scriptures is the *golah* beyond the rivers of Cush, its redemption and return to the Land of Israel. Ethiopia, a land connected with ancient Israel through legend, history, language, and literature has had a special relationship with the Jewish people. It is a land that has preserved ancient Jewish customs, where lost but important Jewish literary works like the *Book of Enoch* and the *Book of Jubilees* have been discovered preserved in their entirety in Ge'ez. It is the land where everyone, including even the non-Jews, calls Friday by no other nomenclature but its Jewish theological term, 'the evening [of Sabbath].'

During the many centuries that Beta Israel lived in Ethiopia they never forgot their tie to the land of Israel. Their places of worship must have at least two entrances (and four big sanctuaries), one facing the east, the other facing northeast to Jerusalem. The priests who officiate in the place of worship must stand beside the Torah facing Jerusalem. Those who enter the place of worship must turn toward Jerusalem and prostrate themselves before entering. The beloved Sabbath is believed to descend to earth in Jerusalem. This commitment to Jerusalem, the heart of the land of Israel, is expressed in the following prayer:

Unite me with your saints and holy ones. Thou, Adonai, your

name is merciful, Adonai, King forever. When your angels rejoice in your kingdom, when you deliver your people Israel and are gracious to Jerusalem, your wife, deliver me also and make me to rejoice together with your chosen Israel.

Thus, on the part of the Ethiopians the *aliyah* generated a feeling of a miraculous return to the land of Israel. On my first meeting with him during my 1985 visit to Israel, my long-time friend, the elderly Ato Yona Bogale, the *de facto* leader of the Ethiopian Jewish community, spoke with some nostalgia, tears in his eyes, of how his life work was at last being fulfilled and rewarded. During the same visit, others with whom I spoke – the new, mostly middle-aged immigrants in the absorption centres – expressed profound gratitude to Israel and world Jewry for the support in their *aliyah* to the land of their forefathers, the ultimate objective of all Jewish people.

With the *aliyah* of Ethiopian Jews, the Land of Israel becomes a veritable museum of living Jews coming together in one place and representing living major Jewish cultural and historical periods: the Western Jews of the post-industrial and technological era; the Middle-Eastern Jews of the medieval era; the Yemenite Jews of the pre-Islamic Rabbinic, Tannaitic, Amoraitic era; and now the Ethiopians of the Israelite priestly Temple era. Jews, the most dispersed nation of antiquity, who today live in every corner of the world and have come together once again in their ancient homeland, know better than any other people that purity of culture or national origin is but self-delusion. The ability of the Jewish people in Israel and the Diaspora to cooperate in solving the seemingly insurmountable problems of the rescue of Ethiopian Jews is a stirring example of Jewish solidarity.

NOTES

1. Hirschberg, H. Z., *Yisra'el Ba'Arab* (Tel Aviv, 1946), pp.40, 49ff; Epstein, Eldad, *Eldad Hadani* [Hebrew] (Pressburg, 1891).
2. Goitein, E.D., 'Note on Eldad,' *JQR*, XVII (1926–27), p.483.
3. Henry Stern's tour of duty, which ended in his imprisonment, did not in fact lead to greater results due to the general Ethiopian suspicion of the intentions of Western missionaries and the strained relations between Ethiopia and the European powers. See his *Wanderings among the Falashas* (1862) which is unfortunately a rather sketchy study.
4. Kessler, David, *The Falashas: The Forgotten Jews of Ethiopia* (London, 1892), p.118.
5. Halévy, Joseph, 'Rapport concernant la mission auprès des Falachas,' *Bulletin of the*

*Alliance Israélite Universelle* (Paris, 1968) and 'Excursion chez les Falachas en Abyssinie,' *Bulletin de la Société de Géographie* (Paris, 1869).
6. Halévy, Joseph, *Prières des Falachas* (Paris, 1877); *Te'ezaza Sanbat* [Sabbath Commandments] (Paris, 1902), and *La guerre de Sarsa Dengel contre les Falachas* (Paris, 1907).
7. Faitlovich, Jacques, *Notes d'un Voyage chez les Falashas*, Paris, 1905; *Jewish Chronicle*, Oct. 1905.
8. *Jewish Chronicle*, 10 Jan. 1908.
9. Kessler, p.150.
10. Messing, Simon D., *The Story of the Falashas; 'Black Jews' of Ethiopia* (Balshon, Brooklyn, 1982), p.3, f.n. 85; Kessler, p.162. There are numerous newspaper accounts. See, for example: *New York Times*, 15 Nov. 1981; the *Jewish-American Examiner*, 2 Feb. 1982; 'Israel at Fault,' the *Jewish Post and Opinion*, 27 June 1980; 'Exodus for a Twice-Lost Tribe,' the *New York Times*, 2 March 1984; 'The Endangered Falashas,' the *Wall Street Journal*, 13 March 1984; 'JCC Series Speaker Urges the Rescue of Ethiopian Jews,' *The Connecticut Jewish Ledger*, 12 March 1981; 'Against Quiet Despair,' *Jerusalem Post International Edition*, 20–26 Dec. 1981.
11. 'Exclusive: Leading Officials Clash on the Falasha Issue,' *Jewish Advocate*, 11 Feb. 1982; 'Call to save Falashas who face Death in Refugee Camps,' the *Jerusalem Post*, 31 March 1983; 'Falashas Emancipated by Ethiopia's Revolution,' the *New York Times*, 4 May 1985.
12. 'Government Forces in Ethiopia Threaten Survival,' *Israel Today*, 16–19 March 1979; 'The Falashas: Doomed to Extinction?,' the *National Jewish Monthly*, May 1981; 'Ethiopic Tortured, Enslaved,' *New York Times*, 21 Oct. 1981; 'Ethiopic Black Jews a Periled Community,' *New York Times*, 21 Oct. 1981; 'Strangers in Their Own Land,' *Washington Post*, 1 Nov. 1983; 'Journey of the Falashas of Ethiopia,' the *Jewish Advocate*, 21 Jan. 1982; 'Journey to Save Falashas,' *San Diego Jewish Press Heritage*, 28 May 1982; 'Ethiopian Journey,' *Hadassah Magazine*, Jan. 1984.
13. Kessler, pp.x-xiv; the *New York Times*, 7 July 1982; *Washington Jewish Week*, 29 Dec. 1983; the *Jerusalem Post International Edition*, 27 March–2 April 1983.
14. 'Ethiopian Jews: Coming Home to the Promised Land,' *Pioneer Woman*, Sept.–Oct. 1983; the *Jewish Advocate*, 5 Dec. 1985; 'Exodus from Ethiopia,' *The Christian Science Monitor*, 3 May 1985.

# NOTES ON CONTRIBUTORS

Avi Beker was born in Tel-Aviv. He studied at Tel-Aviv University and New York University. He is Executive Director in Jerusalem of the World Jewish Congress and Lecturer in Political Science at Bar Ilan University. His recent publications include: *Disarmament Without Order; Politics of Disarmament in the United Nations* (1985); *The United Nations and Israel; From Recognition to Reprehension* (1988); *Jewish Culture and Identity in the Soviet Union* (co-editor, 1989).

Doris Bensimon was born in Vienna. She studied at the Sorbonne and is a professor at the University of Caen and at the Institute of Eastern Languages at the University of Paris. Among her recent publications are: *Judaïsme, Judaïcités* (co-editor with G. Rabinovitch, 1984); *La population juive de France* (with S. Della Pergola, 1984); *Les grandes raufles: Juifs en France, 1940–1944* (1987); *Les Juifs de France et leurs relations avec Israël* (1989); *Juifs d'Algérie: Hier et aujourd'hui* (with J. Allouche-Benayaun, 1989).

Ya'akov Blidstein was born in New York. He studied at Yeshiva University and Columbia University. He is currently Dean of the Faculty of Humanities and Social Sciences at Ben-Gurion University of the Negev and Professor of Jewish Thought and Philosophy in the Department of History where he holds the Hubert Chair in Jewish Law. His recent publications include: *Political Principles in Maimonidean Law* (1983) [Hebrew], for which he was awarded the Jerusalem Prize in 1985.

Phyllis Cohen Albert was born in New York. She studied at the Sorbonne and Brandeis University. She is a Senior Research Fellow at Harvard University. Her publications include: *The Modernization of French Jewry* (1977); *Essays in Modern Jewish History: A Tribute to Ben Halpern* (1982); *Contemporary French Jewry* (working title, forthcoming).

Henry Feingold was born in Ludwigshafen, Germany in 1931. He studied at Brooklyn College and New York University. He is Professor of History at Baruch College and the Graduate Center of the City University of New York. His publications include: *The Politics of Rescue* (1970); *Zion in America* (1974); and *A Midrash on American Jewish History* (1982).

Jonathan Frankel was born in London. He studied at Cambridge University. He is Professor at the Departments of Contemporary

Jewish History and of Slavic Studies at the Hebrew University of Jerusalem. Among his recent publications are *Prophecy and Politics: Socialism, Nationalism and the Russian Jews 1862–1913* (1984); *Studies in Contemporary Jewry* (editor, nos.1 and 4, 1984 and 1988).

Tuvia Friling was born in Beer-Sheva. He studied at Ben-Gurion University of the Negev and the Hebrew University of Jerusalem. He is Director of the Ben-Gurion Archives in Sede Boqer. His recent publications include: 'Examination of a Stereotype: Ben-Gurion and the Holocaust of European Jews 1939–1945,' *Yad Vashem*, 1987; 'Meeting the Survivors: Ben-Gurion's Visit to Bulgaria, December 1944,' *Studies in Zionism*, 1989.

Allon Gal was born in Afulah, Israel. He studied at the Hebrew University of Jerusalem and Brandeis University. He is a Senior Research Fellow at the Ben-Gurion Research Centre at Sede Boqer and Associate Professor of History at Ben-Gurion University of the Negev. His recent publications include *David Ben-Gurion – Preparing for a Jewish State* (1985) [Hebrew] which is being published in English by Indiana University Press in an expanded and revised edition, entitled *David Ben-Gurion and the American Alignment for a Jewish State*.

Ephraim Isaac was born in Ethiopia. He studied at Harvard University. He is Director of the Institute of Semitic Languages at Princeton University. Among his publications include: *The Book of Enoch, A New Translation from the Oldest Known Manuscript with Introduction and Notes in the Old Testament Pseudepigrapha* (1983) which won the Biblical Archaeologist Award; *A History of Religion in Africa* (forthcoming).

Yosef Litvak was born in Melinow, the Ukraine. He studied at the Hebrew University of Jerusalem and the University of Wisconsin. He was Director of the Department of Studies of the Jewish People at the Ministry of Absorption. His recent publications include: *Jews from Odessa and Drop-Outs* (1978) [Hebrew]; *Polish-Jewish Refugees in the Soviet Union 1939–1946* (1988) [Hebrew].

Israel Oppenheim was born in Poland. He studied at the Hebrew University of Jerusalem. He is Professor at the Department of History at Ben-Gurion University of the Negev. His recent publications include: *The 'Hechalutz' in Poland: 1917–1929* (1982) [Hebrew]; *The 'Hechalutz' in Poland: 1929–1939* (forthcoming) [Hebrew]; *Search for Productivisation: Zionist Youth Movements in Poland Between the Two World Wars* (1990); *The*

NOTES ON CONTRIBUTORS

*Attitude of the Polish National Democrats (Andecja) to the Jewish Question in Poland* (forthcoming).

Monty Noam Penkower was born in New York. He studied at Yeshiva University and Columbia University. He is Professor of History and Chairman of the Department of Social Sciences at Touro College, New York. His recent publications include: *The Jews were Expendable: Free World Diplomacy and the Holocaust* (1983); *A Zionist Tapestry* (1984); *The Emergence of Zionist Thought* (1986).

Benjamin Pinkus was born in Warsaw. He studied at the Hebrew University of Jerusalem and the University of Paris. He is Professor of History at Ben-Gurion University of the Negev and Senior Research Fellow at the Ben-Gurion Research Centre at Sede Boqer. Among his recent publications are: *The Soviet Government and the Jews, 1948–1967: A Documented Study* (1984); *Die Deutschen in der Sowjet Union: Geschichte einer Nationalen Minderheit im 20. Jahrhundert* (1987, with I. Fleischhauer); *Jews of Eastern Europe from the Holocaust to Redemption 1944–1948* (ed., 1987) [Hebrew]; *The Jews of the Soviet Union; The History of a National Minority* (1988).

Jehuda Reinharz was born in Haifa. He studied at Brandeis University and is Richard Koret Professor of Modern Jewish History and Director of the Tauber Institute for the Study of European Jewry at Brandeis University. His recent publications include: *Fatherland or Promised Land; the Dilemma of the German Jew, 1893–1914* (1975); *Israel and the Middle East, 1948–1973* (co-editor, 1984); *Chaim Weizmann, The Making of a Zionist Leader* (1985); *Living with Antisemitism: Modern Jewish Responses* (ed., 1987); *The Jews of Poland Between the Two World Wars* (co-editor, 1988); *Hashomer Hatzair in Germany* (1988) [Hebrew]; *Chaim Weizmann: The Making of a Statesman* (1991).

Simon Schwarzfuchs was born in France. He studied at the School for Higher Studies, Paris and at Dropsie College in Philadelphia. He is Professor at the History Department of Bar-Ilan University. His recent publications include: *Les Juifs d'Algérie et la France (1830–1855)* (1981); *The Memoirs of Eliahu Sheid* (ed., 1983); *La Communauté juive au Moyen Age* (1986); *Du Juif à l'Israëlite* (1989).

Selwyn Ilan Troen was born in Boston. He studied at Brandeis University, the Hebrew University of Jerusalem and the University of Chicago. He was formerly Director of the Ben-Gurion Research Centre and is the Sam and Anna Lopin Professor of

Modern History at Ben-Gurion University of the Negev. He was a Fellow of the Davis Centre for Historical Studies at Princeton, Weidenfeld Fellow at St. Antony's College, Oxford and Visiting Fellow of the Oxford Centre for Postgraduate Hebrew Studies. His publications include *The Public and the Schools* (1975); *St. Louis* (1977). He now writes on Israeli social history and his most recent publication is *The Suez–Sinai Crisis 1956; Retrospective and Reappraisal* (co-editor, 1990).

Daphne Tsimhoni was born in Jerusalem. She studied at the Hebrew University of Jerusalem and the University of London. She is Lecturer at Ben-Gurion University of the Negev and Research Fellow at the Ben-Gurion Research Centre at Sede Boqer. This chapter forms part of an extensive research on the Jews of Iraq and their mass immigration to Israel. Among her recent publications are: *The Christian Communities in Jerusalem and the West Bank 1948–1989* (New York: Praeger, forthcoming); 'The Political Configuration of the Christians in the State of Israel,' *Ha-Mizrah He-Hadash*, vol. 32 (1989); and 'The Government of Iraq and the Mass Immigration of the Jews to Israel,' *Pe'amim*, no. 39 (1989).

Moshe Zimmermann was born in Jerusalem. He studied at the Hebrew University of Jerusalem. He holds the Koebner Chair of German History at the Hebrew University of Jerusalem. His recent publications include: *Wilhelm Marr, The Patriarch of Anti-Semitism* (1987).

For Product Safety Concerns and Information please contact our EU
representative GPSR@taylorandfrancis.com
Taylor & Francis Verlag GmbH, Kaufingerstraße 24, 80331 München, Germany

www.ingramcontent.com/pod-product-compliance
Lightning Source LLC
Chambersburg PA
CBHW071235300426
44116CB00008B/1048